FOREIGN RELATIONS IN FEDERAL COUNTRIES

A GLOBAL DIALOGUE ON FEDERALISM
A Joint Program of the Forum of Federations and
the International Association of Centers for Federal Studies

EDITORIAL BOARD

CO-CHAIRS
George Anderson, Forum of Federations
Cheryl Saunders, Australia

SENIOR EDITOR, BOOK SERIES
John Kincaid, United States

Raoul Blindenbacher, Switzerland
Rupak Chattopadhyay, Forum of Federations
David Cameron, Canada
J. Isawa Elaigwu, Nigeria
Thomas Fleiner, Switzerland
Fernando Rezende, Brazil
Horst Risse, Germany
Nico Steytler, South Africa
Ronald L. Watts, Canada

www.forumfed.org
www.iacfs.org

A Global Dialogue on Federalism publications available
BOOK SERIES
Constitutional Origins, Structure, and Change in Federal Countries (2005), Volume 1
Distribution of Powers and Responsibilities in Federal Countries (2006), Volume 2
Legislative, Executive, and Judicial Governance in Federal Countries (2006), Volume 3
The Practice of Fiscal Federalism: Comparative Perspectives (2007), Volume 4
BOOKLET SERIES
Dialogues on Constitutional Origins, Structure, and Change in Federal Countries (2005), Volume 1
Dialogues on Distribution of Powers and Responsibilities in Federal Countries (2005), Volume 2
Dialogues on Legislative, Executive, and Judicial Governance in Federal Countries (2006), Volume 3
Dialogues on the Practice of Fiscal Federalism: Comparative Perspectives (2006), Volume 4
Dialogues on Foreign Relations in Federal Countries (2007), Volume 5
Dialogues on Local Government and Metropolitan Regions in Federal Countries (2007), Volume 6

Select Global Dialogue publications are available in other languages, including Arabic, French, German, Portuguese and Spanish. For more information on what is available, please visit www.forumfed.org.

A Global Dialogue on Federalism
Volume V

FOREIGN RELATIONS IN FEDERAL COUNTRIES

EDITED BY HANS MICHELMANN

Published for

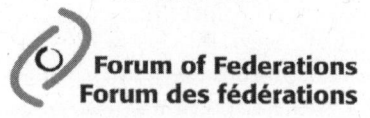

Forum of Federations
Forum des fédérations

and

iacfs
INTERNATIONAL ASSOCIATION OF
CENTERS FOR FEDERAL STUDIES

by

McGill-Queen's University Press
Montreal & Kingston · London · Ithaca

© McGill-Queen's University Press 2009
ISBN 978-0-7735-3501-5 (cloth)
ISBN 978-0-7735-3502-2 (paper)

Legal deposit first quarter 2009
Bibliothèque nationale du Québec

Printed in Canada on acid-free paper that is 100% ancient forest free (100% post-consumer recycled), processed chlorine free

This book has been published with generous financial support from the Government of Canada and the Swiss Agency for Development and Cooperation.

McGill-Queen's University Press acknowledges the support of the Canada Council for the Arts for our publishing program. We also acknowledge the financial support of the Government of Canada through the Book Publishing Industry Development Program (BPIDP) for our publishing activities.

Library and Archives Canada Cataloguing in Publication

Foreign Relations in Federal Countries / edited by Hans Michelmann; senior editor John Kincaid

(A global dialogue on federalism, v.5)
Includes bibliographical references and index.
ISBN 978-0-7735-3301-5 (bnd)
ISBN 978-0-7735-3502-2 (pbk)

1. Federal government. 2. Federal government – Foreign relations.
3. Comparative government. I. Michelmann, Hans II. Kincaid, John, 1946–
III. International Association of Centers for Federal Studies IV. Forum of Federations V. Series: Global dialogue on federalism; v.5

HJ141.P69 2009   321.02   c2009-902348-7

This book was typeset by Interscript in 10/12 Baskerville.

Contents

Preface JOHN KINCAID vii

Introduction HANS J. MICHELMANN 3

Republic of Argentina EDUARDO IGLESIAS / FEDERICO MERKE /
  VALERIA IGLESIAS 9

Commonwealth of Australia ANNE TWOMEY 37

Republic of Austria ANDREAS KIEFER 65

Kingdom of Belgium PETER BURSENS /
  FRANÇOISE MASSART-PIÉRARD 91

Canada ANDRÉ LECOURS 114

Federal Republic of Germany RUDOLF HRBEK 141

Republic of India AMITABH MATTOO / HAPPYMON JACOB 168

Federation of Malaysia FRANCIS KOK WAH LOH 188

Republic of South Africa CHRISTINA MURRAY /
  SALIM A. NAKHJAVANI 211

Kingdom of Spain FRANCISCO ALDECOA / NOÉ CORNAGO 240

Swiss Confederation DANIEL THÜRER / MALCOLM MACLAREN 269

United States of America EARL H. FRY 295

Conclusion HANS J. MICHELMANN 323

Bibliographic Resources for Federalism and Foreign Affairs
  JOHN KINCAID 353

Contributors 385

Participating Experts 391

Index 399

Preface

This volume on federalism and foreign relations in twelve federal countries is the fifth contribution to a series of practical books on federalism being published as a part of the Global Dialogue on Federalism program. The objective of this Global Dialogue is to engage experts from around the world in comparative conversations and debates about core themes and issues of federalism. One of the related goals is to build an international network that enables practitioners, students, scholars, and others to learn from one another, share best practices, and enhance their understanding of the prospects as well as the problems of federalism as a mode of governance in today's world, especially in relation to democracy, freedom, prosperity, and peace.

The Global Dialogue is a cooperative program created and conducted jointly by the Forum of Federations and the International Association of Centers for Federal Studies (IACFS). The Forum is an international network on federalism that seeks to strengthen democratic governance by promoting dialogue on, and understanding of, the values, practices, principles, and possibilities of federalism. The IACFS is an association of centres and institutes throughout the world that maintain a research and teaching focus on political systems that have federal features.

The work of the Forum of Federations and the IACFS is part of a broader endeavour to build and strengthen democracy through federalism when and where appropriate. As a mode of governance that seeks to combine self-rule for regional and minority interests with shared rule for general and common purposes, federalism is necessarily of interest to advocates of democracy. This is particularly true in a world in which the vast majority of nation-states are multinational, multilingual, multireligious, and/or multicultural. Indeed, there has been a tremendous upsurge of interest in federalism since the emergence of a new wave of democratization in the late 1980s. This worldwide interest in federalism is linked directly to movements promoting greater democracy and decentralization and to the simultaneous trends toward globalization and regionalization evident throughout today's world.

Given the dominance of statist ideologies during the past two centuries, however, federalism has often been viewed as a stepchild less worthy of attention and cultivation than the seemingly natural children of modern nationalism. Consequently, although there is a long history of federal-democratic experience in a few countries, such as Australia, Canada, Switzerland, and the United States, there is little practical experience with democratic federalism in most countries, and there are problematic experiences in a number of fledgling federal democracies. In turn, there is a paucity of accessible literature and information on comparative federalism and a dearth of intellectual capital available for investment in research and teaching about the many varieties of federalism worldwide.

This series of books, being published as one important product of the Global Dialogue program, seeks to create informational capital and to fill gaps in our comparative knowledge by providing as balanced a view as possible of theories and practices of federalism in various countries around the world. The series does so by exploring comparative and contrasting theoretical and practical perspectives, with each volume focusing on a particular aspect of federalism through the examples of selected countries that reflect federalism's diversity, including its strengths and weaknesses.

Our aim is to produce books that are accessible to interested citizens, political leaders, government practitioners, and students and faculty in institutions of higher education. Each chapter in this volume, therefore, seeks to provide an overview of its country's arrangements, institutions, and practices regarding foreign relations, especially the international activities of constituent governments, in a way that covers all relevant, important information without overwhelming detail. In doing so, each chapter also provides some analysis of the rationales and workings of federalism and foreign relations while indicating how well or poorly each country's foreign affairs arrangements and institutions function in relation to its Constitution and its society. Foreign relations are a crucial function of all national governments, but in many federal countries there are constituent governments that represent nations within the nation as well as other ethnic, religious, and linguistic groups that desire expression on the world stage. With advancing globalization, moreover, along with free-market economic policies, every constituent government as well as many local governments need to compete in the global economy and also to cooperate with comparable regional and local governments in their immediate neighbourhoods on numerous housekeeping matters of mutual concern.

The first volume, *Constitutional Origins, Structure, and Change in Federal Countries* (2005), began the series with an exploration of the constitutional systems of twelve federal countries. The second volume, *Distribution of Powers and Responsibilities in Federal Countries* (2006), examines the various practices and dimensions of power distribution in eleven federal countries. The third volume, *Legislative, Executive, and Judicial Governance in Federal Countries* (2006), examines the dynamics and interactions of the multiple legislatures, executives, and courts that operate in federations. The fourth volume, *The Practice of Fiscal Federalism: Comparative Perspectives* (2007), examines fiscal structures, practices, and issues in twelve federations. Future volumes will be devoted to local government and metropolitan regions, diversity and unity in federal countries, intergovernmental relations, and other important themes, with a somewhat different mix of countries being represented in each volume. The Global Dialogue program also produces a booklet series that provides an entry point to each corresponding book by highlighting the insights, key issues, and items of international interest that arose at the country and international roundtables. In keeping with their educative and accessible format, each booklet also includes a glossary of country-specific terminology. The corresponding booklet to this volume is available; indeed, the more limited scope of the booklet allows it to be published quickly, in multiple languages, and to be reproduced as changes in the federal countries warrant.

The conceptual framework of the Global Dialogue program can be found in the first volume, *Constitutional Origins, Structure, and Change in Federal Countries,* edited by John Kincaid and G. Alan Tarr. The key idea of the Global Dialogue is to draw on the wealth of others' experiences in order to learn from one another. The program entails a comparative exploration of a dozen core themes in federal governance. Through a series of themed roundtables, participants representing diverse viewpoints in a representative and diverse sample of federal countries search for new insights and solutions. The new information emanating from the roundtables is used to produce comparative materials for worldwide distribution.

Each theme's exploration entails a multistage process. First, a "theme coordinator" is chosen, who makes use of the most current research on the theme to create an internationally comprehensive set of questions covering institutional provisions and how they work in practice. This set of questions, or "theme template," is the foundation of the program, as it guides the dialogue at the roundtables and forms the outline for the theme's book. The theme coordinator also selects a representative sample of federal countries and recommends, for each featured country, a "country coordinator" – each of who is the author of a country chapter in the volume.

Next, each country coordinator invites a select and diverse group of expert practitioners and scholars to participate in a roundtable in his or her country, guided by the theme template. The goal is to create the most accurate picture of the theme in each country by inviting experts with diverse viewpoints and experiences who are prepared to share with and learn from others in a nonpoliticized environment.

At the end of the day, each coordinator is equipped to write a short article that reflects the highlights of the dialogue from each country roundtable. The booklet articles are generated from such exchanges.

Once each country has held its roundtable, representatives of the countries gather at an international roundtable. These representatives are experts who share their varied experiences and perspectives, as well as the knowledge gained from each country's roundtable, to identify commonalities and differences and to generate new insights.

To ensure that the knowledge gained at these events does not end with only those who participated in them, the final stage integrates the reflections from the country roundtables and new insights from the international event into book chapters, thus building on the progress already made and creating opportunities to use the material for further events. The chapters reflect the fact that their authors were able to explore the theme from a global vantage point, resulting in a more informed, comparative analysis of the topic.

Given the extent of the Global Dialogue program, we have many people and institutions to thank. Special appreciation is owed to the editor of this book, Hans J. Michelmann of the University of Saskatchewan, for his invaluable help in organizing and launching this volume. Appreciation is due, as well, to Desneiges Gauthier, a student at the University of Saskatchewan, who helped edit chapters, and to Jodi Bruhn, a translator and editor based in Ottawa, who assisted with chapter editing. Thanks are due also to all the participants in the twelve country roundtables and in the international roundtable, whose input helped to shape the content of this volume's chapters.

We wish to thank, in addition, colleagues who read and critiqued drafts of the chapters contained in this book: Chadwick F. Alger, Ohio State University, United States; Luis Ortega Alvarez, Universidad de Catilla-La Mancha, Spain; Arthur Benz, Fern Universität in Hagen, Germany; Chan Huan Chiang, Universiti Sains Malaysia; Howard Cody, Univeresity of Maine, United States; Timothy J. Conlan, George Mason University, United States; Maureen A. Covell, Simon Fraser University, Canada; Frank Delmartino, Katholieke Universiteit Leuven, Belgium; Thomas Fleiner, Université de Fribourg, Switzerland; Enric Fossas, Letrado del Tribunal Constitucional, Spain; Bede Harris, University of Canberra, Australia; Heidi H. Hobbs, North Carolina State University, United States; Rakesh Hooja, HCM Rajasthan State Institute of Public Administration, India; Sumitrra K. Jain, University of Delhi, India; Nicolas Lagasse, Université Libre de Bruxelles, Belgium; Jan-Erik Lane, University of Geneva, Switzerland; Jean Leclair, Université de Montréal, Canada; Akhtar Majeed, Hamdard University, India; Suresh Narayanan, Universiti Sains Malaysia; Phang Siew Nooi, Universiti Malaya, Malaysia; Horst Risse, Bundesrat, Germany; Cheryl A. Saunders, University of Melbourne, Australia; Sandeep Shastri, International Academy for Creative

Teaching, India; Nico Steytler, University of the Western Cape, South Africa; and Kosie de Villiers, University of Stellenbosch Business School, South Africa. The assistance of these individuals is greatly appreciated, although they are, of course, not responsible for any deficiencies in the chapters.

We also thank our colleagues and associates at the Forum of Federations and at the International Association of Centers for Federal Studies. The program and the present book could not exist without their assistance and expertise. We wish to acknowledge the work of the entire Forum of Federations staff and, in particular, the Global Dialogue staff for technical support: Rupak Chattopadhyay, senior director, global programs; Rhonda Dumas, program assistant; Abigail Ostien Karos, former program manager; Libby Johnston, support officer, global programs; and Chandra Pasma, former program manager. Special appreciation is owed to Raoul Blindenbacher, former vice president of the Forum, who played crucial roles in helping to launch and then guide the Global Dialogue on Federalism program. For their work on behalf of this volume at the Robert B. and Helen S. Meyner Center for the Study of State and Local Government at Lafayette College, Easton, Pennsylvania, thanks are due also to Brandon M. Benjamin and David A. Stamm, former undergraduate EXCEL scholars; Jason C. Pang, student; and Terry A. Cooper, administrative assistant. Finally, we thank the staff at McGill-Queen's University Press for all their assistance in producing the volume and working with us to ensure the success of this fifth book in the Global Dialogue series.

On behalf of the Global Dialogue Editorial Board
John Kincaid, senior editor

FOREIGN RELATIONS IN FEDERAL COUNTRIES

Introduction

HANS J. MICHELMANN

Foreign policy has traditionally been the responsibility of national governments. In countries with a unitary government, this state of affairs is relatively unproblematic because most powers belong to, and most public policy is conducted by, the national government. In federal countries, however, constitutional powers and responsibility for the conduct of public policy are shared between the federal government and the constituent units (e.g., states, provinces, and cantons), with each order responsible for a set of functions. But in federal countries, too, foreign policy has traditionally been considered the constitutional responsibility of the national government because the representation of a country's general collective interests, especially in matters of high politics such as diplomacy, defence, and national security, was seen as transcending the division of powers due to the need to present a common front toward foreign states.

That is not to say that constituent units of federal countries have not in the past undertaken international activities. With some exceptions, these were mostly interactions with neighbouring polities involving practical matters such as cooperation in transportation, flood and pollution control, and even the sharing of services – matters of low politics, conducted primarily in a very limited geographical context. Over time, the scope and nature of "constituent-unit foreign relations," the term used in this book to refer to all aspects of constituent units' engagement with the world beyond their countries' borders, have grown as the volume of international transactions of all kinds (e.g., in foreign direct and portfolio investment, foreign trade, tourism, and illegal migration) has dramatically increased and greatly affected the exercise of constituent governments' constitutional responsibilities. The chapter on the United States discusses clearly how these developments have affected that country's foreign relations, an experience that is mirrored to various degrees elsewhere. In other words, the dramatic increase in international transactions in recent decades, commonly referred to as "globalization," has prompted constituent units to become players, even if minor players, on the international stage.

Globalization has not, of course, had a uniform impact on all federations, nor has the reaction to it been similar in each country. The nature of the foreign relations in which constituent units have engaged, as well as their scope and intensity, vary considerably across and, for that matter, within the twelve countries discussed in this book. Those familiar with the series of which this book is a part, "A Global Dialogue on Federalism," will know that each book in the series includes chapters on Australia, Canada, Germany, Switzerland, and the United States. To these are added other federal countries for a total of twelve in this book. The additional countries are chosen to maximize the variability of factors relevant to an understanding of the book's theme: in our case, foreign relations in federal countries. This introduction is meant to provide an overview of the most important factors and thus to provide a preview of the most important themes discussed in the country chapters.

The geographical setting of each country is one of these factors. The core countries are situated in Europe and North America, and of course, there is Australia. India and Malaysia are Asian federations. The inclusion of South Africa and Argentina means that all inhabited continents are represented in this volume. Three additional European countries, Austria, Belgium, and Spain – all three European Union (EU) member states with features of special interest to the theme of this book – complete the group of twelve.

But representing all continents is not an end in itself. Each continent provides a setting that is relevant to the theme of the book. For example, including South Africa helps to focus attention on the special challenges posed for "constituent diplomacy," as John Kincaid has called the international activities of constituent units, in an environment of economic underdevelopment. This holds true also for Malaysia and India. India, moreover, is adjacent to countries with which relations have often been troubled, with all that this means for constituent-unit foreign relations. Argentina is a member of the Southern Common Market, MERCOSUR, and its experience in that context allows for comparisons with the experiences of constituent units of EU member states. Also, in comparison with Australia, which has no contiguous neighbouring countries, Germany and most other European countries have numerous neighbours, and they are all without exception members of a large number of regional organizations that involve them in a web of relations with numerous European polities.

In Europe regional location blends into political factors because the five European federal countries considered in the following chapters, Austria, Belgium, Germany, Spain, and Switzerland, are either members of or, in the case of Switzerland, closely affiliated with the EU. Dense intra-EU political and economic relations are a distinguishing feature of EU membership and engage constituent units in a multitude of relations with its institutions and with their counterparts in, as well as the national governments of, its member states.

Exploring the geographical setting of the twelve countries, then, introduces factors that affect constituent-unit foreign relations, and these are discussed in the country chapters that follow. But there are other factors that affect foreign relations in federal countries. Ethnicity and culture are important in some countries. Quebec in Canada, Catalonia and the Basque Country in Spain, and Belgium's communities and regions are among the most active constituent units internationally, as they seek not only to serve their economic interests, as do all other constituent units, but also to create and maintain strong links with ethnically or linguistically related communities abroad. In most cases, such activities are not politically charged because they help to forge strong human links across international frontiers. But at times, they have been used to serve, or have been interpreted as serving, separatist goals and have thus become highly controversial at home.

The twelve countries in this book also vary significantly in terms of economic development. Among them are some of the richest countries in the world; these boast developed economies and strong private sectors that foster interaction with partners worldwide and with constituent governments that have the experience and the financial resources to make promoting the economic interests of their citizens a major part of their foreign relations. Others among them are developing countries without such resources, with less sophisticated economies, and with constituent governments that are inexperienced and just beginning cautiously to engage in foreign relations.

Equally important in understanding constituent-unit foreign relations are political factors. For example, among the group of twelve countries are four long-established federations, Australia, Canada, Switzerland, and the United States, in which the relationship between the constituent and federal governments in foreign policy and foreign relations has evolved gradually, and not always harmoniously, over time as conditions have changed. These continuing adjustments were and are politically charged processes, as indeed they were in Belgium, where the present federal constitution came into effect only in 1993 and where relations between the federal and constituent governments in the field of foreign relations had to be fundamentally rethought and recalibrated, and then adjusted again by way of a number of agreements in the light of subsequent experience. In India the complex partisan relationships between the states and the Union government, as well as the reliance of national authorities on political support from regional power brokers to maintain office, allow some state political leaders a say in decisions about India's role in the world, even though states are not constitutionally granted foreign relations powers, even over matters under their jurisdiction. In Malaysia the dominance of an authoritarian national government rules out practically any meaningful foreign relations role for the states. In all countries, partisan politics affects the conduct of foreign relations, as it does other public policy sectors.

Of crucial importance in understanding constituent-unit foreign relations is the constitutional context in which they are conducted. For example, the Indian and Malaysian constitutions explicitly assign the federal government powers over foreign policy and make no reference to any role for constituent units. In others, such as Canada and Australia, the courts have defined the responsibilities of the two orders of government over time, although court rulings have also been important in other countries in clarifying and adjusting the division of powers between the federal and constituent governments in their conduct of foreign policy and foreign relations. At the other end of the spectrum are countries whose constitutions assign them explicit powers over foreign relations, among them Austria, Germany, and Switzerland. It should come as no surprise that the management and conduct of foreign relations in these different settings is strongly affected by this allocation of powers.

The assignment of powers to make and implement treaties is a central feature of the constitutional context of foreign relations. The constituent units of one group, including those in Belgium, Germany, and Switzerland, have been assigned treaty-making powers in their areas of jurisdiction, with the Belgian regions and communities enjoying the broadest powers among the twelve federations; other constituent units, including the Canadian and Spanish, have been assigned none. Clearly, when both the federal and constituent governments have the right to make such binding agreements, there must be close consultation between the two so that a country's engagement with the world is not fraught with confusion and contradictions. In some countries, constituent units have been accorded the right to be consulted on treaties under negotiation by their federal government. Moreover, even in countries where the national government is assigned the lion's share of, or exclusive, treaty-making powers, the implementation of the resulting agreements is often the responsibility of constituent governments because the agreements affect matters over which they have jurisdiction. Hence it is clearly expedient for the national government to take into account their views and interests so that implementation does not become a contentious domestic matter with possibly negative consequences for relations with foreign partners.

Thus federal countries must have a well-functioning system of intergovernmental relations to ensure that the constituent and federal governments act in reasonable harmony when engaging their partners abroad, whether negotiating treaties and less formal agreements or cooperatively managing the day-to-day interactions with these partners at home and abroad. The management of these intergovernmental relations takes on surprisingly different forms in the twelve federations. For example, in Australia judicial interpretation has given the Commonwealth (federal) government powers to implement treaties even in areas under state jurisdiction if the states balk at doing so; thus consultation structures and processes have been created in an attempt to forestall the need for such heavy-handedness. The German and Belgian governments have developed highly complex structures and procedures to manage intergovernmental relations. EU member states have had to develop efficient and flexible structures to manage the very intense interactions between federal and constituent governments in their relations with EU institutions. Governments in India, Argentina, and South Africa are working on the development of consultation procedures as provinces and states gradually become more engaged in foreign relations. In the United States consultation between states and the federal government is minimal, and some observers have expressed concern that the absence of an institutionalized system of intergovernmental relations hurts the country's pursuit of its international interests because the two orders of government do not sufficiently coordinate their actions.

What then of constituent diplomacy? As suggested earlier, economic motivations are central for understanding such activities. They include activities such as travel abroad by political leaders and government officials to promote exports and tourism and to seek foreign investment. Some Canadian provinces, Spanish autonomous communities, and US states, for example, have set up offices abroad to promote commercial ties. Constituent units also seek to be consulted on or to participate in international trade negotiations. They may seek foreign investment through domestic measures such as offering infrastructure enhancements and tax breaks. They meet regularly with their counterparts at home and abroad to exchange information and to establish means of pursuing common interests.

More altruistic motives can also play a role. Constituent governments have expertise in policy fields such as education and healthcare delivery that is not found in the public services of many national governments; thus they can undertake aid projects in less developed countries to transmit such expertise, often as agents of their federal government or its agencies. Such aid can also build government capacity through training public servants and providing policy advice. Many constituent governments engage in cultural diplomacy to showcase their cultural institutions, thus helping to establish an international profile that can serve a number of purposes. As discussed earlier, some also seek to build and maintain ties with polities that are linguistically and culturally similar to their own.

Politicians, while engaged in promoting the interests of their constituent units abroad, can enhance their political profile at home, and partisan political considerations may well play a role in such constituent diplomacy. These are matters of minor importance even if they may raise objections at home. Overtly political actions that stray into the realm of foreign policy are much more controversial. Constituent-unit politicians have been known to make statements, even while abroad, on politically charged foreign policy issues – to the consternation of federal governments. Although such practices are rare elsewhere, US states have sometimes become involved in symbolic or much more aggressive actions that seek to put the spotlight on what domestic lobby groups consider objectionable governmental practices in foreign countries. More generally, the economic, ethnic, cultural, and other interests of one or more constituent units may well clash from time to time with the interests of the country as articulated by the national government.

The conduct and management of foreign relations are sure to become increasingly important in the governance of federal countries in order to avoid such conflicts and, more significantly, to ensure that constituent and federal governments cooperate to maximize the interests of their citizens as their well-being becomes more and more dependent on fruitful interaction with other countries in an ever more complex international environment. In other words, foreign relations in federal countries is a subject well worth studying both because it will continue to be an important part of the literature on federalism and because policymakers will benefit from learning about the experience of federal countries in this regard. It is with these two goals in mind that the following country chapters have been written.

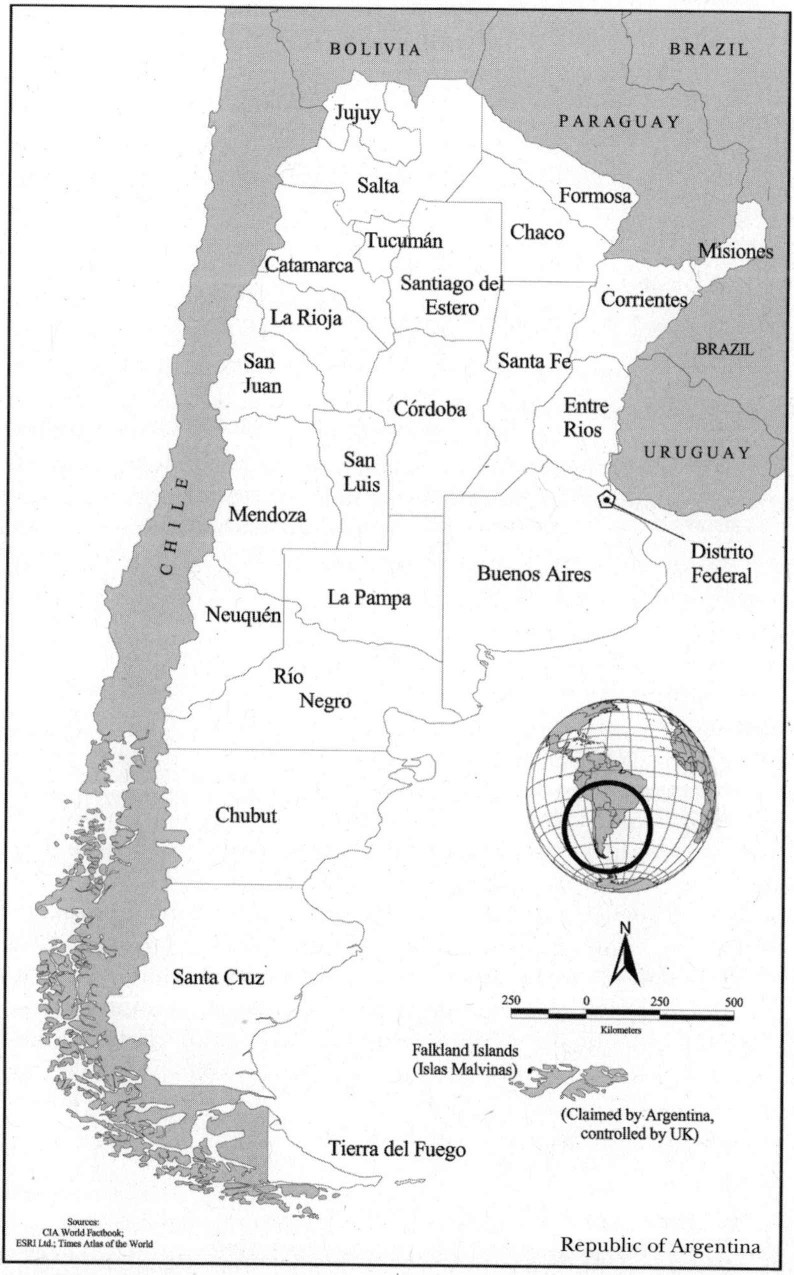

Republic of Argentina

Republic of Argentina

EDUARDO IGLESIAS, WITH FEDERICO MERKE AND VALERIA IGLESIAS

Argentina has one of the most complex and well-developed federal systems in the Southern Hemisphere.[1] This chapter analyzes the participation of constituent governments in shaping Argentina's international relations and also examines the direct international actions of provinces in such diverse policy fields as infrastructure, energy, natural resources, foreign trade, international cooperation, and tourism. Three questions are addressed in particular. First, what characteristics of the politico-institutional context promote provincial involvement in international activities? Second, what incentives encourage provinces to become engaged in international relations? Third, what constraints limit the international activities of the provinces?

The main conclusion is that since the return of democracy in 1983 and the constitutional reforms of 1994, Argentine federalism has taken on an international dimension in its structure and functioning, and the provinces have become involved in foreign relations to different degrees and in different ways. Size, location, level of development, and political will are some of the key variables that differentiate provinces in their degree of participation in foreign relations. Whereas some of the provinces have developed a relatively successful strategy, shortages of institutional memory, financial resources, and expertise remain obstacles for other provinces. Furthermore, the weakness of coordination mechanisms between the federal and provincial governments in some cases limits effectiveness. Although much still needs to be done, there are signs that present efforts are leading to greater effectiveness and efficiency.

THE NATIONAL SETTING

Following the definitive return of democracy in 1983, federalism progressed from "dual" or "competitive" federalism to a more cooperative, consensus-based federal arrangement. This new scheme opened a horizon of opportunities for provinces as a result of the end of the Cold War and the deepening of globalization. Provinces ceased to think and act locally and started to look beyond Argentina's borders, taking into account the new regional and global scenarios. The constitutional reform of 1994 signalled a more flexible and formal approach to international relations, allowing provinces to enter into international agreements provided these do not compromise national foreign policy. Since then, provinces have taken significant steps to make full use of their room to manoeuvre. Although this move toward "internationalization" has led to progress for the provinces, the overall process has been affected by Argentina's economic and political development. Moreover, the size and location of each province have shaped its international outlook and the degree to which it has become active on the international stage. In order to have a better idea of this overall situation, it is necessary first to outline some basic geographic and economic features relevant to understanding the dynamics of federalism in Argentina.

Argentina is located at the southern tip of South America and has a total surface area of 2,331,900 square miles, including the Malvinas Islands, islands of the South Atlantic, and portions of continental Antarctica. With a total population reaching 40.3 million people in 2007, the country is 2,290 miles in length and shares 5,825 miles of borders with Bolivia, Brazil, Chile, Paraguay, and Uruguay. Argentina's gross domestic product (GDP) in 2007 was US$245.6 billion, making it the third-largest economy in Latin America after Brazil and Mexico. Following the economic turmoil of 2001–02, output began to recover in the second quarter of 2002. Real GDP increased by 8.8% in 2003, exceeding the most optimistic predictions, and increased by 9% in 2004. In 2005 the economy continued to grow at a rate of 9%. A similar growth rate was predicted for 2006, which would mean an accumulated economic expansion of 36% from 2003 to 2006.[2] By 2007 the unemployment rate was down to 8.9% – considerably lower than the 24.1% reached in the second quarter of 2002. Also, the poverty rate fell to 31% of the population – a rate that is still considered very high compared with the level of social equity that formerly characterized the country.

In terms of population density, economic development, and international outreach, Argentina displays important regional contrasts. This has obvious implications for foreign relations because widely differing regions put forward different agendas for international relations. The majority of Argentina's population and economic activity is concentrated in less than one-fifth of its territory – an area including the federal district of Buenos Aires (Ciudad Autónoma de Buenos Aires) and the provinces of Buenos Aires, Córdoba, and Santa Fe. As a whole, this area contains 63% of the Argentine population, with the federal district and the province of Buenos

Aires alone accounting for 45.9% of the total, followed by Córdoba with 8.6%, and Santa Fe with 8.3%. Argentina has three international cities: Buenos Aires, Rosario, and Córdoba. Mendoza and Tucumán play a secondary role. As the centre of political and economic power, Buenos Aires has a weight all its own. With its 11.5 million inhabitants, the capital city and the greater Buenos Aires area are at the centre of national life. Yet in terms of agricultural development, industry, and manufactured products, Rosario and Córdoba have also traditionally been considered major cities.

Following this pattern, the economic performance of the Argentine provinces also shows remarkable contrasts. In 2005, for example, Buenos Aires, Chubut, Mendoza, and Santa Cruz accounted for 48% of private investments.[3] There is also great divergence among the productive structures *within* each province – and hence also in the development and exploitation of natural resources. This divergence is reflected in the high concentration of exports in a small group of provinces. In 2005 Buenos Aires, Santa Fe, and Córdoba accounted for 71% of total Argentine exports; Chubut, Catamarca, Mendoza, and Neuquén represented only 12%. There are also discrepancies between provinces in terms of their export markets. The Mercado Común del Sur (MERCOSUR) and the North American Trade Agreement (NAFTA) are the largest markets for products from Buenos Aires, whereas the European Union (EU) and Asia represent the most important markets for Santa Fe. Most exports from Córdoba are concentrated in the EU, NAFTA, and Asian markets.[4]

REGIONAL AND GLOBAL CONTEXT OF THE NATIONAL SETTING

Latin America and MERCOSUR

Regional integration in the Southern Cone gained momentum in the 1980s and 1990s. The restoration of civilian governments in Argentina and Brazil, the adoption of broadly similar economic approaches, and the advancement of trade agreements have led to a remarkable improvement in bilateral relations. Overall, there seems to be a correlation between the reestablishment of democracy, the initial steps toward regional economic integration, and the parallel "desecuritization"[5] of relations between Argentina, Brazil, and Chile.

In 1991 Argentina, Brazil, Paraguay, and Uruguay founded the southern common market, MERCOSUR, which functioned as a common market (involving the free circulation of goods, services, and factors of production) until 1995. Since then, it has also functioned as a customs union with a common external tariff. Under the "four-plus-one scheme," MERCOSUR has two associated partners: Bolivia and Chile. In 2006 Venezuela formally applied to become the first full member to join MERCOSUR since its establishment. Currently, Argentina's gross domestic product accounts for about 20% of the combined GDP of MERCOSUR member states, second after Brazil and ahead of Uruguay and Paraguay.

MERCOSUR is basically an intergovernmental structure without supranational institutions. As such, it lacks a fully institutionalized common foreign policy. Most problems that have arisen within the regional bloc have generally been solved by the members' presidents. This is why Argentine provinces have been striving for greater input on the decisions of a bloc that, on many occasions, has had a direct impact on their affairs. Early in 2000 provincial representatives began attending meetings of the Consultative Council for Civil Society, organized by Argentina's Ministry of Foreign Affairs. Some active provinces have sought to be consulted on the nation's decisions concerning MERCOSUR rather than to be merely informed of them. This situation created pressure to establish more institutionalized participation within MERCOSUR's structure, leading to the creation of the Consultative Forum of Municipalities, Federal States, Provinces, and Departments. Established in December 2004, this forum is intended to serve as the central representative body for constituent governments. It complements another parallel and older structure, the Red de Mercociudades (Merco-Cities Network). According to Article 1 of Resolution 41 of 2004, the forum aims to "stimulate dialogue and cooperation among authorities at the municipal, state, provincial, and departmental level of MERCOSUR's member states." Further, it is mandated to "put forward measures aimed at coordinating policies that promote well being and improve the quality of life of those people inhabiting the municipalities, federal states, provinces, and departments of the region, as well as tabling recommendations through the Common Market Group."[6]

The forum was incorporated into the regional structure in March 2007 during MERCOSUR's Presidential Summit, held in Rio de Janeiro, and in September the Grupo Mercado Comun (MERCOSUR's executive agency) approved the internal regulations of the forum. The available evidence suggests that in its first stage of operations, the forum has offered a venue for sharing experience and discussing common challenges.

Another interesting aspect of provincial regional and transborder relations is the federal-unitary government dimension. Although Argentina is a federal country, it is surrounded, with the exception of Brazil, by neighbours with unitary governments: Uruguay, Paraguay, Chile, and Bolivia. The lack of decision-making powers with respect to the foreign relations of subnational governments in these countries sometimes acts as a disincentive for Argentine provinces to try to establish regional arrangements. Thus in Argentina the usual way to resolve border issues is to look to the national government to deal with its unitary neighbours. Moreover, provinces with MERCOSUR-related problems – with the exception of problems involving the Brazilian states – have made their voices heard mainly in national capitals. These observations demonstrate that the centralized pattern of decision making in foreign policy has generally been reproduced at the regional level.

THE CONSTITUTIONAL SETTING

The Argentine Constitution spells out the powers and jurisdiction of the various orders of government. Originally written in 1853, it was reformed most recently in 1994. Foreign affairs and defence fall within the domain of the national government. Article 121 states that the provinces reserve for themselves all those powers that are not delegated to the federal government. This clause is similar to the Tenth Amendment of the United States Constitution in that, like the states, the provinces retain all powers that have not been expressly relinquished to the federal government.

Legislative powers are assigned to two houses of Congress: the national Chamber of Deputies and the Senate. The Chamber of Deputies is composed of representatives who are directly elected for a term of four years and who may be reelected. Although this chamber is not a provincial representative body, federalism still exerts an influence on its composition and dynamics. Crucially, each province is entitled to at least five deputies – a provision that takes into account the relative weakness of the less populous provinces. For its part, the Senate is a federal chamber representing the provinces that compose the federation. The Senate is composed of three senators from each province as well as three from the city of Buenos Aires. Contrary to the Canadian model, in which senators are not elected but chosen by the federal executive branch, Argentine senators are elected. Two seats are allocated to the winning party; the remaining one goes to the runner-up. Senators hold office for a term of six years and are entitled to indefinite reelection.

Although the allocation of powers among the executive, judicial, and legislative branches is balanced in the constitutional framework, foreign affairs, finances, and defence are centralized for the most part in the hands of the president. In this sense, the executive enjoys a high degree of autonomy in devising and proclaiming Argentina's foreign policy. The Ministry of Foreign Affairs has traditionally served as the gatekeeper of Argentina's international relations. With its body of professionals, the ministry has always had a voice in making foreign policy. In this sense, it has not only implemented the president's vision on foreign policy but has also helped to shape the president's perceptions and orientation in world affairs.

In addition, the president is the commander-in-chief of the armed forces and thus has the overall task of organizing and deploying those forces.

Since the return of democracy in 1983, the executive has tried first to recapture and then to consolidate civilian control of the armed forces. Drawing on these constitutional powers, the president is able to lead major defence initiatives.[7]

Every international treaty approved by Congress subsequently becomes part of federal law.[8] Contrary to the Canadian model – which gives each province the power to decide whether to apply an international treaty affecting one or more of its areas of jurisdiction – Argentine provinces must both respect and implement international treaties. When a provincial law contravenes an international treaty ratified by Argentina, the Supreme Court invokes an extraordinary judicial mechanism by which to ensure effective implementation of the treaty. Likewise, when a province violates a right recognized by an international treaty, its inhabitants are entitled to appeal to the judicial system for a *recurso de amparo*, a kind of injunction or expedited legal action against the province.

Although Congress does not conduct the everyday implementation of foreign policy, it has power over a number of limited yet crucial matters that can affect long-term policies. For example, senators retain the ability to influence foreign policy, and intergovernmental bargaining can play a role. Also, if Congress is to approve international treaties and decisions affecting war or peace as well as the conduct of trade, there is at least a formal possibility that provinces opposing an international treaty, for instance, can have a voice through their senators. Further, in the realm of economics, Congress can settle the payment of the nation's foreign and domestic debts. It is also responsible for regulating trade with foreign nations. In the area of defence, Congress is responsible for securing the integrity of the national boundaries, for determining provincial boundaries, and for creating new provinces. The most important power of Congress with respect to foreign relations is that after the executive has signed an international treaty, Congress is charged with "approving or rejecting treaties concluded with other nations and international organizations, and accords with the Holy See." It is further charged with "approving treaties of integration that delegate powers and jurisdiction to supranational organizations under reciprocal and equal conditions and that respect the democratic order and human rights."[9] This is a matter of central relevance in a system in which treaties and accords have a status higher than that of domestic laws. Yet the reality is much more complex. Interests and alliances are rarely built along provincial lines and are usually subjected to party politics, ideological cleavages, or short-term, electoral-based political bargaining.

The constitutional reform of 1994 involving Article 124 introduced a number of changes aimed at strengthening federalism in the area of international relations. Article 124 reads as follows:

The provinces are empowered to set up regions for economic and social development and to establish entities for the fulfillment of their purposes, and they are also empowered, with the knowledge of Congress, to enter into international agreements provided they are consistent with the national foreign policy and do not affect the powers delegated to the Federal Government or the public credit of the Nation. The City of Buenos Aires shall have a regime which is to be established to that effect.

The provinces have the original dominion over the natural resources existing in their territory.[10]

This article empowers provinces to set up regions for the sake of economic and social development[11] and even to enter into international agreements – provided they do not contravene national foreign policy or affect either the powers delegated to the federal government or the public credit of the nation. Article 124 also establishes that natural resources belong to the provinces. This feature is crucial to understanding the international activities of the provinces because, as a result, they have a strong say in investment, regulation, and infrastructure development in the energy sector, a sector with important international ramifications.

Environmental law is held under concurrent jurisdiction; when exercising their powers in this regard, therefore, the provinces must take into account international treaties signed by Argentina.

Some experts argue that the 1994 reforms represent a qualitative advance for Argentine federalism. They also point out that, in essence, the new Constitution "incorporated" existing practices that had already been implemented by provincial governments. Some analysts cite as evidence the case of Crecenea Litoral, a region created by Salta and San Juan in 1985. Others point out that the provincial constitutions of Salta and San Juan, among others, contained articles on provincial international activities well before the 1994 reform.

Ultimately, both the text of the Constitution and its interpretation have raised a controversial yet unresolved question: specifically, *how and to what extent* should the federal government legally control the actions of provinces in the international arena to avoid contradictions or incompatibilities between national foreign policy and provincial actions? The lines of debate usually revolve around three additional and contentious questions.

First, is it mandatory to regulate Article 124?[12] If so, who should regulate it? On the one hand, a group of provincial representatives and constitutionalists argues that there is no need to regulate Article 124 because such regulation might diminish provincial power. Existing provincial experience in international affairs has proved the redundancy of the attempt to regulate Article 124 in order to ensure that the provinces can be active in the international arena. A more moderate group also opposes formal regulation of

Article 124 but urges the establishment of general guidelines on provincial international relations to avoid potential problems of incompatibility with national policy. On the other hand, there is a group that argues for "the need [formally] to regulate Article 124 in order to safeguard the right of the provinces to enter into international agreements, and to establish very clearly those areas of action that do not comprise the foreign policy or the public credit of the nation as a whole." For this last group, Congress serves as the ultimate representative of the provinces and, as such, is entitled to legislate on this matter.[13] Although the lines of division are not straightforward, it is possible to surmise that advocates for more regulation would restrict the provinces' range of movement, whereas advocates of the *status quo* would seek to maintain it.

The second question is whether provinces should be entitled to sign treaties or agreements. Here, some constitutional experts have proposed a conceptual distinction between treaties and agreements, concluding that provinces are entitled to sign only agreements.[14] Others argue that in practice there is no difference between an international treaty and an agreement, so long as these are limited to specific subjects and do not conflict with the standing of the nation.[15]

The third question is how to interpret the meaning of the "knowledge" of Congress. Some scholars and officials hold that "knowledge" by no means implies "approval" in Congress. They argue that Congress should not decide on provincial competences set out in the national Constitution. Another group contests this position, explaining that if the provinces merely provide information to the federal government on international treaties they conclude, this does not suffice to ensure the unity necessary for conducting foreign policy.

In any case, the reform of the national Constitution in 1994 created a momentum whereby many provinces saw an opportunity to introduce reforms of their constitutions on the basis of those made in the federal document. After providing a detailed analysis of each constitution, a recent study[16] has concluded that the reform process initiated in 1994 marks a growing inclusion of international issues in provincial agendas, particularly issues related to trade, integration, and international cooperation.

The inclusion of references to international matters in the recently reformed provincial constitutions varies considerably. Some provinces (e.g., Salta and San Luis) advocate Latin American integration, whereas others (e.g., Neuquén and San Juan) include the United Nations (UN) Universal Declaration of Human Rights in their provincial constitutions. Still others (e.g., Formosa and Chubut) make reference to Argentina's sovereign claim to the Malvinas Islands. Most important, the majority of provincial constitutions (e.g., La Rioja, Catamarca, Córdoba, Jujuy, La Pampa, and Río Negro) explicitly state their aim to actively influence the formulation of international policy. Yet matching words with deeds is a challenge some provinces still have to face, especially because most of these reforms have been implemented only recently.

INTERGOVERNMENTAL RELATIONS IN FOREIGN AFFAIRS

The Nation-Provinces Relationship and Foreign Policy

Traditionally, local ruling elites in Argentina have perceived foreign policy as a task of the federal government. In addition, diplomacy and international relations have been considered closely related to matters of "high politics" such as national security and the conclusion of political alliances with foreign nations. Therefore, the federal government has been highly skeptical of decentralizing aspects of national foreign policy. The implicit working assumption has been that definition of the "national interest" is a task reserved for the federal government. This has left little room for what have been considered merely parochial or regional interests.

Four processes – empirically interrelated yet analytically distinct – have eroded this centralizing tendency. First, there is a progressive internalization of "the international" by the local orders of government. This means that provinces are increasingly aware of their need to deal with global trends – and, in particular, with regional and neighbouring countries' policies – in terms of their impacts on the constituent units. This awareness has translated into more "internationalized" constitutions and the development of new competences for dealing with international issues within the executive branches of the provinces. The second process is that of region building. Provinces have pressed forward in constituting regions in order to combine their resources for engaging in international activities. This phenomenon is addressed below in the discussion of regional and interregional relations. Third, transformations have occurred within the Ministry of Foreign Affairs itself, demonstrating its aim to "federalize" foreign policy. Fourth, as discussed earlier, the reformed national Constitution authorizes the provinces to sign international agreements. Occurring in the constituent, regional, and federal arenas, these four transformations present new possibilities for a better, substantive articulation of Argentine federalism in international relations.

The Institutional Capabilities of Argentine Provinces

The past decade witnessed an expansion of local capabilities in foreign affairs. That said, this expansion has varied considerably among the provinces.[17] Although a national survey suggests that most provinces have offices that deal to some degree with international matters, very few (e.g.,

Ciudad Autonoma de Buenos Aires, San Juan, Santa Fe, and Corrientes) maintain an agency that deals exclusively with international relations. Another noteworthy aspect is that although provincial agencies in charge of international policies are situated at different official levels – secretariats, undersecretariats, general directions, directions, areas, and so on – the focus is largely on foreign trade at all levels. As in Buenos Aires, Chaco, Salta, and La Pampa, most international agencies operate within the ministries of production. Others are either attached directly to the governor's office (e.g., Corrientes) or are folded into other ministries (e.g., Mendoza and Formosa). One final trend is that national agencies that had traditionally focused on the domestic aspects of tourism, the environment, and infrastructure have increasingly begun to deal with them as aspects also of international and transborder affairs.

Provincial officials tend to agree that, beyond the level of institutional development, the political to-and-fro associated with local elections further conditions the activism of the provinces in international affairs. A change of administration may imply adjustments to institutional structures in general and to the agencies in charge of international affairs in particular.

Finally, it should be mentioned that Argentina possesses no *legal* asymmetries in relations between the federal and the constituent governments that would lead to variations in provincial activity in foreign affairs.

Coordination Mechanisms between the National and Local Governments

Since 1992 the Ministry of Foreign Affairs has dealt with issues related to international trade through its secretary of trade and international economic relations. In addition, the ministry was charged with coordinating the foreign policy efforts and actions of the municipalities, provinces, and national authorities. These new roles prompted a need for heightened coordination between the the Ministry of Foreign Affairs and the provinces – not only in commerce-related matters but also with respect to legal expertise, political affairs, and diplomatic support.

Today, the ministry has a Directorate of Federal Affairs that works as a formal nexus with the provinces and municipalities. In particular, this agency is responsible for (1) advising provinces on matters related to international agreements; (2) helping provinces to organize official trips and trade missions abroad; (3) providing provinces with support in establishing strategic partnerships and in twinning with other constituent units abroad; (4) assisting regions in legal, trade, and diplomatic matters; and (5) articulating the shared interests of the nation and provinces in regulating relations with neighbouring countries.

Recently, the Ministry of Foreign Affairs implemented a number of programs, such as Cancillería en el Interior (2004), Interior: Prioridad para

Exteriores (2004), and Programa de Federalización de Comercio Exterior (2006). These programs had a twofold objective: to "bring the ministry closer to the provinces" and to "bring the provinces closer to the ministry." To further these aims, the ministry took several innovative actions. First, it invited provincial officials to engage in meetings with officials of different ministries so that the former could deepen their knowledge of how international affairs are managed by the federal government. Second, the ministry organized several workshops in the provinces to provide updated information on foreign trade development and to listen to the demands of local officials. The workshops also seek to help provinces to promote their exports and gather commercial intelligence. Finally, in a few cases, diplomats were assigned to certain provinces.

Today, when provinces engage in foreign trade activities, they coordinate their efforts with, and receive the support of, various national agencies. To provide some examples: one such agency is Fundación Exportar, a mixed public-private agency for the promotion of trade that operates with the support of the Ministry of Foreign Affairs. Fundación Exportar helps provinces and local producers to fund stands at trade fairs and to deal with general logistics in foreign countries. Provinces also rely on the support of Argentine embassies and consulates abroad, especially in organizing their governors' trips and short-term missions. Another important support is the Consejo Federal de Inversiones (Federal Council of Investment, or CFI), a regional development agency created by the Argentine provinces and the federal capital city in 1959. Broadly, the CFI acts as a "macro-coordinator" among provinces as well as between provinces and national agencies. The CFI coordinates and finances trade missions abroad, performs commercial intelligence tasks, and provides technical assistance for the formation and functioning of regions.

The Ministry of Foreign Affairs also has a website, the aim of which is to strengthen the involvement of the municipalities in international affairs.[18] The underlying idea is to bring local governments closer to the federal government and thereby to link efforts among municipalities, provinces, nongovernmental organizations (NGOs), businesses, and the federal government. More ambitiously, the program seeks to promote culture, tourism, and other services offered by local governments as well as to twin Argentine cities both with others in the MERCOSUR area and with some in third countries. In advancing these aims, the ministry has committed itself to producing background research on the municipalities and provinces. The ministry is also poised to make agreements with provinces and municipalities so that these can enjoy a greater say and active participation in issues that affect foreign policy. Building on this ongoing initiative, the Ministry of Foreign Affairs signed an agreement as recently as July 2006 with the Federación Argentina de Municipios (Argentine Federation of

Municipalities) to promote local governments' exports. With this agreement, the ministry committed itself to providing the technical and institutional support necessary for improved international outreach – mainly in the sectors of economic development, culture, and tourism.

All these coordination efforts represent an important advance in Argentina's federal form of governance. Yet there is a general understanding that better coordination is needed – not only between the national and provincial governments but also among the provinces and between provinces and municipalities. Principally, four factors seem to hinder the harmonization and coordination of activities: (1) the perception of a lack of a national, strategic, long-term plan for how best to project the regions and provinces into the international arena; (2) the scarcity of financial resources, which sometimes forces programs to end and/or prevents the establishment of new ones; (3) the existence of asymmetries in information on "who does what" among the three orders of government (i.e., nation, provinces, municipalities); and (4) the lack of expertise in international affairs, especially in small provinces.

Provincial officials usually mention a number of measures that could be taken to alleviate some of these deficits. The most salient are: (1) strengthening institutions to avoid a "personalist" policymaking style (i.e., the identification of key policies with individual officers); (2) resolving other important related domestic issues, such as the revenue-sharing tax system known as *coparticipación*, which causes friction between the national government and the provinces and also among the provinces; and (3) increasing the number of visits of national officials and diplomats to the provinces.

Transborder Relations

Most Argentine provinces have long maintained close relationships with adjacent constituent governments in neighbouring countries. In some cases, these relationships started well before the country gained its independence in 1816, and they were encouraged by complementary economic activities, shared idiosyncrasies, and (with the exception of Brazil) a common language. Compared with the long distances that separate some provinces from Buenos Aires, physical proximity inevitably contributed to frequent interaction. This pattern obtained particularly in cases where the constituent units shared similar origins, as seen between some of the northern Argentine provinces and the unitary states of Bolivia, Chile, and Paraguay.

The resolution of pending boundary disputes in the 1980s and 1990s contributed to the adoption of a more cooperative view on the integration of transborder regions. Nowadays, with the greater volume and speed of cross-boundary movements of products, people, and pollutants, the border poses new challenges for the provinces. Issues include the facilitation of trade, construction of roads and bridges, sharing of natural resources, and interconnection of electric systems and communications.[19] Nevertheless, the shared experiences of provincial and national officials have made it evident that each part of the frontier entails its own characteristics and problems.

The Committee of Integration (formerly known as the Frontier Committee) is the formal body for dealing with transborder issues and is coordinated by the Ministry of Foreign Affairs. Basically, it consists of regular meetings in which national and provincial (and in some cases, municipal) authorities on both sides of the frontier negotiate on various aspects of the movement of people and goods into their areas of jurisdiction. Initially, the main attendees were governors, provincial officials, representatives from the different ministries of foreign affairs, and officials working in border services such as customs, immigration, health, transport, and police. In past years, new actors have gained access to these meetings. Whether representatives of tourism, transport, ports, mining, agriculture, or trade, these new actors come principally from the private sector and civil society.

Argentina has three committees of integration with Bolivia, one with Brazil, seven with Chile, six with Paraguay, and a similar mechanism with Uruguay, known as CODEFRO. Both provincial and national officials note that, from time to time, the borders raise some complex issues on the bilateral agenda. Nevertheless, in most cases, there are no major conflicts. In fact, there are significant areas of cooperation on frontier corridors, mining, shared hydro resources, trade, and cultural activities. One of the few important pending problems on the frontier is the regular (and frequently abusive) use by neighbouring communities of free public health facilities located in Argentina.

As mentioned earlier, an important aspect in analyzing provincial transborder relations is whether neighbouring countries are unitary or federal. Generally, when provinces in north-eastern Argentina deal with transborder issues with their counterpart Brazilian states, the negotiation is of a "constituent-constituent government" type. But when Argentine provinces discuss common issues with the neighbouring communities of unitary states (i.e., Chile, Paraguay, Uruguay, and Bolivia), the case is quite different. Very often, the provinces end up dealing with national agencies due to the limited decision-making power of the lower-level governments of these countries.

The Provinces and International Organizations

The economic obligations assumed by the national government in international forums affect the country as a whole. In other words, if Argentina agrees to lower trade barriers for certain products in a World Trade Organization (WTO) negotiation (or any other trade negotiation), provincial policies must adapt accordingly. Despite this requirement, formal participation by the provinces in WTO negotiations is practically nonexistent. In the Doha Round of these negotiations, the provincial representatives were not part of the negotiation team, although there had been provincial representation in trade negotiations with the United States. At most, economically powerful provinces exporting key products – such as grains, meat, sugar, textiles, and automobiles – may have exerted influence in compiling the positive and negative lists used at the national level to identify which products and services will be subject to liberalization. Similarly, no formal agreement or rule enables the provinces to engage directly in negotiations with international organizations, although some provinces have demonstrated a willingness to get involved in some way. An alternative venue for interacting with international organizations is the signing of cooperation agreements. One of the many examples of this practice is the agreement signed by the provinces of Chubut, Rio Negro, and Santa Cruz with the UN Global Environment Facility Trust Fund regarding the prevention of sea contamination and the management of maritime biodiversity.

Since the 1950s Argentina has maintained relationships with international financial institutions (IFIs) such as the Inter-American Development Bank (IADB) and the World Bank. Not until the 1990s did IFIs begin to lend money to Argentine provinces as part of a broader development strategy for developing countries.[20] The autonomy of provinces in contracting credits with IFIs remains quite limited, however, and varies according to the type of credit in question. The national government is the ultimate legal authority entrusted with approving or rejecting credit projects that the provinces present; once a project is in progress, moreover, the national government monitors and evaluates its continuation. Within this legal framework, the provinces can by no means acquire loans from IFIs without gaining prior and explicit consent from the federal government. A similar control mechanism applies when provinces issue bonds for sale in international financial markets. Even the bonds' guarantees must be approved by the national government.

DOMESTIC AND INTERNATIONAL MANIFESTATIONS OF CONSTITUENT DIPLOMACY

The Argentine Provinces in Foreign Affairs

Since the 1990s the provinces have become increasingly aware of their underexploited potential to go abroad. Provinces have engaged in international activities for various case-specific reasons. Some preliminary studies have identified a number of factors that might explain why some provinces are more active than others.[21] Three of the principal factors are as follows.

First, international engagement depends on political will as well as on the institutional capacity to establish and maintain stable international ties.

Some provinces have stable, institutionalized apparatuses that have proven efficient in fostering their international objectives; others have relied more heavily on the vision and will of their governors in adopting international strategies. Increasingly, governors have shown interest in foreign affairs – an interest that extends beyond transborder relations to the organization of official business trips abroad. Governors increasingly regard such trips as a means to establish or strengthen direct contacts with foreign national and constituent governments as well as with technical cooperation agencies.

Second, there is the geopolitical location of each province. As noted above, Argentina borders on five countries – four of them unitary and one federal. Sixteen of a total of twenty-three Argentine provinces are border provinces. The country's geography puts complex issues such as immigration, cross-border infrastructure, security, sanitation, and the fishing and sharing of rivers on the agendas of neighbouring constituent governments on both sides of the border.

A third factor influencing provincial activity internationally is economics. Overall, sound evidence shows that the smaller and poorer the province, the less active it will be in international affairs. Larger and wealthier provinces – particularly those with more mature productive structures and more abundant natural resources – regard export promotion as a key development issue. As the chief nodal points of the so-called Region Centro, the cities of Rosario and Córdoba, for instance, have invested substantial financial and human resources in strengthening their trade position vis-à-vis other world regions and especially Asia.

On this count, the pattern seems to be that provinces having (1) strong political will and institutional capacity, (2) at least one international border, and (3) economic strength show more pronounced activism in international relations.

Regional and Interregional Relations

The dynamics of provincial activism in international affairs cannot be understood fully without considering regional and interregional arrangements with local government units in neighbouring countries.[22] At the first level is the previously mentioned Committee of Integration, a mechanism for helping border provinces to manage their bilateral relationships with neighbouring provinces and localities.

Operating at a second level is the formation and operation of regions. As mentioned earlier, the national Constitution entitles the provinces to sign agreements in order to establish regions with the primary objective of promoting economic and social development. In practice, the formation of regions involves the implementation of common policies by member provinces in diverse areas such as trade, public services, transport, national parks, and environment. In many cases, Argentine regions create their own institutional structures. The effectiveness of regional policies in the international arena varies greatly from region to region and also changes through time. But one clear advantage for provinces of forming regions is the consolidation of a "critical mass" not only to facilitate trips abroad that promote trade, tourism, and investment but also to make demands of the national government from a better position.

Aside from the autonomous city of Buenos Aires (which has a special regime) and the province of Buenos Aires, the provinces are grouped into five regions. Each region presents different particularities in terms both of its formation and institutional development and of its international objectives and strategies. As early as 1984, the provinces of Chaco, Corrientes, Formosa, Misiones, and Santa Fe endorsed the Resistencia Declaration. This declaration formed the basis of the Regional Commission for Foreign Trade of the Litoral-Northeast Region (CRECENEA-Litoral, or NEA). In 1988 Cuyo (a region comprising the provinces of La Rioja, Mendoza, San Juan, and San Luis) signed the Treaty of Economic Integration of the Nuevo Cuyo, with the main objective of consolidating as a bloc. International actions are an important aspect of the treaty. Among its priorities are (1) the opening of corridors to the Pacific via Chile, (2) the development of communication and transportation, (3) the attraction of international capital and financing, (4) the promotion of foreign trade, and (5) the enhancement of shared infrastructure with Chile.[23] A third region was formed by the provinces of the Northwest (Salta, Jujuy, Tucumán, Catamarca, and Santiago del Estero), which signed the Constituent Act of the Northwest Region (Region del Noroeste Argentino, or NOA). Although most coordinated actions of NOA appear to be domestic, functions such as the promotion of tourism and the construction of transborder infrastructure (mainly roads and energy) are important for provincial foreign relations.

In 1996 the provinces of Tierra del Fuego, Santa Cruz, Chubut, La Pampa, Rio Negro, and Neuquen created the Patagonian Region. Most of Patagonia's international actions as a region promote tourism. Among the most important have been the creation of the regional office Patagonia Turistica and the negotiation of integrated tourism itineraries with neighbouring regions in Chile. Following the general trend, the provinces of Córdoba and Santa Fe formed the Region Centro (Centre Region) in 1998; Entre Ríos then joined this region in 1999. Trade, particularly within MERCOSUR and with Asia via Chile, is a key priority for the Centre Region. Another crucial aim is to develop bi-oceanic corridors.

At a third level are what are commonly called "macro-regions," based on regional agreements between contiguous constituent units. One case is the region of Norte Grande, which was joined by those of NEA and NOA. These regions formed a subregion within MERCOSUR called the Zona de

Integracion del Centro Oeste Sudamericano (ZICOSUR). ZICOSUR also includes the Brazilian states of Mato Grosso, Mato Grosso do Sul, and Parana; the Chilean northern regions of Tarapacá, Antofagasta, and Atacama; the Bolivian departments of Potosi and Tarija; the southern regions of Peru; and Paraguay.

In essence, ZICOSUR is a common economic, commercial, and cultural project that involves quite ambitious objectives. These are (1) development of multimodal bi-oceanic corridors; (2) articulation of a subregional project of transport, communications, and logistics; (3) integration of energy supplies; (4) connection of integrated tourist itineraries; (5) exchange of technologic and scientific resources; and (6) incorporation of value added to the available natural resources. ZICOSUR is considered by some to be an alternative project to the metropolitan axis of Buenos Aires, San Paolo (Brazil), and Santiago (Chile). The participants saw it as fitting their economic needs better than MERCOSUR as a whole. One of their greatest motivations to join this zone was that it would allow them to gain access to the Pacific through Chilean ports.

The other macro-regional unit is Crecenea Litoral-Codesul, which includes the north-eastern provinces of Argentina (NEA) and the Brazilian states of Rio Grande do Sul, Parana, and Santa Catarina. With mainly trade objectives, this interregional agreement was institutionalized in 1998 with the signing of the Protocolo Regional Fronterizo 23 (Regional Border Protocol 23). In practice, however, the vitality of Crecenea Litoral-Codesul has not remained constant over the years. At the very beginning, this macro-region initiated relations with countries such as Chile, Paraguay, and Uruguay, as well as with the European Union. A relatively long period of inaction followed, enduring until 2005, when governors apparently decided to relaunch the project with more modest objectives, such as the organization of common trade-promotion activities.

The International Ramifications of Local Policies

The involvement of Argentine provinces in international affairs seems to follow a policy-specific pattern. The provinces do not have their own foreign policies; instead, there are international ramifications of autonomous territorial policies. Overall, the provinces play a marginal role when foreign policy decisions are made. Yet this pattern is more apparent in "high" politics than in "low" political areas such as the environment and development of infrastructure. More important, negotiations with neighbouring countries on matters affecting border provinces usually rely on close provincial involvement. In this context, each policy area differs in the degree of coordination between the various orders of government as well as in the nature of federal-local interaction (e.g., formal vs informal agreements and use of bureaucratic vs political channels).

The use and management of natural resources – rivers, fisheries, oil and gas fields, hydroelectric projects, ecosystems, and so on – is a policy area with significant international dimensions. It has already been noted that the provinces enjoy control over natural resources. This control both justifies and legitimates their participation in the national government's negotiations on natural resources with other countries, particularly neighbouring countries. For the national government, the need to combine provincial interests with its more embracing international relations poses significant challenges. The case of native forests illustrates the conflict between (provincial) interests and (international) commitments. Argentina has 33 million hectares of native forests, but in the past decade the expansion of agriculture, driven largely by the boom in the growth of transgenic soy, has led to the destruction of nearly 300,000 hectares a year, even in protected areas.[24] A crucial case is Salta, rich in native forests, which has authorized logging in formerly protected areas. On the one hand, there is a provincial interest in furthering its development by encouraging agriculture. On the other hand, there is a national (constitutional) commitment to making sustainable use of the environment, although there are difficulties in enforcing this commitment. As a result, relatively weak enforcement powers can lead to a rather ambiguous policy. Notwithstanding this, Argentina formally adheres to the Convention on the International Trade in Endangered Species of Wild Fauna and Flora, the Convention on Biological Diversity, and the Kyoto Protocol on reduction of greenhouse gas emissions.

Straddling Argentina and Chile, the binational mining project of Pascua Lama provides an example of provincial participation in border issues. With Pascua Lama, the province of San Juan was directly involved not only in promoting the mining initiative but also in bilateral negotiations with Chile and in the attendant environmental evaluation process. Another example is provided by the hydroelectric project of Garabi, located between Argentina and Brazil. This initiative relies on active participation by the provinces of Corrientes and Misiones both in technical matters (e.g., assessment of environmental impact) and in political ones (e.g., measuring effects on the provincial power system).[25] Perhaps the most prominent case of cross-border internationalization has been the construction of cellulose plants in Fray Bentos. Although these plants are located in Uruguay, they share a river with Argentina. Building the plants initially provoked criticism and opposition in the province of Entre Rios – particularly in the neighbouring city of Gualeguaychu – and this reaction was later incorporated in the position taken by the national government. One final prominent example is the national law on hydrocarbons, locally known as Ley Corta. In the debate surrounding this law, the Organizacion Federal de Estados Productores de Hidrocarburos (Federal Organization of the Hydrocarbon-Producing States, or OFEPHI) played a major role in building a consensus with the national government on key elements such as the recognition of dominion, exploitation, and foreign investment.

A second major local policy area with international implications is infrastructure. Infrastructure endeavours are considered a fundamental tool for local and regional development, especially for regions distant from Buenos Aires. This explains the strong demands of provinces and regions that the national government provide works of cross-border infrastructure that will allow cheaper and more direct access to neighbouring countries. Building a multimodal transport system that consolidates bi-oceanic corridors from the Atlantic (Argentina) to the Pacific (Chile) is a top priority, one that also benefits Brazil, Uruguay, Paraguay, and Bolivia. A further strategic aim for the Northern Region in particular is to build roads to Bolivia and Paraguay, partner countries in ZICOSUR. Even though border regions share the sense that as many corridors as possible should be opened, each province obviously lobbies for the implementation of those projects planned for its own territory. A similar attitude may be observed for the construction of routes linking Argentina and Chile through the Andes and the resulting access to the Pacific Ocean.

The provinces are also very active in the national definition of priorities within the Iniciativa para la Integración de la Infraestructura Regional Suramericana (Initiative for Integration of the South American Infrastructure, or IIRSA). Broadly, IIRSA aims to promote the development of transport, energy, and communication infrastructure in twelve South American countries in order to integrate them as a region. Currently, 135 potential projects involve Argentine provinces; these projects involve varied processes such as integration in the energy sector, systems of multimodal transport, and border-crossing facilities.[26]

For much of Argentina's history, a federally conceived foreign policy on culture has not been a priority. This has meant that Argentina has not taken advantage of the opportunity to fully exploit its consistently strong soft-power status in the region. Provinces have usually relied on their own strategies and resources to give culture a place in their foreign-outreach programs. A typical pattern has been to link culture with tourism. Argentina is known in the world mainly for its expansive and diverse landscapes, its high-quality food, its tango dance and sports, and its rich provincial traditions in local dances, regional foods, and historical sites. Thus provinces or regions have typically developed their own business plans in line with the areas in which they excel. Patagonia, for instance, is known worldwide for its wilderness and whale-watching attractions as well as for its lakes and mountains. Through the years, this region has developed its own international identity, to the point where many people are aware or have heard of Patagonia without knowing much about it.

In recent years, tourism has proved one of the most dynamic sectors in the Argentine economy. The country's federal character contributes to the development of regional economies that promote private and international investments. In 2004 tourism accounted for more than 4% of GDP. Increasingly aware of the role that tourism might play in regional economies, the federal government promulgated a national law on tourism to establish the Consejo Federal de Turismo (Federal Council of Tourism). Thought to be mainly a consultative body, this council is integrated by representatives of each province plus the city of Buenos Aires.

Foreign Trade

International trade policy has always been an area of provincial concern. With varying degrees of success, the provinces have struggled to have a say both in general trade policy and in specific international negotiations. The general pattern of influence in policy decisions is the following: the more geographically concentrated and horizontally integrated the economic sector at stake in a given international negotiation, the more voice (and lobbying power) the private actors will have. In these circumstances, the role of the provinces appears to be more that of a supporter of private demands than that of a relevant decider of the national stance. This was the case with the sugar negotiations, for example, involving MERCOSUR and the northern provinces.[27]

As for cases in which provinces are directly involved in trade, these are concentrated mainly in commercial promotion. Among the most common actions are the following: assistance to small and medium-sized companies for participation in international trade fairs and exhibitions, organization of trade missions led by governors and joined by businesspeople, coordination of training courses for local businesses interested in exporting, and signing international agreements that promote the exchange of certain goods. It is also important to mention that in some cases when provinces organize trips abroad, the promotion of trade is not the only issue on the agenda. Usually, the governors organize meetings with local authorities and companies to attract foreign investment and promote tourism.

The provinces do not generally have representative offices abroad, although there are a few exceptions. One is the province of Mendoza, which opened two offices – one in San Paolo, the other in Brussels – through Pro-Mendoza, the province's trade-promotion agency. The main purpose of these offices is to develop commercial intelligence and to promote the export of local goods such as wine, juice, fruit, and other agricultural products in its two most important export markets: Brazil and the EU. Authorities of ProMendoza have explained that their offices work in close contact with the network of Argentine embassies. In 2005 and with similar objectives, Entre Rios reopened its Economic Promotion Agency in Brazil, which represents its most important export market. Due to the high costs of maintaining offices abroad, however, such cases are rare.[28] When organizing trade missions or acquiring market information, provincial officials typically rely on the assistance of Argentine embassies and consulates. On some occasions, they also work with the Federal Council of Investment.

Overseas Technical Assistance and International Cooperation

Argentine provinces undertake relations with foreign partners on behalf of the national government by providing overseas technical assistance. In the early 1990s Argentina advanced from being a net beneficiary to being a dual beneficiary and donor. As a donor through the Argentine Fund for International Cooperation (FO-AR), Argentina has undertaken more than 3,558 actions since 1992. The provinces have actively participated mainly in sending local experts abroad. According to information provided by some provinces' webpages, most of these projects are related to technical affairs such as engineering, environment, and agriculture, among others. To cite just two examples, the province of Córdoba arranged a visit of Argentine engineers to El Salvador in order to provide technical assistance in managing waste water. Similarly, the city of Buenos Aires has facilitated visits by technicians to Guatemala, Honduras, Panama, Paraguay, Cuba, El Salvador, the Dominican Republic, Costa Rica, Nicaragua, and Uruguay.

In addition to providing technical assistance, the provinces are also direct recipients of international cooperation. This can take the forms of multilateral, bilateral, or decentralized cooperation. International cooperation usually involves actions like hiring experts, training, and purchasing equipment. Multilateral agencies working with the provinces include the UN Food and Agriculture Organization, the European Union, the Organization of American States, and the United Nations Development Program (UNDP). To provide an example, the UNDP, together with the Committee of Provinces comprising the Consejo Argentino para las Relaciones Internacionales (CARI), implemented a nationwide project that surveys and analyzes the international actions developed by Argentine provinces in the areas of infrastructure, trade, natural resources, and cooperation.

Cities, Municipalities, and Twinning Initiatives

Most of the international activities of cities and municipalities involve twinning and partnership agreements. It is still uncommon to see local governments organize trips abroad, sign international treaties, or open offices abroad. Perhaps the Ciudad Autonoma de Buenos Aires is one of the few exceptions, and this might be due not only to the special regime granted Buenos Aires by the national Constitution but also to its economic leverage.

Twinning initiatives that establish sister-cities have traditionally worked in a highly decentralized, nonpatterned manner. The randomness of this procedure has contributed to some of these initiatives becoming partnerships solely on paper, whereas others have achieved a high level of cooperation.

In response to the growing yet somewhat inarticulated interest in partnering with foreign cities, the Directorate of Federal Affairs is poised to formalize the whole process and thereby to make it more coherent and effective. For instance, it encourages provinces and municipalities to conduct thorough research in order to conclude whether a partnership with a target city will offer concrete benefits. The directorate has also established a ten-step scheme for proceeding with partnerships or twinning agreements. Beginning with the identification of a potential partner, the scheme proceeds through an exchange of notes of intention supervised by the Ministry of Foreign Affairs and concludes with the signing of the partnership and ratification by local legislatures.

Although twinning and partnerships are not new tools, provinces and municipalities have only recently begun to notice their potential. The directorate has undertaken substantial efforts to convince the provinces that it seeks to help them achieve effective partnerships rather than to block their international activities. A small yet significant step toward this goal has been its publication, on a website, of the complete list of partnerships signed by provinces and cities.[29] Whereas this information was hard to obtain even for the provinces, its provision by the directorate marks substantial progress. In this vein, the Committee of Provinces of CARI, together with a number of the provinces and the Federal Council of Investment, has implemented a joint program to digitize all lower-level international agreements, including city partnerships.

Argentine cities have 336 partnerships with forty foreign counterparts. Italy is the preferred partner country, with 32% of total partnerships. This is mainly for historical reasons (migration to Argentina) and because of political incentives. Italian regions, which have been leaders in the internationalization of subnational units, have found in Argentina (this is where history comes in) a country very receptive to further joint interests. Following Italy are Spain (29%), the United States (25%), and Brazil (23%). These four countries account for almost 55% of the total partnerships, followed by Chile (20%), China (13%), Russia (11%), Uruguay (9%), Israel (9%), and Paraguay (7%). This pattern can be understood in terms of history (Spain, Italy, and Israel), power (the United States, Russia, and China), and proximity (Brazil, Chile, Uruguay, and Paraguay). As a result, countries in Africa, Asia, and the Middle East are rarely considered in the search for a partner.

Buenos Aires, Córdoba, Santa Fe, and the capital city account for 78% of total partnerships, reflecting that these are the most internationalized areas of the country. Most agreements are not signed by the provinces as a whole but by municipalities such as Rosario (Province of Santa Fe), Córdoba, and La Matanza (Province of Buenos Aires).

CONCLUSION

Briefly, the responses to four questions summarize the essence of this chapter.

First, what are the characteristics of the politico-institutional context that promote provincial involvement in international activities? Of primary importance is the return of democracy in 1983, which enabled the reconstruction of a more cooperative, consensus-based federal arrangement. At the same time, regional integration in Latin America created a climate and incentives for provinces to look abroad and thus to explore how international engagement could serve their local needs and interests. The constitutional reform of 1994 introduced important changes to Argentine federalism, changes that affected the country's international relations. Finally, more recently, the Ministry of Foreign Affairs gave provinces and municipalities more latitude in policy planning, particularly in matters related to trade.

Second, what are the incentives for provinces to become engaged in international relations? Provincial international engagement depends on political will. Governors and executive authorities must have an international vision and a strong interest in establishing direct contacts with foreign national and constituent governments as well as with agencies that provide technical cooperation. Economic incentives are also crucial. Evidence shows that the smaller and poorer the province, the less active it will be in international affairs. By comparison, larger and wealthier provinces regard the promotion of exports as a key issue for economic development. Furthermore, the geopolitical location of each province matters. Issues such as immigration, developing cross-border infrastructure, providing security and sanitation, and sharing riparian resources offer strong incentives for constituent governments on both sides of an international border to cooperate and to develop common management strategies. Finally, the exploitation of natural resources affects the incentive stucture too. The Argentine Constitution assigns provinces ownership of their natural resources. Hence they have a strong say in investment, regulation, and infrastructure development in the energy sector, a sector that has important international ramifications.

Third, what constraints limit the international activities of the provinces? Four can be mentioned. First, elections are a factor that conditions provincial activism in international affairs. Changes of governments sometimes bring changes in institutional structures, putting institutional memory at risk. Second, the scarcity of financial resources on some occasions forces an end to programs. Third, the shortage of expertise in international affairs discourages forward-looking thinking and planning. Fourth, within the national government, the weakness of coordination mechanisms in some of the key policy areas with important international ramifications limits effectiveness. The problem, a lack of information on "who does what" among the three orders of government, has not yet been completely solved.

Fourth, what are the relevant emerging prospects and trends? In the near future, provincial international activities will grow in number and variety. Currently active provinces will develop a profile as international players as they gain experience and are encouraged by positive results. Smaller provinces will progressively develop international strategies and actions of their own. Also, policy sectors traditionally considered domestic will have more (and new) international ramifications. Policy sectors such as cultural affairs, energy, the environment, tourism, and infrastructure will probably have a greater international profile. Finally, perhaps the medium term will see the consolidation of some regions and macro-regions as alternative (and complementary) integration projects for smaller provinces.

NOTES

1 For background, see also Antonio M. Hernandez, "Republic of Argentina," in Katy Le Roy and Cheryl Saunders, eds, *Legislative, Executive, and Judicial Governance in Federal Countries*, 8–36 (Mon-treal and Kingston: McGill-Queen's University Press, 2006).
2 Centro de Economia Internacional, *Argentine Economic Overview No. 47* (2006), 1–2, http://www.cei.gov.ar/pdf/eco/pea/peaeng.pdf (accessed 1 March 2007).
3 "El 48% de las inversiones se concentra en cuatro provincias," *La Nación* (Buenos Aires), 9 December 2005, 10.
4 Centro de Economia Internacional (CEI), *Exportaciones por Provincia, 2001–2005* (Buenos Aires: CEI, 2006), 6–7.
5 See Barry Buzan, Ole Wæver, and Jaap de Wilde, *Security: A New Framework for Analysis* (London: Lynne Rienner, 1998).
6 Art. 4, Resolution 41/04.
7 For their part, although provinces are not "subjects" in defence policies, when domestic peace is threatened, they become objects. Article 6 of the Constitution establishes that "the federal government may intervene in the territory of the provinces in order to guarantee the republican form of government or to repel foreign invasions; and at the request of their constituted authorities, it may intervene to support or reestablish them, should they have been deposed by sedition or invasion from another province."

8 Constitution, Article 31: "This Constitution, the laws of the Nation enacted by Congress in pursuance thereof, and treaties with foreign powers, are the supreme law of the Nation; and the authorities of each province are bound thereby, notwithstanding any provision to the contrary included in the provincial laws or constitutions, except for the province of Buenos Aires, the treaties ratified after the Pact of November 11, 1859." To be approved, an international treaty needs two-thirds of the votes of the members of each house.

9 Constitution, Article 75.

10 An English version of the Constitution is provided by the Chambers of Senators at: http://www.senado.gov.ar/web/interes/constitucion/english.php (accessed 20 July 2007).

11 The issue related to the regions and its activities is analyzed below in the subsection "Regional and Interregional Relations."

12 Article 124 is legally binding on both the national and provincial governments. However, the Constitution allows a clause to remain "unregulated," meaning that Congress does not pass legislation to specify conditions for its application in the provinces and that provinces do not incorporate the clause into their constitutions or specify how the clause is to be implemented in their jurisdictions. Article 124 has not been regulated in either sense, a state of affairs preferable to the provinces because it allows them maximum flexibility in pursuing their foreign relations. They can thus sign agreements with foreign partners without reference to the national government as long as they deem such agreements not to be in conflict with its powers over foreign policy and external credit or with those powers delegated to it by the provinces in the Constitution.

13 Alberto Dalla Via, "El Marco Jurídico e Institucional para la Gestión Internacional de los Actores Subnacionales Gubernamentales en la Argentina," *Revista Comercio e Integración* 21 (2004): 21–38, at 21.

14 Antonio Hernández, *Integración y globalización: Rol de las regiones, provincias y municipios* (Buenos Aires: Depalma, 2000).

15 Dalla Via, "El Marco Jurídico," 21.

16 See Graciela Zubelzu, "Provincias y Relaciones Internacionales – Primer Informe," in *Consejo Argentino para las Relaciones Internacionales – CARI/UNDP Argentina* (2004), http://www.cari.org.ar (accessed 6 March 2007).

17 See ibid., 28–9.

18 See http://www.promocion.ar (accessed 7 March 2007).

19 Eugenio Valenciano, "La Frontera: Un nuevo rol frente a la integración: La experiencia en el MERCOSUR." Paper presented at the conference "La integración fronteriza y el papel de las regiones en la Unión Europea y en el Cono Sur: experiencias, opciones y estrategias," Centro de Integracion Regional (CEFIR), Montevideo, 23–7 October 1995, 27.

20 Luis Lucioni, "Orientación del financiamiento de organismos multilaterales a Provincias," *Serie de Estudios y Perspectivas / CEPAL Argentina* 17 (2003): 3–22, at 7.

21 Miryam Colacrai and Graciela Zubelzu, "Las vinculaciones externas y la capacidad de gestión internacional desplegadas por las provincias argentinas en la ultima década: Una lectura desde las relaciones internacionales," in Tulio Vigevani, Luiz Eduardo Wandarley, Maria Ines Barreto, and Marcelo Passini Mariano, eds, *A dimensao subnacional e as relacoes internacionais*, 23–45. San Pablo: Puc Editora, UNESP/CEDEC/FAPESP, 2004.
22 Valeria Iglesias, "Las Provincias Argentinas y su accionar en material de comercio exterior," in *Consejo Argentino para las Relaciones Internacionales – CARI/UNDP Argentina* (2005), 23–4, http://www.cari.org.ar (accessed 7 March 2007).
23 Graciela Zubelzu, "Provincias y Relaciones Internacionales – Segundo Informe," in *Consejo Argentino para las Relaciones Internacionales – CARI/UNDP Argentina* (2005), 10, http://www.cari.org.ar (accessed 7 March 2007).
24 See Greenpeace Argentina's website: http://www.greenpeace.org/argentina/bosques (accessed 3 March 2007).
25 Miryam Colacrai, "Subnational Cooperation and Federal Government in Border Areas and the Development of Physical Infrastructure," *Integration and Trade* 21 (2004): 134–55, at 144–5.
26 See the website of Centro de Derechos Humanos y Ambiente (CEDHA): http://www.cedha.org.ar (accessed 5 March 2007).
27 Iglesias, "Las Provincias Argentinas."
28 Little information is available on the budgets for provincial agencies in charge of international activities. One of the most active foreign trade-promotion agencies, Baexporta, had a budget of nearly US$800,000 for export promotion in 2006. See Herán Sánchez, "El destino de los subsidios," *La Tecla* (Buenos Aires), 27 July 2006, 19.
29 See http://www.mrecic.gov.ar (accessed 6 July 2008).

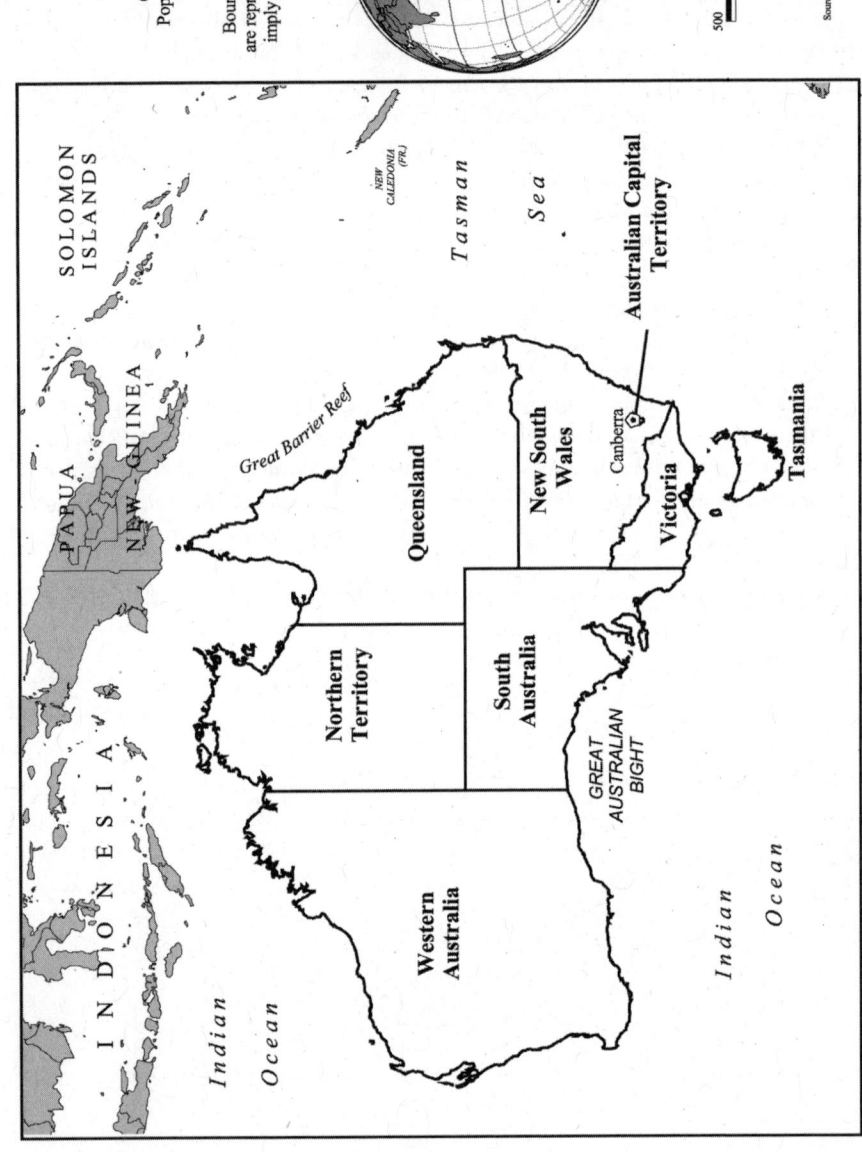

Australia

Capital: Canberra
Population: 20 Million (2004 est.)

Boundaries and place names are representative only and do not imply any official endorsement.

Sources: CIA World Factbook; ESRI Ltd.; Times Atlas of the World

Commonwealth of Australia

ANNE TWOMEY

Power over foreign affairs in Australia has been affected by Australia's colonial background.[1] Even after the Commonwealth of Australia was established in 1901 by the federation of Australian colonies, the treaty power was retained by the British government. It was later devolved upon the Commonwealth government. Although most states have overseas offices and enter into international arrangements concerning trade and exchanges of information and skills, they do not have international personality and play only a minor role in foreign affairs. Instead, the Commonwealth holds the key executive and legislative powers over foreign affairs. Once the Commonwealth enters into a treaty, it obtains the power to legislate to implement it, regardless of whether the treaty's subject matter falls within an area of traditional state jurisdiction. For this reason, the states have focused their attention on reforming the treaty-making process. Significant reforms were made in 1996, enhancing consultation, transparency, and accountability, but there is still room for improvement.

Australia has a largely homogenous population of 21,104,400 people[2] and has, for some decades, supported a policy of multiculturalism. Three-quarters of Australia's population were born in Australia. Of those born overseas, 24% came from the United Kingdom, 9% from New Zealand, 5% from Italy, and 4% each from China and Vietnam. Australia's indigenous people comprise just over 2% of the population.[3]

Although Australia's land mass is large, much of it is inhospitable desert. Australia is one of the most urbanized countries in the world, with three-quarters of the population living in urban areas, primarily on the eastern seaboard. New South Wales is the most populous state, with 6.8 million inhabitants; Tasmania is the least populous, with 482,000 inhabitants.[4]

Australia has the thirteenth-largest economy in the world.[5] Its gross domestic product (GDP) per capita in 2006 was estimated at US$35,311. Its main exports come from mining and agriculture. As a middle-ranking nation with an efficient economy, Australia actively supports trade liberalization through the World Trade Organization (WTO).[6]

Australia is a federation comprising six states – New South Wales, Queensland, South Australia, Tasmania, Victoria, and Western Australia – as well as a number of self-governing and non-self-governing territories. Each state was a self-governing colony of the British Empire with its own legislature and government prior to federation in 1901. After federation, state governments and legislatures continued to operate, and state constitutions were preserved by Section 106 of the Commonwealth Constitution.

There are ten territories that fall under the constitutional responsibility of the Commonwealth government. Both the Northern Territory and the Australian Capital Territory (an area ceded by New South Wales to the Commonwealth for the establishment of the national capital, Canberra) are self-governing territories with their own legislatures and executives. One of Australia's seven external territories, the Australian Antarctic Territory, forms part of Antarctica.

REGIONAL CONTEXT

Border Issues

Australia, as an island nation, does not directly share borders with other nations (except in relation to the Australian Antarctic Territory). However, boundary issues have arisen in two contexts. First, there have been lengthy negotiations with Indonesia, Papua New Guinea, and more recently East Timor about the maritime boundaries to the north of Australia.[7] Maritime boundary delimitations have also been negotiated with New Zealand, the Solomon Islands, and France.

Second, Australia has had problems with smugglers transporting asylum seekers by boat from Indonesia to Australia. Australia has removed from its migration zone certain Australian islands (i.e., islands to the north of Australia, some of which form part of the states of Queensland and Western Australia). "Unlawful noncitizens" who arrive on these islands cannot apply for visas for permanent residence and can be held offshore in detention while claims for refugee status are determined.

Regional Trade and Cultural Relationships

Australia has three main regional relationships. First, it has a close relationship with New Zealand. Australia and New Zealand entered into a Closer Economic Relations Trade Agreement in March 1983 to remove trade barriers between the two nations. The Commonwealth and most states have enacted cooperative legislation concerning the recognition of regulatory standards adopted in New Zealand regarding goods and occupations.[8]

The 1973 Trans-Tasman Travel Arrangement permits Australian and New Zealand citizens to enter, live, and work in either country without applying to the authorities. Since 2001 New Zealanders have been granted a Special Category Visa upon entering Australia. In June 2005, 449,000 New Zealand citizens were living in Australia.

Second, Australia is also a leading power in the South Pacific. It focuses much of its aid on the South Pacific[9] and has provided nations such as the Solomon Islands, Papua New Guinea, Tonga, and East Timor with police and military assistance where needed, as well as other forms of aid and investment. Australia is a member of the Pacific Islands Forum, which is the region's principal institution for cooperation in trade and economic issues, good governance, and security.

Third, Australia is engaged in the Asian region. Australia's closest neighbour is Indonesia, which has 223 million people. The primary Asian regional organization is the Association of South-East Asian Nations (ASEAN), established in 1967. Australia has not been admitted as a member of ASEAN but has, since 1974, been a "dialogue partner" of ASEAN. Annual meetings are held between ASEAN members and its dialogue partners. Australia and New Zealand are currently negotiating a free trade agreement with ASEAN. Australia already has free trade agreements with Singapore and Thailand, and it is negotiating one with Malaysia. Australia also has strong educational links with this area.

In 2005 Australia also participated in the first East Asia Summit. This is a forum for dialogue to advance closer regional integration on economic and strategic issues. Australia's participation in this summit was accepted by ASEAN members only after Australia acceded to ASEAN's Treaty of Amity and Co-operation.[10]

Defence and Security Relationships

Australia's main security alliance is the ANZUS alliance with the United States. It is also a member of the Five Power Defence Arrangement, which facilitates defence cooperation with Malaysia, Singapore, New Zealand, and the United Kingdom. Australia was heavily involved in the negotiation of the Treaty of Rarotonga, which created a South Pacific Nuclear Free Zone in 1986.

Although not a member of ASEAN, Australia participates in the ASEAN Regional Forum, which was established in 1994. The forum comprises twenty-five countries in the Asia Pacific region, including the ten ASEAN members and the ten dialogue partners. It is the principal forum for security dialogue in Asia. It deals with such matters as regional antiterrorism efforts and disaster relief cooperation.

Participation in International Organizations

Australia participates in two areas of economic cooperation. To its east, Australia is a member of Asia-Pacific Economic Co-operation (APEC), which was established in 1989. Its aims are trade and investment liberalisation, business facilitation, and economic and technical cooperation. To its west, Australia participates in the equivalent, but less well-known, Indian Ocean Rim Association for Regional Co-operation, which was established in 1997. Australia is also an active member of many international organizations, including the United Nations, the Organization for Economic Cooperation and Development (OECD), the Commonwealth of Nations, and as noted above, the WTO.

THE CONSTITUTIONAL SETTING

The Development of Australia's Foreign Affairs Powers[11]

The Commonwealth of Australia came into being on 1 January 1901. Prior to federation, the six Australian colonies were self-governing with respect to local matters,[12] but foreign policy was still regarded as an imperial matter and was controlled by the British government. The Australian colonies had no power to declare war, appoint diplomatic representatives, or enter into treaties on their own behalf (although after 1877 they could accede to commercial treaties entered into by the United Kingdom). They were not regarded as having an international personality.

Federation, in 1901, did not transform the Australian colonies into a sovereign nation. It merely joined six colonies into one larger federated colony.[13] Political foreign policy was still conducted by the British government. The Constitution contained no express power to make treaties or any provision giving them binding effect. Instead, in Section 51(xxix), the Commonwealth Parliament was authorized to make laws with respect to "external affairs." The word "external" was used to encompass relations within the empire as well as relations with foreign countries.[14]

After the First World War, the relationship between the United Kingdom and its dominions gradually changed. Australia became a member of both the League of Nations and the International Labour Organization (ILO), with full voting rights. It began, hesitantly, to develop its own foreign policy. At the Imperial Conferences of 1923 and 1926, the empire recognized the power of the dominions, including the Commonwealth of Australia, to enter into treaties on their own behalf. The Statute of Westminster 1931 increased Commonwealth legislative power by allowing the Commonwealth Parliament to make laws with extraterritorial effect and laws that amended or repealed British laws that had previously applied by paramount force. It did not deal with the Commonwealth's executive power, and no formal change was made to the Commonwealth Constitution. Courts have, therefore, been obliged to give an expanded interpretation of the executive power in Section 61 of the Constitution in order to accommodate a treaty-making power that did not exist at federation.[15] The power to declare war was first exercised by Australia in 1941, and Australia's first diplomatic representatives were appointed in 1940.

As this history shows, most powers in relation to foreign affairs were not made exercisable in Australia until well after federation and therefore devolved upon the Commonwealth rather than the states. The absence of any formal constitutional amendment effecting this change has meant that the Constitution has had to be reinterpreted by the courts to conform to reality. Although this has led to disputes about the extent of the Commonwealth's power, particularly in relation to the enactment of legislation that impinges on traditional areas of state jurisdiction, there is a general acceptance in Australia that the primary role in foreign affairs belongs to the Commonwealth.

Foreign Affairs and Commonwealth Executive Power

The power to enter into treaties, appoint diplomatic representatives, and generally conduct foreign policy is now recognized as finding its source in Section 61 of the Constitution, which makes the executive power of the Commonwealth exercisable by the governor general.[16] The governor general's role is purely formal in this regard and is analogous to that of the queen in the United Kingdom. The governor general acts on the advice of Commonwealth ministers. In practice, executive power lies with the Cabinet, which undertakes major policy decisions.

Treaties are not self-executing in Australia. They must be implemented by legislation before they are binding under Australian law. Although there may be legitimate expectations, recognized by administrative law, that the Commonwealth government will take its treaty obligations into account when making administrative decisions, treaties do not have the force of law in Australia unless implemented by Commonwealth or state legislation.[17]

Foreign Affairs and Commonwealth Legislative Powers

The Commonwealth has a range of legislative powers to deal with external matters. Section 51 of the Constitution confers upon the Commonwealth Parliament the power to make laws with respect to various subjects, including trade and commerce with other countries, defence, external fisheries, naturalization and aliens, foreign corporations, immigration and emigration, and external affairs.

In addition, under Section 51(xxxvii), state parliaments may refer matters to the Commonwealth Parliament, giving it power to legislate in relation to them. This mechanism was used to deal with the mutual recognition of standards and qualifications in New Zealand and Australia. Further, under Section 51(xxxviii), the Commonwealth may exercise, at the request of state parliaments, any power that at the time of federation could be exercised only by the Westminster Parliament. This has been used to deal with Commonwealth and state powers with respect to the territorial sea.[18]

Defence Powers

Section 69 of the Constitution required that, after federation, state public-service departments concerning naval and military defence be transferred to the Commonwealth. This occurred on 1 March 1901. From that point, the states lost all power and involvement in defence matters. Section 114 of the Constitution prohibits the states from raising or maintaining any naval or military force without the consent of the Commonwealth Parliament. No such consent has ever been given.

Each state has its own police force but does not have any military or defence personnel. In accordance with an intergovernmental agreement, the state police forces and the Commonwealth armed forces hold regular joint training exercises focused on dealing with potential terrorist threats or civil disorder. Section 119 of the Constitution provides that the Commonwealth "shall protect every State against invasion and, on the application of the Executive Government of the State, against domestic violence."

The Commonwealth's power to legislate with respect to naval and military defence in Section 51(vi) of the Constitution has been held by the High Court to expand in times of war and contract in times of peace.[19] The High Court has recently interpreted it widely to support antiterrorism laws, despite its being implemented in a time of peace.[20]

Section 68 of the Constitution vests control of naval and military forces in the governor general, a civilian, who acts on the advice of Commonwealth ministers. If the governor general dies or is otherwise absent or unavailable, the most senior state governor performs the governor general's functions as administrator of the Commonwealth. Accordingly, from time to time, the titular control of the armed forces is vested in a state governor (albeit while acting in a Commonwealth capacity). Defence decisions are still made by the Commonwealth government.

The External Affairs Power

The external affairs power in Section 51(xxix) has proved to be one of the most controversial powers in the Commonwealth Constitution. This is in part the consequence of the way the federal system was established in Australia. The Constitution does not reserve specific subjects of legislative power for the states. Instead, it lists the legislative powers of the Commonwealth with respect to specific subjects. Most of these legislative powers are concurrent rather than exclusive. State constitutions confer plenary legislative power on state parliaments, subject to any express or implied prohibitions in the Commonwealth Constitution. Section 109 provides that where there is an inconsistency, the Commonwealth law prevails and the state law is ineffective to the extent of the inconsistency.

Early judicial attempts to read Commonwealth powers narrowly so that they would not impinge on matters impliedly reserved for the states (such as agriculture, land management, internal trade, and the criminal law) were overturned by the High Court in 1920.[21] Since then, Commonwealth legislative power has been read broadly, and it is regarded as constitutional heresy to treat traditional areas of state legislative activity as reserved for the states.

Can the "external affairs" power be used to implement treaties on subjects that are "internal" to Australia and fall within traditional areas of state jurisdiction? This question remained unsettled until 1983, when the High Court held that once a bona fide treaty has been entered into by Australia, the Commonwealth Parliament has the power to legislate to implement the treaty obligations, subject to any express or implied constitutional prohibitions.[22] The court was not prepared to draw distinctions based on whether a matter was domestic in nature or of international concern.

In a series of subsequent cases, the High Court developed and refined the limits of the external affairs power with respect to treaty implementation. It is not necessary that the whole of a treaty be implemented. Legislation that partially implements a treaty will be supported by Section 51 (xxix) but not if the implementation is so selective as to deny the law the character of a measure that implements the treaty and not if, in combination with other provisions, the law is substantially inconsistent with the treaty.[23] The treaty itself must impose sufficiently precise obligations, rather than mere aspirations that could be implemented by a variety of possibly contradictory measures.[24] The means chosen by the Commonwealth Parliament to implement the treaty must be "reasonably capable of being considered appropriate and adapted to implementing the treaty."[25] This is sometimes interpreted as requiring reasonable proportionality between the object of the treaty and the means used to implement it. If a Commonwealth law is unnecessarily wide in its purported implementation of a treaty, it may be struck down.

The effect of the High Court's interpretation of Section 51 (xxix) is that the Commonwealth government, by entering into a treaty, may increase the scope of its power to legislate in relation to any subject, as long as its legislation implements the treaty. The Commonwealth may also have the power to legislate to implement the recommendations of international bodies or to legislate with respect to matters of international concern.[26] The consequence has been that through the ratification of treaties, the Commonwealth Parliament has gained new powers to enact laws with respect to human rights, industrial matters, environmental protection, and land management.

The High Court has also interpreted the external affairs power widely with respect to nontreaty matters. In 1991 it held that Section 51(xxix) supports legislation with respect to persons, places, matters, and things that are geographically external to Australia.[27] It therefore supports legislation on subjects such as crimes that occur outside Australia and external petroleum exploration, regardless of the validity of any treaty on the subject.[28] A challenge to the breadth of this interpretation recently attracted some support, but a majority of the High Court upheld the broad "geographical externality" interpretation.[29]

State Foreign Affairs Powers

The states do not have an international personality[30] and cannot enter into treaties on their own behalf.[31] The extent of their powers to enter into agreements of less than treaty status and to participate in international affairs remains uncertain.[32] As a matter of theory, some observers would deny that the states have any such power,[33] but as a matter of practice, states do from time to time enter into memoranda of understanding and other agreements of less than treaty status with national or subnational governments. The most internationally active states are those, such as Queensland and Western Australia, that are trying to expand their export markets and that are therefore seeking cooperation with foreign governments as well as business.

The types of international agreements that states enter into tend to concern matters in which the states have particular expertise. States have entered into memoranda of understanding with neighbouring countries and subnational governments on subjects such as training on bushfire prevention, preservation of flora and fauna, and cooperation in academic and applied research. For example, states such as Western Australia with expertise in agriculture in dry climates and desertification have entered into agreements with countries that have similar climates.[34] States have also entered into agreements concerning areas of trade, industry, and technology where they are seeking to develop markets or expertise. For example, in 2007 the Queensland government entered into an agreement with the US state of South Carolina on cooperative development in biotechnology.[35]

In many cases, agreements may be overseen by state governments and signed by a state premier, but they are actually made between agencies or institutions at a lower level. See, for example, the following agreements in which the Queensland government participated in 2007: a memorandum of understanding between the Queensland Mater Hospital and the Central Java Department of Health, which provides for cooperation in health administration and the exchange and training of staff; an accord between the Queensland Department of Primary Industries and Fisheries and the University of KwaZulu-Natal, South Africa, for exchanges of information and expertise; and an agreement for cooperation in international research between the Queensland Climate Change Centre of Excellence and the Walker Institute for Climate System Research at the University of Reading in the United Kingdom.[36]

In most cases, such agreements are not legally enforceable and merely require states or their institutions to make best endeavours or to open avenues for future projects. In some cases, the agreements are contractual in nature and are enforceable as a matter of private law. In other cases, the status of these agreements remains unclear.[37]

Some foreign relationships relate to the geographical location of the jurisdiction concerned. For example, the Northern Territory entered into a memorandum of understanding with Indonesia on economic development cooperation in 1992 because of its proximity to Indonesia. It later entered into memoranda of cooperation with the Indonesian province of East Kalimantan in 2000 and with the province of Bali in 2001. These agreements pave the way for increased cooperation on infrastructure development, mining, transportation, agriculture, tourism, education, industry, fishery management, and communications.

In 1995 the Northern Territory entered into another major memorandum of understanding with the Philippines. The Northern Territory now participates as a development partner with one of the ASEAN Growth Areas, being invited to meetings of senior officials on trade matters. These agreements have resulted in exchange visits of government delegations, increased trade opportunities, including access to key trade exhibitions, and the promotion of joint projects in areas such as air and sea linkages and educational exchanges between universities. Even though the Northern Territory does not have the status of a state, it is still a self-governing territory with its own legislature and executive, and its efforts to interact with neighbouring countries have been rewarded with a degree of international recognition and significant trade advantages.

The Constitution does not deny the states legislative powers with respect to external affairs. States often legislate to give effect to treaties. Before entering into a treaty, the Commonwealth and the states sometimes agree that it will be implemented by state legislation because the states have the most appropriate institutions or mechanisms to do so. However, if a state law is inconsistent with a valid Commonwealth law, the Commonwealth law prevails under Section 109 of the Constitution. Further, if state legislation attempted to confer treaty-making powers upon the state executive, the validity of such legislation would be highly questionable.[38]

Some doubts existed in the past about whether the Australian states have the power to legislate with extraterritorial effect. The High Court accepted that the states have such a power but required that there be a connection or nexus between a law with extraterritorial effect and the state that enacts it.[39] In 1986 this was confirmed by Section 2(1) of the Australia Acts 1986 (Cth) and (UK), which declares that the states have such a power but maintains the need for a nexus.[40] State laws with extraterritorial effect most commonly apply in other states but have in the past applied to offshore waters or to sailors on ships outside the state that have been registered in the state.[41]

Section 2(2) of the Australia Acts declares that the legislative powers of each state include those that the Westminster Parliament might have exercised in relation to the state before the enactment of the Australia Acts. This was intended to remove any remaining colonial constraints on state legislative power. The Commonwealth, however, was concerned that this provision might be used by the states to support claims to exercise powers associated with national sovereignty. After a great deal of negotiation, a proviso was added to Section 2(2) that "nothing in this subsection confers on a State any capacity that the State did not have immediately before the commencement of this Act to engage in relations with countries outside Australia." This proviso leaves open whether or not the states have such powers. It simply clarifies that Section 2(2) does not enlarge such powers if they already exist.

INTERGOVERNMENTAL RELATIONS IN FOREIGN AFFAIRS

Consultation with the States on Treaty Making

Consultation with the states, prior to the Commonwealth entering into treaties that affected the states, was undertaken as a matter of course throughout most of the twentieth century.[42] Consultation tended to occur through existing federal-state ministerial councils, such as the Standing Committee of Attorneys-General and the Council of Nature Conservation Ministers.[43] The Commonwealth would not ratify treaties concerning subjects of traditional state jurisdiction until all the states agreed. This resulted in a low rate of ratification of ILO conventions and human rights treaties.[44]

In October 1977 the Commonwealth and the states agreed on a set of principles for treaty making. These principles provide for: consultation with states early in treaty negotiations, consultation regarding the implementation of treaties, a first option to the states to legislate to implement treaties within areas of state jurisdiction, the representation of states in delegations to international conferences, and the inclusion of federal clauses in treaties in appropriate cases.[45]

More formal guidelines, known as the Principles and Procedures for Commonwealth-State Consultation on Treaties, were adopted at a premiers' conference in June 1982. These were revised in 1991 and again in 1996 following reforms to the treaty-making system. On each occasion, the revised Principles and Procedures were adopted by an intergovernmental forum, formerly known as the Premiers' Conference and now known as the Council of Australian Governments, which comprises the heads of government of the states, territories, and Commonwealth.

Initially, the Principles and Procedures merely required the Commonwealth to provide information on proposed treaty action to the state premiers' departments. Substantive discussions were left to ministerial councils. The Principles and Procedures provided that the Commonwealth should take into account state views in formulating Australian policy in treaty negotiations and, in appropriate cases, should include state representatives in delegations to international conferences and treaty negotiations. On numerous occasions, state representatives have attended treaty negotiations of significance to the states.[46] For those negotiations that they are able to attend, the states agree among themselves on who will represent them. The states pay the costs of their own representatives.

The Principles and Procedures expressly state that the purpose of inclusion of state representatives on delegations "is not to speak for Australia, but to ensure that the states and territories are well informed on treaty matters and are always in a position to put a point of view to the Commonwealth."[47] However, states do make valuable contributions to treaty negotiations, particularly when the negotiations concern subjects that fall within their expertise.

In July 1991 a Special Premiers' Conference agreed to establish a Standing Committee on Treaties (SCOT) and to revise the Principles and Procedures. The revised version was adopted in 1992. It provided that SCOT would comprise senior officials from the Commonwealth, states, and territories and would meet at least twice a year to:

- identify treaty and other international negotiations of particular sensitivity or importance to the states and propose an appropriate mechanism for state involvement in the negotiation process;
- monitor and report on the implementation of particular treaties where implementation of the treaty has strategic implications, including significant cross-portfolio interests, for states; and
- coordinate as required the process for nominating state representation on delegations where such representation is appropriate.[48]

The Commonwealth secretariat for SCOT is based in the Department of the Prime Minister and Cabinet. However, it also includes representatives of both the Department of Foreign Affairs and Trade and the Commonwealth Attorney-General's Department. Representatives of other Commonwealth departments (such as those concerning the environment, agriculture, and transport) attend when necessary.

At first, in practice, SCOT did not prove to be an effective consultation mechanism. Rather, it was a clearing house for information and facilitated little discussion of matters such as the implementation of treaties. The states remained unhappy about the level of consultation on treaties.[49]

The 1996 Treaty Reforms

Unease about the lack of accountability in treaty making grew in the early 1990s.[50] The subject was referred to the Commonwealth Parliament's Senate Legal and Constitutional References Committee, which in 1995 produced a unanimous report, *Trick or Treaty?* It recommended major reforms to the treaty-making system,[51] most of which were later adopted. The states joined together to make a unanimous submission to the Senate committee. They argued for:

- greater transparency – through the publication of treaty-impact statements showing the benefits and costs of entering into a treaty;
- greater consultation – through improvements to the functioning of SCOT;
- greater political accountability – through the establishment of a Treaties Council comprising the heads of government of the Commonwealth, states, and territories to deal with sensitive treaty issues at the political level; and
- greater involvement of the Commonwealth Parliament – through the formation of a parliamentary committee to monitor and review the treaty-making process and, most controversially, by giving each house of the Commonwealth Parliament a power to veto a treaty or propose reservations to it.[52]

The states did not seek a direct veto over treaties because they knew this was unachievable. Instead, they sought Commonwealth parliamentary involvement so that if a treaty were objectionable to the states, they would have a reasonable chance of convincing the Senate (which is usually not controlled by the government) to reject it.

In 1996 the Commonwealth agreed to publish treaty-impact statements, which it called national-interest analyses. It also agreed to set up a database of treaties to which Australia is a party and to provide greater information on treaties to the public. The Commonwealth agreed to improve consultation with the states through SCOT, including the provision of a schedule every three months that lists current and forthcoming treaty negotiations and matters under consideration for ratification.

The Commonwealth also agreed to establish a Treaties Council consisting of the prime minister, state premiers, and territory chief ministers. The revised Principles and Procedures (adopted by the Council of Australian Governments in June 1996) state that the Treaties Council is to meet at least once a year and that its role is to consider treaties of importance to the states, either of its own volition or when these are referred to it by any jurisdiction. However, since 1996 the Treaties Council has met only once, in November 1997. States have sought to refer treaties to it on a number of occasions,[53] but the Commonwealth has refused to convene it. The Treaties Council is generally regarded as a failure.

On the subject of parliamentary scrutiny, the Commonwealth agreed to establish a Joint Standing Committee on Treaties (JSCOT). This parliamentary committee has now been operating for eleven years. Each treaty is tabled in Parliament at least fifteen (or in some cases, twenty) parliamentary sitting days before ratification. The treaty and its national-interest analysis is then subject to scrutiny by JSCOT, which can call for public submissions and can hold public hearings before issuing its report. Although JSCOT is controlled by government members, it has often been critical of government consultation with the states and others, and it has caused and policed improvements to the consultation process.[54] It has tended, however, to focus on procedural problems rather than on substantive policy concerns. The committee has only once recommended against ratification of a treaty,[55] and its recommendation was accepted by Parliament. Whereas some have criticised JSCOT's effectiveness,[56] others have praised its role in publicizing information about treaties and treaty negotiations.[57]

As for a parliamentary power of veto over the ratification of treaties, the Commonwealth decided to defer consideration of this recommendation. It determined that the other reforms should first be given a chance to operate, as this might resolve concerns about treaty making without the need to take this further step. After a review of the treaty-making process in 1999, the Commonwealth decided that no further reforms were required.[58] A minor change in the treaty-tabling practice was made in 2000: the consultation period between tabling and ratifying treaties of major political, economic, or social significance was increased from fifteen to twenty sitting days (which is approximately eight weeks).

States and Treaty Implementation

Given the uncertainty about the scope of the external affairs power prior to 1983, the Commonwealth tended to take a cautious approach to the implementation of treaties. Where a treaty affected areas of state legislation, the Commonwealth would ratify the treaty only if the states supported ratification or if state laws were otherwise already consistent with the treaty. The Commonwealth regarded the states as under an "honourable obligation not to amend the law so as to infringe the convention save after consultation with the Commonwealth."[59]

Treaties ratified by Australia have often been implemented by the states.[60] This was due not only to uncertainty about the scope of the external affairs power but also to administrative efficiency and convenience. Existing state bodies and systems were used to implement treaties rather than duplicate them at the Commonwealth level.[61]

In some cases, states went further in treaty implementation than the Commonwealth chose to go itself. The Commonwealth Parliament amended the Racial Discrimination Act 1975 (Cth) in 1983 to make it clear that the Commonwealth law was not intended to override state legislation on racial discrimination that furthered the objects of the Convention on the Elimination of All Forms of Racial Discrimination (CERD) and was capable of operating concurrently with the Commonwealth law.[62]

The 1982 version of the Principles and Procedures contemplated the inclusion of federal clauses in treaties[63] and gave states the first opportunity to implement treaty obligations by their own legislation where treaties would affect traditional areas of state responsibility. In 1983 the Hawke Labor Government rejected the use of federal clauses. It favoured the making of a short federal statement upon ratification. It also rejected the notion that the Commonwealth should legislate to implement treaties only once states had failed to do so. Although the Commonwealth agreed to consider relying on state legislation, it reasserted its power to legislate to implement treaties when it so chose.

The Commonwealth has often asserted that any laws inconsistent with a treaty must be amended before the treaty is ratified.[64] In practice, this is not always the case. Inadequate consultation with states on the meaning and effect of treaty obligations may mean that inconsistent state laws are not identified. Further, many treaties, especially those concerning human rights,[65] are not expressly implemented by legislation. The Commonwealth relies on the absence of conflicting state or Commonwealth laws. This can give rise to difficulties. First, states must be aware of all existing treaty obligations when enacting laws in the future, although this is a Herculean task for which they are not resourced. Second, the interpretation of treaty provisions changes over time, so a law that was consistent with a treaty at the time the treaty was ratified may later be considered in breach of the treaty as reinterpreted. Where a state law is identified as being inconsistent with Australia's treaty obligations, the state may not necessarily agree to amend it. The Commonwealth may then choose to legislate to override the state law.

For example, in March 1994 the United Nations (UN) Human Rights Committee published its view, in *Toonen v Australia*, that Australia was in breach of its obligations under the International Covenant on Civil and Political Rights (ICCPR). The offending law was a Tasmanian law that made it a criminal offence to have sexual intercourse with any person "against the order of nature," including consensual homosexual intercourse. The UN Human Rights Committee concluded that this state law breached the right to privacy under the ICCPR.[66] As the Tasmanian government refused to repeal its law, the Commonwealth Parliament enacted the Human Rights (Sexual Conduct) Act 1994 (Cth), which nullified the effectiveness of the Tasmanian law, rather than implementing the right to privacy in the ICCPR. After an unsuccessful legal skirmish,[67] Tasmania eventually repealed its law.[68]

The *Toonen* case arose because Australia had ratified the First Optional Protocol to the ICCPR, allowing complaints to be taken by individuals to the UN Human Rights Committee. This placed states in a vulnerable position when complaints were made about the application of state laws. The states have no standing in the hearing of such complaints; only the views of the Commonwealth and the complainant are heard. In *Toonen*, although the Commonwealth did include some Tasmanian representations in its general submission to the committee, the Commonwealth agreed with the complainant on most significant points, such as admissibility, despite Tasmanian protests.[69]

The Commonwealth has not always legislated to override state laws that conflict with treaty obligations. State and territory laws concerning the imprisonment of children were alleged to breach Australia's obligations under the Convention on the Rights of the Child,[70] but the Commonwealth took no action. In 1999 the Commonwealth contended that the plans of New South Wales to open a medically supervised drug-injection centre breached Commonwealth obligations under narcotic drugs treaties. The International Narcotics Control Board was also critical of the proposal. The state disagreed, producing opinions of eminent international lawyers that the state's proposal was consistent with Australia's treaty obligations and indicating that it would challenge the validity of any Commonwealth legislation to block its proposals. The Commonwealth retreated, and the centre opened in 2001 for a medically supervised trial, which has since been extended.[71]

State Concerns with the Current System

States have long been concerned about the impact upon them of the Commonwealth's ratification of treaties. The subject matter of the most controversial treaties has changed over time from resource issues in the 1970s to environmental protection in the 1980s, human rights and industrial relations in the 1990s, and free trade agreements in the 2000s. All have had important impacts on state laws and policies.

At a seminar in March 2006 to mark the tenth anniversary of the 1996 reforms to the treaty-making process, state representatives accepted that the reforms had greatly improved the process. Subsequent experience had also led to improvements. For example, the problems that occurred during the negotiation of the Australia-United States Free Trade Agreement have not been repeated in more recent free trade negotiations.[72]

However, the states still have some concerns. First, the states want all consultation to take place initially through the premier or the premier's department in order to ensure a "whole of government" approach from each state. Second, states want to be consulted earlier and to receive drafts of the national-interest analysis earlier in the negotiations rather than at the time the treaty is tabled and ready for ratification. Draft national-interest analyses would help the states to identify the potential effects of treaties on them and allow states to raise matters of importance during the negotiation phase. Third, the states want the Treaties Council to be convened when they wish to refer matters to it. They also want a permanent secretariat to be established for the Treaties Council.[73] Finally, the states want greater consultation about the proposed implementation of treaties. They are particularly concerned about how the different free trade agreements are to be given effect by the states and about whose responsibility it is to identify and rectify inconsistencies with treaty obligations.

DOMESTIC AND INTERNATIONAL MANIFESTATIONS OF STATE GOVERNMENT DIPLOMACY

State Bureaucracy and Foreign Affairs

States do not have government departments dedicated to foreign affairs. The subject of foreign affairs is usually dealt with initially by the intergovernmental relations area of the premier's department in each state and then by the department that deals with the substantive subject matter, such as the environment. There are no available figures as to the money and resources dedicated to dealing with foreign affairs matters, as they may be dealt with by any number of government departments and agencies as well as by officials such as the Crown solicitor and parliamentary counsel.

Due to their more limited resources, states pick and choose the subjects to which they will devote their resources according to their particular interests. The states usually agree among themselves in advance on which state will take the lead in relation to a particular treaty or will seek to send a delegate to a negotiation session. Party-political differences rarely affect state cooperation on such matters, particularly at the officials' level.

State and Commonwealth Interaction over Foreign Affairs

Most interaction between the Commonwealth and the states concerning treaties occurs among officials. Political involvement tends to occur only when action is needed to resolve a deadlock or when a treaty is particularly politically sensitive. Despite the failure of the Treaties Council, state ministers may still be involved in briefings on the negotiation of treaty issues but on an ad hoc, unstructured basis. Premiers and state ministers of trade and procurement were briefed on the negotiation of the Australia-United States Free Trade Agreement, as it had a significant impact on state laws as well as state government procurement.

The Commonwealth also seeks state assistance to prepare reports for international bodies on the implementation of particular treaties (such as the ICCPR and the CERD) in Australia. States may be affected as well by the findings of international dispute-resolution bodies.

State governments tend to cooperate with the Commonwealth's Department of Foreign Affairs and Trade (DFAT) concerning international matters. Overseas visits of state officials, ministers, and members of Parliament are arranged in cooperation with DFAT, and guidelines are issued to state governments about official contact with foreign states.[74] Policies concerning foreign aid and cultural matters are primarily developed by the Commonwealth through its agencies. States tend to cooperate with these policies,[75] although they occasionally fund their own programs. States are sometimes called upon to provide police or medical personnel to neighbouring countries in response to emergencies. For example, in June 2006 Victoria sent twenty-three police officers to East Timor, in addition to the forty to sixty Victorian officers serving in international deployment forces in the Solomon Islands, Jordan, and elsewhere.[76] Other states also sent significant numbers of police officers to East Timor and the Solomon Islands. South Australia provided medical and evacuation support to East Timor and sent medical personnel to Banda Aceh after the Boxing Day tsunami of 2004.[77]

DFAT has an office in each state capital. These offices deal primarily with passport issues but also provide a liaison with state ministers, parliamentarians, and officials.[78] On the whole, interaction between the Commonwealth and the states regarding foreign affairs occurs through the central areas of DFAT in Canberra and through the Department of the Prime Minister and Cabinet.

State Parliaments and Foreign Affairs

State parliaments do not often become involved in foreign affairs. The most common involvement is through speeches made during the general debate at the adjournment of each sitting day, which may be on any subject. Members of Parliament then sometimes speak on foreign matters that are of particular significance to ethnic groups within their electorates or on topical matters of public affairs. Motions of condolence are often passed in response to international tragedies such as the Boxing Day tsunami or the London bombings of 2005.[79] Such speeches or debates tend not to be noticed outside the state parliament, although on rare occasions they may give rise to a diplomatic controversy, such as a resolution of the New South Wales Parliament commemorating the Armenian genocide of 1915–18.[80] State parliaments also occasionally discuss international matters that have a more direct impact on state policies, such as climate change and the attraction of skilled workers from overseas.[81]

Members of state parliaments also take study tours abroad through the Commonwealth Parliamentary Association.[82] Sometimes parliamentary committees travel overseas to collect information for particular inquiries. Delegations of parliamentarians have also visited sister-states. These trips tend to come to prominence not because of state involvement in foreign policy but because of allegations of wasted taxpayers' money. Occasionally, delegations of state parliamentarians are invited by foreign governments to visit their countries for diplomatic reasons. For example, after a delegation of South Australian parliamentarians was invited to Taiwan by the Taiwanese government, the South Australian House of Assembly passed a motion supporting the maintenance of the status quo with respect to the relationship between Taiwan and its neighbours. The parliamentarians noted Australia's "one China policy" and saw their visit as an unofficial means to develop economic and cultural contact between Australia and Taiwan.[83]

Issues concerning treaties sometimes come before state parliaments. From 1974 to 1977 Queensland had a Treaties Commission, which advised the Queensland Parliament concerning treaties. It ceased to operate in 1977 when the Commonwealth's Principles and Procedures on treaty consultation came into effect. In 2001 the Queensland premier agreed to table in Parliament communications from JSCOT about a proposed treaty action as well as national-interest analyses.[84] The Queensland Parliament also considered establishing a treaties committee but decided against this, as it can refer treaty matters to existing committees once they have been tabled in Parliament.[85]

In Victoria a parliamentary committee was established in 1996 to deal with federal-state relations. Its first report was *International Treaty Making and the Role of the States*, which recommended greater state parliamentary scrutiny of treaties.[86] The committee was later abolished after a change of government, and no treaties committee was established. Its recommendation that treaties be tabled in the Victoria Parliament was followed until 2001, after which it lapsed.[87]

State Policies and Foreign Affairs

From time to time, state government policies, or indeed the views of state political leaders, have interfered with Australian foreign policy. The former Queensland premier Sir Joh Bjelke-Petersen tended to make statements about foreign policy matters, either to annoy the Commonwealth or to protect Queensland's trade interests, or both. Examples include Queensland's support for South Africa's former apartheid regime, support for recognition of Taiwan, and threats to deny coal licences to Japanese companies because of agricultural trade issues.[88] State "nuclear-free" policies have previously led to attempts to prevent nuclear-powered United States naval vessels from docking in state ports.[89] In November 2006 state attorneys general signed the Fremantle Declaration in support of a fair trial for an Australian detainee at Guantanamo Bay.

The states have also been active on climate change and the establishment of an emissions trading system due to the Commonwealth's previous refusal to ratify the Kyoto Protocol of the United Nations Framework Convention on Climate Change. The states have consulted with like-minded subnational entities, such as the US state of California, in preparing their response to climate-change issues. Victoria, New South Wales, and South Australia entered into a Declaration of the Federated States and Regional Governments on Climate Change in 2005 with other subnational states including California, Quebec, Bavaria, Scotland, Catalonia, and Sao Paulo. The newly formed Council for the Australian Federation, comprised of state premiers, agreed on 13 October 2006 to develop a dialogue between constituent governments in Australia and the United States on policies to address climate change.

State premiers and ministers travel overseas from time to time at government cost. Such trips often involve the announcement of an overseas contract, or a policy to acquire technology or infrastructure (such as trains or water-recycling technology) from the visited country, or a cooperation agreement. For example, in 2005 the Queensland premier opened the Australian International School in Sharjah, United Arab Emirates, which is staffed by Queensland teachers and teaches the Queensland government curriculum. Ministers may also take part in fact-finding missions, attend conferences, or lead trade delegations abroad, such as the BIO 2007 biotechnology fair in Boston. In some cases, states will cooperate and agree not to compete with each other for particular contracts or international events.[90] In other cases, the states do compete against each other, especially in relation to trade and commercial matters, such as securing the head office of an international corporation or an international sporting event.

Municipal governments have become involved, through the Commonwealth Local Government Forum Pacific Project, in international local government development projects that provide technical support in Papua New Guinea, Fiji, Kiribati, and Vanuatu. Many local councils are also closely involved in East Timor through the East Timor Friendship Relationship Program. Its aim is to build capacity through skills development and material aid. Activities include the provision of teachers and project workers, the creation of scholarships, the training and exchange of personnel, study tours, and the provision of material aid, such as education materials, medical equipment, and sewing machines, as well as financial support. The lord mayors of Sydney and Melbourne also attended the C40 Large Cities Climate Summit in New York in May 2007, and the lord mayors of the Australian state capitals all met with the prime minister in 2007 to discuss climate-change concerns. Some local councils remain nuclear-free zones,[91] although their resolutions tend to note their limited powers and responsibilities with regard to the subject and are directed at objecting to the storage and transportation of nuclear or radioactive materials in the municipality, except when used for medical or technological purposes.[92] Their focus tends to be local rather than international.

On the whole, foreign policy issues rank quite low on the list of matters that concern the states and voters in state elections. When global issues such as climate change and terrorism are raised during state elections, the focus tends to be on what the state government itself can do to deal with them. There is generally no expectation that states will have any diplomatic role in dealing with international problems. Domestic matters such as health, transport, education, and law and order are the primary concerns of state ministers and the electorate. The greatest controversy about state involvement in foreign affairs usually arises in relation to the costs of overseas travel by ministers and accusations that they should instead be at home dealing with local problems.

Official Representation of States Overseas

Prior to federation, the Australian colonies were represented in the United Kingdom by agents-general. Some states continue that representation today.[93] Agents-general are accorded a level of consular status[94] due to the longstanding independent relationship between the states and the United Kingdom. State representatives in other countries are not granted diplomatic status.[95] In 1972–73 New South Wales had ninety staff in the office of its agent-general, Queensland had thirty-four, and Western Australia had thirty.[96] The size and nature of state representation in London has since been reduced drastically. Tasmania and New South Wales abolished their offices altogether. Other states now use their agents-general as representatives in Europe as well as the United Kingdom.

States have also long had trade and tourism representation abroad.[97] The first formal overseas state office was opened by New South Wales in New York City in 1958, with offices following in Tokyo and other locations.[98] The level of representation, and its location around the world, has waxed and waned over time depending on economic and political conditions.[99] In some cases, formal state offices are established and staffed with state public servants. In others, local people are asked to represent state interests when they arise, or services are bought from the Commonwealth's Austrade on an ongoing or case-by-case basis. It is therefore extremely difficult to make meaningful comparisons of the extent and cost of state representation abroad.[100]

State overseas offices fill a number of functions, including promoting the state as a tourist destination, promoting it as a location for business headquarters or holding conferences and special events, promoting state exports and culture (such as music and literature), seeking foreign investment, developing collaboration between institutions, universities, and corporations, attracting skilled migrants, and promoting trade. Although there are not great cultural differences between the states, sometimes states will attempt to promote a particular identity. For example, Queensland has promoted itself as the "Smart State" in concert with efforts to build up its biotechnology sector.

According to available information, in 2006 the overseas representation of Australian states was as follows:

New South Wales: trade – none; tourism – Auckland, Los Angeles, London, Tokyo, Hong Kong, and Singapore.
Queensland: trade – London, Los Angeles, Beijing, Shanghai, Guangzhou, Hong Kong, Taipei, Tokyo, Osaka, Riyadh, Abu Dhabi, Seoul, Jakarta, and Bangalore; tourism – Munich, London, Auckland, Los Angeles, Taipei, Hong Kong, Shanghai, Singapore, Tokyo, and Seoul.
South Australia: trade – London, Dubai, Hong Kong, Jinan, Shanghai, and Singapore; tourism – Singapore, Hong Kong, Germany, United Kingdom, France, Italy, Japan, New Zealand, and the United States.
Tasmania: trade – none; tourism – London, Toronto, and Auckland.
Victoria: trade – London, Dubai, Frankfurt, Chicago, New York, San Francisco, Bangalore, Hong Kong, Nanjing, Shanghai, and Tokyo; tourism – London, Frankfurt, Hong Kong, Shanghai, Singapore, Tokyo, Auckland, and Los Angeles.
Western Australia: trade – London, Shanghai, Hangzhou, Mumbai, Chennai, Jakarta, Tokyo, Kobe, Kuala Lumpur, Dubai, Seoul, Taipei, Bangkok, and Los Angeles; tourism – Shanghai, Munich, Tokyo, Seoul, Auckland, Singapore, and London.

The wide variation in level of representation is largely explained by economic factors. Some states with strong export growth need to seek new markets, while those with more established markets do not. New South Wales, for example, decided it was more efficient to run regular trade missions and purchase services from Austrade than to have its own permanent representation abroad.

Sister-State Relationships

The states have formed "sister-state" relationships with a number of other subnational jurisdictions. These relationships are often formalized by a memorandum of understanding that provides the framework for cultural, educational, sporting, and youth exchanges or for trade and business relationships. In some cases, the relationships have ceased to be active. According to available information, in 2006 these relationships included the following:

New South Wales: Guangdong Province, China; Tokyo Metropolitan Government, Japan; California, United States; Special Territory of Jakarta, Indonesia; and Seoul, South Korea.
Queensland: Saitama Prefecture, Japan; Kyonggi Province, South Korea; Province of Central Java, Indonesia; Municipality of Shanghai, China; and South Carolina, United States.
South Australia: Okayama Prefecture, Japan; Chungcheong Province, South Korea; and Shandong Province, China.
Tasmania: Fujian Province, China.
Victoria: Aichi Prefecture, Japan; Busan Metropolitan City, South Korea; Jiangsu Province, China; and Scotland, United Kingdom.
Western Australia: Hyogo Prefecture, Japan; Zhejiang Province, China; East Java Province, Indonesia; and Tuscany Region, Italy.

In addition, there are many sister-city relationships throughout Australia. For example, Sydney has the following sister-cities: San Francisco, Nagoya, Wellington, Portsmouth, Guangzhou, and Florence.

CONCLUSION

Australia's states have little involvement in foreign affairs. Their interests, however, may be seriously affected by Commonwealth foreign activity. In particular, the ratification of a treaty by Australia can result in the Commonwealth Parliament gaining additional powers to legislate in traditional state areas. The states, therefore, have sought to ensure that their interests are represented in treaty making. Great steps were made in the transparency and accountability of the treaty-making system in 1996, but there is still room for improvement.

The underlying complaint of the states is that Commonwealth bureaucrats treat consultation as a tiresome procedure and do not make a genuine effort to use state involvement and expertise to improve both the treaty-making process and its outcomes. Although the procedural reforms protect state interests, attitudinal reform would be in the interests of the whole of Australia.

NOTES

1 For further background on Australia, see Cheryl Saunders, "Commonwealth of Australia," in John Kincaid and G. Alan Tarr, eds, *Constitutional Origins, Structure, and Change in Federal Countries*, 12–47 (Montreal and Kingston: McGill-Queen's University Press, 2005); John Williams and Clement Macintyre, "Commonwealth of Australia," in Akhtar Majeed, Ronald Watts, and Douglas Brown, eds, *Distribution of Powers and Responsibilities in Federal Countries*, 8–33 (Montreal and Kingston: McGill-Queen's University Press, 2006); Cheryl Saunders and Katy Le Roy, "Commonwealth of Australia," in Katy Le Roy and Cheryl Saunders, eds, *Legislative, Executive, and Judicial Governance in Federal Countries*, 37–70 (Montreal and Kingston: McGill-Queen's University Press, 2006); and Alan Morris, "Australia," in Anwar Shah, ed., *The Practice of Fiscal Federalism: Comparative Perspectives*, 44–72 (Montreal and Kingston: McGill-Queen's University Press, 2007).
2 Projected estimate of the Australian Bureau of Statistics as at 4 October 2007.
3 Dennis Trewin, *Yearbook, Australia 2006* (Canberra: Australian Bureau of Statistics, 2006), 121, 134.
4 Ibid., 105, 117.
5 Ibid., 74.
6 Ibid., 80.
7 See, for example, Treaty on Certain Maritime Arrangements in the Timor Sea, 12 January 2006.
8 See, for example, Trans-Tasman Mutual Recognition Act 1997 (Cth); and Trans-Tasman Mutual Recognition (New South Wales) Act 1996 (NSW). Western Australia is the only state that has not enacted such legislation.
9 Trewin, *Yearbook, Australia 2006*, 84–5.
10 See a copy of the treaty and the exchange of letters in the AUSTLII Australian Treaty Series Database at: http://138.25.65.50/au/other/dfat/treaties/2005/30.html (accessed 5 July 2008).
11 See generally, D.P. O'Connell, "The Evolution of Australia's International Personality," in D.P. O'Connell, ed., *International Law in Australia*, 1–33 (Sydney: Law Book Co., 1965); J.G. Starke, "The Commonwealth in International Affairs," in Justice Else-Mitchell, ed., *Essays on the Australian Constitution*, 2nd ed., 343–74 (Sydney: Law Book Co., 1961); Leslie Zines, "The Growth of Australian Nationhood and Its Effect on the Powers of the Commonwealth," in Leslie Zines, ed., *Commentaries on*

the Australian Constitution, 1–50 (Sydney: Butterworths, 1977); Cheryl Saunders, "Articles of Faith or Lucky Breaks?" *Sydney Law Review* 17 (1995): 149–76, at 154–7; and Anne Twomey, "International Law and the Executive," in Brian Opeskin and Don Rothwell, eds, *International Law and Australian Federalism*, 69–76 (Melbourne: Melbourne University Press, 1997).

12 Although self-governing, the states remained subject to the Colonial Laws Validity Act 1865 and could not enact laws that were repugnant to British laws of paramount force.
13 Starke, "Commonwealth in International Affairs," 345.
14 *R v Burgess; Ex parte Henry* (1936) 55 CLR 608, 684–5; and *Victoria v Commonwealth* (1996) 187 CLR 416, 482.
15 See the similar problem faced by Canadian courts, discussed in the chapter on Canada in this book.
16 See generally, Zines, "Growth of Australian Nationhood," 1–50.
17 *Minister for Immigration and Ethnic Affairs v Teoh* (1996) 183 CLR 273, since limited by *Minister for Immigration and Multicultural Affairs; Ex parte Lam* (2003) 214 CLR 1.
18 Coastal Waters (State Powers) Act 1980 (Cth); and Coastal Waters (State Title) Act 1980 (Cth).
19 *Commonwealth v Australian Commonwealth Shipping Board* (1926) 39 CLR 1; *Stenhouse v Coleman* (1944) 69 CLR 457; *Australian Communist Party v Commonwealth* (1951) 83 CLR 1.
20 *Thomas v Mowbray* (2007) 237 ALR 194.
21 *Amalgamated Society of Engineers v Adelaide Steamship Co. Ltd* (1920) 28 CLR 129.
22 *Commonwealth v Tasmania* (1983) 158 CLR 1.
23 *Victoria v Commonwealth* (1996) 187 CLR 416, 459.
24 Ibid., 486.
25 Ibid., 487.
26 Ibid. See also the debate on "international concern" in *XYZ v Commonwealth* (2006) 80 ALJR 1036.
27 *Polyukhovich v Commonwealth* (1991) 172 CLR 501.
28 *Horta v Commonwealth* (1994) 181 CLR 183.
29 *XYZ v Commonwealth* (2006) 80 ALJR 1036.
30 *New South Wales v Commonwealth* (1975) 135 CLR 337, 373.
31 See John Trone, *Federal Constitutions and International Relations* (Brisbane: University of Queensland Press, 2001), 32, and the sources listed there.
32 O'Connell, "Evolution of Australia's International Personality," 16; John Ravenhill, "Australia," in Hans J. Michelmann and Panayotis Soldatos, eds, *Federalism and International Relations*, 77–123 (Oxford: Clarendon, 1990), 83. For contrasting views, see *First Report of the Queensland Treaties Commission*, 1 December 1976, reprinted in Australian Constitutional Convention, *Report of the External Affairs Subcommittee to the Standing Committee*, 129–239 (Brisbane: Government Printer, September 1984); and Henry Burmester, "The Australian States and Participation in the Foreign Policy Process," *Federal Law Review* 9 (1978): 257–83, at 259–62.

33 *New South Wales v Commonwealth* (1975) 135 CLR 337, 506.
34 See, for example, agreements with Libya, referred to in Burmester, "Australian States," 264; and Ravenhill, "Australia," 101-2.
35 Queensland, *Trade Mission Report*, June 2007.
36 Queensland, *Trade Mission Report*, April 2007 and June 2007.
37 Henry Burmester, "Federalism, the States and International Affairs – A Legal Perspective," in Brian Galligan, ed., *Australian Federalism*, 196–217 (Melbourne: Longman Cheshire, 1989), 202.
38 Ibid., 203.
39 *Pearce v Florenca* (1976) 135 CLR 501.
40 *Union Steamship Co. of Australia Pty Ltd v King* (1988) 166 CLR 1.
41 Ibid.
42 A.H. Body, "Australian Treaty Making Practice and Procedure," in D.P. O'Connell, ed., *International Law in Australia*, 52–64 (Sydney: Law Book Co., 1965), 54.
43 Burmester, "Australian States," 281.
44 Kenneth Bailey, "Australia and the International Labour Conventions," *International Labour Review* 54 (1946): 285–308, at 289–90; *First Report of the Queensland Treaties Commission*, 196–203; and Mary Crock, "Federalism and the External Affairs Power," *Melbourne University Law Review* 14 (1983): 238–64, at 246.
45 Burmester, "Australian States," 281. See also the discussion of the Principles and Procedures in Saunders, "Articles of Faith or Lucky Breaks?" 162.
46 For example, Queensland represented the states at the negotiation of the European Union Mutual Recognition Agreement and at the negotiation of a free trade agreement with the United Arab Emirates; the Western Australian solicitor general participated in negotiations on the maritime boundary with Indonesia; Victoria sent a representative to WTO negotiations in Hong Kong; and both New South Wales and Queensland sent representatives to the negotiation of the Rome Statute of the International Criminal Court.
47 Council of Australian Governments, *Communiqué*, 14 June 1996, Attachment C, para. 6.1.
48 Commonwealth, DFAT, *Negotiation, Conclusion and Implementation of International Treaties and Arrangements* (Canberra: DFAT, August 1994), Annexure, 27.
49 Commonwealth, JSCOT, *Report 78: Treaty Scrutiny – A Ten Year Review* (Canberra: Commonwealth Parliament, September 2006), 12, and per Mrs Judge at 75–6.
50 See Philip Alston and Madelaine Chiam, eds, *Treaty-Making and Australia – Globalisation versus Sovereignty?* (Sydney: Federation Press, 1995), where these concerns are discussed throughout.
51 Commonwealth, Senate Legal and Constitutional References Committee, *Trick or Treaty? Commonwealth Power to Make and Implement Treaties* (Canberra: Commonwealth Parliament, November 1995), 300–4.
52 Ibid., 210, 223–4, 252, 260.
53 Commonwealth, JSCOT, *Report 78*, per Mrs Judge at 76, noting that Western Australia had asked on four occasions for the Treaties Council to be convened, and per

Mr Roberts at 68, noting that the Queensland premier had also tried to refer treaties to it.

54 For an analysis of the committee's early reports, see Anne Twomey, "Parliament's Role in Treaty Making and External Affairs," in Geoff Lindell and Robert Bennett, eds, *Parliament – The Vision in Hindsight*, 37–92 (Sydney: Federation Press, 2001), 86–9; and Trone, *Federal Constitutions*, 36.

55 Commonwealth, JSCOT, *Report 11* (Canberra: Commonwealth Parliament, November 1997), 13–14, regarding the Agreement on Economic and Commercial Cooperation with Kazakhstan.

56 Ann Capling, "Can the Democratic Deficit in Treaty-Making Be Overcome?" in Hillary Charlesworth, Madelaine Chiam, Devika Hovell, and George Williams, eds, *The Fluid State – International Law and National Legal Systems*, 57–79 (Sydney: Federation Press, 2005), 74–7; Commonwealth, JSCOT, *Report 78*, per Devika Hovell at 59–61.

57 Joanna Harrington, "The Role of Parliaments in Treaty-Making," in Hillary Charlesworth, Madelaine Chiam, Devika Hovell, and George Williams, eds, *The Fluid State – International Law and National Legal Systems*, 34–56 (Sydney: Federation Press, 2005), 47.

58 Commonwealth, DFAT, *Review of the Treaty Making Process* (Canberra: DFAT, August 1999).

59 Geoffrey Sawer, "Australian Constitution Law in Relation to International Relations and International Law," in D.P. O'Connell, ed., *International Law in Australia*, 35–51 (Sydney: Law Book Co., 1965), 46–7.

60 See Stuart Harris, "Federalism and Australian Foreign Policy," in B. Hocking, ed., *Federal Relations and Federal States*, 90–104 (London: Leicester University Press, 1993), 95; and the examples listed in Trone, *Federal Constitutions*, 59–62.

61 Sawer, "Australian Constitutional Law," 47.

62 The retrospective application of this provision was held to be invalid by the High Court in *University of Wollongong v Metwally* (1984) 158 CLR 447, but its prospective operation remains effective.

63 Such clauses are discussed in detail in W. Bush, "Aspects of Involvement of Australian States with Treaties," in Australian Constitutional Convention, *Report of the External Affairs Subcommittee*, 85–95 (Brisbane: Government Printer, September 1984), 86–93; and Brian Opeskin, "International Law and Federal States," in Brian Opeskin and Don Rothwell, eds, *International Law and Australian Federalism*, 1–33 (Melbourne: Melbourne University Press, 1997), 13–16.

64 Commonwealth, DFAT, *Negotiation, Conclusion and Implementation of International Treaties and Arrangements* (Canberra: DFAT, August 1994), para. 56.

65 See, for example, the International Covenant on Civil and Political Rights (ICCPR) and the Convention on the Rights of the Child, parts of which are implemented through provisions in a range of state and Commonwealth Acts, and parts of which are merely implemented through the absence of infringing legislation.

66 See further Anne Twomey, *Strange Bedfellows: The UN Human Rights Committee and the Tasmanian Parliament* (Canberra: Parliamentary Research Service, 1994).

67 *Croome v Tasmania* (1997) 191 CLR 119.
68 See generally, Hillary Charlesworth, "International Human Rights Law and Australian Federalism," in Brian Opeskin and Don Rothwell, eds, *International Law and Australian Federalism*, 280–305 (Melbourne: Melbourne University Press, 1997), 295–7; Victoria, Federal-State Relations Committee, *International Treaty Making and the Role of the States* (Melbourne: Victorian Parliament, 1997), paras 2.21–2.26; and Hillary Charlesworth, Madelaine Chiam, Devika Hovell, and George Williams, *No Country Is an Island* (Sydney: University of New South Wales Press, 2006), 54.
69 Twomey, *Strange Bedfellows*, 18.
70 Hillary Charlesworth, "Australia's Split Personality: Implementation of Human Rights Treaty Obligations in Australia," in Philip Alston and Madelaine Chiam, eds, *Treaty-Making and Australia – Globalisation versus Sovereignty?* 129–40 (Sydney: Federation Press, 1995), 133.
71 Charlesworth et al., *No Country Is an Island*, 17–19.
72 Commonwealth, JSCOT, *Report 78*, per Mr Roberts at 66.
73 See the discussion of all these points in ibid., per Mr Roberts at 64–8; and per Mrs Judge at 75–9.
74 See, for example, New South Wales, Premier's Department Circular No. 98–12, "Contact with Department of Foreign Affairs Overseas Posts and Guidelines for Contact with Foreign States," 19 January 1998.
75 See further Ravenhill, "Australia," 101.
76 Victoria, *Parliamentary Debates*, Legislative Assembly, 7 June 2006, 1780.
77 South Australia, *Parliamentary Debates*, House of Assembly, 6–7 June 2006 and 8 March 2007.
78 Peter Bassett, "The Australian Federal System and Foreign Policy," in *Australian Foreign Affairs Record* 55 (1984): 322–4, at 324. Note, however, the comment on the ineffectiveness of state offices in Ravenhill, "Australia," 92.
79 See, for example, Victoria, *Parliamentary Debates*, Legislative Assembly, 22 February 2005 and 19 July 2005.
80 New South Wales, *Parliamentary Debates*, Legislative Assembly, 17 April 1997, 7742.
81 Victoria, *Parliamentary Debates*, Legislative Assembly, 7 June 2006, 1754, on migration.
82 In New South Wales each member may take one study tour during his or her time as a member of Parliament. Study tours are more frequent at the federal level.
83 South Australia, *Parliamentary Debates*, House of Assembly, 16 November 2006. State parliamentarians and state ministers are generally not used as an informal diplomatic resource by the Commonwealth.
84 Commonwealth, JSCOT, *Report 78*, per Mr Roberts at 65–6.
85 Queensland, Legal, Constitutional and Administrative Review Committee, Report No. 22, "The Role of the Queensland Parliament in Treaty Making," April 2000, 9.
86 Victoria, Federal-State Relations Committee, *International Treaty Making*.
87 See, for example, Victoria, *Parliamentary Debates*, Legislative Assembly, 20 April 1999, 409; 16 December 1999, 1286; 1 June 2000, 2164; 31 October 2000, 1243; and 16 August 2001, 9.

88 Crock, "Federalism and the External Affairs Power," 243; Peter Boyce, "International Relations of Federal States: Responsibility and Control," in Michael Wood, Christopher Williams, and G. Campbell Sharman, eds, *Governing Federations: Constitution, Politics, Resources*, 187–98 (Sydney: Hale and Iremonger, 1989), 190.
89 Burmester, "Australian States," 258; Ravenhill, "Australia," 103; Allan Gyngell and Michael Wesley, *Making Australian Foreign Policy* (Melbourne: Cambridge University Press, 2003), 181.
90 Most states entered into the Interstate Investment Co-operation Agreement of 2003, which was intended to restrict the use of selective assistance to attract investment. However, as not all states entered the agreement, it has not been effective.
91 See, for example, resolutions of the Randwick City Council (NSW), the Town of Vincent (WA), and the Hobsons Bay City Council (Vic).
92 See, for example, resolutions of the City of Subiaco (WA) and the Hawkesbury Council (NSW), the latter declaring itself a "nuclear free and genetically engineered free zone."
93 See Agent-General for Queensland Act 1975 (Qld); Agent-General Act 1901 (SA); Agent-General's Act 1994 (Vic); and Agent General Act 1895 (WA).
94 Diplomatic Immunities (Commonwealth Countries and Republic of Ireland) Act 1952 (UK), Section 1(2)(b); and Commonwealth Countries and Republic of Ireland Diplomatic Immunities Order in Council 1971 (SI 1971 No. 1237).
95 Crock, "Federalism and the External Affairs Power," 244; Boyce, "International Relations," 191.
96 G. Campbell Sharman, "The Australian States and External Affairs: An Exploratory Note," *Australian Outlook* 27 (1973): 307–18, at 313.
97 Sawer, "Australian Constitutional Law," 38.
98 Ravenhill, "Australia," 97–8.
99 For descriptions of state representation abroad at different times, see Sharman, "Australian States and External Affairs," 314–15; Burmester, "Australian States," 273; Crock, "Federalism and the External Affairs Power," 244; Boyce, "International Relations," 98–9; and Harris, "Federalism and Australian Foreign Policy," 98.
100 See the attempt to do so by a South Australian Parliamentary Committee in 2001: South Australia, Economic and Finance Committee, 35th Report, *South Australian Government Overseas Offices* (Adelaide: South Australian Parliament, October 2001), 13–17. See also Sharman, "Australian States and External Affairs," 314–15; and Ravenhill, "Australia," 98–9.

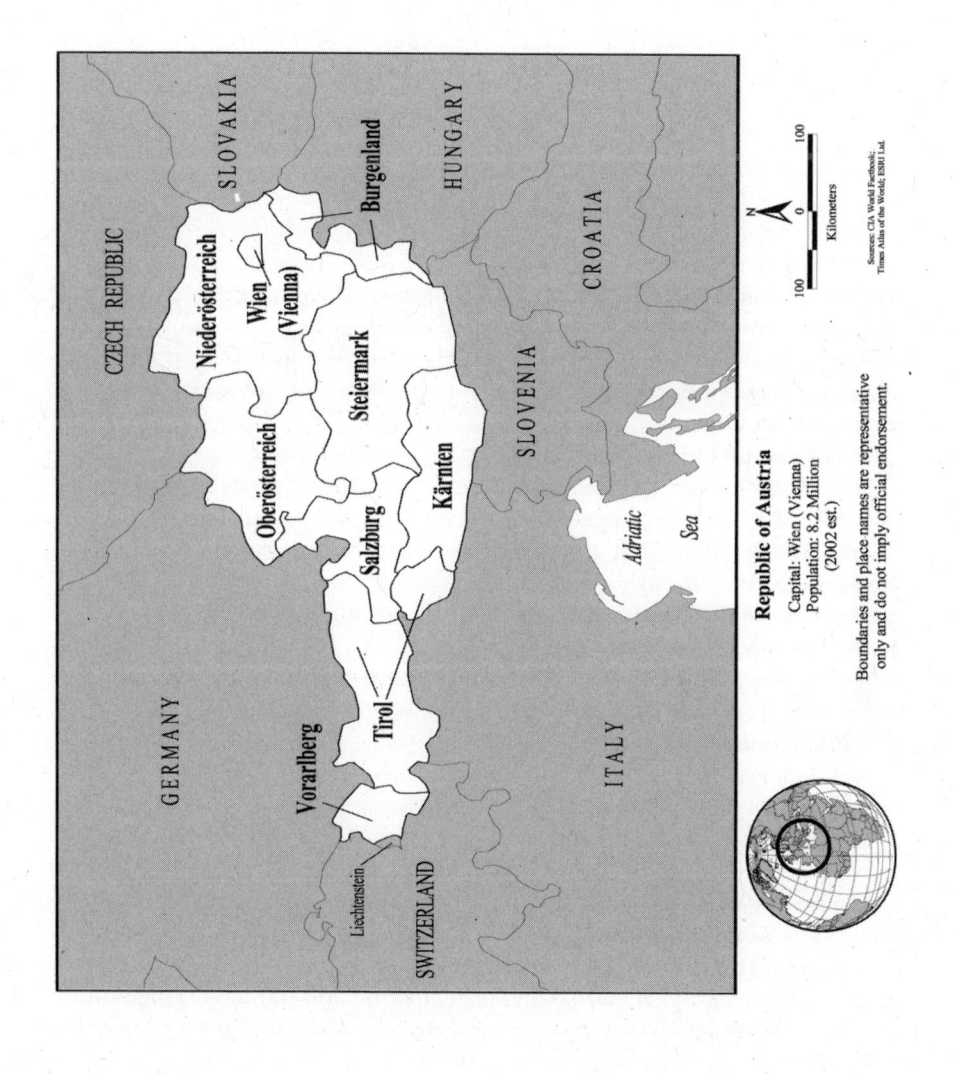

Republic of Austria

Capital: Wien (Vienna)
Population: 8.2 Million
(2002 est.)

Boundaries and place names are representative only and do not imply official endorsement.

Sources: CIA World Factbook;
Times Atlas of the World; ESRI Ltd.

Republic of Austria

ANDREAS KIEFER

Austria's federal Constitutional Act (Bundes-Verfassungsgesetz, or B-VG) of 1920 – considerably amended in 1929 and more than ninety times thereafter[1] – established Austria in Article 1 as a democratic republic and in Article 2 as a federal country "consisting of the autonomous *Länder*[2] of Burgenland,[3] Carinthia, Lower Austria, Upper Austria, Salzburg, Styria, Tyrol, Vorarlberg, and Vienna." The B-VG grants equal powers to all *Länder*.

The *Länder* engage in relations with neighbouring regions through bilateral and multilateral cooperation agreements. Since the late 1980s the *Länder* have entered into numerous associations and regional networks; they now participate in regional bodies of the European Union (EU) and the Council of Europe (COE), namely the Committee of the Regions (COR) and the Congress of Local and Regional Authorities (CLRAE), both established in 1994. The *Länder*, rather small compared to other Europen regions, therefore pursue a policy of networking and of having allies when they are needed for political support.

Both federal external and European relations occur in a highly developed structure. The name change of the federal Ministry for Foreign Affairs to the Ministry for European and International Affairs in 2007 demonstrates the increasing importance of Austria's membership in the European Union and demonstrates that European affairs are no longer seen as strictly international. The *Länder* and municipalities, moreover, share in Austria's financial contribution to the EU,[4] and because they are affected by EU legislation, the *Länder* participate in EU lawmaking, in regulating and implementing bodies such as the Council of Ministers, and in comitology within the Austrian delegation and within consultative bodies such as the COR.

AUSTRIA AT A GLANCE

On 1 January 2007 Austria had 8,298,923 residents.[5] It shares borders with eight other countries. Only 37.4% of its territory (31,355.16 of 83,871.13 km^2)

can be permanently inhabited. The Austrian population is rather homogenous, although at 9.4%, it has the second-highest percentage of foreign residents in the EU. The four largest groups are from Serbia/Montenegro (140,000 persons), Turkey (114,000), Germany (104,000), and Bosnia and Herzegovina (88,000). The official language is German, which, according to the 2001 census, is spoken by 88.6% of the population, although officially recognized minority languages such as Croatian (1.6%), Hungarian (0.5%), and Slovenian (0.3%) are also spoken in parts of the country.[6] For cross-border cooperation by the *Länder* in Euro-regions and especially in multilateral forums, English is increasingly becoming the working language.

In 2006 gross domestic product (GDP) per capita amounted to approximately €31,060 (US$42,293);[7] total GDP constituted 2.3% of the EU-25's GDP. In 2004 GDP per capita ranged from €20,100 (US$27,160) in Burgenland to €31,800 (US$42,960) in Salzburg; in Vienna, the capital, it was €40,300 (US$54,450). Rates of economic growth in recent years have been stable, with 2.4% growth in 2006. *Länder* bordering on the new EU member states show higher rates of economic growth than the western *Länder*, whose economies are oriented toward Germany and Italy. The Austrian Institute for Economic Research expects real GDP growth from 2007 to 2011 to be 2.5% annually, slightly higher than the 2.3% expected for the Euro-area.[8]

Foreign trade figures for 2005 show that the Austrian economy depends more on exports than do the economies of the other member states of the EU. Approximately 84% of its trade is with EU countries.[9]

External relations of the *Länder* complement federal foreign policy. The latter often does not cover all competences, fields of action, or interests of the *Länder*. With their long traditions and identities as former duchies or principalities in the Austro-Hungarian Empire, the *Länder* have always practised cross-border cooperation. Salzburg, for example, became a part of Austria only in 1805. Since the beginning of the thirteenth century, it had been an independent principality ruled by prince-archbishops and had therefore developed its own diplomatic tradition.[10]

As a small country, Austria depends on good relations with its neighbours and the international community. A year after it declared permanent neutrality on 26 October 1955, Austria became a member of both the United Nations (UN) and the Council of Europe. Together with other partners, it co-founded the European Free Trade Association (EFTA) in 1960. After joining the EU in 1995, it held the presidency for two six-month terms in 1998 and 2006.[11]

THE CONSTITUTIONAL SETTING FOR FOREIGN RELATIONS

The Constitutional and Legal Framework

Article 10 of the B-VG assigns the external political and economic representation of Austria to the federation. The federal order also holds the treaty-making power, although it must consult with the *Länder* before concluding international treaties that the *Länder* would be required to implement. The views of the *Länder*, however, are not binding. Only if the federation concludes treaties on matters within the jurisdiction of the *Länder* is the approval of the Federal Council, the second chamber of the federal Parliament, required (B-VG, Art. 50). The Federal Council is composed of members in proportion to the number of inhabitants in the *Länder* elected by their parliaments (*Landtage*). As will be explained below, the role of the *Länder* in Austria's EU policy is much stronger than it is in foreign policy generally.

A 1988 amendment to the B-VG[12] grants the *Länder* treaty-making power. Article 16 enables the *Länder* to conclude international treaties with neighbouring countries or other constituent units in matters falling within their autonomous spheres of action. The procedures require the respective *Land* government to inform the federal government before the start of negotiations. Federal approval must then be obtained prior to conclusion of the treaty. On request of the federal government, a *Land* must terminate negotiations of a particular treaty. Finally, according to Article 66 of the B-VG, the federal president can delegate the power to sign an international treaty to a *Land* government but only where such a treaty does not amend or complement existing laws. Not surprisingly, then, the *Länder* have not yet made use of the new provision.

In addition to this type of limited treaty-making power, Article 9, paragraph 2, of the B-VG could possibly serve as a basis for cross-border and transnational activities as well as for the creation of attendant institutions. Designed for Austria's participation in the activities of intergovernmental organizations, this provision states that federal powers can be transferred to intergovernmental organizations and their authorities after approval by Parliament. The activities of foreign authorities in Austria or the activities of Austrian authorities in foreign countries must be regulated in the same way. As the wording is clearly "federal," there is dispute about whether – in view of recent developments in Europe – it can be applied also to the *Länder*. The (first) additional protocol to the Madrid Convention, which came into force for Austria on 18 June 2004, further developed possibilities for cross-border cooperation by providing for the establishment of cross-border institutions (with or without legal personality) and in Article 4 for the establishment of a public law entity "if the national law allows it." But it is doubtful that this would be the case. Thus the *Länder* have very limited power to conclude agreements that establish transnational public law institutions. The European Outline Convention on Transfrontier Co-operation between Territorial Communities or Authorities of the Council of Europe entered into force in Austria on 19 January 1983 and served as the basis for bilateral agreements with Italy in 1993 and Slovakia in 2003.

Flexibility and Pragmatism: Agreements and Memoranda of Understanding as Subjects of Civil Law

Thus limited in developing external relations as part of their official activity, the *Länder* have done so as subjects of civil law instead. The federation, *Länder*, and municipalities can exercise their powers as public authorities to enact laws or other generally binding regulations or can exercise executive or judicial powers by issuing general executive decrees, individual administrative rulings, or court judgments. Alternately, they can act as "quasi" private persons; in other words, they can act as subjects of the civil law, or the so-called *Privatwirtschaftverwaltung*.

This second kind of exercise of power is of great importance for cross-border and transnational activities. Because many such activities can be considered economic, social, or cultural, they can be undertaken by regional or local authorities acting through the instrumentality of civil law. Accordingly, many memoranda of understanding, cooperation agreements, and so on used in cross-border and interregional activities of both *Länder* and local authorities are based on Article 17 of the B-VG. Although these agreements are not legally binding, they nonetheless express the signatories' commitment to implement common projects. These cases do not require the supervision or approval of the federation. As no registration takes place, the number of these agreements is not documented centrally.

The importance of Article 17 for activities of both the national government and the *Länder* was demonstrated recently in the coalition agreement of the Austrian federal government sworn in on 11 January 2007. The government clearly stated that the content of Article 17 shall be retained unchanged throughout the constitutional reform process foreseen for the 2007–10 legislative period.

ROLE AND STATUS OF THE *LÄNDER* WITHIN THE EU

Role in Forming and Implementing EU Policy

The *Länder* actively promoted Austrian membership in what was then known as the European Communities (EC). On 13 November 1987 the Land Governors' Conference (Landeshauptleutekonferenz) requested that the federal government immediately submit an application for membership. In the run-up to Austria's entry into the European Economic Area (EEA) and the EU, the *Länder* – in a development similar to that of Germany – demanded that their rights to be informed of and to participate in European integration matters be entrenched in the federal Constitution.[13]

This demand was met by the involvement of the *Länder* from 1989 on in the Council for Matters of Integration Policy. In 1992 an amendment was made to Article 16 of the B-VG that introduced information and participation rights of the *Länder* in developing Austria's EU policy. To specify the implementation of the new provisions, two treaties pursuant to Article 15 of the B-VG[14] were concluded on 12 March 1992: one between the federation and the nine *Länder* and another among the nine *Länder*. The 1994 amendment to the B-VG took account of Austria's imminent entry into the EU. A new section entitled "The European Union" established the necessary provisions in Article 23 of the B-VG, replacing and specifying those introduced in Article 16 in 1992.

With the coming into effect of the Maastricht Treaty in 1994, several EU member states introduced constitutionally or legally granted participation rights for their regions. Negotiation of the Maastricht Treaty (concluded on 7 February 1992) led Germany to introduce Article 23 into its Basic Law as well as a new law detailing the cooperation of the federation and *Länder* in EU matters. Coincidentally, the article of the German Basic Law that served as a model for Austria and the corresponding article of the B-VG have the same number.

Under the new Article 23 of the B-VG, the federal government must inform the *Länder* without delay of all projects in the EU framework that affect their autonomous competences or are otherwise of interest to them; it must also allow the *Länder* to present their views within reasonable time. In return, the *Länder* have established coordination mechanisms to allow a swift response. Conferences of *Länder* experts prepare opinions that are presented to the federal chancellery, the Ministry for European and International Affairs, and if applicable, the responsible federal ministry via a liaison office located in Vienna (Verbindungsstelle der Bundesländer, or VST).[15] If the *Länder* present a uniform position (*einheitliche Stellungnahme* – as opposed to the nonbinding common position, see below) on an EU project that falls within their competence, the federation is bound by that position in negotiations and voting in the EU. It may deviate from the agreed position only for compelling foreign and integration policy reasons.

Previously, the *Länder* enjoyed the right only to express an opinion when international treaties affected their autonomous jurisdiction. The federal government was not obliged to heed a unified view of the *Länder*. This new requirement, therefore, brought a considerable increase both in the role of the *Länder* and in their position vis-à-vis the federal government. However, it should not be forgotten that the *Länder* did not gain new competences but only participation rights as a compensation for transfers of some of their sovereign powers to the EU.

From the introduction of this measure in 1992 to December 2007, the *Länder* passed seventy uniform positions. These dealt with such diverse matters as the acquisition of property, the draft guidelines on voting rights for EU citizens in municipalities, the European Commission's green paper on tourism, specific aspects of EU entry negotiations with Hungary, and association talks with Turkey. In 2005 the *Länder* adopted positions on three EU initiatives: (1) a proposal for a directive on access to justice in environmental matters; (2) the draft EU Commission decision adopting the list of sites of European Community importance for the Atlantic biogeographical region, with direct impact on development plans and infrastructure projects in the *Länder*; and (3) the proposal for a directive on services in the Internal Market. In negotiations for the General Agreement on Trade in Services (GATS), the EU represents the member states in the World Trade Organization (WTO). The *Länder* adopted several resolutions seeking to exempt from GATS the opening of markets for services of general interest that are often provided by constituent units, such as water, health, education audiovisual services, urban transport, and social services. The federation respected the binding character of the uniform opinions and defended the *Länder* positions in the EU. The *Länder* also introduced these positions in the deliberations of the COR and in networks of European regional and local authorities.

Because the autonomous legislative powers of the *Länder* are weak, EU legislation affects them only in part while also affecting the federation. Because the Austrian distribution of powers is highly fragmented, EU legislation often requires implementation by both the federation and the *Länder* – each within its sphere of legislation. As a result, the *Länder* often issue common positions (*gemeinsame Stellungnahmen*) that have no binding character. In 2005, 2006, and 2007 they adopted forty-nine common positions that were then generally respected by the federal government.

The reason for this high level of cooperation with the federal government is the strong executive dimension of Austrian federalism. This dimension is characterized both by the *Länder*'s own extensive executive functions and by those transferred from the federal government to the *Länder* in the context of what is called indirect federal administration (*mittelbare Bundesverwaltung*) as outlined in Article 102 of the B–VG, whereby *Land* governments administer federal laws in the *Länder*. The *Länder* are responsible for implementing federal law in areas such as craftsmanship and trade, railway transportation, aviation and shipping, certain areas of environmental protection, health, and water. Further, the *Länder* have to implement legislation pursuant to federal framework laws – for instance, in land reform, provision of electricity, hospitals and nursing homes, and the organization of compulsory schooling. Many of these policies have an international dimension because they must take into account international agreements or EU norms. These responsibilities as well as the strong identities of the *Länder* are reasons for their participation in international and European affairs.

Similarly, the *Länder* are bound by Article 23 of the B-VG to take the necessary measures within their autonomous jurisdictions to transpose and implement EU legislation. Should a *Land* fail to comply expeditiously with this obligation, implementation of EU laws temporarily becomes the responsibility of the federation – but only after a European court has found Austria guilty of failing to implement the legislation. The competence falls back to the respective *Land* once it has passed the required law. Only once (in 2002) has the federation had to act on behalf of a *Land*, when Carinthia failed to incorporate EU labour-protection regulations into its *Land* staff codes.[16]

Länder as Subjects and Objects of European Court Proceedings

Besides introducing and defending *Länder* policy preferences, the federation defends the positions of the *Länder* in infringement procedures. In 2005 the European Commission held Austria responsible for failing to implement 24 of 1,635 directives; 11 of these fell within the jurisdiction of the federation, while 13 fell within the jurisdictions of both the *Länder* and the federation.[17] Over the years, the majority of directives affecting the *Länder* have dealt with nature and wildlife protection, the environment, and ski guides. Conversely, in the case of unlawful action or neglect by EU institutions in matters of *Land* legislation, the federal government – at the request of a *Land* – is obliged by Article 10 of the agreement concluded between the federation and the *Länder* in 1992 to press for appropriate legal remedies before the European Court of Justice (ECJ) — that is, if no other *Land* vetoes the action and no compelling integration or foreign policy reasons are claimed by the federation. The Constitutional Court would decide whether this was claimed rightly. No *Land* has thus far initiated a legal action. The costs of the proceedings are to be borne by the *Länder* that have demanded legal action.

In recent judgments, however, the EU courts have regarded not only member states but also constituent governments as capable of acting in court on matters falling within their legislative responsibility. On 5 October 2005 the Court of First Instance ruled against certain legal provisions issued by Upper Austria prohibiting the cultivation and planting of genetically modified organisms as well as the breeding and release of transgenic animals for the purposes of hunting and fishing.[18] These provisions were held not to comply with provisions of the treaty establishing the European Community and governing the EU's Internal Market.[19] More relevant than the result, however, was the court's acknowledgment of Upper Austria as a directly concerned legislator exercising powers granted to it by the Austrian constitutional system. This trailblazing decision forms the basis for *Länder* and regions to defend their own jurisdictions in European courts and constitutes an approach to a new role for the regions before European courts. If the domestic constitutional system assigns legislative competence to the regions, action by the regions against a negative decision pursuant to EU provisions governing the Internal Market is now admissible.[20]

FEDERATION–*LÄNDER* RELATIONS IN FOREIGN AFFAIRS

The federation's relations with the *Länder* are managed by all federal ministries acting within their particular jurisdictions. There are no federal liaison officers or offices for discussing current domestic or foreign policy issues with the *Länder*. The newly appointed secretary of state for EU-region policy and administrative reforms in the federal chancellery deals largely with the *Länder* in these matters but holds no cross-cutting jurisdiction for general political relations with the *Länder*. If issues need to be discussed, the *Länder* invite the federal chancellor and/or ministers concerned to attend the *Land* Governors' Conference. For fundamental questions of Austria's EU and foreign policy and Austria's defence policy, the Council for European and Foreign Affairs and the National Security Council serve as contacts. The federation also includes representatives of bordering *Länder* in all bilateral commissions with neighbouring countries. Both the *Land* Governors' Conference and the Conference of the Presidents of the *Landtage* present the positions of the *Länder* to the federal government.

Since Austria became an EU member in 1995, European affairs and integration policy have become European domestic policy, and *Länder* participation has become a daily routine. With the increase in EU activities, the *Länder* and federal ministries have established working relations that did not previously exist with much intensity, if at all. The B-VG provides a flexible framework, and Article 22 states the rationale: "All authorities of the federation, the *Länder* and the municipalities are bound within the framework of their legal sphere of competence to render each other mutual assistance." Disputes over foreign policy rarely occur because the federation shares information with the *Länder* and involves them in a timely manner. This procedure leads to a general consensus on Austrian priorities in this field.

Implementation of both bilateral treaties and multilateral ones such as European charters is often a *Land* responsibility. Within their autonomous spheres of competence, the *Länder* are constitutionally bound to take all measures necessary to implement international treaties. Should a *Land* fail to comply punctually with this obligation, the legislative competence for taking these measures passes to the federation – without the requirement for a court ruling or arbitration. That said, any legislative measure the federation takes pursuant to this provision becomes invalid as soon as the *Land* involved takes the required action. This stipulation of Article 16 of the B-VG applies only to non-EU matters.

Land Roles in International Negotiations and Organizations

When the federation negotiates international agreements, the *Länder* exercise most of their influence in the preparatory phases that shape Austria's position. The *Länder* nominate 42 politicians and 197 civil servants as joint representatives[21] for Austrian delegations in the EU, the COE, and the most important international organizations. These delegates must make it clear that they act on behalf of all nine *Länder*. To that end, they must seek a mandate and instructions for their activities and negotiations before meetings. They must also provide the relevant meeting documents and information to the other *Länder* and report back after the meetings.

As for representation in major international forums such as United Nations agencies, the *Länder* nominate joint representatives for bodies dealing with matters of *Länder* relevance (e.g., the World Health Organization (WHO) Charter on transport, environment, and health). In addition, joint representatives participate in the UN Environment Program (UNEP), and *Länder* develop their own strategies to implement the UN's Millennium Goals domestically. Within the Council of Europe, *Land* ministers sit in ministerial conferences such as those for regional planning (Conférence Européenne des Ministres responsables de l'Amenagement du Terrritoire, or CEMAT), local authorities, and the environment. Civil servants – often the sole representatives of Austria – also attend meetings of the Steering Committee on Local and Regional Democracy (CDLR) and its subgroups, committees for the protection of animals in agriculture, the Berne Convention on the conservation of European wildlife and natural habitats, the Pan-European Ecological Network, the European Landscape Convention, and various other committees. But the majority of the 22 politicians and 173 civil servants are appointed to EU bodies, committees, and working parties.

Involvement of Länder in Austrian External Affairs and Defence

Between 1989 and 2001 the *Länder* participated in the Council for Matters of the Austrian Integration Policy, which dealt with EU matters only. The Council for Matters of Austrian Integration and Foreign Policy and the National Security Council were established in 2001, replacing the former Council for Foreign Affairs and the Council for (European) Integration. This reorganization enhanced involvement of the *Länder* and allowed their EU experience since 1995 to be taken into account. The *Länder* send two representatives of the *Land* Governors' Conference and two representatives of their *Landtage* to the Council for Matters of Austrian Integration and Foreign Policy. The council advises the federal government on fundamental questions of foreign policy that have not been reserved for the

National Security Council. The latter advises the federal government on all fundamental matters of foreign, security, and defence policy. A representative of the chair of the *Land* Governors' Conference must sit on the council as an advisory member. If the council deals with issues touching on the interests of a *Land*, the respective *Land* governor must also be invited.

Are the various *Länder* permitted to engage in foreign relations with other countries independently? The policy is quite ambiguous here. In 2002 the Federal Council discussed whether a formal coordination of *Länder* foreign activities with the federal government should take place. Benita Ferrero-Waldner, the foreign minister at the time, stated that no such institutional coordination existed; instead, *Land* governments and federal services held ad hoc meetings when appropriate. As a reaction to a public debate caused by several visits – neither clearly private nor clearly official – of the governor of Carinthia to Libya and Iraq, Ferrero-Waldner addressed the *Land* Governors' Conference. She renewed an earlier offer to use the knowledge and experience of the diplomatic service abroad for visits of *Land* representatives abroad. On 6 March 2002 the conference took note that governors would inform the federal Ministry for Foreign Affairs of political visits abroad and, if required, would make use of the support offered. In practice, Austria's embassies and consulates are frequently asked to prepare official visits of *Land* politicians and delegations.

Joint Initiatives and Projects

Beyond official missions abroad, the federation and *Länder* often implement common projects abroad or joint projects with an international dimension, among them the Austrian School and the Colegio Viena in Guatemala City, Austrian libraries and cultural institutes, and development projects in countries in Asia, Africa, and South America. Directly after the Indian Ocean tsunami of 2004, Austria provided €5.7 million (US$7.7 million) in humanitarian aid, and the federal government, *Länder,* and municipalities prepared a reconstruction program and provided €50 million (US$67.5 million) over three years. The federation contributed €34 million (US$45.8 million), the *Länder* €10 million (US$13.5 million), and the cities and municipalities €6 million (US$8.1 million) for projects like national reconciliation, recovery, tourism, and infrastructure.

A further example of joint international projects is the Reconciliation Fund, involving reparations for an estimated 150,000 persons pressed into forced labour during the Second World War. On 24 October 2000 bilateral agreements were signed with Belarus, Poland, the Czech Republic, Ukraine, and Hungary,[22] as well as an executive agreement with the United States. By the end of 2003 the fund included contributions from the federation totalling €268.9 million (US$363.3 million), from the *Länder* totalling €36.3 million (US$49 million), and from the Austrian private sector totalling €133.8 million (US$180.8 million), as well as funds from other donors.[23]

From 1985 onward, Austrian cities, *Länder,* and the federal government opposed a decision of the minister-presidents of the German *Länder* in 1979 to build a nuclear reprocessing plant in eastern Bavaria. They passed resolutions against this project and made representations to German administrators, arguing that the safety of the citizens was not guaranteed. On 22 July 1998 Austrians presented their concerns at a public hearing in Bavaria. Members of *Land* governments and parliaments, mayors and municipal councillors, and even the federal minister for the environment defended the Austrian position. After the death in autumn 1989 of the main political promoter of the plant, the minister-president of Bavaria, Franz-Josef Strauss, the operating company withdrew the project.[24] Similarly, *Land* governments and *Landtage* adopted resolutions against nuclear plants in the Czech Republic (Temelin and Dukovany), the Slovak Republic (Bohunice and Mochovce), Slovenia (Krsko), and Bulgaria (Kosloduy), asking the federal government to introduce them at the European level. This Austrian antinuclear activity led to considerable tensions with these countries.[25]

DOMESTIC AND INTERNATIONAL MANIFESTATIONS OF *LÄNDER* DIPLOMACY

Size affects external relations. Austria, as a small country, and the *Länder,* as small polities, depend on coexistence, cooperation, and mutual exchange with their neighbours and with partners that have similar interests. *Länder* external relations occur in bilateral, multilateral, and institutional contexts as well as in the framework of Austria's federal foreign policy. The German and Swiss term "*kleine Aussenpolitik*" (minor foreign policy) is not used in Austria.

Foreign and European affairs of a political as opposed to functional nature are the governors' responsibility. They receive ambassadors, pay official visits to other countries, and represent their *Länder* both politically and legally. In most *Länder,* matters such as visits of international dignitaries and general partnership agreements are the responsibility of protocol offices. European affairs offices manage institutional involvement in the COR and the CLRAE as well as in interregional associations. Integrated into the general staffs or the legal and constitutional services of the administration, these offices deal with cross-cutting issues.[26]

Foreign and external activities of the *Länder* are well documented in the annual report on Austrian federalism published by the Innsbruck-based Institute for Federalism, in the annual foreign policy report of the federal Ministry for European and International Affairs, and in many publications of the *Länder* themselves.[27] All these provide a good overview of external activities of the *Länder*, including official visits abroad. Budget data and human resources, however, are not specfied, as foreign activities also occur in the portfolios of the ministers for culture, economy, tourism, agriculture, youth, and most others too. All *Länder* and the federation have agencies to promote investment and/or exports.[28] Subsidies for foreign investments in the *Länder* are limited due to the Internal Market and the state-aid regime of the EU. The *Länder*, therefore, focus their economic development strategies on establishing research clusters, adjusting their educational priorities to take account of the needs of the economy, and offering affordable land with rail, road, and air connections. Because of the party composition of governments and the *Landtage*, external activities are carried out mainly by politicians of the two largest political parties, the Sozialdemokratische Partei Österreichs (SPÖ) and the Österreichische Volkspartei (ÖVP). In the *Land* parliaments, the SPÖ and the ÖVP have 183 and 168 seats, respectively, or 78.3% of the total of 448. The *Land* governments are led by four SPÖ governors, four ÖVP governors, and one Alliance for the Future of Austria (Bündnis Zukunft Österreich, or BZÖ) governor. From 2000 to 2005 *Land* politicians conducted 273 official visits to 49 countries. The majority of these visits (180) were to 18 EU countries – not counting institutional activities in the COR, plenaries and committee meetings in Brussels, and CLRAE activities. The federal president also invites *Land* representatives to join delegations on state visits. Examples since 2000 have included the governors of Burgenland (to Germany and Iran), Salzburg (China and India), Tyrol (India), and Upper Austria (Germany).

In practice, the official foreign activities of legislators are generally limited to acting as speakers and chairpersons of the European and integration committees of the *Landtage*. The annual conferences of the presidents of the constituent-unit parliaments of Germany, Austria, South Tyrol (Italy), and the German Community in Belgium have become valued forums. Some regional parliaments have organized study visits – many to Brussels but also to other parts of Europe. The European Affairs Commission of the *Landtag* of Upper Austria, for example, visited 25 of 27 EU member states and therefore developed European contacts and knowledge of Europe's affairs. All political parties participate. *Landtage*, particularly opposition parties, sometimes raise issues like the cost of official visits abroad, the composition of the delegations, and actual achievements of the objectives of the missions.

The *Länder*, regardless of their size or budget situations, also engage in bilateral cooperation with other regions or countries. This happens in partnerships not only with neighbouring regions but also with regions and sovereign states far from Austria, although their competence to enter into formal state treaties is limited to neighbouring states. The following examples, by no means exhaustive, demonstrate the geographic scope and the nature of the agreements made by virtue of Article 17 of the B-VG: Salzburg and the Republic of Slovenia (common declaration of the governor and the minister-president of Slovenia, 1992), Salzburg and the Chinese province of Hainan (partnership agreement, 2000), Upper Austria and the Western Cape province of South Africa (agreement, 1995), Upper Austria and Israel (memorandum of understanding, 2004), and Styrian cooperation projects with thirty-five countries. Cooperation by *Länder* with constituent units of the Russian Federation is documented on the website of the Austrian embassy in Moscow.[29] Of the thirty-six agreements concluded between the Russian Federation and Austria,[30] several areas – such as tourism, culture, science, technology, and health – affect the jurisdiction of the *Länder*.

After bilateral cooperation and partnership agreements, the *Länder*'s involvement since the 1970s in so-called "working communities" (*Arbeitsgemeinschaft*, or ARGE) has marked a period of growing international activity. ARGE ALP (1972), ARGE Alpen Adria (1978), and ARGE Donauländer (1990) were established with active participation by the *Länder*. The driving force behind these communities was the practice of the principle of subsidiarity, the will to find solutions for common problems without involving the national governments, and the will to present common proposals to them. These working communities also run projects with a people-to-people approach, including family activities and sports events such as the ARGE ALP Trophy, which unites figure skaters from the ten member regions of Austria, Germany, Switzerland, and Italy. A particularly successful network was established in 1972 when the governments of Baden-Württemberg and Bavaria in Germany, the Swiss cantons Appenzell-Außerrhoden, Appenzell-Innerrhoden, St Gallen, Schaffhausen, Thurgau, and Zürich, the Austrian *Land* Vorarlberg, and the duchy Liechtenstein founded the International Conference of Lake Constance (Bodenseekonferenz) to protect and develop the lake area in an environmentally friendly fashion for human use.[31]

Vienna has developed its own external-relations policy to promote the establishment of CENTROPE: an organization involving three Austrian *Länder* and regions from the Czech Republic, the Slovak Republic, and Hungary. As the seat of several international organizations (e.g., UN and OPEC) and their agencies (e.g., the EU's Fundamental Rights Agency, or FRA), Vienna enjoys special support from the federation. Together with the Vienna Chamber of Commerce, the *Land* and city run the Vienna Business Agency, which maintains representative offices for the promotion of commerce and tourism in Brussels, Hong Kong, and Tokyo.

Since Austrian accession to the EU, the *Länder* and municipalities have joined the federal government in cross-border cooperation programs with neighbouring countries. Between 1998 and 2002 Austria seconded experts from federal and *Land* administrations to help implement approximately 160 twinning partnerships with regions and cities in the Czech Republic, Hungary, Slovakia, and Slovenia.

Regions with Legislative Powers, Euro-Regions, and Others

EU regions with legislative powers have established two networks through which to pursue their interests – espcially in institutional matters but also in improved lawmaking, subsidiarity, the safeguarding of regional spheres of legislation, access to European courts, and regional democracy and autonomy. These networks are the Conference of the European Regional Legislative Parliaments (CALRE), founded 1997 in Asturias, Spain, and the Conference of Presidents of Regions with Legislative Powers (REGLEG), established in Barcelona in November 2000. Only 8 of the 27 EU member states – Austria, Belgium, Finland, Germany, Italy, Portugal, Spain, and the United Kingdom – have regions with legislative powers (there are 74 such regions in total).[32] All nine Austrian *Länder* participate in the two networks.

Beginning in 1995, cross-border Euro-regions composed of local authorities have been established in Upper Austria, Salzburg, Tyrol, and Vorarlberg with significant support from the *Länder*. Legally nonbinding development strategies – for example, concerning transport, health, infrastructure, and sports facilities – are being implemented with financial support from the EU, Germany, Austria, and the *Länder*. The fall of the Iron Curtain finally brought new opportunities for the eastern *Länder* to cooperate with their neighbours in the fields of infrastructure, economic development, tourism, and so on. In 2003 Burgenland, Lower Austria, and Vienna joined Bratislava (in Slovakia), Trnava and Brno (in the Czech Republic), and Györ and Sopron (in Hungary) in signing the founding document to create a new Euro-region.

In addition to associations with a broad mandate, there are also networks or associations of regions with a narrower focus – for example, organic farming. In Austria 8% of farming is organic. With the highest rate in the EU, followed by Finland with 6%, it is only natural for Upper Austria, Salzburg, Burgenland, Styria, Carinthia, Tyrol, and Lower Austria to engage actively in a European network of GMO-Free Regions.[33] It comprises forty regions from six countries. These *Land* activities complement the position of the federal government. The federation and the *Länder* share the cost of the required national co-financing for EU subsidies for agriculture at an average ratio of 60:40.

Other significant pan-European regional associations with Austrian membership are the Council of European Municipalities and Regions (CEMR), the Association of European Border Regions (AEBR), the Assembly of European Viticultural Regions (AREV), and the Airport Regions Conference (ARC).

THE EU: A NEW KIND OF DOMESTIC POLITICS

Due to their experiences in interregional associations and networks, the *Länder* were well prepared for Austria's EU membership. EU politics have become regular matters of domestic politics wherever *Länder* competencies are affected. Depending on different *Land* constitutional settings, *Landtage* discuss EU affairs in their EU committees and pass the legislation required for transposition of EU directives. In general, however, foreign and European affairs are the domains of the executives.

Participation in Austrian Delegations and the Council of Ministers

Article 23d, paragraph 3, of the B-VG implements Article 203 of the Treaty Establishing the European Community (TEC)[34] in Austria. In matters of *Land* legislation, the federation can transfer participation in the creation of an opinion in the EU to a representative named by the *Länder*. Due to swift coordination mechanisms between the federation and the *Länder* and the possibility of *Land* participation in all preparatory interministerial meetings, political representatives of the *Länder* have rarely participated in meetings of the Council of Ministers. The federation generally feeds *Land* positions into the official Austrian position. Here, it should not be forgotten that the autonomous legislative competences of the *Länder* are reflected not in a single Council of Minsters committee but only as small elements in several of them. Early participation of *Land* representatives in preparatory meetings has therefore proven to be more effective than single appearances at the council's meetings, where the coordinated position of the member nation-state has to be presented.[35]

The agreement concluded between the federation and the *Länder* on 12 March 1992 calls for *Land* politicians or officials to be included as representatives in the Austrian delegations. For instance, one or two *Land* presidents have participated in ministerial meetings on EU membership negotiations and were able to influence the Austrian delegation's position in important areas such as transalpine transport and secondary residences. At the same time, *Land* representatives were able credibly to explain the Austrian position and negotiation results to their people before the referendum on EU membership of 12 June 1994.

For the 2000 Intergovernmental Conference on institutional reform of the EU (Treaty of Nice), the *Länder* successfully introduced their positions via the federal government as well as via the interregional networks. The treaty extends majority voting to a series of additional areas, whereby Austria – supporting the extension in principle – managed to have unanimous voting retained in particularly sensitive areas touching on *Land* competences such as water management, land use, choice of energy, strategic transport policy, and some environmental questions. Austria is a nuclear-free country. This position is shared by the federation, the *Länder*, and the municipalities and is also defended on the international scene.

The governors of Salzburg and Vorarlberg were nominated to participate in the 1996 and the 2000 Intergovernmental Conferences and to prepare the Austrian position domestically. Only Austria, Belgium, and Germany include representatives of the constituent states in these delegations. On the civil service side, the representative of the *Länder* in Austria's permanent representation to the EU is nominated for all European Council meetings and participates as a member of the Austrian delegation.

Presence of the Länder in Brussels

The *Länder* are entitled to second staff – at their own expense – to Austria's Permanent Representation to the EU in Brussels. Two officers from the staff of the Vienna-based liaison office of the *Länder* work there permanently, with diplomatic status. Their full integration opens early access to nearly all documents that pass from the Permanent Representation to the national capital. Thus the *Länder* receive documents and briefings from their representative in the Permanent Representation, from the Ministry for European and International Affairs, and from their own offices. Between 1992 and 1995, eight of the nine *Länder* established liaison offices to the European Union in Brussels to collect information and lobby primarily the European Commission and the European Parliament for specific projects and policies and for secondments of staff and student internships. Due to the small size of these offices (one to five people), each *Land* focuses on specific topics and develops expertise on these topics, which is then shared among the *Länder*.

Cross-border cooperation between Austrian Tyrol and the autonomous provinces of Bolzano/Südtirol and Trento in Italy provided the motive for establishing a shared liaison office of the Europaregion Tyrol in Brussels in 1995. Although Tyrol ran the office together with the chambers of commerce of the Italian partners, the Italian government considered this an illegal act of regional foreign policy and launched proceedings at the Constitutional Court. In 1997 the court found that cooperation procedures had been ignored, but it also underlined that, according to the principle of subsidiarity, the state could not permanently hinder offices of this kind. In the meantime, a 1996 Italian law permitted all regions to establish liaison offices in Brussels.

The Committee of the Regions (COR)

The COR is the EU counterpart of the CLRAE and became operational in 1994. Because approximately three-quarters of EU legislation is implemented by local or regional governments, local and regional representatives need a voice in developing EU laws. The 344 COR members work in six committees, and preparatory work is done in the 27 national delegations and four political groups. The nine *Länder* nominate one member and one alternate each; local authorities nominate three.[36] In 1994, following the German model, the *Länder* decided to nominate *Land* governors as members of the COR. Alternate members include deputy governors, presidents of regional parliaments, and members of government or Parliament. From 1995 until 2007 Austrian members drafted 21 of 744 opinions adopted by the COR, or 2.82%.[37] Given that the COR is merely advisory, with neither the European Commission nor the European Council being bound by its opinions, it is not always certain how effective in fact the involvement of the *Länder* can be.

An Enhanced Status for Regions

In general, European states have been very reluctant to acknowledge the autonomous activities of regional authorities. However, both EU regional policy and the EU program INTERREG have encouraged them, and future options of territorial cooperation will foster interregional cooperation in a way that member states alone would not have promoted or permitted. Nor would bilateral cooperation alone have achieved such cooperation. European legislation provides the basis for concrete actions across and beyond borders. Effective 1 August 2007, the European Grouping for Territorial Cooperation (EGTC) will enhance this basis by providing a formal cross-border legal structure for the cooperation of member states, *Länder* or regions, local authorities, bodies governed by public law, and the associations of those bodies.[38] By spring 2008, however, Austria had not passed the required domestic legislation, while all others had done so.

In the seven years from 2007 to 2013, EU regional policy will provide €308 billion (US$416.1 billion) for projects stimulating interregional cooperation. That is approximately 36% of the EU budget. The new Objective 3, on "European territorial cooperation," is funded to the extent of €7.75 billion (US$10.5 billion), or 2.4% of the EU budget. Its three components of cross-border cooperation, transnational cooperation, and interregional cooperation will result in a doubling of EU funds, as these initiatives must be co-financed by national and mostly regional contributions.

Presently, the *Länder* participate in two transnational programs (formerly INTERREG III B): Central, Adriatic, Danubian, and South-Eastern European Space (CADSES) and Alpine Space (a program for spatial development in the Alpine region of several adjacent countries).[39]

COUNCIL OF EUROPE

Analogous to the EU scheme but without a specific legal basis, the *Länder* participate in Austrian delegations to both ministerial conferences and bodies of the Council of Europe (COE) such as the Steering Committee for Local and Regional Democracy (CDLR). The *Land* and local authorities also appoint representatives to the CLRAE.

The Congress of Local and Regional Authorities of Europe

The COE was the first European institution to set up a body for matters concerning the regions and local authorities. It began in 1952 with a parliamentary committee for local and regional questions, followed by a committee for local affairs established in 1954. In 1957 the Conference of Local and Regional Authorities was established. But the establishment of the Congress of Local and Regional Authorities of Europe (CLRAE) as a consultative body in the Council of Europe in 1994 marked a breakthrough. Its 315 full and 315 substitute members work in a Chamber of Regions and a Chamber of Local Authorities. As directly elected local and regional politicians, members represent the 200,000 local and regional authorities of the Council of Europe's member states. The *Länder* have three members and three substitute members. In 2007 these represented Tyrol, Lower Austria, Vienna and Carinthia, Upper Austria, and Salzburg.

Because the CLRAE established a working group for regions with legislative powers, it can consider the specific situation of these components better than can the COR. The mandate and composition of this working group are updated and renewed every two years. It addresses, among other things, the role of second chambers of national parliaments as representative bodies for the regions/*Länder*, and it promotes a European charter on regional democracy.

"Proxy Representation"

In 2000 Austrian foreign policy was confronted with extremely difficult and unusual conditions arising from bilateral sanctions imposed by the other fourteen EU member states.[40] These sanctions aimed to undermine the formation of a federal government composed of ministers from the Christian Democratic ÖVP and the right-wing populist Freiheitliche Partei Österreichs (FPÖ) after elections on 3 October 1999. On 31 January 2000, after consultations with the other governments, Portugal announced that the fourteen EU member states would not promote or accept any bilateral official contacts at the political level with an Austrian government integrating the FPÖ. There would be no support in favour of Austrian candidates seeking positions in international organizations, and Austrian ambassadors in EU capitals would be received only at a technical level. Belgium, for example, completely froze military cooperation with Austria. The mayor of Brussels acted to exclude Austrian *Länder* from a tourism trade fair, the

Belgian foreign minister called for a boycott on vacations in Austria, and the French Community placed a ban on school visits there. France cancelled all events that could have had a public effect in the 2000 bilateral program of military cooperation. Individual school and student-exchange programs with France and Belgium were cancelled. Cultural, educational, and scientific cooperation were also affected – especially in Belgium and France but also in Luxembourg and the Netherlands.

Due to its isolation, Austria had difficulty safeguarding its interests in the EU and farther afield. It was also difficult to maintain a degree of objectivity in foreign public opinion, although the federal government immediately issued a clear commitment to Europe's common values and obligations when it took office on 4 February 2000. Austrian federal president Thomas Klestil appealed to the European Parliament on 12 April, asking it "not to lose sight of the principles of objectivity and fairness"[41] and to find a way out of the current situation. The president of the European Parliament, Nicole Fontaine, expressed the hope "that Austria can once again become a full partner in our Union."[42] This statement, later described as a misunderstanding, was regarded in Austria as a deliberate provocation.

Although the opposition in the federal Parliament rejected motions against the sanctions, the *Land* Governors' Conference, representing the three major parties – ÖVP, SPÖ, and FPÖ – issued a joint declaration on 17 May 2000 expressly supporting diplomatic and political efforts by the federal government to lift the sanctions. The *Länder* supported these efforts through their own contributions at the regional level. Thus the regional parliaments of Carinthia, Styria, Tyrol, Salzburg, Vorarlberg, and Upper Austria adopted resolutions demanding that their respective *Land* governments actively work for the lifting of what they described as unjustified and undemocratically imposed sanctions. A number of German *Länder* adopted a noticeably independent and friendly attitude toward Austria in 2000.

The Belgian federal government avoided bilateral political contacts with members of the Austrian federal government, reducing all contact to a technical level. The *Länder* then used their political contacts established in the CoR, the Assembly of European Regions (AER), and the networks of regions with legislative powers (REGLEG and CALRE) to break the ice and attempt to explain the situation to their regional Belgian counterparts. Michael Häupl, governor of Vienna, met Elio di Rupo, the Walloon minister-president on 5 April 2000. Salzburg's governor, Franz Schausberger, was the first senior ÖVP politician to meet officially with the Flemish minister-president, Patrick Dewael, on 11 April 2000. Governor Wendelin Weingartner of Tyrol met with the minister-president of Belgium's German Community on 12 April and 5 August 2000. Finally, following the recommendations of "Three Wise Men,"[43] the sanctions were lifted on

12 September 2000. This cleared the path for a normalization of relations with the other partner countries and led to a new legal procedure in the EU Treaty. The EU Reform Treaty agreed on 19 October 2007 slightly amended the provisions of Article 7, which foresees a mechanism to deal with assumed violations of European values. This is to avoid unilateral political measures without transparent and structured procedures. Austria contributed painfully to the creation of a legal framework for the EU, whose member states have finally learned their lesson. Although the sanctions were felt to be unjust by most Austrians, with opinion polls showing dissatifaction with the EU, the FPÖ could not take advantage in elections. It fell from 26.9% of the vote in 1999 to 10% in 2002 and 11% in 2006.

CONCLUSION

To recapitulate, the foreign relations activities of the *Länder* are frequently based on the flexible Article 17 of the B-VG. This provision has also served as the basis for implementing common projects, although unclear legal provisions sometimes cause obstacles. Success in interregional cooperation is a function not mainly of size but also of priorities and integration into the relevant networks, as well as of the presence of political and administrative structures capable of swift action. Internal intergovernmental and external international activities helped the *Länder* to achieve their policy objectives. In addition to political cooperation, *Land* economic missions are often supported by the Austrian embassies and consulates as well as by the Austrian trade commissioners. Recent examples are missions of Salzburg's minister for economy and tourism to Kuban and Sochi, Russia, and of his Upper Austrian counterpart to Shandong, China, as well as missions of Viennese politicians and representatives of enterprises to Dubai and a delegation of Styria to Dubai and Qatar, all in autumn 2007. Success and cost effectiveness are difficult to evaluate. As economic missions always take place on proposals from economic actors and in close cooperation with the Austrian trade commissioners, and as missions occur repeatedly, the aims seem to be achieved. The same holds true for tourism promotion.

The participation scheme set up for Austria's EU membership marked a compensation for the *Länder* – not a gain of autonomous powers. Participation of senior *Land* politicians in the COR has improved the knowledge and skills of both politicians and civil servants in dealing with EU issues, in establishing and maintaining networks of like-minded regions, and in presenting Europe to the citizenry.

Since 1995 EU politics have increasingly become domestic politics, and the term "*Europäische Innenpolitik*" (European domestic policy) has been introduced. Both ÖVP and SPÖ politicians understand themselves as pro-European, and this attitude is shared by the representative bodies of the municipalities, employers, and employees.[44] With the exeption of transalpine transit traffic of heavy weights governed by EU legislation, international and/or EU issues do not affect *Land* or municipal elections, and they have played a minor role in the federal arena. The discussion of whether to hold a referendum about the EU Reform Treaty, which is strongly demanded by the FPÖ and the BZÖ and by the country's largest newspaper, may be cooled down by the next federal election, scheduled for 2010. On attaining participation rights, the *Länder* have used their possibilities by presenting proposals and positions to be incorporated into Austria's European policies. Although there is no constitutional provision for involvement of the *Länder* in the Council of Europe, the federation and the *Länder* have established a practice analogous to the one used in the EU framework.

Institutional involvement in the EU and financial incentives provided by the EU's regional policy have created the contacts, capacities, and structures necessary for enhanced foreign relations for the *Länder*. Cooperation of the federation and the *Länder* in European and foreign affairs has improved since EU membership, just as the *Länder* have gained significant experience and professionalism through membership.

EU regions, as well as regions and local authorities in neighbouring countries, can expect to gain new impetus from the European Grouping for Territorial Cooperation (EGTC), which began operation in August 2007 (although most member states or their regions had not yet adopted the required national legislation). The EGTC will both facilitate cooperation and help to establish structures with cross-border legal personalities. In the Council of Europe, member states are also negotiating a legal instrument to facilitate interregional and cross-border cooperation in their sphere.

Although membership in the Council of Europe and the EU is limited to member states, federal countries have gradually involved their regions in organizing delegations and preparing European-level legislation on matters affecting subnational government. Together with the federal countries of Belgium and Germany, Austria has contributed its share to establishing the participation of regions in European bodies as a normal procedure.

External activities of the *Länder* are an important element of Austrian federalism, and the federation does support them. Maintaining the key provision in the federal Constitution (Article 17) in the current constitutional reform shows that there is a consensus between the federation, the *Länder*, and the municipalities on external relations and activities both within and beyond the European Union and the Council of Europe. It also has proved useful to include such actors as entrepreneurs, universities, research institutes, and sports and cultural activists in foreign missions. This ensures that travelling does not just serve as end in itself but also achieves broader policy objectives.

NOTES

1 Theo Öhlinger, *Verfassungsrecht* (Vienna: WUV Universitätsverlag, 2005), 26.
2 *Land/Länder* refer to Austria's constituent units. "Regional" refers to the *Länder* and follows the definition of "region" set out in the December 1996 Declaration on Regionalism in Europe issued by the Assembly of European Regions (AER). Here, "region" is described as the first territorial body of public law established immediately below the country and endowed with political self-government. On the role of the AER, consult Lisbeth Weihe-Lindeborg, *Zum regionalen System: Stellenwert der Versammlung der Regionen Europas* (Marburg: Tectum Verlag, 2005).
3 Burgenland became part of Austria after a referendum in 1921.
4 § 9 para 3 of the Financial Equalization Act (Finanzausgleichsgesetz) of 2008, in *Bundesgesetzblatt* [Federal law gazette], part 1, no. 103 (2007), 5, governs the sharing of the costs of Austria's EU membership between the federation, *Länder*, and municipalities.
5 Details from the website of the federal statistical service, Statistik Austria: http://www.statistik.gv.at/web_de/statistiken/bevoelkerung/bevoelkerungsstand_jahres-_und_quartalswerte/bevoelkerung_zu_jahres-_quartalsanfang/022497.html (accessed 23 May 2007).
6 A provision of the Basic Law (Staatsgrundgesetz) of 1867 — "On the General Rights of Nationals in the Kingdoms and *Länder* Represented in the Council of the Realm" – grants the use of these languages. This law from the period of the Austro-Hungarian Empire was transposed to the republican era and granted constitutional status.
7 See Statistik Austria at http://www.statistik.gv.at/web_de/static/volkswirtschaftliche_gesamtrechnung_hauptgroessen_019505.pdf (accessed 5 July 2007).
8 Österreichisches Institut für Wirtschaftsforschung, "Monatsbericht" [Monthly report], February 2007, 121–3, http://www.wifo.ac.at/wwa/jsp/index.jsp?fid=23923&id=28261&typeid=8&display_mode=2 (accessed 15 October 2007).
9 See Statistik Austria at http://www.statistik.at/web_de/services/wirtschaftsatlas_oesterreich/aussenhandel/index.html; and Austrian Chamber of Commerce at http://wko.at/statistik (both accesed 31 January 2007).
10 Johann Kolmbauer, *Von Konsuln und Gesandten: Die Geschichte der Diplomatie in Salzburg*, Sonderpublikationen Nr 116 der Schriftenreihe des Landespressebüros (Salzburg: Land Salzburg, 1998).
11 For a concise discussion of Austria's way into the EU with special attention to the role of the *Länder*, see Andreas Kiefer, "Aspekte der Europapolitik Österreichs," in Martina Haedrich and Karl Schmitt, eds, *Schillerhausgespräche 1999*, 135–70 (Berlin: Schriftenreihe des Hellmuth-Loening-Zentrums für Staatswissenschaften Jena, Band 10, 2000).
12 See *Bundesgesetzblatt* [Federal law gazette], no. 685 (1988), 4495–6.
13 Resolutions of the *Land* Governors' Conferences of 8 June 1990 and 23 November 1990.

14 Article 15a of the B-VG enables the federation and the *Länder* to conclude agreements among themselves about matters within their respective spheres of competence. The principles of international law concerning treaties apply to these agreements.
15 The liaison office of the *Länder* was established in 1951. It serves as the technical platform for coordination of the *Länder* and as a mouthpiece vis-à-vis the federal government in domestic and international matters.
16 173. Verordnung: Schutz von Bediensteten des Landes Kärnten sowie der Gemeinden und Gemeindeverbände dieses Landes gegen Gefährdung durch biologische Arbeitsstoffe, in *Bundesgesetzblatt* [Federal law gazette], part 2, no. 173 (2002), 701. See also Gerhard Hörmanseder, "Probleme der EG-Richtlinienumsetzung aus Ländersicht," in Kärntner Verwaltungsakademie, ed., *4. Klagenfurter Legistik-Gespräche*, 133–50 (Klagenfurt: K-Verlag, 2007).
17 Institut für Föderalismus, ed., *30. Bericht über den Föderalismus in Österreich* (Wien: Braumüller Verlag, 2005), 117.
18 Judgement of the EU Court of First Instance (Fourth Chamber) of 5 October 2005, Joined Cases T 366/03 and T 235/04, Land Oberösterreich and Republic of Austria versus Commission of the European Communities. The question of the admissibility of the action brought by Oberösterreich is dealt with in paragraphs 25 to 30.
19 The judgment referred to Article 95, paragraph 5, of the Treaty Establishing the European Community (TEC), consolidated version published in the *Official Journal of the European Union*, C 321, 20 December 2006, 1–331.
20 Institut für Föderalismus, ed., *30. Bericht über den Föderalismus in Österreich*, 112.
21 A full list of the representatives (*Gemeinsame Ländervertreter*) is provided annually by the liaison office of the *Länder* and communicated to the federation, in addition to the immediate communication of individual nominations.
22 The Russian Federation signed the agreement on 27 November 2000.
23 See http://www.versoehnungsfonds.at (accessed 21 December 2006).
24 The movement against the nuclear reprocessing plant in Wackersdorf is documented at http://www.plage.cc/de/history/history2.shtml (accessed 15 October 2007).
25 Consult http://www.anti.atom.at (accessed 15 October 2007) for documentation of activities especially concerning the Czech Republic.
26 Peter Bußjäger and Andreas Rosner, *Mitwirken und Mitgestalten – Europa und die österreichischen Länder* (Wien: Braumüller Verlag, 2005).
27 The federal legal framework and some practices of Salzburg are documented in Roland Floimair, ed., *Die regionale Außenpolitik des Landes Salzburg* (Salzburg: Salzburg Dokumentationen 108, 1993).
28 All *Länder* agencies are listed on the website of the federal Austrian Business Agency (ABA): http://www.aba.gv.at/de/pages/714D3-227F2.html (accessed 15 October 2007).

29 See the list of cooperation agreements at http://www.aussenministerium.at/ view.php3?f_id=5302&LNG=de&version= (accessed 15 October 2007).
30 A full German-language list of these agreements – as well as of bilateral agreements with almost all countries – can be found at http://www.bmeia.gv.at.
31 See http://www.bodenseekonferenz.org.
32 Descriptions and analysis of the two networks of regions with legislative powers and their activities are published in German in the *Jahrbuch des Föderalismus* for 2004, 2005, and 2006, edited by Europäisches Zentrum für Föderalismus-Forschung (Baden-Baden: Nomos). For the English version, see Andreas Kiefer, "The Contribution of the Regions with Legislative Competences to the European Constitutional Process," in Institute of the Regions of Europe, ed., *Occasional Papers 2/2007: The EU-Constitutional Treaty and the Regions of Europe*, 165–206 (Salzburg: edition pm, 2007).
33 This is a network of regions that want to remain free of genetically modified organisms (GMOs), established in 2003; see http://genet.iskra.net/en (accessed 30 September 2007).
34 Article 203 of the Treaty Establishing the European Community (TEC) reads: "The Council shall consist of a representative of each Member State at ministerial level, authorised to commit the government of that Member State." See *Official Journal of the European Union*, C 325, 24 December 2002, 136.
35 Recent developments in Spain, Italy, and the United Kingdom also seek to involve the regions both in the domestic process and in these states' delegations to the Council of Ministers and its preparatory bodies. For details, see also Committee of the Regions (COR), ed., *Procedures for Local and Regional Authority Participation in European Policy Making in the Member States* (Luxemburg: Office for Official Publications of the European Communities, 2005).
36 For the composition of the Austrian delegation, consult the website of the Committee of the Regions (COR) at http://www.cor.europa.eu/en/presentation/national_delegations.htm# (accessed 15 October 2007).
37 Andreas Kiefer, "Aktivitäten der Länder in europäischen Institutionen, Verbänden und Netzwerken," in Stefan Hammer and Peter Bussjäger, eds, *Außenbeziehungen im Bundesstaat*, 69–85 (Wien: Schriftenreihe des Instituts für Föderalismus, Band 105, 2007).
38 *Official Journal of the European Union*, L 210, 31 July 2006, 19.
39 Participating countries and regions/*Länder*, objectives, and priorities can be found at http://www.cadses.net/en/programme.html and at http://www.alpine-space.eu (both accessed 25 March 2008).
40 See in-depth analysis, documentation, and views of observers from all over the world in Erhard Busek and Martin Schauer, eds, *Eine europäische Erregung: Die "Sanktionen" der Vierzehn gegen Österreich im Jahr 2000: Analysen und Kommentare* (Vienna: Böhlau, 2003).
41 Minutes of the debate in the European Parliament on 12 April 2000, published in English at http://www.europarl.europa.eu/sides/getDoc.do?pubRef=-//EP//

TEXT+CRE+20000412+ITEM-009+DOC+XML+V0//EN&language=EN (accessed 11 August 2008). The statement of Mr Klestil appears in paragaph 12 of his speech.

42 Ibid. The statement of Ms Fontaine appears in paragraph 8 of her closing speech.

43 In July 2000, on request of the governments of the fourteen EU member states, the president of the European Court of Human Rights invited Jochen Frowein, a German expert in international law, Martti Ahtisaari, former president of Finland, and Marcelino Oreja, former foreign minister of Spain, to edit a report about the situation in Austria. On 8 September 2000 the report was presented to the French president, Jacques Chirac, who then chaired the European Council.

44 On its website, the ÖVP calls itself "Europapartei"; see http://www.oevp.at. And the SPÖ has the Austrian flag and the EU stars in its logo; see http://www.spoe.at.

Belgium

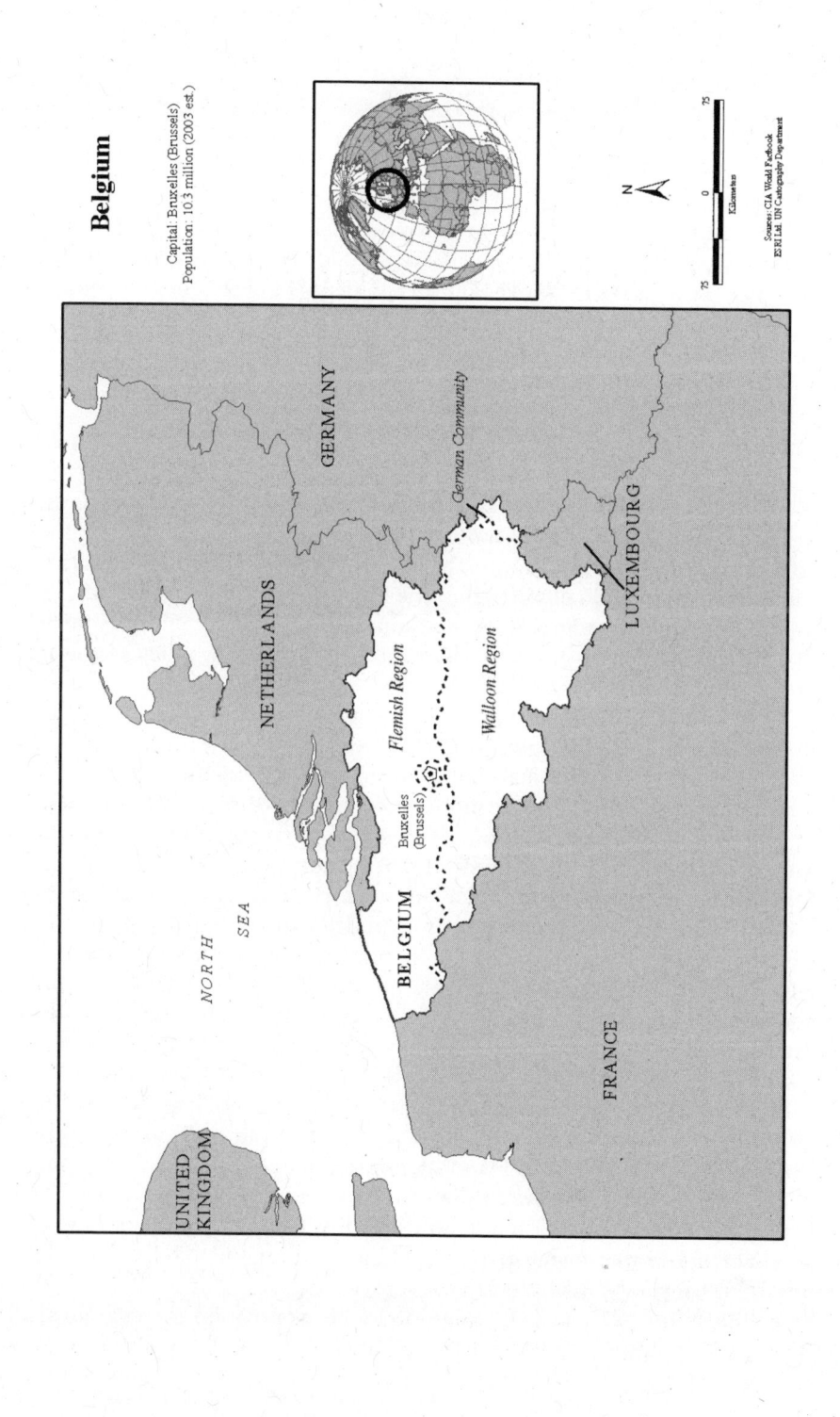

Capital: Bruxelles (Brussels)
Population: 10.3 million (2003 est.)

Kingdom of Belgium

PETER BURSENS AND FRANÇOISE MASSART-PIÉRARD

Belgium was created in 1830 as a unitary state when the southern part of the United Kingdom of the Low Countries (Verenigd Koninkrijk der Nederlanden) seceded from the northern part. Substantial federalization began only in 1970 and culminated in the 1993 Constitution, which officially declared Belgium a federal state. The country's short federal history means that foreign policy up to 1993 was almost exclusively a policy of the national government.

This chapter will discuss the national and international settings of the Belgian federation's foreign relations, as well as its constitutional and political features. It is followed by an examination of Belgium's bilateral and multilateral relations. The ensuing discussion of the constitutional setting of Belgian foreign relations argues that the evolution of Belgium's foreign policymaking was predominantly domestically driven and resulted in a competitive form of federalism. However, intergovernmental relations among the constituent units and the federal government suggest that despite the very strong competences accorded the Communities and Regions, the concrete implementation of foreign relations is of a cooperative kind and approached cautiously. The penultimate section discusses the means used by Belgium's constituent units to represent their interests abroad.

Belgium is a relatively small but densely populated country. Its 10.5 million inhabitants are unequally distributed throughout the country's three Regions. Almost 60% live in Flanders, approximately 30% live in Wallonia, and approximately 10% live in the Capital Region of Brussels (Région de Bruxelles-Capitale or Brussels Hoofdstedelijk Gewest). Exact figures on language use in the various parts of Belgium are unavailable because such questions cannot be asked in censuses. However, estimates are that linguistic composition follows the distribution of the population throughout the Regions quite closely: 60% of Belgians are Dutch-speaking and 40% are

French-speaking, while over 90% of inhabitants of the Capital Region are French-speaking.[1] In addition, about 1% of Belgians speak German as their mother tongue. German speakers are concentrated in the country's east near the German border.

Article 1 of the 1993 Constitution states, "Belgium is a federal State composed of Communities and Regions." It is composed of six different constituent units. According to Articles 2 and 3, these entities are the French Community (Communauté française de Belgique), the Flemish Community (Vlaamse Gemeenschap), the German Community (Deutschsprachige Gemeinschaft), the Walloon Region (Région wallonne), the Flemish Region (Vlaams Gewest), and the Capital Region of Brussels. Thus Belgium has a double federal structure comprised of two types of constituent units. Regions, created for economic reasons because of demands by Wallonia, were granted competences tied directly to territorial space. These include transport, road works, employment policy, industrial policy (economic development), environmental policy, spatial and structural planning, agriculture, housing policy, and trade. Communities, demanded by Flanders for linguistic and cultural reasons, are responsible for education, personalized services, preventive healthcare, culture, media, and use of language ("les matières personnalisables"). The divergent Walloon and Flemish concerns were reconciled through this compromise of establishing the two types of constituent units.

Today, these two types each manage their own sphere of competences and coexist on the same territory. In addition, Communities do not have a fixed territorial base, meaning that Community authorities have jurisdiction in more than one Region. An obvious example is the organization and financing of Dutch-speaking activities and initiatives in the Capital Region of Brussels.[2] In the Flemish part of the country, Community and Region were fused. According to Article 137 of the 1993 Constitution, the Flemish Region's competences are exercised by the council (later called parliament) and the government of the Flemish Community. However, the organization of foreign relations is what makes Belgian federalism most remarkable, as Regions and Communities enjoy full foreign relations powers for the sectors they govern domestically.

THE REGIONAL AND GLOBAL CONTEXT OF BELGIAN FOREIGN RELATIONS

Belgium borders on the Netherlands to the north, Germany to the east, and Luxembourg and France to the south. Regions and Communities have close ties with neighbouring countries whose inhabitants speak the same languages. The resulting cooperation agreements nevertheless diverge depending on the initiating constituent unit and the willingness of international partners to do business with it. The most noteworthy example is Flanders, which enjoys a language union (Taalunie) with the Netherlands as well as with Suriname. (South Africa has associate status.)[3] While the Taalunie is relevant only for Dutch-speaking Flanders, the treaty itself was concluded by the Kingdom of Belgium because it stems from 1980, well before the birth of the new federal Constitution and the accompanying regionalization of foreign relations competences. The Taalunie fosters the development of common dictionaries and rules of grammar but leaves both parties discretion over their own linguistic, cultural, and educational policies. Although the Taalunie serves as a major example of the external activities of Flanders, it does not play a role in the broader institutional discussion. For its part, the German Community prefers international contacts with German-speaking constituent units such as the German and Austrian *Länder*. Overall, these positive relationships between Belgian constituent units and neighbouring states reflect the friendly ties between those states and the Belgian federation as a whole.

The French Community of Belgium concentrates its bilateral and multilateral relations on the Francophonie as an international organization and on its member states. It is one of the prinicpal contributors to this organization. Belgium does not participate in the funding of the Organisation internationale de la Francophonie (OIF), even though it is a member of the Conference at the Summit of Chiefs of States and Governments, which comprises countries that share the French language.[4]

Belgium has always been an enthusiastic supporter of international cooperation and regional integration, even long before external relations became a concurrent power. Two major examples are the Benelux and the European Union. The Benelux is a regional cooperation framework involving Belgium, the Netherlands, and Luxembourg. Still existing today, it began in 1944 and can be considered a forerunner or even laboratory for the later process of European integration. In 1952 Belgium became a founding member of the European Coal and Steel Community (ECSC). From that point on, Belgium has been one of the most prominent supporters of European integration, often initiating – and without exception joining – the consecutive European treaties: the Treaties of Rome, the Single European Act, and the consecutive Treaties of Maastricht, of Amsterdam, and of Nice. It also subscribed early to EU-related policy coordination such as the Schengen Agreements on the free movement of citizens between EU members. In addition, Belgium enjoys no opt-outs, meaning that it participates fully in all EU policy areas. It was a founding member of the Economic and Monetary Union (EMU) and also ratified the draft of the – later rejected – European Constitution in 2005.

While international cooperation within its regional sphere is undoubtedly at the heart of Belgium's foreign policy, cooperation on a wider scale – including the global – has always been part of its external relations. A list of international memberships makes this clear. In addition to its Benelux and EU memberships, Belgium is a member of numerous international organizations, such as the Organization for Economic Cooperation and Development (OECD), World Trade Organization (WTO), United Nations (UN) and its specialized agencies, International Labour Organization (ILO), International Monetary Fund (IMF), and International Organization for Migration (IOM). In addition, Belgium is a member of regional and global security organizations, such as the North Atlantic Treaty Organization (NATO), Interpol, and the Organization for Security and Cooperation in Europe (OSCE).[5]

Not only the federal government but also the constituent units themselves ratify and honour treaties or agreements of international organizations on matters falling within the domestic competences of the constituent units. The basic treaties of the European Union (e.g., Maastricht, Amsterdam, and Nice) are major examples of such "mixed" treaties. The constituent units, while striving to work in concert with the federation as a whole, demand substantial impact on the formation of Belgian preferences in international organizations covering policies that fall within their powers. In some cases, Regions and Communities can even be associate or full members of organizations. One example is the World Tourist Organization; membership of Belgium's constituent units is only logical here, tourism being an exclusively regional competence. In most international organizations that make decisions touching on (nonexclusive) regional competences, Regions and Communities are not formally represented but are required to work through the Belgian delegation. An example is the World Health Organization (WHO), which deals with issues that sometimes fall under the jurisdiction of both the federal and the constituent governments. In addition, Regions from time to time finance projects and programs of UN agencies and global and regional organizations such as the WTO, the OECD, and the Council of Europe. Some organizations are very relevant for Belgium's constituent units. UN institutions such as the ILO, WHO, UNAIDS, and some environmental agencies are a few examples. The OECD and the Council of Europe are also significant partners. Through sponsorship of particular programs, constituent units gain international influence by "buying themselves in." Examples include explicit Flemish sponsorship of certain operational programs of UNAIDS and the WHO. Finally, it should be repeated that, for the French Community of Belgium, the OIF (called La Francophonie since 2005) is a very important multilateral partner.

THE CONSTITUTIONAL SETTING

Article 167 of the Constitution (as amended in 1993) introduced the principle of alignment between internal and external competences. This allowed Hugues Dumont to write, "Belgian constituent units have received treaty-making power in matters under their exclusive jurisdiction."[6] Indeed, according to Article 167, the king (i.e., the federal government) conducts Belgium's international relations "without prejudicing the competency of the Communities and the Regions to deal with international cooperation, including the conclusion of treaties, for the fields that fall within their competences in conformity with the Constitution or by virtue of the latter." The same article also stipulates that "the governments of the Communities and the Regions as defined in Article 121 each conclude, for those areas that concern them, the treaties that fall within the realm of their Council's [i.e., Parliament's] competency." Hence, as is the case, of course, for treaties concluded by the federal government alone, these treaties will take effect only after they have received the approval of the parliament concerned. This provision clearly goes beyond what can be found in other federal countries. In Belgium, the federal government cannot override competences that belong to the constituent units.[7]

From a comparative perspective, this feature makes the Belgian organization of jurisdictions unique. Constituent units are sovereign within the limits of their competences. They are under no form of political tutelage by the federal government in jurisdictions belonging to them alone, including the international aspects of those jurisdictions. At the same time, however, Article 167 is accompanied by a series of mechanisms providing for information, cooperation, and substitution to ensure the coherence of Belgium's overall foreign policy. These accompanying measures are not redundant because competences – and therefore also their international elements – are shared by the constituent units and the federal government. The federal government is exclusively responsible for defence and security policy, whereas trade policy is partly federal and partly regional. Constituent units and the federal government also share development policy, although this is slated to become a regional matter (a plan that is still contested). Furthermore, most EU policies fall under both federal and regional jurisdiction in the Belgian federation.

The constitutional reform of 1988 introduced the *in foro interno, in foro externo* principle for Community competences, which refers to the right of the constituent Communities to create foreign policy for those competences that they have been constitutionally granted domestically,[8] including such policy matters as language, culture, and education. The 1993 constitutional reform expanded this principle to apply to the competences of the constituent Regions. This principle follows from the crucial feature of Belgian federalism: the absence of a hierarchy of legal norms, meaning that federal laws and regional decrees stand on an equal footing and cannot overrule each other. The lack of a hierarchy of norms between the federal and constituent units implies – at least theoretically – that each order must both make and implement international policies falling within its jurisdiction.

Currently, residual powers belong to the federal government. However, it is envisaged by the Constitution that they will be transferred to the constituent units once the competences of the federal government are clearly and restrictively listed in the Constitution and the "special law" – Article 35(2) of the *loi speciale*.[9] By opting for such a solution, the Belgian federation commits itself to the federal philosophy of subsidiarity.[10] This not only brings legal certainty and security into the system but also enables each constituent unit to deal with those fields of international relations for which it has received exclusive domestic competency. Concretely, the federal government lost the privilege of exclusively representing constituent units abroad with respect to a substantial number of policy fields. There are, for example, no longer federal culture or education ministers. Consequently, unlike most other federal governments, the Belgian federal government cannot always play the role of gatekeeper between domestic and international political arenas. On the contrary, Belgian constituent units enjoy fully legitimate and legal direct access to the international stage.

INTERGOVERNMENTAL RELATIONS

Although the *in foro interno, in foro externo* principle looks very simple in theory, its implementation is quite complex. First, international partners need to be informed of the peculiarities of the Belgian system. Above all, they need to be persuaded that international agreements in policy domains such as education and the environment must also be concluded with several constituent governments rather than with the Belgian federal government alone. Second, distinctions must be made to identify policy issues that fall exclusively within the jurisdiction of the constituent units, of the federal government, or of both concurrently. Culture, for example, falls exclusively in the jurisdiction of the Communities, whereas some parts of environmental policy are a federal matter and other parts are a matter of the Regions. Exclusive domestic powers lead to exclusive international competences. The Flemish and the French Communities, for instance, can conclude cultural agreements with other states in their own right. But competences are not clearly divided for the negotiation of many treaties, as well as for representation in most multilateral organizations. As the example of EU policy coordination below illustrates, extensive mechanisms and arrangements with respect to representation had to be installed to ensure that the federation could come up with one representative and a single position.

The authors of the Constitution were already aware of potential coordination problems. The 1993 Constitution therefore lists three limitations to the *in foro interno, in foro externo* principle. The first is the substitution mechanism described in Article 169. This stipulates that if a Region or a Community does not live up to an international or EU commitment and is convicted by an international court such as the European Court of Justice, the federal government can act as a substitute for the constituent unit (but not the other way around) in order to comply with that commitment. The substitution mechanism has never been used; hence the necessary accompanying executive measures have not yet been established. Those opposed to the mechanism argue that it contravenes the absence of a hierarchy of norms. In times of incongruent coalitions (different political parties in power nationally and in one or more constituent units), the chances that the substitution principle will ever be used are even slimmer. It is politically unacceptable for a regional government to be overruled by a federal government (partly) composed of different political parties.

The second constitutional limitation is the provision that regional foreign policy cannot contradict the broad orientations of the commonly agreed foreign policy of the Belgian federation. When, for instance, the federation takes part in an international embargo against a particular state, a Region government – even though chiefly responsible for trade policy – will not export weapons or even dual-use goods (i.e., goods that have both military and civilian application, such as computer components) to that state. Finally, Regions and Communities are obliged to inform federal officials of any foreign agreements and activities. The Flemish government, for instance, must report to the federal government agreements on education made with the Netherlands.

Despite these limitations, the foreign relations aspirations of Belgium's regions paved the way for a heightened involvement of regional authorities in multilateral organizations. The European Union is the most obvious institution. Belgian Regions and Communities take the lead in promoting a "Europe of the Regions." They are very active both in informal networks and in formal European bodies representing regional interests.[11] Belgium's constituent-unit prime ministers, for instance, have a seat in the EU's Committee of the Regions. Other organizations dealing with issues that often fall within regional jurisdictions soon followed suit. These include the United Nations Educational, Scientific and Cultural Organization's (UNESCO) International Convention against Doping in Sport and its Convention on the Protection and Promotion of the Diversity of Cultural Expressions; the French Community of the Belgium delegation within the Belgian Representation was actively involved in the genesis of both. This illustrates that the external affairs component of Belgian federalism has set new procedural standards for the multilateral involvement of constituent units, and it has also created international attention for issues playing out on the subnational level.

Nonetheless, constitutional provisions caused a major institutional misfit in relations between Belgium and the European Union. The absence of a hierarchy of legal norms created a situation in which Belgium's constituent units would be individually responsible for implementing and applying EU legislation without having been extensively involved in the EU's legislative process. This was unacceptable to the constituent units. Yet the solution chosen was not to change the Constitution but to develop a strategy to introduce some changes to the Treaty Establishing the European Union (TEU, or Treaty of Maastricht).

Before 1992, Article 146 of the Treaty on the European Community stipulated that the Council of Ministers of the European Community could be composed solely of national government representatives. Anxious to secure their domestic constitutional prerogatives, constituent units from Germany and Belgium mobilized during the 1991 Intergovernmental Conference (IGC) to change this rule to their advantage. During the IGC, these constituent units forced the Belgian and German delegations to obtain a revision of the disputed article. However, they succeeded only partly. In return for the right to have regional representatives in the Council of Ministers, the French delegation demanded and obtained the guarantee that each representative, setting aside any domestic affiliations, would have to bind the entire member state and not only one part of it. The main significance of the new Article 203 of the TEU lies, therefore, in the access to the Council of Ministers meetings it has created for constituent-unit ministers. In this sense, the article is innovative; it acknowledges that federal executives of member states are not necessarily the most competent negotiating partners in the European arena. Nevertheless, each member-state representative in the Council of Ministers is still considered a unitary actor in the sense of representing a single, united policy position of the member state as a whole – regardless of the constitutional status enjoyed by the representative domestically. In this respect, the European institutional order affirms a traditional principle of international law by requiring that member states act as unitary actors internationally.

At the same time, Article 203 of the TEU generated substantial consequences for the domestic organization of EU policymaking in federal states. It forced national governments to instal coordination mechanisms that would ensure elaboration of a single national position to be negotiated in the Council of Ministers. In this regard, the European level defines European competences as ones shared by federal and constituent units within the domestic constellations. The challenge to comply with this definition is of course much bigger for federal than for unitary member states. For Belgium, it required reconciliation between the domestic *in foro interno, in foro externo* logic and the European rationale of dealing formally only with the member state as a whole. In 1994 this balancing exercise resulted in the conclusion of a cooperation agreement on EU policymaking, which was amended following the recent state reform of 2003. This cooperation agreement describes (1) how Belgium organizes its internal coordination in order to secure the articulation of a single position in the European arena and (2) how the Belgian representative is appointed to European bodies.

Turning to the details of the agreement, the most important body in the coordination process is the Directorate of European Affairs (DEA) within the Federal Public Service Foreign Affairs. This unit organizes coordination meetings with representatives of a wide range of federal and regional executive agencies. Crucially, this federal body needs to reach a consensus in order to back specific negotiation positions. If no consensus is reached, a similar exercise occurs at the Inter-Ministerial Conference for Foreign Policy (CIPE), composed of the ministers themselves; if necessary, it occurs again in the Concertation Committee (CC), composed of the government leaders. In practice, however, consensus is nearly always reached at the sectoral, or DEA, level; only a handful of cases have been discussed at interministerial meetings, and almost no cases have been discussed at the highest political level. Recent exceptions include the EU's Financial Perspectives 2007–2013 and the EU's Services Directive. The 1994–2003 cooperation agreement also makes the Federal Public Service Foreign Affairs a crucial player because it hosts the coordination meetings. Meetings are prepared and chaired by federal administrative and political officials. Despite the *in foro interno, in foro externo* principle, then, the federal government's role in European policymaking remains fairly substantial – although its nature has changed considerably. By incorporating representatives from the Regions and Communities and granting them the same formal position, the Directorate of European Affairs is no longer exclusively a body of the national government; it has become a cooperative intergovernmental agency set within a constitutionally established competitive federal system.[12]

Beyond establishing a coordination mechanism through which to define a joint position, the 1994 cooperation agreement also outlines a system for determining who will represent this position in the European arena. When the Council of Ministers discusses matters belonging exclusively to the Belgian national government, the Belgian delegation is composed solely of representatives from the federal government. When it discusses issues involving the competences of constituent units, Belgium is represented by a delegation led by one of the Regions or Communities (following a rotation system). When the Council of Ministers deals with competences shared by the federal and constituent governments, the delegation is also mixed but is led by the level holding the greatest share of the competences.

To summarize, Belgium has experienced two evolutions over the past decades. On the one hand, a large number of competences have been transferred to the EU; on the other, reform of the Belgian state has led to constituent units gaining a substantial portfolio of policy competences, including foreign relations. Few other states have undergone such extensive reforms. Within a relatively short time, Belgium was transformed from a unitary state into a full-fledged federation – a process that can be seen as an attempt better to reflect Belgium's political and cultural heterogeneity. Yet at the same time, Belgium became intensively involved in and supportive of the process of European integration. Today, it participates fully in all policy areas, including the Monetary Union and the emerging common security and defence policy. Belgium's integration into the EU can be considered an attempt to create policymaking venues that increase the territorial scope of market exchange. In sum, this combination of federalization and European integration has resulted in a far-reaching, complex system of multilevel governance that satisfies two seemingly contradictory considerations: coping with internal heterogeneity on the one hand and reaping the benefits of an expanded economic market on the other.

Somewhat different coordinating mechanisms and arrangements have been established in other policy sectors. As there is no hierarchy in relations between the federal government, the Communities, and the Regions, coordination structures have been put in place to ensure that foreign policy remains coherent. First among these has been a Concertation Committee, established to bring together the senior prime ministers of the federal, Region, and Community governments. The aim of the Concertation Committee is to avert political conflicts and, when necessary, to resolve them. It hosts some fifteen interministerial conferences, including the Inter-Ministerial Conference on Foreign Policy – the sole conference for which there is a legal provision.[13] The CIPE adopts its decisions by consensus, meaning that each party has the right of veto. The CIPE's secretariat is run by Services for Relations with the Federated Authorities, within the the Federal Public Service Foreign Affairs.[14] To ensure that Belgian foreign policy remains coherent, a pragmatic solution has been adopted; it consists of cooperation agreements between the federal government and the constituent units. These cooperation agreements broadly frame the application of Belgium's external relations by involving the various bodies concerned. Belgian foreign affairs are regulated by several cooperation agreements and practices.

Constitutionally empowering its constituent units with a foreign policy power, the Belgian federal government has little choice but to authorize or even encourage its constituent units to adopt cooperation agreements among themselves. Sometimes the federal government is not even involved; the cooperation agreement on regional commercial attachés concluded on 31 December 1993 by the Flemish Region, the Walloon Region, and the Brussels Capital Region is a clear case in which the federal government is left out completely. Despite this, regional commercial attachés and delegates are to be located, wherever possible, in Belgium's consulates and diplomatic representations abroad. According to the December 1993 agreement, "The Belgian Regions undertake to provide for collaboration with the assistance of their commercial attachés in countries or groups of countries where a Region does not have its own attaché." The agreement even stipulates that commercial attachés operating in a country or group of countries where the other two Regions involved are not represented must spend at least 25% of their available work time benefiting those two Regions. Thus the organization of external trade not only forced the three Regions to cooperate in day-to-day commercial representation abroad; it also triggered a profound integration of the Communities' and Regions' international relations services.

Other features also make a cooperative setting necessary. For instance, one finds hardly any place in Belgium where citizens from all three Communities come together. Very relevant in this respect is the absence of political parties organized at the federal level, although power in Belgium is reputed to be party-based. Above all, the international – and especially European Union – requirement to speak with a single voice steers Belgium in the direction of cooperative federalism.

Despite – or some would say because of – the centrifugal nature of Belgian federalism, the principles outlined above require a counterbalance to ensure that the constitutional requirement for a coherent foreign policy is met. It can be argued, especially in foreign relations, that the practical organization of Belgian federalism exemplifies cooperative federalism of a special kind, a kind not always applied to the same degree in practice, often depending on whether the foreign relations at stake are bilateral or multilateral. Where multilateral relations are concerned, the constituent units' autonomy appears to be reduced due to the more official nature of multilateral relations. This makes the federal government more intent on staying in charge, which leads to a more difficult organization within the federal system. Multilateral relations require the various orders of government to coordinate their views in order to determine a single Belgian position. They also require the foreign partners involved to accept the domestic organization of international relations. In addition, the approach differs depending on whether the negotiations involve the European Union or other multilateral international organizations. For the EU, all policies are coordinated by the Federal Public Service Foreign Affairs; all levels concerned assemble to establish Belgium's position before going to the EU's Council of Ministers.

For other international organizations, there is no specific structure that prepares negotiations within the Federal Public Service Foreign Affairs. The presence of Belgium's constituent units on the multilateral stage is of particular interest because it is exceptional. Arrangements for representation in organizations such as UNESCO, the OECD, and the Council of Europe were drawn up between the constituent units and the federal government.[16] Constituent units also take part in the work of the WTO in the fields of agriculture and services and in monitoring the different agreements. An item of particular interest is the OIF, where the diplomatic authority of Belgium's French Community is engaged to the maximum. For the summit meetings of heads of state and government held since 1986, Belgium's French Community, which includes representatives of the Walloon Region, sends its own delegation and has its own seat, while the Belgian federation also has its own representative. This is a case not of joint but of double representation. The two delegations, however, operate jointly based on a distribution of tasks. The federal delegation intervenes with respect to global political issues, while the delegation of the French Community deals with issues of international cooperation falling within its internal competences.

The alignment of internal and external competences can function only because other principles of Belgian federalism support this feature, as do both external and domestic developments. On the one hand, there is an increase in international activity; on the other, there is the ongoing political decentralization in Belgium. The very extensive powers attributed to the constituent units demand that they participate actively in national reforms and in negotiating international agreements that directly concern them.

The application of the principle of the alignment of competences guarantees the constituent units substantial powers. As Renaud Dehousse has rightly stated, "accepting the claims of the federal level with respect to exclusive external competences for the federal level would for the constituent units come down to the acceptance of federal interference in their own exclusive competences."[16] This would endanger the very existence of the constituent units and, *by extension*, of the Belgian federal system and impede the efficient conduct of international relations by the constituent units. At the same time, the Belgian organization of foreign relations also quite clearly demonstrates that alignment of external and internal competences requires a substantial degree of federal comity (or *Bundestreue*; that is, a commitment by both parties to cooperate) to make Belgian foreign relations effective and credible. The Belgian organization of foreign relations grants the constituent units more foreign competences than are granted their counterparts in any other federation. In Belgium constituent units are involved not only in the implementation of treaties and agreements but in their negotiation as well.

Yet there are limits to the application of the *in foro interno, in foro externo* principle. Constituent units do not participate in foreign security policymaking. International diplomacy also involves the *ius tractatis* (the right to conclude treaties) and the *ius legationis* (the right to be represented abroad). These limit the foreign relations of constituent units.

In 1993 the constituent units obtained an "exclusive" right, by virtue of the constitutional revision, to conclude treaties (*ius tractatis*). The special law of 5 May 1993 establishes the rules of negotiating, concluding, accepting, and ratifying treaties falling within the exclusive competences of the federated entities. These rules are also relevant for mixed treaties, namely agreements covering competences that are shared by the federal and constituent-unit governments. Such treaties are subject to a ratification procedure in all parliaments. In this respect, as Eric Philippart has argued, constituent units have the capacity to exercise a right of refusal; that is, they enjoy the right of veto even respecting a treaty that only partially involves their own powers.[17] Thus constituent units sometimes take on the role of veto players, disputing issues that might damage their interests or threaten their values. One prominent example was the Flemish refusal to ratify the draft treaty establishing a European constitution as long as there was no agreement on how to involve regional parliaments in the envisaged system of *ex ante* scrutiny of EU laws by national parliaments.

Diverging preferences make it difficult to define the "Belgian" national interest that lies at the heart of any foreign policy decision. They may also stimulate centrifugal tendencies arising from the frustration of those who feel badly represented by the federation. They could induce constituent units to seek alternative, direct channels to defend their interests internationally, thereby bypassing the federal government. The federal government, however, does well to take into account the interests and sensibilities of constituent units and to establish coordination mechanisms that allow constituent units to join in the policymaking process. One example is the Coordination Committee on International and European Environmental Policy. Because the regional and federal governments share environmental powers, this coordination body seeks to involve all governments in the policymaking process leading up to European and other multilateral negotiations in this field.

Despite the substantial powers of the constituent units, the *ius legationis* is the responsibility of the Belgian federation, thus ensuring the coherence of Belgian representation abroad. However, the constituent units enjoy at least some diplomatic representation as a result of what has become known as the principle of "the unity of the diplomatic post." As far as possible, delegates of the constituent units are invited to participate in Belgian diplomatic missions, which are the responsibility of the federal government. Regional representatives, called attachés, are instructed by their Region or Community authorities but are placed under the diplomatic – not functional – authority of the heads of missions, including both embassies and permanent representations to multilateral organizations with diplomatic status. In 2006 the missions of Wallonia-Brussels were located in France, Switzerland, the EU, the Czech Republic, Quebec, Tunisia, Senegal, the Democratic Republic of Congo, Vietnam, Germany, Morocco, Poland, Romania, Algeria, and Chili. These missions are mostly also accredited with neighbouring countries and international organizations. For example, the mission in Warsaw has also received accreditation from Estonia, Latvia, and Lithuania, while the mission in France has also received accreditation from the OECD, UNESCO, and the Organisation internationale de la Francophonie.[18]

A comprehensive cooperation agreement between the federal government and the Communities and Regions establishes how the constituent units are represented externally. There are plans to review this cooperation agreement in order to allow constituent units to participate in international negotiations on issues for which they have exclusive or partial competences; such a review, however, would not change the practice that they act under the authority of the ambassador or permanent representative. The agreement on representation of the Kingdom of Belgium at the EU Council of Ministers will probably serve as the template for arrangements governing the participation of constituent units' representatives in diplomatic meetings abroad. In addition, the idea of establishing "common delegations" – as is already the case with the Belgian delegation to UNESCO – is also gaining support. Such a system would have mutual advantages. The federal diplomacy would be put at the service of constituent units to defend their interests, while the latter would provide federal diplomats with knowledge of regional issues.

Despite the many efforts to ensure that regional representation in foreign policymaking functions smoothly, some deficiencies have already appeared in practice in four different cases. First, the Flemish Community opposes application of the Convention of the Council of Europe on the Rights of Minorities because it believes that this agreement directly affects its interests and its very identity. Although Belgium signed the convention because its contents affect federal as well as Community competences, it cannot be ratified unless all Communities assent. Second, some political parties resist implementing the transfer of development-cooperation policy to the Communities and Regions because it is considered to be a component of foreign affairs. Third, differing views on the export of arms forced the federal Parliament to pass a 2003 law regionalizing control over the import, export, and transit of arms. Granting the Regions power over arms-trade policies was the only way out of severe differences of opinion within the federal government. Whereas Walloon parties supported the largely Walloon-based arms industry, Flemish parties in the federal government coalition refused to approve arms-export licences for countries involved in armed conflicts. Despite this solution, disputes still occur, particularly when a Region's decisions regarding the arms trade conflict with the overall foreign policy interests of the Belgian federation. A final example involved a foreign affairs minister who condemned a decision made by a constituent unit (within its own jurisdiction) because it was contrary to Belgian foreign policy on the weapons trade.

It is important to note that the overall process of granting the regions more powers has been driven almost exclusively by the domestic political agendas of the major political parties and the two major language communities. The formation of the Belgian federal state reflects the political, cultural, and economic diversity of the Belgian polity rather than a response to European or broader international pressures. Consecutive Belgian state reforms granted competences to Regions and Communities because this fits with the overall logic of state reform – not because European integration had prompted it.

That said, two crucial remarks should be added. First, although the principle of granting Regions and Communities more competences was domestically driven, the European context sometimes provided additional arguments for this transfer of powers. The almost complete regionalization of agriculture policy, for instance, was motivated in part by the changing nature of the European Common Agriculture Policy. It was argued that the European shift to more attention for rural development, animal welfare, and environmental aspects of agriculture policy supported a domestic transfer of powers to the Regions because these were already responsible for spatial planning and environmental regulation. Second, the practical organization of the external and European dimensions of internal policies had to be implemented against the background of EU requirements. Procedures of preference formation and representation rules could not be elaborated without taking into account the European principle requiring a unitary position from member states on the one hand and the opportunities for regional representation on the other. In short, although the formal, autonomous status of Regions and Communities has predominantly been the result of a domestic agenda, it was to some extent reinforced and shaped by European integration.

Overall, the organization of external relations in the Belgian federation is built upon an inductive, pragmatic approach leading to a dynamic elaboration of the system. Many features are built on real situations and formalized by legal arrangements afterwards. This also explains why the external powers of constituent units have evolved progressively – an observation that applies to all dimensions of foreign policy, including the transfer of treaty-making and representational powers. Because the law follows the facts, legal arrangements constantly adapt both to the daily evolving situations and to the demands of those seeking in general more regional autonomy and in particular more autonomy in external relations. In addition, changes to the statutes and regulations of international organizations can trigger new arrangements with respect to the rules governing internal Belgian foreign policy agreements. The new powers of Regions and Communities are reflected in their new, autonomous conduct on the international scene and in international organizations.

COMMUNITIES AND REGIONS ABROAD:
DOMESTIC AND INTERNATIONAL MANIFESTATIONS

In general, the external relations of Belgium's constituent units have developed along two lines. First, since 1970 and especially since 1993, foreign partners have become more numerous and diverse. Belgian Regions and Communities now have partners on all continents; they have targeted many regions, formed interregional associations, and engaged themselves directly with sovereign states as well as with intergovernmental and supranational organizations. Second, Belgian Regions and Communities have dramatically expanded the scope of their foreign actions. These now cover policy areas such as foreign trade and foreign cultural relations – areas that once had been managed solely by the national government.

Flemish foreign relations are directed by a single minister, a single administration (Internationaal Vlaanderen), and a small number of agencies dealing with international cooperation (Vlaams Agentschap voor Internationale Samenwerking), tourism (Toerisme Vlaanderen), and trade (Flanders Investment and Trade, or FIT). In 2007 a total of 495 full-time equivalent (FTE) people were employed in the foreign services of Flanders (as part of the approximately 40,000 civil servants of the Flemish administration).[19] In 2007 the total Flemish budget for external relations was US$219,788,352, or €163,533,000, 0.74% of the total budget of the Flemish Community. In more detail, US$10,277,568 (€7,647,000) was spent on promotion (tourism marketing) and US$29,033,088 (€21,602,000) on support for foreign economic investment in Flanders.[20] Administrative and executive actions are scrutinized by a single parliamentary assembly (Vlaams Parlement) in its committee on foreign relations, European affairs, international cooperation, and tourism.

Flanders is represented abroad by nine official representatives of the Flemish government (in Berlin, Geneva, the Hague, London, Paris, Pretoria, Vienna, Warsaw, and Washington, DC). The Belgian Permanent Representation to the EU hosts ten attachés of the Flemish Community, who cover nearly all EU policies that touch upon Flemish competences. These representatives are perceived as an important tool for Flemish external relations. In recent years, their number has steadily increased, and their activities figure prominently in the policy programs of the Flemish foreign affairs minister.[21] In addition, Flanders Investment and Trade has envoys in more than eighty locations worldwide, and Tourism Flanders has eleven foreign offices.[22] Six agricultural and fisheries envoys also promote Flemish products abroad. Further, Flanders engages in technical assistance programs (i.e., financial support for infrastructure projects and scholarships in developing countries), support for democratization and peace-building programs, initiatives of organizations such as the Council of Europe, and emergency and humanitarian aid in cases of natural disasters.

The French-speaking part of Belgium waited until 1996 to pass a cooperation agreement between the French Community of Belgium and the Walloon Region. This reform, which came into effect only in 1998, is limited to closer ties in international relations between the Commissariat général aux Relations internationales de la Communauté Française (CGRI) and the Direction générale des Relations internationales de la Région Wallonie (DRI). Since 1996 four additional cooperation agreements have been signed by the French Community, the Walloon Region, and the Brussels Capital Region's French Community Commission (Commission communautaire française de la Région de Bruxelles-Capitale, or COCOF). These agreements have reorganized international relations to ensure optimal visibility of the Wallonia-Brussels Community (L'entité administrative dénommée Espace international Wallonie-Bruxelles) internationally. This latter body brings together the international relations services (CGRI-DRI), the Association for the Promotion of Educational Training Abroad (Association pour la promotion de l'éducation et de la formation à létranger, or APEFE), and the Walloon Agency for Export and Foreign Investment (Agence wallonne à l'Exportation et aux Investissements étrangers, or AWEX). The efforts of the different entities, however, are still directed in a different manner toward different countries. The French Community has, for example, concluded more bilateral agreements with countries of northern, central, and eastern Europe than with Arab countries and other countries of the South. In contrast, the Walloon Region has turned more toward countries of the South and countries of central and eastern Europe.

The CGRI-DRI on a daily basis administers the different agreements signed by the three governments (French Community, Walloon Region, and Brussels Capital Region's French Community Commission). Many of these agreements are co-signed; some involve only one of these three bodies. In 2004 the number of bilateral agreements administered by the CGRI-DRI amounted to 67 for the French Community, 50 for the Walloon Region, and 12 in the case of the Brussels Capital Region's French Community Commission, or 129 agreements in total.[23] The total budget allocated to international relations in 2003 differed sightly for the constituent units: 0.33% for the French Community, 0.3% for the Brussels Capital Region, and 0.28% for the Walloon Region. This compares to 0.38% for Flanders and 3.1% for the federal government, if we exclude from the total budget the interest on national debt (or 2.05% if it is included). In absolute terms, the CGRI-DRI budget amounts to US$71.6 million (€61 million), and the APEFE budget is US$12.4 million (€10.6 million).[24]

The organization supports a large network of representatives abroad: sixteen Wallonia-Brussels delegations; seven Wallonia-Brussels offices in southern countries managed jointly with the APEFE; a representation office in Baton Rouge, Louisiana; lecturers and French teachers posted to European states and Israel under CGRI contract; and language lecturers and assistants posted in several bilateral partners within the EU. The CGRI-DRI jointly manages Wallonia-Brussels bilateral relations for the three constituent units of the Walloon Region, the French Community of Belgium, and the Brussels Capital Region's French Community Commission.[25]

In terms of personnel, the CGRI-DRI administration employs 392 individuals (59 of whom are lecturers and trainers). To this should be added 16 persons employed by the APEFE, as well as the so-called *coopérants*, volunteers sent to countries in the South. The number of shared economic and commercial attachés is quite high: 105 posts (about 30 of whom are shared with the Brussels Capital Region and the Flemish Region). In addition to this, the CGRI-DRI administers 26 diplomatic representatives assigned to 15 posts. Among those are the delegates officially accredited with individual international organizations (such as UNESCO and the OECD in Paris) and those accredited with all the international organizations represented in Geneva. In addition, in Lousiana, two cultural centres have been created as well as an education office.[26] Since 2004 the Walloon functions of external trade and attraction of foreign investment – until then managed by distinct departments – have been merged within AWEX. In total, more than 450 individuals (in Belgium as well as abroad) work to promote Walloon exports. When the merger occurred, the economic and commercial attachés were also made responsible for attracting investment. AWEX provides logistic or financial support, subsidizes participation in international trade shows, assists in attracting business from outside of the EU, and provides commercial information. Training activities (for youth and executives) are also supported.[27]

The consolidation of the administration of francophone Belgium reinforces the bipolar character of the Belgian federation. At the same time, it has caused a certain asymmetry between the North and South in managing foreign relations. Whereas in Flanders foreign relations are dealt with by one department, the situation in the Wallonia-Brussels Community is much more complicated. This asymmetry adds to the complexity of Belgium's federal system and makes it difficult for foreigners to deal with Belgian agencies. The asymmetrical organization of the Communities and Regions in the North and South only adds to the difficulty of grasping how Belgian federalism functions in terms of competences, responsibility, and representation. That is why a new cooperation agreement signed on the 20 March 2008 expects to create a general administration named Wallonie-Bruxelles International (WBI). This concerns the Walloon Region, the French Community of Belgium, and the Brussels Capital Region's French Community Commission.[28]

Belgium's population is small, and its cities, in international comparative perspective, are even smaller. With about one million inhabitants, Brussels is by far the largest city. Although it cannot be regarded as a major urban setting, Brussels is a very international city. It hosts most European institutions as well as NATO political headquarters, along with numourous permanent missions to these organizations of states from all over the world as well as numerous public and private representatives. The city itself is not an international player. However, as the city (nineteen municipalities) comprises the territory of the Brussels Region, there is, of course, a "Brussels" foreign policy. This Brussels' regional foreign policy aims to safeguard the city's international status. As indicated above, it does so in close cooperation with the Walloon Region and the French Community (also called the "Wallonia–Brussels Community") in order to take best advantage of the resulting synergies.

CONCLUSION

Compared to their counterparts in other federal countries, Belgian constituent units have a high degree of autonomy in their conduct of foreign relations, with some analysts even detecting elements of a confederal relationship between them and the federal government in this policy sector. Whatever the chararacterization of the relationship, one can argue that it is *sui generis*, combining elements of competition and cooperation that are central features of Belgian federalism. Cooperation is essential both for the daily practice of foreign relations and for guaranteeing the coherence of the Belgian federation's foreign policy. In other words, despite the dualistic nature of Belgian federalism in constitutional terms, the conduct of Belgian foreign relations can be characterized in terms of cooperative federalism because practical arrangements have been devised to ensure that the country's foreign policy remains coherent by virtue of the coordinating role of the federal government. In that light, proposals to transfer additional foreign relations powers to the constituent units have met resistance from the federal government, which argues that substantial areas of foreign relations (such as development cooperation) have traditionally belonged solely to the federal foreign services.

The future formal organization of Belgium's foreign relations will depend on the overall process of institutional reform. Since the latter is a dynamic process, precise predictions are hard to make and can become outdated very quickly. Given that the constituent units already enjoy a high level of constitutional autonomy in foreign relations, one can quite safely say that the limits of regional autonomy have been more or less reached. Except in the contested issue of cooperation with developing countries, the status quo is likely to remain in place. One cannot imagine that matters of security or defence will become regional competences; rather, they will sooner or later be transferred to the EU. Enlargement of regional foreign competences might occur only with respect to the external aspects of potentially new regional competences, congruent with the *in foro interno, in foro externo* principle. Possible examples include science policy and aspects of the justice portfolio. If such transfers occur, the conduct of foreign relations in these fields will also have to be subject to practical cooperation as in other fields in order to ensure coherent Belgian positions when necessary in both bilateral and multilateral relations.

NOTES

1 Edmund A. Aunger, "Regional, National and Official Languages in Belgium," *International Journal of the Sociology of Languages* 104 (1993): 31–48. These figures are also cited in US Central Intelligence Agency (CIA), *World Factbook*, https://www.cia.gov/library/publications/the-world-factbook/geos/be.html (accessed 10 April 2008).
2 For a more detailed overview, see Kris Deschouwer, "Kingdom of Belgium," in John Kincaid and G. Alan Tarr, eds, *Constitutional Origins, Structure, and Change in Federal Countries*, 48–75 (Montreal and Kingston: McGill-Queen's University Press, 2005); and Hugues Dumont, Nicolas Lagasse, Marc Van Der Hulst, and Sébastien Van Drooghenbroeck, "Kingdom of Belgium," in Akhtar Majeed, Ronald L. Watts, and Douglas M. Brown, eds, *Distribution of Powers and Responsibilities in Federal Countries*, 34–65 (Montreal and Kingston: McGill-Queen's University Press, 2006).
3 For details on the Taalunie, see http://taalunieversum.org/taalunie (accessed 15 May 2008).
4 Organisation internationale de la Francophonie (OIF), *Rapport du Secrétaire général de la Francophonie, De Ouagadougou à Bucarest, 2004–2006*, 128.
5 For a full list, see CIA, *World Factbook*, https://www.cia.gov/library/publications/the-world-factbook (accessed 10 April 2008).
6 Dumont et al., "Kingdom of Belgium," 44–5.
7 Godelieve Craenen, "België en de Europese Unie," in Yves Lejeune, ed., *La participation de la Belgique à l'élaboration et à la mise en oeuvre du droit européen*, 39–72 (Brussels: Bruylant, 1999).
8 Literally, the *in foro interno, in foro externo* principle means that whatever applies to the internal arena also applies to the external arena.
9 A "special law" is a peculiar category of Belgian laws. To adopt or change a special law, a special majority is needed in both chambers. It has been created to deal with sensitive issues in the sphere of relations between the Communities and the Regions.
10 Françoise Massart-Piérard, "La Belgique à l'épreuve de l'introduction du principe de subsidiarité au sein de l'Union européenne," *Recherches sociologiques* 31, no. 1 (2000): 67–77.

11. Jan Beyers and Peter Bursens, *Europa is geen buitenland: Over de relatie tussen het federale België en de Europese Unie* (Leuven: Acco, 2006); Jan Beyers and Peter Bursens, "The European Rescue of the Federal State," *West European Politics* 29, no. 5 (2006): 1057–78; Peter Bursens and Kristof Geeraerts, "EU Environmental Policy-Making in Belgium: Who Keeps the Gate?" *Journal of European Integration* 28, no. 2 (2006): 159–79. Françoise Massart-Piérard, "Les entités fédérées de Belgique, acteurs décisionnels au sein de l'Union européenne," *Politique et société* 18, no. 1 (1999): 3–40.

12. "Cooperation agreement relating to the representation of the Kingdom of Belgium within international organisations pursuing activities falling within the scope of the joint responsibilities of March 8, 1994."

13. Article 31bis of the Law of August 8, 1980, on institutional reform. This was later incorporated by the Law of May 5, 1993.

14. Charles-Etienne Lagasse, "Le système des relations internationales dans la Belgique fédérale," CRISP *Weekly Courier*, no. 1549/1550 (1997): 10.

15. "Cooperation agreement relating to the representation of the Kingdom of Belgium within international organisations pursuing activities falling within the scope of the joint responsibilities of March 8, 1994."

16. Renaud Dehousse, *Federalisme et relations internationales* (Brussels: Bruylant, 1991), 108, my translation.

17. Eric Philippart, "Le développement de la 'paradiplomatie' au sein de l'Union européenne et la nouvelle donne belge," *Etudes internationales* 39, no. 3 (1998): 631–46.

18. CGRI-DRI, *Rapport d'activités 2006*, 118–21.

19. E-mail from the communication officer of the Flemish Department of International Relations (Internationaal Vlaanderen), 18 January 2007.

20. Ibid.

21. For the content of the policy programs, see http://docs.vlaanderen.be/buitenland/index.htm (accessed 15 May 2008).

22. See the Flemish Statistical Agency's website: http://aps.vlaanderen.be/statistiek (accessed 15 May 2008).

23. CGRI-DRI, *Rapport d'activitiés 2004*, 11.

24. E-mail from C.-E. Lagasse, directeur général adjoint of the CGRI-DRI, 1 October 2007.

25. Françoise Massart-Piérard, "La projection de la Communauté française de Belgique et de la Région wallonne sur la scène internationale: Une étude comparée," *Studia Diplomatica* 54, no. 5/6 (2001): 81–113; Françoise Massart-Piérard, "Une étude comparée des relations entre entités fédérées au sein du système de politique extérieure en Belgique francophone," *Revue internationale de Politique comparée* 12, no. 2 (2005): 191–206.

26. E-mail from C.-E. Lagasse, directeur général adjoint of the CGRI-DRI, 1 October 2007.

27. AWEX, *Activity Report, 2004*. The obtained results show that federal Belgium remains an exporting country. Wallonia and Flanders sport figures that show dynamic exporting as

well as increasing foreign investments. Belgium as much as its constituent units is obliged to respect the European legislation concerning state support that infringes on competition and could affect trade between member states. Nevertheless, regional aid is sometimes permitted. The policies of commercial promotion by the constituent units should be understood in this light.

28 See *Belgisch Staatsblad – Moniteur Belge*, 23 May 2008, 26.679–26.683, and the website http://www.wbri.be (accessed 1 July 2008).

Canada

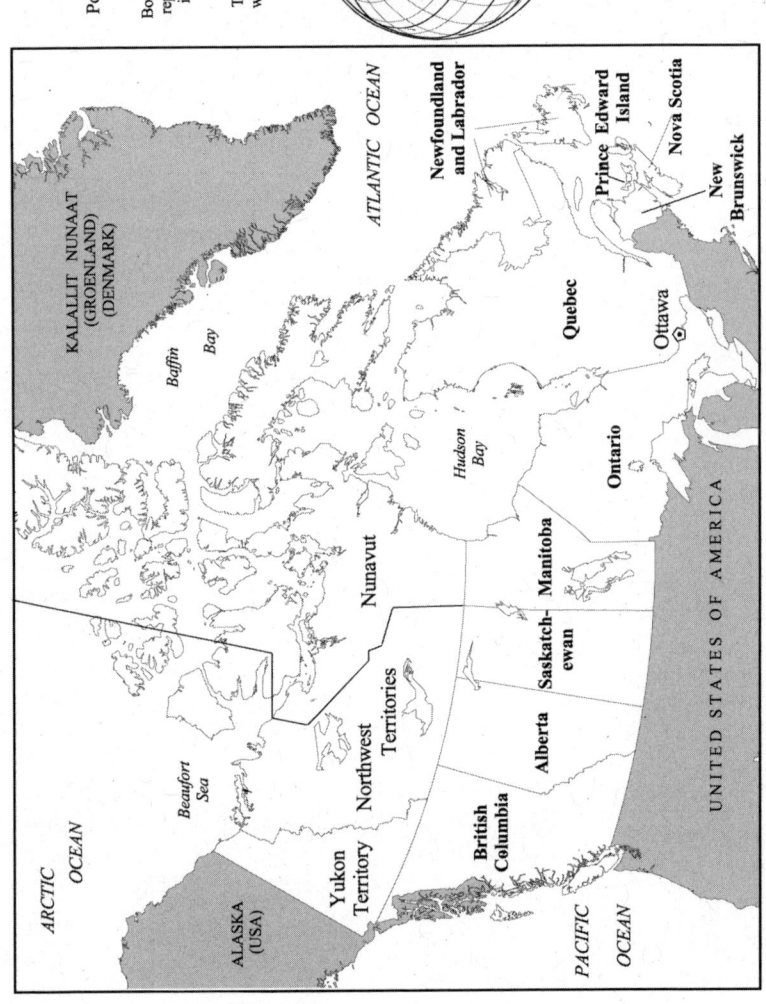

Capital: Ottawa
Population: 31.5 Million

Boundaries and place names are representative only and do not imply official endorsement.

The three northern territories, while adminstrative divisions, are not provinces.

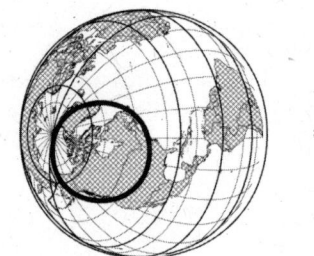

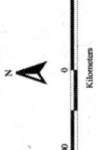

Sources: ESRI Ltd., National Atlas of Canada; Times Atlas of the World

Canada

ANDRÉ LECOURS

The relationship between Canadian federalism and foreign policy is significant for at least three reasons: (1) the provinces play an important role in treaty implementation, which means that there are typically intergovernmental relations surrounding treaty negotiations; (2) the international action of some provinces is quite developed and includes the presence of offices abroad, conducting formal visits and missions, and signing international agreements; and (3) the claims of Quebec for an increased international role pose a serious dilemma for the federal government, even to the point of presenting implications for national unity. Overall, Canadian provinces are active beyond the country's borders, albeit to different degrees and for different reasons, and they are generally keen to present their input when the federal government takes a position internationally on matters that fall, at least partially, within provincial jurisdiction, especially Quebec. This raises two major issues for Canadian federalism when it comes to international relations: to what extent should intergovernmental consultation be formalized, and how should the federal government respond to Quebec's claims for an increased role in foreign affairs?

COUNTRY CHARACTERISTICS

Canada is a vast federal country (9,984,670 km²) of 31,612,897 people.[1] This population is concentrated in the South, especially in the large urban centres of Toronto, Montreal, Vancouver, Ottawa, and Calgary. Linguistic and cultural diversity has always been a defining trait of Canadian society. The country, officially bilingual since 1969, is composed of approximately 76% English speakers and 24% French speakers. Historically, the Catholicism of francophones clashed with the Protestantism of most anglophones, but a decline in religious practice, especially in Quebec, where francophones are concentrated, has considerably lessened the importance of this religious division. There is a strong nationalist movement in Quebec that has translated, since the 1960s, into demands for increased autonomy or outright independence. Political claims that Quebec forms a nation find very strong support in Quebec society, which means that Canada may be called a multinational federation. In addition, Canada has an Aboriginal population making up approximately 3% of the country's total population and comprising many different historical groups that also call themselves nations and are recognized as such by the federal government. Diversity in Canada is also noticeable in its multiple communities stemming from immigration (e.g., Italian, Greek, and Chinese). These communities are formally acknowledged through a multiculturalism policy.[2]

The Canadian federation is composed of ten provinces.[3] There are great variations among these constituent units. In terms of population, Ontario leads the way (12,160,282), followed by Quebec (7,546,131) and Alberta (3,290,350). At the other extreme are Prince Edward Island (135,851), Newfoundland (505,469), and New Brunswick (729,997).[4] From an economic perspective, Alberta, rich in oil, and Ontario, with its strong industrial sector (e.g., the automobile industry), are the two wealthiest provinces, with a nominal gross domestic product (GDP) per capita of US$48,288 and US$36,029 respectively. They are followed by two western provinces: Saskatchewan ($32,817) and British Columbia ($31,292). At the other end are three small Atlantic provinces where seasonal economic activities such as fishing are important sectors of the economy: Prince Edward Island ($25,099), New Brunswick ($26,701), and Nova Scotia ($27,579).[5]

The population and economic discrepancies go some way toward explaining the uneven level of international activity across provinces. Overall, bigger and wealthier provinces (Quebec, Alberta, and to a lesser degree, Ontario) have been the most active internationally and the most interested in having input into positions voiced by Canada internationally about matters that fall into provincial jurisdiction. Meanwhile, the smallest and poorest provinces (Prince Edward Island, Nova Scotia, Newfoundland, and Manitoba) have been less active, with the exception of New Brunswick, which has developed an important international dimension.

More important than size and wealth for explaining the development of international relations in some provinces are political factors. Despite being in the middle of the pack in terms of GDP per capita, Quebec is by far the most active of the Canadian provinces internationally; in fact, it has, along with the Belgian communities and regions, the most developed international relations of any federated or regional unit in the world. This is because nationalism leads Quebec to take the expression of its identity and the promotion of its interests abroad. Alberta is the second most active province. This can be explained chiefly by the province's sentiment of alienation, which features a distrust of the federal government as a defender of Albertan interests. There is no such distrust in Ontario, which explains why, despite the province's size and wealth, the Ontario government has done little internationally. In sum, provinces comfortable with the federal government speaking for all of Canada on the various subjects of international affairs, especially Ontario, tend to have only a modest international dimension themselves.

REGIONAL AND GLOBAL CONTEXT OF NATIONAL SETTING

The international role of provinces is an important question in Canada because the country has always been very active internationally. Until the 1930s Canada's international action was bound by its dominion status in the British Empire, which meant that the country's foreign policy needed to follow that of the United Kingdom. When Canada became a fully sovereign international actor, its foreign policy and international involvement made it a classic middle power. Canadian governments have been quite active in world diplomacy, putting to good use a positive international reputation and strong relationships with the major powers to exercise an influence disproportionate to its size and military capabilities. At the centre of this positive reputation is the role played by Canada in establishing United Nations (UN) peacekeeping missions[6] and in participating in several of these missions thereafter. This stake in peacekeeping and in the United Nations as a privileged forum for world diplomacy and conflict prevention is part of a larger Canadian focus on multilateralism. Canadian governments have invested in a wide array of international organizations such as the World Trade Organization (WTO), the World Health Organization (WHO), and various UN agencies, such as the United Nations Educational, Scientific and Cultural Organization (UNESCO) and the United Nations Conference on Trade and Development (UNCTAD). Also, Canada's French and British heritage means that the country is a member of both the Commonwealth of Nations and La Francophonie.

Canada's most important foreign relationship is with its southern neighbour, the United States. This relationship has been peaceful for almost two centuries, and there are connections of all types between the two countries. Thousands of Canadians and Americans cross the border every day for business and tourism. American popular culture (particularly music and movies) is omnipresent in Canada, but many Canadian artists have become stars in the United States as well. From a political perspective, sharing this long border necessarily involves some degree of cooperation between the two countries. For example, after the attacks of 11 September 2001 in New York City and Washington, DC, the Bush administration made border control a high priority and put pressure on Canada to monitor transborder movement more closely than ever.[7] The American "war on terror" is therefore impacting Canada-US relations. Border control is mostly the exclusive purview of the federal government, although Quebec's formal powers in immigrant selection represent a form of control over population movement.[8] In addition, Canadian provinces have their own direct relations with bordering American states, as demonstrated by the many agreements on various topics that exist between the two.

Indeed, provinces have a major stake in many transborder issues. This is the case for environment and resource management, where provincial voices are being heard. For example, the Great Lakes Conference of the International Joint Commission on Boundary Water Management involves not only the federal minister of environment but also its Ontario counterpart.[9] A recent American plan to steer polluted water from North Dakota into Lake Winnipeg has raised much concern in the Manitoba government and worried other provinces as well.[10] In the field of energy, the National Energy Board of Canada, which regulates the exportation of oil, natural gas, and electricity, coexists with energy boards in Alberta and Ontario that are also responsible for the movement of such resources.[11]

Diplomatically, the two countries have enjoyed a strong relationship based on common commitments to democracy, human rights, economic prosperity, and security despite differences on foreign policy (for example, Canada did not support the US war in Vietnam and, more recently, in Iraq). Canada and the United States are members of many of the same international and regional organizations, including the North Atlantic Treaty Organization (NATO), the Organization of American States (OAS), and the G8. They are also partners in the North American Aerospace Defense Command (NORAD).

The Canada-United States relationship in the context of these organizations has few implications for the provinces. Provincial governments do not seek to have a say in military and defence issues. In contrast, the Canada-United States Free-Trade Agreement (CUSTA), signed in 1988, which became the North American Free Trade Agreement (NAFTA) with the inclusion of Mexico in 1994, has been full of consequences for the provinces. Free trade with the United States reduced the ability of the federal government to regulate commercial flows, as rigid protectionist measures were no longer options. As a result, Canada-US trade increased at the expense of interprovincial trade. By 2004 four-fifths of Canada's exports went to the United States, while two-thirds of its imports came from that country.[12] Ontario is most dependent on the American market, with approximately 90% of its exports going to the United States. It is followed by Alberta, New Brunswick, Prince Edward Island, and Quebec, all with more than 80% of their exports going to the United States. Even provinces that export proportionally less to the United States still rely heavily on that market (e.g., British Columbia, with approximately 65%).[13] In this context of a greater importance acquired by the American market, provinces have developed international operations, if only to help companies take advantage of new opportunities and attract new investment. The global trend toward the liberalization of trade and the free movement of capital has meant that these operations have sometimes acquired a scope beyond the United States.

A more specific consequence of NAFTA for provinces derives from the potential disputes over the extent and limits of free trade. Here, the conflict over softwood lumber is a good example. Canada complained for years that the United States imposed illegal duties on incoming softwood lumber, while the US government justified this practice by arguing that the industry was unfairly subsidized in Canada. NAFTA arbitration panels found mostly in favour of the Canadian position, but both countries sought a negotiated solution to the conflict. Four provinces were directly affected by this dispute because they have significant softwood lumber industries: British Columbia, Quebec, Ontario, and New Brunswick. Of the four, British Columbia had the most at stake because 60% of Canada's softwood exports come from that province. In this context, the BC government requested, and was granted, a "major role" in shaping the Canadian position vis-à-vis the United States while at the same time acting directly in the United States to bring American policy in line with its interests.[14] The other affected provinces were also allowed to offer their input. In the spring of 2006 the Canadian and American governments came to a settlement that was supported by all provincial governments involved. The intergovernmental consultation that occurred during these Canada-United States negotiations was genuine and effective enough to gain the support of the provinces, although the industry in British Columbia was split on the settlement.[15] As such, this consultation could serve as a template for federal-provincial contacts in the context of future international negotiations affecting the provinces.

THE CONSTITUTIONAL SETTING

Canadian federalism was the product of a compromise. In the 1860s projects of political unions involving primarily the two units of the Province of Canada (Canada East, populated by a majority of French-speaking Catholics; and Canada West, composed primarily of English-speaking Protestants) as well as New Brunswick and Nova Scotia surfaced as a result of economic, military, and political imperatives (the instability deriving from the arrangements of the 1840 Act of Union). These projects involved discussions over the specific form of a new state. French Canadian leaders advocated a federal model because they felt it offered the political autonomy necessary for the preservation of their distinct culture, language, and traditional social structure. English Canadian elites favoured a unitary state, which they saw as stronger and more resilient. In the end, Canada was created as a federation in 1867. It was originally a fairly centralized federation that included the provinces of Ontario, Quebec, New Brunswick, and Nova Scotia. Powers over the most important matters of late nineteenth-century public policy were attributed to the federal government: banking, currency, national defence, transportation, and trade and commerce.[16] The federal government was also given the power "to make laws for the peace, order and good government of Canada," except in domains explicitly under provincial jurisdiction. Provinces oversaw such matters as civil and property rights, municipal institutions, and local works.[17] This constitutional arrangement meant that provinces would have authority regarding healthcare and social welfare when these matters became fields of public policy.

Contrary to the constitutional documents of most federations, the British North America (BNA) Act of 1867 did not specifically assign power over international relations to the federal government. Only Section 132 touched on this issue. It specified that Parliament and the Government of Canada were empowered to perform "the Obligations of Canada or any Province thereof, as part of the British Empire, towards Foreign Countries, arising under Treaties between the Empire and such Foreign Countries." This section, however, has fallen into disuse since the 1931 Statute of Westminster gave the dominions formal legislative independence from the United Kingdom and enabled Canada to sign treaties of its own. Power over defence, however, constitutionally rests with the federal government in virtue of Section 91(7). Constitutional changes, including the major reform of 1982, have not altered jurisdiction over international relations. In short, there is nothing in the Canadian Constitution empowering provinces in international relations, nor is there anything preventing them from developing international activities such as striking agreements with foreign governments on matters falling within their own jurisdiction.

In the context of such a silence, courts have been instrumental in specifying the constitutional setting for international relations, at least with respect to the implementation of treaties. After Canada formally acquired its international personality in the 1930s, the federal government assumed the treaty-making powers formerly exercised by the British government.[18] The extent to which Canada's division of power presented a limit on the federal government's ability to implement treaties was tackled in three judgments from the Judicial Committee of the Privy Council (JCPC) in London (the ultimate court of appeal for Canada until this responsibility was given to the Canadian Supreme Court in 1949).

In the *Aeronautics* reference, the JCPC had no difficulty confirming the validity of the Aeronautics Act because it was drafted for the purpose of fulfilling Canada's obligations stemming from a 1922 convention ratified in the context of the British Empire.[19] Therefore, Section 132 applied. Lord

Sankey, who delivered the Privy Council judgment, also made the argument that air regulation "was a matter of such general concern to the whole body politic of Canada that it could be brought under Parliament's power of making laws for the peace, order and good government of Canada."[20] This logic was maintained by Viscount Dunedin in the *Regulation and Control of Radio Communication in Canada* reference,[21] which dealt with the 1927 Radio Telegraph Convention ratified by the Canadian government. In this case, the JCPC rejected Quebec's argument that the implementation of international treaties was subject to the division of power of Sections 91 and 92 of the BNA Act and found instead that this power rested exclusively with the Canadian Parliament.[22] But then, in the 1937 *Labour Conventions* case, the Privy Council, speaking through Lord Atkin, judged that the federal government alone could not enact the labour conventions stemming from Canada's membership in the International Labour Organization (ILO).[23] Lord Atkin found that treaty implementation was not a new matter (as argued in Regulation and Control of Radio Communication) but that it was tied to Sections 91 and 92. Consequently, the logic of the judgment was that if a "treaty dealt with a subject that was normally under section 92, then legislation giving effect to it could be enacted only by the provincial legislatures."[24]

The *Labour Conventions* reference is still the dominant jurisprudence on treaty implementation in Canada. Provinces, particularly Quebec, still refer to the 1937 case to defend the constitutionality of their role in treaty implementation.[25] In fact, Quebec's politicians typically argue that the constitutional division of power should apply not only to the implementation of treaties but also to their negotiation and even their making.[26] This argument is not reflected in current jurisprudence, and most constitutional experts do not find it convincing.[27] Moreover, in international law, responsibility for implementing a treaty falls to the federal government because it is the only government in Canada endowed with an international legal personality. Nevertheless, the notion that domestic powers should be extended onto the international scene, including in the act of treaty making, forms the basis of Quebec's political claims for an increased international role as represented by the so-called Gérin-Lajoie doctrine. In a 1965 speech, then Quebec education minister Paul Gérin-Lajoie suggested there was "no reason for separating the implementation of an international treaty from its making. These are simply two steps of one process."[28]

Disputes over the constitutional possibilities of provincial input into treaty making focus on the interpretation of the formal division of power between the orders of government. This is due partly to the fact that provincial governments do not participate in policymaking within federal institutions. In theory, the Senate serves as the house for territorial representation, but because its members are appointed by the federal government rather than elected or appointed by provincial governments, it does not perform that function. Thus provinces play no formal role in crafting Canadian foreign policy. This constitutes an incentive for them to seek input into treaty making and to develop their own international presence.

INTERGOVERNMENTAL RELATIONS IN FOREIGN AFFAIRS

The crafting and implementation of foreign policy in Canada are not guided by formal political arrangements between the federal and provincial governments insofar as there is not one intergovernmental forum specifically dedicated to international relations. Therefore, the federal government and the provinces do not routinely meet to discuss external affairs. Rather, intergovernmental relations about foreign policy develop when specific questions relating to issues of provincial jurisdiction become the focus of international negotiations. As just discussed, the implementation of treaties whose subject matter falls within provincial jurisdiction requires the participation of provincial governments. Beyond treaty implementation, the constitutional division of power is also central to determining the role of provinces in shaping Canadian foreign policy. Of course, the federal government does not consult provincial governments when deciding on the structure of its diplomatic relations with foreign states or its stance on traditional issues of war and peace, security, and defence; these matters lie within the exclusive jurisdiction of the federal government. For example, the Canadian government's policy of promoting an international ban on land mines was developed without any input from provinces. At the same time, the federal government can be sensitive to public opinion in specific provinces, sometimes expressed by their governments, before deciding on foreign policy. In areas of provincial jurisdiction, however, the federal government must consult the provinces, which leads to the establishment of intergovernmental networks.

Consultation surrounding the implementation of treaties or the definition of Canadian positions on matters of provincial jurisdiction takes place within sectoral intergovernmental forums. These forums may take different forms and have various degrees of formal institutionalization. Typically, discussions of international issues occur in yearly meetings of federal and provincial ministers. In some instances, mechanisms of coordination for the purpose, for example, of treaty implementation are supported by a formal intergovernmental agreement. In the area of labour, the US-Canada agreement that accompanied CUSTA opened the way for ad hoc intergovernmental meetings when international treaties (paralleling other free trade agreements) were negotiated by Canada. In 2005, however, this practice was formalized through "a new Canadian intergovernmental agreement, a framework that establishes a federal-provincial-territorial mechanism for the implementation and operation of international labour-cooperation agreement."[29] In the field of environment, the Canadian Council of Ministers of the Environment (CCME), which typically meets once a year, is the forum for discussing international environmental issues or events. For example, in a June 2005 meeting, the ministers committed to working together to prepare for the United Nations Climate Change Conference held in Montreal later that year.[30] Intergovernmental relations around the international dimensions of agriculture,[31] such as improving foreign-market access for Canadian products, are not stipulated in a distinct agreement but rather written into a larger intergovernmental framework, the Agriculture Policy Framework.

The extent of intergovernmental relations around an international issue involving provincial jurisdiction depends greatly on its salience. In high-profile international negotiations, or negotiations of treaties whose implications raise serious concern for provinces, intergovernmental consultation and coordination may be quite extensive. A few examples follow.

In trade, the federal government did not start consulting provinces until the mid-1970s because, until then, international negotiations focused mainly on tariffs, an area of federal jurisdiction.[32] For example, the 1965 Canada-United States Automotive Products Agreement (Autopact) allowing for duty-free exchanges of motor vehicles and their parts was negotiated without any input from Ontario, although this province had serious stakes in the agreement due to its large automobile industry.[33] With the General Agreement on Tariffs and Trade (GATT) Tokyo round of trade negotiations, however, nontariff barriers such as subsidies were on the table, and provincial governments wanted input. The federal government reacted by creating a federal-provincial committee of deputy ministers and, in 1977, by setting up a Canadian Coordinator for Trade Negotiations office that could channel provincial (and industrial) perspectives.[34]

Negotiations in the mid-1980s over CUSTA were even more consequential for the provinces, and a political decision was made at the November 1985 First Ministers' Conference that provinces would be full participants in the process.[35] For the provinces, full participation meant having input into defining the Canadian position, preferably through formal representation on the negotiating team and oversight of the federal negotiator.[36] The federal government refused to give provinces a formal presence in the negotiations. Instead, the federal and provincial governments agreed to a compromise: first ministers would meet every three months to discuss the negotiations; designated ministers would meet frequently; the federal government would consult the provinces while setting the mandate of the chief negotiator; a Continuing Committee on Trade Negotiations (CCTN) would be created; and the federal government would obtain the views of provinces before accepting any agreement.[37] Opinions differed on the genuine consultative nature of these mechanisms. Provincial representatives complained that their views found their way into the federal position only when it suited the federal government.[38] What is certain is that these consultation mechanisms did not translate into unanimous provincial support for free trade; Manitoba, and especially Ontario, remained opposed until the end. In the face of this opposition, the federal government was careful to craft the language of the treaty in a way that would minimize its apparent encroachment on provincial jurisdiction.[39] At the same time, the intergovernmental relations behind the free trade negotiations highlighted that most provinces backed the agreement, which proved a major asset for the federal government to sell the accord politically.[40] Overall, Canadian federalism was not a major obstacle to signing and implementing CUSTA.

Subsequent international trade negotiations have been accompanied by similar consultation and information-sharing mechanisms.[41] In trade, as in other fields where both federal and provincial governments are active, this is the easiest course for the federal government, although it has at least three other options.[42] The first, which is quite limiting, is to sign treaties only in areas of exclusive federal jurisdiction. The second, dangerous for its potential repercussion for the federal government, is to make a constitutional argument for federal supremacy in the courts. The third is to challenge the provinces to make such an argument against that supremacy. This last course was chosen by Jean Chrétien's government on the Kyoto Protocol.

Intergovernmental relations in the field of environment have been collaborative rather than conflictual, primarily because the federal government has let provinces implement national standards. The 1998 Canada-wide Accord on Environmental Harmonization embodied this cooperative attitude.[43] Initial intergovernmental relations accompanying the federal government's participation in the negotiations on the Kyoto Protocol proved harmonious. Three developments made them acrimonious.[44] First, in 1997 Prime Minister Chrétien presented a Canadian position that lacked provincial support. Second, in 2001 the United States announced it would not ratify Kyoto. This led some provinces, most importantly Alberta, to feel the protocol "would place Canadian business at a competitive disadvantage."[45] Finally, in 2002 Chrétien announced at the September World Summit on Sustainable Development that Parliament would ratify Kyoto in the coming months. For Chrétien, who had announced his retirement from politics, the ratification of Kyoto seemed to be a foremost objective tied to his legacy as prime minister of Canada, and he was determined not to let the provinces block or even slow down the process.[46] This determination angered many provincial governments, which issued a joint condemnation.[47] Moreover, Alberta's premier, Ralph Klein, openly speculated about a judicial challenge to the constitutionality of Kyoto's implementation. Despite this provincial opposition, the federal government proceeded with ratification. The Kyoto case suggests that the constitutional parameter of provincial involvement in the implementation of treaties whose subjects fall at least partially within the jurisdiction of provinces (in the case of the environment, both orders of government can claim to have constitutional authority) gives way to the power politics of intergovernmental relations when it comes to ratification.

In the international politics of culture, the consequence of federalism boils down to the relationship, often tense, between the federal and Quebec governments. The process leading to the adoption in 2005 of the Universal Convention on Cultural Diversity, which was spearheaded by the Canadian government, provides a good example of the dynamics at play. In 1998 the federal government called a meeting in Ottawa of the International Network on Cultural Policy, an informal forum where states discuss issues relating to cultural diversity. These and subsequent discussions centred on the notion of crafting a legal instrument for protecting cultural industries. Federal Heritage Minister Sheila Copps invited her Quebec counterpart, Culture Minister Louise Beaudoin, to attend but with no right to speak. In response, Quebec chose not to attend. In 1999 France invited both Quebec and Canadian ministers to discuss the issue of cultural diversity. This time, Canada refused to attend. This episode shows the deeply political nature of the relationship between the federal and Quebec governments when it comes to a theme like culture in international relations. For then heritage minister Sheila Copps, assuming leadership in an international project on culture allowed for a strengthening of the relationship with France, which seemed to favour Quebec as an interlocutor for this type of topic.[48] Quebec politicians involved in this process felt that they were able to have more influence through their networks in France than through domestic intergovernmental mechanisms.[49] They argue, for example, that the federal government did not take into account Quebec's comments on the proposed convention before sending the Canadian recommendation to UNESCO.[50] They also cite the federal government's refusal to press for arbitration mechanisms to be built into the declaration (as Quebec wished) in deploring Quebec's lack of input on the Canadian position.[51]

On 5 May 2006 the newly elected federal Conservative government signed an agreement with the Quebec government to establish the province's formal position with regards to UNESCO. This agreement constitutes a response to Quebec's claim that the province needs to be in a position to promote its language and culture internationally. Most important, the agreement stipulates that Quebec will have a permanent representative within the Canadian delegation at UNESCO in Paris and that the federal government will consult the Quebec government before taking a formal position in the context of UNESCO's work.

THE DOMESTIC AND INTERNATIONAL MANIFESTATIONS OF CONSTITUENT DIPLOMACY

Canadian federalism also intersects with the international arena through the international activities of provinces. The conduct by provincial governments of international relations, a phenomenon sometimes called "paradiplomacy,"[52] takes many forms, such as the presence of offices abroad, foreign visits and missions (often with business angles), technical cooperation, and cultural exchanges and partnerships. Overall, the federal government accepts this aspect of provincial international relations. Traditional "high politcs" topics are typically not discussed by provincial governments when they go abroad, and the federal government prefers to keep it that way. The international activities of provincial governments do not make the news in most provinces; only in Quebec, and to a lesser extent Alberta, are these activities reported widely. International affairs more generally are typically not big discussion items in provincial politics, although there are some notable exceptions (the signing of the free trade agreement with the United States and, more recently, the participation of Canada's army in military operations in Afghanistan).

The international action of Canadian provinces is not new, and its development is closely linked to changes in federalism. During the first decades following Canada's foundation, provincial governments sought, with some success, to decentralize the federal system. During that time, Quebec sent its first representative to Paris.[53] Offices were subsequently opened in Belgium, the United Kingdom, and the United States.[54] When national leadership was needed in the context of the First World War, the financial crisis of the 1930s, and then the Second World War, the federal government reestablished its prominence vis-à-vis the provinces. Quebec's Belgian and British offices were closed during the Great Depression, in 1933 and 1935 respectively. The next thirty years or so were the heyday of the federal government, as the construction of the Canadian welfare-state through various national social programs consolidated its dominant role within the federal system. In this period, Quebec virtually stopped its international efforts,[55] while the other provinces had yet to develop an international presence. In the 1960s the Quiet Revolution in Quebec led to the formation of Parti libéral du Québec (PLQ) governments that looked to decentralize Canadian federalism and secure the formal recognition of the province's distinctiveness. The Parti québécois (PQ), created in 1968, sought Quebec's independence. In this strongly nationalist context, the Quebec government developed clear international ambitions. It specified, through a 1961 law, the responsibilities of foreign representatives sent to Paris, London, Brussels, New York, Tokyo, and Mexico City.[56] A 1967 law established a department of intergovernmental affairs whose activities included coordination of the province's international activities.

In the case of Ontario, the development of an interest in foreign affairs in the late 1970s and early 1980s was largely the product of concerns over American protectionist measures and the environmental consequences of American industries located close to the border.[57] Although Ontario's international efforts have been strongly oriented toward the United States, it forged, starting in the late 1980s, a partner relationship with the four regions forming the Four Motors of Europe (Rhône-Alpes, Baden-Württemberg, Lombardy, and Catalonia). For the province's Liberal government, association with the Four Motors aimed to promote Ontario as a prime jurisdiction for doing business in North America. In this context, offices were opened in Stuttgart and Milan.[58]

The development of international action by Alberta in the late 1970s also centred on the United States and was spurred by its conflictual relationship with the federal government, particularly over energy. In the context of price control under the National Energy Program, the Alberta government felt that Ottawa did not defend the province's interests in a satisfactory manner and that it therefore needed to have its voice heard in the United States, primarily to communicate that Alberta was dissociating itself from the federal approach to energy.[59] Alberta also invested significantly in developing a presence in Asia, most notably through "twinning" programs with regional governments in Kokkaido (Japan), Kangwondo (South Korea), and Heilongjiang (China).[60]

Since the 1960s, nationalist pressures stemming from Quebec as well as decentralist positions taken by other provincial governments (most notably Alberta) have served to decentralize the Canadian federation. This political dynamic is important for understanding both the intergovernmental relations of foreign affairs in Canada and the international action of the provinces. Facing decentralist pressures on many policy fronts, the federal government has been reluctant to surrender power in the international relations area to provinces, particularly Quebec (the Liberal Party of Canada being much more reluctant than the Conservative Party). Nevertheless, provincial governments such as those in Quebec, Alberta, Ontario, and New Brunswick have established an international presence through, at a minimum, foreign offices, official visits abroad, and cross-border cooperation with American states.

In the case of most provinces, the impetus for this international activity is primarily functional. In this context, it serves to further economic interests through the facilitation of exports and the attraction of foreign investment as well as to share information, and sometimes coordinate policy, with neighbouring US states. From a transborder perspective, these motivations for transnational relations have led to the creation of general coordination bodies (such as the Conference of the New England Governors and the Eastern Canadian Premiers), economic and trade-oriented organizations (e.g., the

Pacific Northwest Economic Region, or PNWER), and sectoral forums (such as the meetings of the Tri-National Agricultural Accord).[61] Alberta has developed a more political dimension in its external activities, with, for example, Premier Ralph Klein making high-profile visits to Washington, DC, in 2001 and 2004 to discuss energy issues and cattle trade with the George W. Bush administration.[62] Quebec stands out among all the provinces for the scope, ambition, and multidimensional nature of its international activities. In addition to having signed international economic and technical-cooperation agreements, Quebec has been active internationally in the field of culture, specifically to promote the French language, and it has developed political relationships with a variety of foreign governments, most notably with France.

Let us now look at the contemporary international activities of all the Canadian provinces. Quebec clearly stands out for the extent and the scope of its international action as well as for the resources allocated to this action by the provincial government. Perhaps most significantly, Quebec's international activities have a definite political dimension insofar as the development of international agency represents for Quebec's political leaders a way to make a statement about the existence of a nation and the power of its government.

Quebec has signed several hundred international agreements since 1964 with both states and regional governments from every continent.[63] These agreements cover virtually all the fields in which the Quebec government is involved domestically: agriculture, economic development, culture, social services, transportation, and so on. Institutionally, Quebec's international activities are crafted and supervised by a government department dedicated to international relations, the Ministère des relations internationales (MRI), which had a budget of US$95,217,018 (0.2% of the province's total budget) in 2005.[64] Quebec has international representation in more than twenty-five countries: it boasts seven "general delegations" (Brussels, London, Paris, Mexico City, Munich, New York City, and Tokyo), five "delegations" (Boston, Chicago, Atlanta, Los Angeles, and Rome), as well as more than a dozen smaller units, including immigration and tourism offices.[65] In the summer of 2006 Quebec announced it was opening offices in India and Brazil, bolstering its presence in Japan and China, and upgrading its Washington, DC, tourist office to a more political role.[66] All in all, Quebec posts more than 250 people abroad.

Ever since the Quiet Revolution, Quebec governments have argued that the province's constitutionally specified powers should extend to the international area (the so-called Gérin-Lajoie doctrine). Of foremost concern to these governments has been the promotion of the French language and culture. In turn, this emphasis determines the types of international partners favoured by Quebec. In bilateral relations, France is the province's crucial partner, while a great number of cooperation agreements with developing countries have been signed with French-speaking Africa. From a multilateral perspective, Quebec focuses its efforts on La Francophonie,[67] an international organization whose members share a connection to the French language. The Quebec government has been able to participate in La Francophonie because the organization accepts membership from constituent-unit governments. As a result, Canada, Quebec, and New Brunswick are all members. For the Quebec government, this arrangement represents a source of inspiration for negotiating a distinct autonomous status among all provinces in the area of international relations.

Why is Quebec the only province to seek such status? For Quebec's politicians, having the opportunity to speak and act internationally is a natural implication of Quebec's nationhood. All the province's parties – the secessionist PQ, the federalist PLQ, and the autonomist Action démocratique du Quebec (ADQ) – seek an increased international role for Quebec.

The PQ ties this issue to its larger objective of independence, arguing that Canadian federalism does not allow Quebec sufficient international expression. The province's 2001–04 strategic plan for international relations, drafted under a PQ government, criticized the "anachronistic character" of the federal government's position on the actors of international relations (favouring states at the expense of substate governments) and dissociated Quebec from the federal objective of furthering Canadian culture, suggesting that this mission involves the negation of Quebec's own culture.[68] This attitude of dissociation from Canadian foreign policy explains the high volume of bilateral agreements and relationships involving Quebec and foreign governments. In the year or so preceding the 1995 referendum on sovereignty, the PQ government's international efforts involved particularly high stakes as it became focused on attempting to secure international recognition following an eventual "yes" majority.[69] More generally, Quebec's diplomacy puts a lot of emphasis on image – that is, on promoting a positive view of Quebec abroad. Since the 1995 referendum, the PQ has made central to its argument for independence the idea that full sovereignty over foreign affairs is crucial in an era of globalization, primarily because of the multiplication of international institutions and negotiations. Quebec, it is argued, needs to be fully sovereign to assume a formal position in these forums in order to effectively defend its interests and present its positions, many of which are said to be distinct from Canada's.[70]

The PLQ, although not seeking independence, adopts a similar reasoning centred on globalization when arguing for increased powers in international relations.[71] After his victory in the 2003 Quebec election, the Liberal premier, Jean Charest, repeatedly signalled his desire for a formalization and expansion of Quebec's autonomy on aspects of international relations touching upon the province's domestic powers. He called for an asymmetrical arrangement with Ottawa. A document signed by Quebec Minister of International Relations Monique Gagnon-Tremblay and issued in October 2005 formally states that Quebec "intends to claim its full constitutional rights on the international stage as a logical extension of its initiatives within the Canadian federation, while fully respecting Canada's foreign policy."[72] The document concludes by summarizing Quebec's claims for an increased role in foreign affairs in five points: (1) full membership in Canadian delegations with the right to appoint its representatives, (2) access to all information and a role in defining the Canadian position prior to international negotiations, (3) the right to speak at international organizations and conferences on matters falling within Quebec's jurisdiction, (4) recognition of a right of Quebec to consent before Canada signs a treaty in such matters, and (5) the right to present its position when Canada appears before international arbitration bodies if Quebec considers its interests to be at stake.[73] In contrast to the PQ, however, the PLQ government has emphasized *l'action concertée* in foreign policy – that is, its desire to collaborate with the federal government.[74]

The ADQ, which jumped from third-party status to official opposition in the 2007 provincial election, also supports an increased role for Quebec internationally.[75]

Claims for a voice in international conferences and organizations are less present in the other provinces, whose international relations focus on trade and the management of common issues with adjacent American states. There are, however, many differences among these nine provinces in their specific approaches to international affairs, the partners they favour, and the institutional importance they give to international relations.

Next to Quebec, Alberta is the most active province in international relations. In Alberta responsibility for foreign affairs lies with an international relations unit nested within the government's Department of International and Intergovernmental Relations. In 2005 this unit had a budget of US$1,540,425, which is 0.009% of the provincial budget.[76] Whereas identity, culture, and language are central to Quebec's rationale for developing an international presence, Alberta's international relations unit presents its international role as one of defending the province's interests abroad.[77] Alberta views its relationship with the United States as the most vital. The United States is Alberta's most important foreign market (90% of its exports abroad go there), and it accounts for two-thirds of foreign investment in the province and for 60% of foreign tourists.[78] There are also historical ties to the United States stemming from emigration to the province.[79] The result is strong bilateral relationships with close to a half-dozen American states and the presence of an Alberta office in Washington, DC. The establishment in March 2005 of this three-person office, located in the Canadian embassy, reflected the growing importance for Alberta of continental issues such as energy and cattle trade. In addition to this heavy investment in the relationship with the United States, Alberta looks strongly toward the Asia-Pacific region, primarily for economic opportunities. From a more cultural perspective, the province has built a special relationship with Ukraine (over 250,000 Albertans have a Ukrainian heritage) and an Advisory Council on Alberta-Ukraine Relations exists to support the government's action in this respect.

Another active province internationally is New Brunswick. Similar to Alberta, this Atlantic province features the Department of Intergovernmental and International Relations[80] and explicitly signals its desire to be an international actor.[81] In 2003 New Brunswick released its first-ever international relations plan, entitled *Prospering in a Global Community: New Brunswick's International Strategy*, which was followed by a progress report issued in January 2006. New Brunswick's international action follows seven strategic sectors: investment and trade, aimed at boosting job creation and economic growth; immigration, where the objective is to attract people to New Brunswick and facilitate their integration; innovation and education, which involves bolstering the number of foreign students in New Brunswick's universities; international development; international environmental stewardship; image and reputation, with a focus on promoting the province's business-friendly environment; and international competencies – that is, sensitizing New Brunswickers to global realities.[82] New Brunswick has been very aggressive in seeking foreign investment, as it must compete with wealthier states and provinces. The province's linguistic duality is central to its international strategy; for example, New Brunswick seeks to open business opportunities in, and attract immigrants from, francophone countries. Moreover, the province has a formal Francophonie Action Plan, "which outlines New Brunswick's interests and potential for growth as a partner in this important multilateral organization."[83]

After Alberta and New Brunswick, the importance of foreign affairs in Canada's provinces goes down one notch. Ontario, although Canada's biggest province, has developed only a modest international presence, which is primarily driven by economic interests. By the early 1990s Ontario boasted seventeen international offices, but these were closed in 1993 for financial reasons. Three "International Marketing Centres" were opened in 2003 (Shangai, Munich, and New York) and then four more in 2005 (Tokyo, London, Los Angeles, and New Dehli).[84] In a pattern similar to Alberta and New Brunswick but different from Quebec, Ontario explicitly seeks the collaboration of the federal government when it comes to its foreign representation – for example, in physically placing its centres within Canadian embassies and in hoping to cash in on the Canada "brand."[85] The bureaucratic unit responsible for overseeing Ontario's international relations is the Office of International Relations and Protocol, which is part of the Ministry of Intergovernmental Affairs.[86] The Ministry of Economic Development and Trade also assumes a function of "marketing Ontario to the world as a preferred business location."[87]

In British Columbia an International Relations Section within the Intergovernmental Relations Secretariat is responsible for the province's foreign affairs.[88] British Columbia's international relations are less developed than Ontario's, focusing primarily on bilateral relationships and multilateral forums with north-western US states. However, the British Columbia government was a vocal opponent of Canada's participation in two major international schemes: continental free trade and the Multilateral Agreement on Investment (MAI). There is also a strong Asian dimension to the province's international interests, as demonstrated by a formal Asia-Pacific initiative, overseen by the minister of economic development.

The remaining provinces have very modest international relations. In Manitoba there is a small unit for Canada-US and International Relations within the Department of Intergovernmental Affairs and Trade.[89] In Saskatchewan there is an International Relations Branch within the Department of Government Relations, whose budget in 2005 was US$723,330, or 0.01% of the province's total budget.[90] In both provinces, cross-border relations represent the bulk of international action. Saskatchewan once had offices abroad (London, New York, Minneapolis, and Hong Kong), but these were closed in the 1990s.[91] The province's energy reserves have sparked some interest from the United States; in February 2005 Premier Lorne Calvert met with the US vice president, Dick Cheney, to discuss oil, gas, and uranium opportunities in the province. For Nova Scotia, Newfoundland, and Prince Edward Island, foreign affairs are understood primarily as contacts with New England states through bilateral relationships and multilateral forums such as the Conference of New England Governors and Eastern Canadian Premiers. Collective efforts at fostering business opportunities in New England also feature trade missions conducted by Team Canada Atlantic, a 1998 initiative supported by a permanent secretariat established in Moncton, New Brunswick. The institutional situation of foreign affairs in these three Atlantic provinces is indicative of its minor political importance, as the relationship with New England states is an extension of intergovernmental relations.[92] In Newfoundland responsibility for this relationship is assumed by an intergovernmental affairs secretariat, with no specific foreign affairs section, nested within the Executive Council. The structure is similar in Prince Edward Island, where this responsibility is exercised by an Intergovernmental Affairs Division within the Executive Council Office. In Nova Scotia there is a Regional Relations Division within the Department of Intergovernmental Relations that coordinates the province's relationship with both Atlantic Canada and New England.

It is also worth mentioning that some Canadian cities have also developed an international dimension. This is particularly the case for Montreal, which can count on Montréal International, an agency supported by the municipal, provincial, and federal governments as well as by private companies, to promote the city's international profile.[93] Other major cities have had more targeted international action. For example, Vancouver is a key partner of the Vancouver Organizing Committee (VANOC), which is in charge of staging the 2010 Winter Games. Meanwhile, Toronto is overseeing the work of the Toronto 2015 World Expo Corporation, which is examining the possibility of a bid for the 2015 World Exposition.

Finally, Aboriginals have often used the international realm to put pressure on federal and provincial governments about what they consider to be breaches of their ancestral rights (e.g., the development of energy-related projects on land claimed by Aboriginal groups). This has sometimes involved formal appeals to the United Nations.

CONCLUSION

Federalism shapes Canada's interactions with the outside world in many different ways. Perhaps most important, the federal government is required to secure the consent of the provinces for the implementation of international treaties whose subject matter falls within provincial jurisdiction (e.g., CUSTA and Kyoto). This means that the federal government has a strong incentive to consult provincial governments before signing such treaties, especially if its provisions are expected to affect the provinces significantly. Even in cases of international negotiations not directed toward the signing of a treaty (e.g., Canada-US negotiations over softwood lumber), provincial governments are likely to attempt to shape Canada's position if they feel their interests are at stake.

The impact of federalism on Canada's international presence is also felt through the international action of provinces. The extent of this action is uneven, although at a minimum all provinces have developed relations with neighbouring US states to manage common resources and problems as well as to boost economic exchanges and attract investment. Alberta has been a particularly noticeable provincial player in the relationship with the United States, having a special interest in issues high on the American agenda such as oil. This being said, the province with the most developed international relations is Quebec. Through its Ministère des relations internationales, Quebec has signed hundreds of agreements with foreign governments in addition to having established a formal presence in several countries. Nationalism in Quebec means that the provincial government is continually seeking to develop its role as the primary agent of foreign representation for Quebec society and to establish itself as the main promoter of its interests abroad.[94]

The process of crafting Canada's international relations within the federal context faces at least two serious questions.

First, what should be the extent of the formalization of the mechanisms for provincial consultation prior to the federal government taking a position internationally in areas of provincial jurisdiction? Such formalization is most important in the area of human rights, where provinces have input in the drafting of the Canadian position and are asked for their consent before signing and ratification.[95] Canada has much to gain from keeping the provinces happy when it negotiates and signs international agreements in areas of provincial jurisdiction because it makes implementation much less problematic. In the case of Kyoto, for example, provincial opposition to the protocol means that implementation is difficult and conflictual. At the same time, formalized and binding consultation mechanisms might take away from the ability of the federal government to adjust its position as negotiations unfold.

Second, what should be the federal government's response to Quebec's claims for a greater role in foreign affairs? These claims are far-reaching, ranging from a right to speak at conferences on topics that affect Quebec's constitutionally specified powers to the opportunity to appear before international arbitration bodies to present its position. Such claims also seem to enjoy strong support among the Quebec population. The potential upside for the federal government reacting positively to at least some of these claims is larger than the substance of these questions. The role that Quebec could play in international relations has become a major issue in the province over the past few years, with the PQ arguing that only independence will allow Quebec to defend its interests and promote its identity abroad. In this context, an accommodation of Quebec's claims in this area could weaken an argument for independence. Such accommodation, however, will not be easy because many view it as a threat to national unity, arguing that it represents a slippery slope toward independence. Moreover, several politicians and commentators are worried about the coherence of Canada abroad if there is a formalization of Quebec's international role and about the message it would send about the nature of the Canadian nation.[96] This being said, Prime Minister Stephen Harper made good on an election promise[97] by specifying a role for Quebec with respect to UNESCO activities, placing the agreement explicitly within the perspective of an "open" and "asymmetrical" federalism. Asymmetry is a controversial concept in Canada because it is viewed by many as undermining Canadian unity by compromising the capacity of the Canadian government to act and by propelling Quebec toward secession.

Thus the issue of provincial involvement in international relations goes beyond the crafting of intergovernmental relations and institutional arrangements. Rather, it plays into the connection between federalism and national unity and how the former can be conceived to secure the latter. Because notions of federalism and nationhood are always evolving and questioned in Canada, it is unlikely that a definitive solution could be found. It is more probable that the issues stemming from the connection between federalism and international relations will require continuing management by federal and provincial politicians and civil servants.

NOTES

1 The population data is drawn from the 2006 census. As of July 2007 the estimated population was 33,390,141.
2 The 2001 census showed that 5,202,245 Canadians had a mother tongue other than French and English.
3 Canada also has three territories (Yukon, Northwest Territories, and Nunavut). They have no constitutional standing and are under the authority of the federal government. On the Canadian federation, see Rainer Knopff and Anthony Sayers, "Canada," in John Kincaid and G. Alan Tarr, eds, *Constitutional Origins, Structure, and Change in Federal Countries*, 103–42 (Montreal and Kingston: McGill-Queen's University Press, 2005); Richard Simeon and Martin Papillon, "Canada," in Akhtar Majeed, Ronald L. Watts, and Douglas M. Brown, eds, *Distribution of Powers and Responsibilities in Federal Countries*, 91–122 (Montreal and Kingston: McGill-Queen's University Press, 2006); Thomas O. Hueglin, "Canada," in Katy Le Roy and Cheryl Saunders, eds, *Legislative, Executive, and Judicial Governance in Federal Countries*, 101–34 (Montreal and Kingston: McGill-Queen's University Press, 2006); and Robin Badway, "Canada," in Anwar Shah, ed., *The Practice of Fiscal Federalism: Comparative Perspectives*, 98–124 (Montreal and Kingston: McGill-Queen's University Press, 2007).
4 These data are for 2005.
5 These data are for 2003. See John R. Baldwin, Mark Brown, and Jean-Pierre Maynard, *Interprovincial Differences in GDP per Capita, Labour Productivity and Work Intensity: 1990–2003*, Statistics Canada, 11–624–MIE, no. 011, 4. The following conversion rate was used to express this information in US dollars: 1 Canadian dollar = 0.893 US dollar.
6 Prime Minister Lester B. Pearson won the 1957 Nobel Peace Prize for creating the first peacekeeping operation.
7 It is in this context that the Canada Border Service Agency was created in 2003.
8 Quebec selects its immigrants, except for refugees and in cases of family reunification, in virtue of the 1978 Cullen-Couture Accord as well as a 1991 agreement with the federal government.
9 Canada Newswire, "Make Big Plans ... to Attend the IJC's Great Lakes Conference and Biennal Meeting," 17 May 2005, 1.
10 Mike de Souza, "U.S. Stand on Water Angers Quebec Minister," *Montreal Gazette*, 27 May 2005, A6.

11 G. Bruce Doern and Monica Gattinger, *Power Switch: Energy Regulatory Governance in the Twenty-First Century* (Toronto: University of Toronto Press, 2003).
12 See Department of Foreign Affairs and International Trade, *Sixth Annual Report on Canada's State of Trade* (April 2005), 4.
13 These percentages were obtained by dividing all provincial exports by provincial exports to the United States using Industry Canada Trade Data Online.
14 Grace Skogstad, "International Trade Policy and Canadian Federalism: A Constructive Tension?" in Herman Bakvis and Grace Skogstad, eds, *Canadian Federalism: Performance, Effectiveness and Legitimacy*, 159–77 (Don Mills: Oxford University Press, 2002), 167.
15 For more details on the British Columbia perspective, see Christopher Kukucha, "Lawyers, Trees and Money: British Columbia Forest Policy and the Convergence of International and Domestic Trade Considerations," *Canadian Public Administration* 58 (2005): 506–27.
16 Other features of the 1867 British North America Act suggest an intention to create a centralized federation. For example, the power of "reservation" allowed the federal government to review provincial legislation, while the power of "disallowance" gave it the right to void such legislation within one year of adoption. See Garth Stevenson, "Federalism and Intergovernmental Relations," in Michael Whittington and Glen Williams, eds, *Canadian Politics in the 21st Century*, 85–110 (Scarborough, ON: Nelson, 2004), 86–7.
17 Immigration and agriculture were created as concurrent powers with federal paramountcy.
18 The 1947 Letters Patent constituting the Office of the Governor General of Canada authorizes the governor general (Canada's formal executive) "to exercise all powers and authorities lawfully belonging to us in respect of Canada." For Peter W. Hogg, "this language undoubtedly delegates to the federal government of Canada the power to enter into treaties binding Canada"; see his *Constitutional Law of Canada* (Toronto: Carswell, 1985), 242.
19 *Regulation and Control of Aeronautics in Canada* (The Aeronautics Reference) [1932] A.C. 54.
20 Peter H. Russell, Rainer Knopff, and Ted Morton, *Federalism and the Charter: Leading Constitutional Decisions* (Ottawa: Carleton University Press, 1989), 86.
21 *Regulation and Control of Radio Communication in Canada* [1932] A.C. 304.
22 Russell, Knopff, and Morton, *Federalism and the Charter*, 93.
23 *Labour Conventions* [1937].
24 Russell, Knopff, and Morton, *Federalism and the Charter*, 104.
25 See the newspaper column signed by Quebec's minister of international relations, Monique Gagnon-Tremblay, titled "Who dares to speak for Canada abroad? We do," *Globe and Mail*, 3 October 2005.
26 Ibid.
27 The arguments of legal experts against the extension of treaty-making power to the provinces are often based on the absence of political precedents. Hogg, for

example, suggests that the federal government has exclusive power to make treaties chiefly because provincial claims to the contrary "never commanded wide acceptance in Canada" and had "never been accepted by the federal government"; see his *Constitutional Law of Canada*, 255.
28 Paul Gérin-Lajoie, quoted in Claude Morin, *L'Art de l'impossible: La Diplomatie québécoise depuis 1960* (Montreal: Boréal, 1987), 28, my translation. The original French: "aucune raison que le fait d'appliquer une convention internationale soit dissocié du droit de conclure cette convention. Il s'agit de deux étapes essentielles d'une opération unique."
29 See the 28 January 2005 news release at http://www.hrsdc.gc.ca/en/cs/comm/hrsd/news/2005/050128a.shtml (accessed 24 January 2006).
30 See the following news release: http://www.ccme.ca/about/communiques/index.html?item=148 (accessed 2006).
31 Agriculture is a shared constitutional jurisdiction.
32 Richard Simeon, "Important? Yes. Transformative? No: North American Integration and Canadian Federalism," in Harvey Lazar, Hamish Telford, and Ronald L. Watts, eds, *The Impact of Global and Regional Integration on Federal Systems: A Comparative Analysis*, 125–71 (Montreal and Kingston: McGill-Queen's University Press, 2003), 154–5.
33 Ibid., 155.
34 Ibid.
35 Douglas M. Brown, "The Evolving Role of the Provinces in Canadian Trade Policy," in Douglas M. Brown and Murray G. Smith, eds, *Canadian Federalism: Meeting Global Economic Challenges?* 81–128 (Kingston, ON: Institute of Intergovernmental Relations and Institute for Research on Public Policy, 1991), 93.
36 Ibid., 94–5.
37 Axel Hülsemeyer, *Globalization and Institutional Adjustment: Federalism as an Obstacle?* (Aldershot, UK: Ashgate, 2004), 94. The contemporary intergovernmental forum for discussing trade issues is CTRADE, which meets four times a year.
38 Ibid.
39 Ibid., 95.
40 Simeon, "North American Integration," 155.
41 Skogstad, "International Trade Policy," 164.
42 The following draws partially from ibid., 163.
43 Quebec's PQ government did not sign the accord, opposing the very idea of national standards.
44 See Christopher J. Kukucha, "From Kyoto to the WTO: Evaluating the Constitutional Legitimacy of the Provinces in Canadian Foreign Trade and Environmental Policy," *Canadian Journal of Political Science* 38 (2005): 129–52, at 146–7.
45 Kathryn Harrison, "Passing the Environmental Buck," in François Rocher and Miriam Smith, eds, *New Trends in Canadian Federalism*, 2nd ed., 313–52 (Peterborough: Broadview Press, 2003), 338.
46 Kukucha, "From Kyoto to the WTO," 148.

47 Ibid., 147.
48 Sheila Copps, *Worth Fighting For* (To-ron-to: McLelland and Stewart, 2004), 166.
49 Interview with Louise Beaudoin, former Quebec culture and international relations minister, Montreal, 20 March 2006.
50 Ibid.
51 Ibid.
52 The term "paradiplomacy" was first used by Ivo Duchacek in his "Perforated Sovereignties: Towards a Typology of New Actors in International Relations," in Hans Michelmann and Panayotis Soldatos, eds, *Federalism and International Relations: The Role of Subnational Units*, 1–34 (Oxford: Clarendon, 1990). See also Francisco Aldecoa and Michael Keating, eds, *Paradiplomacy in Action: The Foreign Relations of Subnational Governments* (London: Frank Cass, 1999).
53 Louis Balthazar, "Les relations internationales du Québec," in Alain-G. Gagnon, ed., *Québec: État et sociétés*, 505–35 (Montreal: Québec/Amérique, 2003), 506.
54 Ibid.
55 Nelson Michaud, with Manon Tessier, "Fédéralisme et politique étrangère: Réponses comparatives à la mondialisation," in Ann L. Griffiths and Karl Neremberg, eds, *Guide des pays fédérés*, 409–37 (Montreal and Kingston: McGill-Queen's University Press, 2002), 424.
56 See http://www.mri.gouv.qc.ca/fr/politique_internationale/historique/historique.asp#Une%20ouverture%20nouvelle (accessed 20 February 2006).
57 James Peter Groen, *Intergovernmental Relations and the International Activities of Ontario and Alberta* (PhD diss., Queen's University, 1995), 173.
58 Ibid., 326.
59 Ibid., 182.
60 Ibid., 279–83.
61 This last forum brings together senior officials from 8 Canadian provinces, 23 US states, and 15 Mexican states.
62 See the website for the Alberta-United States relations section of Alberta's Department of International and Intergovernmental Relations: http://www.iir.gov.ab.ca/international_relations/alberta_us_relations.asp (accessed 2006).
63 Ministère des relations internationales, *Répertoire des ententes internationales du Québec, 1964–2000* (2000).
64 See *2004–2005 Estimates*, vol. 2, 2–134, at http://www.finances.gouv.qc.ca/fr/documents/publications/cp-2004-2005.asp (accessed 23 February 2006).
65 See the MRI's website: http://www.mri.gouv.qc.ca/fr/action_internationale/representations_etranger/representations_etranger.asp.a (accessed 1 February 2006).
66 Rhéal Séguin, "Quebec seeks to raise its profile abroad," *Globe and Mail*, 25 May 2006.
67 Since 1998 the formal name has been Organisation internationale de la Francophonie (OIF).
68 Ministère des relations internationales, *Le Québec dans un ensemble international en mutation: Plan stratégique, 2001–2004* (2001), 23–4.

69 Jacques Parizeau, *Pour un Québec souverain* (Montreal: VLB, 1997), 283–343. The sovereignist "yes" camp fell just short of winning a "50 percent plus one" majority in this referendum.
70 Generally, the PQ argues that Canada is more comfortable with neo-liberal views of globalization than is Quebec. The most recent PQ program states that the party supports "another type of globalization"; see Parti québécois, *Un projet de pays* (2005), 84, http://www.pq.org/tmp2005/programme2005.pdf (accessed 6 February 2006).
71 See Ministère des relations internationales, *Québec in International Forums: Exercising Québec's Constitutional Rights at International Organizations and Conferences* (October 2005), 1.
72 Ibid., 2.
73 Ibid., 8.
74 See Ministère des Relations Internationales, *La politique internationale du Québec: La force de l'action concertée* (2006).
75 Action démocratique du Québec, *Une vision. Un plan. Une parole. Un plan A pour le Québec* (2007), 7.
76 Department of International and Intergovernmental Relations, *2004–05 Annual Report*, 61, http://www.finance.gov.ab.ca/publications/measuring/minann.html (accessed 23 February 2006).
77 See http://www.iir.gov.ab.ca/international_relations (accessed 14 February 2006).
78 See http://www.iir.gov.ab.ca/international_relations/alberta_us_relations.asp (accessed 14 February 2006).
79 Ibid.
80 The total budget of this department is US$2,812,950, with the following breakdown: administrative services, $704,577; North American relations, $594,738; La Francophonie and official languages, $620,635; trade policy, $291,118; and strategic partnership, $601,882. See *Public Accounts 2004–05*, vol. 2, 201, at http://www.gnb.ca/0087/PubAcct/index-e.asp#2005 (accessed 23 February 2006).
81 See Bernard Lord, "Message from the Premier," in *Progress Report on Prospering in a Global Community: New Brunswick's International Strategy* (January 2006), 1.
82 *Progress Report on Prospering in a Global Community: New Brunswick's International Strategy* (January 2006).
83 Ibid., 24.
84 See http://www.ontariocanada.com/ontcan/page.do?page=5930 (accessed 15 February 2006).
85 Ibid.
86 There is no available budgetary breakdown for the Office of International Relations and Protocol.
87 See http://www.ontariocanada.com/ontcan/en/about/a_wwd.jsp (accessed 16 February 2006).
88 There is no available budgetary breakdown for the International Relations section.

89 The budget allocated for trade, federal-provincial relations, and international relations is US$3,924,199. See *2005 Manitoba Estimates of Expenditures*, 105, at http://www.publications.gov.sk.ca/details.cfm?p=11046 (accessed 23 February 2006).
90 *Public Accounts 2004–05*, vol. 2, 20, http://www.publications.gov.sk.ca/details.cfm?p=11046 (accessed 23 February 2006).
91 James Wood, "Saskatchewan urged to be big world player," *Regina Leader Post*, 12 July 2005, B3.
92 There are no specific budgetary entries for international relations in these provinces.
93 See http://www.mon-trealinternational.com/en/accueil/index.aspx (accessed 20 February 2006).
94 André Lecours, "Paradiplomacy: Reflections on the Foreign Policy and International Relations of Regions," *International Negotiation* 7 (2002): 104–10.
95 Ministère des relations internationales, *Québec in International Forums*, 5.
96 Then Liberal prime minister Paul Martin responded to Quebec's claims by arguing that Canada needed to speak with one voice on the world stage. See also former Canadian diplomat Allan Gotlieb, "Only one voice for Canada," *Globe and Mail*, 5 October 2005.
97 Norma Greenaway, "Harper proposes voice for Quebec," *Montreal Gazette*, 20 December 2005, A1, A12.

Germany

Capital: Berlin
Population: 82.5 Million
(September 2003)

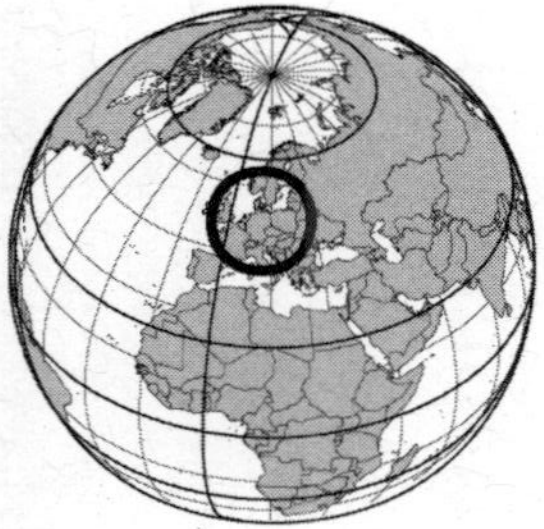

Boundaries and place names are representative only and do not imply official endorsement.

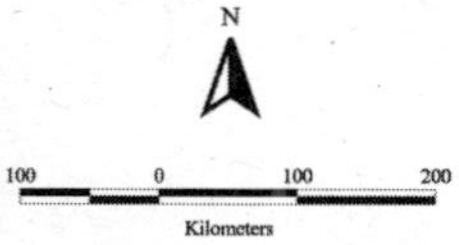

Sources: ESRI Ltd.; CIA World Factbook; Times Atlas of the World

The Federal Republic of Germany

RUDOLF HRBEK

Traditionally, foreign relations have been considered the prerogative of national executives. However, increasingly in federal countries, constituent units, in Germany the *Länder*, have become involved in foreign relations. This is even more the case for Germany because, due to Germany's position in central Europe, the majority of *Länder* have foreign countries as immediate neighbours and because Germany has strong international economic and cultural ties. As a result, *Länder* participate actively in some aspects of foreign relations, particularly in Germany-European Union (EU) relations. EU matters do not belong to the field of foreign relations in a strict sense because they involve the whole range of public policies. Competences in most of these fields are shared between the EU and its member states, among them Germany as a founding member. Given that some of these policy fields fall under the exclusive competence of the *Länder* or affect their interests, both the federation and the *Länder* are involved in EU governance domestically and in Brussels.

This chapter provides an overview of how the conduct of foreign relations, including Germany's relations with the EU, is organized and functions in the Federal Republic of Germany (FRG), examining the roles of both the federation and the *Länder*. Despite occasional disputes between them about (1) the threat to a consistent German foreign policy posed by *Länder* activities and ambitions and (2) the right of the *Länder* to engage in foreign relations, the two sides have found a workable balance in their day-to-day relations in this policy sector.

COUNTRY CHARACTERISTICS

With 82.5 million inhabitants, the FRG is the most populous European country. The proportion of inhabitants of non-German origin is 8.9%. By far, the biggest non-German ethnic group, at 1.9 million, is of Turkish origin;

approximately 40% of foreigners are from EU member states. Linguistically, Germany is homogeneous, and German is the only official language. There are small minorities with a distinct culture and language – the Frisians in the North-West, the Sorbs and Wends (of Slavic origin) in the Centre East; and the German-speaking Danes on the northern border with Denmark. But there are no separatist, not even ethnic nationalist, tendencies.

The level of social development is remarkably high. With a literacy rate of 99%, 85% of Germans have a secondary-school degree, 21% a university degree, and 2.1% a postgraduate degree. The gross domestic product (GDP) in 2005 amounted to US$2.85 trillion, or US$34,580 per capita. The unemployment rate in August 2007 was 8.8%.

Germany's economy shows features typical for developed western European societies. The primary sector has been shrinking steadily, from 22.1% in 1950 to 9.1% in 1970 and to only 2.5% in 2003; the services sector grew from 33.2% in 1950 to 41.5% in 1970 and to 66.4% in 2003; and the secondary sector fell from 49.4% at its peak in 1970 to only 31.1% in 2003. Germany lacks natural resources and is thus highly dependent on imports, especially of oil and gas.

Germany's economy is export-oriented. In 2005 exports stood at US$998.6 billion and imports at US$794.7 billion. One out of five jobs depends on exports. Membership in the EU, and especially in the Internal Market, is of particular importance, as two-thirds of German exports go to other EU countries. The EU's eastern enlargement in 2004 (with eight former Communist countries, plus Cyprus and Malta, joining) and 2007 (Bulgaria and Romania becoming members) has in this context been especially beneficial for Germany (and Austria). Another aspect of integration at the European and global levels for Germany's economy is direct investment. Major target countries for German capital are the EU member states and the United States; the bulk of foreign investment in Germany comes from EU member states, the United States, and Switzerland.

The FRG's constituent units are the *Länder*.[1] There are sixteen *Länder*, compared to eleven before reunification, among them three city-states, Berlin, Hamburg, and Bremen. The *Länder* differ in size, from 404 km² (Bremen) to 70.548 km² (Bavaria), and in population, from 0.66 million (Bremen) to 18 million (Nordrhein-Westphalen). Furthermore, the *Länder* differ in their economic strength and performance. In 2005, GDP ranged from US$23,200 per capita in Mecklenburg-Vorpommern to US$58,425 in Hamburg; the unemployment rate in early 2007 ranged from 5.6% (Baden-Württemberg) to 19.2% (Mecklenburg-Vorpommern). There are disparities in economic strength and prosperity, especially between the East (the five so-called New *Länder*) and West, but also between the North and South, with the most prosperous *Länder*, Baden-Württemberg, Bavaria, and Hessen, being situated in the South.

The FRG belongs to the group of middle powers. Due to its economic strength, however, Germany does belong to the major economic players. The country sees itself primarily as an integral part of the EU and not only in economic terms. Membership in the EU is the major feature of the country's international role, regionally in Europe (not only EU Europe) and globally.[2] The impact of globalization on Germany is very strong.[3]

GERMANY IN THE WORLD

Geographically, Germany is situated in central Europe. In terms of economic development, one group of neighbouring countries – Denmark, the Netherlands, Belgium, Luxembourg, France, Switzerland, and Austria – has a standard of living very similar to that of Germany. Except for Switzerland, all belong to the EU and its Internal Market, which features a high degree of economic integration and close cooperation in a large number of policy fields. In 2005 and 2006 there was an increase in immigration of Germans into Austria and Switzerland, countries that offered better labour opportunities.

Poland and the Czech Republic, however, lag behind considerably. These disparities cause problems, especially in border regions; the provision of low-cost goods and services by the two countries is perceived as unfair competition. Disparities can, however, offer opportunities for division of labour and complementary economic structures that could benefit both sides. Furthermore, disparities attract investments by German firms in their eastern neighbours, which have lower wages combined with remarkably well-qualified workers. Lastly, disparities can lead to migration into German areas, intensifying problems in the German labour market with its relatively high unemployment in some parts of the country, as is particularly the case along the border with Poland. This explains the special provisions in the accession treaties of central and eastern European states, with the EU postponing the right of free movement of labour from these countries into Germany for a period of seven years.

The historic legacy of the two world wars and the Holocaust, as well as that of the banishment of ethnic Germans from former German territories at the end of the Second World War, have always been a disturbing factor in Germany's relations with its neighbours. These legacies seem to have been overcome vis-à-vis the neighbours in the West (including Denmark), primarily as a result of the western European integration process, beginning with the Coal and Steel Community in 1951–52, continuing with the establishment of the European Economic Community in 1957, and extending through the subsequent creation of the EU as the major framework for joint problem solving. They have not yet been overcome vis-à-vis Poland and the Czech Republic; they come to life periodically and generate tensions and conflicts or are a disturbing factor for good neighbourly relations. As concerns Poland, there is an additional factor. In the former German South-West territories (Silesia) live some 173,000 people of German origin, with distinct cultural and linguistic traditions, who look toward the western neighbour expecting closer links that will strengthen their position inside Poland. Although this has nothing to do with separatist tendencies, Polish authorities in Warsaw observe such activities and attitudes in these (border) areas with irritation and distrust.

Linguistic similarities are favourable for communication and cooperation with Austria and the German-speaking Swiss cantons; the same applies to the German Community in Belgium, with approximately 70,000 inhabitants in the area around Eupen. The German language is still well known among some parts of the French population in Alsace and its capital, Strasbourg, and there is a relatively large number of people in Denmark and the Netherlands who have a good command of German, a language not too different from their own.

It is not only the Internal Market that is a major factor in the (economic) relations of Germany with her neighbours. Switzerland, although not a member of the EU, has the de facto status of an "associated" partner by virtue of a series of bilateral agreements in various policy fields. There is also the Monetary Union with the Euro as a common currency, which has the Benelux countries as well as France, Austria, and Germany as members, whereas Denmark, Poland, the Czech Republic, and Switzerland – also immediate neighbours – have stayed outside for various reasons. Also, the so-called Schengen Agreements, in connection with the more comprehensive project to establish an Area of Freedom, Security and Justice in the EU, have created a framework in which Germany, together with her neighbours, cooperates very intensely on domestic and judicial matters, including sensitive issues such as immigration, control of EU-external borders, and combating organized international crime and terrorism.

The *Länder* participate in a relatively large number of cross-border, interregional cooperation projects.[4] Some of them are well developed and date back to the 1960s and 1970s, such as the Upper-Rhine-Valley cooperation project, which includes Swiss cantons, the German *Land* Baden-Württemberg, and French regions. A more recent example, initiated after the end of the Cold War in the 1990s, is the Baltic Sea Cooperation, whose members are German coastal *Länder* and bigger cities and subnational territorial entities of varying legal status in countries around the Baltic Sea, namely Sweden, Finland, the three Baltic states, and Poland.[5] In the management of common resources such as rivers, especially the Rhine, and lakes (Lake of Constance),[6] cooperation and coordination on matters such as ecological concerns are well developed. The EU has set up a special program, INTERREG, to encourage and support cross-border cooperation.[7]

With its strong, outward-looking, and export-oriented economy, globalization is especially important for Germany. German enterprises, although strong in particular sectors, are confronted with growing international competition, which has led them to intensify their activities and efforts worldwide. They are supported by the federal government through its "economic diplomacy." When the chancellor or ministers pay state visits, they are accompanied by (sometimes large) delegations with chief executives as representatives of companies. This applies as well to the *Länder*, with their powers in the field of economic development. *Länder* premiers (or economic ministers) engage in marketing activities in the global market, as does the federal government. Even though the respective *Länder* activities are pursued by private-sector economic development agencies (*Wirtschaftsfördergesellschaften*), they enjoy the active support of the *Länder*.

THE CONSTITUTIONAL SETTING

To properly understand the character and features of Germany's federal system, one has to bear in mind that the reestablishment of the German state after the Second World War was initiated from below. The Allied Powers in their respective occupational zones established *Länder* as territorial entities, each with its own constitution, directly elected parliament, an executive ("government") accountable to this parliament, and its own court system. When the three Western Allies decided in summer 1948 to further stabilize the political situation by establishing a West German state on the territory of the three zones they administered, they called upon the German authorities in the already existing *Länder* to prepare a constitution and demanded that its provisions, among others, introduce a federal structure. The institution set up to draft the new constitution was not a directly elected constituent assembly but was composed of representatives of the *Land* parliaments, selected following party strength. Hence the founding fathers came from the *Länder*.

This helps to explain why the new constitution, or Basic Law as it came to be known, which entered into force in May 1949, stipulates as a general rule that "the exercise of state powers and the discharge of state functions is a matter for the *Länder*" but with an important additional provision: "except as otherwise provided or permitted by this Basic Law" (Article 30). What does this mean for the conduct of foreign relations?

The Constitution gives the federal government the predominant role in foreign relations, but the *Länder* are also given a role.[8] The key clause on foreign relations is Article 32, composed of three paragraphs.[9] Paragraph 1 states: "Relations with foreign states shall be conducted by the Federation." But paragraph 2 adds: "Before the conclusion of a treaty affecting the special circumstances of a *Land*, that *Land* shall be consulted in a timely fashion." This means that, although the federation possesses the power to make treaties, it has to cooperate with the *Land* or *Länder* in such cases. The third paragraph reads: "Insofar as the *Länder* have power to legislate, they may conclude treaties with foreign states with the consent of the federal government." Hence the treaty-making power is not monopolized by the federation. The Constitution extends this power to the *Länder*[10] if these have power to legislate in the relevant policy field. This means that the *Länder* can pursue initiatives in the field of external relations, although they need the explicit consent of the federal government. This again requires mutual cooperation and coordination between the *Länder* and the federation. However, Article 32 lacks clarity. Its provisions do not answer the following two major questions that may arise in the practical conduct of foreign relations:

- Is the Federation authorized to conclude a treaty on matters under *Land* jurisdiction?
- Are the *Länder* obliged to implement treaties concluded by the federation in areas of their exclusive jurisdiction?

The federation and the *Länder* do not agree on the resolution of these issues. Both sides agreed to disagree in principle, but in 1957 they concluded a special agreement, the so-called Lindauer Abkommen, designed to give guidelines for cooperation in the day-to-day conduct of foreign affairs. The major function of this agreement was to be the avoidance of conflicts between the federal government and the *Länder*.[11] Therefore, the agreement stipulates that when treaties with foreign states are under preparation, the *Länder* should be given the earliest possible opportunity to raise their concerns and demands. The agreement provides for the establishment of a special institution composed of *Land* representatives, which functions as a communication partner with the Federal Foreign Office or other federal ministries involved in preparing international treaties. Both sides seem, on the basis of this special agreement, to have been able to come to terms with each other without conflicts. There had been an attempt in the context of considerations on amendments and reforms of the Basic Law in the mid-1970s to find a constitutional solution, but eventually both sides agreed on – and seemed to be satisfied with – the status quo, even though the legality of the procedure remains in question. These rules and procedures reflect the consensus-based interactions typical between the federation and the *Länder* in accordance with the constitutional principle of federal comity or loyalty (*Bundestreue*). This principle, developed and introduced by the Federal Constitutional Court, obliges the federation and the *Länder* to consider and respect the concerns of the other partner when conducting their affairs.[12] Observers as well as participants agree that this principle has been honoured in the conduct of relations between the two orders of government; this applies to the field of foreign relations as well. In other words, both sides have demonstrated their willingness to conduct a fair and balanced relationship.

As opposed to the general provisions on foreign relations – an area much broader than foreign policy, understood as "high politics" – that affect a large number of policy fields and therefore give the *Länder* a role, defence is a matter for the federation exclusively.

The *Länder* have the duty to participate actively in governing the federation in large part because the *Land* governments constitute the membership of the upper house, the *Bundesrat*. Article 50 of the Basic Law reads: "The *Länder* shall participate through the *Bundesrat* in the legislation and administration of the Federation and in matters concerning the European Union." Article 51, paragraph 2, states: "Each *Land* shall have at least three votes; *Länder* with more than two million inhabitants shall have four, *Länder* with more than six million inhabitants five, and *Länder* with more than seven million inhabitants six votes." Article 51, paragraph 3, stipulates that "the votes of each *Land* may be cast only as a unit." This provision causes problems when there are coalition governments in which one partner is part of the federal (coalition) government and the other coalition partner is the opposition party in the federal arena. Coalition agreements usually observe the following rule in such a case: at the demand of one partner, the *Land* will abstain in the *Bundesrat*; this has the effect of a negative vote. According to Article 50 of the Basic Law, international treaties dealing with political relations between Germany and foreign states require the explicit assent of the *Bundesrat*, which is thus involved in exercising the treaty-making power of the federation. Whereas in most *Bundesrat* committees the *Land* governments are represented by civil servants, the committees responsible for foreign policy and defence normally meet at the ministerial level, sometimes at the level of the heads of *Land* governments. As opposed to other committees, the latter two meet only occasionally; "high politics" issues remain more or less the exclusive domain of the federal government.

In addition to the conduct of foreign relations as traditionally understood, EU matters often become part of the political agenda. Although EU policy is not "foreign policy" in the traditional sense, it is also not "domestic" policy. It involves both the federation and the *Länder* and thus requires provisions that take into account their respective rights and regulate their cooperation.[13] It was only after the ratification of the Treaty of Maastricht in 1992 that very detailed provisions in this regard were included in the Basic Law (Article 23). There is a *Bundesrat* committee on EU matters that meets frequently because of its heavy workload, given the large amount of EU legislation requiring implementation by the member states. This means in practice the *Land* governments because it is the *Länder* that are responsible for implementing federal legislation.

The new regulations — Article 23 of the Basic Law (called the "Europe Article"), supplemented by the Law on the Cooperation of Federation and *Länder* in Affairs of the European Union (hereafter Law on Cooperation) and by a special agreement between the federal and *Land* governments — strengthen the position of the *Länder* in dealing with EU matters. The new regulations provide the following:

- The duty of the federal government to maintain existing practice is confirmed: "The Federal government shall keep the *Bundestag* and the *Bundesrat* informed, comprehensively and at the earliest possible time" (Article 23, para. 2).
- Detailed and complex provisions oblige the federal government to observe *Bundesrat* opinions on EU matters. The general rule is that the federal government allows sufficient time for the *Bundesrat* to present its views on matters that touch on the interests of the *Länder*. "Sufficient time" means enough time for the *Bundesrat*'s view to be adequately considered in EU-level negotiations. If the proposed EU measure is in an area of federal competence, the federal government is required merely "to take into account" the *Bundesrat*'s view. By contrast, *Bundesrat* views must be "decisively" taken into account if the EU measure falls within *Land* competence. The federal-*Land* agreement stipulates that in case of disagreement, the two sides should continue in their efforts to reach a compromise. If that fails, and the *Bundesrat* confirms its view by a two-thirds majority vote, the federal government must comply with the *Bundesrat*'s view.
- There are provisions that allow *Land* representatives direct participation in negotiations of the EU Council of Ministers and its committees. To this end, the *Bundesrat* nominates *Land* representatives who then, on a case-by-case basis, are part of the German delegation in EU negotiations. While such cooperation in and of itself is noncontroversial, transferring the lead role in negotiations to *Land* representatives can become a very sensitive and controversial question because the new provisions of 1992 ruled that this would occur whenever the matter under consideration "centrally affects exclusive legislative competences of the *Länder*." In practice, however, the federation and the *Länder* always come to an agreement on how to proceed in individual cases.

Last but not least, an agreement between the federation and the *Länder* authorizes *Länder* to set up their own representative offices in Brussels with the official label "representation" (*Vertretung*). In this context, one should mention that although this is not part of the domestic constitutional setting, the *Länder* are also represented at the EU level in an institutionalized way in the Committee of the Regions, established by the Treaty of Maastricht. This institution, whose functions are only advisory, is designed to give representatives from regional or local entities formal access to EU decision making.

The implementation of all these provisions and arrangements requires coordination between the *Länder* and the federal government. The two sides did not agree on the efficiency of these arrangements in the pursuit of German interests. In the debate on reforming German federalism, which intensified with the establishment of a special commission in late 2003, the federal government made efforts to reduce some of the rights of the *Länder* to deal with EU matters. The *Länder*, however, insisted on maintaining their status and role.[14] The reform package, which was passed with the necessary two-thirds majorities in both the *Bundestag* and the *Bundesrat* in summer 2006, did not reduce the role of the *Länder* in this area but replaced the very vague provision with a clarification specifying that such delegation of functions (to have the lead role in negotiations in the EU Council) to *Länder* representatives is to be restricted to three policy fields: education, culture, and broadcasting. The *Länder* have argued that their constitutional status requires that when EU matters centrally affect their exclusive legislative competences, they must be given the role of representing Germany in the respective EU body.

Another provision (Article 24, 1a) was introduced in connection with the new Article 23 of the Basic Law. It reads: "In so far as the *Länder* are competent to exercise state powers and to perform state functions, they may, with the consent of the federal government, transfer sovereign powers to transfrontier institutions in neighbouring regions." This provision, introduced into the Basic Law in 1992, has never been used.

The constitutional setting described in this section sets the legal framework for the relations between the federation and the *Länder* in the conduct of foreign relations. These provisions, however, represent only a formal and, in many respects, not clearly enough defined framework. It is, therefore, necessary to look at the interaction between the federation and the *Länder* in foreign relations as it takes place in practice.

INTERGOVERNMENTAL RELATIONS

The working relations between the two orders of government in the field of foreign relations, including EU matters, have become intense and routinized. The following analysis deals with and distinguishes between intergovernmental relations in both dimensions – foreign relations in the traditional sense and EU matters – because there is a basic difference. In foreign relations, especially with respect to treaty making, intergovernmental relations are, on the whole, noncontentious; the two sides have established cooperative relations. In contrast with the noncontroversial fields of defence and foreign policy (i.e., those involving non-EU matters), EU matters have become the battlefield, with the federal government and the *Länder* as adversaries; here intergovernmental relations are conflictual.

As concerns foreign policy, the Lindauer Abkommen, mentioned earlier, serves as the formal basis and framework of these interactions whenever an international treaty is to be concluded by the federation. In accordance with the terms of the agreement, the *Länder* have established a permanent body of *Land* representatives – senior civil servants – to communicate with the Federal Foreign Office or other federal ministries, depending on the policy area in question, and there has always been an intense exchange of views when treaties have been negotiated. One aspect of these communication relations is the exchange of information; the other is de facto participation of the *Länder* in conducting foreign relations. There is general agreement that intensive participation by the *Länder* in the preparatory phase of treaty making has been essential for the effective implementation and execution of obligations imposed by international treaties because, as mentioned earlier, the *Länder* are primarily responsible for implementation.

Both sides have managed to come to terms with each other in all practical cases involving *Länder* and federation treaty making because, thus far, there have been no winners or losers. Both sides have disagreed since the outset on the proper interpretation of Article 32, but both sides have viewed the Lindauer Abkommen as equivalent to a memorandum of understanding on cooperation in practice, leaving basic constitutional questions open and unresolved. Interestingly, during attempts at constitutional reform, neither side has pushed for a reformulation of the provisions in Article 32 so that procedures can be regulated legally. This is a further indicator that the status quo of a cooperative relationship has become recognized by both sides as acceptable and functional.

Organization and management of the interaction between federation and *Länder* at the national level are primarily the concern of the Federal Foreign Office. When sectoral fields are at stake, the respective federal ministry is involved, but the Federal Foreign Office always has a coordinating role. In cases of high politics or when issues of national concern appear on the agenda, coordinating functions are performed by the Office of the Chancellor.

The organization of interaction within and among *Länder* is primarily the responsibility of the offices of premiers (*Staatskanzleien* or *Staatsministerien*). Each *Land*, furthermore, has an official representation in Berlin. This office deals primarily with federal issues and EU matters; its mandate and function are to bring to bear the respective *Land*'s interests and points of view. If sectoral policies appear on the agenda, the respective *Land* ministry will become involved in interactions with representatives of the federal government. Smaller and weaker *Länder*, with less administrative capacity, are less active than larger and stronger *Länder* in this respect. An essential feature of German federalism has always been horizontal cooperation and coordination among the *Länder*. There are regular meetings of the heads of governments (*Ministerpräsidenten-Konferenzen*), and there are regular meetings of *Land* ministers responsible for particular policy fields, including EU affairs (*Europaminister-Konferenz*). Issues of foreign relations and EU matters regularly appear on the agendas of these meetings.

The whole network of institutions set up for the day-to-day functioning of "cooperative federalism" serves as a framework for the participation of the *Länder* in foreign relations. Hundreds of committees to foster communication and cooperation between the federation and the *Länder* have been established primarily at the civil-servant level to deal with individual projects and specific questions and issues because many of them have foreign relations dimensions. The interaction takes place not only at the bureaucratic day-to-day level but also at the highest political – that is, the ministerial – level and, if necessary, between the chancellor on the one hand and the premiers of the *Länder* on the other. Because *Land* premiers are also party leaders and representatives, party political considerations can play a role. This is particularly the case if the *Land* politician belongs to a party that is in opposition in the federal arena.

These interactions involve not only individual *Land* but also groups of *Länder*, depending on the nature of the policy field and the different ways *Länder* are affected. The political weight of the *Länder* may be another factor; larger and stronger *Länder* are usually more interested and engaged in foreign relations. As discussed earlier, party political considerations can also play a role.

There are repeated examples demonstrating that the federal government is eager to have *Länder* take an active role on particular issues or in special contexts such as the participation of *Land* ministers in the federal republic's delegation to the Organization for Security and Cooperation in Europe (OSCE), the delegation of Germany to the International Monetary Fund (IMF), and the inclusion of *Länder* in the language-promotion framework of the United Nations Educational, Scientific and Cultural Organization (UNESCO). In these cases, the federal government calls upon the *Bundesrat* to nominate a representative of the *Länder*. Furthermore, *Länder* play an active role in the bilateral relations between Germany and France in the field of culture. The German representative in this field has, from the very beginning, always been a *Land* premier. These examples demonstrate that *Länder* are becoming involved more intensively, especially in fields under their exclusive jurisdiction or where implementation is their responsibility. All these cases of intense cooperation also demonstrate a division of labour. The federal government has always dominated, but the coordination with the *Länder*, either with all, a group, or an individual *Land*, has functioned well and is thus in line with the general pattern of "cooperative federalism."

On EU matters, intergovernmental relations are different. The two sides disagree not only on the extent of *Land* participation, seen as a constitutional issue, but also on how the practical involvement of the *Länder* has affected the promotion of German interests and concerns in the EU context. However, the two sides have managed to come to terms with each other, and the conflict has concentrated largely on how to define the formal rules (in Article 23 of the Basic Law plus complementary provisions) for their behaviour and cooperation. In the context of attempts (from 2003 to 2006) to reform German federalism, the federal government tried to weaken substantially the role of the *Länder* through a reform of Article 23; however, the *Länder* insisted on maintaining or even strengthening their role. The solution found in the reform package of summer 2006 can be seen as a clarification, leaving the *Länder*'s role untouched.

As earlier discussed, one institutionalized framework for this participation of the *Länder* is the *Bundesrat*. First, the committee for EU matters actively represents and promotes special concerns and interests of the *Länder* in European Union issues as a whole vis-à-vis the federal government. Second, most other committees in charge of particular policy fields have become involved in EU matters because the bulk of EU legislation needs to be transformed into domestic legislation. Furthermore, the federal government is obliged to fully inform the *Länder*, in a timely fashion, on all EU issues and to take into account *Bundesrat* opinions in EU Council negotiations in Brussels. These opinions – which amount to approximately 150 per year – are prepared in the respective *Bundesrat* committees, and the *Bundesrat* plenary decides finally (and formally). There are cases where a *Bundesrat* opinion may be very welcome for the federal government because, in the Council negotiations, it can refer to the pressure exerted at the domestic level, which the government cannot ignore, especially if a piece of European legislation subsequently needs the support of the *Bundesrat* (its majority) and of the *Länder* in the implementation phase.

The participation of the *Länder* in European Union matters has, however, again and again given rise to complaints and criticism from both sides. Article 23 of the Basic Law sets the constitutional basis and framework, but the federation and the *Länder* do not agree on the effects of *Länder* participation in this field. The federal government has very sharply criticized the role of the *Länder* and the provisions in Article 23. Its major argument has been that the involvement and participation of the *Länder* in decision making on EU matters on the basis of the provisions in Article 23 would have, and in fact has had, negative effects on pursuing interests and concerns of the federal republic for the following reasons:

- The internal coordination between the federal government and the *Länder*, but among the *Länder* as well, has been cumbersome and time-consuming.
- Agreements on the position to be followed in EU Council meetings arrived at in these coordination processes have prevented the federal government from successful bargaining in the Council because bargaining requires flexibility and the ability to react immediately in the course of negotiation processes, especially if package-deal solutions have to be found.
- The *Länder* are unable to influence issues at an early stage, a precondition for successful participation.
- The *Länder*, furthermore, are not capable of engaging successfully in attempts to bring about coalitions and alliances among member states, which have become more important since the number of qualified majority decisions in the EU has grown.[15]
- There are, as a consequence of the *Länder* presence in Brussels, too many German voices. This has proven to be counterproductive.
- In the implementation of European legislation in Germany, the *Länder* are responsible for frequent delays.
- In this context, the *Länder* must be made co-responsible when EU authorities impose a fine on Germany in cases of noncompliance with the obligation to implement EU decisions properly and in a timely fashion.
- Similarly, the *Länder* must be made co-responsible when Germany violates the fiscal criteria set forth in the Monetary Union's Stability and Growth Pact, particularly the provision that deficits not exceed 3% of GDP.

To deal with these issues, the federal government has demanded the following changes in the discussions on the reform of German federalism. German representation in the EU has to be the sole responsibility of the federal government. This means that only members of the federal government should be authorized to negotiate in EU bodies. Coordination with the *Länder* should take place and be managed domestically in advance. Procedural provisions in Article 23 of the Basic Law should, therefore, be altered. Implementation of European legislation should be the sole responsibility of the federation.

In response to the federal government's criticisms, the *Länder* put forward fundamental arguments related to the very character of Germany's federal system. The *Länder*, given their constitutional status, are constituent parts of the federal republic. As such, they have the right to participate in federal legislation. If *Land*-related functions are to be transferred to the EU, the *Länder* must participate accordingly. The *Bundesrat* has the status of a federal body; as such, it represents the interest not of a single *Land* but of the *Länder* as a whole. The federal government does not have a monopoly in defining Germany's interests; the *Länder* are entitled to define these interests from their perspective also. Both sides, the federal government and the *Länder*, are obliged to adhere to the principle of federal comity (*Bundestreue*) – that is, to properly take into account the interests and concerns of the other side. Given that EU affairs no longer belong to the area of "foreign policy," the federal government cannot claim preferential status or dominance. The *Länder* have insisted that their participation on the basis of Article 23 has never led to disadvantages for Germany. Deficiencies in the coordination processes can be attributed to unsatisfactory communication between the federal government on the one hand and the *Länder* or the *Bundesrat* on the other, primarily caused by poor (or even nonexistent) coordination between the various departments of the federal government.

Given this state of affairs, the *Länder*, during the debate on reforming German federalism in 2003–04, put forward two reform options ranging from the demand for sole responsibility in all areas in their legislative domain, as is the case in Belgium, to the more moderate option, sometimes referred to as the "status quo plus," in which Article 23 would be maintained but its wording made more precise. Such modifications would have to be made in the Law on Cooperation and in the complementary agreement between the federal and *Land* governments.

It quickly became clear that only the second option could be the basis for an agreement. Toward this end, the *Länder* argued in favour of maintaining Article 23 and strengthening their position especially in areas of their exclusive competence. They also indicated that some of the points under discussion could be dealt with at a level below that of constitutional law, namely in the Law on Cooperation and its attendant agreement. Finally, they suggested improvements in the conduct of day-to-day European business. Such measures were to include, among others, an upgrading of the *Länder* representations in Brussels so that the heads of these offices should as early as possible become involved in cooperation and coordination processes between the federal government and the *Länder*. It was also suggested that some representatives of the *Länder* participate in COREPER[16] and that *Länder* representatives should be included in the Permanent Representation of the Federal Republic in Brussels, the mission of Germany to the EU. Further proposals and demands of the *Länder* were related to the participation of *Länder* in intergovernmental conferences and/or in future constitutional conventions. Such participation has already been shown to work well.

The key issue concerning *Land* participation in EU matters has to do with the special bargaining and negotiation context of EU Council meetings. These negotiations have a give-and-take pattern during which a new situation requiring an immediate and flexible response may arise, which in most cases can and will not be identical with the position agreed to in the preparatory coordination efforts between the federal government and the *Länder*. The federal government, therefore, demanded that the *Länder* appoint a representative authorized to give the opinion of the *Länder* as a whole, whereas otherwise the federal government representative would act without being able to take into account the position of the *Länder*. Because the position of such a representative, in the view of the majority of the *Länder*, would be rather precarious, they were not willing to accept such a procedure. The solution, finally arrived at in the first stage of the reform of German federalism in summer 2006, was that the right of the *Länder* to represent Germany in Council meetings is, in the future, to be restricted to the three areas that belong to the exclusive competences of the *Länder*: education, culture, and broadcasting. In all other cases, Germany will be represented solely by a member of the federal government, and coordination with the *Länder* will have to occur in advance. The new formula provides greater clarity; however, it will not prevent all conflicts between the federal government and the *Länder*.

The 2006 reform package also included an agreement on federation-*Land* cost sharing. The agreement contained:

- a new paragraph (6) in Article 104a of the Basic Law dealing with internal cost sharing between the federation and the *Länder* in cases of violations of international or European commitments. (The federation has to bear 15% of the burden, and the *Länder* 85%; the latter's share is to be divided so that 35% is borne by all and the remainder by the *Länder* responsible for the costs.)
- a new paragraph (5) in Article 109 of the Basic Law relating to the obligation for fiscal and budgetary discipline in the framework of the EU's Monetary Union. The new clause declares the federation and the *Länder* to be jointly responsible for adhering to these convergence criteria. In case of sanctions from the European Union, 65% of the burden is the federation's, and the *Länder* are responsible for the remaining 35%, with (as in the previous case) all the *Länder* jointly contributing 35% of their burden and 65% being paid by the *Länder* responsible for violating the European rule.

It will be interesting to see how the new rules work and whether both sides will really recognize them as an improvement, making the relationship between the federation and the *Länder* in EU matters less conflictual. The need for cooperation and mutual respect, in accordance with the principle of *Bundestreue*, will continue to require that both sides draw on their experience in dealing with each other.

LÄNDER AS ACTORS IN FOREIGN RELATIONS AND EU POLITICS

The *Länder* do not conduct foreign policy in its traditional sense, but they are actors in external relations and, as a consequence of European integration, in EU politics. The senior representative of each *Land* is its premier. That ambassadors to the Federal Republic of Germany pay inaugural visits to all *Land* premiers is an indication of both the *Länder*'s constitutional status and their status as actors in foreign relations. There are no foreign ministries in the *Länder.* External relations are managed in the central offices of premiers. These have only a very small budget for foreign activities; the bulk of financial resources spent by the *Länder* for their international activities are included in other budgets, such as those for cultural activities and economic promotion. There is no grand design for the foreign relations activities of the *Länder;* rather, they are conducted on an ad hoc basis in response to particular situations and in relation to particular interests. A broad spectrum of such activities can be identified.[17]

The first of these are treaties that individual *Länder* have concluded with foreign states in accordance with Article 32, paragraph 3, of the Basic Law. As earlier discussed, such treaties require the explicit approval of the federal government, which has the right, taking into account the political interests of Germany as defined by the federal government, to approve or disapprove. Such a case has not arisen. This is not surprising given the fields in which these treaties have been concluded. A compilation of these treaties[18] covering 1949 to 1993 identifies the following fields: cooperation in general; administrative cooperation in border areas; police cooperation; hunting and fishing; water, waterworks, and dikes; traffic, road construction, and maintenance of bridges and roads; environmental protection and conservation of nature; science, education, and culture; and health. Because treaties in these fields deal with very practical problems and tasks, and because they have not negatively affected national political interests, the federal government's approval was obtained easily.

The number of such treaties is (at first glance) surprisingly low: 144 treaties from 1949 to 2004. The author of the compilation identifies the following four major reasons for the low number of treaties concluded by *Länder.*[19]

- The *Länder* lack many legislative powers because the federation has monopolized resort to concurrent powers.
- Most western European regions, as potential treaty partners, are not authorized to conclude international treaties. Belgian regions and communities, with their vast legislative powers, have become more visible and active in this respect.

- Since EU legislation has expanded, covering an ever-broader field of policies, there is little functional need to have additional treaties.
- As concerns practical issues in border areas, municipalities have become very active; hence no *Land* treaties are required.

In addition, the author tries to explain the obviously low interest of the *Länder* in concluding international treaties. He argues that *Land* governments no longer perceive international treaties as a means to represent the *Länder*. The situation with respect to the EU is of course different.

A comparative look at the *Länder* shows that only 5 (out of 16) have been relatively active, concluding 119 of the total of 144 treaties: Rheinland-Pfalz (with 44) and Baden-Wuerttemberg (30) lead this group, followed by Saarland (18), Nordrhein-Westfalen (15), and Bavaria (12). This picture – at first sight, unexpected and astonishing – can be explained by referring to specific administrative traditions and experiences that differ among the *Länder* for various reasons. Furthermore, to get the approval of the federal government is seen as time-consuming and complicated. The *Länder*, therefore, prefer to find an understanding or to bring about an agreement below the treaty level with foreign states or constituent units, including regions.

In this second dimension of autonomous *Land* activities fall joint declarations, memoranda, protocols, and the like, which are not binding legally and, therefore, do not require formal approval by the federal government. They are signed by the *Land* premier or by a *Land* minister and a representative either of the foreign state or of the region in a foreign state. They deal with a whole range of policy fields, such as cross-border and inter-regional cooperation; promotion of economic development, trade, and tourism; cooperation in education, research, and culture; and even development aid. Some recent examples include a joint declaration of the governments of Bavaria and Quebec (May 2003), a memorandum between the Hamburg Ministry of Education and its counterpart in China (September 2002), a cooperation agreement between Rheinland-Pfalz and the Republic of Rwanda (May 2002), and a joint declaration on cooperation in research and culture of Sachsen-Anhalt and Israel (October 1997). All these correspond to the general foreign policy outlook and orientation of the federal government.

Such written agreements may have political substance, even if formulated only in rather general terms, such as a joint declaration on cooperation between Bavaria and the Republic of Serbia (March 2001) and a similar document between Saxony and the Czech Republic (December 1992). Again, these have been in line with the foreign policy orientation of the federal government either in mentioning that good and close relations should be strengthened and extended to all areas of common interest or in simply emphasizing good neighbourly relations.

Other activities that also fall within the second dimension are public or publicized political statements of *Land* politicians, primarily premiers whose party is at the time not a government party in the federal arena. Their actions form part of an opposition strategy, and they are designed to make publicly known those positions that the respective opposition party or politician wants to use in the competition among parties domestically. This, however, means that the respective actor is primarily to be perceived as an (opposition) party representative and not so much as a *Land* representative; he or she uses the office only for such purposes.

Examples include meetings (and accompanying statements) of Christian Democratic premiers with the then Christian Democrat Austrian chancellor, Wolfgang Schuessel, who had been "sanctioned" by the Social Democrat-led federal government (and governments of other EU member states) for having formed a coalition with the populist Freiheitliche Partei Österreichs (FPÖ), led by Jörg Haider,[20] and criticism by Christian Democrat premiers of Chancellor Gerhard Schroeder's EU enlargement policy concerning Turkey. These are, however, exceptions, and they fall primarily in the field not of intergovernmental relations but of party competition.

The normal pattern of such activities involves public speeches by members of *Land* governments, especially premiers, when abroad. They travel to foreign countries, sometimes with relatively large delegations that include representatives of enterprises and other private organizations located in their *Land*. On such occasions, *Land* politicians sometimes make statements related to foreign policy issues. During the preparations for such "state visits," *Land* officials contact their federal counterparts; during the visit, the German ambassador accompanies the representative of the *Land*, and upon the delegation's return, there is always an official report to the Federal Foreign Office. Only in very rare cases has the federal government perceived public statements by *Land* representatives to be challenges to the diplomatic representation of Germany in a foreign country.

However, *Land* representatives are politicians, not experienced diplomats, and if a political statement of a *Land* representative does not comport with the position adopted by the federal government, or if a statement is made before the German government's "official" view has been expressed, such an activity may have an impact on German foreign policy. A precommitment by a *Land* or a group of *Länder* or by a plurality of German voices abroad may be confusing and negatively affect a uniform representation of German interests in foreign countries. One cannot argue that such public statements are illegal, but the federal government would prefer a code of conduct between the federal government and the *Länder* as a means to avoid conflicts of this nature. The latter do not see a need for such a formalized agreement. They claim that they carefully observe the principle of *Bundestreue* and that their representatives have the democratic mandate for political activities of this kind. A statement made by the premier of a large *Land* in a smaller foreign country – for example, in the Balkans – might be perceived as an authoritative German voice. Autonomous *Land* activities in foreign relations, therefore, can generate problems from time to time. As in the past, this would be an exception to the well-respected rule that *Land* politicians abroad should be in agreement with the foreign policy of the federal government.

Autonomous activities of the *Länder* play a much greater role in the context of EU politics and decision making. The provisions in Article 23 of the Basic Law, discussed above, stipulate the rules and procedures for *Land* participation in dealing with EU matters. But there are, beyond this framework, autonomous *Land* activities. In the mid-1980s all *Länder* began to establish representations to the European Union in Brussels.[21] Initially, they were called information offices, but they have since been formally upgraded to official representations. Their functions are diverse. They collect and pass on information about all aspects of EU affairs; they promote the economic interests of their *Land* and assist firms or other organizations in the development of projects in which EU institutions play a role; they perform representational functions; and they are an important forum for discussion and thus are essential parts of networking activities of the *Länder*. These activities can be considered lobbying. Over the years, the *Land* representations have been recognized as influential actors in the larger Brussels arena. Given that they represent the diversity of the German federal state in many respects, the choir of all *Land* voices does not always sound harmonious. When it comes to the special interests of individual *Länder*, they behave like competitors. The federal government, especially the Permanent Representation at the EU, is not always very happy with this variety of voices, but, pragmatically, it recognizes their presence and activities in Brussels as an established fact.

A further aspect of such networking is the membership of *Länder* in European-wide associations of constituent units such as the Assembly of the European Regions (AER)[22] and the more ambitious group Regions with Legislative Powers (REGLEG), which affiliates constituent units that have their own legislative powers within different EU member states. In addition to German *Länder*, the members include Austrian *Länder*, Belgian regions, Spanish autonomous communities, and Scotland.[23] The Committee of the Regions, established by the Treaty of Maastricht, offers institutionalized access to the decision-making system of the EU. This relatively new institution, however, has only advisory functions; therefore, it plays only a marginal role in autonomous *Land* activities within the EU system.[24]

Furthermore, *Länder*, represented by ministers and civil servants, actively participate in a large number of cross-border cooperation schemes. The federal government is not involved in such activities, and the *Länder* enjoy considerable latitude to set up and further develop such links and forms of cooperation, already referred to above. There are a large number of these regional cooperation schemes, and they are organized both bilaterally and multilaterally. Civil-society organizations participate as well. Interregional cooperation has developed and intensified because the number of issues of common concern to the participating partners has grown considerably. Policy sectors addressed in such contexts include regional planning, infrastructure development, tourism, cultural relations, education (including language training), environmental protection, and other issues of practical concern. Because this cooperation is seen as fruitful, *Länder* have continued to take initiatives to establish, strengthen, and further develop such links. Responsibility for cooperation projects lies with the respective ministry, and such projects are but one aspect of a *Land*'s policy in this field. Multiple-field coordination is done in the *Land* premier's office, where one division with only a few civil servants is responsible for all the *Land*'s external relations, of which cross-border and interregional cooperation is only one element. Such autonomous *Land* activities are seen as unproblematic as far as relations with the federation are concerned, and there are many instances of *Land* activities supporting the federal government's political initiatives. Thus *Länder* have organized and carried out training programs for civil servants in the new EU member states in central and eastern Europe (e.g., Baden-Württemberg in Hungary).

In addition to cross-border regional cooperation, there are bi- and multilateral cooperative relations between *Länder* and regions in countries with which Germany does not share a common border. One such cooperation scheme is the Four Motors network that affiliates Baden-Württemberg in Germany, Catalonia in Spain, Lombardy in Italy, and Rhône-Alpes in France.[25] Such schemes normally focus on particular policy areas. The Four Motors network focuses on high technology and postsecondary education. It is noteworthy that the Canadian province of Ontario has entered into a partnership with this network. These functionally focused activities do not involve foreign relations in the traditional sense; therefore, they do not create problems for relations between the *Länder* and the federation. In this context, one should note that there are a number of activities that have only symbolic value.

There is another field in which the *Länder* are international actors. Most *Land* governments engage in marketing activities worldwide, thus paying tribute to the emergence and existence of a global market. It is primarily the larger and economically stronger *Länder* that are very active in this respect. When premiers pay state visits to other continents and countries, their delegations are composed of representatives of the larger export-oriented enterprises. Such state visits, therefore, partly have the character of promotional tours. Furthermore, *Länder* that can afford such measures have set up or supported the establishment of offices and independent agencies abroad (sometimes called "German House," as in Singapore and Cairo) designed to help primarily small and medium-sized enterprises to establish themselves abroad. Such activities do not generate conflicts with the federal government.

Land parliaments have been trying to play a role in external relations, too. Delegations of *Land* parliamentarians visit parliaments – national and/or regional assemblies – in other countries, and they have tried to build up a network of regional parliamentary assemblies with the goal of strengthening their role and visibility.[26] The results, however, have been very modest because, clearly, the administrative and executive branches of government have an advantage over legislatures in the conduct of foreign relations.

Autonomous *Land* activities in the field of external relations need to comply with provisions of the legal setting, be it German constitutional law or EU treaty law. When, for example, in the 1950s a *Land* government tried to launch a referendum against nuclear armament of German troops, the Federal Constitutional Court – called upon by the federal government – ruled this initiative to be illegal because it interfered with the exclusive foreign policy responsibilities assigned to the federation. The same applies, logically, to similar local or municipal initiatives. To take a different field, economic sanctions against a foreign country can be enacted neither by a *Land* – let alone a municipal government – nor even by the federal government because trade policy, with its various instruments, has long since been an EC/EU responsibility. In its efforts to promote a *Land*'s economic development, the *Land* government has to observe the very rigid competition-policy regime of the EU, which does not allow direct subsidies in any form.

To deal here with what can be called "municipal diplomacy" would go far beyond this chapter's scope and would require an explanation of the status and role of local government – on the basis of the constitutional principle of local self-administration (Article 28 of the Basic Law) – in the framework of Germany's federal system. This is a very complex issue, as are activities of municipalities in the broad field of external relations. Within the realm of their competences, they can conclude agreements with public authorities in foreign countries (primarily in areas close to borders) in order to pursue specific functional goals (such as in the fields of traffic, environment, education, and culture). Thus they have acquired the role of actors in external relations.

There exist thousands of municipal-twinning agreements, which have a political function as well, and it is primarily in this field that municipalities appear in the international arena. As concerns the European Union, which affects local politics in many respects, municipalities have become active in lobbying in Brussels via their own representations (either of a larger city or of associations of local entities), similar to the ones of the *Länder*.

CONCLUSION

Both the federation and the *Länder* play a role in the conduct of foreign relations. The Constitution gives the federal government the predominant role; this has been recognized by the *Länder*, and political practice confirms this pattern. But the *Länder*, possessing exclusive juridiction in a number of policy fields and the right to participate in the legislation and administration of the federation through their membership in the *Bundesrat*, as well as in matters concerning the EU, are entitled and authorized to play a role as well. The term "the open federal state" (*Der offene Bundesstaat*)[27] tries to draw attention to factors, trends, and developments that affect the character of the federal system, especially in the fields of foreign policy and external relations. Article 32 of the Basic Law, complemented by provisions of the Lindauer Abkommen, impart a spirit of mutual cooperation and coordination in relations between the two orders of government. The experience of the past decades shows that these provisions have, in general, worked well and that both sides have managed successfully to use their respective powers and to cooperate effectively.

But foreign relations do not involve just the negotiation of legally binding treaties. *Länder* are active in other capacities, too. There are fields of foreign relations in which the *Länder* (i.e., the heads of *Land* governments) participate as political actors. Whenever *Land* politicians perform as (political) players in these fields, they are to be perceived as party representatives competing with the federal government, which is composed of rival parties. It is in this dimension of foreign relations that the federation and the *Länder* occasionally – and only when party politics is the dominant factor – clash, the federal government arguing that *Land* activities, especially autonomous activities, are a threat to a consistent foreign policy and Germany's capacity to perform successfully on the international stage. In response, the *Länder* insist on their right to engage in foreign relations. This exchange of arguments shows that it will remain a challenge for both sides to find a proper balance in day-to-day relations between the two orders of government. Both are, however, committed to the constitutional principle of federal comity, and observers conclude that this principle has never been in real danger.

A special case is the role that the federal government and the *Länder* play in EU matters. The *Land* role has expanded considerably to encompass most policy fields during the past twenty years. *Länder* have acquired the role of very influential, efficient, and highly recognized (institutional) actors in the Brussels arena and at the domestic level as well when EU issues appear on the policy agenda. The exercise of their rights of participation requires prior coordination between both orders of government, although they occasionally disagree on how such coordination should function and on how it affects efficiency in the pursuit of German interests. The 2006 constitutional reforms had as their goal the clarification of the respective responsibilities of both sides. One cannot expect, however, that the new procedures will rule out disagreements at all times. It will remain a challenge for the two orders of government to find a proper balance within the pattern of cooperative federalism characterizing intergovernmental relations in Germany.

NOTES

I wish to acknowledge the contribution of all participants in the national roundtable on this project in Tübingen, 12 May 2006. I am especially grateful for the many examples given primarily by the practitioners, who provided illustrations that were particularly helpful in my quest to better understand the conduct of foreign relations in the FRG, including the problems that occasionally arise within Germany's "cooperative federalism."

1 Hans-Georg Wehling, ed., *Die deutschen Länder: Geschichte, Politik, Wirtschaft* (Opladen: Leske & Budrich, 2000).
2 Rudolf Hrbek and Wolfgang Wessels, eds., *EG-Mitgliedschaft: Ein vitales Interesse der Bundesrepublik Deutschland?* (Bonn: Europa Union Verlag, 1984); Wolfgang Wessels and Udo Diedrichs, eds, *Die neue Europäische Union: Im vitalen Interesse Deutschlands? Studie zu Kosten und Nutzen der Europäischen Union für die Bundesrepublik Deutschland* (Berlin: Europäische Bewegung Deutschland, Europa-Union Deutschland, 2006).
3 Rudolf Hrbek, "The Effects of Global and Continental Integration on Cooperation and Competition in German Federalism," in Harvey Lazar, Hamish Telford, and Ronald L. Watts, eds, *The Impact of Global and Regional Integration on Federal Systems: A Comparative Analysis*, 329–71 (Montreal and Kingston: McGill-Queen's University Press, 2003).
4 Bernd Groß and Peter Schmitt-Egner, *Europas kooperierende Regionen: Rahmenbedingungen und Praxis transnationaler Zusammenarbeit deutscher Grenzregionen in Europa* (Baden-Baden: Nomos, 1994), gives an overview of such projects. The authors analyzed fourteen such cooperation projects with 214 territorial units and private-law organizations as participants.
5 Thomas Pfannkuch, "Ostseekooperation: Ein Phänomen, das seinesgleichen in Europa sucht," in Europäisches Zentrum für Föderalismus-Forschung Tübingen, ed., *Jahrbuch des Föderalismus 2001: Föderalismus, Subsidiarität und Regionen in Europa*, 379–91 (Baden-Baden: Nomos, 2001).
6 Roland Scherer and Klaus Dieter Schnell, "Die Stärke schwacher Netzwerke – Entwicklung und aktuelle Situation der grenzübergreifenden Zusammenarbeit in der REGIO Bodensee," in Europäisches Zentrum für Föderalismus-Forschung Tübingen, ed., *Jahrbuch des Föderalismus 2002: Föderalismus, Subsidiarität und Regionen in Europa*, 502–18 (Baden-Baden: Nomos, 2002).

7 Wolfgang Petzold, "Kooperation ohne Grenzen: Die EU-Gemeinschaftsinitiative INTERREG III," in Europäisches Zentrum für Föderalismus-Forschung Tübingen, ed., *Jahrbuch des Föderalismus 2003: Föderalismus, Subsidiarität und Regionen in Europa*, 407–19 (Baden-Baden: Nomos, 2003).

8 Gernot Biehler, *Auswärtige Gewalt: Auswirkungen auswärtiger Interessen im innerstaatlichen Recht* (Tübingen: Mohr, 2005); Kai Hailbronner, Rüdiger Wolfrum, Luzius Wildhuber, and Theo Öhlinger, "Kontrolle der auswärtigen Gewalt," in *Veröffentlichungen der Vereinigung der Deutschen Staatsrechtslehrer*, vol. 56, 7–158 (Berlin: Walter de Gruyter, 1997); Hans-Jürgen Papier, "Abschluss völkerrechtlicher Verträge und Föderalismus: Lindauer Abkommen," in Wolfgang Knippel, ed., *Verfassungsgerichtsbarkeit im Land Brandenburg: Festgabe zum 10-jährigen Bestehen des Verfassungsgerichts des Landes Brandenburg*, 91–101 (Baden-Baden: Nomos, 2003).

9 Hans D. Jarras, "Art. 32," in Hans D. Jarras and Bodo Pieroth, eds, *Grundgesetz für die Bundesrepublik Deutschland: Kommentar*, 8th ed., 582–8 (München: Beck, 2006); Bernhard Kempen, "Art. 32," in Hermann von Mangoldt, Friedrich Klein, and Christian Starck, eds, *Kommentar zum Grundgesetz*, 5th ed., vol. 2, 735–78 (München: Vahlen, 2005).

10 Matthias Niedobitek, "Rechtliche Probleme für die Außenbeziehungen von Regionen, dargestellt am deutschen Beispiel," in Rudolf Hrbek, ed., *Außenbeziehungen von Regionen in Europa und der Welt: External Relations of Regions in Europe and the World*, 17–31 (Baden-Baden: Nomos, 2003).

11 Bardo Fassbender, *Der offene Bundesstaat: Studien zur auswaertigen Gewalt und zur Voelkerrechts-Subjektivitaet bundesstaatlicher Teilstaaten in Europa* (Tuebingen: Mohr, 2007), deals comprehensively with this agreement as well.

12 Hans-Jochen Vogel, "Die bundesstaatliche Ordnung des Grundgesetzes," in Ernst Benda, Werner Maihofer, and Hans-Jochen Vogel, eds, *Handbuch des Verfassungsrechts der Bundesrepublik Deutschland*, 805–62 (Berlin and New York: Walter de Gruyter, 1984), esp. 824–7; Hartmut Bauer, *Die Bundestreue: Zugleich ein Beitrag zur Dogmatik des Bundesstaatsrechts und zur Rechtsverhältnislehre* (Tübingen: Mohr, 1992).

13 Rudolf Hrbek, "The Effects of EU Integration on German Federalism," in Charlie Jeffery, ed., *Recasting German Federalism: The Legacies of Unification*, 217–33 (London and New York: Pinter, 1999).

14 Rudolf Hrbek, "Der deutsche Bundesstaat in der EU: Die Mitwirkung der deutschen Länder in EU-Angelegenheiten als Gegenstand der Föderalismus-Reform," in Charlotte Gaitanides, Stefan Kadelbach, and Gil Carlos Rodriguez Iglesias, eds, *Europa und seine Verfassung: Festschrift für Manfred Zuleeg*, 256–73 (Baden-Baden: Nomos, 2005).

15 The EU Council, composed of member-state representatives, takes unanimous decisions only in a small number of cases of particular saliency for the member states (such as social and welfare policies and tax matters). In the majority of cases, which have increased in number as a result of treaty reforms since the mid-1980s, the Council decides by qualified majority. In this procedure, the votes of the member states are weighted based on demographic and economic considerations (e.g.,

Germany and France have 29 votes each, Belgium and Portugal 12 each, and Malta 3). The total number of votes is 321, and the threshold for qualified majority voting is 232 (72.3%) and a majority of the twenty-five member states.

16 This is the Committee of Permanent Representatives of the member states, which is entrusted to deal with all EU matters and either prepare decisions to be taken in formal EU Council meetings (always at ministerial level) or decide on behalf of the Council.

17 Karl Greißing, "Die Außenbeziehungen der deutschen Länder: Das Beispiel Baden-Württemberg," in Rudolf Hrbek, ed., *Außenbeziehungen von Regionen in Europa und der Welt: External Relations of Regions in Europe and the World*, 53–68 (Baden-Baden: Nomos, 2003); Hans-Mayer, "Die Beziehungen Bayerns zu Ländern und Staaten Mittel-, Ost- und Südosteuropas," in Europäisches Zentrum für Föderalismus-Forschung Tübingen, ed., *Jahrbuch des Föderalismus 2005: Föderalismus, Subsidiarität und Regionen in Europa*, 587–96 (Baden-Baden: Nomos, 2005).

18 Ulrich Beyerlin and Yves Lejeune, *Sammlung der internationalen Vereinbarungen der Länder der Bundesrepublik Deutschland* (Berlin: Springer, 1994). Fassbender, *Der offene Bundesstaat*, updates (through 2004) the compilation of such treaties concluded by the *Länder*.

19 Fassbender, *Der offene Bundesstaat*.

20 See the chapter on Austria in this volume.

21 Martin Große Hüttmann and Michèle Knodt, "Diplomatie mit Lokalkolorit: Die Vertretungen der deutschen Länder in Brüssel und ihre Aufgaben im EU-Entscheidungsprozess," in Europäisches Zentrum für Föderalismus-Forschung Tübingen, ed., *Jahrbuch des Föderalismus 2006: Föderalismus, Subsidiarität und Regionen in Europa*, 595–605 (Baden-Baden: Nomos, 2006).

22 See note 4.

23 Andreas Kiefer, "Informelle effektive interregionale Regierungszusammenarbeit: REGLEG – Die Konferenz der Präsidenten von Regionen mit Gesetzgebungsbefugnissen und ihre Beiträge zur Europäischen Verfassungsdiskussion 2000–2003," in Europäisches Zentrum für Föderalismus-Forschung Tübingen, ed., *Jahrbuch des Föderalismus 2004: Föderalismus, Subsidiarität und Regionen in Europa*, 398–412 (Baden-Baden: Nomos, 2004).

24 Thomas Wiedmann, "Der Ausschuss der Regionen nach dem Vertrag von Amsterdam," *Europarecht* 1 (1999): 49–86; Annegret Eppler, "Der Ausschuss der Regionen im Jahr 2004 – Zukünftiger Mittelpunkt eines 'Netzwerks' zwischen EU-Institutionen und Regionen?" in Europäisches Zentrum für Föderalismus-Forschung Tübingen, ed., *Jahrbuch des Föderalismus 2005: Föderalismus, Subsidiarität und Regionen in Europa*, 620–31 (Baden-Baden: Nomos, 2005).

25 Petra Zimmermann-Steinhart, "Interregionale Kooperationen am Beispiel der Initiative 'Vier Motoren für Europa,'" in Rudolf Hrbek, ed., *Außenbeziehungen von Regionen in Europa und der Welt: External Relations of Regions in Europe and the World*, 69–82 (Baden-Baden: Nomos, 2003).

26 Peter Straub and Rudolf Hrbek, eds, *Die europapolitische Rolle der Landes-und Regionalparlamente in der EU* (Baden-Baden: Nomos, 1998); Andreas Kiefer, "Gesetzgebende Regionalparlamente und ihr europäischer Verband: Die CALRE," in Europäisches Zentrum für Föderalismus-Forschung Tübingen, ed., *Jahrbuch des Föderalismus 2006: Föderalismus, Subsidiarität und Regionen in Europa*, 606–29 (Baden-Baden: Nomos, 2006).
27 Fassbender, *Der offene Bundesstaat.*

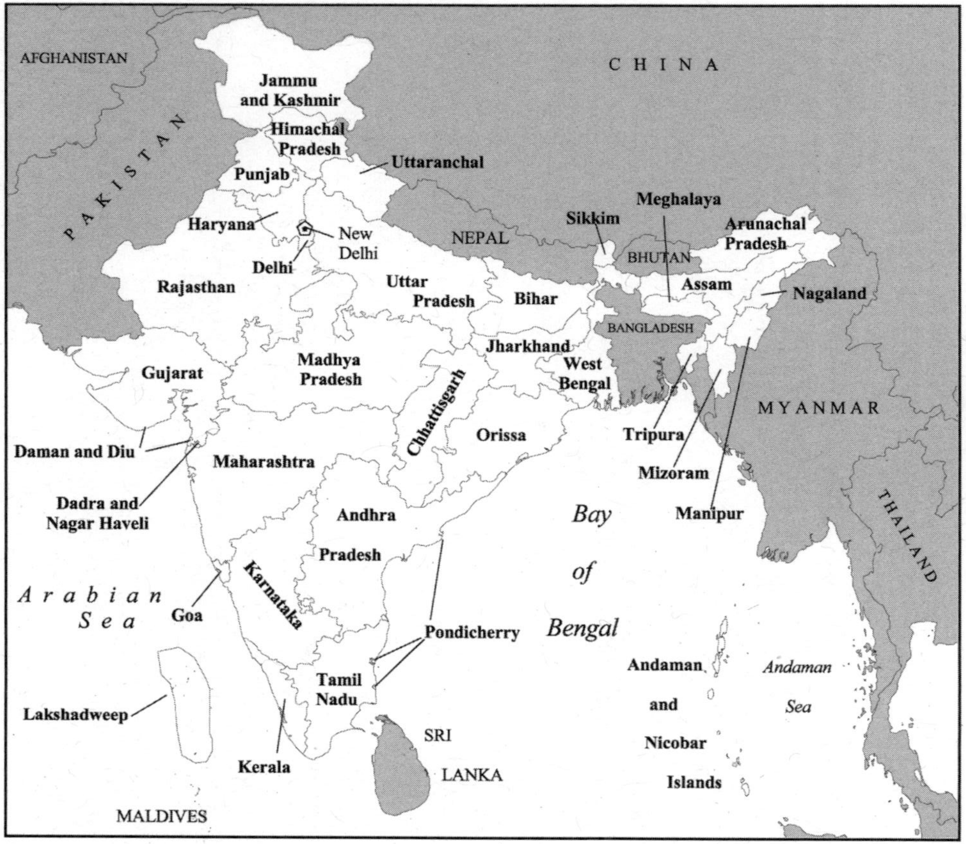

India

Capital: New Delhi
Population: 1 Billion
(2002)

Boundaries and place names are representative only and do not imply any official endorsement.

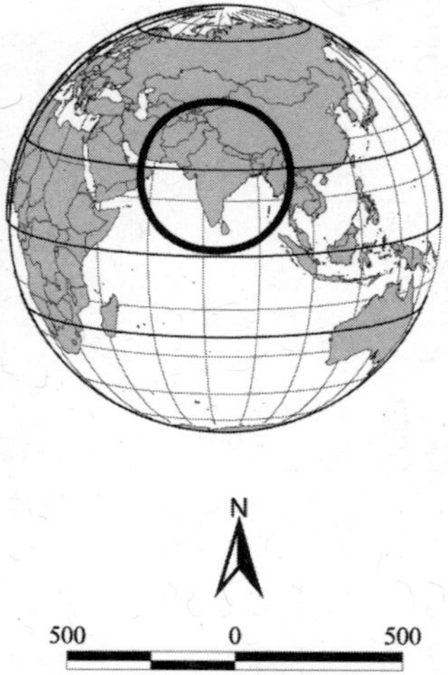

Sources: Times Atlas of the World; ESRI Ltd.; CIA World Factbook

Republic of India

AMITABH MATTOO AND HAPPYMON JACOB

The Constitution of India gives the Union government in New Delhi virtually exclusive jurisdiction over foreign and defence policy. Prior to India's independence in August 1947, foreign relations and defence were managed by the British colonial government. Indian political leaders played virtually no direct role in the conceptualization, formulation, and conduct of foreign policy. However, the Imperial Civil Service, which was bifurcated into the Indian Administrative Service and the Indian Foreign Service shortly after independence, provided a sense of continuity, especially in terms of procedures, if not always in policy.

In practice, the central government has exercised strong control over India's external relations since the Constitution came into force in 1950. The constituent states have, with some notable exceptions, played little role in the formulation or implementation of the country's foreign relations. However, this centralized control has begun to weaken over about the past decade. A variety of factors are responsible, and this gentle erosion of central authority, *de facto* if not *de jure*, is likely to continue in the future. This gradual loosening of the centralized control over foreign relations, of course, is not always a conscious or voluntary act by the Union government. By focusing on the roles of the states, this chapter provides an understanding of how federalism affects foreign relations in India by examining how the formulation and practice of India's foreign relations are changing.[1]

India is a union of twenty-eight states and seven centrally administered Union Territories. It has a land area of 490,048 square miles (788,656 km^2) and a coastline of more than 4,500 miles (7,200 km), with the Indian Ocean to the south, the Arabian Sea to the west, and the Bay of Bengal to the east. India borders Pakistan in the west; China, Nepal, and Bhutan in the northeast; and Bangladesh and Myanmar in the east. It had a population in 2006 of about 1,129,866,154 people, of whom 75% lived in rural areas. It is the world's seventh-largest country by geographical area and the second most populous country. With a gross domestic product (GDP) in 2006 of US$806 billion and GDP per capita of US$730,[2] it was the second fastest growing large economy in the world. India's labour force was estimated to be 496 million. Around 9% of Indians are unemployed, while 25% are estimated to live below the poverty line. India's literacy rate is 59.5%, the male rate being 70% and the female rate 48%. As reported in the 2001 census, Hindus constitute 80.5% of the population, Muslims 13.4%, Christians 2.3%, and Sikhs 1.9%. There are strong regional disparities among the states, particularly economically and educationally.

THE REGIONAL AND GLOBAL SETTINGS

India's geopolitical status in the South Asia region is one of natural predominance. Its geography, economy, military power, and population make it the most influential country in a region that is weighed down by interstate and intrastate conflicts, economic underdevelopment, and a colonial legacy. India's cultural predominance in the region also arises from the fact that prior to independence, two of the subcontinent's powerful nations, Pakistan and Bangladesh, were part of British India. In many ways, the extent of cultural affinity that India shares with the rest of the subcontinent (Pakistan, Bangladesh, and Nepal) is often greater than the cultural affinity that the north Indian states share with those in the south of India.

The country has long-lasting conflicts with some of its neighbours. Most significant among them is the one with Pakistan, involving more than fifty years of clashes over Kashmir and other, smaller bilateral issues. India also has bilateral irritants with Bangladesh, including the sharing of water resources and illegal immigration from Bangladesh to India. There is limited transborder migration within the region and little migration between Pakistan and India. Migrants (mostly illegal) come from Bangladesh into India, and India has an open border with Nepal. India has also been a host to refugees from Sri Lanka, Bhutan, Tibet, and Myanmar. Although cross-cutting ethnic and religious affinities would suggest considerable movements of people and transport linkages within the region, and even though these existed before 1947 when the subcontinent was partitioned between India and Pakistan, the existing political realities have ensured that there is now limited movement. There are traditional transportation routes in the South Asia region, but they are little used. The governments in the South Asia region are now negotiating to open many of those traditional routes. Lack of such physical links among the countries of the South Asia region has ensured that there is no unified economy in the region. Legal trade between India, Pakistan, and Bangladesh is much lower than its potential. Trade with Nepal is facilitated by open borders.

There have been some common initiatives for regional cooperation. For example, the Agreement on South Asian Free Trade Area (SAFTA) was signed by all seven member states of the South Asian Association for Regional Cooperation (SAARC) during the Twelfth SAARC Summit, held in Islamabad in January 2004. The agreement came into force on 1 January 2006. Along with SAFTA, SAARC strives to bring about cooperation among its members in the fields of agriculture, rural development, science and technology, culture, health, population control, narcotics control, and antiterrorism. A free trade agreement between Sri Lanka and India has also been signed to increase trade between the two countries. There are also other cooperation initiatives. The Kunming initiative, for instance, envisages integrating Yunan Province in China, Myanmar, India's northeast, Bangladesh, Bhutan, and Nepal into one unit of mutually benefiting communication networks, trading links, and transportation arteries, along with links to the outside world.

India has also been an active member of the Bay of Bengal Initiative for Multi-Sectoral Technical and Economic Cooperation (BIMSTEC), a regional organization involving Bangladesh, India, Myanmar, Sri Lanka, Thailand, Bhutan, and Nepal that works toward greater regional cooperation. It has endorsed a plan for a free trade pact by 2017. The three most advanced countries of the area – India, Sri Lanka, and Thailand – are committed to trade liberalization by 2012. Further development of most of these organizations and initiatives has been hampered by bilateral issues.

Like all South Asia states, India does not share its military powers with any regional organizations, nor has India ever entered into a military alliance with another country.

INDIA'S FOREIGN POLICY

Independent India's foreign policymakers had to deal with a host of challenges: partition of the country and creation of a hostile Pakistan, extreme poverty, military weakness, underdevelopment, backwardness in the core sectors of industry, and simmering regional and religious tensions. India's policy toward its neighbours – especially in terms of defining its boundaries – mimicked British colonial policy. New Delhi also pursued an independent approach to foreign policy by choosing to remain nonaligned in the rivalry between the Eastern and Western blocs during the early years of the Cold War. A key characteristic, however, has been the centralization of foreign policy decisions as envisioned in India's Constitution, with New Delhi providing little space for states.

Jawaharlal Nehru, India's first prime minister, was the most influential thinker on foreign policy. Virtually single-handedly, he defined the main contours of India's foreign policy in the first decades after Independence. His control of foreign and defence policy played an important role in strengthening the control of the Union government over the country's foreign and defence policymaking. Nehruvian ideas had a lasting impact on the country's foreign policy. Nehru's grand strategy rested on two pillars: self-reliance and nonalignment. As India was a militarily and economically weak state, he believed it was important to avoid entrapment in Cold War rivalries while simultaneously becoming self-reliant internally. Nehru's nonalignment was, however, far from neutrality. India was active in the movement for disarmament, in decolonization, and in the campaign for more equitable international economic development. Nehru sought to make Indian foreign policy adopt the role almost of being the conscience of the world.

The limits of Nehruvian "idealism" were demonstrated by India's military defeat during the Sino-Indian war of 1962. Gradually, even while the Nehruvian legacy survived in many other ways, the reality of power politics injected itself into Indian policymaking. It was Nehru's daughter, Indira Gandhi, who became prime minister after Nehru's death. She conducted India's first nuclear test in 1974, intervened in East Pakistan to help create Bangladesh, and established a close relationship with the former Soviet Union. It was not, however, until 1998 that *realpolitik* became the defining feature of India's foreign policy. The dominating influence of Nehru and then Indira Gandhi meant that there was limited space for other leaders and even less for individual states to intervene in foreign policy issues.

The watershed in India's foreign policy came in May 1998, when – defying traditional assumptions, analytical predictions, and international opinion – New Delhi conducted a series of nuclear-bomb tests. This was the beginning of what has been widely described as a new phase of realism in India's foreign policy. This decision was, however, taken in secret by Prime Minister Atal Behari Vajpayee and his closest advisers and without the knowledge of even the Cabinet, let alone leaders from the states.

Despite this new phase, India's fundamental foreign policy goals had not changed very much. These objectives formed the bedrock of India's engagement with the outside world. It was primarily India's search for security and stability in South Asia and its quest to influence international politics – beyond the immediate neighbourhood – through its growing "hard" and "soft" power that formed the mainstay of New Delhi's foreign policy. Faced with the necessity of an accelerated and multifaceted engagement with the outside world, India also sought to retain the autonomy to make decisions on key issues of national interest without capitulating to international pressure or being crushed by globalization. This was most strikingly evident in India's position in multilateral trade talks as well as in New Delhi's unwillingness to support the US-led war in Iraq or to let Indian soldiers be deployed there as part of the multinational force.

THE CONSTITUTIONAL SETTING

The Constitution of India came into effect on 26 January 1950. Federalism, secularism, popular sovereignty, fundamental rights, directive principles of state policy (guidelines in the Constitution to the government of the day on certain things to do and achieve that are, nonetheless, not enforceable), judicial independence, and a cabinet form of government are the basic principles enshrined in the Constitution. Even though federalism is one of the basic features of the Constitution, the word "federalism" is not mentioned in the document. Article 1(1) of the Constitution calls the country "a union of states." Each of India's twenty-eight constituent states has its own legislature (some of them have both upper and lower houses), executive, and judiciary. India's Parliament has two houses: Lok Sabha (lower house) and Rajya Sabha (upper house, or council of states). Because the upper house consists of the representatives of the states and the Union Territories, besides those nominated by the president of India, states can influence legislative proceedings on foreign and defence policy by raising and discussing such issues.

That the Union government has ultimate authority over the foreign relations of the country is evident from the fact that even if a majority of states, theoretically speaking, oppose a particular foreign policy, the Union government is not constitutionally bound to take this opposition into account.

The states have policing powers within their own territory and do not possess anything akin to an organized military apart from the state police, whose senior officers are selected, trained, and called to its service by the central government. Although Parliament has the authority to make decisions regarding foreign and defence policy, in practice the Union Cabinet makes the actual decisions. Parliament can discuss these decisions, review them, and vote against them. If the decisions of the Cabinet were overturned not only would they be reversed but, because of the conventions of parliamentary government, the government would fall. This never happens because the central Cabinet enjoys the support of the majority in Parliament. Parliament also has various committees on foreign and defence policy, but their powers are merely recommendatory and not enforceable. Such committees are comprised of members from both houses, although the majority are from the lower house. The permanent civil service in the foreign office is drawn from the Indian Foreign Service (IFS). Its officials are specially recruited through a federally appointed body, the Union Public Service Commission (UPSC), and their cadre management is with the central government.

On balance, India has a strong central government.[3] The centralizing features of the Constitution are evident from the following powers of the Union government: it has major taxation powers; it has the power to reorganize the states through an act of Parliament, a power it has exercised in the past; state governors, who are appointed by the central government, have the power to delay consent to legislation passed by a state legislature; state governors can play a role in the formation of state governments, and the central government is vested with the power to dismiss state governments by virtue of Article 356;[4] and Parliament can override legislation passed by the states, citing national interests.

Legislative powers under the Constitution are divided into three lists under Article 246 of its seventh schedule, namely the Union list, the state list, and the concurrent list. Only the central government has the authority to pass legislation on items listed under the Union list. State governments make laws on items listed under the state list. The concurrent list contains items on which both the state and Union governments can enact legislation. However, in the event of a conflict between a state and the centre on any item under the concurrent list, the writ of the central government prevails. The central government, not the state governments, holds the residuary power. The following powers are all unambiguously part of the Union list and thus outside the jurisdiction of state governments: defence of India; matters regarding naval, military, and air forces and other forces of the country; deployment of any armed force of the country in any state as an aid to civil power; delimitation of cantonment areas; foreign affairs and all matters that bring India into relation with any foreign power; diplomatic, consular, and trade representation; the United Nations; participation in international conferences, associations, and other bodies and implementing decisions made thereof; entry into treaties and agreements with foreign countries; implementation of treaties, agreements, and conventions with foreign countries; war and peace; foreign jurisdiction; extradition and admission, immigration and expulsion, passports and visas; and foreign loans. As regards trade and commerce, not only international trade but even interstate trade are the subject matter of the Union government. Treaties with foreign governments can be concluded only by the Union government, and more important, it does not need to have the treaties ratified by Parliament. Parliament may discuss any treaty or agreement entered into by the executive but may not affect its finality or enforceability. The Constitution, then, gives the central government in New Delhi virtually exclusive jurisdiction over foreign and defence policy. The states have, with some notable exceptions, played little role in formulating or implementing the country's foreign relations.

The Indian government's order of business, in allocating functions to each ministry, invariably contains the rider that anything to do with international relations and foreign affairs is not to be dealt with by the concerned ministry but by the central Ministry of External Affairs. As regards the bureaucracy, whether working in the central government or in governments of the various states, its members are forbidden to interact with any multilateral or bilateral agency without the formal knowledge and consent of the concerned agency of the central government. In fact, even for private companies, the maximum extent of foreign direct investment (FDI) and the degree of foreign ownership permissible in different categories of private companies are limited by laws of the Union government.

CENTRE VERSUS STATES

Despite a strong central government, the relationship between India's states and the central government has been an evolving one. This process of evolution has gone through various phases of cooperation and confrontation. The period until the late 1960s was characterized by extreme centralization. It was in 1967, three years after the death of Jawaharlal Nehru, that one-party rule in India started breaking down. The rise of regional parties in the 1970s and 1980s led to demands for the transfer of more powers to the states. The Union government relented by appointing the Sarkaria Commission to review centre-state relations in 1983.

The rise of regional parties to power at the centre had to wait until the general elections of 1989, which saw the establishment of the National Front coalition government led by Vishwanath Pratap Singh. Singh set up the long-awaited Inter-State Council in 1990, a forum for which provision had already been made in the Constitution. Even the Congress government that succeeded the National Front government had to depend on regional parties to gain and remain in power. This became a regular feature after the formation of the United Front government in 1996. In other words, ever since the 1989 general elections, no single party has won a majority in Parliament. Whereas in the 1989 election, 27 regional parties gained seats, 43 did so in the 1991 election. Many of these small parties' agendas are limited to highlighting only state-specific issues.

The demand for decentralization by the states is further augmented by two factors that play themselves out in the Indian political arena: the movement for local governance (through *panchayati raj*[5] and urban local bodies, namely municipalities) and demands for further reorganization of India's states. The movement for local governance is enshrined in the 73rd and 74th Amendments to the Constitution, which were passed by Parliament in 1992. These call for further decentralization of state power to local elected bodies, although this provision is not implemented by many Indian states. The movement for further reorganization of states based on regional identities has already seen results in the recent creation of an additional three states. All these factors appear to have strengthened regional forces asking for more and more decentralization of political power and resources. Although this renegotiation of centre-state relations had no direct implication for foreign relations, it did pave the way for the new assertiveness that the Indian states are showing today vis-à-vis the country's foreign policymaking.

INTERGOVERNMENTAL RELATIONS IN FOREIGN AFFAIRS

The centralized control of foreign and defence policy long exercised by the Union government has begun to weaken over the past decade or so. There are four interrelated reasons for this growing influence of constituent units on foreign relations. First, the special constitutional status given to some states (as in the case of Jammu and Kashmir) may give the states' political leadership a voice in the country's foreign policymaking. Second, the political weight of a leader of a particular state can also influence foreign policymaking, albeit in an informal manner. Third, coalition governments at the centre have provided space for state governments and leaders to exercise greater say on foreign policy issues because coalition Union governments are formed by regional parties, many of which are based exclusively in one state. Finally, although the Constitution has not undergone change, the forces of globalization have created new practices and possibilities that have already given the states a greater role and will continue to do so in the future. This is especially evident in the case of foreign economic policymaking. Many international financial agencies and institutions, for instance, are negotiating directly with the state governments in India.

These trends suggest that this gradual erosion of central authority, *de facto* if not *de jure*, is likely to continue over the next decade. The loosening of centralized control of foreign policy is not a conscious or voluntary act by the Union government but a result of the convergence of a number of factors. However, it is necessary here to point out that (1) the central government is not constitutionally bound to consult states on matters of foreign policy, (2) the states do not have any place in foreign policymaking meetings or during negotiations of international treaties and other agreements, and (3) there is not yet any formal structure to consult states on matters of foreign and defence policy. If any state has a concern in this regard, it is usually taken up at the highest political level (the chief minister conveying it to the prime minister). No bureaucratic mechanism exists to channel any such concerns. Rarely are any meetings called even at the political level to discuss foreign policy matters with states. The exceptions are when the prime minister meets with the chief ministers of states to discuss their concerns regarding foreign economic policies. States do not have offices or representatives abroad to pursue foreign policy, economic policy, or even cultural policy. Foreign missions setting up consulates in various parts of India need to liaise with and obtain clearance from the Union government, not from the state governments. It is for the central government to interact with state governments in this regard.

As the Constitution is clear about the centralized control of foreign and defence policymaking, it is necessary to look for evidence outside the constitutional framework to see whether the states have been able to influence such decisions through extraconstitutional means and practices. The following sections look at how globalization and coalition politics have affected the making of India's foreign economic policy and how border states and the political weight of state leaders have affected India's foreign and security policy.

DOMESTIC AND INTERNATIONAL MANIFESTATIONS OF CONSTITUENT DIPLOMACY

The 1990s were of great importance for centre-state relations in foreign policy. The ninth general election to Parliament saw a coalition government come to power, with regional parties, some even single-state parties, playing decisive roles in forming and running the government in New Delhi. This meant political decentralization. The years that followed also witnessed an unprecedented phase of liberalization leading to the opening up of the Indian economy. India's experiment with globalization and privatization meant the gradual abolition of the autarkic "permit-licence raj," characterized by bureaucratic red tape, that had been typical of the Indian economy since independence. This translated into economic decentralization. As Lloyd I. Rudolph and Susanne Hobber Rudolph point out, "economic liberalization, the dismantling of the 'permit-license raj' and an increasing reliance on markets, proved to be an enabling factor for the emergence of the federal market economy."[6] The coming together of these two factors forced a redefinition of centre-state relations in an unprecedented manner. The earlier decades had been characterized by constitutional rigidity, whereas the new era ushered in creative and accommodative federalism. In short, economic liberalization and coalition politics in the country provided the space for the states to confidently participate in the nation's foreign economic policymaking, which earlier had been the exclusive role of the central government.

The states' new role in foreign economic policymaking is demonstrated by the fact that many international financial agencies and institutions, for instance, are directly negotiating with state governments. Independent discussions and negotiations are held between international agencies and organizations – such as the World Bank, the Asian Development Bank, UNICEF, and the United Nations Development Program (UNDP) – and the various state governments, even though the state governments require permission from the centre to conclude agreements reached in this fashion. If these organizations wish to approach the various state governments, they must do so through the Ministry of External Affairs and the Department of Economic Affairs of the Ministry of Finance. However, if the states approach them, they can do so independently, but a memorandum of understanding

(MOU) would require the approval of the Union government. This means that the central government does have the wherewithal to control such negotiations if it wants to do so.

However, on many occasions, the central government is constrained from controlling such activities due to the compulsions of coalition politics. The states of Andhra Pradesh and Maharashtra, among others, have World Trade Organization (WTO) departments to deal with WTO-related issues, and their functioning has been rated innovative. With the southern Indian states becoming the hubs of software development and focal points for foreign investment, the Union government has to consider their policy preferences in making foreign economic policy. Moreover, with the competition for FDI increasing among the states, top state officials often travel abroad to negotiate terms and conditions for such investment with the organizations concerned. Antiglobalization movements in various parts of the country too have exhibited the power to influence the terms and conditions of investment and production in particular regions.

Political and economic structural changes have led the states to become increasingly involved in the world economy. State officials have signed a range of agreements with foreign economic institutions for purposes of collaboration and financial borrowing. There have been visits abroad by state leaders as well as visits of influential political and corporate leaders such as Bill Clinton, Bill Gates, George W. Bush, Yoshiro Mori, and Li Peng to various state capitals. No longer can the central government's prerogative or acts of favoritism determine the destination of FDI. Not only do the states understand that the central government is no longer an all-powerful entity that can bail them out of any financial problems, but they also understand that they need to compete with each other to get investment if they are to survive in the era of economic globalization. State representatives undertake missions abroad to advertise to the world that attractive investment opportunities exist in their states and that the states provide infrastructural support such as roads and low-cost power, capital and interest subsidies, and a stronger enforcement of law and order. Sometimes incentives take the form of special economic zones, software technology parks, reformed labour policies that permit downsizing and more flexible hiring and dismissal practices, tax concessions such as tax-free zones, and more relaxed environmental laws. As early as 1993, this new activism of the states was demonstrated by a deal struck between the Government of Maharashtra and the Enron Corporation to build a 2000–megawatt power plant, with the government of India providing financial guarantees to Enron. This was the first agreement of its kind in the history of independent India.

As the states established their standing among the country's important economic actors, the state chief ministers became the new role models of the new India's economic strength and development. State leaders such as Chandrababu Naidu (former Andhra Pradesh chief minister), S.M. Krishna (former Karnataka chief minister), and to some extent, Buddhadeb Bhattacharjee (presently West Bengal's chief minister) transcended their traditional role — which had been limited essentially to maintaining law and order and managing the state – to aggressively woo investment and capital. It was Naidu who started off this process by negotiating with the World Bank for a loan. Some chief ministers have even participated in the World Economic Forum meetings in Davos, Switzerland. Naidu has visited many foreign capitals to woo investment. In August 2002, for example, he visited Singapore to attract investments in the Special Economic Zone set up in Vishakapatanam in Andhra Pradesh.

In subsequent years, many state governments signed agreements with international economic institutions and aid agencies such as the Asian Development Bank and the World Bank. This is in addition to the many deals that various states struck with multinational companies. Important also are the negotiations conducted by state governments with foreign firms and governments to set up "smart cities" in the high-tech area in their states in order to promote international collaboration and attract investment. Recently, the Government of Kerala negotiated with a Dubai-based firm to set up such a smart city in Cochin. It is pertinent to note that in all these initiatives by the states, the Union government tried to facilitate only due to coalition pressures and because these initiatives were seen as part of its overall economic-development vision.

There have also been differences of opinion between the Union government and the states on a variety of issues. One of the major issues of concern for many states was the signing by the central government of the WTO agreement. Many states claimed that by signing the WTO agreement on agriculture, for example, the Union government had in fact usurped the states' power over agricultural policy. Some state governments took "the GOI [government of India] to court demanding a reinstatement of the constitutionally mandated division of powers between the central and state governments, in which agriculture is categorized as a subject."[7] In another instance of confrontation between states and the central government, the Government of Chhattisgarh opposed the Union government's plans to sell a publicly owned enterprise to a private firm, the Bharat Aluminum Company (BALCO). The state government approached the Supreme Court, but it ruled in favour of the central government. Such aggressive actions by state governments have forced the Union government to consult with them, as did Atal Behari Vajpayee, who held a meeting of state chief ministers in 2001 to discuss with them their concerns regarding the WTO and its impact on agriculture.[8]

THE LIMITS OF STATES' FOREIGN ECONOMIC DIPLOMACY

The new activism of the states has not been without the imposition of many constraints and limits by the various central governments that have come to power. Rob Jenkins, having looked closely at what has become known as foreign economic diplomacy, argues that the newfound activism of the states has not been very successful. Jenkins claims that states' encounters with external actors "do not constitute 'foreign economic policy' so much as domestic policies with implications for the possibility of transacting business with transnational capital and international financial institutions."[9]

Jenkins points out that the central government has not been particularly accommodating of state participation in the decision-making process in the country's foreign economic policy. He writes that "the general trend is the ability of central government officials responsible for the implementation of trade policy to remain substantially impervious to the entreaties of state governments representing key trade-affected constituencies."[10] This has been amply evidenced in the fact that the central government, heedless of repeated requests from many states, did not raise tariffs on certain imported commodities despite evidence that their import had an adverse impact on domestic agricultural producers. Jenkins also points out that the Government of India has not even included the states in the discussions under the WTO-mandated Trade Policy Review Mechanism (TPRM), in which the states' involvement would have served them well.[11] The WTO does not provide any mechanism that allows states to influence agreements signed with the Union government. Furthermore, the complexities of the behind-the-scene politics of most international financial organizations are well beyond the reach and understanding of the state governments. Most of the WTO cells established by state governments have not been able to contribute much to the states' involvement in decision making about foreign economic policy[12] – this despite the fact that the central government has encouraged the states to set up such bodies.[13] One of the reasons for this is that these cells are often headed by civil servants who are reluctant to undertake initiatives on their own; a second is that their agenda has been limited. A cursory glance at the objectives of the Andhra Pradesh WTO cell, for example, demonstrates that there is nothing radical in its action program.[14]

Moreover, the central bureaucracy has not been very positive about the states' participation in the decision-making process of the country's foreign economic policy even as the political leadership seems to be more open and encouraging. In fact, the central bureaucracy does everything to ensure that the states do not bypass the interests and influence of the Union government when negotiating with international organizations and agencies. Even though politically there may be a willingness to demonstrate greater flexibility, the bureaucracy is unwilling to share turf or to change the status quo. In any case, structural problems inhibit states from taking loans from international organizations, agencies, and states because the central government often has a decisive say in such transactions. A good example is World Bank loans. These always identify the central government as the principal borrower even when the loan is to go to a state government. The central bureaucracy, more often without the explicit consent of the political leadership, also tries to place legal impediments in the way of independent state negotiations with international organizations. Therefore, organizations asked to provide loans almost always try to negotiate with the central government before finalizing the agreement with a particular state. Jenkins puts it well: "Through the considerable leverage it possesses with foreign agencies, the Government of India is able to influence the shape of states' multilaterally funded assistance packages even before the draft programmes are brought to state governments themselves."[15]

Be that as it may, it is now widely recognized that there is increasing collaboration and consultation between the Union government and states on matters of economic diplomacy. On the one hand, the central government recognizes that it is better to be understanding of the demands of states because the stability of the central government in the era of coalition politics depends much on the regional parties. The outlook and attitudes of the politicians at the centre also have changed regarding how far they should accommodate regional views. Today's political leadership draws its power from the regional parties and has a thorough understanding of the demands and aspirations of the country's regions. What perhaps has not changed is the central bureaucracy. The real managers of power in the Union government, the bureaucrats, do not like to delegate their power to the states, especially in the absence of clear legislation requiring them to do so.

BORDER STATES AND FEDERAL RELATIONS

India's border states have special problems, two of which are dealing with illegal migration and cross-border terrorism. Because of these problems, they have negotiated special treatment with or have behaved differently from other states vis-à-vis the central government. Debates and arguments about illegal migration from Nepal and Bangladesh have been especially strong in India's north-eastern states. Rafiq Dossani and Srinidhi Vijayakumar point out that, "as the state parties have increased their voice in government, they have demanded an increased role in controlling migration into their states. Nowhere is the ambiguity of federal jurisdiction more apparent than in the case of border patrol. In West Bengal, the state police and the Border Security Force [a centrally-controlled paramilitary force] often work together to control the movement of migrants and goods from Bangladesh."[16]

Although the legal power over border control and regulation lies with the Union government, it is often not in a position to carry these out effectively without the cooperation of the state governments. This has prompted the central government to delegate powers to them. In one such instance, L.K. Advani, the then Union home minister, asked the states to take the necessary steps to stop illegal migrants.[17] In another instance, the West Bengal government opposed a move by Maharashtra and the central government to expel some alleged illegal Bangladeshi migrants through the territory of West Bengal.[18]

The border states have also had to deal with cross-border terrorism. States like Jammu and Kashmir have designed their own ways to do so and have at least sometimes come into conflict with the central government. The disbanding of the Special Operations Group (SOG) by the Mufti Mohammad Sayeed government in Jammu and Kashmir, opposed by the central government, is such an instance. Although SOG was a state-run organization and therefore operated by virtue of the policing powers of Jammu and Kashmir state, the Union government had definite interests in the matter because it affected the country's internal security. The Mufti government also had adopted a "healing touch" approach to the Kashmir problem and had decided to release from confinement many persons accused of indulging in acts of militancy despite the central government's displeasure.

In the recent past, Sayeed was also able to have an impact on India's policy toward Pakistan. Sayeed is widely regarded as the architect, although indirectly, of several confidence-building measures that were introduced between the two countries. These include the resumption of the Srinagar-Muzaffarabad bus service across the volatile line of control that divides Jammu and Kashmir between India and Pakistan, as well as the unprecedented collaboration between Islamabad and New Delhi after the devastating earthquake in Jammu and Kashmir in fall 2005. Since then, a large number of initiatives vis-à-vis Pakistan have been undertaken in Jammu and Kashmir. The Poonch-Rawalkot bus service has already begun, and bus services are proposed between Kargil and Skardu in Pakistan-administered Kashmir and between Jammu and Sialkot, also in that part of Kashmir. There have been many debates in the Jammu and Kashmir Legislative Assembly on the role of Pakistan in sponsoring terrorism in the state. For example, in March 2000, speaking in the state assembly, the then chief minister, Dr Farooq Abdullah, stated that "Pakistan was bent upon destabilizing peace in India. He said he had requested the US President, Mr. Bill Clinton, that he should tell Islamabad, during his ensuing visit, that it should stop exporting terrorists to Jammu and Kashmir. He said that Mr. Clinton should assert his authority and force Pakistan to end its 10-year-long proxy war which had resulted in the death of several thousand people in the State. Dr. Abdullah said the USA should declare Pakistan a terrorist state and impose sanctions against it."[19]

The political weight of a particular state leader can also influence foreign policymaking, albeit informally. This is illustrated by the example of Amrinder Singh, the chief minister of Punjab, who reached out to Pakistan's Punjab on the basis of a shared cultural tradition, Punjabiyat. This policy received considerable popular support in Indian Punjab. Another such instance occurred in 1964 when the Kashmiri leader, Sheikh Abdullah, went to Pakistan as Prime Minister Nehru's emissary, where he is believed to have even worked out an understanding with President Ayub Khan. This understanding, however, was not translated into action because Nehru passed away while the sheikh was still in Pakistan. Similarly, political heavyweights from the southern state of Tamil Nadu have been able to exercise considerable influence on New Delhi's policy toward Sri Lanka. Indeed, the Tamil Nadu legislature has often in the past passed resolutions on the situation of Tamils in Sri Lanka. On 17 August 2006 the Tamil Nadu Assembly condemned attacks on Tamils in northern Sri Lanka by government forces. When Sri Lanka criticized the resolution, Tamil Nadu's chief minister, M.K. Karunanidi, retorted that "if Tamils condemning the killing of their Tamil brethren was dubbed a mistake, then they [Tamil Nadu Assembly] would continue to commit it."[20] Again, in December 2006, the Tamil Nadu Assembly resolved that "this house is deeply concerned about the travails of the Tamils in Sri Lanka because of lack of protection to life and property. We request the central government to take necessary steps to alleviate the situation to the satisfaction of all concerned."[21]

The forces of regional integration in South Asia have also created opportunities for states to play a role. After the chief minister of Sikkim, Pawan Chamling, set up a study group that strongly recommended the opening of the route, pressure from the Government of Sikkim helped to speed up the opening of the traditional trade links between Sikkim and China across the Nathula Pass, which was closed in the 1960s. Similarly, West Bengal has supported the Bay of Bengal Initiative for Multi-Sectoral Technical and Economic Cooperation (BIMSTEC), which links South Asia to South East Asia and seeks to create a Bay of Bengal economic community. This would have the potential to make Kolkata (the capital of West Bengal) once again the hub of trade and commerce, as it had been until the early years of the twentieth century.

The Kunming initiative, discussed earlier, will undoubtedly require removing existing bilateral irritants between India and its neighbours. Indeed, linking the northeast of the country with the neighbouring countries would be extremely beneficial for that region, as it would benefit from a sea link as well as trade links with the rest of the region. River-water management, border management, and energy production in the region also require regional collaboration between India, Nepal, and Bangladesh. As far-fetched as many of these developments may be, that there is thinking along these lines is of great significance.

Indeed, the Union government is considering many more such trade and other links, which will strengthen the country's regional engagements and enable the states to have more say in the establishment and management of the country's trade and links with neighbouring countries. The following are some of them. Integrated check points (ICPs) are being negotiated with Nepal, along with upgrading of highways and train links between the two countries. Border links with Bhutan, Bangladesh, and Myanmar are also being pursued seriously.[22] Given the importance that successive Indian governments have attributed to neighbourhood diplomacy over the past few years, it is likely that most of these initiatives will see the light of day. What needs to be noted here is that such links with the neighbouring states will certainly increase the role of the Indian states in policy formulation vis-à-vis their foreign neighbours. However, all these links first have to be approved by the Union government.

It is worth considering what would happen if India gave more freedom to its states to engage the international arena in the same manner as, for example, Canadian provinces, Belgian regions and communities, Swiss cantons, or even US states. Can India take the risk of allowing such freedom? If not, why not? Such counterfactual analysis could provide a clue about the health of India's recent federalism. When the Indian National Congress was the dominant party in Indian politics, a period referred to by many as the "Congress system," giving Indian states more freedom to engage the international arena may not have made much of a difference because the centralized Congress party's high command would not have let the state governments exercise such powers in the first place. However, the state of affairs is different in today's coalition era, when states are vying to influence Indian foreign policy, including foreign economic policy. Regional parties and their leaders, without whose support no Union government can today be formed or sustained, have certainly used such constitutional provisions to influence the country's policies toward its neighbours, and state governments have independently negotiated with foreign governments and firms regarding FDI, joint business ventures,[23] border trade, border patrolling, people-to-people engagements, and matters regarding the Indian diaspora.[24]

States have also been more vocal about expressing their foreign and defence policy preferences to the central government.

However, it may not be in the larger interests of the country and its unity to allow a great deal of freedom to its states given their wide-ranging and at times conflicting interests. A strong central government may be necessary to hold together a country that has great diversity and constitutes a subcontinent. It should be said that India is still in the process of state building and consolidation. There are regions and subnationalities in the country that have not yet fully accepted the unity of the country. Under such circumstances, it might be rash to grant constituent units such freedoms. Despite the moderately increasing role of the states in decision making on foreign policy, it is curious that there is hardly any discussion of the need to give a greater role to the state governments in the country's foreign relations.

CONCLUSION

The Constitution of India gives the Union government virtually exclusive jurisdiction over matters of foreign and defence policy. In practice, too, the central government has exercised strong control over India's external relations since the Constitution came into force in 1950. Even before then, there were very marked centralizing tendencies due particularly to the British tradition of a strong central government that did not permit state governments to get involved in defence and external affairs during the period of British rule. Although the states have virtually no direct constitutional jurisdiction over foreign relations, in practice the emerging reality is somewhat different. Since the early 1990s there has been a gradual weakening of the central government's tight grip on the country's foreign relations.

This is being made possible by a variety of factors despite the absence of constitutional change. First, the special constitutional status given to some states, such as Jammu and Kashmir, seems to have accorded their political leadership a voice in the foreign policymaking of the country. Second, the political weight of a leader of a particular state has also influenced foreign policymaking in many cases. Third, coalition politics and its ramifications at the centre have provided space for state governments and leaders to exercise greater say on foreign policy issues. Finally, opportunities provided by opening the Indian economy to globalization have created new practices and possibilities that have given the constituent units a greater role. In fact, the happy coincidence of the opening of India's economy and the arrival of coalition politics in India in the early 1990s paved the way for an increased state role in making the country's foreign and defence policy.

The slow and indirect but steady change that the country is witnessing in its foreign policy formulation is widely welcomed. A diverse, plural country such as India must allow change in its style of policy formulation so that it is really in tune with its heterogeneity. A more consultative, organic, and creative style of foreign policy would be more in line with the needs of the people and could become the basis of a real national consensus.

NOTES

1 For other chapters on India, see Akhtar Majeed, "Republic of India," in John Kincaid and G. Alan Tarr, eds, *Constitutional Origins, Structure, and Change in Federal Countries*, 180–207 (Montreal and Kingston: McGill-Queen's University Press, 2005); George Mathew, "Republic of India," in Akhtar Majeed, Ronald L. Watts, and Douglas M. Brown, eds, *Distribution of Powers and Responsibilities in Federal Countries*, 155–80 (Montreal and Kingston: McGill-Queen's University Press, 2006); Rajeev Dhavan and Rekha Saxena, "Republic of India," in Katy Le Roy and Cheryl Saunders, eds, *Legislative, Executive, and Judicial Governance in Federal Countries*, 165–97 (Montreal and Kingston: McGill-Queen's University Press, 2006); and Govinda Rao, "Republic of India," in Anwar Shah, ed., *The Practice of Fiscal Federalism: Comparative Perspectives*, 151–77 (Montreal and Kingston: McGill-Queen's University Press, 2007).
2 The Economist, *Pocket World in Figures, 2008 Edition* (London: Profile Books, 2007), 156.
3 India's government has also been called a "quasi-federal system," "centralized federalism," and "the union system of Indian federalism."
4 Amal Ray, with John Kincaid, "Politics, Economic Development, and Second-Generation Strain in India's Federal System," *Publius: The Journal of Federalism* 18 (Spring 1988): 147–67.
5 Local self-government institutions.
6 Lloyd I. Rudolph and Susanne Hoeber Rudolph, "The Iconization of Chandrababu: Sharing Sovereignty in India's Federal Market Economy," *Economic and Political Weekly*, 5 May 2001, 1542.
7 Rob Jenkins, "How Federalism Influences India's Domestic Politics of WTO Engagement (and is itself affected in the process)," *Asian Survey* 43, no. 4 (2003): 598–621, at 607.
8 P.K. Vasudeva, "Chief Ministers' Conference on WTO Mixed Results," 2 July 2001, http://members.tripod.com/israindia/isr/july3/vasu.html (accessed 1 February 2008).
9 Rob Jenkins, "India's States and the Making of Foreign Economic Policy: The Limits of the Constituent Diplomacy Paradigm," *Publius: The Journal of Federalism* 33 (Fall 2003): 63–81, at 69–70.
10 Ibid., 79.
11 Ibid.
12 WTO cells are set up by state governments to assess the impact of the WTO regime on their economies. Andhra Pradesh, West Bengal, Madhya Pradesh, Karnataka, Delhi, Tripura, Nagaland, Haryana, and the Union territory of Dadra and Nagar Haveli have established WTO cells so far. Punjab has also constituted a high-powered committee to look into the impact of the WTO regime.
13 "Centre to continue talks with states on WTO," 20 March 2001, http://www.rediff.com/money/2001/mar/20wto.htm (accessed 1 December 2007).

14 The key objectives are: preparation of the WTO Strategy Document for Agriculture in Andhra Pradesh; regular documentation of WTO impacts on agriculture and allied sectors; advice and guidance to senior management of the concerned departments on WTO-related strategies; determining the communication strategies to advise stakeholders, especially farmers, on WTO-related aspects; and keeping the agriculture sector in Andhra Pradesh in pace with the changing world in the wake of the WTO. See http://agri.ap.nic.in/wto.html (accessed 1 December 2007).
15 Jenkins, "India's States," 73.
16 Rafiq Dossani and Srinidhi Vijayakuamr, "Indian Federalism and the Conduct of Foreign Policy in Border States: State Participation and Central Accommodation since 1990," Shorenstein APARC Working Paper, Walter H. Shorenstein Asia-Pacific Research Center, Stanford University, 5.
17 Ibid., 10.
18 Ibid.
19 "J&K House resolves to banish terrorism," 24 March 2000, http://www.tribuneindia.com/2000/20000324/j&k.htm#1 (accessed 1 December 2007).
20 M. Mayilvaganan, "Uncertainty in Sri Lanka and a Possible Thaw in Indian Perception," 12 December 2006, http://www.idsa.in/publications/stratcomments/Mmayilvaganan121206.htm (accessed 15 October 2007).
21 "Tamil Nadu house passes resolution on Sri Lankan Tamils," 7 December 2006, http://in.news.yahoo.com/061207/43/6a3sj.html (accessed 15 October 2007).
22 Shyam Saran, "Connectivity as India's neighbourhood policy," http://www.himalmag.com/2006/october/opinion_1.htm (accessed 15 October 2007).
23 The Jammu and Kashmir Bank has been planning to open branches in Pakistan-controlled Kashmir. The matter is pending with the central government in Delhi, which has not yet given permission. If the state government had been invested with powers to negotiate independently with the Government of Pakistan, things would have been different.
24 One would have to consider the outbursts of the Tamil Nadu government in response to the alleged human rights violations against its Tamil population by the Malaysian government. Only the Government of India can formally lodge a protest with the Malaysian government.

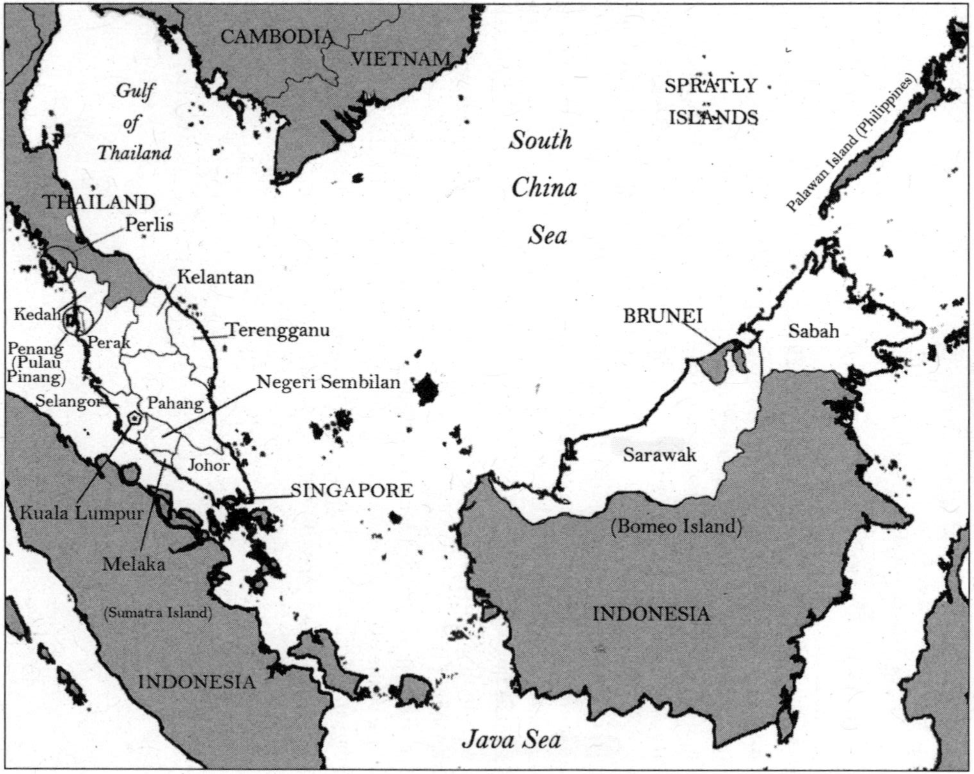

Federation of Malaysia

Capital: Kuala Lumpur
Population: 24.3 Million (2002)

Boundaries and place names are representative and do not imply any official endorsement.

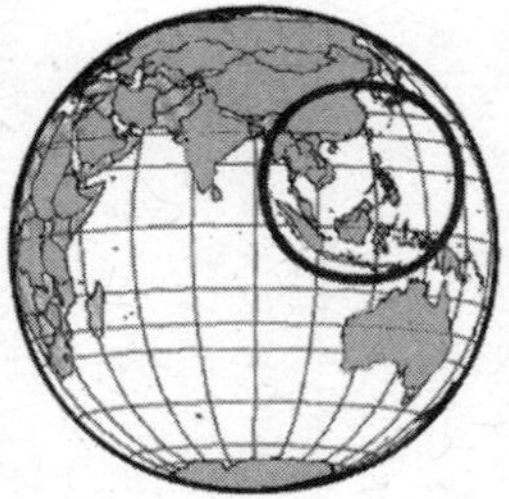

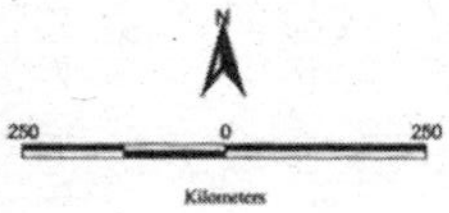

Sources: ESRI Ltd.; CIA World Factbook; Times Atlas of the World

Federation of Malaysia

FRANCIS KOK WAH LOH

Globalization has made economic issues ever more central to foreign relations and foreign policy. In most federal countries, formal or informal restructuring of federal-state relations has occurred to accommodate the enhanced roles of constituent units in foreign trade and foreign investment. However, no formal restructuring of these relations has occurred in Malaysia. The scope of new, informal intergovernmental arrangements that link the states to foreign policymaking has also been limited.

There are several reasons why Malaysia's states play such limited roles in foreign affairs, notwithstanding globalization. First, the Constitution clearly favours the central over the state governments. Second, the political process has been dominated by a single political party, the Barisan Nasional (BN) coalition, which has held power at the centre for fifty years, facilitating BN control uninterruptedly over most of the constituent states. Only three of the thirteen states have been governed by the opposition and, except in one case, only for short periods. This domination coincides with the increased role of the executive in decision making. In turn, centralization has been legitimized in terms of the need to combat subversion and terrorism – once associated with communists, nowadays with extremist Muslims – and to preserve ethno-religious harmony in multiethnic, multireligious Malaysia. In pursuit of the latter, the New Economic Policy (NEP), an affirmative-action policy that discriminates in favour of the Malays and Indigenous peoples, was launched in 1971, further contributing to the expansion and consolidation of the BN government. Consequently, although it maintains a formal federal and parliamentary structure, Malaysia has been described as a "semidemocratic" country, a "statist democracy," and a "centralized unitary system with federal features." That said, conflicts and tensions in intergovernmental relations have occurred from time to time.

This chapter traces changes in Malaysia's foreign relations, which culminated in the adoption of an economic foreign policy in 1985. It then discusses how this change in policy had an impact on interdepartmental relations at the centre and on intergovernmental relations as well, without, however, resulting in formal restructuring. The constraints and inefficiencies arising from a centralized federalism in an era of globalization are then investigated and evaluated via two examples of state-led efforts, namely to promote Penang as a regional hub of the global information and communication technology (ICT) industries and to develop the cross-border Association of South-East Asian Nations (ASEAN) Growth Areas, particularly in East Malaysia.

MALAYSIA: AN OVERVIEW

At independence in 1957, the Federation of Malaya, a former British colony, comprised the eleven states of the Malayan peninsula. In 1963 the federation was expanded to include Singapore, along with Sabah and Sarawak in northern Borneo, and was renamed the Federation of Malaysia. Due to various disagreements, Singapore withdrew from the federation in 1965. Today, Malaysia comprises the eleven peninsular states of West Malaysia, the states of Sabah and Sarawak in East Malaysia, and three federal territories (Kuala Lumpur, Putra Jaya, and Labuan).

Malaysia's multiethnic society comprises 25 million people. Malays constitute the major ethnic group, most residing in the peninsula. The largest Native group in Sabah is the Kadazandusun, while Dayaks predominate in Sarawak. Malays, Kadazandusuns, Dayaks, and the members of other smaller Indigenous communities are categorized as *bumiputeras* (sons of the soil) and account for 65% of the population. The two principal non-*bumiputera* groups are the Chinese (about 26%) and Indians (about 8%), who immigrated to Malaysia during colonialism. Linguistic, cultural, and religious differences distinguish the ethnic groups from one another. Malays are invariably Muslim; Chinese are predominantly Buddhist or Taoist; and Indians are mostly Hindu, with smaller numbers of Muslims and Sikhs. About half the Natives of Sabah and Sarawak are Christian, and another one-third are Muslim.

Due to a consociational arrangement among the three major ethnic-based political parties that formed the Alliance coalition at independence, Malay was adopted as the national language; the Malay sultans were acknowledged as the heads of state and Islam as the official religion; and "special rights" were reserved for Malays in land allocation, bureaucratic appointments, and scholarship awards. In exchange, non-Malays were offered citizenship and allowed to practise, study, and promote their languages, cultures, and religions. Except for a brief period during 1969–71, following ethnic riots in Kuala Lumpur, Malaysia has maintained political stability and enjoyed economic growth. It has been moving up the Human Development Index (HDI) of the United Nations Development Program

(UNDP) since the 1990s. In 2004 it ranked number 59, putting it among the top medium HDI-ranking countries. According to official estimates, gross domestic product (GDP) per capita in 2005 was approximately US$10,300. That year access rates to education were 96% for primary schools, 85% for secondary schools, and 30% for tertiary-level institutions. The infant mortality rate (per 1,000 live births) was only 5.8%, while the absolute poverty rate was down to 5.7% (in 2004).[1]

Beginning from the early 1970s, Malaysia embarked on a policy of export-oriented industrialization (EOI), which emphasizes electrical and electronic components, textiles and garments, and resource-based industries. EOI resulted in increased foreign exchange earnings and employment opportunities. Following a recession in the mid-1980s, the Malaysian government identified the private sector as the new engine of growth and promoted economic deregulation, liberalization, and privatization in keeping with global neo-liberal trends. The result was a spectacular increase in foreign direct investment (FDI), especially from the East Asian countries, which promoted steady economic growth with low inflation until a regional financial crisis occurred in 1997–98.[2]

In response to the crisis, Malaysia introduced a package of initiatives in 1998 that included pegging the Malaysian ringgit to the US dollar and introducing currency controls. Beginning in 2002, currency controls were eased, and in 2005 they were lifted completely. During that latter year, the ringgit was also depegged. Consequently, FDI again flowed in (increasing from US$2.473 billion in 2003 to $4.624 billion in 2004 and to $6.06 billion in 2006), thus underlining growing confidence in Malaysia as an investment destination.[3] Meanwhile, due to the earlier growth and the current growth, the structure of the Malaysian economy was transformed from one dependent on raw materials (e.g., tin ore, natural rubber, palm oil, and tropical timber) to one based on EOI, the export of petroleum and natural gas discovered in the early 1970s, and services. All told, Malaysia possesses strong economic fundamentals and is regarded as East Asia's "fifth tiger," or a second-generation Newly Industrialized Country (NIC).

Following the 1969 ethnic riots, various measures were introduced to restrict political participation and to resolve ethnic conflict. As mentioned, the affirmative-action NEP was adopted in 1971. It sought to eradicate rural Malay poverty and to restructure the ethnic division of labour. Accordingly, the state intervened in the economy in unprecedented ways. It established statutory bodies and public corporations and appointed *bumiputeras* to head them. *Bumiputera* individuals and companies were also given preferential treatment in the awarding of government contracts, licences, and loans. Special education institutions catering exclusively to young *bumiputeras* were created, while ethnic quotas were introduced to increase their intake into the universities and their receipt of scholarships.

The goal was to create a *bumiputera* commercial and industrial community as a means to reduce inequalities and thereby foster national unity.

No doubt, *inter*ethnic inequalities have been reduced since the 1970s. However, because of the emergence of "money politics" and nepotism related to the expansion of the public sector, *intra*ethnic inequalities have also increased, especially within the Malay community.[4] Regional inequalities have also widened. According to the Ninth Malaysia Plan (2006–10), whereas the overall rate of poverty in peninsular Malaysia was 3.6% in 2004, it was 23% in Sabah, 15.4% in Terengganu, 10.6% in Kelantan, and 7.5% in Sarawak. Hence the NEP's results have been mixed. More important for this study, implementation and monitoring of the NEP required the expansion of the public sector and tight control by the central authorities, measures that have had an impact on federal-state relations.

THE REGIONAL AND GLOBAL CONTEXT

By constitutional design, foreign relations and foreign policymaking fall under the purview of the federal government. In the early decades after independence, Malaysia's role in international relations was quite inconsequential. During the leadership of the first prime minister, Tunku Abdul Rahman (1957–69), which coincided with the height of the Cold War, Malaysia adopted a pro-West, anticommunist stance. Under the second prime minister, Tun Abdul Razak Hussein (1969–76), the policy shifted to one of nonalignment, neutrality, and peaceful coexistence. Like the United States, which pushed for rapprochement with China, Malaysia, too, established diplomatic relations with Beijing. Under the auspices of ASEAN, Tun Razak led an initiative to declare Southeast Asia a Zone of Peace, Freedom, and Neutrality (ZOPFAN). These foreign policy orientations were consolidated under the third prime minister, Tun Hussein Onn (1976–81).

However, major changes in foreign policy occurred under the fourth prime minister, Tun Dr Mahathir Mohamad (1981–2003). First, Malaysia began to prioritize its relations with ASEAN partners, the Organization of the Islamic Conference (OIC), and the Non-Aligned Movement (NAM). Second, while developing these ties, a new assertive role with regard to regionalism and South-South cooperation was discerned as well. This new assertive role coincided with a shift from traditional geo-political diplomacy to geo-economic considerations.[5] As shown below, these changes were in response to economic globalization, which had been spurred by the end of the Cold War on the one hand and by the rise of political Islam globally on the other.

Kuala Lumpur pushed for a number of changes within ASEAN during the 1980s and 1990s, among them drawing Vietnam, Laos, Cambodia, and Myanmar into the group. It further promoted the ASEAN Free Trade Area as a means to engage with globalization. Mahathir also pushed for closer ties with Japan, China, and South Korea, initially via his proposal to form an East Asia Economic Community and later by setting up the ASEAN Plus Three grouping.

Beginning from the 1980s, Malaysia also reached out to Muslim countries partly in response to Islamic resurgence in the OIC countries as well as in Malaysia. The plight of Muslims in war-torn Palestine and Afghanistan and also in nearby Cambodia, southern Thailand, and southern Philippines, where they were discriminated against as minorities, was especially highlighted. Malaysia also deployed officers as part of the UN Protection Force (UNPROFOR) in Bosnia-Herzegovina and hosted a meeting of the OIC to discuss the role of UNPROFOR in 1995. Such initiatives shored up Mahathir's credentials as a leader among the heads of Islamic countries.[6]

In fact, Mahathir's ties with Islamic countries were also economically motivated. He courted the oil-rich Arab countries in order to finance the establishment of the International Islamic University and other development projects in Malaysia. Regarding the OIC as a somewhat cumbersome grouping, Mahathir supported the Turkish initiative to establish the Developing Eight (or D-8), which comprises more-developed OIC countries, in order to promote economic and technical cooperation. Hence the symbolic and economic interests converged.

Involvement in NAM was useful for promoting common stances in multilateral trade negotiations such as the Uruguay Round of talks, the United Nations Conference on Trade and Development (UNCTAD), and meetings of the World Trade Organization (WTO). However, NAM was too unwieldy when it came to promoting trade, education, and technical cooperation. Consequently, Malaysia pushed for the formation of the Group of 15, which comprises the more economically dynamic NAM countries.[7]

Apart from these initiatives, Malaysia also established bilateral relations with many developing countries for the first time, all with an eye to promoting investment and commerce. In this regard, Malaysian companies invested in forestry in Guyana and Papua New Guinea, infrastructure projects in South Africa and Uruguay, power generation plants in Kazakhstan and Cambodia, and oil-field development in Iran and Vietnam.[8] The corollary to these trade and investment ties was the Malaysian Technical Cooperation Programme (MTCP), under which auspices Malaysia provided human resource development aid to about eighty developing countries.[9]

This stance in foreign policy continued under the fifth prime minister, Datuk Seri Abdullah Badawi. Until 2006 Malaysia chaired both the OIC and NAM. In December 2006 Kuala Lumpur hosted the first Asian Summit, which brought together the ASEAN 10, China, Japan, and Korea, as well as India, Australia, and New Zealand. Nowadays, Malaysia is considered a champion of the developing countries and is dubbed a "middle-range power" in international relations.

However, Malaysia's championing of the South did not imply shunning the developed countries, which would have proven disastrous economically. Its new thrust toward geo-economic considerations included consolidating its ties with the developed countries too. Malaysia's new Foreign Economic Policy, enunciated for the first time in 1985, identified three principal objectives: to expand its markets with the United States, Japan, and the European Union (EU); to look for new markets for Malaysian exporters; and to encourage South-South cooperation.[10]

THE CONSTITUTIONAL SETTING AND SEMIDEMOCRATIC POLITICAL PROCESS

Article 74 of the federal Constitution is explicit about the federal government's preeminence in foreign relations. The ninth schedule further details the distribution of legislative powers and responsibilities between the federal and state governments. Apart from foreign affairs, defence, internal security, and law and order, the purview of the federal government includes trade, commerce and industry, physical development like communication and transport, and human development (e.g., education, health, and medicine). By contrast, the state governments' purview is restricted to areas like lands and mines, Muslim affairs and customs, Native laws and customs, agriculture and forestry, local government and public services, burial grounds, markets and fairs, and licensing cinemas and theatres. The concurrent list covers social welfare, scholarships, town and country planning, drainage and irrigation, housing, culture and sports, and public health.[11]

Apart from the federal bias in the constitutional design, the political process wherein the Barisan Nasional coalition has controlled the federal Parliament and most of the state assemblies uninterruptedly since independence further ensures the states' compliance with federal priorities. Hence the federal government has been able to dictate the pace and direction of development in the constituent states via its control of development funds (as provided for under the Constitution),[12] even when state governments are held by the opposition parties, as in Kelantan state (1990 till today), Terengganu state (1999–2004), and Sabah state (1985–94). Additionally, the federal executive may invoke party discipline and removal of the *menteri besar* (chief minister) of any constituent state that challenges the prerogatives of the centre.[13] With the abolition of local government elections in the early 1970s, the BN federal government's reach penetrated even deeper through appointments of its functionaries to municipal, town, district, and local authorities. With privatization of public utilities, beginning from the late 1980s, these local and municipal authorities have been charged largely with monitoring local development planning (especially building activities), petty business licensing, and maintenance of local authority properties. Their roles being largely inconsequential in scope politically speaking, it follows that they hardly ever play any role in foreign affairs.

The federal executive has further consolidated power at the expense of the legislature, the judiciary, and civil society generally through the use of the Internal Security Act (which allows for detention without trial) and other coercive laws like the Official Secrets Act and the Printing Presses and Publications Act that actually circumscribe civil liberties and political rights enshrined in the Constitution. In short, the government resorts to "coercive legalism," which is why researchers have described Malaysia as a semidemocracy or a statist democracy. Hence, by constitutional design and a process dominated by a strong executive, Malaysia's federalism has evolved into a centralized one.[14] To some observers, Malaysia might better be described as a centralized unitary state with some federal features. It is therefore not surprising that foreign affairs, even under increasing globalization, remain the prerogative of the central government. The constituent states (let alone local authorities) have virtually no say on foreign affairs even when they are drawn into economic, social, and cultural relations with foreign third parties.

Moreover, decision making on foreign policy and security matters, as well as on foreign trade and investments, is not only a federal prerogative but also a particularly elitist federal-executive affair. It has been noted that "debates on foreign policy in the Malaysian Parliament have been generally scanty and sparse."[15] Likewise, the media controlled by the government and BN parties do not foster debate on foreign policymaking or, indeed, on policymaking generally.[16] Hence, contrary to the more pluralistic process in Western democracies, the foreign policymaking process in Malaysia is a top-down one dominated by the prime minister and an elitist group within the Cabinet, who are assisted by a specialized group of administrative elites in the Ministry of Foreign Affairs. That said, it is not suggested that the idiosyncracies of the prime ministers have prevailed. Rather, as Joseph Liow recently emphasized, foreign policymaking is determined by the preferences of the prime minister as well as by international exigencies and domestic contingencies.[17] The external exigencies in particular have contributed to a more assertive foreign policy anchored in geo-economic considerations.

Although the shift carried Mahathir's imprint, two other agencies were increasingly consulted as this shift occurred. One, the Economic Planning Unit (EPU), is attached to the Prime Minister's Department and is the central planning agency responsible for formulating policies, strategies, and programs for economic development of the country, especially the preparation of five-year plans. Its input on foreign economic policymaking is crucial. The other, the Institute of Strategic and International Studies (ISIS), a think-tank, was established with a government grant in 1983. It was tasked with conducting policy-oriented research in the realm of strategic and international relations. These, then, were the main actors in the development of a new economic foreign policy beginning in 1985.

Beginning from 1990, other stakeholders like the Malaysian Business Council (MBC)[18] became involved in foreign policymaking. MBC members frequently accompanied Mahathir on his overseas trips to look for investment opportunities. Over time, other government agencies, semigovernmental bodies, and even nongovernmental organizations (NGOs) were drawn into the web of foreign policymaking during Mahathir's tenure, without, however, playing any direct role in the process.

INTERGOVERNMENTAL RELATIONS THROUGH INCREASED INTERDEPARTMENTAL CONSULTATIONS

The organizational structure and role of the Ministry of Foreign Affairs, often referred to as Wisma Putra in reference to the building it occupies, also changed with the adoption of an economic foreign policy. Promoting trade and investment, educational and technical exchanges, and active involvement in various international forums became integral parts of conducting diplomacy.[19] Since many of these nontraditional diplomatic activities come under the purview of other ministries and departments, interdepartmental meetings become an important feature of policymaking in Wisma Putra. It is only because of such increased interdepartmental consultations, especially in the realm of economic and investment matters, that the constituent states began to be drawn into foreign policymaking, albeit indirectly.

Whenever Wisma Putra performs the role of lead agency on a matter involving other government agencies like the EPU and ISIS, or perhaps the MBC and other interested NGOs, consultations with these bodies are conducted prior to submitting the recommendations to the secretary general of Wisma Putra, who then forwards them to the foreign minister. Once approved, the resolutions are moved downward to the Wisma Putra division responsible for execution. The foreign minister subsequently briefs the prime minister either immediately or during the weekly Cabinet ministers' meeting.

Not infrequently, the lead agency, especially concerning foreign economic policy, is no longer located in Wisma Putra. For instance, the lead agency for the MTCP is the EPU. Its section on external assistance acts as the MTCP secretariat. Given that the principal function of the MTCP pertains to education and training, the Training Division of the Public Services Department and the Ministry of Education are also consulted; so too are the directors of various training institutes and universities. Meanwhile, Wisma Putra, acting as gatekeeper, is responsible via its embassies for disseminating information from the MTCP and for collecting and forwarding applications and project proposals from the many developing countries to the EPU. Once the decisions on the applications have been made, the MTCP's assistance is offered via Wisma Putra.[20]

Hence the constituent states are drawn into the web of foreign policymaking indirectly. As clarified, this development is not due to any new initiative on the part of Wisma Putra. Rather, it results from increased interdepartmental consultations involving Wisma Putra with other federal government agencies. For instance, during negotiations with the WTO, the Department of Trade in the Ministry of International Trade and Industry (MITI) consults with the state governments (and the corporate sector). Likewise, in deliberations about foreign investments, the Malaysian Industrial Development Authority (MIDA) of MITI consults with the state development authorities.

Foreign trade missions to woo investors to Malaysia and also to seek investment opportunities, particularly in developing countries, are now commonplace. Often led by the federal minister, and sometimes by the prime minister, these missions, conducted by MITI, include local industrialists and entrepreneurs as well as state government leaders and officials. Some state governments, such as those of Penang, Selangor, Sabah, and Sarawak, occasionally organize their own trade missions. Invariably, these missions are conducted with the cooperation of MITI. To date, no state government has established its own offices abroad, conceivably because they are expensive to maintain but also perhaps because the states might not be allowed, legally speaking, to utilize public funds to do that. In any event, the states depend on MIDA, which has established offices abroad – initially in the United States, Europe, and Japan, later in other Asian capitals, and even in Johannesburg and Dubai – to sell themselves as investment centres. It is also MITI's Department of ASEAN Economic Cooperation that functions as the lead agency on the ASEAN Free Trade Agreement (FTA), and it is the EPU, which is the lead agency for the ASEAN Growth Areas, that draws in the states for consultations, not Wisma Putra.

In the case of illegal immigration, it is the Department of National Security (involving the home affairs, defence, and foreign ministries) that oversees the problem. In this regard, it consults with the chief ministers and *menteri besars*,[21] who head their respective state security committees. There are also occasions when the state governments (and business and civil society groups) are invited to participate in closed-door meetings on global and security issues organized by ISIS. However, unlike in some countries, state governments rarely ever comment on foreign policy matters, even in support of federal government stances, let alone in opposition to them.[22]

As the shift to a more economic-oriented foreign policy occurs, existing or new federal lead agencies are identified to oversee new concerns. However, because state governments do not become involved in foreign policy matters, it is simply particular departments, units, or officers that are identified or assigned to work with the federal lead agencies, often on an ad hoc basis, or as more often is the case, as an add-on to existing functions.

The above shows that, at best, the state governments play rather passive and limited roles in foreign economic policymaking. This is also true vis-à-vis socio-cultural foreign affairs. For instance, in the 1980s and early 1990s a few municipal authorities like Georgetown (in Penang) twinned with sister-cities elsewhere – in this case with Adelaide, Medan, and Xiamen – and began to establish cultural, educational, sports, and trade ties with them. Ostensibly on the ground that the local authorities might be held liable under common law for not fulfilling provisions contained in the memoranda of understanding (MOUs) signed with their foreign counterparts, the local authorities were advised by Wisma Putra not to formalize those ties, an argument that might have carried additional weight especially following the 1997–98 regional financial crisis when the country, generally, was strapped for funds. Apparently, the substantive question of whether local authorities have a legal basis to sign MOUs with foreign counterparts was not raised directly; the issue was certainly not debated openly.[23] In any event, many of these twinning arrangements persist and the exchanges continue, although the former hype surrounding them appears to have been muted.

As well, it appears that the seemingly innocuous effort of the Penang Heritage Trust, an NGO, in collaboration with the Penang state government to have the historic city of Georgetown listed as a United Nations Educational, Scientific and Cultural Organization (UNESCO) World Heritage site has also come under the scrutiny of federal authorities. Belatedly, the federal Ministry of Culture, Heritage and the Arts has suggested that the NGO and the Penang authorities work in cooperation with counterparts in Malacca, another historic city, as well as with ministry officials, to seek a joint listing as "Straits Settlements twin sites" instead of seeking a separate listing. To persuade the Penang NGO and authorities, the ministry offered to provide federal funds and expertise for restoration and remedial measures to prevent the deterioration of heritage buildings, which is a requirement for UNESCO listing.[24]

All told, therefore, the roles of the state and local authorities in foreign economic and even socio-cultural policymaking remain indirect and very limited, notwithstanding their being drawn into the web of foreign affairs following globalization. Although they are consulted, their suggestions are seldom given the serious attention they deserve. Consequently, conflict has occasionally occurred between the federal and state governments. That said, these conflicts do not raise questions of competing jurisdictions. On no occasion have any of the state governments demanded that the foreign policymaking process be revamped so that the states can play increased roles. In this regard, all but one (i.e., Kelantan) of the state governments currently belongs to the BN ruling coalition. There have been demands by opposition parties and critical NGOs for amendments to one or another constitutional provision on several occasions. Invariably, these demands have been rejected, often on the basis that they have "hidden ethno-religious agendas" that might generate conflict; this is so even when the intent might be to preserve civil liberties or to deepen democratic practices.[25] In any event, there has been no demand by the states, opposition parties, or NGOs for comprehensive constitutional reform, even though the Malaysian Constitution is fifty years old.

Instead, the focus of the state governments has been on improving federal bureaucratic procedures by removing some of the many rules and conditions, control points, and layers of approvals or by countering the nonaction, delay, and corruption that currently characterize their dealings with the federal authorities. Alternatively, on the basis of personal relations with federal leaders, the chief minister might seek "special considerations" in order to expedite specific requests within the existing framework.[26] Apparently, the states consider it fruitful to make gains in this manner, rather than demanding constitutional reform. In the early 1990s several opposition leaders calling for greater autonomy for Sabah were detained without trial on the ground of fostering secession,[27] and on other occasions BN state leaders who questioned BN federal leaders have been put into political limbo.

MANIFESTATIONS OF INTERGOVERNMENTAL ENGAGEMENT: SCOPE OF THE PROBLEMS

In this section, two different but related issues in foreign relations during Mahathir's tenure are discussed as examples of the tight rein kept by the national government over the state governments: the Penang state government's attempt to promote itself as the regional hub for the global ICT industries; and joint efforts by the federal and several state governments to promote the so-called ASEAN Growth Areas. These cases highlight how the constituent states have been drawn into foreign relations, defined broadly, yet are not able to play meaningful roles in resolving problems occasioned by foreign relations due to the centralized federal system. Consequently, the inefficiencies of centralized federalism emerge, while tensions in intergovernmental relations fester.

Promoting Penang as a Regional Hub of the Global ICT Industries

The Penang state government was the first to embark on export-oriented industrialization in a comprehensive manner during the early 1970s. Under the auspices of the predecessor to the Foreign Investment Act, a federal law, it set up free trade zones (FTZS) that offered multinational corporations (MNCS) tax incentives to invest in the island. A statutory body, the Penang Development Corporation (PDC), was established and put in charge of planning, implementing, and monitoring development in the state, especially in the FTZS.[28] A special relationship between the then longstanding Penang chief minister and the federal executives (first Abdul Razak, then Hussein Onn, followed by Mahathir Mohamad) promoted good relations between the state and federal governments (both belonging to the BN coalition) and facilitated ties between the PDC and various federal agencies, especially MIDA, responsible for approving foreign direct investments (FDIs). The special relationship also facilitated Treasury and EPU approval of various incentives and exemptions granted to the MNCS under the Foreign Investment Act.[29]

By the 1990s Penang had already built up impressive manufacturing capabilities for producing electrical machinery and for assembling and testing various electronic products. Hence it desired to attract high value-added ICT investments to transform Penang into a regional ICT hub. However, this goal has proven difficult. The major problem relates to developing the necessary technological capability. Apparently, the Penang government is keen to adopt the strategies undertaken by the Singapore government; this means encouraging the MNCS to bring successive waves of new technologies into their subsidiary operations, thereby inducing technological capabilities among local subcontracting firms, promoting the adoption of new technologies among the local small and medium-sized enterprises (SMEs), and advancing technical manpower training programs. These strategies require sustained government intervention.[30]

In 1990 a new chief minister was appointed in Penang. Aware of the need for government intervention, he has undertaken measures to maintain Penang's competitive edge in the ICT industries. The task of attracting a new round of FDIs has been given to InvestPenang, a PDC subsidiary created in 2001. Like the PDC previously, it regularly conducts trade missions overseas, sometimes led by the chief minister, to attract investors. In the past, these missions visited the United States, Great Britain, Europe, Japan, Korea, and Taiwan regularly. Recently, China, India, and eastern Europe have been included in the itineraries. As evidenced by the wide scope of FDIs in Penang, these missions have been fruitful.[31] However, attracting more value-added FDIs in the current competitive environment has proven more difficult.

Nowadays, it is InvestPenang that helps these investors to apply to MIDA for approvals and to the Ministry of Finance for tax incentives. Seeking these approvals from federal authorities results in delays and has hampered Penang's competitiveness because competitors like China, India, and Vietnam, apart from Singapore and Thailand, have reportedly decentralized decision making with regard to these matters.[32] Due to a labour shortage, it has also become necessary to import foreign workers, necessitating an additional approval from the Immigration Department of the Ministry of Home Affairs.[33]

Another initiative undertaken by the Penang government in 1989 was to establish the Penang Skills Development Centre (PSDC), with the collaboration of industry and the local public university. Setting up the PSDC was no mean achievement because human resource development falls under the purview of the federal authorities, specifically the Ministry of Education, the Ministry of Higher Education, and the Ministry of Human Resources. This means that the PSDC receives no federal funding. Yet the PSDC has trained about 2,400 students to date, most of whom have been absorbed into the electronics and electrical industries in Penang.[34]

However, the level of support required cannot be met by the Penang government alone. Federal support is critical not only to produce skilled workers and to attract FDIs but also to promote global marketing and branding, as well as research and development. Yet the latter has not been forthcoming for several reasons, the most important being the federal government's own development of Cyberjaya, touted to become a "world-class ICT hub" connected to the Multimedia Super Corridor (MSC), which in turn is linked to the new administrative capital of Putrajaya, the new Kuala Lumpur International Airport, and the new Kuala Lumpur City Centre, where the major Malaysian corporations are located. By 2006 about 1,621 companies had registered in Cyberjaya, allowing them to take advantage of the incentives offered to MSC-status companies. Several major Penang-based MNCs like Intel and Motorola have also registered in Cyberjaya. It was only after much lobbying by the Penang government that the MSC's "roll-out program" was extended to Penang-based companies, allowing them to enjoy the same incentives. By 2005 there were about sixty such companies based in Penang, lagging far behind Cyberjaya.

In spite of Penang's headstart and initial advantages in the ICT industries, it is clear that Cyberjaya will emerge as a more important regional ICT hub. The domination of the federal over the state authorities in the area of foreign ICT investments, the federal government's enormous financial outlay for Cyberjaya, and the close connections between the federal departments and the MSC authority ensure this outcome. More likely, Penang will consolidate as a regional manufacturing centre for the ICT hardware supply chain, apart from being an extension of the MSC via its roll-out program. Even here, the Penang government continues to face obstacles.[35]

A case in point is the proposal by a Penang government unit, the Collaborative Resource and Research Centre (CRRC), to the federal government that called for revising the scheme of incentives offered to the MNCs. The CRRC argued that it should no longer be based on the volume of products exported; rather, it should encourage higher value-added production activities.

One proposal was that the MNCs should be offered incentives for retraining the workforce (as in Singapore and Taiwan) to encourage the MNCs to relocate product research and development activities to Penang. Under the auspices of the CRRC, several rounds of dialogue between the MNCs and various federal agencies were held with no progress made. Related attempts to work with the local public university to introduce new courses in order to meet the needs of industry have not been encouraging either, not least because higher education and human resource development come under the purview of federal bodies. Consequently, the MNCs and the Penang government complain that the overly centralized federal system is compromising Penang's competitiveness, not only vis-à-vis Cyberjaya but vis-à-vis its foreign competitors too.[36] Here, then, is a case of how the centralized federal system constrains the ability of state governments like Penang to respond to the needs of the global ICT industries adequately, in the process threatening Penang's competitiveness.

Promoting the ASEAN Growth Areas in Cross-Border Regions

The notion of ASEAN Growth Areas is based on transborder economic cooperation at the subregional level. Compared to the proposed ASEAN Free Trade Area, a Growth Area would be a looser arrangement requiring fewer trade-barrier adjustments on the part of three to four, rather than all ten, ASEAN countries. Presumably, the Growth Areas should be more easily realized than the ASEAN FTA. The focus of this section is on the Indonesia-Malaysia-Thailand Growth Triangle (IMT-GT), proposed by Malaysia in 1991, and on the Brunei-Indonesia-Malaysia-Philippines East ASEAN Growth Area (BIMP-EAGA), proposed by the president of the Philippines, Fidel Ramos, and launched in 1994.[37]

Far from the capital cities, it was hoped that joint efforts could promote economic development in ASEAN's subregional border areas, which are rich in resources. As well, it was hoped that economic integration would be accelerated and that security and stability in the transborder regions would be enhanced.

Central to the success of the Growth Areas is the role of the private sector as the engine of growth, while the public sector facilitates the effort through infrastructure development. Coordination is at the level of the ASEAN Ministers Meeting (MM), which convenes annually, and at the Senior Officials Meeting (SOM), which convenes once or twice a year. The Asian Development Bank (ADB) was appointed to conduct investigative studies into the viability of the proposal and to identify policies, programs, and projects. Based on the ADB studies, joint working groups involving the subregional authorities (the federal/central officials of participating countries) and business communities were set up, and countries were identified to take charge of each working group.

The ADB completed its study of the IMT-GT in 1994. The proposal included new forms of government cooperation at the subregional level involving joint policy formulation and consultation and collaboration on transport and communications, agriculture and fisheries, trade investment and labour mobility, and tourism.

A major goal was to develop the Seamless Songkhla-Penang-Medan (SSPM) Economic Corridor. To achieve this goal, a "land bridge" consisting of six major components – namely oil and gas pipelines; road, rail, and sea links; and electricity interconnection – was proposed. Major infrastructure projects such as the development of ports, highways, railways, and ferry services were identified. In-situ development projects were geared toward developing the IMT-GT into a "regional hypermarket" that would necessitate harmonization of customs, immigrations, and quarantine (CIQ) requirements and the creation of "special trade zones" incorporating border towns, among other initiatives. Tourism development was to be promoted by the tourist associations acting jointly to market the region as a common destination. A final goal was to link up to the hinterland of the SSPM Economic Corridor via agriculture and fisheries projects.

In Malaysia's case, an IMT-GT Liaison Secretariat was established in Alor Setar, Kedah, following a meeting of the chief minister of Penang and the *menteri besars* of the other three northern peninsular states. The secretariat, headed by an official from the Economic Planning Unit (EPU) in the Prime Minister's Office, liaises with the economic planning units of the concerned states (UPEN). In the initial stages, there appeared to be much interest in the IMT-GT on the part of the federal authorities, perhaps because the establishment of the Growth Area coincided with Mahathir's foreign policy notion of "prosper-thy-neighbour." If the IMT-GT proves successful, the Muslim-majority population in the two strife-ridden regions of southern Thailand and northern Sumatera would be helped as well. Success could also stem illegal immigration into Malaysia. However, the 1997–98 regional financial crisis caused most plans to be scuttled as Thailand and Indonesia refocused their attention at the national level. Meanwhile, public security in southern Thailand and in Acheh worsened due to the insurgencies there. Since the December 2004 tsunami, rehabilitation of Acheh, rather than realizing the IMT-GT, has been the focus of Jakarta's attention in the region. For its part, Malaysia has also refocused attention on the problem of forced migration from Indonesia and Thailand.

The BIMP-EAGA[38] has made more progress than the IMT-GT. As for the latter, the ADB proposed that governments provide the policy framework, build the necessary infrastructure, and facilitate the freer movement of people, goods, and services in the BIMP-EAGA. A BIMP-EAGA Facilitation Centre comprising one minister and one senior official from each country was set up. In turn, country secretariats linked the centre to working-group clusters in each country. As for the IMT-GT, the BIMP-EAGA national secretariat in

Malaysia was run by an EPU unit located in Kota Kinabalu, Sabah. An East ASEAN Business Council (EABC) comprising business associations in the subregion was also established. As it turned out, it was the EABC, with the support of the subregional authorities, that pushed hardest for the realization of the EAGA.

Some gains were made during 1994–97, noticeably in liberalizing air and sea transport policies, which resulted in the establishment of new commercial sea and air routes between Indonesia, the Philippines, and Malaysia. Within the area, tariff charges on long-distance calls were reduced, while the travel tax was waived. However, due to the 1997–98 financial crisis, there was little progress in promoting manufacturing.

The most significant gains were in tourism and trade: EAGA-wide trade fairs, tour exchanges, sports events, and investment in hotels. Significantly, many of these projects drew from special funds made available by the states rather than by the federal government. Even so, the 1997–98 financial crisis caused major plans to be shelved. It was only in November 2001 at the Seventh ASEAN Summit that a decision was taken to revitalize the Growth Areas, and the ADB was asked to conduct a follow-up study.

It was obvious from the earlier experience that the push for the EAGA had come from the respective subregional authorities – in Malaysia's case, the Sarawak and especially Sabah state governments – and from their private sector counterparts. Based on such observances, one researcher concluded that although "central government control and decision making appear crucial to the ebb and flow of regional cooperation, a certain degree of independence is nevertheless necessary for enhancing socioeconomic results. A decentralization of authority would ensure that subunits are able to gear to changes in the economic environment and seek to adjust accordingly. The leadership of the sub-region may also be more aware of the specific needs of the varied constituents in their locality."[39]

Yet when the BIMP-EAGA Facilitation Centre was established in August 2003 in Kota Kinabalu, it was made responsible to the ASEAN governments in the capital cities rather than to the constituent governments. In this regard, many researchers have commented that ASEAN regional cooperation is readily supported only when it coincides with national interests. In other words, there was the usual fear that one's country might not benefit equitably from specific EAGA projects even though these projects might be supported by one's own subregional authorities. Hence, in Malaysia's case, the chain of control flowed from the national EAGA secretariat down to the state EAGA coordinators in the Sabah and Sarawak governments. The implementation of EAGA-wide programs, projects, and activities in Malaysia was also coordinated by the national secretariat. These vertical links within Malaysia were clearly evident, less so the horizontal links between Sabah and Sarawak with their subregional counterparts. Paradoxically, this might work out for the better because the EAGA's success has necessitated greater intervention by the central governments, especially in promoting the development of land, sea, and air linkages and other social infrastructure, as well as in helping to attract non-ASEAN foreign investors to participate in the EAGA. However, the sustainability and further promotion of the EAGA requires that initiatives ultimately be passed down to the subregional level.

CONCLUSION

During the tenure of Mahathir Mohamad as prime minister, Malaysia championed the South and prioritized relations with ASEAN, the OIC, and NAM at the expense of the Commonwealth and the West. However, its new Foreign Economic Policy of 1985 highlighted the importance of consolidating its economic ties with the United States, the EU, and Japan while promoting regional economic cooperation and seeking out new markets in the South. A more assertive foreign policy anchored in geo-economic considerations was henceforth discernible. This shift coincided with the end of the Cold War, which facilitated economic globalization, which in turn was considered to have been responsible for Malaysia's recession in the mid-1980s and, later, for the 1997–98 financial crisis.

After adopting a more economic-oriented foreign policy, the organizational structure and role of Wisma Putra changed to include nontraditional diplomatic activities, particularly the promotion of trade and foreign investments and educational and technical exchanges. Given that many of these activities came under the purview of other ministries and departments, interdepartmental meetings became an important feature of policymaking in Wisma Putra. Through consultation with the other ministries and departments like MITI, MIDA, and the EPU or with the semigovernment think-tank ISIS, the states were drawn into foreign policymaking, albeit indirectly. Due to the constitutional design of a centralized federal system, as well as a political process dominated by a single ruling party for fifty years, the state governments still play rather limited and passive roles. As well, central control is considered necessary for implementing and monitoring the New Economic Policy (NEP). Given the circumstances, no formal restructuring of federal-state relations has occurred, nor have there been sustained pressures by the states to usher in a more cooperative federalism.

This is not to say that no conflicts of interests have arisen in federal-state relations since the federal government adopted a more assertive and geo-economic-oriented foreign policy. This chapter has discussed how the Penang state government was unable to transform the state into a regional hub of the global ICT industries because of the federal government's own plan to develop Cyberjaya and the MSC on the one hand and because of Penang's inability to overcome various federal bureaucratic obstacles and inefficiencies on the other. The chapter has also demonstrated that, despite a desire on the part of the state governments in the border regions to promote the ASEAN Growth Areas, there has been limited progress. The regional financial crisis of 1997–98 and the worsening security situation in neighbouring Thailand, Indonesia, and the Philippines are partly to blame. However, it also appears that the federal government via the EPU is keen to maintain control of the entire project. Consequently, horizontal linkages between the Sabah and Sarawak state governments and their subregional counterparts remain very limited in scope.

The overall lack of change in federal-state relations in a multiethnic developing country like Malaysia is not surprising. In fact, much centralization of power has occurred not only in terms of federal-state relations but also in terms of the relationship between the federal executive and the two other branches – indeed, between the state and civil society generally. A major theme arising from previous research in developing countries is the so-called issue of the "democratic trade-off" – that is, the idea that democracy is usually sacrificed for the sake of development. In Malaysia this appears to be the case. Although parliamentary rule has persisted and the formal structures of a federal system have been adopted, Malaysia is better characterized as a semidemocracy or a statist democracy and as a centralized unitary system with federal features. Recent globalization has accentuated the tensions in intergovernmental relations. Although nowadays there is more consultation with the constituent states, their involvement remains limited and indirect via increased interdepartmental consultation between the Ministry of Foreign Affairs and other ministries, resulting no doubt in a certain amount of inefficiency on the part of the federal authorities. However, if Malaysia continues to register respectable economic growth and if there are no sustained pressures from either the constituent states or civil society to redress the situation, executive dominance and centralized federalism will persist, with foreign affairs largely determined by a small group of political elites at the centre.

NOTES

1 United Nations Development Program, *Human Development Report 2004* (New York: United Nations, 2005), 140; and United Nations Development Program, *Ninth Malaysia Plan 2006–2010* (Kuala Lumpur: Government Printers, 2006), 6–12.
2 K.S. Jomo, *Growth and Structural Change in the Malaysian Economy* (London: Macmillan, 1990); and R. Thillainathan, "Malaysia and the Asian Crisis: Lessons and Challenges," in Colin Barlow and Francis K.W. Loh, eds, *Malaysian Economics and Politics in the New Century*, 13–28 (Cheltenham: Edward Elgar, 2003).
3 Bank Negara, *Annual Economic Report*, various years.

4 Edmund Terence Gomez and K.S. Jomo, *Malaysia's Political Economy: Politics, Patronage and Profits* (Cambridge, UK: Cambridge University Press, 1997).
5 Ahmad Faiz Abdul Hamid, *Malaysia and South-South Cooperation during Mahathir's Era* (Subang Jaya: Pelanduk, 2005), 18.
6 Sheila Nair, *Islam in Malaysian Foreign Policy* (London: RoutledgeCurzon, 1997), 83–5; Mohd Abu Bakar, "Islam in Malaysia's Foreign Policy," in Mohammed Azhari Karim, Llewellyn Howell, and Grace Okuda, eds, *Malaysian Foreign Policy: Issues and Perspectives*, 77–88 (Kuala Lumpur: National Institute of Public Administration Malaysia, 1990).
7 Ahmad Faiz, *Malaysia and South-South Cooperation*, 97.
8 Ibid., 45.
9 Ibid., 55–67.
10 Minister of Foreign Affairs, "Malaysia's new foreign economic policy," *Foreign Affairs Malaysia*, March 1985, 21–3.
11 See Mohamad Agus Yusoff, *Malaysian Federalism: Conflict or Consensus* (Bangi: Penerbit Universiti Kebangsaan Malaysia, 2006), 68–76; Tan Sri Datuk Mohd. Salleh bin Abas, "Federalism in Malaysia – Changes in the First Twenty Years," in Tun Mohamed Suffian, H.P. Lee, and F. A. Trindade, eds, *The Constitution of Malaysia: Its Development 1957–1977*, 163–91 (Kuala Lumpur: Oxford University Press, 1978); Jeffrey G. Kitingan, "Thorny Issues in Federal-State Relations," in Tan Chee Beng, ed., *Reflections on the Malaysian Constitution*, 149–68 (Penang: Aliran, 1987); and Shafruddin Hashim, "Thirty Years on the Road between Centre and States in Malaysia," in Tan Chee Beng, ed., *Reflections on the Malaysian Constitution*, 169–85 (Penang: Aliran, 1987).
12 See Yusoff, *Malaysian Federalism*, 76–83; and Shankaran Nambiar, "The Practice of Fiscal Federalism in Malaysia," in Anwar Shah, ed., *The Practice of Fiscal Federalism: Comparative Studies*, 178–203 (Montreal and Kingston: McGill-Queen's University Press, 2007).
13 Lim Hong Hai, "Sabah and Sarawak in Malaysia: The Real Bargain, or What Have They Gotten Themselves Into?" in Francis K.W. Loh, ed., *Sabah and Sarawak: The Politics of Development and Federalism*, special issue of *Kajian Malaysia* 15, no. 1–2 (January and December 1997): 21–5.
14 See Francis K.W. Loh, "National Security, the Police and the Rule by Law," in Jayadeva Uyangoda, ed., *Militarising State, Society and Culture in Asia*, 179–208 (Hong Kong: ARENA, 2005); and Rais Yatim, *Freedom under Executive Power in Malaysia: A Study of Dominance* (Kuala Lumpur: Endowment 1995).
15 M. Pathmanathan, "Formulation and Administration of Malaysian Foreign Policy," in Mohammed Azhari Karim, Llewellyn Howell, and Grace Okuda, eds, *Malaysian Foreign Policy: Issues and Perspectives*, 17–30 (Kuala Lumpur: National Institute of Public Administration Malaysia, 1990), 28.
16 J. Saravanamuttu, *The Dilemma of Independence: Two Decades of Malaysia's Foreign Policy, 1957–1977* (Penang: Penerbit Universiti Sains Malaysia, 1983); J. Saravanamuttu, "Malaysia's Foreign Policy in the Mahathir Period, 1981–1995: An Iconoclast Come

to Rule," *Asian Journal of Political Science* 4, no. 1 (June 1996): 1–16; M. Pathmanathan, "The New Dimensions of Malaysia's Foreign Policy," in M. Pathmanathan and D. Lazarus, eds, *Winds of Change: The Mahathir Impact on Malaysia's Foreign Policy*, 28–55 (Petaling Jaya: Pelanduk, 1984); Pathmanathan, "Formulation and Administration," 17–29; Ahmad Faiz, *Malaysia and South-South Cooperation*.

17 Joseph Liow, "Personality, Exigencies and Contingencies: Determinants of Malaysia's Foreign Policy in the Mahathir Administration," in Ho Khai Leong and James Chin, eds, *Mahathir's Administration: Performance and Crisis in Governance*, 120–60 (Singapore: Times Books International, 2001), 126.

18 The MBC was set up in February 1991, bringing together corporate leaders, Cabinet ministers, and top officials involved in foreign affairs and international trade and investment. The MBC's role was to facilitate cooperation between the public and private sectors via exchange of information and ideas and to propose trade and investment policies. A back-up research centre was subsequently established in ISIS to service the MBC. It was at the inaugural meeting of the MBC that Mahathir delivered his keynote address titled "Malaysia: The Way Forward," which became the basis of "Vision 2020," his strategy to promote Malaysia's emergence as a developed nation by 2020. See Khoo Boo Teik, *Paradoxes of Mahathirism* (Kuala Lumpur: Oxford University Press), 227–38.

19 Ahmad Faiz, *Malaysia and South-South Cooperation*, 68.

20 Ibid., 58–9.

21 Chief ministers and *menteri besars* perform essentially the same functions, but the first term refers to the chief executives of the former Straits Settlements (e.g., Penang), whereas the latter refers to the heads of former Federated Malay States (e.g., Kedah).

22 See below for a discussion of Sabah's criticism of the worsening security problem in the state posed by the influx of illegal immigrants, an area that falls under the federal government's purview.

23 Wisma Putra's stance on local authorities signing MOUs with foreign counterparts was clarified by a senior official who participated in the Penang Roundtable. Apparently, there is no public documentation of this stance.

24 "Federal govt to aid UNESCO listing application," *TheSun* (Kuala Lumpur), 3 May 2007.

25 For instance, opposition parties and prodemocracy NGOs have been calling for the repeal of coercive laws, including the draconian Internal Security Act (ISA), for inclusion of proportional representation in the simple-majority electoral system, and for the reintroduction of local government elections. With a stronger opposition and more democratic space, there would presumably be greater scope for constitutional reform, including changes that would allow states and local authorities to play increased roles in foreign policymaking and foreign affairs.

26 The problem of bureaucratic obstacles and weaknesses is linked to the politicization of the bureaucracy itself under the NEP. Among others, promotions and recruitment were based on ethnic quotas rather than on meritocracy. Reforms were

slow in coming not least because of the political costs involved in removing the entrenched, politicized, and predominantly Malay bureaucracy. See Lim Hong Hai, "Public Administration: The Effects of Executive Dominance," in Francis K.W. Loh and Khoo Boo Teik, eds, *Democracy in Malaysia: Discourses and Practices*, 165–97 (Richmond, BC: Curzon, 2002).

27 Francis K.W. Loh, "A New Sabah and the Spell of Development: Resolving Federal-State Relations in Malaysia," *Southeast Asia Research* 4, no. 1 (March 1996): 63–84.

28 Chan Huan Chiang, "The Penang Economy: Rapid Growth and Its Implications," in Tan Pek Leng, ed., *Agenda 21: Building a Fully-Developed Penang*, 10–25 (Penang: Penang State Executive Committee for Education, Economic Planning and Information, 1996); Chong Eu Choong, "Perindustrian Pesat dan Perhubungan Persekutuan-Negeri di Malaysia: Kajian Kes Negeri Pulau Pinang" [Rapid industrialization and federal-state relations in Malaysia: A case study of Penang State] (MA thesis, Universiti Sains Malaysia, 1997), 72–114.

29 Chong, "Perindustrian Pesat," 61–70.

30 On difficulties in moving up the value chain of the ICT industries, see Lai Yew Wah, "Pemindahan Teknologi di Sektor Elektronik dan Elektrik di Malaysia: Paras, Takat dan Kekangan" [Transfer of technology in the electronic and electrical sectors in Malaysia] (Professorial Public Lecture, School of Social Sciences, Universiti Sains Malaysia, 2001). On the need for more proactive state interventions to further the competitiveness of Penang, see Wong Poh Kam, "Technological Capability and Development Strategies in Asian NIEs: Possible Lessons for Penang," in Tan Pek Leng, ed., *Agenda 21: Building a Fully-Developed Penang*, 26–43 (Penang: Penang State Executive Committee for Education, Economic Planning and Information, 1996).

31 Apart from political leaders and PDC/InvestPenang officials, these missions usually include local industrialists looking for foreign partners or for investment opportunities in the countries visited. Similar trade missions are conducted by other states. All venture to neighbouring ASEAN and regional countries, while some others, say Selangor, Johore, Sarawak, and Sabah, like Penang, venture farther, travelling to the United States, the United Kingdom, and Europe.

32 This point was made by several participants from the private sector during the Penang Roundtable. Their complaints are supported by a recent World Bank report which claimed that a potential investor in a factory had to undergo 25 procedures that would take 281 days, whereas the same required 17 procedures in 140 days in Australia, 11 procedures in 129 days in Singapore, and only 9 procedures in 127 days in Thailand. On the basis of this report, the prime minister set up a task force called Pemudah, jointly headed by the chief secretary to the government and a corporate leader, to look into the matter. See "Govt heeds World Bank report, cuts red tape," *TheSun* (Kuala Lumpur), 12 January 2007.

33 Numerous complaints have been raised in private as well as in the media about irregularities and the incompetence of the Immigration Department officers. See for instance, Joachim Xavier, "Let's Put Our House in Order First," *Aliran Monthly* 25, no. 1 (2005): 25–8; and Michelle Lee Guy, "'Globalization Dilemma': Immigrants

in Malaysia," in Bridget Welsh, ed., *Reflections: The Mahathir Years*, 417–27 (Washington, DC: Southeast Asia Program, Johns Hopkins University, 2004), 423–4.

34 "PSDC – history of achievements," *The Star* (Kuala Lumpur), 20 September 2006.

35 Perhaps this is why the Penang government has been promoting the state as a biotechnology centre more recently. This shift is in line with the goals of the latest five-year development plans of the federal government. See "Biotechnology Push," *The Star* (Kuala Lumpur), 6 December 2006.

36 This section is based on an interview with the former coordinator of the CRRC. On the existing scope of tax incentives offered, see United Nations Conference on Trade and Development, *Foreign Direct Investment and Performance Requirements: New Evidence from Selected Countries* (New York and Geneva: United Nations Conference on Trade and Development, 2003), 176–80.

37 It was Goh Chok Tong, then Singapore's prime minister, who first proposed an ASEAN Growth Area – in this case, the SIJORI Growth Triangle involving Singapore, Johore (in Malaysia), and the Riau Islands (in Indonesia) – in the late 1980s.

38 More has been written on the BIMP-EAGA than on the IMT-GT. See for instance, Mohd Yusof Kasim and Mohd Shukri Haji Noor, "Sabah dan Sarawak dalam Konteks Kawasan Pertumbuhan Asean Timur" [Sabah and Sarawak in the context of the East ASEAN Growth Area], in Mohd Yusof Kasim and Sabihah Kasim, eds, *Sabah dan Sarawak dalam Arus Globalisasi* [Sabah and Sarawak under globalization], 39–51 (Bangi: Penerbit Universiti Kebangsaan Malaysia, 2002); Pushpa Thambipillai, "Competing Interests in Regional and Sub-Regional Cooperation: ASEAN and BIMP-EAGA," in Abdul Maulud Yusof, Dg Suria Mulia, and Rosazman Hussin, eds, *Proceedings A Regional Conference on Academic Cooperation in BIMP-EAGA: Prospects and Challenges*, 38–43 (Kota Kinabalu: School of Social Sciences, Universiti Malaysia Sabah, 1999); Bilson Kurus, "The East ASEAN Growth Area: Prospects and Challenges," in Mohd Yaakub Hj Johari, Bilson Kurus, and Janiah Zaini, eds, *BIMP-EAGA Integration: Issues and Integration*, 17–30 (Kota Kinabalu: Institute of Development Studies, Sabah, 1997); Bilson Kurus, "The BIMP-EAGA: Growing Pains and Teething Problems," in Mohd Yaakub Hj Johari, Bilson Kurus, and Janiah Zaini, eds, *BIMP-EAGA Integration: Issues and Integration*, 31–44 (Kota Kinabalu: Institute of Development Studies, Sabah, 1997); and Asia Development Bank, *East ASEAN Growth Area* 4, no. 2 (1996).

39 Thambipillai, "Competing Interests," 42–3.

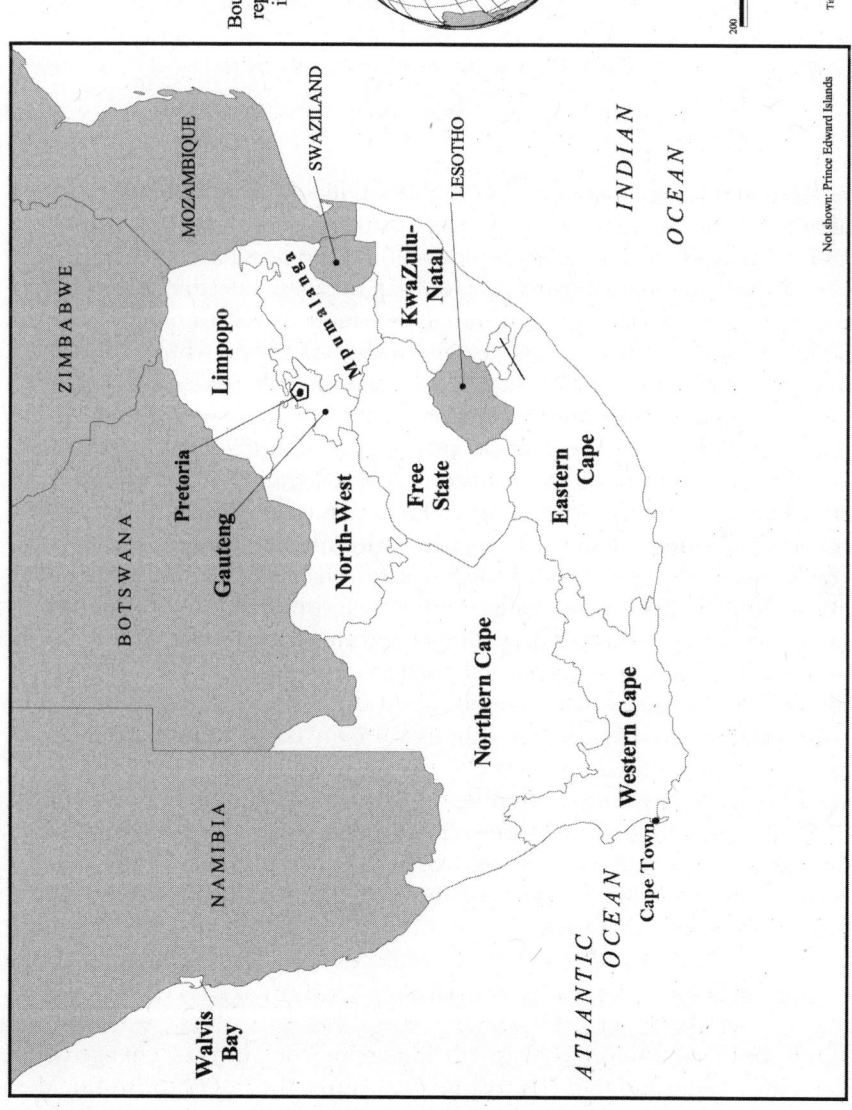

Republic of South Africa

Capital: Pretoria
Population: 43.5 Million (2002 est.)

Boundaries and place names are representative only and do not imply official endorsement.

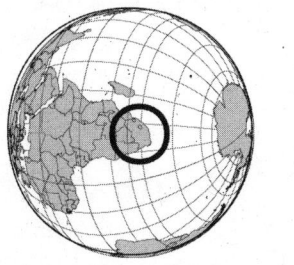

Not shown: Prince Edward Islands

Sources: CIA World Factbook; ESRI Ltd;
Times Atlas of the World; UN Cartographic Dept.

South Africa

CHRISTINA MURRAY AND
SALIM A. NAKHJAVANI[1]

Emerging in 1994 from decades of international isolation and eager to surmount the socio-economic legacy of apartheid, South Africa's new provinces and municipalities were as enthusiastic about the possibility of foreign relations as the national government. However, the extent to which the constituent governments can engage in foreign relations is far from clear, and the national government's response to international initiatives by provinces and municipalities varies from indulgence to disapproval. The conduct of international relations affecting matters of concurrent competence underscores the uncertainty about the roles of provinces and municipalities in international relations. In particular, the constitutional framework intended to secure a provincial voice in international relations is not being used effectively. Indeed, with the notable exception of environmental matters, the national government seldom consults with provinces on international matters relating to their competences. Thus South Africa's international relations take place in a system that is but partially formed and characterized by more questions than answers, few established practices, and perhaps more uncertainty than is found in many older federal countries.

In practice, this means that although provincial and municipal officials may travel abroad and host foreign visitors (usually in the interest of developing trade links), enter twinning agreements, and receive international development aid, these activities remain haphazard. The national government has successfully asserted control of the most important international relations matter, development aid, and only the wealthiest province, Gauteng, has foreign trade offices.

THE COUNTRY, PEOPLE, AND PROVINCES

South Africa's transition from apartheid to democracy in 1994 changed both domestic politics and the country's relationship to the rest of the world. Most significantly on the domestic front, the extension of the franchise to all adult South Africans and a commitment to constitutionalism were entrenched in an interim constitution and then in the "final" Constitution of 1996. The constitutional settlement also divided the country into provinces and municipalities with protected powers. At the same time, South Africa engaged constructively with the regional and international organizations of which it is now a full member, such as the Southern African Development Community (SADC), the Organization of African Unity (now the African Union), the Commonwealth of Nations, and the United Nations (UN). The country also seized the opportunities for international trade arising from the abundance of international goodwill created by the peaceful transition to democracy.

South Africa's political history is one of the separation of white people and black people by a white elite and the deliberate neglect of the needs of black people.[2] This meant that, when the interim constitution was negotiated in 1993, the primary concern was to unite the country across colour lines. The nine provinces were not intended to have distinct ethnic identities, nor were they to have significant autonomy. South Africa is accordingly best described as a weak federal system. Some refer to it as a quasi federation. The bitter legacy of "separate development" – manifested through the proliferation of ethnically distinct "homelands" – accounts, at least in part, for strongly centralizing tendencies in South Africa's federal structure.

In practice, the dominance of the national sphere of government inscribed in the Constitution is compounded by the dominance of the national party of liberation, the African National Congress (ANC), which commands more than 70% of the vote in the National Assembly and controls all nine provinces. During the drafting of the Constitution, the ANC did not favour the creation of provinces, and the prospect of their consolidation into purely administrative "regions" was once again mooted within party structures in 2006.[3]

There remain significant differences in the racial composition of South Africa's nine provinces. In seven, black South Africans make up over 75% of the national population[4] of 47.9 million people,[5] but in the two others, the "coloured" (i.e., mixed-race) population, constitutes the majority. Linguistic diversity provides a second dimension of difference. English is the first language of only 8.2% of the population, and it is one of eleven official languages, but it can be considered the de facto national auxiliary language. IsiZulu is the most widely spoken home language (23.8%), followed closely by IsiXhosa (17.6%). Other languages are spoken by much smaller numbers. Language use varies across provinces.[6] However, the divisions between black, coloured, Indian, and white still dominate politics, while differences in language use and ethnicity play little role.

South Africa's nine provinces differ enormously in terms of territorial size and population density. Just 1.8% of the people live in the largest province, the Northern Cape, while Gauteng, the smallest province, comprises only 1.4% of the surface area but is the second most populous province with 19.7% of the population.[7]

Overall, South Africa's gross domestic product (GDP) is US$201 billion,[8] or US$11,417 per capita.[9] Provincial development levels and GDP contributions vary substantially. Gauteng is by far the greatest contributor to GDP, accounting for 33% of the national total. The Northern Cape accounts for a mere 2.4%.[10] Six major cities contribute 55% of the country's GDP.[11]

Foreign trade amounts to about 50% of GDP, indicating strong integration into the world economy.[12] Just over 27% represents export revenue,[13] mostly supplied from the primary sector (i.e., minerals, commodities, and agriculture).[14] Although manufacturing represented only 19% of total merchandise exports in 1993, this figure rose to about 33% in 2000. There has been a corresponding decline in the share of mineral exports.[15] Foreign direct investment accounts for around 2% of GDP.[16]

SOUTH AFRICA IN ITS INTERNATIONAL CONTEXT

South Africa was isolated economically and politically during most of its apartheid years. Although the United Nations condemned South Africa's racial policies in 1946 and forty-six countries cut arms links in 1963, the major powers would not condone South Africa's expulsion from the UN. Thus from 1974, a frustrated General Assembly simply rejected the credentials of the South African delegation, effectively excluding its participation. An OPEC oil embargo was imposed in 1973. Private disinvestment started during the 1960s and peaked in 1985 when a state of emergency was imposed in many parts of the country.[17] In some countries, including the United States and Canada, constituent governments engaged in antiapartheid disinvestment.[18] In 1977 the UN Security Council banned arms sales to South Africa – the first mandatory sanctions against a full UN member.[19] However, South Africa remained the tenth-largest arms producer in 1994.[20] Perceived as a US ally against communism, South Africa's international isolation was never absolute.[21]

South Africa is bordered by Namibia, Botswana, Zimbabwe, Mozambique, and Swaziland. It also surrounds Lesotho. Under apartheid, South Africa had a strained relationship with its neighbours – the "frontline states" – including Angola and Zambia, which openly supported South African liberation movements against the apartheid regime. As community links across these borders have always been close and many languages are shared, it is unsurprising that struggles for independence in the region strengthened transborder links. For example, in the 1970s displaced people from the Mozambican civil war – a conflict fuelled by the apartheid government – found refuge in Mpumalanga and Limpopo in South Africa. In the postapartheid era, South Africa's regional relationships are completely different and its cross-border military activities have been limited to a 1998 intervention to restore law and order in Lesotho, at the request of SADC.[22]

South Africa's strong role in Africa is similar to that of India in Asia and Brazil in South America.[23] It aligns itself with developed liberal states like Sweden, Norway, and Canada[24] but seeks, generally successfully, to represent the South, aiming to bridge the North and South divide while pressing a southern agenda. It is broadly acknowledged to be an "emerging" middle power – a "good citizen" that punches above its weight in the international arena and with international standing above countries with comparable development indicators.[25]

Political factors linked to its transition to liberal democracy have contributed to South Africa's rapid integration into the international community, but "hard" factors such as its economic and development status have played a role too. It has 40% of Africa's gross national income, its trade surplus dominates Africa, and it is the major source for foreign direct investment in Africa, with a threefold increase from US$1 billion in 1996 to US$3.4 billion in 2001.[26] Its GDP per capita in 2004 exceeded that of its poorest neighbour, Lesotho, by a factor of seven, and that of Namibia by 160%, falling just shy of Botswana.[27] It is also the highest-ranking Sub-Saharan country in the UN Human Development Index (HDI),[28] ranked 121st in the 2006 report (with an HDI of 0.653).[29] The South African literacy rate of 86% outranks that of most SADC countries.[30]

Since the end of apartheid, South Africa has forged significant commercial and trade links with neighbours in SADC and farther north. It enjoys a favourable SADC trade balance, with exports accounting for US$2.45 billion of US$2.95 billion in total trade.[31] South African businesses and joint ventures have been active in acquiring interests in African countries and are responsible for the national railway in Cameroon and for airports serving seven African capitals. A subsidiary of the national electricity supplier is responsible for state electricity utilities in Tanzania, Rwanda, Malawi, and Zanzibar while managing power plants in six nations from Zimbabwe to Morocco. South African businesses have controlling shares in Telecom Lesotho and provide cellular services in six African nations.[32] Retail stores have also crossed borders.[33] This corporate expansion makes South Africa the single biggest source of foreign direct investment (FDI) in southern Africa, pouring more money into the SADC region since 1994 than Britain and the United States combined.[34]

South Africa's economic strength makes it an influential member of both the African Union (AU) and SADC.[35] The fifty-three-member AU aims to create a peaceful, democratic, and developed African continent with an effective common market. SADC aims to achieve a regional peace and security community with an integrated regional economy, and it is working toward a free trade zone with common external tariffs and no internal tariffs by 2012. Both institutions enjoy the support of government and the business community and are seen as contributors to stability and economic development in Africa.

Aside from a good road network and the ubiquity of cellular phones among the urban poor and rich alike, transport and communications infrastructure in South Africa still bears the divisive imprint of the apartheid era. Commuter links, for example, were designed to ferry black workers to and from white centres of industry on working days only. Travel by bus remains the most affordable and popular mode of transborder public transport. The railroad operation is the largest in southern Africa, with 31,700 kilometres of single rail track. However, the only operational transborder rail route is between Pretoria and Maputo, Mozambique. The national airport agency manages three international and six national airports and projects 30% growth per year in the air transport market to 2030.[36] The so-called "low-cost" airline market has also taken root, and although most travel is internal, transborder flights are increasingly available to the middle class.

In 2001 South Africa had 52 land border posts, over a total border distance of 3,500 kilometres, of which 19 were open for the movement of commercial goods. There were 10 air border posts and 8 sea border posts. Borders are considered porous, and besides illegal immigration, cross-border criminal activity includes a flow of illegal weapons, drugs, diamonds, and stolen vehicles.[37]

After the transition to democracy, it was feared that South Africa would be overwhelmed with migrants and refugees alike, aggravating the acute skills shortages of its neighbours. Accordingly, from 1994 to 2000, restrictive immigration policies sought to circumvent any "threat" to the new polity through mass migration from southern Africa.[38] Census data indicate that these fears did not materialize.[39] However, recent research by the Southern African Migration Project suggests that mass-skills migration to South Africa may be on the horizon, as "skills acquisition" dominates the domestic regulatory agenda and as the economic and political situation of neighbouring countries – especially Zimbabwe and the Democratic Republic of Congo – continues to deteriorate.[40]

A 2001–02 migration survey indicated that almost half the migrants from South Africa's neighbours came from Lesotho, and 28% from Swaziland.[41] Causes are complex and interwoven, but general reasons include cross-border trading, poor economic conditions in the countries of origin (including unemployment, low wages, expensive consumer goods, and the low value of local currencies), employment opportunities in South Africa, and border penetrability.[42] Notably, any immigrant absorption burden is likely to fall not on the poorer frontier provinces but on tiny, highly urbanized Gauteng. With a median annual income of US$3,404 for working-age adults, Gauteng remains attractive to economic migrants despite its 25.8% unemployment rate.

South Africa and its neighbours have a generally good record of cooperation on environmental conservation and sustainable development, particularly through the promotion of eco-tourism. The region includes five transfrontier parks and conservation areas, crossing parts of four provinces.[43] These areas are governed by bilateral or multilateral treaties, and in one case they provide an implementing role for the provincial authorities of KwaZulu-Natal. The mountainous border of Lesotho and KwaZulu-Natal includes the most significant water catchments for the region, and two bilateral civil engineering projects supply water to major industrial and population centres in Gauteng while generating hydroelectric power for Lesotho.[44]

Finally, South Africa is significantly involved in peacekeeping operations in Africa, with troops in Burundi and the Democratic Republic of Congo under UN command and in Sudan as part of the AU peacekeeping effort.

Despite the country's increasing political and economic integration in the international community, the role of South Africa's provinces in international relations is often underestimated. In practice, provinces and municipalities have interacted enthusiastically with foreign counterparts in a number of different areas. Nico Steytler observes that "the South African provinces are slowly but surely pushing open the door to the international community."[45] As discussed below, most foreign relations of provinces are modest at present. But the seven frontier provinces are increasingly involved in what John Kincaid has called cross-border "housekeeping."[46] That South Africa's borders cut across ethnic and linguistic communities suggests that these arrangements are likely to expand, perhaps including cultural links in the future.[47] In addition, as provinces and the national government come to understand the role of provinces more clearly, provinces are also likely to be more directly involved in international relations driven by the national government.

CONSTITUTIONAL SETTING

Under the South African Constitution, provinces and municipalities have only those powers that are expressly stipulated. They fall into three categories: (1) so-called "concurrent," or "Schedule 4," powers that provinces and municipalities share with the national government; (2) exclusive provincial and municipal powers in Schedule 5; and (3) a limited number of other constitutional powers. All other powers vest in the national government. Both the national government and the provinces have legislative authority over the concurrent powers, but the national government's power to override provincial legislation and municipal bylaws is strong. In case of conflict, provincial legislation prevails over national law unless the national law deals with a matter that provinces cannot effectively regulate on their own or if it is necessary for "national security," "economic unity" and the common market, the promotion of equal opportunity and equal access to government services, or the protection of the environment.[48] Such legislation must operate uniformly across the country. In areas of concurrent and exclusive provincial competence alike, national legislation can trump provincial initiatives if necessary, *inter alia*, to maintain national security, economic unity, and "essential national standards" or to "prevent unreasonable action taken by a province which is prejudicial to another province or the country as a whole."[49]

Enumerated provincial powers do not include international relations, treaty making, foreign policy, or the like. Thus the prevailing understanding is that these matters are entirely and exclusively a national concern. The Constitution seems to support this view with respect to treaty making because Section 231(1) states that "[t]he negotiating and signing of all international agreements is the responsibility of the national executive."[50] However, this apparently unambiguous statement of national control of international agreements is undercut immediately by the requirement in the following subsection that international agreements be approved by both houses of Parliament. Hence an international agreement can be vetoed by the vote of five of the nine provincial delegations in the National Council of Provinces (NCOP), the second chamber of the national Parliament.[51] This power is considerable, as it extends to matters that fall outside the usual competence of provinces and is greater than the power that the NCOP has over national legislation.

The collective power of South Africa's provinces to veto international agreements in the NCOP is limited in only one way: agreements of a "technical, administrative or executive nature" and agreements that "[do] not require either ratification or accession" must be tabled in Parliament but need not be approved by Parliament and so, presumably, cannot be vetoed by the NCOP. The Constitution does not define "technical, administrative, or executive" agreements; the executive defines these as agreements that are departmentally specific or politically insignificant or that carry no financial or domestic legal consequences.[52] In law, the only authoritative interpretation of what agreements fall under this provision lies with the Constitutional Court. In the absence of judicial determination, because Parliament has the inherent power to control its own procedure, it is responsible for deciding whether specific agreements require Parliament's approval.[53] In practice, the executive arrogates to itself the power to make a determination of which procedure to invoke in Parliament, leaving the decision to the substantive department negotiating the agreement in consultation with legal advisers from the ministries of justice and foreign affairs.[54]

The constitutional framework also anticipates a role for provinces in international relations. For instance, chapter 3 of the Constitution sets out principles of cooperative government applicable to relations among the three spheres of government and requires consultation "on matters of common interest" and coordination of "actions and legislation."[55] The national government and provinces share concurrent jurisdiction on matters such as trade, the environment, and agriculture, all of which are frequent subjects of international agreements. Although Section 231 might reserve the right to sign international agreements for the national government, the requirement of cooperative government clearly requires provinces to be consulted. This is a "soft" requirement. Although provinces can insist that they be consulted, and there is some indication that courts would enforce this right,[56] they cannot insist that their views be accepted. Moreover, the constitutional provisions that give the national government precedence in protecting national security, the economic unity of the country, "the common market in respect of the mobility of goods, services, capital and labour," and the environment[57] suggest that the Constitution contemplates the dominance of national policies.

The requirement of consultation is not a mere constitutional gesture. The Constitution anticipates that provinces will implement not only provincial but also national legislation that falls within concurrent areas. If provinces are to implement the laws that result from international agreements, it is obvious that they should be involved in the preceding negotiations. Despite this, an examination of current practice indicates that provinces have – and expect – little involvement in international negotiations.

Precisely which agreements may be entered into on the sole prerogative of provincial and local governments remains contentious.[58] The *Manual on Executive Acts of the President of the Republic of South Africa* states that "[p]rovinces may not enter into agreements governed by international law except as agents of the National Executive." But, it adds, "[t]hey may of course conclude contracts with foreign companies *or constituent unit entities.*"[59] This approach seems right. It assumes that when provinces (or municipalities) enter agreements with counterparts in other countries, they do not have the capacity to bind the state under international law and are not concluding international agreements per se. Of course, the principles of cooperative government set out in the Constitution apply here too. Just as the national government must, in principle, consult with provinces when engaging in international relations on matters of concurrent jurisdiction, provinces must, in principle, keep the national government abreast of their international activities.

There are two areas in which the limits on provincial engagement in international relations are clear: international borrowing and defence. First, the Constitution permits provinces and municipalities to take out loans "in accordance with national legislation,"[60] but national law enacted pursuent to these provisions prohibits international borrowing by provinces or municipalities.[61] Second, with two exceptions, full responsibility for defence vests in the national government.[62] The exceptions relate, first, to the use of the defence force "in cooperation with the police service" in defence of the country and in fulfilment of an international obligation; and second, to a declaration of "a state of national defence." In these circumstances, both houses of Parliament must be informed and, in the second case, must approve the declaration.

Finally, provinces have some involvement with policing. For instance, they can monitor the effectiveness of policing, but the Constitution gives the National Executive ultimate authority over all policing; thus the national government is responsible for international policing activities.[63]

Under the Constitution, then, the most significant provincial involvement in international relations will be, first, their engagement and conclusion of agreements with constituent units in other countries and, second, their participation as partners in a system of multisphere government, deeply implicated in the exercise of concurrent powers. However, as shown below, national, provincial, and municipal officials and politicians are confused about the legitimate and appropriate roles of different spheres of government in foreign relations. First, the national government has not developed an understanding of the constitutional framework within which provinces and municipalities may engage in international relations. Second, with very limited exceptions, national departments do not engage the provinces in the development of international relationships and agreements in matters that affect the provinces directly. Third, the provinces do not exercise their right to review international agreements in the NCOP.

INTERGOVERNMENTAL RELATIONS IN FOREIGN AFFAIRS

Intergovernmental relations in South Africa have developed rapidly over the past fourteen years. However, the assumption that international relations are a national prerogative has meant that foreign affairs matters are not often raised in the "mainstream" intergovernmental forums such as meetings of ministers and of officials serving particular portfolios. With the notable exception of environmental matters, the national government seldom consults with provinces on international matters relating to provincial competences and frowns upon uncoordinated foreign ventures by provincial and municipal governments. Moreover, as the agendas of intergovernmental fora are determined and dominated by the national government, the provinces rarely use them to raise issues related to their international activities.

The first clear manifestation of these realities was the production of a policy framework on municipal international relations in 1998 by the national Department of Provincial and Local Government (DPLG). The framework was intended to help all spheres of government develop "sound, efficient and effective" municipal international relations programs that support both "internal developmental priorities" as well as South Africa's "approach to foreign relations."[64] As early as 1997, the self-defined role of the DPLG extended to "managing," "coordinating and facilitating" the conduct of municipal international relations, the establishment of learning networks between municipalities, and the encouragement of "affordable and beneficial" twinning arrangements.[65]

In addition, and consistent with the centre's intention of controlling these matters, provinces have been encouraged (perhaps instructed) to set up units to deal with international relations. All provincial governments now include a small, dedicated directorate for "intergovernmental relations," "international relations," and/or "protocol," typically within the immediate Office of the Premier or the larger Department of the Premier, comprising up to seven staff members.[66] Each either has a separate budget or depends on the overarching office or department for budget management. These units act as provincial "points of entry" for the national government. Otherwise, their role seems to be limited. Provincial officials may see their role as including the management of development grants from foreign sources, but this is not always the case. Although about seven out of nine donors approach provinces first, provinces are now instructed to direct these donors to the National Treasury.[67] Sometimes fairly detailed programs are developed before this happens, but the current policy is that no formal agreements may be concluded without the National Treasury's approval, and provinces appear to adhere to this requirement.

The system has both benefits and drawbacks. Once the National Treasury approves an agreement, lawyers in the Department of Justice and the Department of Foreign Affairs (DFA) ensure compliance with domestic and international law. The president then signs a Presidential Minute authorizing the relevant national minister, under domestic law, to conclude an "international agreement." The National Treasury is responsible for meeting increasingly stringent donor accounting and reporting requirements attached to official development assistance under all "international agreements." This system is intended to allow the national government to ensure that national and broader regional development priorities[68] are addressed properly and that the benefits of donor largesse are distributed equitably. Curtailed provincial autonomy to pursue development priorities is an intended consequence, given the Treasury's practice of meeting annually with potential donors to identify areas for new agreements.

The national government has attempted to ensure coordination of provincial and municipal international relations through the establishment of International Relations Coordinating Groups for each sphere.[69] These bodies bring together the key national departments (i.e., the provincial and local governments, Treasury, and DFA) with constituent-unit international relations practitioners and the South African Local Government Association, an organization established under the Constitution to represent municipalities. Assertions that better coordination is needed are not unfounded. For instance, although the national policy is for officials to visit Taiwan when visiting the People's Republic of China, the flow of South African municipal officials to Chinese sister-cities shows little awareness of foreign policy directives. Also, without proper diplomatic notice, local delegations attempting to enter the Palestinian territories have had their passports confiscated at Israeli border posts. Nevertheless, provincial and municipal governments complain of inadequate support from the DFA. This could be a result of the DFA's view that constituent governments should really not engage in international relations at all, although it is more likely caused by the allocation of responsibility for provincial and municipal international relations in the DFA to relatively low-ranking officials and by the DFA's own limited capacity.

The efforts of the national government to supervise the international activities of provinces and municipalities have not been matched by a concomitant willingness to consult with provinces on international matters that affect the areas over which provinces have competence. The obvious forums for such consultation are the MinMECs. These are regular meetings of the national minister and provincial executive council members (MECs) held in each area of concurrent responsibility, including the environment, health, agriculture, and trade.[70] Clearly, many matters relating to international relations arise in fields of concurrent responsibility, yet all available evidence suggests that – with one notable exception – national departments make little effort to consult with their provincial counterparts on international matters. This is partly explained by the limited capacity of provincial governments to engage on these matters, although as provincial capacity strengthens, practices may change. However, the firmly held idea that international relations are beyond provincial concern contributes at least equally to this approach.

The exception is the environment, where intergovernmental practice emerges as a source of best practice. The main reason for this seems to be that a number of provinces, but most notably KwaZulu-Natal, have sophistication in this area that is not matched in the national sphere. The provinces are, in short, essential to the effective implementation of international environmental arrangements.

The NCOP should provide provincial checks and balances on international agreements that engage the concurrent competences of the provinces. While the threat of an NCOP veto has not yet encouraged a more cooperative attitude from the National Executive, this may change as the NCOP's perception of its role develops. Currently, international agreements are tabled at the NCOP without comment, even when they involve key provincial interests such as health.[71] What discussion there may be relates to general national issues, not to specific provincial interests.

Several factors strengthen the hand of the national government over provincial and municipal international relations. First, as noted above, there is constitutional uncertainty concerning the allocation of responsibility for international relations. Second, the ANC's control of every province and most municipalities, together with the very limited capacity of most of the provinces and municipalities, has meant that there has been little resistance to national supervision and ready acquiescence to assertions that national (and nationally determined) priorities must underpin all decisions. Third, in discussions of appropriate roles and relationships in matters of international relations, the national government's rhetorical justifiers – rationalization and efficiency – go unchallenged. An additional justifier – risk of diplomatic incident – is readily deployed by the Department of Foreign Affairs.

DOMESTIC AND INTERNATIONAL MANIFESTATIONS OF DIPLOMACY BY PROVINCES AND MUNICIPALITIES

As noted in the introduction, in the first years after the 1994 elections, South Africa's nine provinces as well as many of its municipalities stumbled enthusiastically into international relations, excited by the sudden interest paid to them by the international community. At the same time, they had little understanding of their overall role in South Africa's new constitutional framework and even less grasp of the full burden of their domestic responsibilities. During this honeymoon period, many international agreements were concluded by provinces and municipalities, but most focused more on "trips, toasts and twinning," as Steytler observes, than on substantive projects. Despite good intentions, following initial visits and exchange of cards, many arrangements became dormant.[72]

Now all provinces are demonstrating more systematic approaches to international relations, promoted in part by national control over international relations. As described above, the national government now insists that most forms of development aid – the subject of many agreements – be channelled through the National Treasury and that there be a clearly identified national liaison point in each province that benefits from development aid. Provinces and municipalities seem to share the national government's concern that their international ventures should contribute in concrete ways to developmental priorities identified by the national government. To this end, in 2006 most provinces had already developed or were in the process of developing some form of framework or policy within which to conduct international relations.[73]

As noted earlier, provincial directorates for international relations serve as liaisons between the national and provincial governments and are intended to coordinate the international activities of all provincial departments and to interact with other bodies such as provincial agencies responsible for trade. They are usually also specifically mandated to manage twinning agreements. There are some indications that, in some provinces at least, the appointment of staff dedicated to managing international relations is starting to bear fruit and, for instance, that dormant agreements are being revived and exploited by provincial departments. Provincial international relations activities – whether mere travel or the conclusion of arrangements – usually also require the approval of the relevant provincial cabinet committee. Nonetheless, insiders acknowledge that provincial line-function departments do engage overseas counterparts in international relations without alerting either the relevant Cabinet committee or the international relations directorate, demonstrating a disregard for harmonization with national or broader regional developmental objectives. Expressing a sentiment that probably holds for all provinces, one provincial bureaucrat noted that "other departments have their own agendas." This may help to explain why the role of the directorates is at times limited to arranging trips.

It is difficult to ascertain the budgets of the provincial directorates, but generally they appear to be relatively small, and most international activities are paid for by the line-function departments concerned. So, for example, staff appointed to a directorate might facilitate international relations for a provincial department of health, with that department carrying the costs.

Major cities, including Tshwane (Pretoria), Johannesburg, eThekwini (Durban), Ekuhurleni (East Rand), and Mogale City (Krugersdorp), employ dedicated international relations personnel in small units that function as a protocol officer and an international media adviser to the mayor while also advising line-function departments on the implementation of international relations projects. Smaller municipalities do not deploy dedicated staff. Municipal officials in major cities are aware of the need to cooperate with national departments – especially the Treasury, which, as indicated above, channels and monitors international development aid received under "international agreements."[74] Although the more cosmopolitan municipalities know how to leverage their international reputations, they demonstrate awareness of the policy directives of the national government. As one municipal international relations officer commented, "there is one national interest, implemented at local, provincial and national levels."[75] It is also safe to assume that the national government occupies the field where international relations are especially delicate.

There is no reliable information about the frequency with which provincial and municipal politicians and bureaucrats travel abroad or how many foreign delegations visit South Africa's provinces and municipalities. Members of provincial legislatures do occasionally visit their counterparts in other countries, but any significant international parliamentary events are hosted by the national Parliament. Provincial officials report meeting many foreign delegations, and at least one province, KwaZulu-Natal, has developed a framework for hosting international delegations.[76] Trips abroad by provincial and municipal politicians and officials are attracting increased public scrutiny, leading to reduced travel. For instance, a 2005 parliamentary policy allows NCOP committees to undertake only two trips during each five-year term. The KwaZulu-Natal draft "Framework for Provincial International Relations" also discourages large delegations because they are expensive, difficult to arrange, and "can easily create a wrong perception with overseas hosts."[77]

Delegations abroad vary in their composition and often include representatives from business and the tourism industry. These participants are usually expected to pay their own way. Anecdotally, municipal officials tend to see themselves as informal "practitioners of goodwill"[78] for South Africa in their overseas engagements – although not as *de jure* representatives of the state with powers to generate international obligations.[79]

Elections in South Africa are dominated by national parties and issues, and very few specifically provincial or municipal issues are raised. Moreover, international issues play virtually no role in national elections. However, in speeches to the provincial legislatures and the NCOP, provincial politicians refer quite frequently to international issues, including development aid, trade, culture, and sport. But such speeches present information rather than debate provincial foreign relations policy. Provincial politicians and NCOP members alike see themselves more as implementers of national policies for the provinces. Because the NCOP is intended to "represent the provinces in the national sphere of government,"[80] one might expect delegates to raise matters concerning international relations that have a direct impact on the provinces. Similarly, one might expect reports of study tours abroad to comment on the relevance of the trip to the concerns of South Africa's provinces. Instead, debates and reports on international matters are of a general nature and reflect the attempts of NCOP delegates to emulate their counterparts in the National Assembly rather than to identify themselves as provincial representatives.

As one might expect in a country struggling to provide adequate services at home, South Africa's provinces do not have significant engagements in technical assistance or democratization projects abroad, nor do they provide financial aid to other governments or communities.

*Trade and Development Aid:
The International Focus of Provinces and Municipalities*

The combination of the constitutional arrangement that binds provinces to national policy on economic matters, the general lack of capacity of provinces, and the current dominance of the ANC means that provinces (and municipalities) seek to conform to national economic policies in their international endeavours and make little attempt to influence these domestically. Although national economic policies and the demands of the global economy are hotly debated, these debates do not have an obvious provincial dimension.

All but one of the provinces have established independent agencies to represent their commercial interests.[81] These agencies offer services both to foreign investors seeking business opportunities in the provinces and to provincially based businesses seeking export or trade opportunities abroad. However, not all of these agencies operate abroad, and the nature and extent of their operations vary. Only the Gauteng agency has its own dedicated offices abroad, while the Western Cape has forged "strategic partnerships" with the foreign offices of the national Department of Trade and Industry (DTI) and with South African embassies abroad. Other provincial agencies undertake trade missions to foreign countries and participate in trade exhibitions organized by the DTI, but they do not maintain a permanent presence overseas. The agencies that do operate abroad are not accredited diplomatic representatives of the provinces but private companies, incorporated in terms of the laws of South Africa or established by statute in South Africa. They do not have the legal status or authority to bind provincial governments to agreements with foreign entities but rather see themselves as conduits for businesses in the province to enter key world markets.[82]

As might be expected, the most ambitious of these agencies is located in Gauteng – the most economically productive province.[83] The Gauteng Economic Development Agency (GEDA) is a company registered as an association not for gain.[84] It is mandated to "implement and promote the economic development policies" of Gauteng "in the areas of economic production, investment and trade."[85] GEDA has two foreign offices – in Sao Paolo, Brazil, and in London, UK – as well as representation in San Jose, California. The aim of these offices is to facilitate access for Gauteng-based companies to markets in South America, Europe, and the Silicon Valley. GEDA also has links with the trade offices of a number of foreign countries and US states.[86] In addition, it has undertaken a number of missions to other countries, including Uruguay, Japan, the United States, and Nigeria. In contrast to the approach of most provincial politicians, GEDA expressly links its activities to South Africa's role as a strategic access point for other African markets.

The Western Cape Investment and Trade Promotion Agency (Wesgro) offers a slightly different model. It is incorporated as a private and independent company, entirely owned by the Western Cape government and the City of Cape Town.[87] It reports to the provincial member of the Executive Council (MEC) for Economic Development and to the corresponding portfolio in the Cape Town City Council. Like its counterparts in other provinces, Wesgro's primary task is the promotion of business in the province. Both provincial and municipal politicians and officials participate in its activities. Although Wesgro states that it operates with the provincial context in mind, it takes its lead from national economic strategy and from the national Department of Trade and Industry.

The agencies established to promote investment in the other provinces are more modest in their activities. Most are intended to facilitate trade and fixed direct investment opportunities both locally and internationally. They conduct trade missions abroad and participate in trade fairs either at the invitation of the DTI or in their own right. The agencies of the Free State and the Eastern Cape have a predominantly domestic focus. In the Northern Cape the provincial Department of Economic Affairs itself promotes international investment.[88]

Overseas trade missions often result in agreements between the provincial agency and foreign entities to stimulate relationships between individual businesses and commercial interests. In those rare cases where such "memoranda of understanding" have legal implications,[89] it seems likely that only the entity itself, as a juristic person with separate legal personality, will be bound to that agreement.

As described above, the national government now manages most forms of development aid, and provinces are required to direct most donors to the National Treasury. Insistence that the national government control development aid reached international headlines in 2002 when the national government blocked a major UN grant to KwaZulu-Natal for AIDS prevention, care, and treatment. The national minister for health claimed that the Global Fund had tried to bypass the national government by awarding the grant to the province. The national government's failure to approve the grant led to its revocation.[90] Available information does not establish how the national government's management of international development aid since 2002 has affected the flow of aid to the provinces.

Accountability issues are raised both in the context of the provincial entities intended to promote commerce and in respect to the use of development aid. The universal problem with institutions intended to promote commerce is that they are rarely called to account, and in any event, it is hard to measure their success. The problems with accountability for development aid are just as acute. Where such aid is "off budget" and therefore not considered in the routine auditing and accounting processes, there is always a danger that it will not achieve its intended goals.[91] The practice of channelling such money through the National Treasury may ensure that it is not mismanaged but does not require the provincial officials who spend it to engage with the people of the province concerning its use.

Twinning and Other Agreements

In 2004, 53 of the 284 municipalities in South Africa were parties to formal international relationships. However, only better-established municipalities have been able to form these relationships. In fact, just 13 of these municipalities account for two-thirds of such relationships.[92] The municipalities of Buffalo City, Johannesburg, and Cape Town together are responsible for half.[93]

South Africans have learned, however, that it is difficult to realize the promise of twinning. At least in part, this is due to inadequate capacity to manage such relationships. At least thirty-five of the relationships entered into by municipalities since 1988 have lapsed,[94] and many more exist only on paper.[95] The experience in provinces is similar, and both provinces and municipalities have realized that, for the energy expended on such relationships to pay off, they need to be more focused. For instance, in Mpumalanga, no new twinning agreements have been concluded since 2002, and the current approach is to activate those already in place. The long lists of objectives found in these older agreements will also not be replicated in the future. Instead, Mpumalanga officials say that future agreements must be focused on matters that can secure real benefits. This view is widely shared by provincial and municipal officials who claim that more recent agreements are focused on development objectives.[96]

The medium-sized municipality of Buffalo City, in the Eastern Cape, is notable for its early efforts to engage in substantive international relations aimed at attracting development assistance. The municipality has received funding from Swedish and Dutch development agencies, coordinated through twinning agreements with the cities of Gavle and Leiden, for training and capacity building for municipal councillors and officials, urban renewal, spatial development, disaster and environmental management, and student exchanges.[97] As a quick starter in the arena of international development aid, Buffalo City experienced difficulty in channelling funds from overseas donors through the National Treasury's database in 2004,[98] although national systems appear to be functioning more effectively at present.

As with most other cities, Cape Town municipal officials, finding that symbolic and ceremonial relationships lack sustainability and cannot weather political change, have refocused their activities on development projects. Current projects in Cape Town include local economic development and HIV/AIDS projects funded by Monaco – in its capacity as a city rather than a state, municipal officials note – as well as a partnership between schools in Arcueil, France, and the historically "coloured" neighbourhood of Athlone, in honour of the local ANC activist Dulcie September, who died in exile in France.[99]

Although the South African Municipal International Relations (MIR) Policy encompasses a broad range of international relationships, including links that involve "local non-governmental organizations, community-based organizations or private associations,"[100] municipal governments have emerged as key facilitators in these agreements. This is because they are in a better position than members of civil society or business to access and develop organizational resources needed to foster international urban relations.[101] Unsurprisingly, then, much of the content of over three-quarters of these agreements lies in the "soft" areas of citizen participation, exchange of information and expertise, exchange of officials and politicians, and symbolic exchange. Only half the agreements include provisions directed at the "hard" areas of business or industry and tourism.[102] Indeed, participation by the business community in these twinning agreements is limited.[103]

A 2005 study found that municipalities are often assisted by outside bodies – usually national and provincial governments – in concluding their agreements. Of 37 agreements reviewed, 21 were supported either by the national Department of Foreign Affairs or by the national Department of Provincial and Local Government Affairs. A further 8 were assisted by their respective provincial Department of Provincial and Local Government Affairs.[104] Perhaps in keeping with the largely ceremonial rather than commercial nature of these agreements, the national Department of Trade and Industry assisted in only a handful of cases. Although cultural links rank high in the priorities of these agreements, the national Department of Arts and Culture does not seem to have been involved at all. Similarly, although the environment is an area of concern in 41% of agreements and tourism in 56%, the national Department of Environmental Affairs and Tourism does not appear to have participated.

Regional development priorities, expressed in instruments such as the Windhoek Declaration on South-South Relations,[105] add weight to the national government's encouragement of municipal and provincial international relationships with their counterparts in the region – in Lesotho, Mozambique, and Zimbabwe, for instance. These agreements are increasing. Some flow from agreements between the national governments. For instance, the Maputo Development Corridor agreement between Mozambique and South Africa was the catalyst for an agreement between the province of Maputo in Mozambique and Mpumalanga in South Africa. Other transborder agreements in the region appear to have been driven by constituent governments themselves. Steytler provides the example of the Trans-Limpopo Spatial Development Initiative, which includes Limpopo province in South Africa and both the Bulawayo City Council and Matabeleland South and Matabeleland North provinces in Zimbabwe. Its goal is to foster cooperation in tourism, wildlife conservation, disease control, and agriculture.[106] Limpopo also has an agreement with the Mozambican province of Gaza, and Mpumalanga has agreements with both Gaza and Maputo. Municipalities – particularly those adjacent to South Africa's borders – have also started to establish relations with their neighbours across the border. Most of these concern general "twinning" matters, cooperation on tourism and other business matters, and cultural links. But some are more specific and seek cooperation on matters such as stock theft, the movement of people, the use of shared resources such as water, and road building.[107]

Other municipal South-South twinning agreements extend beyond the region, such as that between eThekwini in Durban and Mombasa in Kenya. The idea of tripartite agreements is a yet more ambitious manifestation of the same idea. These agreements would link a South African city, another developing African city, and a developed city in the North.

Examples of particularly effective provincial and municipal international relations arise in the areas of environmental conservation and sustainable development, where transboundary thinking is an operational requirement and where the national government has consented to extensive constituent-unit involvement. As noted above, South Africa is involved in a set of ambitious regional initiatives to create transnational parks with five of its neighbours. The provincial wildlife authorities in KwaZulu-Natal initiated two such engagements with their cross-border counterparts. A memorandum of understanding between the KwaZulu-Natal Nature Conservation Services and the Lesotho Ministry of Environment, Gender and Youth Affairs was a key stage in the establishment of the Maloti-Drakensberg Transfrontier Park through an agreement between the national government and Lesotho. KwaZulu-Natal is now South Africa's implementing agent and is party to the "project agreement." KwaZulu-Natal environmental authorities have played a similar role in the development of the Lubombo Transfrontier Conservation and Resource Area, which, when fully established, will span parts of South Africa, Mozambique, and Swaziland.

Informal International Relations

Perhaps the most significant foreign relations of South Africa's provinces and municipalities are informal and deal with cross-border "housekeeping."[108] Health officials in KwaZulu-Natal routinely spray malaria mosquitoes across the border in Mozambique. They have commented that "South Africa's ability to control malaria will depend on the successes of its neighbours in combating mosquitoes."[109] Officials also report that residents of Lesotho obtain heath services in neighbouring South African district hospitals by informal acquiescence, as identity documents are not routinely checked. Under these circumstances, linkages between health authorities across the border are essential. Officials also point to agreements related to firefighting between Lesotho firefighting authorities and the Free State province in South Africa. It is more difficult to establish the degree to which transborder migration is dealt with informally, but it is likely that provincial offices of the national Department of Home Affairs liaise with provincial officials on the matter.

South Africa's Provinces and Municipalities in International Forums

Like the national government, South Africa's provinces and municipalities have been active in international organizations. All nine provincial legislatures are members of the Commonwealth Parliamentary Association, and provinces and municipalities are members of a variety of other international organizations, including the World Association of Major Metropolises (Johannesburg is a member) and the International Council for Environmental Initiatives (ICLEI). The South African Local Government Association (SALGA) is a member of United Cities and Local Governments (UCLG).[110] SALGA, the national Department of Provincial and Local Government, and the national Municipal Demarcation Board are among the South African members of the Commonwealth Local Government Forum. The Western Cape is a partner in a grouping of five regions – the others are Quebec (Canada), Shandong (China), Bavaria (Germany), and Upper Austria – linked by an agreement focused on such areas of cooperation as tourism, agriculture, trade, health, and education.[111] Steytler suggests that the driving force behind this partnership may be a shared desire for greater autonomy. It may also be a sense that a small grouping like this can achieve concrete results.

Provinces also participate in international conferences. For instance, in Montreal, Canada, in 2005 members of provincial environment ministries were included in the South African delegation to the first joint Conference of the Parties to the United Nations Framework Convention on Climate Change and Meeting of the Parties to the Kyoto Protocol. Delegates from the Western Cape took this opportunity to attend climate-change meetings specifically for regions, convened by Quebec, as well as meetings of the Steering Committee of Regions for Sustainable Development (nrg4sd), where the Western Cape and the Basque Country hold the joint chair.[112]

CONCLUSION

To a close observer of South African politics, the preceding description of the international relations of South Africa's municipalities and provinces contains few surprises. The most striking feature of these relations is the degree of control asserted by the national government and the extent to which the provinces and municipalities allow such control. Because most people consider provinces and municipalities firmly subordinate to the national government and due to the very limited capacity of these constituent governments, the national policy is seldom challenged. Instead, provinces and municipalities are generally content to allow the national government a considerable degree of say in their foreign relations (most obviously in the area of overseas development aid) and to entrust international negotiations to the national government, even on matters that fall squarely within provincial and municipal jurisdictions.

However, globalization constantly exposes provinces and municipalities to the attractions of international engagement, and those constituent units that have greater capacity, including the larger metropolitan centres and provinces such as the Western Cape and Gauteng, are responding. The most obvious developments are the establishment of agencies to promote the commercial interests of provinces and cities. It is likely that, if these agencies become successful, constituent-unit international relations will increase and expand to other issues. In addition, the excitement of the opening of South Africa's borders to its neighbours in the region at the end of apartheid provokes a strong desire to engage in the region, and the national government is generally in support of such regional, South-South relations. Regional international relations between South African municipalities and provinces and their counterparts in SADC are modest at the moment but are likely to grow as the region stabilizes.

It is impossible to predict when, if ever, provinces will engage as partners with the national government in international negotiations or demand more autonomy in negotiations involving aid and other international links. This depends both on political decisions concerning the future of the provincial system and on the role that provinces themselves assume. However, it seems certain that both municipalities and provinces will respond to the allure of international engagement in some way and gradually develop increasing commercial and cultural links with the outside world.

NOTES

1 The authors are grateful to Michelle Oliver for critical comments, to Rachel Logan, Paula Youens, Richard Stacey, Jewel Amoah, and Andrea M'Paradzi for invaluable research assistance, and to the participants at the South African Roundtable for their contributions. For background, see Nico Steytler, "Republic of South Africa," in John Kincaid and G. Alan Tarr, eds, *Constitutional Origins, Structure, and Change in Federal Countries*, 311–46 (Montreal and Kingston: McGill-Queen's University Press,

2005); Christina Murray, "Republic of South Africa," in Katy Le Roy and Cheryl Saunders, eds, *Legislative, Executive, and Judicial Governance in Federal Countries*, 258–88 (Montreal and Kingston: McGill-Queen's University Press, 2006); and Bongani Khumalo and Renosi Molcate, "Republic of South Africa," in Anwar Shah, ed., *The Practice of Fiscal Federalism: Comparative Perspectives*, 262–86 (Montreal and Kingston: McGill-Queen's University Press, 2007).

2 Recognizing this, Statistics South Africa classifies the population by racial group using the old apartheid classifications of black, coloured, Indian, and white.

3 Vicki Robinson, "ANC move to scrap provinces," *Mail and Guardian online*, 28 July 2006, http://www.mg.co.za/articlePage.aspx?articleid=279004&area=/insight/insight_national (accessed 31 October 2006).

4 Limpopo, Mpumalanga, the North West, the Free State, Eastern Cape, Gauteng, and KwaZulu-Natal.

5 Statistics South Africa, midyear population estimates 2007, Statistical Release P0302, 3, http://www.statssa.gov.za/PublicationsHTML/P03022007/html/P03022007.html (accessed 1 October 2007). The country's surface area is 1,219090 km^2.

6 In the Eastern Cape, more than 80% speak isiXhosa as their home language, while in KwaZulu-Natal the same percentage speak isiZulu. Afrikaans is the majority language in the Western Cape and Northern Cape. In Gauteng no single language commands a majority. See Statistics South Africa, *Census 2001*, http://www.statssa.gov.za/publications/Report-03-02-01/Report-03-02-012001.pdf (accessed 4 October 2006).

7 Ibid.

8 Department of Trade and Industry, "Financial and Economic Data," http://www.thedti.gov.za/econdb/sddsdata.html (accessed 4 October 2006).

9 National Advisory Council on Innovation (NACI), "The South African National System of Innovation: Structures, Policies and Performance," Background Report to the OECD Country Review of South Africa's National System of Innovation, ed. David Walwyn (July 2006), http://www.naci.org.za/OECD/OECD%20Report%2021Aug.pdf (accessed 2 January 2007), 6.

10 Statistics South Africa, "Gross Domestic Product Annual Estimates: 1993–2003; Annual estimates per region: 1995–2003; Third Quarter: 2004," 76, http://www.statssa.gov.za/publications/P0441/P04413rdQuarter2004.pdf (accessed 4 October 2006).

11 Johannesburg and Cape Town together account for nearly 30% of national GDP; see South African Cities Network, http://www.sacities.net/downloads/cities_gdp.doc (accessed 6 October 2006).

12 "South Africa Fast Facts," http://www.southafrica.info/ess_info/sa_glance/facts.htm (accessed 4 October 2006).

13 Andre Roux, *Everyone's Guide to the South African Economy* (Cape Town: Zebra Press, 2005), 97.

14 NACI, "South African National System of Innovation," 7.

15 Michael Nowak, "The First Ten Years after Apartheid: An Overview of the South African Economy," in Michael Nowak and Luca Antonio Ricci, eds, *Post-Apartheid South Africa: The First Ten Years*, 1–11 (Washington, DC: International Monetary Fund, 2005), 8.
16 The average over the last five years is 2.1%, the highest figure being 8.41% in 2001; see NACI, "South African National System of Innovation," 7.
17 Between 1 January 1984 and 14 April 1989, 155 US companies and 122 companies based in other countries disinvested from South Africa. Chase Manhattan Bank led the refusal of many to renew loans in 1985. See Philip Levy, "Sanctions on South Africa: What did they do?" Economic Growth Center, Yale University, Center discussion paper no. 796, 5, http://www.econ.yale.edu/growth_pdf/cdp796.pdf (accessed 25 September 2006).
18 See Linda Freeman, "All but One: Britain, the Commonwealth and Sanctions," in M. Orkin, ed., *Sanctions against Apartheid*, 142–56 (Cape Town: David Philip, 1989), 149.
19 Resolution 418. See also Human Rights Watch, "South Africa, A Question of Principle: Arms Trade and Human Rights, II. The Apartheid Era," http://www.hrw.org/reports/2000/safrica/index.htm#TopOfPage (accessed 15 May 2006).
20 Human Rights Watch, "South Africa."
21 President Ronald Reagan tried to prevent full sanctions and instead promoted "constructive engagement" until the US Comprehensive Anti-Apartheid Act was adopted in 1986; see Levy, "Sanctions on South Africa," 7.
22 This has been described nonetheless as an action of "dubious legality"; see John Dugard, *International Law from a South African Perspective*, 3rd ed. (Landsdowne: Juta, 2005), 521.
23 This is reflected in the short time it took for South Africa to play a leadership role in a number of international organizations. For instance, it represents Africa as one of the permanent governors of the International Atomic Energy Agency (IAEA), has occupied a nonpermanent seat on the UN Security Council since January 2007, chaired the 54th session of the United Nations Commission on Human Rights (UNCHR) in 1998, chaired the United Nations Conference on Trade and Development (UNCTAD) from 1996 to 1999, chaired the G77 in 2006, chaired the Commonwealth Heads of Government Meeting from 2000 to 2002, and chaired the Non-Aligned Movement from 1998 to 2003.
24 J. Cilliers, "An Emerging South African Foreign Policy Identity," Institute for Security Studies (ISS) papers no. 39 (April 1999), 10, http://www.iss.co.za/Pubs/Papers/39/Paper39.html (accessed 4 October 2006).
25 See Maxi Schoeman, "South Africa as an Emerging Middle Power: 1994–2003," in J. Daniel, A. Habib, and R. Southall, eds, *State of the Nation: South Africa 2003–2004*, 349–67 (Cape Town: HSRC Press, 2003); and Janis van der Westhuizen, "South Africa's Emergence as a Middle Power," *Third World Quarterly* 19, no. 3 (1998): 435–55, at 435.
26 S. Naidu, "South Africa and Africa: Mixed Messages?" in E. Sidiropoulos, ed., *Apartheid Past, Renaissance Future: South Africa's Foreign Policy 1994–2004*, 205–19 (Johannesburg: SAIIA, 2004), 214.

27 US$4574 (South Africa) as compared with $598 (Lesotho), $2749 (Namibia), and $4959 (Botswana) according to official figures of the Southern African Development Community; see http://www.sadc.int (accessed 10 October 2006).
28 The HDI is calculated on a scale of 0 to 1.0. The United Nations Development Program, *Human Development Report 2006*, describes the HDI as a broad definition of well-being; see http://hdr.undp.org/hdr2006/statistics/countries/country_fact_sheets/cty_fs_ZAF.html (accessed 28 November 2006).
29 Ibid.
30 Ibid.
31 Data from 1999; see J. Daniel, V. Naidoo, and S. Naidu, "The South Africans Have Arrived: Post-Apartheid Corporate Expansion into Africa," in J. Daniel, A. Habib, and R. Southall, eds, *State of the Nation: South Africa 2003–2004*, 368–90 (Cape Town: HSRC Press, 2003), 375–6.
32 Ibid., 376–7.
33 Ibid., 380.
34 Ibid., 379.
35 SADC's members are Angola, Botswana, Lesotho, Malawi, Mozambique, Swaziland, Tanzania, Zambia, Zimbabwe, Namibia, South Africa, Mauritius, Democratic Republic of Congo, and Madagascar.
36 Daniel, Naidoo, and Naidu, "South Africans Have Arrived," 379.
37 Analysis of post-1994 regional police cooperation initiatives shows notable, if temporary, success in countering cross-border criminal activity; see F. Msutu, "Responses to Organized Crime in SADC: INTERPOL and SARPCCO," Monograph no. 56, Institute for Security Studies (2001), http://www.iss.co.za/Pubs/Mongraphs/No56/Chap2.html (accessed 10 October 2006).
38 J. Crush, "Vulnerable States," in J. Crush et al., eds, *States of Vulnerability: The Future Brain Drain of Talent to South Africa*, 1–7 (Cape Town: Southern African Migration Project, 2006), 3.
39 The number of SADC citizens in South Africa increased by only 40,000 from 1996 to 2001; see ibid.
40 Ibid., 5.
41 Marie Wentzel, Johan Viljoen, and Pieter Kok, "Contemporary South African Migration Patterns and Intentions," in Pieter Kok, Derik Gelderblom, John Oucho, and Johan van Zyl, eds, *Migration in South and Southern Africa: Dynamics and Determinants*, 171–204 (Cape Town: HSRC Press, 2006), 175.
42 Ibid., 172–4.
43 These transfrontier parks are lAi-lAis/Richtersveld (Namibia and Northern Cape), Kgalagadi (Botswana and Northern Cape), Limpopo/Shashe (Botswana, Zimbabwe, and Limpopo), Great Limpopo (Zimbabwe, Mozambique, Limpopo, and Mpumalanga), and Maloti-Drakensberg (Lesotho and KwaZulu-Natal).
44 The Tugela-Vaal Scheme and the Lesotho Highlands Water Project.
45 Nico Steytler, "Cross-Border External Relations of South African Provinces," in Rudolf Hrbek, ed., *External Relations of Regions of Europe and the World*, 247–56 (Baden-Baden: Nomos, 2003), 247.

46 Ibid., 253.
47 The Basotho live in both the Free State province and Lesotho; the Swati live in Mpumalanga and Swaziland; and the Tswana live in the North West province and Botswana; see Steytler, "Cross-Border External Relations," 253.
48 Constitution, Section 146.
49 Constituion, Section 44(2).
50 Steytler has suggested that Section 84(2)(h) and (i) of the Constitution, which gives the president responsibility for "receiving and recognizing foreign diplomatic and consular representatives" and for "appointing ambassadors, plenipotentiaries and diplomatic and consular representatives," makes the president responsible for conducting foreign relations. However, these powers are relics of the old prerogative powers and are better interpreted as part of the apparatus of statehood than as the political function of conducting international relations and determining foreign policy.
51 The Constitution requires most NCOP decisions to be supported by the vote of five provincial delegations. Under Section 65(2), each provincial delegation must vote as instructed by its legislature. Certain constitutional amendments need the support of six provinces, and decisions on certain national bills are taken not by provincial delegations acting as units but by the individual delegates to the NCOP. For a description of the role of the NCOP, see Murray, "Republic of South Africa," 266–70.
52 Office of the Chief State Law Adviser (International Law), *Practical Guide and Procedures for the Conclusion of Agreements* (Pretoria: Department of Foreign Affairs, 2004), 10.
53 Constitution, Section 57.
54 *Manual on Executive Acts of the President of the Republic of South Africa*, compiled by N. Haysom, G. Wissing, V. Kahla, and H. Masondo (Cape Town: Executive and Legal Services, Office of the President, March 1999), para. 5.5.
55 Constituion, Section 41(1)(h).
56 *National Gambling Board v Premier, Kwazulu-Natal, and Others* 2002 (2) SA 715 (CC); and *Uthukela District Municipality and Others v President of the Republic of South Africa and Others* 2003 (1) SA 678 (CC).
57 Constitution, Section 146(2)(c)(i), (iii), and (iv).
58 *Harksen v President of the Republic of South Africa and Others* 2000 (2) SA 825 (CC), paras 18–27.
59 *Manual on Executive Acts*, ch. 5, 29, emphasis added. Chapter 5 is titled "International Agreements and Representation of the Government at International Level."
60 Constitution, Sections 230 and 230A.
61 Public Finance Management Act 99 of 1997, Section 67 (for provinces); and Municipal Finance Management Act 56 of 2003, Section 163 (for municipalities).
62 Constitution, Sections 198 and 199. In addition, under Sections 44(2) and 146(2), the national government can always override provinces on grounds of national security.
63 Constitution, Sections 205 to 208.

64 Ministry for Provincial and Local Government, *Municipal International Relations: A Policy Framework for South Africa* (Pretoria: Ministry for Provincial and Local Government, 1999), 1.
65 Department of Provincial and Local Government, *Annual Report 1997* (Pretoria: Department of Constitutional Development, 1997), 19, http://www.dplg.gov.za/documents/annualreport/reports/arindex.htm (accessed 12 October 2006).
66 Some work well, but others are barely functional.
67 The chief directorate of the International Development Cooperation, within the National Treasury, is responsible for the policy framework and procedural guidelines for the management of official development assistance. This body's Development Cooperation Information System is available at http://www.dcis.gov.za (accessed 12 October 2006).
68 These include the UN-sponsored Millennium Development Goals, the New Partnership for African Development (NEPAD), and SADC priorities and national initiatives.
69 These are the Municipal International Relations Coordinating Group (MIRCG) and the Provincial International Relations Coordinating Group (PIRCG); see E. Gqabaza, *Federalism and External Relations in South Africa* (King William's Town: Litha Institute, 2006), 24.
70 Dirk J. Brand, "The Role of Provinces in International Relations," in H-J Cremer, T. Giegrich, D. Richter, and A. Zimmerman, eds, *Tradition und Weltoffenheit des Rechts Festschrift für Helmut Steinberger,* 667–79 (Berlin: Springer, 2002), 675.
71 See, for example, parliamentary records surrounding the ratification of the WHO Framework Convention on Tobacco Control, which was tabled in the NCOP without debate: Hansard, National Council of Provinces Debates, 26 October 2004, 51.
72 Steytler, "Cross-Border External Relations," 252.
73 The most sophisticated of these is KwaZulu-Natal's draft "Proposed Framework for Provincial International Relations," Intergovernmental Relations Unit, Office of the Premier, KwaZulu-Natal, May 2006.
74 Interview with Denise Marais, National Treasury, 16 November 2006.
75 National Roundtable, Cape Town, 2 June 2006.
76 "Checklist for Hosting International Visitors and for Convening Formal Meetings – Guide 'C'," in KwaZulu-Natal, "Proposed Framework," 4, which sets out the roles and responsibilities of the provincial unit for liaison with the national Department of Foreign Affairs and for missions abroad and also provides a detailed checklist for logistics and protocol purposes. The existence of a company established to manage visits to South Africa by delegations of Chinese politicians and officials suggests that the Chinese are frequent visitors.
77 Ibid.
78 J. Kincaid, "The International Competence of US States and Their Local Governments," in F. Aldecoa and M. Keating, eds, *Paradiplomacy in Action: The Foreign Relations of Subnational Governments,* 111–33 (Portland: Frank Cass, 1999), 132.
79 Ibid.

80 Constitution, Section 42(4).
81 The Northern Cape is the exception. Its economic development is handled by the provincial Department of Economic Affairs.
82 Gauteng Development Agency, "Gauteng Development Agency Annual Report 2005–2006" (2006), 15, http://www.geda.co.za/X_Files/News/GEDA%202006%20AR_151106.pdf (accessed 30 December 2006).
83 See note 10.
84 Despite its apparent status as a private company representing the Gauteng government, GEDA is recognized as a "provincial public entity" in terms of Schedule 3C of the national Public Finance Management Act 1 of 1999.
85 Gauteng Development Agency, "What is GEDA," http://www.geda.co.za/Default.asp?index=47&ID=37&sub=2 (accessed 30 December 2006).
86 Gauteng Development Agency, "Foreign Offices," http://www.geda.co.za/Default.asp?index=53&ID=161&sub=2 (accessed 30 December, 2006).
87 Interview with Rifquah Jappie, Wesgro trade economist, 6 October 2006.
88 See http://www.northern-cape.gov.za/index.asp?inc=departments/economic/main.html (accessed 30 December 2006).
89 Wesgro recently entered an agreement with a Spanish organization called Promo Madrid, which involves an exchange of employees and a consequential need for legal regulation of the relationships flowing from the exchange.
90 South African Press Association, "Health Ministry Blocks UN Aids Grant to KZN-TAC," 11 July 2002, http://www.aegis.org/news/sapa/2002/SA020707.html (accessed 13 October 2006); Lynne Altenroxel, "KZN did try the right channels," *The Star* (Johannesburg), 2 August 2002, http://www.hivan.org.za/arttemp.asp?id=1615&netid=403&search=KZNdidtrytherightchannels (accessed 14 October 2006).
91 In practice, "off-budget" international donor funding is not subject to external auditing unless a "special purpose audit" is requested by the auditee or if the funds are considered income and selected in the audited sample of ordinary income and expenditure. See correspondence with Cobus Botes, senior manager, Office of the Auditor-General, 21 November 2006 (on file with the authors).
92 J.C. de Villiers, "Strategic Alliances between Communities, with Special Reference to the Twinning of South African Provinces, Cities and Towns with International Partners" (PhD diss., Stellenbosch University, 2005), 300. These thirteen municipalities are the only municipalities that have entered into more than three international relationships. They account for 113 of 171 relationships.
93 Ibid.
94 Ibid., 288–9.
95 Of 37 such agreements investigated, 4 are described as "dead," a further 4 as "stagnant and living off past performance," 2 as "need to jumpstart immediately or will be defunct" and as "declining," and 1 as "never got off the ground" (ibid., 310–11).
96 See also Brand, "Role of Provinces," 678, which explains the rationale behind the twinning agreements entered into by the Western Cape.
97 See E. Gqabaza, *Federalism and External Relations*, 26–32.

98 Ibid., 31.
99 Interview with Sindiswa Mququ, manager, International Relations in the City of Cape Town, 7 November 2006.
100 Ministry for Provincial and Local Government, *Municipal International Relations*, 3.
101 Y. Hsu, "Montreal's Twinning with Shanghai: A Case Study of Urban Diplomacy in the Global Economy" (PhD diss., Concordia University, 2003), 153, cited in De Villiers, "Strategic Alliances between Communities," 251. De Villiers notes that in South Africa just over half of these relationships are described as "municipal-to-municipal," about 40% involve the community as well as the municipality, and only the remaining 10% or so are "community-to-community" (306).
102 De Villiers, "Strategic Alliances between Communities," 311.
103 Ibid., 314.
104 Ibid., 309.
105 The South African Local Government Association (SALGA) represented municipal interests in the negotiation of this nonbinding instrument.
106 Nico Steytler et al., "Transfrontier Cooperation: Towards a Provincial Strategy," Discussion Document prepared for the Premier's Office, Government of KwaZulu-Natal, November 2004, 37.
107 Ibid., 38–9.
108 Steytler, "Cross-Border External Relations," 253.
109 Steytler, "Transfrontier Cooperation," 32.
110 Until 2004 this body was called the International Union of Local Authorities (IULA).
111 Steytler, "Cross-Border External Relations," 251.
112 See http://www.nrg4sd.net.

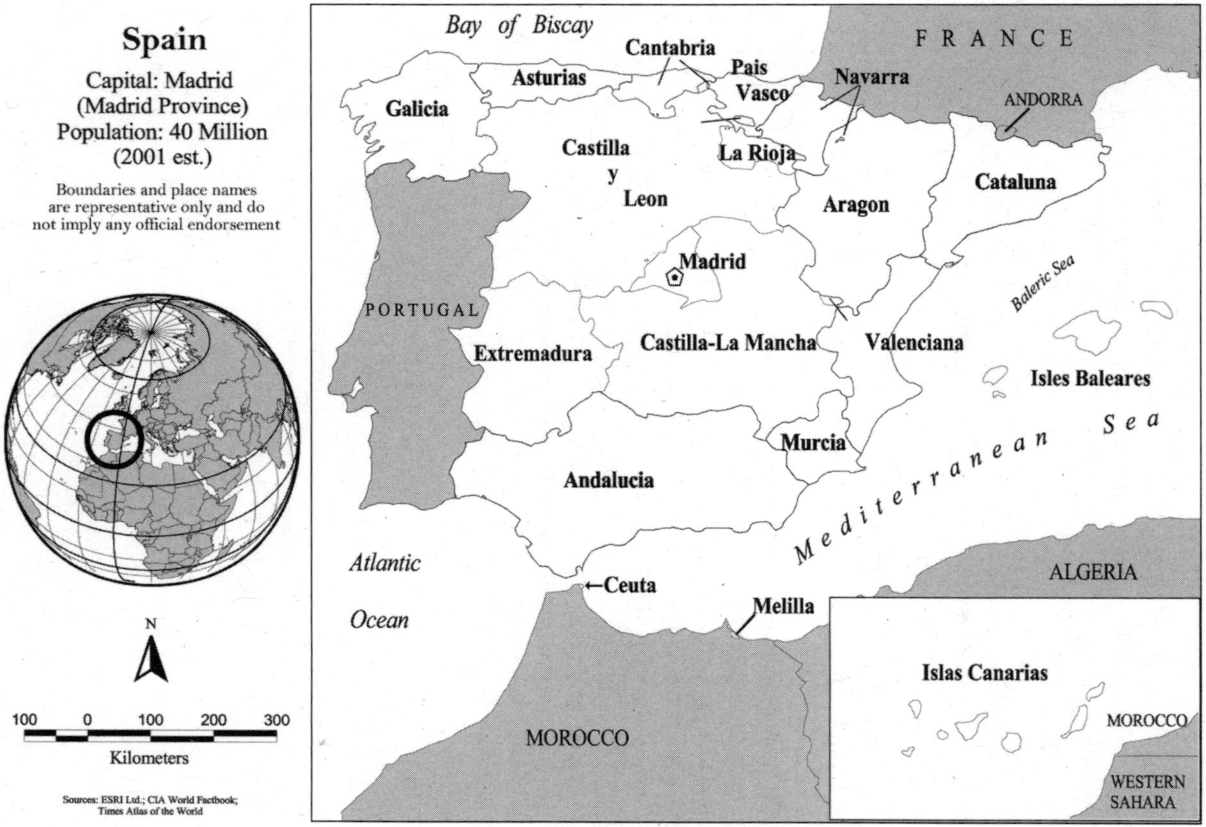
Spain
Capital: Madrid
(Madrid Province)
Population: 40 Million
(2001 est.)
Boundaries and place names
are representative only and do
not imply any official endorsement
N
100
0
100
200
300
Kilometers
Sources: ESRI Ltd.; CIA World Factbook;
Times Atlas of the World
Bay of Biscay
FRANCE
ANDORRA
Galicia
Asturias
Cantabria
Pais
Vasco
Navarra
La Rioja
Castilla
y
Leon
Aragon
Cataluna
Madrid
PORTUGAL
Extremadura
Castilla-La Mancha
Valenciana
Baleric Sea
Isles Baleares
Murcia
Andalucia
Mediterranean Sea
Atlantic
Ocean
Ceuta
Melilla
ALGERIA
MOROCCO
Islas Canarias
MOROCCO
WESTERN
SAHARA

Kingdom of Spain

FRANCISCO ALDECOA AND NOÉ CORNAGO

Although not formally a federal country, Spain, the so-called State of the Autonomies, is a highly decentralized political system.[1] Its uniqueness is largely due to the complex territorial organization that was created during the post-1975 transition to democracy, when Spain achieved a new and widely shared legitimacy. After decades of dictatorship, the most influential political forces agreed on the need to significantly decentralize political power in order to contain separatist trends as well as to try to win the widest popular support for the new democracy. As an outcome of this political climate, the framers of the Spanish Constitution of 1978 established a quasi-federal system, albeit with significant asymmetric features.[2] Nonetheless, for more than two decades, the Spanish political system has quite successfully managed the political tensions between centralist forces and ethno-territorial demands. More recently, however, the situation changed dramatically. A wave of new legal reforms and political decisions is challenging the Spanish political model and engendering significant political debate.

The Spanish Constitution stipulates that international relations are the exclusive competence of the central government, but from the very first moment, the new political system revealed a quite unexpected foreign dimension when regional governments tried to develop a presence abroad. Reasons for this development are very diverse, depending on the different specific cases, but in broad terms, it is the result of a more or less balanced combination of both functional and symbolic concerns. For some regions, such as Catalonia and the Basque Country, both governed by nationalists for a prolonged period, developing a presence abroad was from the outset of democracy very important because it made possible symbolic representation of these regions as political entities differentiated from the rest of Spain. Rarely spectacular in form and content, this international activism has, however, provoked considerable concern among more centralist political forces. But generally, economic reasons are the most powerful motives for autonomous communities' international activism. The impact of globalization and more specifically the effects of European integration have induced all subnational governments, not only those with an ethno-nationalist profile, to look abroad and to intensify international economic and political relations. As a result of this trend, a combination of legal and intergovernmental mechanisms has been created during the past decades to facilitate the necessary policy learning among the different orders of government, with the aim of assuring institutional stability and democratic legitimacy.[3]

COUNTRY OVERVIEW

The Kingdom of Spain is formally a unitary yet decentralized state. Although the 1978 Constitution emphasizes the indissoluble unity of the Spanish nation, it also expresses the need to protect cultural diversity and the right to territorial self-government. The Constitution does not specify the identity and number of constituent units, but it does establish the distinction between the so-called *nationalities* and mere *regions*. Until very recently, it was generally accepted that the nationalities were the Basque Country and Catalonia, which already enjoyed autonomy during the Spanish Second Republic (1931–39), as well as Galicia, which came close to attaining this status at the end of this period. But the situation has changed recently because Article 1 of the new Statute of Autonomy of Andalusia, formally adopted in 2007, establishes that Andalusia is also a historic nationality. However, in spite of the ambiguity of the constitutional text, between 1979 and 1983, seventeen autonomous communities and two autonomous cities were created, each with its own specific statute of autonomy.[4] These are Andalusia, Aragon, Asturias, the Basque Country, the Balearic Islands, the Canary Islands, Cantabria, Castille-LaMancha, Castille-Leon, Catalonia, Extremadura, Galicia, La Rioja, Madrid, Murcia, Navarre, Valencia, and two African enclaves, the autonomous cities of Ceuta and Melilla.[5]

Each autonomous community has a parliament or legislative assembly, elected by direct universal suffrage. The parliament elects the president of the community, who later appoints the Regional Government Council. Within the limits established by Articles 148 and 149 of the Spanish Constitution, each autonomous community holds all the powers that are listed in its own Statute of Autonomy and effectively transferred by the national state in fields such as organization of the institutions of autonomous government, land-use planning, town planning, housing, public works, agriculture, fisheries, culture, economic development, and tourism, among others. In the case of the Basque Country and Navarre, for historical reasons, the powers are also extended to regulation and tax collection. The communities wield legislative power in their areas of both exclusive and shared authority. A delegate of the central government represents the state's central administration within each autonomous community.[6]

Spain is a country of great cultural diversity that lacks a single and all-embracing national identity. Although Spanish is the only official language for the whole state, it shares its official status with others such as Catalan, Basque, and Galician in their respective autonomous territories.[7] In these regions, significant parts of the population have developed a strong nationalist feeling that questions the idea of a fully coherent and unanimously shared Spanish national identity. In addition, as a way to show refusal with the proverbial Spanish rightist national patriotism that characterized Francisco Franco's dictatorship (1939–75), the Spanish left has usually been quite sympathetic to ethno-national claims. But interestingly, the result of this pluralism has not been a growing social or political polarization because even in those regions in which ethno-nationalist feelings are widely shared, most of the population shows what has been called a dual identity. According to a 2002 survey, 78% of Spain's people define themselves in dual terms (e.g., Basque and Spanish, Catalan and Spanish, Galician and Spanish, and Andalusian and Spanish) but only 22% as simply Spanish, Basque, Catalan, Galician, or Andalusian. Even in the Basque Country, in which nationalist feelings are particularly salient, only around 25% of the people define themselves as simply Basque, against more than 40% who prefer to identify as both Basque and Spanish. As Luis Moreno has rightly pointed out, the pervasiveness of this dual identity explains the fact that Spanish citizens generally feel loyalty to both orders of government without perceiving this dual loyalty as contradictory.[8]

More recently, however, the situation has changed considerably because the political system established by the Constitution of 1978 is being widely questioned, particularly by Basque and Catalan nationalists. In addition, the two major political parties – the Socialist Party and the centre-right Popular Party – have such different understandings of the issue that achieving consensus for any constitutional reform seems almost impossible. But while resistance to constitutional reform is strong, changes have already begun from below. In 2004, after the accession to power of President[9] José Luis Rodriguez-Zapatero with the conditional support of Catalan left-wing nationalists, a new era of significant changes began. In 2005 the Basque government proposed a new framework for bilateral relations between the Basque Country and Spain, aiming to achieve a new, more loosely structured model of association, but the so-called Ibarretxe Plan was abruptly turned down by the Spanish Parliament. The Basque case stands in contrast to the successful adoption of new statutes of autonomy in Andalusia, Catalonia, and Valencia. Moreover, at present, various autonomous communities, such as Aragon, the Balearic Islands, and the Canaries, are also formally involved in their own reform processes.

In some political quarters, these statutory reforms are seen simply as an opportunity for the autonomous communities to slightly increase their level of autonomy, but for ethno-nationalists, the current process could open the way to full constitutional recognition of Spain as a *plurinational* state, although this is much more controversial. The idea of a plurinational state is certainly gaining recognition in some academic and political circles, not necessarily ethno-nationalist, as a way to renew the grammar of the political legitimacy of Spain, but it also provokes resistance among those who understand Spain as a unitary nation-state.[10]

Finally, in addition to the political and institutional context, and to understand the growing international activism of the Spanish regions, it is worth noting Spain's economic transformation over the past decades. Until 1978 Spain was officially regarded as an underdeveloped country by the Organization for Economic Cooperation and Development (OECD), but in the short time since the restoration of democracy, it has acquired the features of a middle power whose economic, political, and cultural influence in the world is growing rapidly.[11] With a population of around 44 million inhabitants[12] and a gross domestic product (GDP) of more than US$1.4 trillion in 2007,[13] Spain is presently the eighth-largest economy in the world as well as one of the most dynamic within the European Union (EU). According to a recent OECD survey,[14] Spain has managed a remarkable performance in terms of growth, employment, public finances, foreign trade, and inward and outward investment since the early 1990s. Spanish corporations have made a global name for themselves in crucial sectors such as banking, textiles, energy, construction, and telecommunications. This corporate international presence has added a new economic dimension to Spanish foreign policy, advancing the international position of Spain in the global market. But these favourable developments are threatened by weaker performances in the control of inflation, competitiveness, household debt, external deficits, and territorial economic imbalances. Another weakness of Spain's economy lies in its dependence on foreign supplies of energy. Because Spain produces less than a quarter of its energy needs, access to secure supplies of energy while keeping consumption in line with its Kyoto commitment is an important foreign policy priority. This is a major issue that has only recently begun to attract the attention of the autonomous communities.

In addition to good economic performance, the positive effects of EU membership have also facilitated the improvement of social welfare and domestic political cohesiveness. The 2006 United Nations' Human Development Index, for instance, places Spain in nineteenth position, immediately after France, Italy, and the United Kingdom and before Germany. However, Spain's GDP per capita, now US$25,600, remains 7% below the OECD average and more than 17% below that of the EU. Further, important territorial inequalities exist among the autonomous communities. A small group of regions have average incomes considerably above the EU average. This is the case for the Balearic Islands, the Basque Country, Catalonia, La Rioja, Madrid, and Navarre, while others like Andalusia, Extremadura, and Castille-La Mancha have significantly lower values. Economic dynamism is also concentrated in some regions. Andalusia, the Basque Country, Catalonia, Madrid, and Valencia produce more than 70% of Spain's GDP. These imbalances are at the base of the increasing competition among the autonomous communities, and they act as an incentive for political mobilization at both the domestic and international levels.

SPAIN'S CHANGING ROLE IN THE WORLD

Since the transition to democracy, Spanish foreign policy has been characterized by a firm determination to avoid direct involvement in armed conflict, as well as the will to make its diplomatic resources and negotiation capabilities available to the service and promotion of international cooperation. During the past decades, this peaceful approach to foreign policy – only recently interrupted – greatly facilitated widespread acceptance of Spain as a legitimate member of the democratic world, but it contrasts significantly with the long historical tradition of war and conquest that characterizes Spain's imperial past from its early beginnings to its final decline.

In 1898, after the Spanish-American War and the consequent loss of Cuba, Puerto Rico, and the Philippines, Spain's international ambitions declined dramatically. Absorbed first by domestic problems and later by a long civil war, Spain remained formally neutral during both the First World War and, albeit more disputably, the Second World War. After Franco's victory in 1939, the Republican government in exile was quickly disappointed in its expectations of obtaining the international support required to overturn Franco's regime. But for more than a decade, Spain experienced almost total international isolation. Both the Soviet Union and the United States, as well as their allies, rejected Franco's dictatorship and promoted the diplomatic isolation of Spain, even exclusion from United Nations (UN) membership. Only Argentina offered limited support in the early years of the Franco regime. During this period, both the Basque and Catalan governments in exile enjoyed a certain degree of international legitimacy, although in practice they lacked any substantial political influence. After many previous failed attempts, Spain became a member of the UN in 1956, and in 1969 Spain was even elected, somewhat unexpectedly, as a nonpermanent member of the UN Security Council. But the diverse efforts employed by the regime to obtain international recognition usually failed. However, the ideological climate of the Cold War and Franco's resolute anticommunism facilitated escape from this isolation. In 1953 a bilateral military treaty with the United States set the stage for a long and tedious process of gaining diplomatic recognition across the world.

After Franco's death in 1975, Spain's transition to democracy was widely celebrated around the world, but for many years its foreign policy remained particularly discreet. The adaptation of Spanish foreign policy to the standards of Western democracies was even characterized by continuity more than renewal. In this context, only the rapid signing and ratification of some of the most important international legal agreements on human rights in 1979, the establishment of diplomatic relations with the Soviet Union in 1977 and with Israel in 1986, and membership in NATO in 1981 and in the European Communities in 1986 marked a long awaited break with the past. With the exception of the somewhat controversial process of gaining membership in NATO, these achievements were widely supported by the main political parties, and it can be said that for more than three decades, the successive centrist, socialist, and centre-right governments generally formulated and implemented Spanish foreign policy in a climate of national consensus.

In this context, the leading role of Spain in both the Central American and Middle East peace processes in the 1980s as well as the institutionalization of both the Iberoamerican Summits and Euro-Mediterranean Conferences by the early 1990s fulfilled Spain's international ambitions in record time. But surprisingly, most of the international priorities of the new democratic Spain look almost the same as those that for many years characterized the Franco dictatorship's international efforts: deeper participation in European integration; commitment to Western security schemes under the leadership of the United States; and special attention to economic and political developments in Latin America and, to a lesser extent, in the Arab states.[15]

Nonetheless, the Popular Party's second period in office, under the leadership of Jose María Aznar, led to changes in Spanish foreign policy that resulted in the breaking of the so-called national consensus in foreign policy. Aznar's alleged ambition was to achieve international visibility and influence for Spain, which would correspond to its increasing economic weight and cultural presence around the world, through the adoption of a more active and aggressive international role. His staunch alignment with President George W. Bush and Prime Minister Tony Blair in the global "war on terror" and more specifically in the 2003 invasion of Iraq, in contrast with the more moderate position adopted by Germany and France, among others, provoked massive street demonstrations. Later, in March 2004, the tragic train bombings in Madrid three days before the Spanish elections, and the immediate decision by the newly elected President Zapatero to withdraw Spanish troops from Iraq, brought Spanish foreign policy into the international spotlight. The new socialist government adopted a new foreign policy discourse under the rubric of the so-called Alliance of the Civilizations, a global invitation to promote intercultural dialogue launched by Zapatero and the Turkish premier, Recep Tayyip Erdogan, which immediately received the support of the UN's secretary general, Kofi Annan. However, as discussed below, the most significant source of renewal for Spanish foreign policy has been EU membership.

THE SPECIAL RELEVANCE OF THE EUROPEAN CONTEXT

As in other policy domains, the most important force behind the transformation of Spanish foreign policy has been Spain's membership in the EU. Of course, the way that this influence has worked has varied, depending on both the successive stages in the integration process and the changing domestic economic and political factors. But in broad terms, it can be said that the EU and to a lesser extent the Council of Europe have provided international legitimacy and credibility to Spanish foreign policy efforts, helping to promote its national interests, particularly with respect to the relationship with its Atlantic partners and with Latin American, eastern European, and Mediterranean countries, thus maximizing its economic, political, and cultural influence.[16]

The implications of EU membership have been even more decisive for the internationalization of the autonomous communities. The initial erosion of regional governments' authority across Europe as a result of integration soon provoked the political mobilization of regional elites in Spain, as it did in countries like Austria, Belgium, and Germany. This subnational mobilization has facilitated the establishment of both formal and informal mechanisms for regional participation in the EU's political process, creating the basis for policy learning and domestic administrative adaptation in member states. There have been three milestones in the EU's political recognition of the regions: first, the 1994 creation of the Committee of the Regions with a consultative role on issues such as territorial and social cohesion, education and culture, public health, transport, and infrastructure; second, the recruitment of regional authorities as partners in implementing European policies; and third, the provision that member states can be represented in the Council of Ministers by ministers of their respective regional governments.[17] As this chapter shows below, the political debate about the establishment of this policy was particularly intense in Spain because the autonomous communities have always considered gaining access to European institutional resources and decision-making procedures their international priority.

EU membership has been a particularly important source of revenue for Spanish regions and municipalities. As the largest net beneficiary of European structural and cohesion funds in absolute terms, Spain received more than US$72.5 billion – that is, more than 25% of total net EU subsidies – from 2000 to 2006. Due to the most recent EU enlargement, however, Spain will eventually become a net contributor to the EU budget and will thus lose one of the driving forces behind its economic success. This scenario is causing increasing concern among regional elites, but in the meantime European programs have provided strong incentives for autonomous communities to participate in activities across Europe and beyond.

The EU's important domestic implications for Spain contrast with NATO's weak impact on the Spanish political system. Spanish participation in the Western alliance has been largely irrelevant in shaping the autonomous communities' international role. Although the accomplishment of Spanish NATO membership was preceded by significant popular opposition – particularly in the Basque Country – the Constitution explicitly reserves military and defence powers to the national government, and none of the autonomous communities has ever questioned this seriously. Occasionally, however, there has been some controversy between the central government and some autonomous communities about the utilization of American military bases in Spain, particularly during the Iraq and Afghanistan wars. In addition, in the context of the "war on terror," some autonomous communities that have their own autonomous police forces, such as Navarre, Catalonia, and especially the Basque Country, have explored, albeit without success, the possibility of participating in cross-border operations in the framework of Interpol cooperation. More recently, other issues with implications for security, illegal immigration, and organized crime have given rise to increasing concern in some autonomous communities, especially in Andalusia and the Canaries.

THE CHANGING CONSTITUTIONAL SETTING

The Spanish quasi-federal political system is not a fully accomplished political project but an evolving reality. The Spanish transition to democracy produced a constitutional arrangement that allows each of the regions subsequently to decide its own model of autonomy within Spain. Once a statute of autonomy is enforced, the fulfilment of its provisions is subject to continuous negotiation between the constituent government and the central government in order to determine the specific terms and character of the devolution process. In this context, therefore, the international role of the State of the Autonomies is certainly an issue open to negotiation. Of course, the Constitution of 1978 establishes the base in this regard, as do, more modestly, the statutes of autonomy, but the final model is far from being built because its construction is evolutionary by nature.

The Constitution of 1978 does not refer explicitly to any foreign activity of the autonomous communities. Rather, it establishes very concisely and without further explanation that the domain of "international relations" is an exclusive power of the state (Art. 149.1.3). The state also has exclusive power over foreign and defence policy (Art. 97), foreign representation and diplomacy (Arts 56.1. and 63.1), treaty making (Arts 93, 94, and 96), and many other domains, such as nationality, migration, status of aliens, asylum, foreign trade, currency and monetary policies, customs, public health measures, air space, flag shipping, and licensing of aircraft (Art. 149.1). However, in contrast with other countries where federal institutions have power to implement foreign policy domestically regardless of the division of powers, the Spanish model requires the cooperation of the autonomous communities to implement any foreign policy measure or international law (including European law) that affects regional powers. In addition, in accordance with the evolving jurisprudence of the Constitutional Court, the autonomous governments are entitled to become engaged internationally insofar as this serves the management of the foreign aspects of their own areas of jurisdiction. However, to understand the Spanish political process, it is important to note that, in contrast with federal countries such as Germany and Austria, Spain's constitutional system does not provide for the effective representation of the autonomous communities at the national level. Although there is a territorial chamber, the Senate, it lacks clout and is basically irrelevant in the decision-making process. Consequently, reform of the lower house is one of the most important constitutional issues.[18]

In addition to the constitutional provisions, the legal framework for the autonomous communities' foreign relations also depends on the specific provisions contained in the different statutes of autonomy.[19] For purposes of clarity, four types of provisions can be identified here:

1 Some statutes include the right of the autonomous communities to be informed about international treaties signed by the central government when they could have binding implications for them. This is the case of Andalusia (Art. 240), Aragon (Arts 41 and 97), Asturias (Art. 34.3), Balearic Islands (Art. 102), Basque Country (Art. 20.5), Canary Islands (Art. 37.1), Catalonia (Arts 187 and 191), Madrid (Art. 33.1), Murcia (Art. 12.2), Navarre (Art. 68), and Valencia (Arts 22 and 62). In contrast, the issue is ignored in the statutes of Galicia, Cantabria, La Rioja, Castilla-La Mancha, Castilla León, and Extremadura.
2 Some statutes also recognize the right of autonomous communities to ask the central government to enter into international negotiations on matters affecting their interests or concern: Andalusia (Arts 240 to 243), Aragon (Art. 97), Balearic Islands (Art. 102), Basque Country (Art. 6.5), Cantabria (Art. 6), Castille-La Mancha (Art. 7), Castille-Leon (Art. 6), Catalonia (Arts 195 to 197), Extremadura (Art. 3.3), Galicia (Art. 7.2), and Valencia (Art. 62). Some statues even allow for the possibility of participation in international negotiations within the Spanish delegation: Balearic Islands (Art. 102), Catalonia (Arts 185 to 187), and Valencia

(Art. 62). In contrast, both are ignored in the statutes of La Rioja, Murcia, Canary Islands, Madrid, and Navarre.

3 Other statutes of autonomy include measures to facilitate the implementation of international treaties and conventions in areas of a community's own jurisdiction: Andalusia (Arts 240 to 243), Aragon (Art. 97), Asturias (Art. 12), Balearic Islands (Art. 102), Basque Country (Art. 20.3), Canary Islands (Art. 37.2), Castille-La Mancha (Art. 34), Castille-Leon (Art. 28.7), Catalonia (Arts 195 and 196), Extremadura (Art. 9.1), Madrid (Art. 33.2), Murcia (Art. 12.2), Navarre (Art. 58.2), and Valencia (Art. 62). The issue, however, is ignored in the cases of Galicia, Cantabria, and La Rioja.

4 Finally, some statutes include special provisions on very diverse issues such as the foreign promotion of culture or vernacular languages: Andalusia (Art. 68), Catalonia (Arts 6, 50, and 127), and Galicia (Art. 7.1); international contacts with overseas migrant communities: Andalusia (Art. 6), Asturias (Art. 8.3), Catalonia (Art. 13), Basque Country (Art. 6.5), Extremadura (Art. 3.3), and Galicia (Art. 7); and foreign aid: Andalusia (Arts 220 to 245), Catalonia (Art. 197), and Valencia (Art. 62).

However, beyond the formal provisions initially adopted, it has been actual practice and the evolving jurisprudence of the Constitutional Court that has established what can be called the "constitutional framework" for the foreign relations of the autonomous communities. Although the content of the statutes of autonomy differs, Constitutional Court decisions apply to all the constituent units, not only to those affected by each specific case, because they create binding precedents.

The evolution of Constitutional Court jurisprudence on this issue has been particularly relevant. The different judgments produced by the court about the scope and limits of the international activities of the autonomous communities reveal very significant change across time. During the 1980s the court maintained a very restrictive position regarding the autonomous communities' involvement in foreign relations. These initial judgments display a restrictive interpretation of Article 149.1.3^a of the Spanish Constitution, which closes almost any avenue for constituent-unit involvement in foreign affairs. Illustrative of this trend is Judgment 137/89, in which the Constitutional Court considered illegal a simple joint communication signed by the Autonomous Government of Galicia's Ministry of Environmental Affairs and the Kingdom of Denmark's General Directorate for Environmental Affairs.

Subsequently, however, the Constitutional Court significantly changed its position. This change was evident in Judgments 153/1989, 17/1991, and 80/1993, but the most significant step in the new direction was taken in Judgment 165/1994, when the court established, against the Spanish government's claims, that the Basque Government Delegation in Brussels could be considered official because relations with the EU could no longer be considered "international." Although controversy remains regarding overseas offices established beyond the EU, this judgment, which was unanimously welcomed by the autonomous governments regardless of their political orientation, clarified the scope and limits of the autonomous communities' involvement in foreign affairs. Since then, it has become widely accepted that the autonomous communities are entitled to develop diverse international activities as far as these activities are instrumental for the effective exercise of their own powers, are not invasive of the powers that the Constitution assigns exclusively to the national government, and neither affect the national government's international responsibilities nor create new obligations. Consequently, the involvement of autonomous communities in international relations is in line with the constitutional framework as long as it serves to better accomplish the functions assumed by the autonomous communities resulting from the powers granted to them by the statutes of autonomy.

The implementation of treaties is also an important issue. In strictly legal terms, the Spanish Constitution does not explicitly include the implementation of treaties within the international relations domain; consequently, it does not establish the power to implement treaties either for the central government or for the autonomous communities. In contrast, various autonomous communities include in their own constitutions some provisions regarding the implementation of treaties in the areas of their own competence, including the possibility of adopting further legislation. However, according to Constitutional Court jurisprudence, the most important aspect regarding this issue is not the distribution of powers but the idea that both the central government and the autonomous communities are obliged to comply with international treaties adopted by Spain. Otherwise, noncompliance would affect the international responsibilities of Spain as a whole. Consequently, in case of controversies regarding implementation or lack of cooperation by the autonomous communities, the central government exercises its surveillance responsibilities through ordinary legal mechanisms, not merely through its decree-making powers or through ad hoc executive measures.

Certainly, the new Catalan Statute that came into effect in August 2006 opened a new era in this regard, adopting a much more ambitious approach to international issues that others will no doubt emulate. For this reason, it deserves more attention. The 2006 statute establishes a bilateral commission between Catalonia and the Spanish government, which, among other tasks, will monitor both the participation of Catalonia in the EU as well as central-government international action in any area under Catalonia's jurisdiction. This bilateral approach has always been sought by both Catalan and Basque nationalists, but its extension to other new statutes seems unlikely. According to the new statute, Catalonia shall be informed by the central government of EU treaty-reform initiatives (Art. 187). Moreover, the position taken by Catalonia shall be decisive for the development of Spain's position if it affects Spain's exclusive powers and if the European proposal or initiative could lead to especially important financial or administrative consequences for Catalonia.

In other cases, this position is to be taken into account by the national government (Arts 185 and 186). Catalonia can engage in foreign relations and promote its interests in this area while respecting the powers of the state in foreign affairs, and it may also establish offices abroad as well as sign international collaboration agreements in areas falling within its powers (Arts 193 to 195). It must be informed in advance by the national government of the signing of treaties that could have any direct effects on its powers, and it is entitled to forward its views to the central government. Moreover, in the case of treaties having a direct effect on its exclusive powers, Catalonia may request to have its own representatives included in the negotiating delegation (Arts 195 and 196).

Furthermore, according to the new statute, the central government shall adopt, in coordination with the Government of Catalonia, the necessary measures to carry out any international legal obligation that affects matters under Catalonia's jurisdiction (Art. 196). In addition, Catalonia shall promote cooperation and establish relations with the European regions with which it shares economic, social, environmental, and cultural interests as well as promote cooperation with other territories through development-cooperation programs (Art. 197). In a provision that seems to take its inspiration from recent developments in Canada,[20] the new statute establishes that Catalonia shall participate in international bodies in matters of major interest, especially the United Nations Educational, Scientific and Cultural Organization (UNESCO) and other cultural bodies "in the manner established by the corresponding regulations" (Art. 198). Finally, the new statute provides that Catalonia shall promote the international activities of its social, cultural, and sporting organizations (Art. 200).[21]

The practical and legal scope of these provisions remains to be seen, but the new Catalan statute has established a model for the new wave of statutory reforms currently in progress. Although the new Catalan statute is already in force, the Spanish Constitutional Court is presently considering its content, following a petition by the Popular Party alleging that the new Catalan statute contains unconstitutional elements. However, it is interesting to note that although the text manifests a clear desire for autonomy in the international sphere, it also indicates a resolve for a renewed cooperation with the Spanish government and emphasizes the importance of intergovernmental mechanisms.

MECHANISMS OF INTERGOVERNMENTAL COOPERATION

The legal framework previously outlined neither assures autonomous communities' participation in the Spanish foreign policy process nor impedes its implementation. To explore concrete possibilities in this regard, a number of intergovernmental mechanisms for collaboration have been established in recent years. Of course, the likelihood of support for the central government by the autonomous communities at critical moments has varied significantly depending on political circumstances and changing electoral results at both the national and constituent-unit levels. At the same time, autonomous governments' chances of increasing their international profile with the support of the central government have always depended on the windows of opportunity opened by diverse political developments. As a result, for many years the real template for discussions about foreign relations of the autonomous communities has been the EU and, more specifically, the controversy surrounding the place of regional governments in the new European polity.

Spain's membership in the EU since 1986 has significantly eroded the distinction between domestic and foreign matters, thus challenging the constitutional division of powers and existing domestic mechanisms for accommodating national differences. Despite the strong opposition of regional elites, many areas that were previously under the jurisdiction of the constituent units have been transferred to the EU by the central government by virtue of its exclusive foreign policy powers. This process eroded the legislative powers of autonomous communities while simultaneously requiring their collaboration in implementing EU legislation. The increasing concern about this trend encouraged regional elites to mobilize their efforts to secure greater participation in EU policymaking. Regional participation in the EU has also become a common topic for political debate between centralist and ethno-territorial forces during electoral campaigns. The Basque Country and Catalonia have been the most active regions in this regard, but the issue of direct participation in the EU decision-making process is a concern of every autonomous community. As a result, some demands are widely shared among them: first, participation in the elaboration of Spain's position before the EU Council of Ministers as well as in its working groups when the shared or exclusive competences of the constituent units are directly affected; second, co-management and co-decision in the distribution of the European funds; third, official recognition and institutional support for the autonomous communities' delegations in Brussels; and finally, direct access to the European Court of Justice in matters of their own jurisdiction and concern.

However, due to the asymmetrical character of the Spanish political system, attempts to institutionalize general standards have always been complicated by the tensions existing between the most powerful and influential autonomous communities and the rest. For instance, the Basque and Catalan nationalists' demand for the creation of distinct autonomic electoral constituencies for European parliamentary elections, instead of the current single country-wide constituency, is supported by Galicia and the Canary Islands but rejected by the rest. This example shows that relations among autonomous communities are becoming more competitive and less cooperative.

In addition, in contrast with their Austrian, Belgian, and German counterparts, successive Spanish governments have been reluctant to proceed through legal reforms, preferring instead to establish informal mechanisms for intergovernmental collaboration and consultation. However, the model that finally emerged is largely the result, both in its formal and informal profiles, of the lessons learned by the central government and the regions from earlier failed attempts.

The most important intergovernmental mechanism has been the so-called sectoral conferences. Departing from previous practice, the central government in 1992 promoted the establishment of a series of thematic multilateral conferences designed to foster intergovernmental cooperation. These conferences are issue-specific – education, agriculture, education, environment, culture, and health, among others – and always constitute representatives of each autonomous community and the corresponding central-government minister. Presently, only one of these conferences, the Sectoral Conference Relating to European Union Affairs (SCREU), which was later institutionalized by Law 2/1997, is explicitly international, albeit only European, in scope, and it works in close collaboration with the other issue-specific sectoral conferences. Whereas the SCREU discusses general EU matters, specific issues are dealt with at the regular meetings of the various sectoral conferences. The SCREU was established as a forum for consultation between the central government and autonomous communities, with the aim to enhance regional participation in the implementation, management, and monitoring of EU policies as well as to facilitate the formulation of common positions on EU matters. Meeting at least twice a year, it serves as a forum where the autonomous communities can exchange views about their European concerns in close cooperation with central-government representatives. In spite of its basically multilateral character, the SCREU permits the establishment of bilateral cooperative mechanisms so as to allow any single autonomous community to participate in dealing with EU matters directly affecting its specific interests. Catalonia and the Basque Country have availed themselves of this procedure, although without substantial results.

Furthermore, Law 2/1997 allows for the participation of constituent-unit representatives alongside central-government representatives in the complex network of EU working groups. Constituent-unit representatives do not speak for the Spanish state but accompany central-government civil servants and support the position previously agreed to by all autonomous communities in the sectoral conference. Recently, thanks to the willingness of the Zapatero government to advance in this direction, some sectoral conferences have served as venues for intergovernmental information sharing and consultation on international topics beyond those in the European domain, such as the Kyoto Protocol and some matters related to the World Trade Organization (WTO). In addition, although far from being perfect, the SCREU experience will probably serve as a model for the future creation of a Sectoral Conference for Foreign Affairs. In sum, although the SCREU model is a modest achievement and its use has not produced tangible results, it has served as an avenue for developing experience in intergovernmental policymaking for both the central government and the autonomous communities.[22]

More recently, however, after the accession to power of President Zapatero with the support of Catalan left-wing nationalists and in a context of statuary reforms, new steps have been taken to recognize the international relations of the autonomous communities. The most important is without doubt the adoption in December 2004, within the framework of the SCREU, of an agreement granting the autonomous communities direct representation in the EU Council of Ministers on matters affecting their powers. These are employment, social policy, education, culture, youth, health, agriculture, fisheries, the environment, and consumer affairs. Moreover, the autonomous communities are allowed to designate two officials in Spain's Permanent Representation to the EU. The agreement also makes it the responsibility of the relevant sectoral conferences to designate representatives of the autonomous communities.

Almost two years after this mechanism was established, the first evaluations are possible. The absence of any formal rule guiding the appointment of these representatives has provoked serious criticism. Diverse procedures have been adopted by the different sectoral conferences. Sometimes representatives have been appointed because of the length of their personal experience. In other cases, the criterion has been the representation of a sector of the population or the relevance of a particular issue to a specific autonomous community. Political convenience has also played a role. Even balloting has been employed. This absence of well-specified criteria has engendered strong concerns in some autonomous communities while reinforcing the preference of the Basque and Catalan nationalists to pursue special bilateral relations with the central government. Although the system has many shortcomings, it has afforded the constituent units practice in direct participation in the EU Council of Ministers and in Spain's Permanent Representation.[23]

Finally, two other initiatives adopted by Zapatero deserve attention. The first was the launching in October 2004 of the Conference of Presidents. Holding periodic multilateral meetings between the prime minister of the national government and the premiers of constituent units has a long tradition in some federal countries like Canada, but the practice was completely new to Spain. Even so, it was initially welcomed by different political parties and the autonomous communities, although the Basque and Catalan nationalists were less than enthusiastic. The results have, however, been very poor. Three meetings had been held by 2007, and none seemed to have been fruitful. Many autonomous communities have complained that the meetings lacked a serious agenda, especially in matters of substantial political interest. The opposition also argues that they have served merely to increase Zapatero's public profile. But given the importance of similar initiatives elsewhere, the Conference of Presidents could become a significant forum for public discussion of relevant domestic and international matters.

The second and more modest initiative has been to invite presidents of the autonomous communities on the Portuguese border, such as Galicia, Castilla-Leon, Extremadura, and Andalusia, and those on the French border, such as the Basque Country, Navarre, Aragon, and Catalonia, to participate, although merely as guests, in the periodic Spanish bilateral summits with France and Portugal. This initiative has also been criticized by the Basque and Catalan nationalists as mere political marketing intended to promote the image of a central government sensitive to regional concerns, but in the near future such participation could become more important.

THE AUTONOMOUS COMMUNITIES ON THE WORLD STAGE

In a country with a history as long as that of Spain, it is not difficult to find, even in the most remote past, precedents for the current involvement of the autonomous communities in foreign affairs. A simple reference to the Kingdoms of Castilla, Aragon, or Navarre, among others, and even Al Andalus long before the others, would remind us of the deep historical roots of the plurality of voices existing in Spain. However, the most influential regions in setting the pace for current autonomous communities' international activism have been the Basque Country, Catalonia, and to a lesser extent, Galicia.[24] In addition to their equally ancient cultures and roots, the reason for this influence is that in the nineteenth century these three regions developed a sense of national belonging that strongly differentiates them from Spain. Later, during the interwar years from 1919 to 1938, the Basque, Catalan, and Galician nationalist elites were particularly active in the international field promoting the cause of national minorities across Europe and beyond.[25] During the Second Republic, the Spanish government tried to facilitate the accommodation of these regions through a devolution process. The unfortunate outbreak of the Civil War in 1936 forced the recently created autonomous governments of Catalonia and the Basque Country into exile. During the decades that preceded the restoration of democracy, the Basque Country and Catalonia were very active internationally. However, resource shortages as well as the international consolidation of Franco's regime kept them from obtaining strong or enduring foreign support.

Given these historical precedents, it is not surprising that after the transition to democracy, both the Basque Country[26] and Catalonia[27] were, from the outset, particularly active internationally. In addition to their political motivations, they are both wealthy regions with powerful economies. They also share international borders with France and are located next to the sea. For the Basque Country and Catalonia, developing a presence abroad was from the outset very important because it made possible the symbolic representation of their own cultural distinctiveness.[28] Certainly, other autonomous communities also have symbolic concerns. Andalusia, Galicia, Extremadura, and the Canary Islands, among others, have found the promotion of their distinctive cultures a valuable instrument for asserting themselves politically and institutionally, both within and beyond Spain. But it is indisputable that political symbolism is particularly important in some regions. It is worth remarking, for instance, that only the Basque and, less frequently, the Catalan governments officially use the expression "diaspora" in dealing with their expatriate communities. Other autonomous communities with a sizable population living abroad, like Andalusia, Asturias, the Canary Islands, and Extremadura, call them simply "communities abroad." This difference, however, is based not solely on political preferences but also on deep cultural reasons because Basque and Catalan people living abroad frequently maintain a highly shared sense of belonging to a distinctive collective identity. Particularly important is the Basque case. Presently, nearly 200 organized Basque communities in twenty-two countries maintain a dense network of relationships among themselves, receiving the institutional and economic support of the Basque government.[29] In the case of Catalonia, 116 foreign private entities are presently officially recognized as Catalan Communities Abroad (CCA).[30] Finally, Galicia has formally recognized 154 communities abroad, but according to some registers, there are more than 400 such Galician communities.[31]

In addition to symbolic and cultural concerns, more functional motivations always drive autonomous communities' foreign relations. Foreign trade, international fairs, tourism, and foreign investment all apply in the Spanish case, as they do elsewhere. Autonomous communities have, in addition, signed hundreds of international-collaboration agreements of different types with diverse partners: subnational governments all over the world, central governments, international organizations, corporations, and international nongovernmental organizations (NGOs). This practice was quite controversial two decades ago but is widely accepted now so long as the agreements respect certain conditions. First, such agreements cannot incur international obligations that are binding on the Spanish state. Second, they are not to affect Spanish foreign policy adversely. Third, as entities, autonomous communities entering into international agreements cannot be considered subjects of international law.

Not all autonomous communities have established offices abroad, but all seventeen communities have delegations in Brussels. At first, these offices were established as private-law entities, but following a decision of the Constitutional Court regarding the status of the Basque delegation in Brussels, it is possible to establish official delegations abroad while also maintaining other arrangements under the guise of private law. Presently, only the Basque Country and Catalonia have established official delegations abroad. As discussed earlier, in 1994 the Constitutional Court ruled against the central government, holding that the Basque Government Delegation in Brussels can be considered official because interactions with the EU can no longer be seen as "international relations." Although controversy remains regarding the overseas offices established outside the EU, this judgment has served to clarify the scope and limits of the autonomous communities' involvement in foreign affairs insofar as they do not seek to encroach upon the central government's exclusive domains.

In addition to their delegation in Brussels, all autonomous communities maintain a more or less dense network of trade offices or business delegates abroad to attract investment and to promote the international competitiveness of their local economies. Enumerating them all would lead to an expansive list, but as an illustration of this trend, it can be mentioned that Andalusia maintains fourteen offices abroad through the so-called EXTENDA network; Aragon has a delegation in Brussels and ten business centres; Asturias has a delegation in Brussels and ten business centres; the Basque Country maintains official delegations in Brussels, Mexico, Caracas, Bogotá, Santiago de Chile, Buenos Aires, New York, and Paris as well as eleven business and trade centres through its SPRI network; the Canary Islands has a delegation in Brussels and seven business and trade offices in Miami, Caracas, Sao Paulo, Praia, Agadir, Nouakchott, and Dakar, constituting the PROEXCA network; Catalonia has official delegations in Brussels, Paris, and Perpignan as well as five cultural centres, two information centres, and thirty-eight business and trade offices abroad through the so-called COPCA; Extremadura maintains a delegation in Brussels and business and trade offices in Lisbon, London, New York, Buenos Aires, and Shangai; and the Community of Valencia has delegations in Brussels, Prague, Warsaw, and Vienna as well as twenty-three trade offices abroad. These networks are generally established through the initiative of the respective autonomous government, in partnership with chambers of industry and commerce, major regional business associations, universities, and banking institutions, among other private-sector organizations. The establishment of these networks has not been particularly controversial. With the exception of the Basque and Catalan official delegations, all these offices abroad adopt various vehicles of private law to avoid controversy and to facilitate more fruitful public and private partnerships.

In budgetary terms, the amount dedicated to international activities by the various autonomous communities is proportional to their respective economic strength but also determined by their international ambitions. In terms of public expenditure, Andalusia, Catalonia, and the Basque Country are particularly relevant. In 2006 Andalusia dedicated more than US$93 million to its international program, including $88 million solely to development aid. Also in 2006 Catalonia spent approximately US$84 million, including $66 million for development aid, and directly employed around 250 persons in the international field.[32] In the same year, the Basque Country spent US$70 million, including $50 million on development aid, and employed fifty staff members.[33]

A salient feature of the autonomous communities' international activism in the economic field is its competitive character. Cooperation among different communities rarely happens, except when they participate with other European regions in cross-border or interregional cooperation schemes. This competition is accentuated because the most dynamic communities – Catalonia, the Basque Country, and even Andalusia and the Canary Islands – prefer bilateral rather than multilateral negotiations with the central government. Aggressive competition among the communities is also growing in the field of business promotion and in the provision of incentives for foreign investment, frequently provoking complaints because of alleged violations of European competition law. Attempts to coordinate central-government trade policy more closely with autonomous communities' promotional activities have failed so far. This is because business associations and firms expect to obtain better treatment and more incentives when the communities compete among themselves. Consequently, multilateral lobbying of the central government has rarely been attempted by the autonomous communities, except in the case of more direct participation by the autonomous communities in the EU decision-making processes. Autonomous communities' international activities have generally been funded by public resources, but more recently some autonomous communities, particularly Madrid and Catalonia, have entered into partnerships with private firms having or seeking greater international exposure in a campaign to compete aggressively on the international scene. For instance, through close collaboration with the private sector, Catalonia mobilizes more than US$350 million for business and trade promotion abroad.

Another field in which autonomous communities are very active is cross-border relations. Relationships of Galicia, Castilla-Leon, Extremadura, and Andalusia with their various Portuguese counterparts are particularly extensive, as are relationships of the Basque Country, Navarre, Aragon, and Catalonia with French departments. Although these initiatives are generally very pragmatic and technical in the case of the Basque Country and Catalonia, and to a lesser extent Galicia, symbolic dimensions are also relevant because in both cases recognizable cultural affinities exist across the border. In addition to the existing bilateral agreements with France and Portugal, the legal basis of autonomous communities' involvement in cross-border relations is the Council of Europe's European Convention for Transborder Cooperation. This legal framework has greatly facilitated the establishment of transborder relations across Europe. However, the most important driving force for such initiatives is currently the European Union by virtue of programs like INTERREG, an initiative aimed at strengthening economic and social cohesion as well as balanced development in the EU by promoting cross-border, transnational, and interregional cooperation. Actions in relation to the borders between member states and between the EU and nonmember countries are therefore at the heart of such initiatives, particularly in the context of successive EU enlargements. The INTERREG initiatives are always co-financed by both the EU and the member states. Although the specific projects proposed by local and regional governments are submitted by the member states, the European Commission makes a financial allocation to each of them. The allocation is based primarily on border regions' population but also on other social indicators of the internal border areas of the EU, such as the border regions between Spain and France and between Spain and Portugal. But other priorities have been set for the so-called (in EU parlance) *ultraperipheral* regions like the Canary Islands, in the case of Spain, and the French overseas territories. For the period 2000–06, INTERREG III had a budget of more than US$5 billion, of which the amount initially proposed for Spain exceeded US$1 billion.[34]

Autonomous communities have also increasingly and innovatively become involved in development aid. According to a recent OECD survey on so-called "decentralized cooperation," the Spanish autonomous communities are the world's most active subnational units in this field. One-fifth of Spain's bilateral Official Development Assistance (ODA) is provided by regional governments (e.g., US$321 million in 2003), two-thirds of which is provided by autonomous communities and one-third by local governments. Data for 2003 identify more than 1,800 initiatives in eighty-one recipient countries, generally with the participation of NGOs. The Spanish Law on Development Cooperation of 1998 provides that Spanish local authorities can conduct "decentralized cooperation activities consistent with the international cooperation instituted by the Spanish State." This law stipulates that the Ministry of Foreign Affairs is to coordinate such initiatives by local authorities. Various mechanisms have been established to ensure the coordination and coherence of aid provided by the central administration and other actors. The Interterritorial Commission of Development Cooperation is the most important of these. In recent years, there has been a notable increase in development assistance from the autonomous communities, municipalities, and other local entities, to the extent that they represent more than one-third of Spain's nonreimbursable foreign aid. Nine of the seventeen autonomous communities have their own annual or multiyear development cooperation plans. Five autonomous communities, and some municipalities, have decided to earmark 0.7% of their budgets for development assistance.[35]

Catalonia, the Basque Country, Andalusia, Madrid, and Valencia are the most active in this field. In addition to offering funding for NGOs, some autonomous governments have established strong relationships with various UN agencies such as the UNDP, the UNHCR, UNITAR, UNESCO, and UNIFEM.[36] Contrary to the wishes of the central government, autonomous communities' involvement in foreign aid is rarely coordinated with national development aid programs. Their officials distrust the intentions of the central government, and they try to maintain their own programs free from the control and influence of the Spanish Agency for International Cooperation. In this field, it is worth mentioning that in contrast to some cases in the United States, the autonomous communities in Spain have never attempted to apply economic sanctions as a form of political pressure against foreign states or firms. However, they participate actively through different technical programs in institutional and democratic capacity building in the developing world. This is the case with Catalonia's cooperation with the UNDP in Colombia in the field of peace education and the Basque Country's partnership with UNITAR in the field of new information technologies and local and regional governance.

However, the international activities of the autonomous communities have generally not been impressive. Catalan and Basque efforts have generated resentment by the central government, but in most instances these initiatives have been deliberately discreet to avoid direct conflict with the Spanish government's foreign policy. In some cases, close collaboration among different orders of government has indeed been the best possible recipe. The 1992 Barcelona Olympic Games demonstrated close collaboration between the central and autonomous governments, resulting in a very successful outcome for both parties. Only very few exceptions have created serious political concern in Madrid, such as the failed attempt of the Basque Parliament to host a meeting of the Kurdish Assembly in Exile in 1999, which strongly irritated the Turkish ambassador to Spain. The case immediately provoked a conflict over competences between the central government and the Basque government that was later resolved when, as a result of the political controversy, the Kurdish Assembly formally declined to accept the Basque Parliament's invitation. More recently, Catalonia's decision to open an office in Warsaw devoted to selective contracting of Polish workers at their place of origin provoked some controversy. Given that legislation governing migration and aliens is an exclusive power of the state, the central government has expressed its concern, asking that this facility be closed or reorganized.

Finally, in contrast with Canada, Australia, and the United States, where the domestic implications of the WTO have been highly controversial, the implications for the constituent units of the new global trade regime remain almost completely ignored in the Spanish political debate. In a similar vein and in contrast with the cases of India, Argentina, and Brazil, Spanish constituent governments have not been affected in any specific form by the decisions of either the International Monetary Fund (IMF) or the World Bank.

In sum, until very recently, the international agenda of Spanish local and regional governments was concentrated almost exclusively on the controversies surrounding the EU integration process and the prominent attention devoted to development aid. They have addressed other international issues only rarely. But it can be said that over the past decades, Spain's constituent units have been involved in a learning process. As a result, their foreign relations are becoming more ambitious, more sophisticated, and more effective.

CONCLUSION

Although far from being exceptional in either form or content, the growing involvement of autonomous communities in foreign affairs is becoming an important feature of the Spanish political system. The Constitution indicates very clearly that international relations are the exclusive competence of the central government, but it seems that for both normative and functional reasons, this position will be difficult to sustain. The evolving jurisprudence of the Constitutional Court has increasingly opened new spaces for constituent-unit international activities. Moreover, a combination of legal and intergovernmental mechanisms has been created during the past decades to facilitate the necessary policy learning and to assure that these developments will not affect institutional stability and democratic legitimacy.

For some regions, developing a strong presence abroad has important symbolic appeal. But economic motivations have been the most powerful reasons behind autonomous communities' international activism. The impact of globalization and, more specifically, the implications of European integration have propelled all subnational governments, not only those with an ethno-nationalist profile, to intensify economic and political involvements abroad. Unlike constituent units in federal countries such as Germany and Belgium, Spain's autonomous communities have neither the political influence nor the legal power to veto any central-government foreign policy decisions, even when these fall within areas of their competence or affect their crucial interests. Consequently, they can address such issues only through intergovernmental coordination and institutional dialogue.

As in other European countries, constituent governments' participation in EU decision making has been at the heart of discussions over the foreign relations of the autonomous communities and has been mooted as a model for their international relations more generally. Spain's membership in the EU has significantly eroded the distinction between domestic and foreign matters and has resulted in challenges to the constitutional distribution of powers, thereby affecting previous attempts to accommodate territorial differences. Many powers previously held by autonomous governments have been transferred to the EU by the Spanish government by virtue of its exclusive powers over foreign policy. The increasing concern about this trend has encouraged regional elites to secure greater participation in EU matters. As a result of the learning process associated with these developments, autonomous governments have also urged the establishment of intergovernmental mechanisms that allow them to participate more or less directly in the foreign policy process, particularly when their own powers are affected. The formal establishment of the Sectoral Conference Relating to European Affairs in 1997 is at present the most relevant achievement, but new mechanisms are under development. Although for a long time the central government was reluctant to accede to such developments, the conduct of international relations by the autonomous communities is becoming a more accepted feature of the Spanish political system.

NOTES

1 Following the Spanish practice, we use the terms "Spain," "State of the Autonomies," or simply "state" as synonyms. "Central government" is equivalent to "federal government." "Autonomous communities" is the name for Spain's constituent units or regions. "Statutes of autonomy" is the term for the constituent units' own formal constitutions, which were all negotiated and approved after the adoption of the 1978 democratic Constitution by virtue of its provisions for territorial self-government.
2 As Luis Moreno has pointed out, Spain does not fully qualify as a federation, but certain features of the Spanish constitutional system lend support to its

quasi-federal nature: (1) Spain's autonomous system combines both "self-rule" and "shared rule"; (2) Spain is a democracy where two orders of government – central and regional – enjoy constitutionally separate powers and representative parliamentary institutions; (3) the Spanish Constitution is the source for the right of self-government by the autonomous communities whereby the authority of the regional layer is not a surrogate of the central government; (4) Spain is composed of seventeen autonomous communities, each and every one having democratic constitutional statutes of autonomy for their internal organization; (5) Spain's Constitutional Court is the ultimate arbiter for the demarcation of concurrent powers and government competences; and (6) the Spanish Parliament is bicameral with a Senate envisaged as a "territorial upper chamber." For the full elaboration of this argument, see Luis Moreno, *The Federalization of Spain* (London: Frank Cass, 2001).

3 Among the most relevant works, see Gurutz Jáuregui, *Comunidades Autónomas y Relaciones Internacionales* (Oñate: IVAP/HAEE, 1989); Manuel Pérez González, Fernando Mariño, and Francisco Aldecoa, eds, *La acción exterior y comunitaria de los Länder, Regiones, Cantones y Comunidades Autónomas* (Oñate: IVAP/HAEE, 1994); Jose Luis Prados Cuerdo, *La acción exterior de las comunidades autónomas: Teoría y práctica* (Madrid: Escuela Diplomática, 1995); Jorge Pueyo Losa and Maria Teresa Ponte Iglesias, *La actividad exterior y comunitaria de Galicia: La experiencia de otras comunidades autónomas* (Santiago de Compostela: Fundación Alfredo Brañas, 1997); Pablo Perez Tremps, ed., *La participación europea y la acción exterior de las Comunidades Autónomas* (Madrid: Marcial Pons, 1998); Carlos Conde, *La acción exterior de las Comunidades Autónomas: La institucionalización de gobiernos territoriales y la integración internacional* (Madrid: Tecnos, 2000); José Manuel Sobrino Heredia, ed., *La acción exterior de las Comunidades Autónomas* (Santiago de Compostela: Fundación Galicia Europa, 2001); and Carlos Fernández Casadevante, *La acción exterior de las comunidades autónomas: Balance de una práctica consolidada* (Madrid: Dilex, 2001).

4 For a basic but reflective overview of the Spanish constitutional system, see Shioban Harty, "Spain," in Ann L. Griffiths and Karl Nerenberg, eds, *Handbook of Federal Countries 2005*, 324–42 (Montreal and Kingston: McGill-Queen's University Press, 2005); Enric Argullol and Xavier Bernadí, "Kingdom of Spain," in Akhtar Majeed, Ronald L. Watts, and Douglas M. Brown, eds, *Distribution of Powers and Responsibilities in Federal Countries*, 238–64 (Montreal and Kingston: McGill-Queen's University Press, 2006); and Julio López-Laborda, Jorge Martínez-Vázquez, and Caralos Monasterio, "Kingdom of Spain," in Anwar Shah, ed., *The Practice of Fiscal Federalism: Comparative Perspectives*, 287–316 (Montreal and Kingston: McGill-Queen's University Press, 2007).

5 Spain regards the small African enclaves of Ceuta and Melilla as integral parts of its national homeland, not as colonial possessions. They are surrounded by Morocco, which views the Spanish presence as a colonial residue and claims sovereignty. Both enclaves acquired a new prominence in the 1990s as a result of the dramatic increase in illegal immigration from Africa and Asia. Spain also controls some tiny islets along the North African coast, including uninhabited Perejil, which was at the

centre of a serious diplomatic conflict in 2002 when Moroccan soldiers occupied it but were later removed by the Spanish army. However, these differences have not prevented the strengthening of relations between Morocco and Spain in recent years. In 2005 Spain and Morocco agreed to deploy extra troops to try to secure the borders.

6 In addition to the seventeen autonomous communities and two autonomous cities, Spain is also organized into fifty provinces. Provinces are responsible for coordinating local and central administration, but they also have their own fields of authority in areas such as judicial, economic, and technical assistance. Spain also has 8,092 local governments or municipalities.

7 Approximately one-fourth of Spain's population of 44 million are bilingual. Catalan and its variations are spoken by 4.2 million in Catalonia, 2.1 million in Valencia, and 0.2 million in the Balearic Islands; Basque is the language of 0.7 million in the Basque Country and 0.05 million in Navarre; and Galician is spoken by 2.3 million Gallegos. See José Carlos Herreras, *Lenguas y normalización en España* (Madrid: Gredos, 2006).

8 For more elaboration, see Luis Moreno, "Federalization in Multinational Spain," in Michael Burgess and John Pinder, eds, *Multinational Federations*, 86–107 (London: Routledge, 2007).

9 In Spain, the official title of the chief of government, or prime minister, is "president of government."

10 Enric Fossas has pointed out: "The main conditions for a political consensus in the current circumstances would basically be those which might contribute to ensuring a commitment between the nationalist minorities – Basque, Catalan, and Galician – and the Spanish nationalist majority. The idea of a *plurinational* state would be a solution because the nationalist minorities would be obliged to clarify their political demands, articulating them in a constitutional project … while the latter should recognise without reservation the necessary accommodation within the State of the historical nationalities and guarantee their right to make use of real political capacity for self-government." See Enric Fossas, "Asymmetry and Plurinationality in Spain," *Universitat de Barcelona/Institut de Ciencies Politiques i Socials Working Papers*, no. 167 (1999): 12. For contrasting positions on a plurinational Spain, see Francisco Javier Corcuera, "La articulación del Estado plurinacional desde el punto de vista constitucional," *Ebro: Revista aragonesista de pensamiento*, no. 2 (2000): 67–81; and Ferran Requejo, "Federalismo plurinacional y Estado de las Autonomías," *Ebro: Revista aragonesista de pensamiento*, nos 4–5 (2005): 99–108.

11 This brief economic overview is based on the very comprehensive insights in William Chislett, *The Internationalization of the Spanish Economy* (Madrid: Real Instituto Elcano, 2006).

12 In 2005 the autonomous communities' shares of Spain's population in decreasing order were Andalusia (7.9 million), Catalonia (7.1 million), Madrid (6 million), Valencia (4.8 million), Galicia (2.7 million), Castille and Leon (2.5 million), Basque Country (2.3 million), Canary Islands (1.95 million), Castille La Mancha

(1.93 million), Murcia (1.3 million), Aragon (1.2 million), Extremadura (1 million), Asturias (1 million), Balearic Islands (1 million), Navarre (0.6 million), Cantabria (0.5 million), La Rioja (0.3 million), and finally, the small autonomous cities of Ceuta (0.075 million) and Melilla (0.065 million). See the website of the Spanish National Institute for Statistics (INE): http://www.ine.es (accessed 20 December 2007).

13 In 2005 the autonomous communities' shares of Spanish GDP were Catalonia (18.6%), Madrid (17.7%), Andalusia (13.8%), Valencia (9.7%), Basque Country (6.1%), Galicia (5.1%), Castille and Leon (5.4%), Canary Islands (4%), Castille La Mancha (3.4%), Aragon (3.1%), Murcia (2.5%), Balearic Islands (2.5%), Asturias (2.2%), Extremadura (1.7%), Navarre (1.7%), Cantabria (1.3%), La Rioja (0.7%), and finally, the autonomous cities of Ceuta (0.1%) and Melilla (0.1%). See the website of the Spanish National Institute for Statistics (INE): http://www.ine.es (accessed 16 December 2007).

14 See OECD, *Economic Survey of Spain* (January 2007), http://www.oecd.org (accessed 13 December 2007).

15 This was pointed out in, among others, Benny Pollack, *The Paradox of Spanish Foreign Policy* (New York: St Martin's Press, 1987).

16 For a thoughtful analysis, see José I. Torreblanca, "Ideas, Preferences and Institutions: Explaining the Europeanization of Spanish Foreign Policy," *University of Oslo – ARENA Working Papers*, no. 26 (2001): http://www.arena.uio.no/publications/working-papers2001/papers/01_26.xml (accessed 13 December 2007).

17 See Frederik Fleurke and Rolf Willemse, "The European Union and the Autonomy of Sub-National Authorities: Towards an Analysis of Constraints and Opportunities in Sub-National Decision-Making," *Regional and Federal Studies* 16, no. 1 (2006): 83–98.

18 See Elise Roller, "Reforming the Spanish Senate: Mission Impossible?" *West European Politics* 25, no. 4 (2002): 69–92.

19 A comparative overview of the statutes of autonomy is available at the website of the Spanish Ministry for Public Administration: http://www.map.es/documentacion/politica_autonomica/estado_autonomico/estatutos_materias.html (accessed 20 December 2007).

20 In May 2006 the Canadian prime minister, Stephen Harper, and the Quebec premier, Jean Charest, signed an agreement between the two governments that will give Quebec an official representative in Canada's UNESCO office in Paris.

21 The English version of the new statute is available on the Government of Catalonia website: http://gencat.net (accessed 20 December 2007).

22 A critical but thoughtful account is given by Elisa Roller, "Conflict and Cooperation in EU Policy-Making: The Case of Catalonia," *Perspectives on European Politics and Society* 5, no. 1 (2004): 81–110.

23 According to the Spanish Ministry of Public Administration, in 2005 the pattern was as follows: Castilla-Leon participated five times in the EU Council of Ministers,

Catalonia four times, Andalusia and Madrid three times, Galicia and the Basque Country twice, and Asturias, Aragon, and Extremadura once. See http://www9.map.es/documentacion/politica_autonomica (accessed 10 December 2007).

24 See Caterina Garcia i Segura, "La participación de las comunidades autónomas españolas en las relaciones internacionales: Reflexiones sobre la presencia internacional de las comunidades autónomas históricas: Cataluña, Galicia y el País Vasco," in Tullo Vigevani, Walter Wanderley, and Marcelo Passini, eds, *A Dimensão Subnacional e as Relações Internacionais*, 211–49 (São Paulo: EDUC/Fundação Editora da UNESP, 2002).

25 See Alexander Ugalde Zubiri, "The International Relations of Basque Nationalism and the First Basque Autonomous Government (1890–1939)," in Francisco Aldecoa and Michael Keating, eds, *Paradiplomacy in Action: The Foreign Relations of Subnational Governments*, 170–84 (London: Frank Cass, 1999).

26 For a systematic account of the Basque Country's international relations, see José Luis de Castro and Alexander Ugalde, *La acción exterior del País Vasco (1980–2003)* (Oñati: IVAP/HAEE, 2003).

27 For Catalonia, see Caterina García i Segura, "Les stratégies internationales de la Catalogne: Nationalisme politique et pragmatisme économique," *Bulletin d'Histoire Politique* 10, no. 1 (2001): 99–109; and Stephane Paquin, *Paradiplomatie identitaire en Catalogne* (Quebec: Les Presses de l'Université Laval, 2003).

28 On international relations as a tool for nation building, see for the case of the Basque Country, André Lecours and Luis Moreno, "Paradiplomacy: A Nation-Building Strategy? A Reference to the Basque Country," in Alain-G. Gagnon, Montserrat Guibernau, and François Rocher, eds, *The Conditions of Diversity in Multinational Democracies*, 267–94 (Montreal: Institute for Research on Public Policy and McGill-Queen's University Press, 2003).

29 See Gloria Totoricagüena, "Diasporas as Non-Central Government Actors in Foreign Policy," *Nationalism and Ethnic Politics* 11, no. 1 (2005): 265–87.

30 See more detailed information at the website of Catalonia's Secretariat for Foreign Affairs: http://www.gencat.net/cooperacioexterior/cce_cast/index.htm (accessed 21 December 2007).

31 See the complete information at the website of Galicia's General Secretariat for Emigration: http://www.galiciaaberta.com (accessed 20 December 2007).

32 More detailed institutional information about Catalonia's international presence is available at http://www.gencat.net/cooperacioexterior/cce (accessed 13 December 2007).

33 See César Colino, "La acción internacional de las comunidades autónomas y su participación en la política exterior española," *OPEX Working Paper*, no. 10 (2007): 50–1. This document is available at the Fundacion Alternativas website: http://www.falternativas.org (accessed 20 December 2007).

34 See http://ec.europa.eu/regional_policy/interreg3/foire/faq1_en.htm (accessed 13 December 2007).

35 See OECD, "Aid Extended by Local and State Governments," *DAC Journal* 6, no. 4 (2005): 98. This document is also available at http://www.oecd.org/dataoecd/47/62/35935258.pdf (accessed 20 December 2007).
36 The United Nations Development Program, the United Nations High Commissioner for Refugees, the United Nations Institute for Training and Research, the United Nations Educational, Scientific and Cultural Organization, and the United Nations Development Fund for Women.

SWITZERLAND

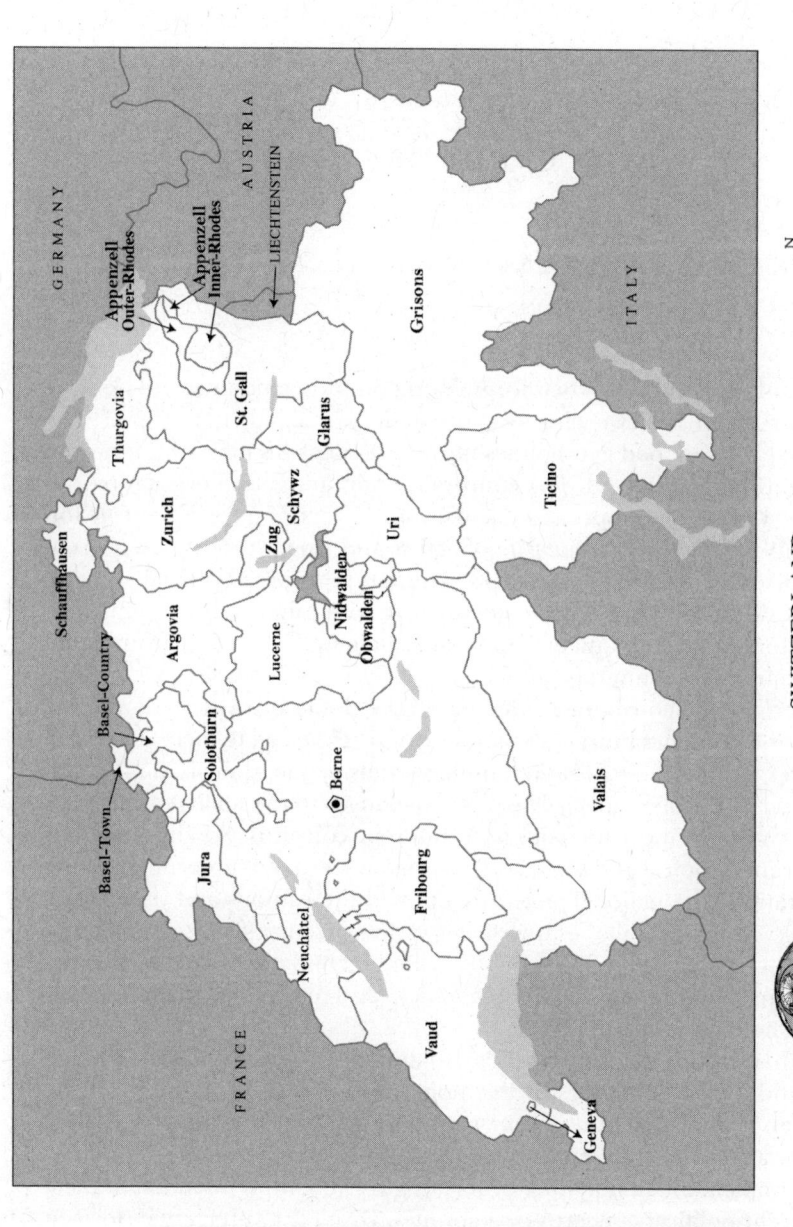

Capital: Bern
Population: 7.2 million (2002 est.)

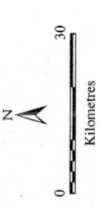

Swiss Confederation

DANIEL THÜRER AND MALCOLM MACLAREN

Switzerland was long renowned for insisting on independence and neutrality in its foreign policy, being described as "an island in Europe." The forces that have shaped geo-politics in the past decades have not, however, left Switzerland unaffected. The country is integrating itself ever more into the wider world. The approach taken by all orders of government to foreign relations has been increasingly active and open, moving away from isolationism and toward engagement. There is widespread official recognition that Switzerland will have to collaborate with other states and international actors in order to meet new policy challenges, from environmental threats to increasing migration.

As international collaboration increases, the domestic contestation of the conduct and content of foreign relations can be expected to increase as well. The forces of internationalization, multilateralism, and globalization[1] – and integration in Europe especially – pose challenges to the ability of the Swiss political system to meet the country's different concerns. Foreign relations have become a topical and sensitive issue for each order of government – the confederation (the national government) and the cantons and municipalities (the constituent units) – as well as for the citizenry. Their conduct and content directly concern Switzerland's self-perception as a member of the international community, as a democracy, and most important for our purposes here, as a federation.[2]

Foreign relations are in principle a national matter. Switzerland being Switzerland, however, powers in this policy area are also conferred on the cantons and municipalities as well as on "the people" (*das Volk*). A federal system, by allocating competences for the forming of opinion, decision making, and implementation among orders of government, is intended to meet the different political concerns in a country. Divided sovereignty in foreign relations has the potential, however, to become a source of tension in a federation and an obstacle to international cooperation. Switzerland has avoided these fates so far. The confederation, cantons, and municipalities have been considerate of each others' competences and interests in their dealings and have worked together to coordinate policy design and delivery. Where necessary, new arrangements have been created and existing powers modified. The question going forward is whether the relevant authorities will continue to demonstrate the reciprocity that the Swiss federal system demands and make use of the flexibility that it offers, especially if the country joins the European Union (EU).

More generally, the conduct and content of foreign relations in Switzerland are also important issues for the citizenry. Citizens are in this regard little concerned with traditional concepts of federalism and more concerned with the real effectiveness and ongoing democratic basis of government policies. As Switzerland engages ever more with the wider world, the country's political system may have to be reformed so that foreign relations do not give rise to serious citizen dissatisfaction.

THE SITUATION OF SWITZERLAND AND A HISTORY OF ITS FOREIGN POLICY

To understand the conduct and content of foreign relations in Switzerland, it is necessary to understand the domestic context. The country is above all characterized by diversity. Switzerland is not a nation in the traditional, ethnic-based sense; it is a *Willensnation*, crafted by the desire of its inhabitants to live together peacefully in their diversity. This diversity motivated the choice of political system upon the founding of the federal state in 1848 and has subsequently defined the politics of Switzerland, described as one of "overcoming divisions, fragility and internal conflict."[3] This desire and its institutional expressions must be renewed in keeping with changing circumstances to ensure the country's continuing success.

The nation's 26 cantons and 2,867 municipalities reflect a mosaic of languages (officially German, French, and Italian; semiofficially Romansh), religions (largely and evenly Roman Catholic and Protestant), and more broadly, cultures.[4] These divides in the Swiss citizenry contribute to different political concerns among the constituent units. The cantons (and municipalities) are, moreover, the product of different historical processes. Some have enjoyed a degree of sovereignty since the Middle Ages, while others were dependent on powers inside or outside present-day Switzerland into the nineteenth century. Finally, the cantons vary greatly in terms of territory, population, and economy; for example, the smallest canton in terms of territory (Basel-City) is more populous and economically powerful than the largest (Grisons). Although these differences among constituent units can cross-cut and offset one another, they can also exacerbate one another. There are, for example, clear fault lines in attitudes regarding integration in Europe between the smaller, rural, and conservative cantons (largely German-speaking) and the bigger, urban, and progressive cantons (especially French-speaking).

The country's geographical situation has also defined the conduct and content of foreign relations. In light of its relatively small area of 15.9 million square miles and population of 7.3 million people as well as its location in the centre of Europe, foreign policy has necessarily been made with Switzerland's larger neighbours in mind. This reality has had particular importance for constituent units that border Germany, France, Italy, and Austria due to natural social, economic, and environmental ties.

The diversity and location of Switzerland led in the past to foreign policymaking that emphasized the country's sovereignty. Extensive freedom in both external and internal decision making was considered necessary to maintain the country's identity. Although Switzerland was founded as a federal state, an extensive foreign policy competence was accorded to the confederation. The confederation was to shield the country from outside threats and entanglements through the army and diplomacy so that the country could attend domestically to its federal tradition. The cantons were to enjoy broad competences in many policy areas in recognition of their importance for Swiss citizens.

THE REGIONAL AND GLOBAL CONTEXT

Whereas the country's size and location traditionally led to an isolationist policy in matters of security and diplomacy, they have led in economic, cultural, and environmental policy areas to a more cooperative approach internationally. This duality in Swiss foreign policy is manifested in Swiss membership – or rather nonmembership – in various international intergovernmental organizations (IGOs).[5]

To elaborate, a fear of foreign threats from and of entanglements with other states led to a longstanding insistence on reciprocal noninterference in internal affairs. Potential centrifugal influences in the federation from culturally related neighbours were also to be minimized thereby.[6] Independence and neutrality became so integral to the country's legal order, political system, and sense of self that this policy has proven difficult to redefine in recent decades. With the revision of the Federal Constitution in 1999, however, Swiss foreign policy moved decisively from an exclusive concern with safeguarding the country's independence and welfare to broader concerns with alleviating world poverty; promoting respect for human rights, democracy, and the peaceful coexistence of nations; and preserving natural resources.[7] These broader concerns are considered to contribute to, not compromise, Swiss security.

Although Switzerland has sought to keep pace with the global geo-political changes following the Cold War and to play a role internationally, it has also sought to avoid being drawn into compromising military commitments. For example, although Switzerland signed onto the North Atlantic Treaty Organization's Partnership for Peace in 1996 to promote peace and security, it will withdraw if Swiss neutrality is threatened. Subsequent government proposals to deploy fully armed Swiss peacekeepers on missions of the United Nations and the Organization for Security and Cooperation in Europe as well as to cooperate more closely in military training with other countries provoked heated debate domestically and were only narrowly approved in a popular referendum in 2001.

The historic insistence on independence and neutrality, which long kept Switzerland out of many IGOs, has obscured the high degree of integration (especially economic) that has actually occurred. In matters of "low" as opposed to "high" politics, realism regarding the situation of Switzerland has demanded engagement by all orders of government with the wider world. From a functional perspective, it is no accident that Switzerland is a major international partner and player in economic and financial policy.[8] Switzerland has an inherent interest in promoting free trade, as it is located "at the crossroads of Europe" and is relatively poor in natural resources. This engagement contributed to an enviable per capita gross domestic product in 2007 of US$39,800. Likewise, cross-border environmental cooperation is well developed; ecological and other concerns call for joint management of internationally shared rivers and lakes.

This dualist approach to foreign policy and to membership in IGOs is most obvious in Switzerland's integration in Europe and in attitudes toward joining the EU. Switzerland is surrounded by EU member states[9] and is a close political, cultural, and economic[10] partner of the EU. Nonetheless, Switzerland is not a member. Switzerland has dealt with the supranational organization bilaterally, concluding a series of carefully negotiated agreements on defined areas of common interest.[11] Switzerland is a member of the European Free Trade Agreement, but its voters rejected membership in the European Economic Area (EEA) in 1992, which would have enabled Switzerland to participate in the Internal Market. This restrained integration in Europe in the form of traditional treaties concerned with trade and not politics is believed to best protect the country's freedom to act.

Swiss citizens, who have the last word on decisions about joining important IGOs, continue to be wary about membership in IGOs and about integration in Europe in particular, many strongly preferring that the country guard its distinctiveness and independence. Swiss citizens may be outward-looking on an individual basis (e.g., trading globally, travelling widely, and learning foreign languages eagerly), but they have been inward-looking in referenda regarding international integration, repeatedly rejecting or approving by narrow margins foreign policy proposals of the confederation. There has been a shift in their attitudes in the past years toward more interest in and engagement with the wider world.[12] Nonetheless, popular perceptions of contemporary reality and the appropriate policy response can still diverge sharply from official perceptions. As the capture of the largest share of the national vote in 2003 and 2007 by the isolationist Swiss People's Party (Schweizerische Volkspartei) demonstrated, the traditional governing parties have been unable to make the case for a fundamental reorientation of foreign policy. There continues to be a widespread belief in Switzerland as a politically unique country (*Sonderfall*). Popular support in favour of international integration is accordingly not guaranteed but must be fought for by governments each time anew.

THE CONSTITUTIONAL SETTING

The changed circumstances in which foreign relations are conducted were partly responsible for the revision of the Federal Constitution in 1999. As noted, Switzerland was founded as a federal state, and cantonal autonomy remains the basis of the federation. Article 3 of the Constitution has not been changed in the course of 150 years and 150 other partial revisions. It reads: "The Cantons are sovereign insofar as their sovereignty is not limited by the Federal Constitution; they shall exercise all rights which are not transferred to the Confederation."

The Constitution accordingly sets out the competences of the different orders of government. As also noted, an extensive foreign policy competence was exceptionally accorded to the confederation. Distinctions between foreign and domestic policy have, however, proven hard to maintain in the face of prevailing geo-political forces; today, "[v]irtually all political problems have a foreign policy dimension, whether with regard to their content or to the decision-making process."[13] From the 1980s at the latest, the danger that the cantons' competences would be hollowed out through the confederation's competence to conclude treaties concerning matters normally resting with the cantons became clear and pressing.[14] For example, the cantons feared (and continue to fear) that their competences in taxation, public procurement, and business support would be circumscribed through the confederation's extensive foreign policy competence and the country's international economic integration.[15] They accordingly began to exercise their rights in the federation more strongly, asserting that they have, and should have, powers and identities of their own. They demanded that their foreign policy role, particularly their participation in the foreign relations of the confederation, be systematized and strengthened. The cantons were closely involved in the revision of the Federal Constitution that ensued.

The new Constitution seeks to buttress the federal character of the country in the foreign policy area, as in others. The revision was concerned less with the allocation of competences in the federation and more with intergovernmental cooperation and the practical fulfilment of responsibilities.

In the first paragraph of the section concerning authority over relations with foreign countries, the new Constitution provides that foreign relations are a national matter (Art. 54, para. 1). Although this was effectively the case prior to the revision, the 1874 text did not contain such an explicit statement. There is no list of all matters belonging to "foreign relations" in the Constitution, but Article 54, paragraph 2, gives an indication of their breadth. One matter undoubtedly resting with the confederation is defence. As elaborated in Article 185, the Federal Council[16] is entitled to take measures to secure the external security, independence, and neutrality of Switzerland, including mobilizing the armed forces. Military matters are effectively national; only traces of cantonal sovereignty in this regard remain. In contrast, the cantons are primarily responsible for applying national law and enforcing law and order, and each canton maintains a police force. This traditional division of responsibilities for security between orders of government seems increasingly anachronistic. Inner security must to an extent be considered a military task today. Swiss security is threatened not by other countries' armed forces (particularly no longer by its neighbours) but by machinations of nonstate groups and asymmetric forms of fighting.

Despite the general rule that foreign relations are a national matter, the cantons' concerns about and openness to foreign relations are acknowledged in the Constitution. Indeed, the cantons made their approval of Article 54, paragraph 1, contingent on provisions for a right of consideration and, where appropriate, of participation in the confederation's conduct of foreign policy as well as for a certain leeway for their own foreign policy being included. The resultant power of the cantons regarding the conduct of foreign relations is among the most extensive of subnational units anywhere. Specifically,

- Article 54, paragraph 3, states that the confederation is, in its foreign relations, to take the competences of the cantons into consideration and to protect their interests. The principle of cooperative federalism and existing practice already foresaw the participation of the cantons in the *grosse Aussenpolitik* (the major foreign policy of the confederation). Nonetheless, the revised provision is a fundamental statement on the exercise of the confederation's power that informs the other provisions in the section and marks a decisive shift from dual to cooperative federalism.
- Article 55 requires the participation of the cantons in foreign policy decisions of the confederation that affect them. This implicitly includes those regarding the EU. In this circumstance, the confederation must inform the cantons fully and in a timely fashion and must solicit their opinion. The cantons' opinion is to be given particular weight when their competences are concerned; indeed, the cantons

are then entitled to participate in international negotiations in an appropriate manner (Art. 55, para. 3). This participation is not to inhibit the confederation's ability to conduct foreign policy.
- Article 56 allows the cantons to pursue their own relations abroad, a so-called *kleine Aussenpolitik*, or minor foreign policy. Cantons can deal directly with lower-ranking foreign authorities; in other cases, the relations of the cantons with foreign countries are to be[17] intermediated by the confederation. Cantons can also conclude treaties in conformity with their internal competences. Any such treaty must not be contrary to the laws and interests of the confederation and to the laws of other cantons, and the signing canton must inform the confederation prior to the treaty's conclusion. Although the cantons were allowed to pursue a *kleine Aussenpolitik* prior to 1999, this power was circumscribed.

Given this allocation of competences and these provisions for cooperation, what procedures for decision making in foreign affairs and defence in national institutions are foreseen in the Constitution? Foreign relations are primarily the responsibility of the federal Department of Foreign Affairs (EDA),[18] which is headed by the Swiss foreign minister. (Within the EDA, responsibility for coordinating the confederation's European policy rests with the Integration Office.) The Federal Council represents Switzerland abroad, including in the negotiation of treaties. It nominates and instructs the Swiss delegation, provides delegation members with signing authority, and is entitled to ratify the signed treaty (Art. 184).

The Federal Assembly for its part has the constitutional right only to accept or reject the treaty in question (Art. 166). The Federal Assembly and its foreign affairs committees are otherwise entitled to participate in Swiss foreign policymaking by virtue of rights to be informed and heard on the entire range of matters in this policy area. Due to the growing importance of foreign policy in government activities, the Federal Council has effectively gained power at the expense of the Federal Assembly. This power shift to the executive from the legislature appears to constitute a serious loss of democracy in the political system.

Be that as it may, these participatory rights of the Federal Assembly do not ensure constituent-government representation in foreign policymaking in national legislative institutions. Members of the Council of States, the second chamber of the Federal Assembly, are not under instruction from cantonal governments but are popularly elected. As a result, cantonal interests find expression at most in the Council of States generally. More significant is the right that cantons have to be consulted regarding important treaties, just as they do during the preparation of important legislation or other substantial projects (Art. 147). The cantons can make their position(s) in this framework clear.

A special feature of the Swiss political system as regards the conduct of foreign relations is that important decisions may be subject to a referendum. Proposals to join organizations for collective security or supranational communities are automatically subject to a referendum. Certain categories of treaties are subject to a referendum at the request of 50,000 eligible voters or eight cantons. The citizenry's and the cantons' role in the confederation's foreign policymaking is thereby strengthened, especially in the case of the mandatory referendum, as it requires a double majority of the people and the cantons for approval.

In the area of foreign policy, as in other policy areas, the confederation largely delegates the implementation of its laws (including treaties that it has concluded)[19] to the cantons.[20] The cantons must undertake in due time the measures necessary to conform to international laws that concern them,[21] as they must do regarding national legislation.

The confederation is generally obligated to respect cantonal autonomy and is in the present context obligated to leave the cantons with as much leeway as possible and to take into account differences among them (Arts 47 and 46 respectively). The key role of the cantons is made clear by the choice of the term implementation (*Umsetzung*) rather than execution (*Vollzug*) in the Constitution, which foresees a policy-formation task and not mere administration.

Whereas the cantons are subject to national lawmaking internationally, the confederation is practically dependent on the cantons domestically. Federal institutions do not generally have the means to implement foreign policy; they must rely on cantonal cooperation. Swiss federalism functions in this respect, as in others, primarily according to co-responsibility and dialogue. Constitutional principles such as *Bundestreu* (federal comity) affect in turn the constituent governments' propensity to implement treaties concluded by the confederation.

INTERGOVERNMENTAL RELATIONS IN FOREIGN AFFAIRS

The constitutional articles prescribing the conduct of foreign relations would be worth little more than the paper that they are written on without complementary legislation, arrangements, and capacities. These structures must in turn remain adaptable to changes wrought by prevailing geopolitical forces. Integration in Europe has in particular shaped relations between the confederation, the cantons, and the municipalities, leading to the modification of existing structures and to the creation of new ones.

Before these structures are examined, it must be emphasized that the success of Swiss federalism depends not only on such "tangibles" but also on "intangibles." To be efficient and effective, the constitutional and legal provisions must be applied by each order of government in keeping with the principles of subsidiarity[22] and cooperative federalism,[23] as well as with mutual consideration and support.[24] These principles constitute long-standing ideals of the political system, but they have grown in importance as cantonal autonomy has diminished. In short, without the *esprit fédérale* (i.e., the internalization of these principles by the different orders of government in their interactions), federalism cannot succeed in meeting the different concerns of the country.

Relations between the Confederation and the Cantons

The 1999 constitutional revision was accompanied by a legislative revision in this policy area, namely the Federal Law on the Participation of the Cantons in the Foreign Policy of the Confederation (BGMK). This law provides for intergovernmental cooperation in foreign relations, as codified in Article 55 of the new Constitution. It attempts to balance interest in an effective and efficient foreign policy with respect for cantonal opinions and for Swiss federalism more generally.

The second dimension of the foreign policy role of the cantons is complemented by another formal, but nonconstitutional, arrangement. Article 56's provisions regarding a *kleine Aussenpolitik* have been realized by international agreements that Switzerland, with the consent of the cantons, has signed obligating countries to facilitate cross-border collaboration between their constituent territorial bodies, including granting them the right to conclude agreements. The foundational international agreement in this respect is the Madrid Agreement.[25] In the Karlsruhe Agreement, Switzerland, Germany, France, and Luxembourg went further, recognizing territorial bodies' right to conclude agreements without additional authority or approval of other orders of government.[26]

Various institutional mechanisms have been developed to ensure effective cooperation between the confederation and the cantons as a whole. These include the Confederation-Canton Contact Body, the Coordination Commission, and the Conference of Cantonal Governments (CdC). Their development has been spurred by the issue of Swiss integration in Europe.

As noted, the confederation is obligated to provide the cantons timely information about any foreign policy plans it has that are of significance for them. It sends the cantons a list of such plans every half-year, and the cantons are entitled to request particulars. The Federalist Dialogue – a regular meeting between a confederal delegation and cantonal representatives – also plays an important role in meeting the confederation's obligation to provide the cantons with information (and vice versa).

The confederation consults with the cantons prior to and during negotiations in IGOs or with other states when the cantons are affected or sometimes on its own initiative. The way that the cantons participate in international negotiations is determined by the confederation in widest possible agreement with the cantons. When cantonal representation in a Swiss negotiations delegation is considered appropriate, the cantons propose and the confederation decides the staffing (Art. 5 BGMK). Direction of the delegation remains with the confederation, even if a cantonal representative is appointed its head.

The confederation and individual cantons can engage in foreign activities together – for example, when the activity in question affects only particular regions of the country. Since Swiss federalism is based on the equality of the cantons, however, the confederation cannot exclude other cantons in a comparable position that wish to join in.

Direct participation of the cantons in IGOs is little to nonexistent. Even in the EU, the possibilities for cantons to formally influence supranational decision making are limited. The cantons accordingly prefer membership to bilateralism as an approach to Switzerland's integration in Europe. Membership would, they believe, open channels of influence for them at the European level: the EU would be receptive to making provision for cantonal concerns, as it seeks to be closer to the citizens and to allow expression of national identities.

In short, the confederation and the cantons depend on one another for the coming into being, approval, and implementation of treaties with the EU or other countries. They must rely heavily on cooperative federalism working effectively. The reality of these intergovernmental relations is illustrated by the history of the aforementioned Bilateral Agreements. In the context of the Bilateral Agreements I, the confederation included cantonal representatives in the negotiations delegations from the outset. Moreover, the cantons were offered – and accepted – the possibility of accrediting a liaison officer in the Integration Office of the confederation. In the context of the Bilateral Agreements II, the cantons closely followed the negotiations in Berne and Brussels and engaged in consultations about them through the CDC. The cantons then came out strongly in favour of the agreements, helping the confederation to win parliamentary and public votes. Today, the confederation depends on the cantons for the practical (as well as legal) implementation of the Bilateral Agreements II, especially as regards police cooperation.

Relations between the Cantons

The cantons have responded to the foreign policy challenge in keeping with their interests and capabilities, individual and collective. Here, the great differences in situation and size between the cantons come into play.

Individually, the cantons show varying degrees of interest in foreign affairs, with many cantons long being little interested. Even today, the importance that they as a whole accord foreign affairs is limited; only a few cantons have, for example, created a separate department of foreign affairs headed by a senior civil servant (e.g., Vaud and Jura).

However strong their interests may be, actual engagement of the cantons in foreign policy is conditioned by their resources and capacities. Cantonal collaboration with the confederation in the framework of Article 55 typically occurs through special coordination units found in the cantonal chancellery (*Staatskanzlei*). Herein lies potential for problems in intergovernmental relations. The provision for extensive cantonal participation in the confederation's foreign policy risks preventing the confederation from reacting quickly enough to developments internationally, especially if the responsible cantonal personnel are not "up to speed." The cantons must support the confederation through competent and informed personnel as well as through reliable structures for cooperation.

The cantons are constitutionally prohibited from entering joint agreements if these are contrary to the rights of other cantons (Art. 48, para. 3). Regardless, the tendency has been for the cantons to exercise their rights to participate in the foreign policy decisions of the confederation collectively due to their commonality of interests, the need for consensus, and the resultant gains in efficiency and expertise.

The cantons coordinate their transborder activities within Switzerland in various conferences. Foremost among these is the CdC. The cantons set up the CdC in 1993 to develop common positions and present them to the confederation, especially regarding European policy. They also wished then, as now, to be considered real partners, co-responsible for Swiss foreign policy. At first, there was general skepticism about the CdC's ability to develop common positions. Foreign policy matters, especially integration in Europe, can produce tensions between cantons due to the cantons' often fundamentally divergent individual interests.

During the negotiation of the Bilateral Agreements II, however, the CdC demonstrated an ability to react quickly and to speak with one voice. Since the CdC has become a successful lobbyist for the cantons and an important dialogue partner of the confederation, attention has shifted to the legitimacy of its role in the confederation's foreign policy. The goals, aims, and workings of the CdC have been defended by some as legally consistent with the constitutional mandate of the cantonal governments and as an efficient and effective institution of intercantonal collaboration. In contrast, the emergence of an institution that is based on a contractual agreement among cantonal governments, that operates largely among them to the exclusion of cantonal assemblies, and that is little known by the public as a pivotal player in a policy area already renowned for thin popular bases has been criticized by others as democratically unsupportable. This difference of opinion concerning the CdC's legitimacy has taken concrete form in debates over making formal provision for the cdc in the federation and over including more than just the cantonal executives in its operation.

Relations between the Confederation, Cantons, and Municipalities

Two of every three Swiss live in an urban agglomeration, and six of the eight largest agglomerations border on foreign countries. The increased importance of the municipalities in the political life of Switzerland was formally acknowledged in the revision of the Constitution. The new Article 50 makes the tripartite federation explicit. Paragraph 1 guarantees municipal autonomy if a population centre is granted the status of a municipality by cantonal law. The confederation is obligated to take into consideration the effects of its activities on municipalities (para. 2) and in particular on cities and agglomerations (para. 3). This obligation encompasses the confederation's conduct of foreign relations.

The municipalities' transborder cooperation has contributed to the denser networks between Switzerland and other countries. Swiss cities and communes have pursued public transport, sewage, and similar projects with their neighbours on an administrative level and are positioning themselves internationally as places to live, work, and study. As with the cantons, the growing number and range of the municipalities' foreign activities are explained largely by functional concerns. The transborder nature of contemporary public issues favours transborder cooperation in their management, and global pressures demand that municipalities' interests be deliberately promoted abroad as well as at home.

This *ganz kleine Aussenpolitik* (very small foreign policy of the municipalities) is also significant for the federation, especially as regards European integration. Indeed, given the commonality of concerns and the requirement for close cooperation among orders of government, there is arguably now one foreign policy and no longer three. The municipalities must be careful not to exceed their authority. Just as they expect not to be unduly hindered by the confederation and cantons, they must heed the laws and interests of the federal and cantonal governments in their efforts at transborder cooperation.

CONSTITUENT GOVERNMENT DIPLOMACY

The cantonal governments have pursued their own foreign relations in diverse ways. Some cantonal governments appreciate the opportunities provided them by the Constitution and the confederation. These engage in cross-border "housekeeping" and pursue economic interests internationally rather than assert their cultural or political identity abroad.[27] The cantons as a whole have not, however, made full use of their powers. The primary aim of the cantons as regards foreign policy seems to be to maintain their influence in domestic policy. For their part, citizens show limited interest and are little involved in their cantonal governments' foreign activities, viewing such efforts generally with skepticism.[28]

Historical and Contemporary Context

As noted, the revision of the Constitution represented more a confirmation of existing practice and doctrine than a reallocation of competences in the area of foreign policy. The previous constitutional provision regarding transborder cooperation by the cantons had been circumscribed. (Such cooperation was to relate to a limited range of subject matters, and any treaties resulting from it required the confederation's approval.) In practice, however, the cantons already had various possibilities for transborder cooperation, the confederation had adhered to a generous policy in this regard, and the resultant cooperation had in some cases been many-sided and intense. Nonetheless, the cantonal desire for an explicit, wider-reaching foreign policy competence grew as cantonal autonomy diminished in other respects. This desire was fanned by the rejection of Swiss membership in the EEA in the 1992 referendum, which shifted the focus to developing other forms of transborder cooperation.

Since the 1999 revision, the confederation has continued to give the cantons leeway in their direct dealings with foreign authorities, recognizing that their concerns may be thereby better dealt with. The *kleine Aussenpolitik* is considered to produce policy that is more custom-tailored than that designed in Berne. Indeed, the confederation is active only in a few areas of regional, cross-border cooperation. The EDA tends to restrict itself to providing political assistance. It signs international treaties in the name of or together with the cantons, strives for optimal framework conditions (e.g., through the conclusion of the Karlsruhe Agreement), supports projects with bilateral and multilateral political instruments (e.g., the INTERREG-Framework Credit),[29] and meets with the foreign ministries of neighbouring countries to facilitate information flow and dispute resolution.

Having said that, there are clear bounds to how active a foreign policy role the confederation will allow the cantons. The confederation has made little use of the possibility of delegating to the cantons the authority to conclude treaties with foreign states or of mandating a cantonal representative to represent its interests at the European level when the discussions concern the cantons. Cantonal representatives are not located in Swiss diplomatic missions, and the missions do not have officers responsible for working with the country's constituent governments.

More significant, as the confederation is legally responsible internationally for the treaties of the cantons, it must oversee them. Cantonal treaties once had to be approved by the confederation. The cantons are now obligated merely to inform the confederation prior to their conclusion (Art. 56, para. 2). The Federal Council retains the right, however, to raise objections to cantonal treaties.[30] The protection of the interests of the confederation extends beyond a ban on treaties that are contrary to the Constitution or federal law to include the requirement for a "certain foreign policy appropriateness." The treaties are not to stand in the way of the interests of Switzerland as a whole. They are to be limited to traditional functions, especially to matters of local concern, and are not to attempt a *grosse Aussenpolitik.*

The foreign activities that the cantons undertake individually can be competitive, in that some are zero-sum games (e.g., attracting particular foreign enterprises and individuals to their jurisdictions).[31] Governments are also naturally concerned to outperform other cantons in any comparison lest their popularity suffer. Cantonal agreements may not, however, be contrary to the law of other cantons (Art. 56, para. 2).

In terms of the permissible content of cantonal foreign activities, the power to conduct foreign economic policy rests with the confederation. It is founded upon the confederation's general competence to make treaties and to conduct foreign policy, and it includes competence for trade measures and economic sanctions. Concurrent cantonal powers exist only within precise limits, which comprise supporting humanitarian organizations and assisting developing countries. Participation of the cantons in the formulation of foreign economic policy, let alone formal participation in related IGOs, is not foreseen. Constituent governments (collectively or individually) must lobby the confederation to get their views heard on international commercial negotiations.[32] Likewise, the legality of constituent-government efforts to project influence internationally on normative issues is highly doubtful. The aspirations expressed in the constitutions of various cantons to contribute to understanding and cooperation among peoples beyond their borders seem unobjectionable. When, however, such efforts *in concreto* infringe an exclusive competence of the confederation, they are forbidden, as the cantons are not to prejudice the relations of Switzerland with foreign states.[33]

Domestic and International Manifestations

Some cantons, especially those bordering on foreign countries, highly value the ability to pursue cross-border cooperation projects actively, in a targeted manner, and with maximum flexibility. These cantons see the *kleine Aussenpolitik* as a means not merely to solve problems but to realize common opportunities. Nonetheless, the cantons in general have far from exhausted the extensive possibilities provided them by the Constitution and the confederation of engaging in relations with international actors. The conclusion of treaties and other official business of the cantons with foreign jurisdictions takes place principally via the confederation. Given that smaller and weaker cantons are less able to pursue an active foreign policy, more telling is the priority that their representatives attach to this policy area. The cantons as a whole are not concerned with the "wide world." For example, executive speeches and proclamations dealing directly with international political issues tend to be exceptional. The cantons do participate in European institutions, especially in the Assembly of European Regions. Their foreign activities tend to focus, however, on regional and cross-border themes, as manifested in the typical allocation of competence for the conduct of such activities to the relevant domestic departments (e.g., justice and economic development) rather than to a separate department. Further, international agreements concluded by the cantons remain few in number in absolute terms; represent a very small share of cantonal laws; concern a limited range of matters, namely the living and working environment; and are concluded almost exclusively with neighbouring jurisdictions. Finally, although the cantons have the constitutional opportunity to pursue foreign contacts, including official visits and permanent representatives, their governments have made little to no use of this opportunity. Swiss cantons as such are, for example, not represented abroad.

Although the cantons have not made full use of their powers to pursue a *kleine Aussenpolitik*, their exercise of these powers does take many forms. Unfortunately, it is not possible here to list all regional and cross-border organizations in which constituent governments participate[34] or to detail all their foreign activities.[35] General remarks and some illustrations will be offered instead.

The agreements of the cantons take a variety of forms, extending well beyond the traditional international legal form of the treaty to include everything that is practically necessary for the fulfilment of responsibilities, for collaboration, and for partnership. (Indeed, the legal status of some constituent governments' agreements with foreign jurisdictions is unclear.) The agreements can prescribe the rights and duties of the relevant authorities or of private parties. As regards signatories, agreements may be reached between governments or administrations. The subject matter can be factual or organizational. Finally, the attributes themselves of individual agreements may change over time.

In addition to collaboration foreseen in individual agreements concluded by the cantons, considerable collaboration occurs within cross-border government commissions and cross-border agencies set up by the confederation and foreign jurisdictions or by the cantons and foreign jurisdictions, respectively. To be more specific:

- Joint government commissions exchange information and make recommendations to their respective national authorities. Two categories of commission exist. Consultative commissions are based on international agreements and deal with regional topics and relations between neighbours in a border region. There are currently consultative commissions for the Geneva and the Upper Rhine regions. They have no decision-making powers. The confederation in the form of the EDA provides administrative services. Special commissions are based on bilateral treaties and deal with specific, clearly delineated tasks (such as cultural exchanges and public-transport fare partnerships). They meet as and when required. Around forty of these commissions exist today, and the EDA is a member of some.
- Within the cross-border agencies, the cantons pursue joint projects and conduct a regular dialogue with the territorial authorities of neighbouring states. Some agencies include parliamentary bodies. Their primary concerns are matters for which the cantons are wholly or partly responsible (e.g., transport, environmental protection, infrastructure, and disaster relief). The EDA is generally represented in these agencies as an observer or a permanent guest. Cross-border agencies have been created for the following regions: Upper Rhine, Lake Constance, Grisons, Ticino, Valais, Lake Geneva, and Jura. The International Lake Constance Conference is particularly noteworthy. This border region, which comprises constituent units of Switzerland, Germany, and Austria, as well as Liechtenstein, has long been engaged in a broad and deep integration, and the extent of integration today demonstrates the potential of the *kleine Aussenpolitik*.

The subject matter of constituent-government diplomacy differs according to the level at which the diplomacy occurs. At the European level, the cantons are part of wider efforts to develop a "Europe of the Regions," a governance arrangement that speaks to Swiss concepts of citizen proximity, subsidiarity, and federalism. At the regional level, themes such as regional planning, education, environment, and tourism constitute the focus of representatives. At the cross-border level, matters include urban and rural development, infrastructure, resource use, and interpersonal contacts.[36]

Some of these policy concerns are also cross-cutting (implicating different orders of government), such as cultural and economic promotion. Promotion of culture in Switzerland is entrusted largely to the cantons and municipalities. Article 69, paragraph 1, states that culture is a cantonal matter. The Constitution does, however, provide that the confederation may support cultural activities of nationwide interest beyond cantonal borders (Art. 69, para. 2). The public actors in Swiss cultural diplomacy comprise Pro Helvetia (the Arts Council of Switzerland), which works directly with foreign partners; the EDA, which supports cultural activities through project funding as well as through its diplomatic missions and transport facilities; the constituent units themselves, which facilitate international partnerships; and related cantonal and municipal organizations like universities and museums, which engage in their own cooperation.[37] Although cultural promotion by the constituent units gives expression to local identity, these units are not seeking to achieve recognition abroad of distinct "national" identity.

As noted, the power to conduct foreign economic policy rests with the confederation. The constituent governments can nonetheless promote themselves by various means as a place to do business. Within the leeway granted them to implement the treaties of the confederation liberalizing trade (e.g., the Bilateral Agreements), they can more or less proactively remove border obstacles for their citizens and the local economy, thereby encouraging the free movement of goods, services, capital, and people. Further, they are entitled to enact laws and promulgate relations to attract investment, enterprises, and individuals from abroad as expressions of their longstanding authority over business support, taxation, and citizenship. Finally, the cantons can and do undertake these activities on their own as well as with national officials, the private sector, and nonprofit and civic organizations.

The approaches of Basel-City and Zurich to foreign activities are illustrative of those cantons pursuing an active foreign policy but not, as noted, of all cantons.

- The canton of Basel-City cooperates above all with its neighbours in various cross-border institutions. These institutions concern themselves with the local universities, regional planning, and transport, among other policy areas. They bring together a mix of parliamentarians, government leaders, municipal representatives, and administrators, with or without the participation of private parties. The cooperation that takes place varies from one institution to another, as does the geographical range of the institutions.
- The canton of Zurich is of particular interest in this context for its foreign commercial strategy. The canton's cross-border cooperation is principally aimed at making the area more attractive for business and for realizing mutual projects with neighbouring regions. (Zurich cooperates closely with Baden-Württemberg, jointly organizing annual conferences for Swiss and German enterprises.) Cooperation with other regions is intended to broaden perspectives, build contacts, and open

doors for local business. (The canton is notably a member of the World Cities Alliance.) Finally, the canton cooperates with other cantons and local enterprises in the framework of the Greater Zurich Area AG, a public-private partnership that promotes the eponymous economic area abroad through offices in Germany, the United States, and Japan.

Public Participation and Public Attitudes

The foreign activities of cantons tend to be executive-driven. The participation of cantonal parliaments is limited, and these rarely discuss and pass resolutions on international political issues. Indeed, members of cantonal governments have been accused in this context of confusing themselves at times with the cantons as a whole.

The way that foreign policy is conducted in the constituent units (and, as noted, in the confederation) raises concerns about democracy in the political system. Not only has there been a power shift to the executive from the legislature, but there also seems to be a discrepancy between the actual international cooperation of Swiss governments at all levels and the official explanation of and the public participation in this cooperation. Government representatives have been unable to engage citizens consistently in foreign policy discussions and to convince them of the need to reorient the policy itself.

Citizens are much attached to their cantons, but they attach little importance to their cantons' foreign activities. When public debates on issues of international relations do take place within cantons, they relate to particular local concerns that have an international dimension. Cantons (and municipalities) have yet to arouse real interest among their citizens in their foreign activities. Indeed, they must fight against the considerable public perception that the additional effort and expense involved in transborder cooperation is a waste of their taxes. When developing cooperation structures, authorities are accordingly advised to prioritize projects that the public can appreciate and to maintain a sense of proportion and efficiency.

The changing circumstances in which foreign policy is conducted demand greater accountability on the part of the bodies responsible. The foreign activities of Swiss governments are increasingly numerous and have become increasingly important for the everyday life of citizens. Considerations of effectiveness also advise greater accountability. As the head of the department responsible for the foreign activities of Basel-City observed, "[t]rans-border cooperation may be so important and good, but that is of little use if it has a bad reputation in the media and the population."[38] Foreign policy should no longer be treated as special among government competences but should be opened up like domestic policy through mechanisms for public participation, transparency, and official justification.

The preceding has in fact been perceived by some constituent-unit authorities. They realize that the public must be convinced of the rationale for and the goals of transborder cooperation and that it must be integrated into and actively support related efforts. These authorities accordingly take pains to explain why the government is engaging in transborder cooperation and to include all parties affected, such as business and community organizations, in policymaking.

OUTLOOK

Swiss federalism attempts to strike a balance between self-rule and shared rule. The constitutional revision of 1999 sought to counter a centralization induced by Switzerland's increasingly active and open foreign policy that threatened to upset this balance. Above all, it provided the cantons with more opportunities to participate in the confederation's conduct of foreign relations. The tension in the early 1990s between the confederation and the cantons regarding foreign policy seems to have been resolved for the time being; intergovernmental relations are again working according to the principle of cooperative federalism. The conduct and content of foreign relations are today contentious issues more in civil society; many citizens feel they are not participating in and benefitting from the activities of all three orders of government as they should be. Swiss foreign policy must prove itself to be representative as well as coherent and effective.

To be more specific, foreign relations are a national matter in Switzerland. The confederation, particularly the Federal Council, has the responsibility for and leadership in their conduct. This mandate, however, is an "integrated" mandate. A role for the cantons is foreseen in revised constitutional provisions regarding relations with foreign countries. These provide for the confederation to respect cantonal competences and interests, for the participation of the cantons in foreign policy decisions of the confederation, and for relations between the cantons and foreign countries. The constitutional provisions supplement the instruments traditionally available to the cantons to influence domestic policymaking by the confederation.

The Federal Council has generally viewed self-rule and shared rule in foreign relations as advantageous for both the confederation and the cantons. A recent Swiss foreign minister described this divided sovereignty in the forming of opinion, decision making, and implementation as a win for all Swiss citizens and a loss for none.[39] For their part, the cantons believe that their participation in the confederation's foreign policy and their relations with foreign countries enhance democratic co-determination, the attachment of citizens to their local authority, and the legitimacy of foreign policy generally.

If, as argued, prevailing forces have led to a reform of Swiss foreign relations in general, the country's integration in Europe is doing so in particular. Switzerland's relationship with the EU has been and will for the foreseeable future remain the major concern of foreign policy. It could have dramatic effects on Swiss federalism. In light of the confederation's comprehensive treaty-making competence, the broad scope of matters concerned, and the EU's own legislative and quasi-legislative power, integration in Europe again raises the specter of centralization in the Swiss federation. (Specifically, the cantons fear they will not be able to control developments or to maintain their autonomy but will be reduced to the role of administrators, taking instructions from Berne and Brussels. They fear even more that cantonal competences may be transferred wholesale to the confederation and the EU.) Accordingly, representatives of the cantons argue that upon joining the EU, the institutional foundations of the Swiss political system will have to be reformed to compensate the cantons for lost policymaking leeway.

At all events, the success of Swiss federalism in coping with internationalization, multilateralism, and globalization will depend in part on how well the mechanisms for the conduct of foreign relations function. Federalism cannot be allowed to interfere with Swiss governments' ability to act internationally. In this policy area, as in others, tasks in the federation must be executed efficiently and policies developed that meet the needs of the citizenry. The relevant authorities are, at a minimum, called upon to show pragmatism in the conduct of foreign relations. This means being open to dealing with concerns in ways that may not strictly conform to existing laws but that are functionally effective. (The benefits of *sui generis* rules or gentlemen's agreements in intergovernmental arrangements have, for example, been demonstrated as regards constituent units' cross-border cooperation.) Foreign policy might then be made that is more appropriate to the matters concerned and more expressive of citizens' wishes.

Traditional concepts of federalism and the conventional way of conducting foreign relations in Switzerland are being challenged not only by the pressure of practical problems and the popular concern for their solution but also by a worrying power shift in government. As the country's international collaboration increases, so does the power of the executive and the administration at the expense of the legislature and by extension the *Volk*. Many Swiss accordingly feel that they are being deprived of their right to form an independent opinion in foreign policy by elites and impersonal forces. They express a widespread lack of trust in the country's foreign policy mechanisms. This power shift and the popular concern with it have to be addressed through a reform of prevalent concepts and institutions in order to ensure the democratic legitimacy of governance in this policy area.

NOTES

1 We mean by "internationalization" the new penetration of state borders and growing international interdependence; by "multilateralism," the legalization and institutionalization of international politics; and by "globalization," the increase in and intensification of borderless interactions (e.g., economic, social, and technological). Further, see Bernhard Ehrenzeller, Rudolf Hrbek, Giorgio Malinverni, and Daniel Thürer, "Federalism and Foreign Relations," in Raoul Blindenbacher and Arnold Koller, eds, *Federalism in a Changing World*, 53–73 (Montreal and Kingston: McGill-Queen's University Press, 2003), 57–60.

2 Generally on Swiss federalism, see Nicolas Schmitt, "Swiss Confederation," in John Kincaid and G. Alan Tarr, eds, *Constitutional Origins, Structure, and Change in Federal Countries*, 347–80 (Montreal and Kingston: McGill-Queen's University Press, 2005); Thomas Fleiner, "Swiss Confederation," in Akhtar Majeed, Ronald L. Watts, and Douglas M. Brown, eds, *Distribution of Powers and Responsibilities in Federal Countries*, 265–94 (Montreal and Kingston: McGill-Queen's University Press, 2006); Wolf Linder and Isabelle Steffen, "Swiss Confederation," in Katy Le Roy and Cheryl Saunders, eds, *Legislative, Executive, and Judicial Governance in Federal Countries*, 289–315 (Montreal and Kingston: McGill-Queen's University Press, 2006); and Gebhard Kirchgassner, "Swiss Confederation," in Anwar Shah, ed., *The Practice of Fiscal Federalism: Comparative Perspectives*, 317–43 (Montreal and Kingston: McGill-Queen's University Press, 2007).

3 Jürg Martin Gabriel, *The Price of Political Uniqueness: Swiss Foreign Policy in a Changing World*, Beiträge Nr 38, Center for International Studies, ETH Zürich (December 2002), 4.

4 According to the Federal Census of 2000, among the resident population of Switzerland, 63.7% speak German, 20.4% French, 6.5% Italian, 0.5% Romansh, and 8.9% other languages, while 41.8% are Roman Catholics, 35.3% Protestants, 7.5% hold other religious affiliations, and 15.4% have no religious affiliation.

5 For a list of Swiss IGO memberships, see http://www.ch.ch/behoerden/00328/00337/index.html?lang=en (accessed 14 December 2006).

6 It was often said that the best foreign policy was no foreign policy at all, the so-called *keine Aussenpolitik*.

7 As per Article 54, paragraph 2, of the Federal Constitution of Switzerland (hereafter "the Constitution"). All citations of legal provisions refer to the Constitution unless indicated otherwise. The Constitution was adopted by popular vote on 18 April 1999 and entered into force on 1 January 2000. For an English version with amendments to 2002, see http://www.admin.ch/org/polit/00083/index.html?lang=en (accessed 14 December 2006).

8 In this policy area, Switzerland is a member *inter alia* of the World Bank, the International Monetary Fund, and the Organization for Economic Cooperation and Development.

9 Except for Liechtenstein.

10 For example, more than two-thirds of Swiss exports are destined for the EU, and more than four-fifths of Swiss imports originate from the EU, Germany being the principal trading partner. Over 800,000 EU citizens live and work in Switzerland, and many more cross the borders of the country regularly.

11 In 1999 Switzerland and the EU concluded the Bilateral Agreements I, which primarily regard matters of market access, and in 2004 they concluded the Bilateral Agreements II, which primarily regard security and asylum policy, environment, statistics, and cultural affairs. The Swiss Federal Council confirmed this bilateral approach in its *2006 Report on Europe*; see http://www.europa.admin.ch/europapol/off/europa_2006/e/index.htm (accessed 14 December 2006). Nonetheless, the Swiss application to join the EU, filed in 1992, has not been formally withdrawn.

12 In 2002, for example, voters narrowly approved full membership in the United Nations, whereas in 1986 they had rejected it by a 3-to-1 margin. Similarly, since 2000 the Federal Council has enjoyed success in referenda broadening and deepening the bilateral relationship with the EU.

13 Ehrenzeller et al., "Federalism and Foreign Relations," 61.

14 Specifically, the issue of cantonal participation in the foreign policy of the confederation came to the fore during the General Agreement on Tariffs and Trade (GATT)-Uruguay Round of negotiations and during the discussions regarding EEA membership.

15 Not to be overlooked is that by concluding treaties, and more specifically through membership in an IGO, countries in principle agree to an ongoing development of their (and their constituent units') international obligations, most notably through the legislative and judicial organs provided therein. Swiss cooperation in the framework of the UN Human Rights Committee has, for example, had a centralizing effect on cantonal procedural and administrative law.

16 The government of the confederation is comprised of a legislature and an executive. The legislature (Federal Assembly) is popularly elected and consists of two equal chambers. The National Council is elected from twenty-six constituencies corresponding to the cantons. Seats are divided according to population shares, with each canton having at least one member, resulting in a total of 200 members. The Council of States is comprised of 2 members from each full canton and 1 member from each half-canton, which totals 46 members. For its part, the executive is the 7–member Federal Council, which is *sui generis* in its power and makeup. Although its members are individually elected by the Federal Assembly, the Federal Council cannot be dissolved by the Federal Assembly. Moreover, it operates on a collegial basis, with decisions on all important issues being made collectively and members taking turns in the *primus inter pares* role of president.

17 "Lower-ranking foreign authorities" are understood as offices of territorial bodies of a foreign country; direct dealings with the national government of a foreign country are forbidden.

18 Some relations are handled by other departments within the Federal Council (e.g., international environmental matters by the Department of the Environment,

Energy, Transport and Communications; and world cultural heritage matters by the Department of Home Affairs). This division of responsibilities poses a challenge for the coordination and coherence of Swiss foreign policy.

19 Self-executing treaty provisions gain binding force for the individual upon the treaty's publication in the systematic collection of federal laws. If the treaty provisions are not self-executing and concern a federal competence, the confederation decides which order of government is to implement them domestically. If they are not self-executing and concern a cantonal competence, implementation lies with the cantons.

20 The confederation is nonetheless responsible vis-à-vis other signatory countries for the fulfilment of treaty obligations.

21 As per Article 7 BGMK. The cantons are also responsible for implementing any treaties that they themselves conclude and are co-responsible for implementing any concluded by their municipalities.

22 This principle is implicit in Article 42, paragraph 2, which states that the confederation is to exercise only those "tasks that require uniform enforcement."

23 See Article 44, paragraph 1. "Cooperative federalism" refers to the collaboration between the confederation and the cantons and among the cantons themselves in the conduct of their affairs.

24 See Article 44, paragraph 2.

25 Formally, the European Framework Agreement on Transfrontier Co-operation between Territorial Bodies or Authorities of 21 May 1980; see http://www.eda.admin.ch/eda/de/home/topics/intla/scoop/sclaw.html#0002 (in German, accessed 12 March 2007). Switzerland has also ratified the two optional protocols.

26 Formally, Agreement between Germany, France, Luxembourg, and Switzerland on Cross-Border Co-operation between Territorial Bodies and Local Public Authorities of 23 January 1996; see http://www.eda.admin.ch/etc/medialib/downloads/edazen/topics/scoop/sclaw.Par.0001.File.tmp/KarlsruherAbkommen.pdf (in German, accessed 12 March 2007).

27 Following the distinctions of John Kincaid, "Foreign Relations of Sub-National Units," in Raoul Blindenbacher and Arnold Koller, eds, *Federalism in a Changing World*, 74–96 (Montreal and Kingston: McGill-Queen's University Press, 2003), 81–3. To these may be added constituent units' development cooperation, such as technical assistance to foreign governments in democracy and rule-of-law projects.

28 The following section discusses ways that the cantonal governments have pursued their own foreign policy; it only touches upon the municipalities' efforts. Some findings regarding the cantons, however, hold true also for the municipalities. Typically, Swiss municipalities have not been proactive in foreign relations; to the extent that municipal civil servants have taken up contact with colleagues abroad, it has been in an uncoordinated fashion; and such activities are dismissed by many inhabitants as "bureaucrats' junkets." See Daniel Kübler and Nico van der Heiden, "Warum Städte aussenpolitisch tätig werden," *Neue Zürcher Zeitung*, 6 August 2007, 9.

29 Since 1991 the cantons have participated in the Integration of the Regions in the European Area program of the European Commission, and since 1995 their participation has been financed by the confederation. INTERREG supports cross-border cooperation in order to achieve a balanced development of the regions in Europe. Further, see http://www.interreg.ch/index_e.php?lang=e (accessed 26 August 2007).

30 In such a case (or when another canton does the same), the Federal Assembly is to decide on the impugned treaty's approval (Art. 172, para. 3). Since in Article 56, paragraph 1, treaties are considered cantonal law, they can also be subsequently abrogated by contrary treaties concluded by the confederation or by contrary national legislation passed in cognizance of the existing cantonal treaty.

31 International economic activities can also present opportunities for cantons to cooperate with other cantons or with the confederation in order to enhance the activities' effectiveness.

32 For example, various meetings regarding the ongoing negotiations on the World Trade Organization (WTO) and the General Agreement on Trade in Services (GATS) have been held within Switzerland. Participants included the confederation and CdC officials, who presented the cantons' common position on the confederation's offer in the negotiations. Decisions taken in the framework of the WTO can be of special concern for individual cantons as well as of general collective concern. Those cantons with, for example, an important agricultural sector lobby the confederation particularly hard to see that their interests are protected during any multilateral discussions about liberalizing agricultural trade.

33 Cantonal participation in the Organisation internationale de la Francophonie (OIF) exemplifies the limits placed on cantonal foreign policy. The organization was originally intended to encourage cultural and technical cooperation among its members but has become increasingly political in its activities. The confederation alone among Swiss governments is a full member of the OIF and represents the country at its various conferences. The confederation does, however, permit cantons to be associate members of the OIF's consultative institution, the Parliamentary Assembly. At present, Geneva, Valais, and Vaud are associate members.

34 For a list, see the EDA website: http://www.eda.admin.ch/eda/en/home/topics/intla (accessed 14 February 2007).

35 Figures on the costs of these efforts cannot be provided because the respective budget lines are lacking. In this respect, as in others, the distinction between external and internal policy has been blurred; many of these efforts are financed together with other expenditures.

36 Cantonal engagement in development cooperation is relatively rare and small in scale. For example, the canton of St Gall, in addition to pursuing a regional policy (vis-à-vis the Lake Constance and Alps regions), seeks to contribute to the establishment of stable structures in eastern Europe. It has concluded cooperation agreements with administrative authorities in Poland, Hungary, and the Czech Republic,

and in the framework of the EU-stability pact, it assists with a cooperation project with the Serbian education ministry.

37 These and other actors work together in Presence Switzerland, an organization that coordinates the presentation of the country around the world. Presence Switzerland is mandated to convey knowledge about Switzerland, to create understanding and empathy for Switzerland, and to highlight the diversity and attractiveness of Switzerland. Administrative responsibility for the organization lies with the secretary of state in the EDA, and the organization acts abroad primarily through Swiss missions.

38 Hans Martin Tschudi, "Chancen und Probleme regionaler Außenbeziehungen aus der Sicht der politischen Praxis," in Rudolf Hrbek, ed., *Aussenbeziehungen von Regionen in Europa und der Welt*, 45–50 (Baden-Baden: Nomos, 2003), 49, our translation.

39 Joseph Deiss, "Federalism in Swiss Foreign Policy," in Raoul Blindenbacher and Arnold Koller, eds, *Federalism in a Changing World*, 534–8 (Montreal and Kingston: McGill-Queen's University Press, 2003), 536.

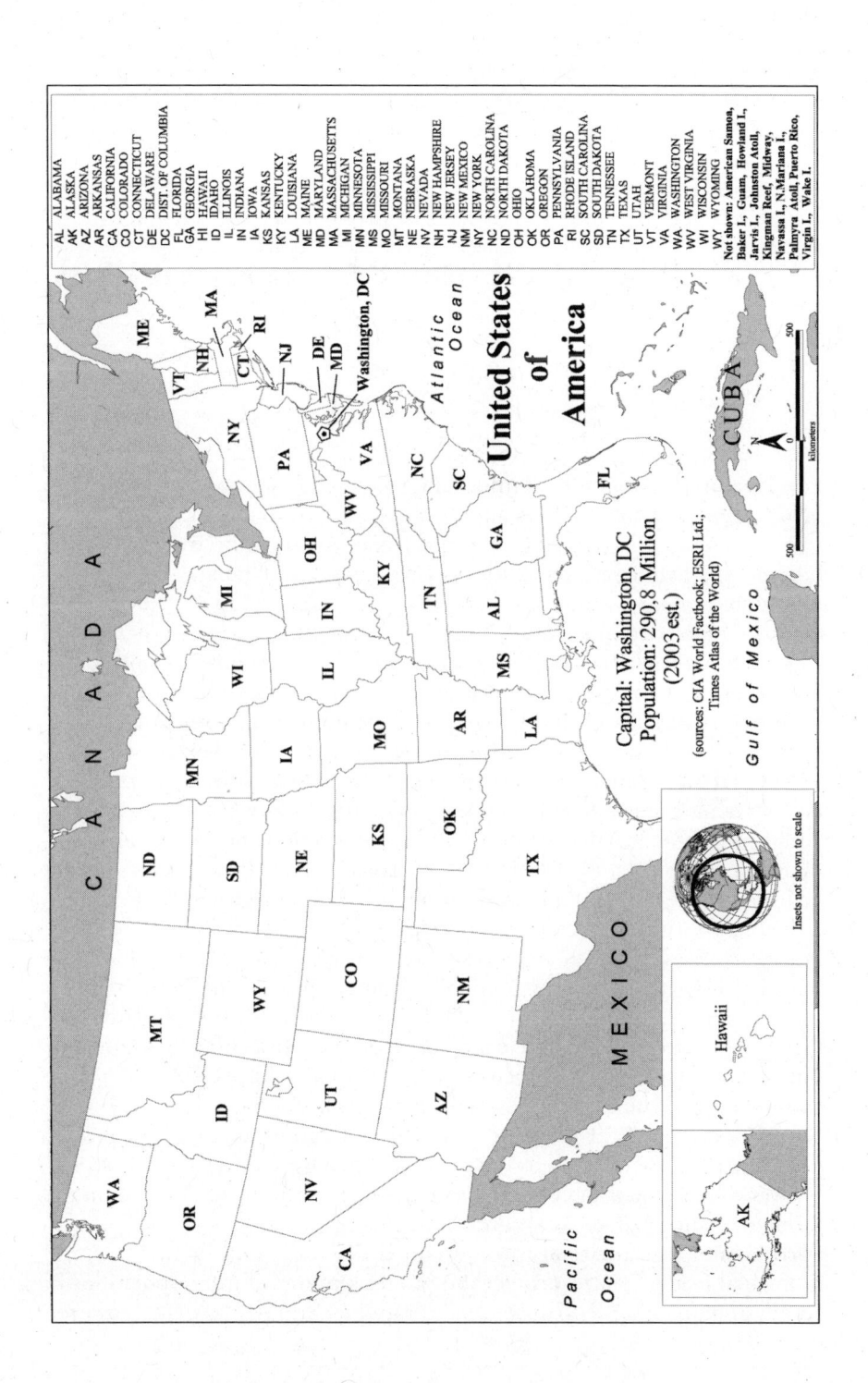

United States of America

Capital: Washington, DC
Population: 290,8 Million (2003 est.)

(sources: CIA World Factbook; ESRI Ltd.; Times Atlas of the World)

AL	ALABAMA
AK	ALASKA
AZ	ARIZONA
AR	ARKANSAS
CA	CALIFORNIA
CO	COLORADO
CT	CONNECTICUT
DE	DELAWARE
DC	DIST. OF COLUMBIA
FL	FLORIDA
GA	GEORGIA
HI	HAWAII
ID	IDAHO
IL	ILLINOIS
IN	INDIANA
IA	IOWA
KS	KANSAS
KY	KENTUCKY
LA	LOUISIANA
ME	MAINE
MD	MARYLAND
MA	MASSACHUSETTS
MI	MICHIGAN
MN	MINNESOTA
MS	MISSISSIPPI
MO	MISSOURI
MT	MONTANA
NE	NEBRASKA
NV	NEVADA
NH	NEW HAMPSHIRE
NJ	NEW JERSEY
NM	NEW MEXICO
NY	NEW YORK
NC	NORTH CAROLINA
ND	NORTH DAKOTA
OH	OHIO
OK	OKLAHOMA
OR	OREGON
PA	PENNSYLVANIA
RI	RHODE ISLAND
SC	SOUTH CAROLINA
SD	SOUTH DAKOTA
TN	TENNESSEE
TX	TEXAS
UT	UTAH
VT	VERMONT
VA	VIRGINIA
WA	WASHINGTON
WV	WEST VIRGINIA
WI	WISCONSIN
WY	WYOMING

Not shown: American Samoa, Baker I., Guam, Howland I., Jarvis I., Johnston Atoll, Kingman Reef, Midway, Navassa I., N.Mariana I., Palmyra Atoll, Puerto Rico, Virgin I., Wake I.

Insets not shown to scale

The United States of America

EARL H. FRY

For most of the twentieth century, "international relations" were viewed by many scholars as interactions among the leaders of national governments, with the ultimate goal being to protect and enhance the interests of the nation-state. Scholars such as Richard Neustadt and Graham Allison, however, were among the first to illustrate that this leadership actually consists of many parts (e.g., executive, bureaucratic, legislative, and judicial) and that each part may have differing priorities in the formulation and implementation of a nation's foreign policy.[1] Robert Keohane and Joseph Nye went even further and questioned whether international relations should even be considered the exclusive domain of national governments. They began to refer to official exchanges between representatives of national governments as "interstate interactions" and differentiated this activity from "transgovernmental interactions," which link subunits of different governments, and from "transnational interactions," which involve cross-border activities wherein at least one actor is not an agent of a government.[2]

Within this context, a country's "foreign policy" will be defined here as embracing "the goals that the nation's officials seek to attain abroad, the values that give rise to those objectives, and the means or instruments used to pursue them," while admitting that the national government consists of many parts that may or may not be united in ascertaining what official priorities should be pursued internationally.[3] The cross-border activities sponsored by officials in constituent governments such as states and cities in federations, which may be considered a hybrid of Keohane and Nye's transgovernmental and transnational interactions, will be referred to as "foreign affairs" or "foreign relations."

Over the past quarter-century, there has been a sharp acceleration in the foreign relations of US state and municipal governments. This trend toward greater international involvement is likely to continue as state and municipal leaders act to protect the interests of their local populations in an era of expanding globalization and rapid technology change. However, this accelerated engagement abroad will be hampered at times by the low priority often accorded such programs, periodic budget crises, the lack of institutionalization in many of these programs, and tenuous intergovernmental cooperation within the US federal system. The population of the United States of America was 303.6 million in early 2008. The United States ranks as the world's third-largest nation-state in population and is the fourth-largest in territory. Only the rudimentary elements of its federal system are readily understood by its own population, namely a rather vague division of government authority between one national government and fifty state governments.[4] In reality, in 2002 there were 87,576 distinct governmental units within the US federal system, including 3,034 county and 19,429 municipal governments.

In political terms, only the state governments can formally share authority with Washington, DC, because the Tenth Amendment to the Constitution stipulates that all power not explicitly delegated to the national government is "reserved" to the states and the people. From its beginnings as a relatively small nation with thirteen states sequestered along the Atlantic seaboard, the United States grew immensely in territory through wise expenditures such as the Louisiana and Alaska purchases, through exploration and claiming of new lands to the west, and at times through the threatened or actual use of military force, such as stripping Mexico of half its land and then annexing it into the United States. Many people are unaware that the "fruits" of Manifest Destiny[5] have also left Washington with authority over Puerto Rico, the US Virgin Islands, Guam, American Samoa, the Northern Mariana Islands, and a few other overseas possessions, such as the controversial Guantanamo Bay in Cuba. In most instances, the 4.4 million residents of these commonwealths or territories or possessions are either citizens or nationals of the United States. Puerto Rico, the US Virgin Islands, and Guam each elect a delegate to the US House of Representatives, but they have no formal vote in Congress, giving them the same status as the delegate elected from the District of Columbia, home to the nation's capital. This vast assemblage of states, commonwealths, and territories stretches more than 9,400 miles from the US Virgin Islands in the East to Guam in the West.

The US federal system is complicated even further by the presence of 562 federally recognized tribal governments, each exercising some degree of sovereignty and autonomy and many being formally recognized as "domestic dependent nations."[6] As Erich Steinman asserts, "tribal governments are now visible and active as a category of government within the boundaries of the United States," even though "tribes have long been anomalies within American governance."[7] The sovereignty of Native American tribal governments is also linked to foreign relations because the Jay Treaty of 1794, signed between the United States and Great Britain, provides Native groups near the border with what is now Canada the free right of passage across the boundary line established by Europeans who had settled in the New World and encroached on Native lands. Some tribal units, such as the Mohawks on the Akwesasne reserve near Montreal, Quebec, actually straddle the current Canada-US border, and they insist on the right not only to cross the border freely but also to transport goods for personal and community use without undue interference from Canadian or US authorities. On the southern border, the Tohono O'odham occupy the second-biggest reservation in the United States, larger than the state of Connecticut, and its boundaries straddle the international border that was established with Mexico in 1853. Recently, the way of life of this tribal group has been adversely affected by illegal immigration and drug trafficking, which have sparked cross-border frictions between the United States and Mexico.

Contemporary federalism rarely generates headlines in the United States, unlike the situation in Canada, Spain, and several other federal or quasi-federal nations. Nevertheless, the US system continues to evolve, and intergovernmental tensions arise from time to time, in part because state and even municipal governments are now exercising what they consider their constitutional right to be engaged not only in domestic activities but also increasingly in international affairs.[8] This chapter highlights what these constituent governments are doing and analyzes the overall implications of these activities on the US system of government. In effect, state and local governments have significant leeway to engage in a wide array of international activities, but some of these activities, combined with contentious policies enacted by the national government, exacerbate intergovernmental relations and challenge the overall effectiveness of the US federal system.

US FEDERALISM IN PERSPECTIVE

Is US federalism exceptional? To a certain extent it is, as emphasized by Samuel Krislov: "American federalism emerges as exceptional, and not only in its inception, inventiveness, and derivation. It has also been truly exceptional in its emergent qualities, its ability to maintain itself, and to transform and recreate itself as a system both legally and in fact."[9]

Most exceptionally, the United States was the first nation-state to adopt a federal system of government in 1787, even though confederations have roots in ancient Greece and what today constitutes Switzerland. During the period when the American revolutionaries were fighting the British for independence, the Articles of Confederation of 1781 was adopted as the country's original constitutional document. The new state governments granted most authority to themselves, leaving the national government extremely weak and consisting of a unicameral legislature without functioning executive or judicial branches or the ability to raise most revenues without the prior permission of the states. The Articles of Confederation was effective enough to carry the country through the Revolutionary War, but then its decentralizing tendencies began to fragment the new nation into its constituent parts, and unity was badly frayed. A sense of urgency over this fragmentation prompted many political leaders to gather in Philadelphia in the late spring of 1787. Behind closed doors in Independence Hall, these delegates from the states made the momentous decision to tear up the Articles of Confederation and begin anew. From late May until mid-September, the delegates pieced together a new constitution and then sent it to the states for formal ratification by popularly elected conventions. The document went into effect in March 1789 and succeeded in preserving the very fragile union. The hallmarks of the new constitution were scrapping the confederal system in favour of a federal system dividing authority between the national and state governments, a viable national government divided into three branches with separation of powers and checks and balances in place to ensure that no one branch would become predominant, and the establishment of a national economic system that frowned upon protectionism by the state and local jurisdictions.

The Constitution of 1787 and the federal system it created suffered through numerous tribulations as the decades passed. The War of 1812 was a miserable experience for the country, and only British magnanimity allowed the United States to preserve its territory. The war was fought in part because many members of Congress, backed by some officials in state governments, wanted to bring British North America under US control. US troops and state militias invaded what is now Canada, and the British retaliated by occupying Washington, DC, in August 1814, forcing President James Madison to vacate the White House and run for his life.

A much more serious challenge to US unity and federalism occurred in the late 1850s and early 1860s. Southern states were unhappy with developments in the north of the country and wanted to preserve their largely agrarian system based on slavery. They proclaimed that states' rights were being trampled by Washington and decided to secede from the Union, an action vehemently rejected by President Abraham Lincoln. The international dimension was important to the confederacy because the British were initially supportive of its goals, in part because they wanted continued access to cheap raw materials provided by the southern states for British textile mills, and in part because they perceived that a weakened and divided United States would be in their own best interests. The North and the South engaged in the bloodiest conflict in US history, with almost a million soldiers and civilians killed during the Civil War period of 1861–65.

States' rights would continue to be a major federalist issue through the 1960s, especially in the arena of civil and voting rights. Many proponents of states' rights also worried that President Franklin D. Roosevelt's New Deal regime from 1933 to 1945 spelled the beginning of the end for true federalism, insisting that Washington had taken control of most important government functions and that federalism was beginning to exist in name only. Decades later, in 1995, two moderate governors, Republican Michael Leavitt of Utah and Democrat Ben Nelson of Nebraska, attempted to organize a Conference of the States that would demand the strengthening of the Tenth Amendment and push for a transfer of authority away from Washington and toward the state capitals. The meeting was to be convened in Philadelphia with each state represented by its governor and four legislators. This meeting would have been the first full conference of the states to discuss constitutional issues since the historic 1787 meeting in Philadelphia. Initially, momentum seemed to be on the side of these governors because many leaders in the states and even some in Washington were advocating a "devolution revolution." However, both the left and the right on the political spectrum began to have second thoughts after the announcement of the Philadelphia meeting, and eventually the organizers had to scale back their expectations and agree to a watered-down States' Federalism Summit that met in Cincinnati in the autumn of 1995.[10] Critics worried that the proposed Philadelphia meeting, which would bring together the fifty constituent state governments, could be transformed into a constitutional convention resulting in major changes to the Constitution, much as had occurred in 1787 when the Articles of Confederation was replaced by an entirely new document. Municipal government representatives were also unhappy because they were not invited to join the proceedings.

Today, most governors and state legislative leaders would agree with the premise that Washington has usurped too much authority that should rightfully belong to the states in education, health care, the environment, regulation, control over the National Guard, and several other areas.[11] They also continue to complain about the periodic preemption of state laws and unfunded mandates in which Washington orders the state governments to do something without sufficient financial compensation to carry out the mandates. In addition, they argue that the explosive issue of illegal immigration is a federal responsibility but that state and local governments are being saddled with most of the financial burden of educating and providing medical care and other services to the estimated 12 million undocumented immigrants residing in the country. One of the most vitriolic rebukes by state officials of federal attempts to strip the states of constitutional powers occurred during the summer of 2006 when a clause was added at the last moment to the National Defense Authorization Act, subsequently passed by the US Congress. This clause gave the president the authority to control the National Guard in case of "a serious natural or manmade disaster, accident, or catastrophe that occurs in the United

States, its territories and possessions, or Puerto Rico." This legislation prompted a unanimous response from all fifty governors and the governor of Puerto Rico condemning the clause and demanding it be removed. However, even in the face of the united opposition of the governors, the controversial legislation became law.

One final area of growing disagreement relates to what role state and local governments can play in the domain of US foreign relations in an increasingly complex and interdependent global setting.

THE REGIONAL AND GLOBAL PRESENCE OF THE UNITED STATES

Since the end of the Cold War, the United States has been widely perceived as the world's only superpower. In the aftermath of national government policies enacted after the horrific events of 11 September 2001, the perception that many other nations have of the United States has become more negative than at any other time over the past half-century. The Pew Global Attitudes Project, which conducts periodic surveys in sixteen nations, has found that residents of most countries have far more negative attitudes than positive ones toward the United States. This growing anti-Americanism reflects not just an antipathy toward the US government but also a growing disenchantment with the American people themselves.

Over the past two centuries, American power has been used wisely and unwisely at home and abroad, and the nation's power base still remains very formidable. In 2006 the US gross domestic product (GDP), representing the sum of the goods and services produced each year, reached US$13.1 trillion, almost 2.5 times the size of the second-largest national economy, Japan, and roughly equal to the output of the twenty-seven-nation European Union.

The global presence of the United States is more pervasive than at any time since the zenith of the British Empire. It is also complicated and controversial. Naturally, the US government will quickly defend from an external threat its own constituent parts from the US Virgin Islands to Guam. However, treaty obligations also commit it to defending from external threat many nations in Europe, the Middle East, Asia, Oceania, and North and South America to the same extent that it would defend its own territory. This is referred to as a forward-defence obligation and is very costly in money and personnel.

Regionally, the United States has entered into a free trade arrangement with the two other major nations of North America: Canada and Mexico. The North American Free Trade Agreement (NAFTA) represents the largest free trade area in the world and brings together not only three national governments but also approximately 100 states, provinces, districts, and territories in countries that all have federal systems. The United States is also a recent signatory to the Central American Free Trade Area (CAFTA) and a prime supporter of the Free Trade Area of the Americas (FTAA), which, if ever enacted, would comprise all the nations in the Western Hemisphere except for Cuba.

As will be discussed in greater detail later, officials in state and local governments do not always agree with administrations in Washington over regional and global policy initiatives. Several constituent governments have pledged to uphold Kyoto Protocol standards even though the federal government has rejected this treaty. Scores of local governments have passed resolutions opposed to US policies in Iraq and elsewhere in the world. Some state and local governments are also implementing their own sanctions against other nations, with the most recent cases targeted against Sudan. Others now oppose certain parts of NAFTA and have concerns about CAFTA. Constituent governments perceive at times that they suffer the repercussions of a national government that is so actively involved globally, and now they also want the right to be engaged internationally, a pursuit that causes some dismay among officials in the nation's capital. These frictions involve the intersection of the global with the local, as well as differing perceptions concerning the distribution of authority within the contemporary US federal system and how one should differentiate between "foreign policy" and "foreign affairs."

THE CONSTITUTIONAL SETTING

At first glance, the commerce and supremacy clauses in the US Constitution appear to grant all important foreign policy and foreign relations functions to the national government. Article 1, Section 8, stipulates that Congress "shall regulate commerce with foreign nations ...; declare war ...; make all laws which shall be necessary and proper for carrying into execution the foregoing powers." Section 10 adds that "No state should, without the consent of Congress, lay any duty of tonnage, keep troops, or ships of war in time of peace, enter into any agreement or compact with another state, or with a foreign power, or engage in war, unless actually invaded, or in such imminent danger as will not admit of delay."

In Article 6, the supremacy clause was designed to permit the federal government to act within its areas of jurisdiction without undue state government interference: "This constitution, and the laws of the United States which shall be made in pursuance thereof, and all treaties made, or which shall be made, under the authority of the United States, shall be supreme law of the land; and the judges in every state shall be bound thereby, anything in the constitution or laws of any state to the contrary notwithstanding." This clause was not widely used until the twentieth century, but in recent decades, bolstered by federal court decisions, it has been used by the national government to strengthen federal control and to preempt certain state laws.

Twentieth-century interpretations of the Constitution by federal courts have also reinforced national government control of foreign policy. *Missouri v. Holland* (1920), *Zschernig v. Miller* (1968), and the Massachusetts-Vietnam War controversy of 1970 are among the court cases that have strengthened Washington's control over major foreign and defence policy initiatives.[12]

In the current decade, the US Supreme Court ruled in *Crosby v. National Foreign Trade Council* (2000) that the 1996 Burma law, passed by Massachusetts, was unconstitutional. This law limited access to state procurement contracts for any company that did business in Burma (Myanmar). The law was patterned after several state and local government sanctions placed on South Africa during the 1980s and was also similar to earlier sanctions imposed by a few state and local governments on Nigeria, Indonesia, Cuba, and Northern Ireland. The Supreme Court ruled that the federal government had already implemented economic sanctions against Burma and, therefore, that the supremacy clause rendered the Massachusetts law null and void.

The *Crosby* decision does leave some manoeuvring room for state and local governments. In the earlier *Barclays Bank PLC v. Franchise Tax Board* (1994) case, the Supreme Court ruled that states could impose their own unitary tax formula on companies doing business in the United States as well as other countries, so long as the national government was "silent" on the issue.[13] This implies that if the Bill Clinton administration (1993–2001) had not moved to place restrictions on new investment activity in Burma by US companies, perhaps the Massachusetts law might have been constitutional. In addition, various constituent governments, including Illinois, have or are in the process of placing sanctions on Sudan, arguing that Washington has been "silent" on the issue or that their actions are different from what Massachusetts had done toward companies doing business in Burma.[14] Inevitably, the Supreme Court will be asked to decide cases involving what actions can be taken by state and local governments that have a direct effect on international relations.

Since 1994 the United States has entered into several international accords or agreements and has joined the World Trade Organization (WTO), NAFTA, CAFTA, and a variety of other international or regional trade organizations. Many state attorneys general have argued that federalism is being watered down by these US treaty or "pact" obligations and that authority exercised by state and local governments is being eroded because Washington can always invoke either the commerce clause or supremacy clause to preempt activities by constituent governments.[15] For example, Chapter 11 in NAFTA provides companies in Canada, the United States, and Mexico with right of establishment and national treatment guarantees in all three member countries. Methanex, a Canadian corporation, sued the United States for US$970 million under Chapter 11 because California banned the use of its product MTBE. This product, a fuel component of gasoline, was phased out in California in 1999 and banned outright in 2004. California authorities claimed that MTBE was a suspected cause of cancer and also that it contaminated ground waters. Methanex claimed that California was discriminating against Canadian products because it banned methanol that contained MTBE but did not ban ethanol, which was primarily fabricated from US farm products. A NAFTA binational panel finally ruled in August 2005 against Methanex and ordered it to reimburse the United States US$4 million for legal fees. Various other challenges to state and provincial government actions in the three member countries are now pending before NAFTA panels, and their policymaking latitude in a variety of domains is now subject to scrutiny by these international panels.

Many state and local governments are also convinced that the WTO ignores the division of powers within federal systems and is eroding their ability to govern. In a case initiated in 2003, the nation of Antigua and Barbuda, with a population of 69,000 people, sought redress against the United States before a WTO tribunal because Utah and Hawaii do not allow any form of gambling. Antigua and Barbuda argued that this ban discriminates against its companies, which run Internet gambling operations, and that under the General Agreement on Trade in Services (GATS), Washington must force its state governments to comply. The final WTO panel ruling recommended that Washington permit, at a minimum, electronic betting on horse races, an action in clear violation of state regulations in Utah and Hawaii. In reaction to the GATS decision, twenty-nine state attorneys general sent a letter to the Office of the US Trade Representative (USTR) in May 2005. It stated: "The prospect of [future] WTO challenges to [state-level gambling] prohibitions should alone be sufficient to give U.S. negotiators enormous motivation to use the current GATS negotiations to secure a rule change that makes explicit the right of a WTO signatory to ban undesirable activity in a GATS covered sector."[16]

In effect, state and local government leaders fear that international agreements entered into by the US government may eventually inhibit anything they do that might be construed as restricting or distorting trade and investment activity. This might include environmental regulations, labour laws, preferences given to local contractors, and a host of other functions. They insist that this may cripple the federal system and violates protections provided to the states in the Tenth Amendment. Federal officials are usually sensitive to these concerns, but when push comes to shove, they can preempt state and local government actions by invoking the supremacy and commerce clauses, and the federal courts have usually supported the national government's authority to do so.

In terms of the constitutional division of authority, as the world becomes more globalized, the United States may become less federalized. The late Daniel J. Elazar warned over two decades ago about the dangers of globalization for US state governments: "The threat to the states is not simply a question of dramatics or imagery. It may be that, as the United States becomes more deeply entangled with the world, it is less likely to have the time or the energy to exercise the self-restraint needed to maintain a domestic system of noncentralization that requires a certain amount of time-consuming bargaining and negotiation to make it function."[17] With this in mind, the president of the National Conference of State Legislatures warned at that organization's 2005 annual meeting: "There is an effort within the halls of Congress to centralize public policy decision-making within the Washington Beltway. When Congress imposes a one-size-fits-all approach to a policy problem, they fail to recognize the individualism and uniqueness of each state, threatening the collective strength of the states."[18] However, with state and some municipal governments becoming more engaged internationally as a result of globalization, it is possible that these activities could strengthen some aspects of federalism as all governments increasingly recognize the need to collaborate in order to maintain America's competitiveness. Nonetheless, there remains a strong temptation in Washington to strengthen centralized policy control in the face of escalating international challenges.

INTERGOVERNMENTAL RELATIONS AND US FOREIGN RELATIONS

Intergovernmental cooperation and coordination in foreign relations have been sporadic among national, state, and local governments, even though a number of intergovernmental groups exist to foster dialogue within the US federal system. For example, the Office of the US Trade Representative is the lead agency for the national government in its interaction with states over trade policy, and it does meet with state officials infrequently through the Intergovernmental Policy Advisory Committee (IGPAC), which was established by Congress in 1974. In his examination of IGPAC, Robert Stumberg concluded that it was not viable, and officials at the USTR generally ignored or did not act on the issues of major concern to state representatives.[19] The USTR also has an Office of Intergovernmental Affairs and Public Liaison, which theoretically interacts with single points of contact in each state government when pertinent issues arise. However, federal officials rarely contact these people, and as administrations change within states, the designees often leave government or are assigned to new duties that have little to do with intergovernmental relations. From the national government's standpoint, whether under Democratic or Republican administrations, Washington is ascendant in all aspects of foreign policy and will ultimately make the final decision. If state governments are unhappy with an action or pending decision, they are welcome to express their objections but preferably through their states' elected members in the US House of Representatives and the US Senate.

State governments do coordinate at times with some of their own local governments in an effort to set up programs that encourage small businesses to export, to convince business leaders to participate in international trade missions, and to facilitate the attraction of foreign direct investment (FDI). The attraction of FDI, however, is a very difficult issue in terms both of state and local government cooperation and of cooperation among state governments. State governments often walk on egg shells in the FDI arena because they do not want to be perceived as favouring one municipality in their state over others. As for state-to-state cooperation in attracting FDI, it rarely occurs because FDI is perceived as a zero-sum game with only one winner. Consequently, each state goes it alone in an effort to attract direct investment from abroad, and this spawns bidding wars among the states and even local communities, helping major foreign auto companies in particular to reap hundreds of millions of dollars in incentives. In one case, the executives of a German auto company and the German chancellor actually requested that governors from south-eastern states travel to Germany and, while there, present their final incentive packages to the German automaker.[20] This is a very serious game because the United States has been the recipient of US$2.1 trillion in FDI, and foreign investors control over US$16.3 trillion in US assets.[21] More than 6 million Americans also work for foreign-controlled companies on US soil, and these subsidiaries of foreign corporations are much more likely to export than are their American-owned counterparts and to pay higher hourly wages. State and local governments distribute roughly US$50 billion in incentives to domestic and foreign-owned companies each year, and their right to do so was upheld in a Supreme Court decision rendered in May 2006.[22] Although the decision was a victory for states' rights, it is regrettable that so many incentives are handed out by these constituent governments because (1) in almost all cases, FDI will come to the United States without any incentives so that foreign businesses can secure or expand their positions in the world's largest national market, (2) incentives invariably favour one company over other companies in the same or related business sectors, (3) incentives are given at the expense of taxpayers and public-sponsored programs such as education, and (4) government incentives clearly distort the market system, which most Americans consider to be the hallmark of the US economy.

Those who work on state and municipal foreign relations progams are able to gather occasionally in meetings sponsored by the National

Governors' Association, the Council of State Governments, the National Conference of State Legislatures, the State International Development Organization, the National Association of Counties, the National League of Cities, the US Conference of Mayors, and a few other organizations. Some of these associations also have specialists who coordinate projects related to international affairs and even sign contracts with foreign governments to foster cross-border exchanges among constituent units. Most of these programs are economic in nature, and these associations have provided much-needed continuity, which compensates somewhat for the rapid turnover in personnel in individual states and municipalities. Some of these state and municipal associations also attract the active participation of officials from US overseas commonwealths and territories. For example, the Western Governors' Association consists of eighteen states plus American Samoa, Guam, and the Northern Mariana Islands, and the Southern Governors' Association includes fifteen states plus Puerto Rico and the US Virgin Islands. A few of these associations also permit some of the Canadian provinces to be associate members in an effort to spur greater cross-border cooperation among constituent governments. The annual meeting of the Council of State Governments was actually held in Quebec City in 1999, with the Quebec government providing significant financial and logistical support for the conference.

In foreign relations, intergovernmental cooperation and coordination among national and constituent units has been modest at best and has simply not been a major priority of most government leaders. Without any doubt, state governments are increasingly frustrated with Washington because international treaty or pact obligations are perceived as limiting the exercise of state and local authority. Yet even in this contentious policy area, the intergovernmental dialogue has been far from robust.

THE DOMESTIC AND INTERNATIONAL MANIFESTATIONS OF STATE AND LOCAL GOVERNMENT FOREIGN RELATIONS

Under the Articles of Confederation, several state governments engaged in their own international diplomacy and maintained their own representation abroad. When the founders gathered in Philadelphia in 1787, they began the process of transformation from a confederation to a federation and put an end to almost all state forays abroad.

However, we now fast-forward 221 years and find that most state governments and even some larger municipal governments are once again actively engaged in the international arena and claiming "competence" in foreign relations.[23] State governments currently operate approximately 230 offices abroad, and most governors lead state delegations abroad every year.[24] In contrast, only four states had opened international offices in 1980 and none prior to the late 1960s.[25] Perhaps the first governor to lead an international mission in the post-Second World War period was Luther Hodges of North Carolina, who directed such a mission to Europe in 1959 in search of FDI. A decade later, Virginia stationed a representative in Brussels, hoping to cash in on the major economic revival under way in western Europe. At the time, the US Department of Commerce had only one person assigned to work full time on attracting inward FDI, and this was considered insufficient by some state officials. As governor of Georgia from 1971 to 1975, Jimmy Carter became perhaps the most active state chief executive in foreign relations. He estimates that he spent nearly one-fourth of his time as governor recruiting new direct investment and promoting Georgia's exports. He also visited about a dozen foreign countries and directed the opening of state offices overseas.[26]

The initial thrust of states was to attract FDI. Attention then shifted gradually to export promotion. Export activity expanded dramatically from the mid-1980s to the mid-1990s, with most states doubling their export volume. Governor Tommy Thompson of Wisconsin proclaimed that governors had become "the trade ambassadors of the United States," adding that "the world has become smaller, so governors' economic development strategies have become more far-reaching. Now that economic opportunities are more international in scope, governors' efforts must extend beyond state and national boundaries."[27] Thompson also observed that "the federal government is so big it often does not get the job done on the issues of trade, and governors need to be involved in expanding trade relationships with other countries."[28] He listed the basic tools governors can use in promoting economic development at home and abroad as trade and investment promotion, education and workforce training, innovation, and infrastructure development and modernization.[29]

States are potentially powerful actors in the global economy, especially in terms of facilitating the efforts of their resident companies to engage in international commerce and in attracting hundreds of billions of dollars in investment from around the world. In 2005 the World Bank provided annual GDP estimates for 183 nations. In terms of the individual US states, three would have ranked in 2005 among the 10 largest nations measured by GDP, 14 among the top 25, 38 among the top 55, and all 50 states among the largest 77 national economies in the world.

The growth in their own economic capacities is only one reason why many state governments have decided to become so much more actively engaged internationally over the past quarter-century. Traditionally, state officials have viewed their purpose as enhancing and safeguarding the interests of the people they represent. This effort, however, has become much more complicated as a result of globalization and what the economist Joseph

Schumpeter referred to as "creative destruction." With reference to globalization, approximately 18 million US jobs are now tied to exporting, inward FDI, and visits by foreign tourists, representing over 12% of employment in the civilian sector. Each state wants its share of these jobs and desires that its own business community will be globally competitive. State leaders also perceive that value-added benefits are derived from setting up their own offices abroad and sponsoring periodic international economic missions, rather than being satisfied with allowing the more than 240 US embassies, consulates, and diplomatic missions scattered around the world to promote the states' collective interests. In addition, many state and local leaders perceive that Washington has botched opportunities to enhance international economic linkages; thus they must take matters into their own hands. As an example, 51 million foreign residents visited the United States in 2000. In 2003, 10 million fewer visitors came, even at a time when world tourism in general had recovered from the traumas of 11 September 2001.[30] Finally, in 2006 the number of foreign visitors equalled the levels of 2000, but in the interim the US share of total international tourism revenues had fallen from 17.1% to 12.0%, a difference equating to roughly US$35 billion in lost revenue in 2006 alone.[31] Leaders in states and cities reliant on foreign tourism for a healthy share of their revenues have blamed Washington for instituting onerous visa policies and giving the perception that the welcome mat has been removed for visitors residing outside the United States. Some states and cities have reacted by advertising internationally and setting up special programs catering to overseas visitors.

States and communities along the 49th parallel also marshalled their resources in an effort to convince Washington not to impose new passport requirements on both Canadians and Americans beginning in 2008. With 100 million two-way crossings each year along the Canada-US border, and only two-fifths of Canadians and one-fifth of Americans holding passports, border communities could lose hundreds of millions of dollars in revenue annually if the passport requirement is implemented as planned under provisions in the Western Hemisphere Travel Initiative (WHTI).[32] The same passport requirement for land travel between the United States and Mexico will have a negative effect on San Diego, El Paso, and other cities scattered along the 2,000–mile southern border.[33] Sarcastically, some local officials hint that the US Department of Homeland Security's "war on terror" has now been extended to include a "war on tourism," with border cities and states bearing the brunt of the financial consequences.

State governments also want to be on the right side of creative destruction. Each year in the United States, almost 600,000 new businesses are created, but almost as many close their doors.[34] In 2005, 55 million Americans, or 40% of the workforce, either lost or left their jobs, but because it was a relatively good year economically, 57 million found jobs.[35]

Silicon Valley can do exceedingly well in the era of creative destruction, but Detroit, Newark, St Louis, and several other communities have struggled to keep up. States understand that both domestic and global conditions can affect how they will fare economically, and they have reacted accordingly by becoming more involved internationally.

In 2002 state governments spent a record $190 million on their international programs and assigned approximately 1,000 employees to work in these programs, although both numbers represent a very small proportion of overall government spending and employment.[36] Typical programs include the sponsorship of "how to export" seminars for small businesses, arranging international economic missions heavily laden with local business leaders, hosting foreign missions and visiting dignitaries, overseeing international offices or coordinating with foreign nationals hired to represent the state in various countries, and attracting FDI. Some states take advantage of their geographic positions to emphasize relations with constituent governments in neighbouring countries. Texas has significant ties with some of the states of Mexico, exemplified by George W. Bush's relationship with Vicente Fox when they were respectively governors of Texas and Guanajuato.[37] New York and Quebec officials have met annually over the past several years to discuss border challenges and other issues of mutual interest. Some national and regional organizations also emphasize cross-border cooperation with Mexico and Canada such as the Border Governors' Conference, the Border Legislative Conference, the Council of Great Lakes Governors, the Conference of New England Governors and Eastern Canadian Premiers, and the Pacific NorthWest Economic Region. Issues commonly discussed by these groups include regional trade, investment, tourism, the environment, energy, infrastructure development, and security.

The challenges of globalization depicted in figure 12.1 indicate the intersection of the local with the global and show why state and even local governments are involved in what John Kincaid calls "constituent diplomacy," even when they are simply fulfilling their traditional role of protecting and enhancing the interests of the people whom they represent.[38] During the 2001–02 legislative year, 886 bills and resolutions linked to some aspect of foreign relations were introduced in state legislatures, and 306 were adopted. This type of activity is up dramatically from the beginning of the 1990s.[39]

Governors may also be actively engaged abroad, meeting not only with their counterparts in other countries but even occasionally with leaders of national governments. In May 2006 President Vicente Fox came to the United States for formal visits with governors in California, Washington, and Utah. His visit with Governor Jon Huntsman Jr in sparsely populated Utah was prompted by Huntsman's meeting with Fox in Mexico City a year earlier and by Huntsman's willingness to sponsor a resolution passed by

Figure 12.1
International decisions and events affecting governance in US states and cities

INTERNATIONAL SECTOR

weapons proliferation, conflict, sports and entertainment, economics, cyberspace, terrorism, immigration, energy, religion and ideology, environment, culture, resources, crime, disease

U.S. STATE AND LOCAL GOVERNMENTS

the Western Governors' Association that supports a guest-worker program with Mexico. Utah is also one of several states that allow undocumented residents to attend public colleges and universities at in-state tuition rates and that have issued special permits authorizing them to drive motor vehicles. Governor Arnold Schwarzenegger of California has expressed reservations about Washington's proposal to beef up US security along the southern border by deploying National Guard troops, echoing Fox's own line of thinking. Mexico's national government also recognizes that some state governments are potential allies in convincing Washington to endorse more pro-Mexico policies, especially in the area of immigration and guest workers. This rationale helps to explain why Mexico operates forty-seven consulates spread around the United States, far more than any other nation. Not only do these consular officials serve the needs of the more than 10 million Mexican citizens who live in the United States and send US$20 billion in remittances back to their home country annually, but they also lobby US state and local government officials on behalf of the Mexican national government. In a similar vein, other foreign governments have almost 1,500 consular offices or honorary consuls to represent their interests outside of Washington, DC, and their duties include maintaining close contacts with state and local governments.[40]

Some of the foreign relations issues discussed by state legislatures during the current decade are focused on this rapid rise of immigrants in the United States. This issue, above all, illustrates why, in an age of globalization, state and local officials must be involved in foreign relations whether they like it or not. The US Bureau of the Census estimates that at the end of 2004, 34.2 million residents of the United States were foreign-born, representing 12% of the US population. The peak level occurred in 1910, when 14.7% of residents came from other countries. This then began a steady decline to reach 4.8% in 1970, only to reverse and climb again to 8.7% in 1994 and to 12% a decade later. The most contentious issue is illegal immigration, with most coming from Latin America, especially from Mexico. Currently, it is estimated that 10% of Mexico's population resides in the United States, including roughly 15% of Mexico's overall labour force.[41] Many of these people are undocumented, and their number doubled during the 1990s. State and local leaders want help from Washington to defray the significant health, education, infrastructure, and other costs associated with this dramatic rise in undocumented immigrants, pointing out that immigration is exclusively in the domain of the national government and that Washington should ultimately bear the financial burden.

FEDERALISM AND US FOREIGN RELATIONS: A FOCUS ON THE MAJOR CHALLENGES

Various challenges now confront federalism as it relates to US foreign affairs. The first challenge is differentiating between foreign policy and foreign relations. Washington has not been overly concerned about states engaging in the international economy, establishing special relationships with other constituent governments abroad and signing international accords, or even solidifying international ties that go beyond the economic dimension. However, the national government wants the states and cities to stay out of foreign policy as defined at the beginning of this chapter. Incidents of foreign policy include the unilateral sanctions brought by Massachusetts against Burma and the current sanctions of Illinois against Sudan.

The growing mélange of international and domestic issues also provokes intergovernmental tensions, such as when cities instruct their officials not to assist federal officials in tracking down undocumented immigrants, even though the Illegal Immigration Reform and Immigration Responsibility Act of 1996 mandates such cooperation. More than 120 cities have enacted a type of sanctuary policy that negates cooperation with federal authorities, including New York City, Chicago, Miami, Los Angeles, Houston, and San Francisco.[42] Maywood, California, is one of these sanctuary cities for undocumented immigrants. Maywood is a suburb of Los Angeles with 45,000 residents; 96% are Latino, over 50% are foreign-born, and roughly 35% are purportedly undocumented.[43] The city councils of San Francisco and Berkeley (California), Madison (Wisconsin), and Burlington (Vermont) have historically passed numerous resolutions that approve city sanctions against other countries, declare themselves nuclear-free zones, and oppose various policies supported by administrations in Washington.[44]

Most of these resolutions are relatively innocuous, except when they attempt to limit certain activities, such as a prohibition on any vehicle entering city limits with nuclear-related material on board or any ship visiting their ports that is equipped with nuclear weapons. In these rare cares, Washington acts swiftly and requests federal court judges to nullify these policies, almost always successfully. Various constituent governments have also been actively involved in opposing US policy in Iraq and in voting to support Kyoto Protocol objectives. In a ballot measure presented to San Francisco's voters in November 2004, two-thirds supported bringing US troops home from Iraq. In early 2006, forty-six Vermont towns passed resolutions demanding the same thing, and they have been joined by numerous other cities and towns across the nation.[45] At the 2005 annual meeting of the US Conference of Mayors, 168 mayors from cities in thirty-seven states committed their cities to upholding Kyoto Protocol environmental standards. In a historic meeting at the Port of Long Beach on the last day of July 2006, Governor Schwarzenegger of California signed a bilateral environmental accord with Prime Minister Tony Blair of Britain aimed at curbing emissions of greenhouse gases within their two jurisdictions. Schwarzenegger complained that the Republican administration in Washington "lacked leadership" on protecting the environment and said that it was time for California, the world's twelfth-largest source of greenhouse gases in 2005, to act to protect its own interests.[46] A month later, the California legislature imposed the most stringent controls on carbon dioxide emissions in the United States, pledging to cut such emissions by one-quarter by 2020. In August 2007 the Western Climate Initiative was formalized, which commits six US western states and the Canadian provinces of British Columbia and Manitoba to cutting greenhouse gas emissions to 15% below 2005 levels by no later than 2020.[47] This international accord involving federated units in the United States and Canada differs dramatically from the environmental policy positions of the George W. Bush administration in Washington and the Stephen Harper government in Ottawa.

The White House, of course, argues that foreign policy remains constitutionally in the exclusive domain of the national government and that the nation must speak with a unified voice on key foreign policy issues, even though such unity is usually more of a myth than a reality in the institutions of power within Washington's celebrated Beltway.[48] Some state and local governments, citing what they consider to be the success of their sanctions on companies doing business with South Africa during the apartheid period, beg to differ. However, most business associations are squarely on the side of Washington on this issue, claiming that both national and constituent-government sanctions and related activities hinder the market system at home and abroad and end up hurting US companies and workers more than the targeted countries. The National Foreign Trade Council and its affiliate, USA Engage, have been the focal point for major companies to express their displeasure with any state or local government intrusion into the realm of foreign policy.

To place this issue in proper perspective, only a distinct minority of state and local governments have actively engaged in foreign policy, whereas most engage in foreign relations and use international engagement primarily as a means to improve economic development within their state or municipal boundaries. At the municipal level, many partner through Sister Cities International or other groups or mechanisms to establish an international voice.[49] Sister Cities International, which was inspired by the vision of President Dwight D. Eisenhower in 1956 and split off from the National League of Cities in 1967, now helps to coordinate ties between almost 700 US municipalities and 1,750 foreign communities located in 134 countries.[50] It remains a good entry point for many towns and cities that are just getting their feet wet in terms of international engagement. Other cities or groups of neighbouring cities provide even more ambitious models for pursuing foreign affairs. The city of San Antonio, Texas, has operated an international affairs department for a quarter-century and has maintained an office in Japan for more than two decades. Its Casa San Antonio Program has also established close working relations with constituent government units in Mexico. The Greater Seattle Alliance is a public-private sector partnership encouraging export and investment activity and sponsoring periodic trade and investment missions abroad. The Kansas City Gateway project is another public-private sector program that works to build midcontinent commercial and transportation ties from Canada to Mexico, with Kansas City serving as a US hub for North American exchanges. Both the National League of Cities and the US Conference of Mayors have a variety of targeted programs to encourage these types of international activities on the part of municipal governments.[51] On the whole, however, in a nation where four of every five people live in urban settings, most US municipalities are not actively engaged in foreign affairs, and even the largest cities are only modestly engaged.[52]

For the most part, the vast majority of constituent governments will be able to find common ground on what constitutes foreign policy versus foreign relations, and state and local governments will continue to have tremendous discretionary latitude within the realm of foreign affairs. For the very few areas of disagreement that must still be resolved, either Congress or the federal courts will act as the final arbiter, and they will overwhelmingly tilt in favour of the national government's position.

The second challenge is the perceived erosion of state powers as a result of US international treaty and international accord obligations. As discussed previously, various state officials have argued that US commitments to the WTO, NAFTA, CAFTA, and other groupings of nations have stripped the states of some of the authority guaranteed to them by the US Constitution. This is especially the case in Chapter 11 of NAFTA, which may limit what state governments can do to protect the environment and the health of their citizens if such actions are construed by binational NAFTA panels as inhibiting or distorting North American trade and investment flows.

The third challenge is the dearth of intergovernmental cooperation in coping with the effects of globalization and creative destruction. State government representatives complain that they need good data on export and import activity at the local level but that Washington is actually cutting back on data gathering instead of expanding it. The same officials add that there is no effective dialogue with Washington over such issues as NAFTA's Chapter 11 and that inadequate consultation occurs with the states before the national government commits itself to international treaties or accords. State leaders, who actively seek grants-in-aid and other financial inducements from the national government, are beginning to think that their states are treated as any other interest group that lobbies in Washington rather than as constituent units deemed to be co-equal with the national government in the US Constitution.[53]

The fourth challenge is for all orders of government to engage in more effective public-private sector collaboration. The United States is a major underachiever in the export field, and most companies do not ship their products abroad. State and municipal governments are best equipped to work with small and medium-sized businesses locally and to establish world-class infrastructures, including vastly improved public education systems, that would assist these businesses in producing globally competitive goods and services and then in beginning to export their production overseas.

The fifth challenge is common to all federal systems. Is federalism a plus or a minus in coping with the exigencies of globalization and unprecedented technology change? Are unitary systems better equipped to react quickly and uniformly to international conditions? In the United States some states still engage in local protectionist practices that may alienate foreign investors. These investors would also prefer to see one set of laws governing business activity instead of fifty different state laws and one national law. States may also have widely different positions on key international issues. For example, some state governments might want price controls on gasoline and more federal spending on alternative energy sources. In contrast, major oil and gas producers such as Alaska and Texas would oppose some of these actions. In a country with 304 million people spread across the fourth-largest territorial expanse in the world, would an enhanced role for state and municipal governments in foreign relations actually benefit the individual American citizen in the long run?

The final challenge is for state governments to stop vacillating and finally decide what level of commitment they are willing to provide to their international programs beyond the next budgetary cycle. It is impressive that states now operate 230 offices abroad, compared to 4 in 1980. However, in 2002 states operated 243 offices in thirty different countries. During the administration of Governor Gray Davis, the predecessor to Arnold Schwarzenegger, all twelve state offices overseas were closed, and even the California Technology, Trade and Commerce Agency was disbanded. One governor may be enthusiastic about international programs, whereas his or her successor could care less about such involvement. Moreover, staffing levels and funding for programs falling within the realm of foreign affairs are insignificant in terms of overall state employment and expenditures. Even more ominously, staff assigned to international programs often perceive that they are the last hired and the first fired when states face periodic budgetary problems. Most state programs have also failed to engage in any serious long-range planning or to produce strategic papers focusing on their individual state's relationship to the regional and international economies, a situation that stands in stark contrast to the planning undertaken by the major provincial governments in Canada. Most states also lack sophisticated evaluation processes to ascertain the relative success or failure of their international pursuits. Even the term "foreign office" is somewhat of a misnomer because many states simply hire on a part-time or commission basis a contractor in another country to represent their interests. Many of these local contractors have full-time jobs elsewhere and work only occasionally to promote state activities. Frankly, state governments may give lip service to the notion of "thinking globally and acting locally," but their journey into the realm of US foreign relations has thus far been sporadic and largely devoid of long-term vision and institutional continuity.

CONCLUDING OBSERVATIONS

Elazar argued that "the virtue of the federal system lies in its ability to develop and maintain mechanisms vital to the perpetuation of the unique combination of governmental strength, political flexibility, and individual liberty that is the central concern of American politics."[54] This "virtue" will be tested significantly in the decades ahead. Already, the phenomenon known as "intermestic politics" is a fact of life in the United States. The term refers to the growing overlap of the domestic and international, with many policy decisions consisting of both dimensions.[55] Furthermore, globalization and unprecedented technology change have contributed to the acceleration of creative destruction and to a proliferation of intermestic issues. This rather volatile combination of forces means that governance in states and municipalities is more difficult than ever.

Globalization is here to stay and will intensify in the decades ahead. If it does not, this will probably be due to some horrible war or other cataclysmic event or due to a return to 1930s-style rampant protectionism, all of which would have dire consequences much worse than entrenched globalization. State and local government leaders must adjust to the changing circumstances and be cognizant of the fact that all nations, including a superpower, will be increasingly effected by decisions made and actions that occur beyond the frontiers of their nation-state.

For their own sakes and for the long-term vitality of the nation, both state and local governments should refrain from engaging in foreign policy, even though the number of times they have done so in the past has been very limited. They have every right to object to the policies of Washington, and this can be trumpeted through resolutions or initiatives. They should also act boldly to convince officials elected from their states to the US House of Representatives and the US Senate to overturn misguided national policies and laws. Nevertheless, the nation does need to speak at times with at least a somewhat unified voice on important issues in a very complicated world, and this should be the prerogative of national government leaders and institutions. In particular, the imposition of unilateral sanctions on foreign countries, whether put into effect by national or constituent governments, is rarely effective and tends to hurt the US business community and workers more than the targeted country.

Even so, state and local government involvement in a wide range of foreign relations activities should be encouraged and will undoubtedly accelerate in the future. As nations become more vulnerable to what transpires outside their frontiers, all orders of government will have to prepare to act and react. For states and municipalities, the world outside the United States contains almost 96% of global consumers and 75% of the global production of goods and services. This must be the target for local private companies, which provide most of the jobs in the United States and which must produce globally competitive goods and services to maintain or expand their operations. Constituent governments should assist the efforts of the private sector by providing a world-class infrastructure, a reasonable regulatory environment, a high quality of life, and top-ranked primary, secondary, and postsecondary education institutions and research laboratories. Helping to attract direct investment domestically and internationally, without resorting to market-distorting incentives, is another worthy activity for constituent governments. Providing basic information on how small companies can begin to export, arranging periodic trade and investment missions abroad, maintaining selective overseas offices or hiring contractors abroad, and other related activities are also worthwhile endeavours.

State and local governments desiring to be engaged internationally must commit themselves to long-range programs providing institutional continuity that will successfully bridge changes in elected leadership. They should also take better advantage of the expertise available through their regional or national organizations such as the National Governors' Association, the Council of State Governments, the National League of Cities, and the US Conference of Mayors. There are many areas where state and local offices can work together and across state lines, with only the attraction of FDI remaining a widely perceived zero-sum game. Intergovernmental cooperation can be improved substantially, and public-private sector collaboration must also be strengthened.

US constituent governments spent US$1.5 trillion from their own sources in 2006 and also received transfers from the national government of US$434 billion. Figuratively, only a few pennies of expenditures were devoted to international activities. Quebec, Ontario, Alberta, and to a lesser extent British Columbia spend far more on their international programs, devote many more people to these operations, and are far more sophisticated in planning and strategizing than are their counterparts in the United States. Of course, almost 40% of Canada's GDP is linked to international trade and investment activity, with more than 80% of all exports destined for only one foreign market, the United States. America's dependence on the outside world for growth in GDP and for jobs is only a fraction of Canada's, which helps to explain, up to a point, why the international programs of the US states are less developed. However, this reliance on the international economy to enhance the well-being of the citizens that the states represent will continue to grow, and state and local governments must be better prepared in the future to think globally, act locally, and stand up for the integrity and vitality of the US system of federalism.

NOTES

1 Richard Neustadt, *Alliance Politics* (New York: Columbia University Press, 1970); and Graham Allison, *Essence of Decision* (Boston: Little, Brown, 1971).
2 Robert Keohane and Joseph Nye, *Power and Interdependence: World Politics in Transition* (Boston: Little, Brown, 1977).
3 Eugene R. Wittkopf, Charles W. Kegley Jr, and James M. Scott, *American Foreign Policy*, 6th ed. (Belmont, CA: Thomson Wadsworth, 2003), 14.
4 For more background on the United States, see G. Alan Tarr, "United States of America," in John Kincaid and G. Alan Tarr, eds, *Constitutional Origins, Structure, and Change in Federal Countries*, 381–408 (Montreal and Kingston: McGill-Queen's University Press, 2005); Ellis Katz, "United States of America," in Akhtar Majeed, Ronald L. Watts, and Douglas M. Brown, eds, *Distribution of Powers and Responsibilities in Federal Countries*, 295–321 (Montreal and Kingston: McGill-Queen's

University Press, 2006); John Dinan, "United States of America," in Katy Le Roy and Cheryl Saunders, eds, *Legislative, Executive, and Judicial Governance in Federal Countries*, 316–43 (Montreal and Kingston: McGill-Queen's University Press, 2006); and William Fox, "United States of America," in Anwar Shah, ed., *The Practice of Fiscal Federalism: Comparative Perspectives*, 344–69 (Montreal and Kingston: McGill-Queen's University Press, 2007).
5 Manifest Destiny refers to a nineteenth-century belief held by many Americans that the United States was naturally destined to expand its territory from the Atlantic Ocean to the Pacific Ocean.
6 Ann O'M. Bowman, "American Federalism on the Horizon," *Publius: The Journal of Federalism* 32 (Spring 2002): 3–22, at 20.
7 Erich Steinman, "American Federalism and Intergovernmental Innovation in State-Tribal Relations," *Publius: The Journal of Federalism* 34 (Spring 2004): 95–114, at 113–14. Within the court system, *Cherokee Nation v. Georgia*, 30 US 1 (1831) provides significant insights on future intergovernmental relations involving tribes.
8 The title of the following article sums up some of the uncertainty among scholars of US federalism: Dale Krane and Heidi Koenig, "The State of American Federalism, 2004: Is Federalism Still a Core Value?" *Publius: The Journal of Federalism* 35 (Winter 2005): 1–41. To examine the issue in comparative perspective, consult Hans J. Michelmann and Panayotis Soldatos, eds, *Federalism and International Relations: The Role of Subnational Units* (New York: Oxford University Press, 1990); and Raoul Blindenbacher and Arnold Koller, eds, *Federalism in a Changing World* (Montreal and Kingston: McGill-Queen's University Press, 2003).
9 Samuel Krislov, "American Federalism as American Exceptionalism," *Publius: The Journal of Federalism* 31 (Winter 2001): 9–26, at 26.
10 The results of the Cincinnati meeting are detailed in Council of State Governments, *Restoring Balance to the American Federal System* (Lexington, KY: Council of State Governments, 1996).
11 A recent discussion of the Tenth Amendment is found in Mark R. Killenbeck, ed., *The Tenth Amendment and State Sovereignty: Constitutional History and Contemporary Issues* (Lanham, MD: Rowman and Littlefield, 2002).
12 In *Missouri v. Holland*, 252 US 416 (1920), the US Supreme Court decided that the national government's right to enter into treaties is supreme, even if such treaties interfere with the exercise of state authority. In *Zschernig v. Miller*, 389 US 429 (1968), the court threw out an Oregon probate statute that denied inheritance rights to residents of certain foreign countries. In *Massachusetts v. Laird*, 400 US 886 (1970), the Court nullified a Massachusetts law which stated that no resident of the state who was a member of the armed forces could be forced to fight in a hostile environment abroad (i.e., Vietnam) unless Congress first issued a formal declaration of war as outlined in Article 1, Section 8, Clause 11, of the US Constitution.
13 The unitary taxation formula was used by certain states to tax multinational corporations on the basis not only of their business activity within the affected state but

also of their entire activity around the world. The rationale for this formula was to prevent corporations from using accounting legerdemain to show a profit outside of the state but little or no profit in terms of their specific business pursuits within the state.

14. The Illinois law requires state pension funds to divest from companies doing business in Sudan. This prohibited list includes such companies as Eastman Kodak, Toyota, and Verizon Communications.

15. A thorough legal treatise on this issue is provided by Peter J. Spiro, "Globalization and the (Foreign Affairs) Constitution," *Ohio State Law Journal* 63, no. 2 (2002): 649–730. The federal courts have done little to differentiate between US treaties and what might be termed international pacts or accords. A treaty is negotiated by the executive branch and must be ratified by at least a two-thirds vote in the US Senate. Under fast-track or trade-promotion authority, which has been in effect for most, but not all, of the years since the presidency of Gerald Ford (1974–77), a pact or accord such as NAFTA or the WTO requires a majority vote in both the House of Representatives and the Senate. Thus far, these pacts or accords have been treated as functional equivalents to treaties in making the federal action supreme over any state laws or practices that run counter to provisions in these pacts or accords.

16. This letter is quoted in the testimony of Georgetown University law professor Robert Stumberg before the US Senate's Subcommittee on Federal Financial Management, Government Information, and International Security, 15 July 2005.

17. Daniel J. Elazar, *American Federalism: A View from the States*, 3rd ed. (New York: Harper and Row, 1984), 255.

18. "Federal Preemption of State Authority a Disturbing Trend," *NCSL News* (Denver), 16 August 2005.

19. Stumberg's testimony before US Senate, as cited at note 16.

20. Earl H. Fry, *The Expanding Role of State and Local Governments in U.S. Foreign Affairs* (New York: Council on Foreign Relations Press, 1998), 117.

21. These figures are for the end of 2004 and were compiled by the Bureau of Economic Analysis in the US Department of Commerce.

22. Peter Fisher and Alan Peters, "The Failure of Economic Development Incentives," *Journal of the American Planning Association* 70, no. 1 (2004): 27–38; and Dennis Cauchon, "Business Incentives Lose Luster for States," *USA Today*, 22 August 2007. In *DaimlerChrysler Corp. v. Cuno and Wilkins (Ohio Tax Comm.) v. Cuno*, 547 US (2006), the US Supreme Court ruled 9-0 that Ohio taxpayers had no right to challenge the state government's granting of US$300 million in tax breaks to entice DaimlerChrysler to build a new assembly plant in Toledo.

23. John Kincaid, "The International Competence of U.S. States and Their Local Governments," *Regional and Federal Studies* 9 (Spring 1999): 111–30.

24. State International Development Organization, *SIDO Survey 2006: Emerging Trends in State International Business Development* (Washington, DC: State International Development Organization, 2006); and Adrienne T. Edisis, "Global Activities by U.S. States: Findings of a Survey of State Government International Activities," paper

prepared for the Elliott School of International Affairs, George Washington University, July 2003.
25 Fry, *Expanding Role*, ch. 4; and John M. Kline, "The International Economic Interests of U.S. States," *Publius: The Journal of Federalism* 14 (Fall 1984): 81–94.
26 Fry, *Expanding Role*, 67–8. See also, John Kincaid, "The American Governors in International Affairs," *Publius: The Journal of Federalism* 14 (Fall 1984): 95–114.
27 Tommy G. Thompson, "Governors Are the Trade Ambassadors of the United States," *Governors' Bulletin*, 22 July 1996, 6; and Tommy G. Thompson, "Going Global: A Governor's Perspective," *Intergovernmental Perspective* 16 (Spring 1990): 15–17, at 15.
28 National Governors' Association, *Governors' Bulletin*, 8 July 1996, 1–2.
29 Thompson, "Going Global," 15–16.
30 US Department of Commerce, International Trade Administration, Office of Travel and Tourism Industries. See http://tinet.ita.doc.gov.
31 US Department of Commerce, International Trade Administration, Office of Travel and Tourism Industries, "Historical U.S. Travel and Tourism Statistics," http://tinet.ita.doc.gov/outreachpages/inbound_historic_visitation_2007.html (accessed 7 July 2008).
32 The US Council of State Governments, Eastern Regional Conference, uses data collected by the Conference Board of Canada and estimates that the United States would lose US$785 million in revenues because of fewer cross-border visits by Canadians. See the Council of State Governments, Eastern Regional Conference, "A Resolution Regarding the Western Hemisphere Travel Initiative," Halifax, Nova Scotia, 22 October 2005.
33 The San Diego Association of Governments estimates that fewer border crossings from Mexico, combined with the slow movement of tourism and commercial traffic at the border, results in US$1.3 billion in lost revenues annually in the San Diego region. See Brady McCombs, "Squeezing Border Business," *Arizona Daily Star*, 24 September 2006.
34 In 2004, 581,000 businesses or "employer firms" were created, and 576,000 were terminated. See US Small Business Administration, *The Small Business Economy: A Report to the President* (Washington, DC: US Government Printing Office, 2005), 7.
35 Data from Job Openings and Labor Turnover Survey (JOLTS), US Bureau of Labor Statistics, quoted in Robert M. Kimmitt, deputy secretary of the US Treasury, "Why Job Churn Is Good," *Washington Post*, 23 January 2007.
36 Edisis, "Global Activities"; Council of State Governments, *The Book of the States*, 2006 ed. (Lexington, KY: Council of State Governments, 2006), 353, 443. Spending on international programs represented 0.02% of total state expenditures, and employees engaged in international activities represented 0.04% of total state workers in noneducation sectors.
37 A detailed examination of the complex Texas-Mexico relationship is presented in Julia Melissa Blase, "Has Globalization Changed U.S. Federalism? The Increasing Role of U.S. States in Foreign Affairs: Texas-Mexico Relations" (PhD diss., University of Texas at Austin, 2003).

38 John Kincaid, "Constituent Diplomacy: U.S. State Roles in Foreign Affairs," in Daniel J. Elazar, ed., *Constitutional Design and Power-Sharing in the Post-Modern Epoch*, 107–42 (Lanham, MD: Jerusalem Center for Public Affairs and University Press of America, 1991).
39 Timothy J. Conlan, Robert J. Dudley, and Joel F. Clark, "Taking on the World: The International Activities of American State Legislatures," *Publius: The Journal of Federalism* 34 (Fall 2004): 183–201.
40 US Department of State, *Consular Offices in the United States* (Washington, DC: Government Printing Office, 2006). This list was compiled in August 2006.
41 Carolyn Lochhead, "Give and Take across the Border," *San Francisco Chronicle*, 21 May 2006.
42 "Sanctuary City, USA," http://www.ojjpac.org/sanctuary.asp (accessed 8 January 2008). Some city officials may argue that they do cooperate to a certain extent with federal officers and have set limits only on the degree of cooperation.
43 *Los Angeles Times*, 21 March 2006, A1, A18.
44 Heidi H. Hobbs, *City Hall Goes Abroad: The Foreign Policy of Local Politics* (Thousand Oaks, CA: Sage, 1994). These cities are exceptional in their stances on foreign policy. For example, only a handful of US cities have actually declared themselves nuclear-free zones. See also, John Kincaid, *American Cities in the Global Economy: A Survey of Municipalities on Activities and Attitudes* (Washington, DC: National League of Cities, 1997).
45 Consult http://www.citiesforpeace.org.
46 Edwin Garcia and Paul Rogers, "Governor, Blair Sign Warming Accord," *San Jose Mercury News*, 1 August 2006.
47 The six states are California, Oregon, Washington, Arizona, New Mexico, and Utah.
48 Michelle Sager, *One Voice or Many? Federalism and International Trade* (New York: LFB Scholarly Publishing, 2002).
49 A discussion of involvement by local authorities internationally is found in Chadwick F. Alger, "Searching for Democratic Potential in Emerging Global Governance," in Bruce Morrison, ed., *Transnational Democracy in Critical and Comparative Perspective*, 87–106 (Aldershot, UK: Ashgate, 2003), esp. 96–103.
50 See the Sister Cities International website: http://www.sister-cities.org.
51 The National League of Cities has an International Council composed of local elected officials who guide the development of international programs. The US Conference of Mayors has an International Affairs Committee that carries out similar functions.
52 Peter Karl Kresl and Earl H. Fry, *The Urban Response to Internationalization* (Cheltenham, UK: Edward Elgar, 2005), ch. 3.
53 The Sixteenth Amendment to the US Constitution, ratified in 1913 and authorizing income taxation, has greatly strengthened Washington's role in fiscal issues, to the disadvantage of state and local governments. The Seventeenth Amendment, also ratified in 1913, provides for the direct election of the two senators from each

state. Previously, senators were selected by the state legislatures. Although this amendment strengthened democracy, it has resulted in senators being less inclined to follow the policy recommendations of governors and state legislative leaders in dealing with the national government.
54 Elazar, *American Federalism*, 257.
55 The term "intermestic" was coined by Bayless Manning, "The Congress, the Executive and Intermestic Affairs: Three Proposals," *Foreign Affairs* 55 (January 1977): 306–24.

Conclusion

HANS J. MICHELMANN

The previous chapters demonstrate considerable diversity in the conduct of constituent-unit foreign relations in twelve federal countries. This chapter provides an overview and synthesis. Perforce, it cannot go into great detail. The reader will have discovered or is invited to discover the richness of the stories told in the previous country chapters to get a more complete picture; it is part of the goal of this chapter to provide a guide to the essentials and an overview of the range of foreign relations carried out by the constituent units of the countries featured in this book.

These countries vary significantly in many important attributes: size, wealth, ethnic composition, geographical context, history, constitutional and legal provisions affecting the management of foreign relations, and the extent of constituent-unit international activity. The latter varies from active participation in an increasingly complex international environment to an almost insignificant presence on the world stage.

Constituent units in the long-established federal countries have historically been involved in some form of foreign relations. Those adjacent to foreign countries have long been engaged in cross-border interactions with neighbouring polities involving practical "housekeeping" matters, as John Kincaid has labelled them, such as cooperation in transportation, flood and pollution control, and even the sharing of services – matters of low politics conducted primarily in a very limited geographic context. Of course, there have also been a few more prominent instances of constituent units' presence abroad; for example, some Canadian provinces and Australian states have long had offices in London, but these manifestations of "constituent diplomacy," also Kincaid's term, have been very much the exception.

Practical cooperation across national borders continues to be important. However, the scope and nature of constituent-government involvement with other polities (primarily other constituent units but also from time to time national governments), regional and international organizations, businesses, educational and cultural organizations, and so on have increased, although very modestly in some countries, in most federations during the past four decades. This has been due, among others factors to be explored below, to a variety of constitutional and political developments. In recent decades, the development of ever more sophisticated worldwide electronic communications has permitted increasingly efficient worldwide financial transactions and personal and commercial communication. Faster and more efficient transportation has allowed an ever increasing volume of goods and number of people to travel long distances cheaply and efficiently. The common term used collectively for these phenomena is "globalization," and globalization has accelerated the pace and broadened the scope of constituent-unit foreign relations. As Daniel Thürer and Malcolm MacLaren argue in their chapter on Switzerland, nowadays no policy sector in Switzerland is not in one way or another affected by international developments. This holds true, of course, in other federations. Hence, in some countries, constituent governments on an almost daily basis have to look beyond the borders of their countries to carry out their responsibilities. However, this is less common in other settings where the constituent units are rather less exposed to the world. It is part of the goal of this chapter to examine why.

THE DOMESTIC AND INTERNATIONAL SETTINGS OF CONSTITUENT-UNIT FOREIGN RELATIONS

Level of Economic Development

A first attempt to generalize, then, must examine the relationship between the level of economic development and the extent of constituent-unit foreign relations, although doing this is not to suggest that economic factors alone determine constituent-unit foreign relations. Such an examination leads to the conclusion that there is a positive correlation between these variables. The United States, Australia, Canada, Austria, Belgium, Germany, Spain, and Switzerland – all of them among the most wealthy countries – provide evidence of active constituent-unit foreign relations. In Argentina, with an intermediate level of wealth, this scope and intensity have not been attained to the same degree, and among the less developed countries – India, South Africa, and especially Malaysia – constituent diplomacy is considerably more limited, although developing gradually.

There is also considerable evidence that the direct relationship between wealth and international activity holds among constituent units within countries. Other variables can and do complicate the matter, and the correlation is not perfect, but such a relationship is highly plausible: wealthy countries and constituent units are usually more highly integrated into the global economy and more active in constituent diplomacy than are those with lower levels of economic development. Thus the scope and intensity of these constituent units' international transactions are greater in areas such as foreign trade, finance and investment, cultural exchanges, and international tourism.

Ethnic and Cultural Factors

Ethnic and cultural factors play a strong role in constituent-unit foreign relations in some countries. A prime example is Canada. There, Quebec, with its majority French-speaking population, is by a considerable margin the province most actively engaged in foreign relations. Its constituent diplomacy seeks to forge and strengthen relationships with francophone and other communities abroad and to ensure a high profile for the province internationally. In the past, under separatist governments, Quebec has sought to make a political statement about its potential to become an independent country. In Spain it is the constituent units populated by ethnic minorities, the Basque Country and Catalonia, that are most active in foreign relations. In the Basque case, this leads to close relations with the adjacent Basque community in France. In both cases, it gives a higher profile to the special nature of their regions and also builds relations with diasporas. Ethnicity also plays a part in the intensity and direction of constituent-unit foreign relations in Belgium. Wallonia's ties with France and those between Flanders and the Netherlands demonstrate the effects of such affinity, as do Swiss cantons' more intense relations with constituent units in adjoining countries that share their language. Relations among constituent units in Germany and Austria are facilitated and strengthened by a common language and culture. In Latin America, Argentine states' relationships with adjacent Spanish-speaking countries are stronger than with the Portuguese-language Brazilian states. In South Africa provinces' relations with adjacent jurisdictions are facilitated if cultural groups straddle the international border. In India common ethnicity in the past has on very rare occasions facilitated a hesitant constituent diplomacy between Indian and Pakistani states where the Punjabi community straddles the border between them, although historical animosity has made constituent diplomacy next to impossible. Thus ethnic affinity, in many instances reinforced by geographic proximity, affects the direction and intensity of constituent-unit foreign relations. In some contexts, such as Quebec and Catalonia, it also helps to strengthen a sense of national identity.

The Regional Context

The characteristics of the regional context in which a country is situated, including the extent and strength of regional organization, help to shape constituent diplomacy because where regional organization is prevalent, it involves constituent units in a network of cooperative relations with adjacent polities. "Region" denotes geographic proximity, an important consideration in itself for foreign relations because the most intense interactions, all things being equal, tend to be among neighbouring polities, if only because of the need to perform "housekeeping" functions discussed earlier. But these functions are only part of the story. For example, Argentina's provinces cooperate with neighbouring polities in projects to develop regional transportation infrastructure. Also, "region" does not refer only to immediate proximity. On a continent like Europe with a large number of smaller countries, environmental protection can, and typically does, involve more than just two countries, as does the management of infrastructure such as roads and railways. Regional organizations focus on other functions as well. The Four Motors of Europe brings together constituent units in Germany, France, Italy, and Spain to further cooperation in science, research, education, and culture.

As the country chapters demonstrate, other regional organizations affiliate with constituent units in deliberations about and the pursuit of common political interests – for example, in the Assembly of European Regions (AER) and in the networks of regions with legislative powers. The INTERREG intiative in the European Union (EU) serves to further economic and social cohesion among constituent units and provides substantial funds matched by member states. The Council of Europe's European Convention for Trans-Border Cooperation has promoted cross-border cooperation among constituent units. The chapters on the European countries, especially the Austrian chapter, demonstrate the large number of regional organizations in which the European constituent units participate and the broad scope, collectively, of these organizations' mandates. In North America, US states are affiliated with their constituent-unit counterparts in Mexico and Canada through regional organizations that treat subjects such as regional trade, investment, and tourism. But these regional organizations are not nearly as prevalent as those in Europe, nor are their mandates as strong.

Regional organizations are less prevalent in the developing world, although they are being established in eastern and northern South Africa under the tutelage of the national government. In India there are hesitant developments toward the creation of transborder regional organizations that would affiliate constituent units in the country's Northeast to develop regional infrastructure and to promote economic growth, although great potential for such cooperation does not yet exist along its borders with Pakistan for political reasons. Finally, Malaysia is a member of a number of regional organizations; however, these organizations are dominated by national governments and involve state governments only in a very limited way.

In developing countries, cooperation among constituent units lags considerably behind that in the economically more developed countries. Relations with neighbouring polities are more intense in the developed countries in Europe and North America than they are in Malaysia, India, and South Africa because vibrant private sectors that help spur governments to undertake foreign relations are less advanced in these developing countries and because they are situated in regions where neighbouring countries are very poor. That these neighbouring countries are so poor, even when compared with these three countries, creates some troubling problems for constituent units. The relative prosperity of India and Malaysia, as well as South Africa, attracts large numbers of economic migrants to constituent units adjacent to the poorer neighbours. For South African provinces, given the desperate economic and political plight of neighbouring Zimbabwe, one can even speak of refugees. In turn, these migrants and refugees give rise to attendant problems, such as resentment among the host countries' citizens that the newcomers are willing to work for very low wages, problems of sanitation and accommodation, and so on. Attempts to resolve these problems mean, among other things, negotiating with the federal government for financial help that may be slow in coming. In short, this puts public services under great stress.

All things being equal, in the wealthy federations the foreign relations between constituent units and other polities in their regions are more broad and intense and not nearly as problematic, not only because of government resources available to conduct foreign relations but also because private-sector organizations on both sides of the border interact frequently and because citizens cross borders to engage in recreation, to shop, and in some instances even to work. These private-sector interactions bring with them the need for cooperation among governments of adjacent jurisdictions.

The Special Case of EU Member States

A "regional organization" in its broadest sense can be based on more than geographic proximity and functionally delimited interactions among constituent units. Notably, constituent diplomacy in EU member states is embedded in a supranational organization, the EU, that is characterized by a high degree of economic, political, and policy integration. This has had a major impact on the foreign relations of Austrian, Belgian, German, Spanish, and even Swiss constituent units. Relations between constituent units and federal governments in all four EU states considered in this book have also been strongly and uniquely affected by their membership in the EU and have effectively increased constituent units' foreign relations roles in a manner not found in other federal countries. It is necessary to remember here, as noted in the relevant country chapters, that EU matters fall in a unique way between domestic and international matters in the sense that EU decisions and regulations integrally bind member states into the EU system, creating a hybrid system in which the distinction between the domestic and foreign is transcended in a manner not found anywhere else. Still the constituent units' relationships with the EU, and their interactions with their federal governments in this context, project their activities beyond national frontiers to Brussels, the EU capital, and involve them intensively in collective decision making with foreign national and constituent-unit governments.

Through participation in EU institutions and an increased role in developing their countries' positions before EU deliberations take place, constituent units are compensated for their loss to the supranational level of parts of their domestic powers in the affected policy sectors, powers that were (and continue to be) transferred during the integration process. When this transfer of powers took place, national governments took on the role of representing their countries' interests vis-à-vis the EU; hence constituent units lost any meaningful jurisdiction over these policy sectors. This practice was changed during the 1990s by the insistence of Belgian and German constituent units that their national governments involve them in the preparation of their countries' positions on EU decisions and allow them to participate directly in the EU decision-making process even to the point of representing their countries in the Council of Ministers when matters under their jurisdiction are considered. In Germany these changes were brought about through a change in the country's Constitution. Austrian *Länder* benefited from these developments, which helped to prompt similar changes in their relationship with Vienna. Here also, these changes were formalized through constitutional amendment. Spain's constituent units were the last to be granted consideration of their case for the right to participate in EU decision making in Madrid and Brussels, but they too are now actively engaged in both the national and supranational arenas.

After the decision-making powers affecting a policy sector are transferred to the EU, its policies become applicable to the member states. These are implemented by the member states' public services, especially those of constituent governments because so many EU laws and regulations fall into policy sectors under their jurisdiction. In carrying out these responsibilities, constituent governments develop further ties with European institutions. On a regular basis, they must cooperate with the EU Commission, which is responsible, among other matters, for policing the implementation of EU law. They also serve on numerous advisory committees to the commission and have representative offices in Brussels. What is more, they are members of a body, the Committee of the Regions, that has advisory functions vis-à-vis the EU institutions. In all these capacities, constituent-government officials interact in a complex web of relations with their counterparts' officials as well as with officials and politicians of other member states. These developments constitute a significant and unique role for constituent units on the international stage and, given the transfer of jurisdiction to the supranational level, have attenuated and otherwise transformed the constituent units' relationship with their citizens in ways not found in other settings.

Even Switzerland, which is not an EU member, has many bilateral agreements with the EU; hence cantons are actively engaged in relations with constituent units in EU member states. In comparison, the functions of other essentially regional intergovernmental organizations (as opposed to the supranational EU) – such as South America's Southern Common Market (MERCOSUR), where constituent units collectively are only beginning to play an advisory role, and the North American Free Trade Agreement (NAFTA) – are more modest, and their impact on constituent units is concomitantly substantially lower.

The Impact of History

The past, of course, conditions the conduct of politics and government in all countries. But history, particularly recent history, has had a special impact on constituent diplomacy in some countries. In Argentina and Spain, particularly, constituent-unit foreign relations must be seen in the context of their countries' recent past: in Spain the demise of the fascist dictatorship in 1975; and in Argentina the return of democracy in 1983 after a period of military rule. These two countries only reengaged fully in the international system after the stigma of dictatorship and the attendant isolation had passed; thus a tradition of constituent-unit foreign relations is not as established as it is in other federations.

The legacy of the Second World War has negatively affected relations across the Polish-German border and, thus, relations between German *Länder* and their counterparts in that country. By comparison, the end of the Cold War has encouraged relations between western European constituent units and their counterparts in central and eastern European countries as well as in Russia. Apartheid in South Africa made that country an international pariah, which left it isolated in the world while most of its people remained subject to a dictatorship. The overthrow of that system had major repercussions. South Africa is now very active internationally, although developing a fully functioning federation with strong provinces that are politically more independent of the national government and thus more likely to engage in foreign relations is still a work in progress. India's postindependence legacy of import-substitution industrial development contributed to its economic isolation, which began to disappear only with the implementation of liberal economic policies in the early 1990s, leading to the gradual abolition of impediments to foreign trade and investment. Liberalization of economic policy has opened up the states to the world and to the hesitant beginnings of participation in foreign relations.

As just discussed, the process of European integration, begun in 1951 with the establishment of the European Coal and Steel Community to help overcome the legacy of the Second World War, and progressing to the establishment of the EU, has had significant implications for constituent diplomacy in its member states. Moreover, as some European country chapters demonstrate, a constituent unit's historical legacy as an independent or quasi-independent political entity before, sometimes even well before, federation (e.g., Bavaria in Germany, Salzburg in Austria, and a number of Spanish autonomous communities) has led to a sense of identity that often seeks to find expression in constituent diplomacy.

Dominant Political Parties

Partisan politics is pervasive in democratic countries, with the party system playing a particularly strong role in the foreign relations of a number of countries as a backdrop to the functioning of other factors affecting the conduct of constituent-unit foreign relations. In Malaysia the dominance of the Barisan Nasional coalition in the country's politics, including in the states, when added to the centralizing features of the Constitution, helps to explain the tight control exercised from the centre and the almost complete lack of international activity by the states. Similarly, in India the long-time dominance of the Congress Party, together with a constitution that assigns only the Union government a role in foreign relations, once reinforced the almost complete lack of international activity by the states. It was only after that party no longer had the votes to dominate Parliament and after state politicians acquired the political clout to have some say in national politics that the states became more involved in limited, primarily economic foreign relations. In South Africa the dominance of the African National Congress in the political life of the country and the resulting centralization of government has meant that the provinces play a limited role in foreign relations. In the other countries not dominated by one party either presently or in the recent past, party politics is a normal part of political life. It has effects for the conduct of foreign relations without being a primary factor.

THE CONSTITUTIONAL SETTING

Assignment of Foreign Relations Powers

Constitutions provide the legal framework for constituent diplomacy and for the relations between constituent units and their federal government.

The constitutions of one group of countries assign only the federal government responsibility for foreign affairs and defence, either in a written constitution or through court interpretation as in Canada and Australia, without explicitly assigning constituent units any powers. The rest of the members of this group are India, Malaysia, and Spain. However, as demonstrated below, such a lack of powers does not necessarily impede constituent-unit foreign relations.

The second group of countries encompasses those whose constitutions explicitly assign constituent units some powers over foreign relations: the United States, Switzerland (since 1999), the Federal Republic of Germany, Austria, Argentina, Belgium, and South Africa (through the constitutional provision that the National Council of Provinces ratifies international agreements). The degree of the constituent units' empowerment in these countries varies considerably, ranging from making treaties in their areas of jurisdiction without the tutelage of the federal government, as in Belgium, to the authorization of Argentine provinces to sign agreements of limited scope with foreign partners as long as these agreements do not conflict with the national government's powers over foreign policy.

Trends in the Assignment of Constituent-Unit Powers Is there evidence that constituent units have been assigned greater foreign relations powers in constitutions recently enacted than in those enacted in previous times? Among the four oldest constitutions, the American, Australian, Canadian, and Swiss (when initially enacted in 1848), three grant the federal government, but not constituent units, powers over foreign relations; in the United States, states are allowed to enter into agreements and compacts with foreign powers with the assent of Congress, and at one time, through their direct representation in the Senate, they could influence the conduct of American foreign policy, although after 1913 senators were directly elected and the ability of state governments to affect national policy diminished because senators could no longer be directly instructed by state governments. In the constitutions that came into effect in the post-Second World War period before the mid-1960s – Austria, Germany, India, and Malaysia – constituent units are accorded foreign relations powers in the first two countries but not in the other two. As for the most recently enacted constitutions – Spain, Argentina, South Africa, and Belgium – the Belgian assigns such powers to constituent units, the broadest powers in all twelve countries, while in South Africa provincial representation in the National Council of Provinces means that provinces participate in the legislative approval of treaties. Neither in Spain nor in Argentina were such powers explicitly granted to constituent units. Hence constituent units were granted foreign relations powers by four of the eight constitutions enacted after the Second World War – two in the immediate postwar years and two in the period after 1965. There is, then, a slight trend toward an increase in the assignment of foreign relations powers to constituent units (one of four among the older federations and four of eight among those established after the Second World War), although no positive trend is discernable when comparing the two periods after the Second World War.

Constituent units in five countries, then, were assigned foreign relations powers when their constitutions were first enacted: the United States, Austria, Germany, South Africa, and Belgium. Such powers were granted to cantons by a 1999 constitutional amendment in Switzerland. Argentina's provinces, through a 1994 constitutional amendment, have been accorded the power to make agreements with international partners, although subject to some constraints. In Germany and Austria constitutional amendments were made in the 1990s to allow constituent units enhanced participation in EU decision making both domestically and in Brussels, thus enhancing their foreign relations powers.

The role of Belgian constituent units in EU decision making was enhanced by a 1994 agreement through which constituent governments are accorded the right to speak for Belgium in the Council of Ministers on matters under their exclusive jurisdiction and to participate in the Belgian delegation in matters of concurrent jurisdiction. Spain's constitution initially provided the autonomous communities no legal basis to participate in foreign policy. As is the case for their counterparts in the three other EU member states, they have recently seen their powers increase in EU decision making, again both domestically and in Brussels. What is more, although in the early years after 1978 the Constitutional Court rulings allowed the autonomous communities almost no role in foreign affairs, a subsequent judgment has loosened these restrictions significantly so that they are now allowed to undertake international activities in their areas of jurisdiction as long as these do not encroach on the powers of the national government or create new obligations for it. Finally, a 1996 Australian amendment to the agreements between the Commonwealth government and the states on treaty making enhances their foreign relations role. There has been no increase for constituent units in powers over foreign relations in five countries: Canada, India, Malaysia, South Africa, and the United States.

Thus, through the assignment of powers in constitutions enacted after the Second World War (Austria, Belgium, Germany, and South Africa) and/or through constitutional amendments or legal changes since then (Argentina, Australia, Austria, Belgium, Germany, Spain, and Switzerland), constituent units have been accorded foreign relations powers or increased foreign relations powers in eight of the twelve countries. This is a significant trend toward initial or further empowerment of constituent units in foreign relations in the post-Second World War period.

Constituent Units and Treaties

Assignment of Treaty-Making Powers Treaties and treaty making are at the heart of much of the process of intergovernmental relations between constituent units and their federal governments in the management of foreign relations. The constitutions of only four of the twelve countries discussed in this book explicitly grant constituent units powers to make treaties. Those of Germany and Austria provide constituent units treaty-making powers in areas of their exclusive jurisdiction. But in both countries federal consent is required before a treaty is concluded.

In the case of Germany, there have been numerous such treaties, but all of very limited importance, dealing with cross-border matters such as cooperation in management of the environment, in building and maintaining physical infrastructure, and in education and culture. In Austria the *Länder* have thus far concluded no treaties. However, in both countries the federal government is required to consult the constituent units before concluding treaties in policy fields under their jurisdiction: in Germany such treaties include those that affect the constituent units' particular interests, and in Austria, more restrictively, they include those that must be implemented by the constituent units. In Austria, if treaties are concluded by the federal government in areas under *Land* jurisdiction, assent of the Federal Council, in which *Land* parliaments are represented, must be sought. In Germany the *Bundesrat*, which represents *Land* governments, must assent to treaties, a significant constitutional feature in the conduct of German foreign policy.

In Switzerland the confederation (federal government) is required to take into account the cantons' powers and interests and must provide for their participation in treaty negotiations. The cantons may deal directly with foreign constituent polities and conclude treaties in areas of their jurisdiction, provided that these are not contrary to the confederation's laws and interests, and the confederation must be notified prior to the treaty's conclusion.

Belgian constituent units have been accorded treaty-making powers, without federal oversight, in the large number of fields of their exclusive jurisdiction, and they participate with the federal government in areas of concurrent jurisdiction. These very broad powers, the most extensive in the twelve countries, are tempered somewhat by the requirement that constituent-unit actions should not contradict the general orientation of Belgian foreign policy and that the federal government should be informed of any treaties that the constituent units are negotiating. As demonstrated below, an elaborate system of consultation, found also in the other four members of this group, is meant to help ensure that Belgium's relations with the world are not rendered incoherent.

The country chapters show that constituent-unit powers to make treaties are correlated with active constituent diplomacy. The exercise of such powers has the potential to lead to conflicts with federal governments because these see it as their role to represent their countries abroad and because the line between what is federal and what is constituent-unit territory is often difficult to draw. The following sections, including especially that on intergovernmental relations, demonstrate what mechanisms have been devised toward ensuring that interactions between constituent and federal governments are managed peacefully and productively.

The Role of Upper Houses Each of the federations considered in this book has a bicameral legislature and thus an upper house whose responsibilities typically include the formal representation of constituent units in the federal government's decision-making process. Do these upper houses give constituent governments a role as participants in the formulation of national foreign policy, including treaty making, when such policy affects their own foreign relations interests?

The short answer is that they are not given a great role, with three exceptions where constituent governments are represented either by the political executive directly or by contingents of legislators. The absence of reliable and effective links between the constituent governments and the representatives of constituent units in upper houses, because of the way that these representatives are elected or appointed and because of partisan politics, often undermines this means of participation by constituent governments in decision making on national foreign policy. The constituent-unit representatives in an upper house may reflect the views of constituent governments, but there is no guarantee that they will. Hence, although upper houses have committees on foreign relations, and even though in some countries the upper house is called upon to ratify treaties, the positions they take are not guaranteed to reflect those of constituent governments.

In Argentina, Australia, Switzerland, and the United States, members of the upper house are directly elected; that is, constituent governments per se are not represented, and members of the upper house can thus not be held accountable by them. Partisan and other political considerations are often more important than the representation of constituent governments, and although members can choose to speak on their behalf, they will normally represent the interests of their constituent unit as they interpret them – which may or may not accord with the position taken by constituent governments. In Canada the Senate is not considered a body of regional representation, primarily because its members are appointed by federal governments and thus have no democratic legitimacy. Provincial governments, therefore, have no effective representation in that institution. In

Malaysia a weak parliament very rarely considers international relations in a system in which the conduct of these matters is monopolized by the executive. In India the states are directly represented in the upper house, and Parliament votes on matters of foreign policy and defence, but governments have a parliamentary majority, which means that, although debates and committee deliberations on these matters take place, it is the political executive that makes final decisions in matters of foreign policy. In Spain the upper house is weak and has no effective influence over foreign policy.

Only in Germany, Austria, and South Africa are constituent governments represented in the upper house. The means of representation vary. In Germany *Land* executives are represented and have an effective role in decision making on foreign policy. Ratification of international treaties requires the consent of the *Bundesrat*, and the importance of this role is demonstrated by the participation of *Land* premiers in major deliberations on foreign policy. South Africa's provinces are represented in the National Council of Provinces by delegations headed by their premiers and instructed by their legislatures, and with a simple majority, they can thwart ratification of treaties. In Austria the Federal Council, composed of *Land* representatives elected by their parliaments, must approve treaties only in areas of *Land* jurisdiction, which means that they do not have as strong a role in national foreign policymaking as do their German counterparts. What is more, because they are elected by their parliaments, there is no guarantee that the representatives of any one *Land* will speak with one voice. It is only in Germany and South Africa, then, that the constituent governments participate directly in foreign policymaking. The German *Länder* have taken full advantage of these powers and have exercised their influence openly and repeatedly. The South African provinces have been more reticent to exercise their powers independently of their federal government because of the African National Congress's all-pervasive role in politics.

Treaty Negotiation Austrian, Belgian, German, and Swiss constituent governments, in addition to their right to make treaties in their areas of jurisdiction, are accorded the right to be consulted about treaties made by their federal governments. This right strengthens their treaty-making role. In South Africa provinces have the right to be consulted by virtue of the constitutional provisions for cooperative government.

But even if there are no explicit constitutional provisions for consulting with constituent units on treaties in policy sectors under their exclusive or concurrent jurisdiction, it is prudent for a federal government to engage them meaningfully in the process of devising a national position on negotiations or even in the negotiating process itself. This is so for practical reasons. First, constituent governments have valuable expertise that is often lacking in the federal public service. Second, each will know the special circumstances of its province, state, or canton, and thus collectively they will be able to provide insights about how a treaty will affect the entire country. Third, friction between the two orders of government that may arise out of the implementation process is likely to be reduced or avoided if constituent units have participated in the negotiating process both to represent their interests and to gain a clearer understanding of the issues and complexities involved.

Constituent units have good reason to press their federal governments for participation in treaty making because treaties signed by federal governments can whittle away or restrict the exercise of their powers. For example, as the chapter on Switzerland demonstrates, this was a concern shared by Swiss cantons, and it prompted the 1999 constitutional amendment that accords the cantons a greater role in the foreign policy process. It is a continuing concern of US states and Canadian provinces. Constituent governments in EU member states saw some of their powers erode when these were transferred to the EU by their federal governments. These issues, then, provide a strong rationale from the perspective of constituent governments for well-functioning systems of intergovernmental relations that can take their concerns into account when foreign policy decisions that affect them are made by their federal governments.

Federal governments, by comparison, are inclined to be concerned about the restrictions imposed on them in the management of national foreign policy by the often cumbersome process that results from the need to consult a large number of constituent governments and the need to arrive at negotiating positions that represent a compromise among their various positions and interests. They are inclined to be concerned about an inability to react expeditiously to an often rapidly changing international environment, especially to quickly and decisively engage in the horse trading that characterizes international negotiations, and are also likely to have some doubt about the experience of constituent-government officials. A clear example of the clash between the perspectives of a federal government and constituent units is the attempts by the German federal government to bring about reforms of the process of intergovernmental relations established in the early 1990s in order to give the *Länder* a greater role in EU decision making both in Berlin and in Brussels. Such stresses and strains are features as well of intergovernmental relations in other countries; for example, in Canada and the United States it is the constituent units that are calling for a more elaborate and structured process of intergovernmental relations, while the federal governments are unwilling to cede them competences in this area.

Implementation of Treaties The foregoing discussion demonstrates that the implementation of treaties is potentially a divisive issue because it may impose unwanted obligations on constituent governments and impinge on or even erode their powers. How, then, can it be assured that obligations that federal governments incur in signing treaties are carried out when implementation falls to constituent units? Constitutional practice in this regard ranges from legal compulsion of constituent governments to implement treaties, to constituent-government discretion in implementing treaties signed by their federal government, to the right to refuse implementation. The following discussion will be summary, although it will highlight some significant peculiarities.

In two countries, India and Malaysia, the national governments legislate the states' implementation of treaties. In another group, Argentina, Austria, and Switzerland, constituent units are also required to implement treaties. In the United States treaty obligations become binding on states. In Australia, if after attempts at negotiation and persuasion states do not implement treaties, the Commonwealth can pass laws to ensure they do so. In South Africa provinces are constitutionally required to implement treaties that affect provincial and concurrent jurisdiction. Spain's Constitutional Court has ruled that both the national and constituent governments must comply with international treaties adopted by Spain, and in case of partial or total noncompliance by autonomous communities, action can be taken against them by the central government in the Constitutional Court or the Council of State.

In three countries the practice is not as straightforward. In Germany the question of implementation of treaties concluded in areas of exclusive *Land* jurisdiction is legally unresolved. However, an agreement between the federal government and the *Länder* in effect since 1957, the Lindauer Abkommen, has been followed in regulating the interactions between the two orders of government. As a result, major controversies have been avoided. In Belgium, in a reversal of what happens in other federations, the constituent-unit legislatures must ratify treaties negotiated by the national government in their areas of jurisdiction or in areas of concurrent jurisdiction; hence constituent units can refuse to implement such treaties. They will, of course, implement treaties that they have negotiated themselves. Finally, in Canada it is the provinces' responsibility to pass legislation to implement treaties whose subject matter is under their jurisdiction; they can thus choose whether or not to implement. Nonimplementation has been largely avoided by virtue of federal-provincial consultation, although in some instances, notably in the dispute about implementation of the Kyoto Protocol discussed in the Canadian chapter, relations can become fractious.

Other International Agreements Limiting the discussion to treaties would give a restrictive view of commitments made by constituent governments to foreign partners. Far outnumbering treaties is a range of agreements not subject to international law. What Thürer and MacLaren in their chapter on Switzerland characterize as "gentlemen's agreements" are used by constituent units to establish and maintain relations in many policy fields – tourism, culture, cross-border "housekeeping," promoting and cooperating in economic development, and so on. The country chapters demonstrate that such agreements are commonly used, although their number and significance vary among the twelve countries. Their use brings a degree of pragmatism and flexibility to the foreign relations of constituent units and allows them to expand their range of actions beyond what would occur if such relations in every instance required the lengthy and tedious process of negotiating a treaty.

INTERGOVERNMENTAL RELATIONS

Three patterns of intergovernmental relations can be distinguished among eleven of the twelve countries: one in which the federal government controls the process and constituent units are subordinate; one in which relations between the two orders of government are more evenly balanced, although the federal government has the greater role and procedures are only partly formalized; and one characterized by an elaborate and institutionalized set of structures and regularized procedures in the relations between the federal government and the constituent units, where federal government actions are circumscribed by constitutional or legal provisions and the two partners are, at least in terms of intergovernmental relations, on a more or less equal footing. Intergovernmental relations in Argentina, India, Malaysia, and South Africa conform to the first pattern; in Canada and Australia to the second; and in Austria, Belgium, Germany, and Switzerland to the third. Spanish intergovernmental relations are moving in the direction of the third pattern and hence are discussed in that context. The United States does not fit any of these patterns well.

Group One: National-Government Dominance

The federal government has the preeminent role in intergovernmental relations in the first group of countries. Contacts between constituent units and the federal government on foreign relations, when they occur, are limited mostly to discussions of technical issues, provision of training and support by the federal government, and supervision of constituent units in their international activities. Discussions rarely take place at the political level, if at all. No specialized structures have been established for ongoing consultation or negotiations between the two orders of government, although in both Argentina and South Africa the federal government's foreign affairs ministry has a unit with responsibility to liaise with the provinces. Constituent units are engaged in foreign relations to only a very limited degree, although in Argentina such activity is increasing.

Intergovernmental relations in Malaysia, whose states are not active in foreign relations, are very limited in scope and conducted in the context of a process dominated by the national government. Its ministries and agencies from time to time consult the states on various matters, primarily foreign economic policy, but this consultation is initiated and controlled by the central government and is conducted at the civil-service level.

Intergovernmental processes are somewhat more complex in India. Chief ministers from both orders of government occasionally meet to discuss foreign economic policy, but no structures or processes for regular interaction have been established. Federal civil servants maintain control of the consultation process.

The South African system operates in a similarly top-down fashion. Foreign relations are considered the prerogative of the national government. It seldom consults with provinces on international matters relating to provincial competences, and these matters are infrequently raised, if at all, in intergovernmental meetings at the political and senior-official levels.

In Argentina the federal government's role is also preeminent. Within the Ministry of Foreign Affairs, the Directorate of Federal Affairs interacts with the provinces on the whole range of issues relevant to provinces' foreign relations and provides training and assistance to their officials. It helps to facilitate cooperation between provinces and goes further to include municipal governments as it seeks to engender cooperation among the three orders of government in their engagement with the international community. Intergovernmental relations are conducted almost exclusively at the civil-service level.

Group Two: Loosely Structured Interaction, Federal Government in Leading Role

In Australia, Canada, and Spain consultation between the federal and constituent governments is not constitutionally mandated, but structures and practices have nonetheless developed to foster cooperation. With some exceptions, constituent units are not as engaged in foreign relations as those in group three. The national government and constituent governments cooperate in a loosely structured framework where the federal government is in a senior position and can exercise a good deal of discretion in its interactions with constituent units.

There is no single Canadian intergovernmental forum that regularly brings together representatives of the federal and provincial governments. There are annual federal-provincial ministerial meetings in the policy sectors most affected by international relations, and depending on need, periodic meetings occur between federal and provincial officials, as do contacts between their ministries. In other policy sectors, meetings are less frequent. Provinces are consulted on matters affecting provincial jurisdiction in policy-specific forums operating with varying degrees of institutionalization and organizational support. In the negotiations of treaties of greatest significance to provinces, federal officials consult with them, allow them to participate in developing the Canadian position, and keep them regularly informed during the negotiations. Provinces have urged the federal government to institutionalize these procedures more thoroughly and to give the provinces a formal role in treaty negotiations, but there has been no positive response so far. On a day-to-day basis, regular consultation takes place between federal ministries and provincial offices responsible for foreign affairs.

Australia's intergovernmental relations in foreign affairs are somewhat more structured. Consultation is institutionalized at the highest level through a committee of senior Commonwealth and state officials from key departments, including that of the prime minister. The committee meets at least biannually. A formal statement of guidelines for Commonwealth-state relations in the field has been approved by the heads of government. It provides that states' views be taken into account in formulating Australia's position in negotiations. The Commonwealth government regularly provides state governments with information about treaties and an evaluation of their impact on Australia. State representatives frequently attend treaty negotiations as observers when these involve issues important to them in order to keep states informed and to provide information and advice to Commonwealth negotiators. Day-to-day consultation is carried on between the Commonwealth and the states through regular interactions between departments at both levels responsible for individual policy sectors and at the highest levels between the offices of the prime minister and the state premiers.

The Spanish system of intergovernmental relations fits uneasily into this classification scheme because it takes on two quite different forms. One is geared toward Spanish participation in the EU, where relations between the central and constituent governments are structured and frequent. Consultation between constituent units and Madrid by civil servants is organized around "sectoral conferences." Only one of these conferences, that dealing with the EU, has an explicit foreign relations mandate, and given the breadth of European policies, it works closely with other conferences. Some of the latter, however, are beginning occasionally to discuss international issues beyond the EU. What is more, intergovernmental relations are complicated by the lack of a uniform relationship between the central government and the autonomous communities, each having its own constitutional agreement with Madrid; hence consultation on foreign relations is often conducted bilaterally. But there are signs that a more uniform system could be developing based on the new statute to govern relations between Madrid and Catalonia, which may well become a model for a more systematized approach to intergovernmental relations.

Group Three: Highly Formalized Procedures, Strong Role for Constituent Units

Intergovernmental relations in the third group of countries are much more structured and subject to formal agreements than in the countries in groups one and two, and they often involve national and constituent government ministers, frequently at the head-of-government level. In each country, a system of committees has been established where politicians and/or public servants meet regularly. In each EU member state, the most active and structured network is that dealing with EU policies. The constituent units of all three EU countries in this group, although to a more limited degree in Switzerland, are more actively engaged in foreign relations on a wider range of issues than those in other countries, making cooperation between them and their federal governments a necessity.

Austrian intergovernmental relations operate at both the administrative and political levels. *Land* governors and presidents of *Land* parliaments meet regularly with their federal counterparts. Consultation between the *Länder* and the federal government on fundamental questions of EU policy and foreign policy is conducted in a number of councils dealing with European and foreign policy. The cooperation between the two orders of government on EU matters is intense and continuous. *Länder* participate in the preparations for EU negotiations, and both *Land* politicians as well as senior public servants serve as representatives of the *Länder* on Austrian delegations to the EU, the Council of Europe, and other international organizations such as United Nations (UN) agencies, where they speak on behalf of all *Länder* and report back to them.

Belgium's elaborate system of coordination is necessary to ensure a coherent foreign policy in a setting in which the constituent units have very broad foreign relations powers. At the highest level, a coordinating-committee structure brings together federal and constituent-unit heads of government. Sectorally specific consensus-based interministerial conferences include the statutorily established Inter-Ministerial Conference on Foreign Policy. A series of cooperation agreements between the federal government and the constituent units regulates intergovernmental relations in the formulation and implementation of Belgian foreign policy. The foreign affairs ministry organizes the interaction between federal and constituent officials in EU policy sectors, involving heads of government if necessary, so that they can work toward consensus. Cooperation agreements among constituent governments facilitate coordination on EU policies.

The preparation of the Belgian position in other fields is not as formally organized. It involves a coordinating committee, operated by the Ministry of Foreign Affairs, whose sectoral subcommittees of federal and constituent-unit civil servants work toward a consensus on foreign policy issues affecting constituent-unit interests. A series of cooperation agreements between the national and constituent governments institutionalizes cooperation among them to work toward establishing coherent Belgian positions vis-à-vis the world.

German intergovernmental relations regularly involve both politicians and public servants. An agreement, the Lindauer Abkommen, regulates interaction between the two orders of government on the disputed matter of treaty making and implementation in policy sectors under *Land* jurisdiction, leading to generally harmonious relations. Extensive interaction between the federation and *Land* governments takes place in the *Bundestag*'s Committee on Foreign Policy, Defence and EU matters, which deals with, among other issues, German policies toward the EU. Numerous committees have been established primarily at the civil-service level, but if necessary these involve political leaders to foster communication and cooperation in that context. *Länder* participate in the federal government's delegation to the international organizations whose mandates affect their jurisdiction. Participation by *Land* governments in EU decision making in Brussels, which includes representing Germany on matters in their exclusive jurisdiction, is contentious because the federal government feels that their participation has made representing the German position cumbersome, inefficient, and less effective. The federal government's attempts to reform the process have not met with success. Organizing the day-to-day interaction between the federal and *Land* governments is the responsibility of the Ministry of Foreign Affairs and may involve participation of the chancellor's office and other ministries depending on the policy sectors involved. In the *Länder* relevant ministries and the premier's office deal with foreign affairs. Each *Land* has a representative office in Berlin. At their frequent meetings, the *Land* premiers regularly address EU matters and foreign relations.

Switzerland's Federal Law on the Participation of the Cantons in the Foreign Policy of the Confederation operationalizes the constitutional provision that there be intergovernmental cooperation in foreign relations. An elaborate system of intergovernmental relations is mandated, and a system of bodies that institutionalize confederation-canton relations as well as relations among cantons has been set up to foster cooperation between the confederation and the cantons and among the cantons. There is regular consultation between the confederation and the cantons before the negotiation of treaties with other states and with international organizations, and cantonal representatives can participate in international negotiations as part of the Swiss delegation. Cantons wish to be seen as partners with the federal government in making, and being co-responsible for, foreign policy. The confederation is also obligated to take into account the interests of municipalities in the conduct of foreign relations.

The United States as a Special Case

Speaking of a system of US intergovernmental relations would be misleading because, as Earl Fry argues, communications between the states and the federal government on foreign relations are intermittent at best. The few federal agencies with responsibility for liaison with states infrequently interact with them, in good part because the federal government views foreign policy as its domain. If there is conflict, it is ultimately subject to resolution on Washington's terms. Here, then, is a pattern of intergovernmental relations unique among the twelve countries. As in the countries of group one, there is a dominant federal government with the final say on all aspects of foreign policy. But there is not even the loosely structured system of intergovernmental relations that exists in Australia and Canada, let alone the highly structured system characteristic of the countries in group three that affords constituent units regular consultation and negotiation with their federal governments and among themselves. Nonetheless, many states are actively engaged in foreign relations. That such a system does not serve states' interests well is evident in their requests that there be a better developed system of intergovernmental relations so that there is systematic interaction with Washington. This objective is pursued for essentially the same reasons that such systems have developed in other countries, namely the protection of constituent-unit constitutional interests and the practical benefits of cooperation on the world stage.

Intergovernmental Relations: An Assessment

What can be learned from this overview of intergovernmental relations in the twelve countries? Among the countries with the least developed intergovernmental structures are the lower-income cases: Argentina, India, Malaysia, and South Africa. The common factor in all these cases is a strong national government and a constitution that gives the predominant role in foreign relations to the national government. In all countries a strong national government is seen as essential to economic development. At the same time, constituent units generally do not yet have the expertise and financial resources to become actively engaged in foreign relations. Hence there is no great need for highly developed intergovernmental relations.

Another common factor in two cases, Malaysia and South Africa, is one-party dominance. In Malaysia this reinforces the already strong centralization bias in the constitution. In South Africa such dominance overshadows constitutional provisions for a more decentralized system of government and a more federalized structure than have evolved in practice. Argentina's states are still finding their way in foreign relations – hence the federal government's central role – but they are becoming more active, and there are signs that intergovernmental relations may well be developing toward a more decentralized system in which provinces will gain a greater role. In short, intergovernmental relations in Argentina are highly centralized and less complex than those in the other federations.

Intergovernmental relations in group two countries can in part be explained by the more limited degree of constituent diplomacy when compared with that in group three, with the notable exception of the Canadian province of Quebec and some Spanish autonomous communities. In these countries' constitutions, there is no explicit provision for constituent-unit foreign relations or provision for participation in the foreign policy process, although the three governments involve their constituent units in the treaty-making process. Constituent units, when compared with those in group one, have been longer established – in the case of Canada and Australia, much longer – and have developed strong identities. They have greater powers and function in less centralized constitutional and political settings than do those countries in group one. Canada has always lacked structured intergovernmental relations; thus the pattern in foreign relations is not unexpected. In Spain the lack of homogeneity in constitutional arrangements between Madrid and the autonomous communities has made the development of a highly structured system of intergovernmental relations difficult.

The defining characteristic of group three is the dense network of institutionalized structures and processes for intergovernmental relations. These can be explained mostly by the constitutional provisions that constituent units be closely involved in formulating their countries' relations with international partners in policy sectors under their jurisdiction and that they be engaged in treaty negotiations in their own right. The three EU members are heavily engaged in the EU decision-making process and must in that context cooperate with their federal governments in a highly structured system. In Austria, Germany, and Switzerland the pattern of intergovernmental relations mirrors that in other policy sectors. However, in Belgium, where on domestic matters the constituent units operate quite independently, the need to arrive at a common national position on foreign policy matters requires a degree of structured relations equal to that in Austria, Germany, and Switzerland. Intergovernmental relations regularly involve not only senior public servants but also federal and constituent-unit ministers, even up to the level of heads of government. In Austria, Belgium, and Germany the most highly structured subsystem is that established to manage relations with the EU in order to ensure a coherent national position in EU decision making.

The pattern of relations between the two orders of government in these countries varies, with bilateral relations between federal ministries in charge of policy sectors and constituent units being the norm in some settings, whereas in others the foreign ministry plays a coordinating role. The most highly formalized systems of intergovernmental relations also result from constitutional and legal provisions entitling constituent units to be consulted when their federal governments are involved in treaty negotiations in their areas of jurisdiction. In all four countries, constituent units regularly discuss common interests in conferences of constituent-unit heads of government. The German and Belgian systems provide constituent units with arguably the strongest roles in intergovernmental relations but for quite different reasons. In Germany *Land* governments are integrated into national decision making through their membership in the powerful *Bundesrat*, which helps to shape German foreign policy. In Belgium the constituent governments' strong domestic and concomitant foreign relations powers give them a role equal to that of the federal government in intergovernmental relations.

CONSTITUENT DIPLOMACY

The country chapters demonstrate the diversity of international activity undertaken by constituent units and how the policy sectors for which they are responsible are affected by developments and forces from beyond their national borders. Their reaction to these and, indeed, the actions they initiate themselves vary for constitutional and legal, political, and economic reasons as well as for reasons having to do with the features of their environment. The chapters also demonstrate that constituent units are not all equally active in constituent diplomacy; for example, Gauteng is by some measure the most active province in South Africa, and Zürich is more engaged than other Swiss cantons.

Even cities become engaged internationally. Twinning and sister-city agreements with foreign cities are common in many countries and do much to foster good will as well as allow partners to exchange experience in local government and to establish commercial ties. In some cases, cities cooperate with their constituent units to engage in development aid, as the chapters on Austria and Spain demonstrate. Australian local councils have been active in areas such as providing skills training, medical supplies, and financial aid to countries in the South Pacific. Management of cross-border relations with neighbouring polities is part of municipal diplomacy in Switzerland and elsewhere. The promotion of economic interests abroad is an important feature of municipal diplomacy, especially in the United States and in cities such as Montreal and Zürich.

If one set of activities is preeminent in constituent-unit foreign relations, it is that centred on the promotion of economic interests. Such activities constitute almost exclusively the very limited involvement of Malaysian states in foreign relations, as they do for Indian states, and they are also at the core of South African provinces' foreign relations. The constituent units of these countries are becoming engaged in the world only hesitantly. The activities of Argentine states in promoting their economic interests are of an order of magnitude higher than those of the former three, but the Argentine states are becoming involved in other forms of constituent diplomacy only gradually. As for Australia, the United States, and Canada (with the exception of Quebec), constituent-unit promotion of economic interests is front and centre. Much the same can be said of the constituent units of the remaining countries – Austria, Belgium, Germany, Spain, and Switzerland – whose range of activities is also broader than that of practically all constituent units in the other countries. As argued earlier, the extensiveness and intensity of these activities are directly related in most instances to the constituent units' level of economic development.

The promotion of economic interests takes on a number of forms. The attraction of foreign investment is typically a top priority. Improving infrastructure to attract direct foreign investment is common in contexts as varied as Indian, American, and Malaysian states, Swiss cantons, German *Länder*, and Canadian provinces. American states compete with each other to provide tax and other financial incentives, including direct subsidies, to firms willing to invest in their jurisdictions, as do Canadian provinces. Such competition also takes place across the US-Canada border. In the EU, by comparison, competition regulations do not allow direct subsidies. Export counselling for small and medium-sized firms is provided by constituent units in most countries. Trade missions, led by heads of constituent governments or other senior politicians, typically involving representatives of the business sector, are a common form of constituent diplomacy for Malaysian, Indian, and American states, Spanish autonomous communities, German *Länder*, Canadian provinces, and so on. These missions are in most instances supported by federal foreign-service officers stationed in the destination country. Many constituent units, although not, for example, Swiss cantons, have representative offices abroad to seek investments, attract foreign business, promote exports and tourism, and seek economic intelligence – in short, to support the business sector at home. Although some are run directly by the home government, these offices are often operated in cooperation with private-sector organizations or have been entrusted to specialized organizations that operate on a contractual basis. Another option frequently pursued is to engage agents abroad. The establishment and maintenance of representative offices is costly, and as the Canadian and American chapters demonstrate, some constituent units close such offices when the costs of maintaining them outweigh the perceived benefits. Hence they are normally maintained by only a subset of constituent units in individual countries. Only some Canadian provinces have offices abroad, whereas maintaining such offices is more common among Australian states and more common still for German *Länder*, US states, and Spanish autonomous communities. Belgian regions also have numerous offices and envoys in many parts of the world. When such offices are operated directly by constituent governments, they frequently also perform functions such as the maintenance and furthering of cultural and educational ties as well as direct liaison with constituent units and occasionally even national governments. EU member-state constituent-unit delegations in Brussels have responsibilities not only for political representation but also for the promotion of economic interests through lobbying EU institutions, seeking economic intelligence, and interacting with umbrella groups of European businesses.

One may ask why constituent units undertake such economic diplomacy at all. The answer is that their governments are often not certain that their interests are given as much attention by their federal governments as they think they deserve, an attitude particularly prevalent in the United States. However, most often the relationship between representatives of the two orders of government is one of cooperation, with federal officials providing logistical support and advice to constituent-government representatives abroad. In Belgium and Canada such cooperation is visible because constituent-government officials are often housed in their countries' embassies. Although relations among constituent units abroad are often characterized by competition, as seen among American states and Australian states, there is also cooperation – for example, when representatives of one constituent unit make those of another aware of opportunities of which the former cannot take advantage, as has occurred not infrequently among representatives of Canadian provinces. Cooperation among constituent units housed in Belgian embassies is institutionalized by an agreement that a region's officials represent not only their own region's interests but also those of other regions when these regions are not represented in a particular embassy. As for the overall picture, there is a strong argument to be made that the economic interests of a country are furthered when constituent-unit representatives enhance and complement the federal presence abroad, in part because there are more boots on the ground but also because constituent-unit representatives are knowledgeable about the special needs and circumstances at home.

Constituent diplomacy is not limited to economic concerns. Active participation in regional organizations is a striking feature of European federations' constituent diplomacy. Leaving aside cooperation in the EU setting, which is magnitudes greater in scope and depth than in other organizations, and focusing on regional organizations with less ambitious goals, one tends to find a direct relationship between geographical proximity and intensity of interaction as well as between the geographic extent of a regional organization and the scope of its functions. Cooperation in small regional contexts is intense and focused on practical concerns such as education, tourism, and economic development, whereas the focus in regional organizations having a wider geographic scope and greater heterogeneity among participating polities is less on practical matters and more on abstract themes such as the Assembly of European Union's emphasis on promotion of political dialogue and democracy as well as the transfer of knowledge about best practices in governance. European constituent units participate much more frequently in regional organizations than do their counterparts elsewhere. They need to do so not only because of geography (and thus the need to cooperate across national borders in order to solve practical problems on a continent where countries are small and borders are many) but also because, compared with other settings, there exist in Europe many more regional organizations focusing on more abstract and political themes.

As the country chapters demonstrate, constituent units also participate in development projects. Among the most prominent examples are the Spanish autonomous communities, which spend considerable sums on foreign aid and provide technical assistance to developing countries. Belgian regions contribute to the development programs of UN agencies and also undertake their own projects. Typically, constituent units can send experts to developing countries to train government officials and other government employees. Thus some Canadian provinces have provided assistance to strengthen governance in developing countries, such as the training of Namibian municipal officials by provincial government experts from the province of Saskatchewan. Argentina's provinces have provided technical assistance to less developed Latin American countries. Austrian *Länder* have cooperated with federal and municipal governments to provide foreign aid, and German *Länder* have signed cooperation agreements with developing countries for the same purpose.

Given that constituent units are typically responsible for education and culture, they have initiated and carried out a wide variety of projects and programs in these fields with foreign partners. Quebec is among the few constituent units that make culture and education their first international priority. German *Länder* have signed numerous protocols on culture and education with foreign polities, and a large number of the regional organizations in Europe to which the five European federations belong have the promotion of culture as one of their goals. EU constituent units also take the lead in representing their countries when culture and education are on the Brussels agenda. Belgian and German constituent units share representation with their federal governments in the United Nations Educational, Scientific and Cultural Organization (UNESCO), and the Quebec government has recently been accorded status as a permanent member of the Canadian delegation to that organization. The Taalunie involves linguistic and cultural cooperation between the Belgian region of Flanders, the Netherlands, Suriname, and South Africa.

International activities such as these by constituent units rarely lead to conflicts with their federal governments. As is the case for the promotion of economic interests, their activities enhance efforts by their federal governments to provide development aid. Indeed, the Swiss confederation and cantons cooperate formally in cultural promotion. The experience and skills required to train public administrators in the developing countries are often found only in constituent-government agencies; training for education or healthcare administration, for example, as well as for other services with direct impacts on people's lives, can typically be done only by these agencies' experts because federal governments do not deliver such services. Not infrequently, the two orders of government cooperate in such efforts, with the federal government helping to provide funding and the constituent units providing expertise.

Constituent-unit politicians sometimes travel abroad for political reasons. They may hope that the attention from press coverage of a trip abroad will make them appear to be sophisticated statespersons, an asset at election time, or they may have aspirations to hold federal office, especially in countries like Germany and the United States where politicians frequently make the jump from constituent-unit to federal politics. Delegations of constituent-unit parliamentarians attend international meetings with their counterparts from other countries or visit sister-states. Such visits can build good will and allow participants to broaden their horizons. They are also often strategically targeted to complement efforts at economic promotion.

The country chapters demonstrate that matters of high politics are very rare themes in constituent elections and are infrequently discussed in constituent-unit legislatures. There are some exceptions. The Kyoto Protocol has been discussed in Canadian provincial legislatures, and a federal-provincial dispute has arisen over its implementation. International cooperation on climate change has also engaged members of legislatures. More dramatically, the India-Pakistan dispute over Kashmir has been addressed in the Jammu-Kashmir legislature because of the ongoing conflict in that state and the immediate danger it poses to citizens. But the themes in constituent-unit elections and legislative debates are almost exclusively more practical, tending to focus on citizens' immediate concerns about such matters as education, infrastructure, and taxation.

Conflict between constituent and federal governments can occur. There is always the conflict typical of everyday political life that differing views on foreign relations will inevitably entail. Or interests may clash, such as disagreements between some provincial governments and the Canadian federal government over the negotiation of the North American Free Trade Agreement (NAFTA). As this example and the other country chapters demonstrate, it is impossible to isolate domestic policy from foreign policy. Federal government foreign policy can have major implications for domestic policies within the constituent governments, even to the extent of restricting constituent-unit powers, as shown in the American and Swiss chapters. Potential friction of this type is often forestalled in the intergovernmental relations processes discussed earlier, although the United States, in the absence of well-developed procedures and structures, appears to be an exception.

Occasionally, conflicts become more acute. They are often played out domestically, but they can also be carried onto the international stage if partisan politics or domestic issues are projected abroad, as a number of examples from the country chapters demonstrate. The US chapter discusses instances when state governments have shown their disapproval of pariah regimes – Burma, the Sudan, Nigeria, and Cuba, for instance – by threatening or even implementing financial sanctions against American firms dealing with these countries. Such actions can clearly be considered interference in American foreign policy and have been outlawed by American courts when the federal government has chosen to quash them by resort to legal action. Serious disagreements arose in Belgium when regional decisions about the arms trade were in conflict with Belgian foreign policy. As the chapter on Spain relates, a controversial invitation for a visit by a delegation of the Kurdish assembly in-exile to the Catalonian Parliament had to be called off because of the predictably strong objections by the Turkish ambassador to Spain. *Land* premiers of parties in opposition in the German federal government have made pronouncements on foreign policy, although these can best be seen in the light of domestic party competition rather than understood as direct interference in German foreign relations. A dramatic example of domestic conflicts being carried onto the international stage occurred when Quebec (at the time ruled by the separatist Parti québécois), sought to demonstrate to its citizens and the world that it could conduct its own foreign policy if it were to become independent by establishing a large network of offices abroad that were encouraged to make contact with public officials and to put as much of a political slant on constituent diplomacy as possible. It even attempted, with some success, to develop a state-to-state relationship with France. German *Land* politicians occasionally have made statements abroad that fall clearly in the domain of foreign policy and embarrass Berlin. But such cases are exceptional.

The challenge, then, in each federal country is to ensure that the foreign relations of constituent units and the foreign policy articulated by their national governments do not clash. Both orders of government can contribute to developing an effective foreign presence. Constituent-unit governments have much relevant technical expertise and a detailed understanding of the interests and concerns of private-sector actors who are or wish to become engaged internationally. National governments can bring greater experience to bear in dealing with the international environment, and they can wield greater political and economic clout than can individual or even groups of constituent units. The cooperation of the two orders of government requires consultation through durable and adequately conceptualized institutions of intergovernmental relations, and it requires the willingness to make compromises. Effective cooperation is essential as effective foreign relations become increasingly important in a highly interdependent world.

Bibliographic Resources for Federalism and Foreign Affairs

JOHN KINCAID

Abelson, Donald E., and Michael Lusztig. "The Consistency of Inconsistency: Tracing Ontario's Opposition to the North American Free Trade Agreement." *Canadian Journal of Political Science* 29 (1996): 681–98.

Abgrall, Jean-Francois. "The Regional Dynamics of Province-State Relations: Canada and the United States." *Horizons* 7 (2004): 50–4.

Aguirre, Inaki. "Making Sense of Paradiplomacy? An Intertextual Enquiry about a Concept in Search of a Definition." *Regional and Federal Studies* 9 (Spring 1999): 185–209.

Akinyemi, A.B. "Federalism and Foreign Policy." In A.B. Akinyemi, P.D. Cole, and Walter Ofonagoro, eds, *Readings on Federalism*, 36–43. Lagos: Nigerian Institute of International Affairs, 1979.

Aldecoa, Francisco. "Towards Plurinational Diplomacy in the Deeper and Wider European Union (1985–2005)." *Regional and Federal Studies* 9 (Spring 1999): 82–94.

– and Michael Keating, eds. *Paradiplomacy in Action: The Foreign Relations of Subnational Governments*. London: Frank Cass, 1999.

Alger, Chadwick F. "Searching for Democratic Potential in Emerging Global Governance." In Bruce Morrison, ed., *Transnational Democracy in Critical and Comparative Perspective*, 88–105. Aldershot, UK: Ashgate, 2003.

– "Quali sono le implicazioni, sia a livello regionale che globale, del coinvolagimento delgi attori localia nell'ambiato della governance futura?" *Futuribili*, nos 1–2 (2004): 38–52.

Allee, D.J. "Subnational Governance and the International Joint Commission: Local Management of United States and Canadian Boundary Waters." *Natural Resources Journal* 33 (1993): 133–51.

Alm, Leslie R., and Leah Taylor. "Alberta and Idaho: An Implicit Bond." *American Review of Canadian Studies* 33 (2003): 197–218.

Alper, D.K. "The Idea of Cascadia: Emergent Regionalism in the Pacific Northwest-Western Canada." *Journal of Borderlands Studies* 11 (1996): 1–22.

Alston, Ona. "Promoting an African-American Foreign Policy Agenda: A Municipal Strategy." *Urban League Review* 16 (1993): 45–56.
Angus, H.F. "The Canadian Constitution and the U.N. Charter." *Canadian Journal of Economics and Political Science* 12 (1946): 127–35.
Appadorai, A. "Impact of Federalism on India's Foreign Relations." *International Studies* 13 (1974): 389–423.
Archer, Stephen H., and Steven M. Maser. "State Export Promotion for Economic Development." *Economic Development Quarterly* 3 (August 1989): 235–42.
Aspaturian, Vernon V. *The Union Republics in Soviet Diplomacy*. Geneva: Droz, 1960.
Atkey, Ronald G. "Provincial Transnational Activity: An Approach to a Current Issue in Canadian Federalism." In Ontario Advisory Committee on Confederation, ed., *Background Papers and Reports*, vol. 2. Toronto: Queen's Printer, 1970.
– "The Role of the Provinces in International Affairs." *International Journal* 26 (Winter 1970–71): 249–73.
Avery, William P. "Domestic Interests in NAFTA Bargaining." *Political Science Quarterly* 113 (Summer 1998): 281–305.
Ayers, Caroline. "Australian Intergovernmental Relations and the National Emissions Trading Scheme." *Melbourne Journal of Politics* 31 (2006): 36–56.
Badiello, Lorenza. "La Representación Regional en Bruselas." In Francesc Morata, ed., *Gobernanza multinivel en la Unión Europea*, 327–68. Valencia: Tirant lo Blanch, 2004.
Bailly, Antoine S. "A Geopolitical Study of the Regio Genevensis." In Ivo D. Duchacek, Daniel Latouche, and Garth Stevenson, eds, *Perforated Sovereignties and International Relations: Trans-Sovereign Contacts of Subnational Governments*, 189–98. New York: Greenwood, 1988.
Baldersheim, Harald, and Krister Ståhlberg. "The Internationalization of Finnish and Norwegian Local Government." In Harald Baldersheim and Krister Ståhlberg, eds, *Nordic Region-Building in a European Perspective*, 121–50. Aldershot, UK: Ashgate, 1999.
– Jan Bucek, and Pawel Swianiewicz. "Mayors Learning across Borders: The International Networks of Municipalities in East-Central Europe." *Regional and Federal Studies* 12 (Spring 2002): 126–37.
Balthazar, Louis. "Quebec's Triangular Situation in North America: A Prototype?" In Ivo D. Duchacek, Daniel Latouche, and Garth Stevenson, eds, *Perforated Sovereignties and International Relations: Trans-Sovereign Contacts of Subnational Governments*, 83–9. New York: Greenwood, 1988.
– "The Quebec Experience: Success or Failure?" *Regional and Federal Studies* 9 (Spring 1999): 153–69.
– "Les relations internationales du Québec." In Alain-G. Gagnon, *Québec: État et sociétés*, 505–35. Montreal: Québec/Amérique, 2003.
– Louis Bélanger, and Gordon Mace, eds. *Trente ans de politique extérieure du Québec 1960–1990*. Ste-Foy: Centre québécois de relations internationales; Sillery: Éditions du Septentrion, 1993.

Barfield, Claude E. "Free Trade, Sovereignty, Democracy: The Future of the World Trade Organization." *Chicago Journal of International Law* 2 (Fall 2001): 403–16.
Bassett, Peter. "The Australian Federal System and Foreign Policy." *Australian Foreign Affairs Record* 55 (1984): 322–4.
Beaudoin, Louise. "Origines et développement du role international du gouvernement du Québec." In Paul Painchaud, ed., *Le Canada et le Québec sur la scene internationale*, 441–71. Quebec: Presses de l'Université du Québec, 1977.
Beaufays, Jean. "Bicommunal Belgium and Its International Dimension." In Ivo D. Duchacek, Daniel Latouche, and Garth Stevenson, eds, *Perforated Sovereignties and International Relations: Trans-Sovereign Contacts of Subnational Governments*, 3–28. New York: Greenwood, 1988.
Beaumont, Enid F. "Domestic Consequences of Internationalization." In Jong S. Jun and Deil S. Wright, eds, *Globalization and Decentralization: Institutional Contexts, Policy Issues, and Intergovernmental Relations in Japan and the United States*, 373–87. Washington, DC: Georgetown University Press, 1996.
Beckman, Norman. "The Governors and the National Guard in *Perpich v. Defense*." *Publius: The Journal of Federalism* 21 (Summer 1991): 109–23.
Bélanger, Louis. "The United States and the Formative Years of an Independent Quebec's Foreign Policy." *American Review of Canadian Studies* 27 (Spring 1997): 11–25.
– "The Domestic Politics of Quebec's Quest for External Distinctiveness." *American Review of Canadian Studies* 32 (Summer 2002): 195–216.
Berck, Jonathan S. "Immigration Law: Local Enforcement of Federal Immigration Laws." *Harvard International Law Journal* 25 (Spring 1984): 477–83.
Berensen, Judy S. *Nonstate Nations in International Politics: Comparative System Analyses*. New York: Praeger, 1977.
Bernier, Ivan. *International Legal Aspects of Federalism*. Hamden, CT: Archon Books, 1973.
– ed. "Numéro special: Les politiques extérieures des états non souverains: Convergences et divergences." *Études internationales* 25 (Septembre 1994).
Bernier, Luc. "The Foreign Economic Policy of a Subnational State: The Case of Quebec." In Ivo D. Duchacek, Daniel Latouche, and Garth Stevenson, eds, *Perforated Sovereignties and International Relations: Trans-Sovereign Contacts of Subnational Governments*, 125–39. New York: Greenwood, 1988.
– *De Paris à Washington: La politique internationale du Québec*. Quebec: Presses de l'Université du Québec, 1996.
– "Mulroney's International 'Beau Risque': The Golden Age of Quebec's Foreign Policy." In Nelson Michaud and Kim Nossal, eds, *Diplomatic Departures: The Conservative Era in Canadian Foreign Policy, 1984–93*, 128–41. Vancouver: University of British Columbia Press, 2001.
Bildre, Richard. "The Role of States and Cities in Foreign Relations." *American Journal of International Law* 83 (1989): 817–35.
Bissonette, Lise. "The Evolution of Quebec-American Diplomacy." In Calvin Veltman, ed., *Contemporary Quebec*, 160–72. Montreal: Presses de l'Université du Québec, 1981.

- "Orthodoxie fédéraliste et relations régionales transfrontieres." *Études internationals* 12 (1981): 635–55.
Blanco, Frank. *State Export Promotion Programs: A Look at Maryland and Texas.* Washington, DC: Foreign Service Institute, March 1997.
Blatter, Joachim. "Cross-Border Cooperation and Sustainable Development in Europe and North America." *International Journal of Economic Development* 2 (2000): 402–39.
- "Debordering the World of States: Toward a Multilevel System in Europe and a Multi-Polity System in North America." *European Journal of International Relations* 7 (2001): 175–209.
Bojar, E. "Euroregions in Poland." *Tijdschrift voor economische en sociale geografie* 87 (1996): 442–47.
Border Governors' Conference. *First International Meeting of the Border Governors of the United States and Mexico.* Ciudad Juarez, Chihuahua, 26–7 June 1980.
Borras, Susanna. "The Four Motors of Europe and Its Promotion of R&D Linkages Beyond Geographic Contiguity in Interregional Agreements." *Regional Politics and Policy* 3 (Summer 1993): 163–76.
Börzel, Tanja. "From Competitive Regionalism to Cooperative Federalism: The Europeanization of the Spanish State of the Autonomies." *Publius: The Journal of Federalism* 30 (Spring 2000): 17–42.
Bosold, David. *Transatlantische Paradiplomatie.* Marburg: Schriften der Marburger Universitätsbibliothek, 2004.
- "Deutsch-kanadische Paradiplomatie: Erfolgsmodell subnationaler Zusammenarbeit?" In Lothar Zimmerman, Hartmut Fröschle, and Myka Burke, eds, *German-Canadian Yearbook 2004/2005*, 69–100. Toronto: University of Toronto Press, 2005.
Bradley, Curtis A. "The Treaty Power and American Federalism." *Michigan Law Review* 97 (1998): 390–461.
- "*Breard*, Our Dualist Constitution, and the Internationalist Conception." *Stanford Law Review* 51 (1999): 523–59.
- "The Treaty Power and American Federalism, Part II." *Michigan Law Review* 99 (2000): 98–133.
- "World War II Compensation and Foreign Relations Federalism." *Berkley Journal of International Law* 20 (2002): 282–95.
- and Jack L. Goldsmith. "The Abiding Relevance of Federalism to U.S. Foreign Relations." *American Journal of International Law* 92 (October 1998): 675–9.
Brand, Dirk J. "The Role of Provinces in International Relations." In Hans-Joachim Cremer, Thomas Giegrich, Dagmar Richter, and Andreas Zimmerman, eds, *Tradition und Weltoffenheit des Rechts: Festschrift für Helmut Steinberger,* 669–82. Berlin: Springer, 2002.
Brilmayer, Lea. "Federalism, State Authority, and the Preemptive Power of International Law." In Dennis J. Hutchinson, David A. Strauss, and Geoffery R. Stone, eds, *1994: The Supreme Court Review,* 295–343. Chicago: University of Chicago Press, 1995.

Brown, Douglas M. "The Evolving Role of the Provinces in Canadian Trade Policy." In Douglas M. Brown and Murray G. Smith, eds, *Canadian Federalism: Meeting Global Economic Challenges?* Kingston: Institute of Intergovernmental Relations, Queen's University, 1991.
– and Earl H. Fry, eds. *States and Provinces in the International Economy.* Kingston: Institute of Intergovernmental Relations, Queen's University, 1993.
Brunet, Nunez, Laura Segú, Grau Segú, Marti Stelios, and Stavridis Stelios, "Los parlamentos regionales como actors internacionales: El Parlament de Catalunya y el espacio euromediterraneo." *Cuadernos Constitucionales de la Catédra Fadrique Furió Ceriol,* no. 47 (2004): 133–53.
Bucar, Bojko. "The Emergence of International (Legal) Obligations between Subnational Territorial Units – Illusion or Reality?" In Renate Kicker, Joseph Marko, and Michael Steiner, eds, *Changing Borders: Legal and Economic Aspects of European Enlargement,* 32–42. Frankfurt/Main: Peter Lang, 1998.
Burmester, Henry. "The Australian States and Participation in the Foreign Policy Process." *Federal Law Review* 9 (1978): 257–83.
– "Federal Clauses: An Australian Perspective." *International and Comparative Law Quarterly* 34 (July 1985): 522–37.
– "Federalism, the States, and International Affairs – A Legal Perspective." In Brian Galligan, ed., *Australian Federalism,* 197–211. Melbourne: Longman Cheshire, 1989.
Busygina, Irina. "Russia's Regions in Shaping National Foreign Policy." In Jackie Gower and Graham Timmins, eds, *Russia and Europe in the Twenty-First Century: An Uneasy Partnership,* 75–88. London: Anthem Press, 2007.
– ed. *External Relations of Russian Regions.* Moscow: Moscow State Institute of International Relations, 2001.
Butler, Rohan. "Paradiplomacy." In Arshag O. Sarkissian, ed., *Studies in Diplomatic History and Historiography in Honour of G.P. Gooch, C.H.,* 12–25. London: Longmans, 1961.
Byrnes, Andrew C. "The Implementation of Treaties in Australia after the Tasmanian Dams Case: The External Affairs Power and the Influence of Federalism." *Boston College International and Comparative Law Review* 8 (Summer 1985): 275–340.
– and Hilary Charlesworth. "Federalism and the International Legal Order: Recent Developments in Australia." *American Journal of International Law* 79 (July 1985): 622–40.
Campbell, Tim, and Harald Fuhr. *Leadership and Innovation in Subnational Government: Case Studies from Latin America.* Washington, DC: World Bank, 2004.
Cappellin, Riccardo, and Peter W.J. Batey, eds. *Regional Networks, Border Regions, and European Integration.* London: Pion, 1993.
Carnago, Noé. "Diplomacy and Paradiplomacy in the Redefinition of International Security: Dimensions of Conflict and Co-operation." *Regional and Federal Studies* 9 (Spring 1999): 40–57.
Casadevante, Carlos Fernández. *La acción exterior de las comunidades autonomas: Balance de una práctica consolidada.* Madrid: Dilex, 2001.

Chafee, Zachariah, Jr. "Federal and State Powers Under the U.N. Covenant on Human Rights." *Wisconsin Law Review* (May 1951): part 1, 389–473; part 2, 623–56.

Chaudhuri, Joyotpaul. "Federalism and the Siamese Twins: Diversity and Entropy in India's Domestic and Foreign Policy." *International Journal* 48 (1993): 448–69.

Chernotsky, Harry I., and Heidi H. Hobbs. "Responding to Globalization: State and Local Policy Initiatives in the Southeast." *Passages: The Journal of Transnational and Transcultural Relations* 3 (Spring 2001): 57–82.

Church, Andrew, and Peter Reid. "Local Democracy: Cross-Border Collaboration and the Internationalization of Local Government." In Robin Hambleton, H.V. Savitch, and Murray Stewart, eds, *Globalism and Local Democracy: Challenge and Change in Europe and North America*, 201–18. Basingstoke: Palgrave, 2002.

Clarke, Susan E. "Regional and Transnational Discourse: The Politics of Ideas and Economic Development in Cascadia." *International Journal of Economic Development* 2 (2000): 360–78.

Cohen, L.J. "Federalism and Foreign Policy in Yugoslavia: The Politics of Regional Ethnonationalism." *International Journal* 41 (1986): 624–54.

Cohn, Theodore H., and Patrick J. Smith. "Subnational Governments as International Actors: Constituent Diplomacy in British Columbia and the Pacific Northwest." *British Columbia Studies* 110 (Summer 1996): 25–59.

Colgan, Charles S. *Forging a New Partnership in Trade Policy between the Federal and State Governments*. Washington, DC: National Governors' Association, 1992.

Colson, David. "The Impact of Federalism and Border Issues on Canada/U.S. Relations: Pacific Salmon Treaty." *Canada-United States Law Journal* 27 (Annual 2001): 27–32.

Compton, Arthur A. "Activities of a State Overseas Office." *State Government* 48 (Winter 1975): 12–13.

Conde, Carlos. *La acción exterior de las Comunidades Autónomas: La institucionalización de gobiernos territoriales y la integración internacional*. Madrid: Tecnos, 2000.

Conlan, Timothy J., and Michelle A. Sager. *International Dimensions of American Federalism: State Policy Responses to a Changing Global Environment*. Washington, DC: US-Asia Environmental Partnership, November 1997.

– Robert L. Dudley, and Joel F. Clark. "Taking on the World: The International Activities of American State Legislatures." *Publius: The Journal of Federalism* 34 (Summer 2004): 183–99.

Cooper, Andrew Fenton. "Subnational Activity and Foreign Economic Policy Making in Canada and the United States: Perspectives on Agriculture." *International Journal* 41 (1986): 655–73.

Cowles, W.B. "International Law as Applied between Subdivisions of Federations." *Hague Recueil: Académie de droit international: Recueil de cours* 74 (1949): 659–754.

Cremer, R.D., Anne de Bruin, and Ann Dupuis. "International Sister-Cities: Bridging the Global-Local Divide." *American Journal of Economy and Sociology* 60 (January 2001): 377–401.

Criekemans, David. "The Case of Flanders (1993–2005): How Subnational Entities Develop Their Own 'Paradiplomacy.'" In Kishan S. Rana and Jovan Kurbalija,

eds, *Foreign Ministries: Diplomatic Networks and Optiomizing Value*, 118–56. Msida, Malta: DiploFoundation, 2007.
Crock, Mary. "Federalism and the External Affairs Power." *Melbourne University Law Review* 14 (1983): 238–64.
Cuerdo, Luis Prados. *La acción exterior de las comunidades autonomas: Teoría y práctica.* Madrid: Escuela Diplomática, 1995.
Dale, William B., and David C. Fulton. *Do the States Have a Role to Play in Foreign Aid?* Menlo Park, CA: Stanford Research Institute, January 1961.
De Boer, Stephen. "Canadian Provinces, US States and North American Integration: Bench Warmers or Key Players?" *Choices: Canada's Options in North America* 8 (2002): 2–24.
De Castro, José Luis, and Alexander Ugalde. *La acción exterior del Pais Vasco (1980–2003).* Oñate: IVAP/HAEE, 2003.
Dehousse, Renaud. "Fédéralisme, asymétrie et interdependence: Aux origins de l'action internationale des composantes de lÉtat federal." *Études internationales* 20 (June 1989): 283–309.
– *Fédéralisme et Relations Internationales.* Bruxelles: Bruylant, 1991.
Deiss, Joseph. "Federalism in Swiss Foreign Policy." In Raoul Blindenbacher and Arnold Koller, eds, *Federalism in a Changing World: Learning from Each Other*, 534–8. Montreal and Kingston: McGill-Queen's University Press, 2003.
Delagran, Leslie. "Conflict in Trade Policy: The Role of the Congress and the Provinces in Negotiating and Implementing the Canada-U.S. Free Trade Agreement." *Publius: The Journal of Federalism* 22 (Fall 1992): 15–29.
Denning, Brannon P., and Jack H. McCall Jr. "The Constitutionality of State and Local 'Sanctions' against Foreign Countries: Affairs of State, States' Affairs, or a Sorry State of Affairs?" *Hastings Constitutional Law Quarterly* 26 (1999): 1–8.
– and Jack H. McCall Jr. "States' Rights and Foreign Policy: Some Things Should Be Left to Washington." *Foreign Affairs* 79 (January/February 2000): 9–15.
Diedrichs, Udo, and Wolfgang Wessels. "Federal Structures and Foreign Policy of International and Supra-National Organisations." In Raoul Blindenbacher and Arnold Koller, eds, *Federalism in a Changing World: Learning from Each Other*, 130–48. Montreal and Kingston: McGill-Queen's University Press, 2003.
Dijkink, Gertjan, and Constance Winnips. "Alternative States: Regions and Postfordism Rhetoric on the Internet." *GeoJournal* 48 (August 1999): 323–35.
Doeker, Günther. *The Treaty-Making Power in the Commonwealth of Australia.* The Hague: Nijhoff, 1966.
Dolan, Edward. "The Member Republics of the USSR as Subjects of the Law of Nations." *International and Comparative Law Quarterly* 4 (1955): 629–36.
Dossani, Rafiq, and Srinidhi Vijaykumar. *Indian Federalism and the Conduct of Foreign Policy in Border States: State Participation and Central Accommodation since 1990.* Stanford, CA: Asia-Pacific Research Center, Stanford University, March 2005.
Drezner, Daniel W. "On the Balance between International Law and Democratic Sovereignty." *Chicago Journal of International Law* 2 (Fall 2001): 321–36.

Duchacek, Ivo D. "The International Dimension of Subnational Self-Government." *Publius: The Journal of Federalism* 14 (Fall 1984): 5–31.
– "The International Competence of Subnational Governments: Borderlands and Beyond." In Oscar J. Martinez, ed., *Across Boundaries: Transborder Interaction in Comparative Perspective*. El Paso: University of Texas at El Paso, Texas Western Press, 1986.
– *Toward a Typology of New Subnational Governmental Actors in International Relations.* Berkeley: Institute of Governmental Studies, University of California, 1987.
– "French Views of Quebec in 1984 and 1985: A Survey." In Ivo D. Duchacek, Daniel Latouche, and Garth Stevenson, eds, *Perforated Sovereignties and International Relations: Trans-Sovereign Contacts of Subnational Governments*, 119–24. New York: Greenwood, 1988.
– "Multicommunal and Bicommunal Polities and Their International Relations." In Ivo D. Duchacek, Daniel Latouche, and Garth Stevenson, eds, *Perforated Sovereignties and International Relations: Trans-Sovereign Contacts of Subnational Governments*, 3–28. New York: Greenwood, 1988.
– "Perforated Sovereignties: Towards a Typology of New Actors in International Relations." In Hans J. Michelmann and Panayotis Soldatos, eds, *Federalism and International Relations: The Role of Subnational Units*, 1–33. Oxford: Clarendon, 1990.
– Daniel Latouche, and Garth Stevenson, eds. *Perforated Sovereignties and International Relations: Trans-Sovereign Contacts of Subnational Governments*. New York: Greenwood, 1988.
Dudziak, Mary L. "The Little Rock Crisis and Foreign Affairs: Race, Resistance, and the Image of American Democracy." *Southern California Law Review* 70 (September 1997): 1641–1716.
– *Cold War Civil Rights: Race and the Image of American Democracy*. Princeton: Princeton University Press, 2000.
– "Birmingham, Addis Ababa and the Image of America: International Influence on U.S. Civil Rights Policy during the Kennedy Years." In Brenda Gayle Plummer, ed., *Window on Freedom: Race, Civil Rights and Foreign Affairs, 1945–1988*, 181–200. Chapel Hill: University of North Carolina Press, 2003.
– "*Brown* as a Cold War Case." *Journal of American History* 91 (June 2004): 32–42.
Dunning, John H., ed. *Regions, Globalization, and the Knowledge-Based Economy*. Oxford: Oxford University Press, 2002.
Dyment, David M. "The Ontario Government as an International Actor." *Regional and Federal Studies* 11 (Spring 2001): 55–79.
Earle, Karl M. "Cousins of a Kind: The Newfoundland and Labrador Relationship with the United States." *American Review of Canadian Studies* 28 (1998): 387–411.
Eayrs, James. "Canadian Federalism and the United Nations." *Canadian Journal of Economics and Political Science* 16 (1950): 172–83.
Edisis, Adrienne T. *Global Activities by U.S. States: Findings of a Survey of State Government International Activities*. Washington, DC: George Washington University, 2003.

Ehrenzeller, Bernhard, Rudolf Hrbek, Giorgio Malinverni, and Daniel Thürer. "Federalism and Foreign Relations." In Raoul Blindenbacher and Arnold Koller, eds, *Federalism in a Changing World: Learning from Each Other*, 53–73. Montreal and Kingston: McGill-Queen's University Press, 2003.

Eisenger, Peter, and Charles Smith. "Globalization and Metropolitan Well-Being in the United States." *Social Science Quarterly* 81 (June 200): 634–44.

Enokido, Keisuke. "Searching for Partners across Borders: A Literature Review on Cross-Border Cooperation." *Journal of Tourism Sciences* 1 (March 2007): 55–79.

Europäisches Zentrum für Föderalismus-Forschung Tübingen. *Jahrbuch des Föderalismus 2004: Föderalismus, Subsidiarität und Regionen in Europa*. Baden-Baden: Nomos, 2004.

– *Jahrbuch des Föderalismus 2005: Föderalismus, Subsidiarität und Regionen in Europa*. Baden-Baden: Nomos, 2005.

– *Jahrbuch des Föderalismus 2006: Föderalismus, Subsidiarität und Regionen in Europa*. Baden-Baden: Nomos, 2006.

Ewen, S., and M. Hebbert. "European Cities in a Networked World during the Long 20th Century." *Environment and Planning C: Government and Policy* 25 (2007): 327–40.

Feldman, Elliot J., and Lily Gardner Feldman. "Canada." In Hans J. Michelmann and Panayotis Soldatos, eds, *Federalism and International Relations: The Role of Subnational Units*, 176–210. Oxford: Clarendon, 1990.

– and Lily Gardner Feldman. "The Impact of Federalism on the Organization of Canadian Foreign Policy." *Publius: The Journal of Federalism* 14 (Fall 1984): 33–59.

– and Lily Gardner Feldman. "Quebec's Internationalization of North American Federalism." In Ivo D. Duchacek, Daniel Latouche, and Garth Stevenson, eds, *Perforated Sovereignties and International Relations: Trans-Sovereign Contacts of Subnational Governments*, 69–80. New York: Greenwood, 1988.

Fischer, Thomas, and Siegfried Frech. *Baden-Württemberg und Seine Partnerregionen*. Stuttgart: W. Kohlhammer GmbH, 2001.

Fitzgerald, Gerald F. "Educational and Cultural Agreements and Ententes: France, Canada, and Quebec – Birth of a New Treaty-Making Technique for Federal States?" *American Journal of International Law* 60 (1960): 529–37.

Flaherty, Martin S. "Are We to Be a Nation? Federal Power vs. 'States' Rights' in Foreign Affairs." *University of Colorado Law Review* 70 (Fall 1999): 1277–1316.

Floimair, Roland, ed. *Die regionale Außenpolitik des Landes Salzburg*. Salzburg: Salzburg Dokumentationen 108, 1993.

Fleurke, Frederik, and Rolf Willemse. "The European Union and the Autonomy of Sub-national Authorities: Towards an Analysis of Constraints and Opportunities in Sub-national Decision-Making." *Regional and Federal Studies* 16 (2006): 83–98.

Fosler, R. Scott. "The Global Challenge to Governance: Implications for National and Subnational Government Capacities and Relationships." In National Institute for Research Advancement and National Academy of Public Administration, eds, *The Challenge to New Governance in the Twenty-First Century: Achieving Effective*

Central-Local Relations, 494–524. Tokyo: National Institute for Research Advancement, 1999.

Frankman, Myron J. *World Democratic Federalism: Peace and Justice Indivisible.* New York: Palgrave Macmillan, 2004.

Frazier, Michael. *Implementing State Government Export Programs.* Westport, CT: Praeger, 1992.

Freudenwald, David. "Hometown Diplomats Link Counties to Foreign Policy." *County News* 36 (15 November 2004): 3.

Friedman, Barry. "Federalism's Future in the Global Village." *Vanderbilt Law Review* 47 (October 1994): 1441–83.

Fry, Earl H. "The Economic Competitiveness of the Western States and Provinces: The International Dimension." *American Review of Canadian Studies* 16 (Fall 1986): 301–12.

– "Trans-Sovereign Relations of the American States." In Ivo D. Duchacek, Daniel Latouche, and Garth Stevenson, eds, *Perforated Sovereignties and International Relations: Trans-Sovereign Contacts of Subnational Governments*, 53–67. New York: Greenwood, 1988.

– "Foreign Direct Investment in the United States: The Differing Perspectives of Washington, D.C., and the State Capitals." *Brigham Young University Law Review* 2 (1989): 373–91.

– "State and Local Governments in the International Arena." *Annals of the American Academy of Political and Social Science* 509 (May 1990): 118–27.

– "The United States of America." In Hans J. Michelmann and Panayotis Soldatos, eds, *Federalism and International Relations: The Role of Subnational Units*, 276–98. Oxford: Clarendon, 1990.

– "U.S.-Canada Economic Relations: The Role of the Provinces and the States." *Business in the Contemporary World* 3 (Autumn 1990): 120–6.

– "The International Relations of Provinces and States: Federalism in an Age of Economic Interdependence." In A.R. Riggs and Tom Velk, eds, *Federalism in Peril: National Unity, Individualism, Free Markets, and the Emerging Global Economy*, 103–17. Vancouver: Fraser Institute, 1992.

– "North American Municipalities and Their Involvement in the Global Economy." In Peter Karl Kresl and Gary Gappert, eds, *North American Cities and the Global Economy*, 21–44. Thousand Oaks, CA: Sage, 1995.

– "Quebec, Canada, and the United States: The Economic Dimension." *American Review of Canadian Studies* 25 (Winter 1995): 497–517.

– "Regional Economic Development Strategies in Canada and the United States: Linkages between the Subnational, National, and Global Settings." *International Journal of Canadian Studies* 16 (Winter 1997): 69–91.

– *The Expanding Role of State and Local Governments in U.S. Foreign Affairs.* New York: Council of Foreign Relations Press, 1998.

– "Quebec's Relations with the United States." *American Review of Canadian Studies* 32 (Summer 2002): 323–42.

- "Federalism and the Evolving Cross-Border Role of Provincial, State, and Municipal Governments." *International Journal* 60 (Spring 2005): 471–82.
- "U.S.-Canada Economic Relations: Interactions among the States and Provinces." In Keon Chi, ed., *The Book of the States, 2006*, 545–9. Lexington, KY: Council of State Governments, 2006.
- and Gregory A. Raymond. *Idaho's Foreign Relations: The Transgovernmental Linkages of an American State.* Boise, ID: Center for Research, 1978.
- Lee H. Radebaugh, and Panayotis Soldatos, eds. *The New International Cities Era: The Global Activities of North American Municipal Governments.* Provo, UT: David M. Kennedy Center for International Affairs, Brigham Young University, 1989.

Furmankiewicz, Marek. "International Co-operation of Polish Municipalities: Directions and Effects." *Tijdschrift voor economische en sociale geografie* 98 (July 2007): 349–59.

Gambari, Ibrahim A. "Federalism and the Management of External Relations in Nigeria: Lessons from the Past and Challenges for the Future." *Publius: The Journal of Federalism* 21 (Fall 1991): 113–24.

Ganster, Paul, Alan Sweedler, James Scott, and Wolf Dietre-Eberwein, eds. *Borders and Border Regions in Europe and North America.* San Diego: San Diego University Press and Institute for Regional Studies of the Californias, 1997.

Ghosh, R.C. *Treaties and Federal Constitutions: Their Mutual Impact.* Calcutta: World Press Private, 1961.

Gibbins, Roger. "Canadian Federalism: The Entanglement of Meech Lake and the Free Trade Agreement." *Publius: The Journal of Federalism* 19 (Summer 1989): 185–98. .

Gildner, Jay W. *Activities of American States Abroad: Purposes, Operations, and Policy Questions.* Washington, DC: US Department of State, Senior Seminar in Foreign Policy, Eighteenth Session, 1975–76.

Gilhooly, John. *State Government Roles in Exporting Manufactured Products, Importing Foreign Capital.* Washington, DC: US Department of State, Senior Seminar in Foreign Policy, Nineteenth Session, 1976–77.

Glaser, Robert E. "Foreign Investment in the United States: Ohio's Limitations on Foreign Investment." *Canada-United States Law Journal* 4 (Summer 1981): 102–43.

Goldsborough, James O. "California's Foreign Policy." *Foreign Affairs* 72 (Spring 1993): 88–96.

Goldsmith, Jack L. "Federal Courts, Foreign Affairs, and Federalism." *Virginia Law Review* 83 (November 1997): 1617–1715.

González, Manuel Pérez, Fernando Marino, and Francisco Aldecoa, eds. *La acción exterior y comunitaria de los Länder, Regiones, Cantones y Comunidades Autónomas.* Oñate: IVAP/HAEE, 1994.

Gordon, Mark C. *Democracy's New Challenge: Globalization, Governance, and the Future of American Federalism.* New York: Demos, 2001.

Gordon, Michael R. "With Foreign Investment at Stake, It's One State against the Others." *National Journal* 12 (18 October 1980): 1744–8.

Gress, Franz. "Interstate Cooperation and Territorial Representation in Intermestic Politics." *Publius: The Journal of Federalism* 26 (Winter 1996): 53–71.
Greve, Michael S. "Federalism Values and Foreign Relations." *Chicago Journal of International Law* 2 (Fall 2001): 355–64.
Groen, James P. "British Columbia's International Relations: Consolidating a Coalition-Building Strategy." *British Columbia Studies* 102 (Summer 1994): 54–82.
Gross, Bernd, and Peter Schmitt-Egner. *Europas kooperierende Regionen: Rahmembedingungen und Praxis transnationaler Zusammenarbeit deutscher Grenzregionen in Europa.* Baden-Baden: Nomos, 1994.
Gunlicks, Arthur B. *The Länder and German Federalism.* New York: Manchester University Press, 2003.
Habegger, Beat. "Participation of Sub-National Units in the Foreign Policy of the Federation." In Raoul Blindenbacher and Arnold Koller, eds, *Federalism in a Changing World: Learning from Each Other,* 159–68. Montreal and Kingston: McGill-Queen's University Press, 2003.
Halberstam, Daniel. "The Foreign Affairs of Federal Systems: A National Perspective on the Benefits of State Participation (Symposium: New Voices on the New Federalism)," *Villanova Law Review* 46 (2001): 1015–68.
Hansen, Niles. "Transboundary Cooperation in Centralist States: Conflicts and Responses in France and Mexico." *Publius: The Journal of Federalism* 14 (Fall 1984): 137–52.
Harguindeguy, Jean-Baptiste. "Cross-Border Policy in Europe: Implementing INTERREG III-A, France-Spain." *Regional and Federal Studies* 17 (September 2007): 317–34.
Harris, Richard G., ed. *North American Linkages: Opportunities and Challenges for Canada.* Calgary: University of Calgary Press, 2003.
Hartman, F.L. "Federalism as a Limitation on the Treaty-Making Power of the United States, Western Germany, and India." *Western Reserve Law Review* 18 (1966): 134–56.
Harwell, James. "The States' Growing International Role." *State Government* 48 (Winter 1975): 2–5.
Hauslohner, Paul. "Prefects as Senators: Soviet Regional Politicians Look to Foreign Policy." *World Politics* 33 (January 1981): 197–232.
Hay, Peter. *Federalism and Supranational Organizations.* Champaign: University of Illinois Press, 1966.
Heberlein, Horst Christoph. *Kommunale Aussenpolitik als Rechtsproblem.* Köln: W. Kohlhammer/Deutcsher Gemeindeverlag, 1989.
Hellwig, Renate. "Die Rolle der Bundesländer in der Europa-Politik." *Europa Archiv* 42 (October 1987): 297–302.
Hendry, James McLeod. *Treaties and Federal Constitutions.* Washington, DC: Public Affairs Press, 1955.
Henkin, Louis. *Foreign Affairs and the Constitution.* Mineola, NY: Foundation Press, 1972.

- "International Law as Law in the United States." *Michigan Law Review* 82 (1984): 1555–69.
- "Provisional Measures, United States Treaty Obligations, and the States." *American Journal of International Law* 92 (1998): 679–83.

Henrikson, Alan K. "Facing across Borders: The Diplomacy of Bon Voisinage." *International Political Science Review* 21 (2000): 121–47.

Hero, Alfred O., and Marcel Daneau, eds. *Problems and Opportunities in U.S.-Quebec Relations*. Boulder, CO: Westview Press, 1984.

Hewitt, W.E. "Municipalities and the 'New' Internationalism: Cautionary Notes from Canada." *Cities* 16 (December 1999): 435–44.

Hobbs, Heidi H. *City Hall Goes Abroad: The Foreign Policy of Local Politics*. Thousand Oaks, CA: Sage, 1994.

Hocking, Brian. "Pluralism and Foreign Policy: The States and the Management of Australia's External Relations." In George Keeton and Georg Schwarzenberger, eds, *Yearbook of World Affairs*, 143–4. London: Stevens and Sons for London Institute of World Affairs, 1984.
- "Regional Government and International Affairs: Foreign Policy Problem or Deviant Behaviour?" *International Journal* 41 (Summer 1986): 477–506.
- *Localizing Foreign Policy: Non-Central Governments and Multilayered Diplomacy*. London: Macmillan, 1993.
- "Les intérets internationaux des gouvernements régionaux: Desuetude de l'interne et de l'externe?" *Revue Etudes Internationales* 25 (1994): 404–20.
- "Patrolling the 'Frontier': Globalization, Localization and the 'Actorness' of Non-Central Governments." *Regional and Federal Studies* 9 (Spring 1999): 17–39.
- "Regions and International Relations." In Michael Keating and John Loughlin, eds, *The Political Economy of Regionalism*, 90–111. London: Frank Cass, 1997.
- ed. *Foreign Relations and Federal States*. London: Leicester University Press, 1993.

Holden, Robert J. "Governor Ninian Edwards and the War of 1812 – The Military Role of a Territorial Governor." In *Selected Papers in Illinois History, 1980*, 1–8. Springfield: Illinois State Historical Society, 1982.

Holsti, Kai J., and Thomas Allen Levy. "Bilateral Institutions and Transgovernmental Relations between Canada and the United States." In Annette Baker Fox, Alfred O. Hero Jr, and Joseph S. Nye, eds, *Canada and the United States: Transnational and Transgovernmental Relations*, 283–309. New York: Columbia University Press, 1976.

Hooghe, Liesbet, and Gary Marks. "'Europe with the Regions': Channels of Regional Representation in the European Union." *Publius: The Journal of Federalism* 26 (Winter 1996): 73–91.

Hopkins, William John. "Foreign Relations of Sub-National Units." In Raoul Blindenbacher and Arnold Koller, eds, *Federalism in a Changing World: Learning from Each Other*, 149–58. Montreal and Kingston: McGill-Queen's University Press, 2003.

Horn, Jörg. "Asymmetric Federalism: Are Federated Micro-Regions Viable?" *Asia Europe Journal* 2 (December 2004): 573–87.

Hornsby, Stephen J., and John G. Reid, eds. *New England and the Maritime Provinces: Connections and Comparisons.* Montreal and Kingston: McGill-Queen's University Press, 2006.

Hoshino, Shinyasu. "Japanese Local Government in an Era of Global Economic Interdependency." In Jong S. Jun and Deil S. Wright, eds, *Globalization and Decentralization: Institutional Contexts, Policy Issues, and Intergovernmental Relations in Japan and the United States,* 359–73. Washington, DC: Georgetown University Press, 1996.

Hrbek, Rudolf. "The Effects of EU Integration on German Federalism." In Charlie Jeffery, ed., *Recasting German Federalism: The Legacies of Unification,* 217–33. London: Pinter, 1999.

– "Der deutsche Bundesstaat in der EU: Die Mitwirkung der deutschen Länder in EU-Angelegenheiten als Gegenstand der Föderalismus-Reform." In Charlotte Gaitanides, Stefan Kadelbach, and Gil Carlos Rodriguez Iglesias, eds, *Europa und seine Verfassung: Festschrift für Manfred Zuleeg,* 256–73. Baden-Baden: Nomos, 2005.

– ed. *Europapolitik und Bundestaatsprinzip: Die "Europafähigkeit" Deutschlands und seiner Länder im Vergleich mit andrren Föderalstaaten.* Baden-Baden: Nomos, 2000.

– ed. *Aussenbeziehungen von Regionen in Europa und der Welt.* Baden-Baden: Nomos, 2003.

– and U. Thaysen, eds. *Die deutschen Länder und die Europäischen Gemeinschaften.* Baden-Baden: Nomos, 1986.

– and Sabine Weyand, eds. *Betrifft: Das Europa des Regionen.* München: C.H. Beck, 1994.

Hülsemeyer, Axel. *Globalization and Institutional Adjustment: Federalism as an Obstacle?* Aldershot, UK: Ashgate, 2004.

Hynek, Nikola. "Federalism, Internationalization and the Phenomenon of Paradiplomacy: A Conceptual and Empirical Analysis." In Maxmillián Strmiska, Roman Chytilek, and Nikola Hynek, eds, *Federalism and Multi-Level Polity: The Canadian Case,* 69–104. Brno: Anton Pasienka, 2007.

Hynes, Cecil V. *Michigan and Ontario: Trade and Transport Reciprocity.* East Lansing: Michigan State University Press, 1966.

Ingram, Helen M. "State Government Officials' Role in U.S./Mexico Transboundary Resource Issues." *Natural Resources Journal* 28 (Summer 1988): 429–41.

Ishiguro, Kazunori. "Technology Transfer from Iowa to Japan: Internationalization and the Quality of Life in Rural Areas." In Jong S. Jun and Deil S. Wright, eds, *Globalization and Decentralization: Institutional Contexts, Policy Issues, and Intergovernmental Relations in Japan and the United States,* 347–58. Washington, DC: Georgetown University Press, 1996.

Jain, Purnendra. *Japan's Subnational Governments in International Affairs.* London: Routledge, 2005.

Jans, M. Theo, and Patrick Stouthuysen. "Federal Regions and External Relations: The Belgian Case." *The International Spectator* 42 (June 2007): 209–20.

Jeffery, Charlie. "Regional Information Offices in Brussels and Multi-Level Governance in the EU: A UK-German Comparison." In Charlie Jeffery, ed., *The Regional Dimension of the European Union*, 183–203. London: Frank Cass, 1997.

Jenkins, Rob. "How Federalism Influences India's Domestic Politics of WTO Engagement (and Is Itself Affected in the Process)." *Asian Survey* 43 (July-August 2003): 598–621.

– "India's States and the Making of Foreign Economic Policy: The Limits of the Constituent Diplomacy Paradigm." *Publius: The Journal of Federalism* 33 (Fall 2003): 63–81.

Jensen, Nathan, and Fiona McGillivray. "Federal Institutions and Multinational Investors: Federalism, Government Credibility, and Foreign Direct Investment." *International Interactions* 31 (October 2005): 303–25.

Jha, Nalini Kant. "Foreign Policy Making in Federal States: The Indian and Canadian Experiences." *India Quarterly* 55 (1999): 1–18.

Joenniemi, Pertti. "Accounting for the Role of Cities in Regional Cooperation: The Case of Europe's North." In Christopher S. Browning, ed., *Northern Europe after the Enlargements*, 143–60. Aldershot, UK: Ashgate, 2005.

Johannson, Peter R. "Provincial International Activities." *International Journal* 33 (Spring 1978): 357–78.

– "British Columbia's Relations with the United States," *Canadian Public Administration* 21 (Summer 1978): 212–33.

Jones, Benjamin J. "The Effects of Free Trade Agreements on State Sovereignty." In Council of State Governments, ed., *Book of the States 1994/95*, 616–21. Lexington, KY: Council of State Governments, 1995.

Kaiser, Robert. "Paradiplomacy and Multilevel Governance in Europe and North America: Subnational Governments in International Arenas." *Participation* 27 (2003): 17–19.

– "Sub-State Governments in International Arenas: Paradiplomacy and Multi-Level Governance in Europe and North America." In Guy Lachapelle and Stéphane Paquine, eds, *Mastering Globalization: New Sub-States' Governance and Strategies*, 90–103. London and New York: Routledge, 2005.

Kastor, Peter J. "'Motives of Peculiar Urgency': Local Diplomacy in Louisiana, 1803–1821." *William and Mary Quarterly* 58 (October 2001): 819–48.

Keating, Michael. "Regions and International Affairs: Motives, Opportunities and Strategies." *Regional and Federal Studies* 9 (Spring 1999): 1–16.

Keating, Tom, and Don Munton, eds. *The Provinces and Canadian Foreign Policy: Proceedings of a Conference*. Edmonton: University of Alberta, 28–30 March 1985.

Keck, Margaret E., and Kathryn Sikkink. *Activists beyond Borders: Advocacy Networks in International Politics*. Ithaca: Cornell University Press, 1998.

Kellenberger, Jakob. "Federalism and Foreign Relations." In Raoul Blindenbacher and Arnold Koller, eds, *Federalism in a Changing World: Learning from Each Other*, 189–93. Montreal and Kingston: McGill-Queen's University Press, 2002.

Kelman, Illan, Megan Davies, Tom Mitchell, Iain Orr, and Bob Conrich. "Island Disaster Para-Diplomacy in the Commonwealth." *The Round Table: The Commonwealth Journal of International Affairs* 95, no. 386 (2006): 561–74.

Keohane, Robert, and Joseph Nye. "Transgovernmental Relations and International Organizations." *World Politics* 27 (October 1974): 39–62.

Khan, Rahmatullah. "Implementation of International Law and Supra-National Law in Sub-National Units." In Raoul Blindenbacher and Arnold Koller, eds, *Federalism in a Changing World: Learning from Each Other*, 115–29. Montreal and Kingston: McGill-Queen's University Press, 2002.

Kincaid, John. "The American Governors in International Affairs." *Publius: The Journal of Federalism* 14 (Fall 1984): 95–114.

– "State Offices in Europe." *Comparative State Politics Newsletter* 6 (August 1985): 22–8.

– "Constituent Diplomacy in Federal Polities and the Nation-State: Conflict and Co-operation." In Hans J. Michelmann and Panayotis Soldatos, eds, *Federalism and International Relations: The Role of Subnational Units*, 54–75. Oxford: Clarendon, 1990.

– "State and Local Governments Go International." *Intergovernmental Perspective* 16 (Spring 1990): 6–9.

– "Constituent Diplomacy: U.S. State Roles in Foreign Affairs." In Daniel J. Elazar, ed., *Constitutional Design and Power-Sharing in the Post-Modern Epoch*, 107–42. Lanham, MD: University Press of America, 1991.

– "Sharing Power in the Federal System: The American States in World Affairs." In John M. Bryson and Robert C. Einsweiler, eds, *Shared Power*, 291–308. Lanham, MD: University Press of America and Hubert H. Humphrey Institute, 1991.

– "The International Competence of US States and Their Local Governments." *Regional and Federal Studies* 9 (Spring 1999): 111–33.

– "Foreign Relations of Sub-National Units." In Raoul Blindenbacher and Arnold Koller, eds, *Federalism in a Changing World: Learning from Each Other*, 74–96. Montreal and Kingston: McGill-Queen's University Press, 2002.

– "Globalization and Federalism in the United States: Continuity in Adaptation." In Harvey Lazar, Hamish Telford, and Ronald L. Watts, eds, *The Impact of Global and Regional Integration on Federal Systems: A Comparative Analysis*, 37–85. Montreal and Kingston: McGill-Queen's University Press, 2003.

– "U.S. State and Local Governments in International Affairs." In Rudolf Hrbek, ed., *Außenbeziehungen von Regionen in Europa und der Welt*, 257–76. Baden-Baden: Nomos, 2003.

– with Joshua L. Handelsmann. *American Cities in the Global Economy: A Survey of Municipalities on Activities and Attitudes*. Washington, DC: National League of Cities, 1997.

Kirk-Green, A.H.M. "Foreign Policy and Federalism (the Nigerian Experience)." *African Affairs* 75 (1976): 258–9.

Kline, John M. *State Government Influence in U.S. International Economic Policy.* Lexington, MA: Lexington Books, 1983.

– "The International Economic Interests of U.S. States." *Publius: The Journal of Federalism* 14 (Fall 1984): 81–94.

- "State and Local Boundary-Spanning Strategies in the United States: Political, Economic, and Cultural Transgovernmental Interactions." In Jong S. Jun and Deil S. Wright, eds, *Globalization and Decentralization: Institutional Contexts, Policy Issues, and Intergovernmental Relations in Japan and the United States*, 329–46. Washington, DC: Georgetown University Press, 1996.
- "Australian Federalism Confronts Globalisation: A New Challenge at the Centenary." *Australian Journal of Public Administration* 61 (2002): 27–37.

Koh, Harold Hongju. "Is International Law Really State Law?" *Harvard Law Review* 111 (1998): 1824–61.

Kresl, Peter Karl. "The Response of European Cities to EC 1992." *Journal of European Integration* 15 (1992): 151–72.
- and Earl H. Fry. *The Urban Response to Internationalization*. Cheltenham, UK: Edward Elgar, 2005.
- and Gary Gappert, eds. *North American Cities and the Global Economy: Challenges and Opportunities*. Thousand Oaks, CA: Sage, 1995.

Kübler, Daniel, and Jolita Piliutyte. "Intergovernmental Relations and International Strategies: Constraints and Opportunities in Multilevel Polities." *Environment and Planning C: Government and Policy* 25 (2007): 357–73.

Kukucha, Christopher J. "The Role of the Provinces in Canadian Foreign Trade Policy: Global Governance and Sub-National Interests in the Twenty-First Century." *Policy and Society* 23 (2004): 113–34.
- "From Kyoto to the WTO: Evaluating the Constitutional Legitimacy of the Provinces in Canadian Foreign Trade and Environmental Policy." *Canadian Journal of Political Science* 38 (March 2005): 1–24.
- "Lawyers, Trees, and Money: British Columbia Forest Policy and the Convergence of International and Domestic Trade Considerations." *Canadian Public Administration* 58 (2005): 506–27.
- "Expanded Legitimacy: The Provinces and Canadian Foreign Policy." In Duane Bratt and Christopher J. Kukucha, eds, *Readings in Canadian Foreign Policy: Classic Debates and New Ideas*, 214–35. Don Mills: Oxford University Press, 2006.
- "The Federal-Provincial Committee System on International Trade: CTRADE – An Extension of Executive Federalism?" In Luc Bernier and Nelson Michaud, eds, *The Administration of Foreign Affairs: A Renewed Challenge?* Toronto: University of Toronto Press, 2006.

Kuzman, Eduard. "Russia: The Center, the Regions, and the Outside World." *International Affairs* (Moscow) 45 (1999): 26–8.

Laskin, Bora. "Some International Legal Aspects of Federalism: The Experience of Canada." In D.P. Currie, ed., *Federalism and the New Nations of Africa*, 389–414. Chicago: University of Chicago Press, 1964.
- "The Provinces and International Agreements." In Ontario Advisory Committee on Confederation, ed., *Background Papers and Reports*, 101–13. Ottawa: Queen's Printer, 1967.

Latouche, Daniel. "State Building and Foreign Policy at the Subnational Level." In Ivo D. Duchacek, Daniel Latouche, and Garth Stevenson, eds, *Perforated Sovereignties and*

International Relations: Trans-Sovereign Contacts of Subnational Governments, 29–42. New York: Greenwood, 1988.
Laux, Jeanne Kirk. "Expanding the State: The International Relations of State-Owned Enterprises in Canada." *Polity* 15 (Spring 1983): 329–50.
– "Public Enterprises and Canadian Foreign Economic Policy." *Publius: The Journal of Federalism* 14 (Fall 1984): 61–80.
Lazar, Harvey, Hamish Telford, and Ronald L. Watts, eds. *The Impact of Global and Regional Integration on Federal Systems: A Comparative Analysis*. Montreal and Kingston: McGill-Queen's University Press, 2003.
Lecours, André. "Paradiplomacy: Reflections on the Foreign Policy and International Relations of Regions." *International Negotiation* 7 (2002): 91–114.
– "Diversité culturelle et relations internationals: Les cas du Québec et de la Région Wallone/Communauté française de Belgique." In Pierre Noreau and José Woerling, eds, *Appartenances, institutions et citoyenneté*, 207–18. Montreal: Wilson and Lafleur, 2005.
– *Basque Nationalism and the Spanish State*. Reno: University of Nevada Press, 2007.
– and Luis Moreno. "Paradiplomacy: A Nation-Building Strategy? A Reference to the Basque Country." In Alain-G. Gagnon, Montserrat Guibernau, and François Rocher, eds, *The Conditions of Diversity in Multinational Democracies*, 267–92. Montreal: Institute for Research on Public Policy and McGill-Queen's University Press, 2003.
– and Luis Moreno. "Paradiplomatie et nationalisme: Le cas basque." In Jean Tournon and Ramon Maiz, eds, *Ethnicisme et politique*, 277–307. Paris: L'Harmattan, 2005.
Leeson, Howard. "Alberta/Saskatchewan Transborder Contacts with US States: A Survey and Analysis Revisited." In J. Peter Meekison, Hamish Telford, and Harvey Lazar, eds, *Reconsidering the Institutions of Canadian Federalism*, 315–39. Kingston: Institute of Intergovernmental Relations, Queen's University, 2004.
Lefevre, C., and E. d'Albergo. "Guest Editorial: Why Cities are Looking abroad and How They Go about It." *Environment and Planning C: Government and Policy* 25 (2007): 317–26.
Leisner, Walter. "The Foreign Relations of the Member States of the Federal Republic of Germany." *University of Toronto Law Journal* 16 (1996): 346–60.
Lejeune, Marc. *Les Relations Internationales des Communautés et des Régions*. Namur: Faculté de Droit, 1983.
Lejeune, Yves. *Recueil des accords internationaux conclus par les cantons suisses*. Bern: Peter Lang, 1982.
– "Belgium." In Hans J. Michelmann and Panayotis Soldatos, eds, *Federalism and International Relations: The Role of Subnational Units*, 142–75. Oxford: Clarendon, 1990.
– "Participation of Sub-National Units in the Foreign Policy of the Federation." In Raoul Blindenbacher and Arnold Koller, eds, *Federalism in a Changing World:*

Learning from Each Other, 97–114. Montreal and Kingston: McGill-Queen's University Press, 2002.

Leonardy, Uwe. "Treaty-Making Powers and Foreign Relations of Federated Entities." In Bruno Coppetiers, David Darchiashvili, and Natella Akaba, eds, *Federal Practice: Exploring Alternatives for Georgia and Abkhazia*, 151–68. Brussels: VUB University Press, 1999.

Leslie, Peter M., and Keith Brownsey. "Constitutional Reform and Continental Free Trade: A Review of Issues in Canadian Federalism in 1987." *Publius: The Journal of Federalism* 18 (Summer 1988): 153–74.

Letamendia, Francisco. "Basque Nationalism and Cross-Border Co-operation between the Southern and Northern Basque Countries." *Regional and Federal Studies* 7 (Summer 1997): 25–41.

Levine, Jerry, with Fabienne Vandenbrande. "American State Offices in Europe: Activities and Connections." *Intergovernmental Perspective* 20 (Fall 1993 – Winter 1994): 43–6.

Levy, Thomas Allen. "International Legal Aspects of Federalism." *Dalhousie Law Journal* 1 (2003): 634–8.

– and Don Munton. "Federal-Provincial Dimensions and State-Provincial Relations." *International Perspectives* (March-April 1976): 23–7.

Lewis, Kevin. "Dealing with South Africa: The Constitutionality of State and Local Divestment Legislation." *Tulane Law Review* 61 (1987): 469–517.

Li, Luis. "State Sovereignty and Nuclear Free Zones." *California Law Review* 79 (1991): 1168–1203.

Liang, Yuen-Li. "Colonial Clauses and Federal Clauses in UN Multilateral Instruments." *American Journal of International Law* 45 (1951): 108–28.

Liner, E. Blaine. "States and Localities in the Global Marketplace." *Intergovernmental Perspective* 16 (Spring 1990): 11–14.

– Thomas O. Singer, and Harry P. Hatry. *International Business Development and Marketing in Illinois: A Review of the State's Performance*. Washington, DC: The Urban Institute, February 1989.

Looper, Robert B. "Federal States Clauses in Multilateral Instruments." *British Yearbook of International Law* 32 (1955–56): 162–203.

– "The Treaty Power in India." *British Yearbook of International Law* 32 (1955–56): 300–7.

– "The Treaty Power in Switzerland." *American Journal of Comparative Law* 7 (1958): 178–94.

– "Limitations on the Treaty Power in Federal States." *New York University Law Review* 34 (1959): 1045–66.

Lordkipanidze, Gocha. "Segmentation and Integration: Proposals for a Federalisation of Foreign Policy in Georgia." In Bruno Coppetiers, David Darchiashvili, and Natella Akaba, eds, *Federal Practice: Exploring Alternatives for Georgia and Abkhazia*, 169–78. Brussels: VUB University Press, 1999.

Lubin, Martin. "Quebec-United States Relations: An Overview." *American Review of Canadian Studies* 16 (Spring 1986): 17–31.
– "New England, New York, and Their Francophone Neighborhood." In Ivo D. Duchacek, Daniel Latouche, and Garth Stevenson, eds, *Perforated Sovereignties and International Relations: Trans-Sovereign Contacts of Subnational Governments*, 143–62. New York: Greenwood, 1988.
Lutter, Randall. "Sovereignty, Federalism, and the Identification of Local Environmental Problems." *Chicago Journal of International Law* 2 (Fall 2001): 447–56.
MacFarlane, John. *Ernest Lapointe and Quebec's Influence on Canadian Foreign Policy*. Toronto: University of Toronto Press, 1999.
Maier, Harold G. "Preemption of State Law: A Recommended Analysis." *American Journal of International Law* 83 (1989): 832–9.
Maillat, Denis. "Transfrontier Regionalism: The Jura Arc from Basle to Geneva." In Ivo D. Duchacek, Daniel Latouche, and Garth Stevenson, eds, *Perforated Sovereignties and International Relations: Trans-Sovereign Contacts of Subnational Governments*, 199–211. New York: Greenwood, 1988.
Makarychev, Andrey S. "Russian Regions as International Actors." *Demokratizatsiya* 7 (1999): 501–26.
Malchus, Viktor V. *Partnerschaft an europäischen Grenzen*. Bonn: Europa Union Veerlag, 1975.
Marin, Anaïs. "The International Dimension of Regionalism – St. Petersburg's 'Para-Diplomacy.'" In Katri Pynnöniemi, ed., *Beyond the Garden Ring: Dimensions of Russian Regionalism*. Helsinki: Aleksanteri Institute, University of Helsinki, 2002.
Marks, Gary, Richard Haesly, and Heather A.D. Mbaye. "What Do Subnational Offices Think They Are Doing in Brussels?" *Regional and Federal Studies* 12 (Autumn 2002): 1–23.
Martin, Pierre. "When Nationalism Meets Continentalism: The Politics of Free Trade in Quebec." *Regional and Federal Studies* 5 (Spring 1995): 1–27.
Mashaw, Jerry L. "Federal Issues in and about the Jurisdiction of the Court of Justice of the European Communities." *Tulane Law Review* 40 (1965–66): 21–56.
Massart-Piérard, Francoise. "Politique des relations extérieures et identité politique: La stratégie des entités fédérées de Belgique." *Études internationales* 30 (December 1999): 701–27.
– "La projection de la Communauté francaise de Belgique et de la Région wallonne sur la scene internationale: Une étude comparee." *Studia Diplomatica* 54 (2001): 81–113.
– "Une etude comparée des relations entre entités fédérées au sein du systeme de politique exterieure en Belgique francophone." *Revue internationale de Politique comparée* 12 (2005): 191–205.
Massell, David. "Governors and Premiers Practice International Cooperation." *Canadian Studies Update* 22 (2003): 6–8.
McMillan, Samuel Lucas. "Subnational Foreign Policy Actors: How and Why Governors Participate in U.S. Foreign Policy." *Foreign Policy Analysis* 4 (July 2008): 227–53.

McWhinney, Edward. "Canadian Federalism and the Foreign Affairs and Treaty Power: The Impact of Quebec's Quiet Revolution." *Canadian Yearbook of International Law* 7 (1967): 3–32.
Medeiros, Marcelo de A. "Subnational Dynamics vs. Center-Periphery Logic: The Impact of Mercosur on the Political Economy of Pernambuco, Bahia, São Paulo and Rio Grande do Sul. Revista Brasileira." *Política Internacional* 49 (June 2006): 43–67.
Melvin, N. *Regional Foreign Policies in the Russian Federation.* London: Royal Institute of International Affairs, 1995.
Mettger, H. Philip. "Foreign Relations at the State Capital." *State Government* 28 (October 1955): 237–40.
Michaud, Nelson. "Quebec and North American Integration: Making Room for a Sub-National Actor?" In J. Peter Meekison, Hamish Telford, and Harvey Lazar, eds, *Reconsidering the Institutions of Canadian Federalism*, 377–409. Kingston: Institute of Intergovernmental Relations, Queen's University, 2004.
Michelmann, Hans J. "Federalism and International Relations in Canada and the Federal Republic of Germany." *International Journal* 41 (Summer 1986): 539–71.
– "Länder Paradiplomacy." *German Politics and Society* 15 (October 1988): 22–31.
– "The Federal Republic of Germany." In Hans J. Michelmann and Panayotis Soldatos, eds, *Federalism and International Relations: The Role of Subnational Units*, 211–44. Oxford: Clarendon, 1990.
– "Paradiplomacy in Germany and Canada." *ACS Bulletin/Bulletin AEC* (Association for Canadian Studies/Association d'études canadiennes) (1999): 24–7.
– "Federalism and Paradiplomacy." In Thomas Jäger, Gerhard Kümmel, and Maria Lerch, eds, *Sicherheit und Freiheit*, 188–205. Baden-Baden, Nomos, 2004.
– and Panayotis Soldatos, eds. *Federalism and International Relations: The Role of Subnational Units.* New York: Oxford University Press, 1990.
Mingus, Matthew. "Transnationalism and Subnational Paradiplomacy: Are Governance Networks Perforating Sovereignty?" *International Journal of Public Administration* 29 (2006): 577–94.
Mitchell, James. "Lobbying Brussels: The Case of Scotland Europa." *European Urban and Regional Studies* 2 (1995): 287–98.
Montero, Alfred P. "After Decentralization: Patterns of Intergovernmental Conflict in Argentina, Brazil, Spain, and Mexico." *Publius: The Journal of Federalism* 31 (Fall 2001): 43–64.
Moore, John Norton. "Federalism and Foreign Relations." *Duke Law Journal* 1965 (Spring 1965): 248–321.
Morin, Claude. *L'Art de l'impossible: La Diplomatie québécoise depuis 1960.* Montreal: Boréal, 1987.
Morris, Gerald L. "The Treaty-Making Power: A Canadian Dilemma." *Canadian Bar Review* 45 (1967): 478–512.
Morrow, Duncan. "Regional Policy as Foreign Policy: The Austrian Experience." *Regional Politics and Policy* 2 (Autumn 1992): 27–44.

Motomura, Hiroshi. "Federalism, International Human Rights, and Immigration Exceptionalism." *University of Colorado Law Review* 70 (Fall 1999): 1361–94.

Mumme, Stephen P. "Regional Power in National Diplomacy: The Case of the U.S. Section of the International Boundary and Water Commission." *Publius: The Journal of Federalism* 14 (Fall 1984): 115–35.

– "State Influence in Foreign Policymaking: Water-Related Environmental Disputes along the United States-Mexico Border." *Western Political Quarterly* 38 (December 1985): 620–40.

Nadelmann. Kurt H. "Ignored State Interests: The Federal Government and International Efforts to Unify Rules of Private Law." *University of Pennsylvania Law Review* 102 (1953–54): 323–66.

Naftzger, David. "The States' Role (if any) in Foreign Affairs." *State Legislatures* 26 (December 2000): 24.

Nagata, Naohisa. "The Impact of Globalization on Domestic Administration and its Influence on Local Governance." In National Institute for Research Advancement and National Academy of Public Administration, ed., *The Challenge to New Governance in the Twenty-First Century: Achieving Effective Central-Local Relations*, 466–93. Tokyo: National Institute for Research Advancement, 1999.

Nass, Klaus Otto. "The Foreign and European Policy of the German *Länder.*" *Publius: The Journal of Federalism* 19 (Fall 1989): 165–84.

Nasyrov, Il'dar. "The International Activity of Federal Subjects: Reasons, Objectives and Form." *Kazan Federalist* 4, no. 8 (Autumn 2003): 122–42.

National Governors' Association, Committee on International Trade and Foreign Relations. *Export Development and Foreign Investment: The Role of the States and Its Linkage to Federal Action.* Washington, DC: National Governors' Association, 1981.

National League of Cities, International Economic Development Task Force. *International Trade: A New City Economic Development Strategy.* Washington, DC: National League of Cities, 26 November 1983.

Nedbailo, P.Y., and V.A. Vassilenko. "Soviet Union Republics as Subjects of International Law." *Soviet Yearbook of International Law* (1963): 85–108.

Neuse, Steven M. "State Activities in International Trade." *State Government* 55 (Summer 1982): 57–64.

Nothdurft, William E., and Ilene K. Grossman. *Small Firm Export Assistance in Europe: Lessons for States.* Lombard, IL: Council of State Governments, Midwestern Office, 1996.

O'Toole, Kevin. "Kohusaika and Internationalization: Australia and Japanese Sister City Type Relationships." *Australian Journal of International Affairs* 55 (2001): 403–19.

Oneal, Frances H. "U.S. State Government Responses to EC-1992." In Dale L. Smith and James Lee Ray, eds, *The 1992 Project and the Future of Integration in Europe*, 163–77. Armonk, NY: M. E. Sharpe, 1993.

Opeskin, Brian R., and Don Rothwell. *International Law and Australian Federalism.* Melbourne: University of Melbourne Press, 1997.

Oyebode, A. "Treaty-Making Powers and their Implementation Under a Federal Constitution." In A.B. Akinyemi, P.D. Cole, and Walter Ofonagoro, eds, *Readings on Federalism*, 52–62. Lagos: Nigerian Institute of International Affairs, 1979.

Painchaud, Paul. "Territorialization and Internationalism: The Case of Quebec." *Publius: The Journal of Federalism* 7 (Fall 1977): 161–76.

– "L'Etat du Québec et le systéme international." In Gérard Bergeron and Réjean Pelletier, eds, *Le'Etat du Québec en devenir*, 351–69. Montreal: Boréal Express, 1980.

– "The Epicenter of Quebec's International Relations." In Ivo D. Duchacek, Daniel Latouche, and Garth Stevenson, eds, *Perforated Sovereignties and International Relations: Trans-Sovereign Contacts of Subnational Governments*, 91–7. New York: Greenwood, 1988.

– ed. *Le Canada et le Québec sur la scene internationale*. Quebec: Presses de l'Université du Québec, 1977.

Palermo, F. *Die Aussenbeziehungen der Italienischen Regionen in Rechtsvergleichender Sicht*. Frankfurt/Main: Lang, 1999.

Palumbo, Dennis J. "The States and the Conduct of Foreign Relations." In Daniel J. Elazar, R. Bruce Carroll, E. Lester Levine, and Douglas St Angelo, eds, *Cooperation and Conflict: Readings in American Federalism*, 377–87. Itasca: F.E. Peacock, 1969.

Paquin, Stéphane. *La paradiplomatie identitaire en Catalogne*. Quebec: Presses de l'Université Laval, 2003.

– "La paradiplomatie identitaire: Le Québec, la Catalogne et la Flandre en relations internationals." *Politique et Sociétés* 23 (2004): 176–94.

– "Les actions extérieures des entités subétatiques: Quelle signification pour la politique comparée et les relations internationales?" *Revue internationale de politique comparée* 12 (2005): 129–42.

Pascoe, James J. "Time for a New Approach? Federalism and Foreign Affairs after *Crosby v. National Foreign Trade Council* (Massachusetts Law Restricting Purchases from Firms Doing Business in Burma)." *Vanderbilt Journal of Transnational Law* 35 (January 2002): 291–320.

Patry, André. *Le Québec dans le monde*. Montreal: Leméac, 1980.

Paul, Darel E. *Rescaling International Political Economy: Subnational States and the Regulation of the Global Political Economy*. London: Routledge, 2005.

Pelinka, Anton. "Austria." In Hans J. Michelmann and Panayotis Soldatos, eds, *Federalism and International Relations: The Role of Subnational Units*, 124–41. Oxford: Clarendon, 1990.

Perkmann, Markus and Ngai-ling Sum, eds. *Globalization, Regionalization and Cross-Border Regions*. Hampshire, UK: Palgrave Macmillan, 2002.

Pfisterer, Thomas. "Auslandbeziehungen der Kantone." In Daniel Thürer, Jean-Francois Aubert, and Jörg Paul Müller, eds, *Verfassungsrecht der Schweis*, 525–46. Zurich: Schulthess, 2001.

Philippart, Eric. "Le développement de la 'paradiplomatie' au sein de l'Union européenne et la nouvelle donne belge." *Études internationals* (Quebec) 39 (1998): 631–46.

Pickering, Margaret S. "Acts by State Governments Affecting Foreign Relations." *Harvard International Law Journal* 25 (Winter 1984): 200–5.

Pilcher, Dan. "The States and Mexico: An Experiment in Cooperation." *State Legislatures* 7 (March 1981): 17–22.

– and Lanny Proffer. *The States and International Trade: New Roles in Export Development – A Legislator's Guide.* Washington, DC: National Conference of State Legislatures, 1985.

Podolak, Martha M. "The Availability of a Jury Trial in Federal Courts: Suits against Foreign Sovereign-Owned Instrumentalities." *Hastings International and Comparative Law* 6 (1982): 185–209.

Polaschek, Martin F. "Implementation of International and Supra-National Law in Sub-National Units." In Raoul Blindenbacher and Arnold Koller, eds, *Federalism in a Changing World: Learning from Each Other*, 169–78. Montreal and Kingston: McGill-Queen's University Press, 2002.

Policy Research Initiative. *The Emergence of Cross-Border Regions: Interim Report.* Ottawa: Policy Research Initiative, November 2005.

Porterfield, Matthew C. "State and Local Foreign Policy Initiatives and Free Speech: The First Amendment as an Instrument of Federalism." *Stanford Journal of International Law* 35 (1999): 1–48.

– "International Expropriation Rules and Federalism." *Stanford Environmental Law Journal* 23 (January 2004): 3–7.

Portes, Jacques. "Paris-Ottawa-Quebec: A Unique Trangle." In Ivo D. Duchacek, Daniel Latouche, and Garth Stevenson, eds, *Perforated Sovereignties and International Relations: Trans-Sovereign Contacts of Subnational Governments*, 103–18. New York: Greenwood, 1988.

Posner, Alan R. *State Government Export Promotion: An Exporter's Guide.* Westport, CT: Quorum Books, 1984.

Price, Daniel M., and John P. Hannah. "The Constitutionality of United States State and Local Sanctions." *Harvard International Law Journal* 39 (1998): 443–99.

Québec, Ministere des relations internationales. *Le Québec dans le monde – Le défi de l'interdépendence.* Quebec: Ministere des relations internationales, 1985.

Quigley, Harold S. "Federalism and Foreign Relations in China." *Political Science Quarterly* 42 (December 1927): 561–70.

Ramsey, Michael D. "The Power of the States in Foreign Affairs: The Original Understanding of Foreign Policy Federalism." *Notre Dame Law Review* 75 (1999): 341–431.

Rand, Michael C. "International Agreements between Canadian Provinces and Foreign States." *University of Toronto, Faculty Law Review* 25 (1967): 75–86.

Ravenhill, John. "Australia." In Hans J. Michelmann and Panayotis Soldatos, eds, *Federalism and International Relations: The Role of Subnational Units*, 76–123. Oxford: Clarendon, 1990.

– "Federal-State Relations in Australian External Affairs: A New Co-operative Era?" *Regional and Federal Studies* 9 (Spring 1999): 134–52.

Rémillard, Gil. "Quebec's Role in Relations between Canada and the United States." In Elliot J. Feldman and Priscilla Battis, eds, *New North American Horizons: Conference and Survey Report of the Harvard Project on Canadian-United States Relations*, 18–27. Cambridge, MA: University Consortium for Research on North America, 1987.

Resnik, Judith. "Law's Migration: American Exceptionalism, Silent Dialogues, and Federalism's Multiple Ports of Entry." *Yale Law Journal* 115 (2006): 1564–1671.

– "Foreign as Domestic Affairs: Rethinking Horizontal Federalism and Foreign Affairs Preemption in Light of Translocal Internationalism." *Emory Law Journal* 57 (December 2007): 31–92.

– "Law as Affiliation: 'Foreign' Law, Democratic Federalism, and the Sovereigntism of the Nation-State International." *International Journal of Constitutional Law* (2008): 33–66.

Roberts, John W. "Cold War Observer: Governor Adlai Stevenson on American Foreign Relations." *Journal of the Illinois State Historical Society* 76 (Spring 1983): 49–60.

Rodgers, Raymond S. "The Capacity of States of the Union to Conclude International Agreements: The Background and Some Recent Developments." *American Journal of International Law* 61 (1967): 1021–8.

– "Conclusion of Quebec-Louisiana Agreement on Cultural Co-operation." *American Journal of International Law* 64 (1970): 380.

Rose, John. "Foreign Relations at the State Level." *Journal of State Government* 64 (1991): 110–17.

Rothstein, Morton. "The American West and Foreign Markets: 1850–1900." In David M. Ellis, ed., *The Frontier in American Development*, 381–406. Ithaca: Cornell University Press, 1969.

Rowswell, Ben. "The Federal Context: Ottawa as Padlock or Partner?" *American Review of Canadian Studies* 32 (2002): 215–39.

Rutan, Gerard F. "Legislative Interaction of a Canadian Province and an American State." *American Review of Canadian Studies* 11 (Autumn 1981): 66–79.

– "British Columbia-Washington State Governmental Interrelations: Some Findings upon the Failure of Structure." *American Review of Canadian Studies* 15 (Spring 1985): 97–110.

– "Micro-Diplomatic Relations in the Pacific Northwest: Washington State-British Columbia Interactions." In Ivo D. Duchacek, Daniel Latouche, and Garth Stevenson, eds, *Perforated Sovereignties and International Relations: Trans-Sovereign Contacts of Subnational Governments*, 163–88. New York: Greenwood, 1988.

Salomon, Mónica, and Carmen Nunes. "A Acao Externa dos Governos Subnacionais no Brasil: Os Casos do Rio Grande do Sul e de Porto Alegre: Um Estudo Comparative de Dois Tipos de Atores Mistos." *Contexto Internacional* 29 (January-June 2007): 99–147.

Sample, Steven B., and Eugene P. Trani. "The Foreign Policy of Nebraska." *Washington Quarterly* 3 (Summer 1980): 6–71.

Sancton, Andrew. "Municipalities, Cities, and Globalization: Implications for Canadian Federalism." In Herman Bakvis and Grace Skogstad, eds, *Canadian Federalism: Performance, Effectiveness and Legitimacy*, 261–77. Don Mills, ON: Oxford University Press, 2002.

Schindler, Benjamin. "Federal Structures and Foreign Policy of International and Supra-National Organisations." In Raoul Blindenbacher and Arnold Koller, eds, *Federalism in a Changing World: Learning from Each Other*, 179–88. Montreal and Kingston: McGill-Queen's University Press, 2002.

Schlegel, John P. "Federalism and Canadian Foreign Policy." *Round Table* 282 (April 1981): 179–92.

Schmahmann, David, and James Finch. "The Unconstitutionality of State and Local Enactments in the United States Restricting Business Ties with Burma (Myanmar)." *Vanderbilt Journal of Transnational Law* 30 (March 1997): 184–202.

Schmitt, Nicolas. "The Foreign Relations of Swiss Cantons – Within the Frame of the New 1999 Swiss Constitution." In Lidija R. Basta and Thomas Fleiner, eds, *Federalism and Multiethnic States – The Case of Switzerland*, 2nd ed., 182–91. Basel: Helbing and Lichtenhahn, 2000.

Schmitt, William. *Border Governors Conference – A State Level Foreign Policy Mechanism*. Washington DC: Executive Seminar in National and International Affairs, Foreign Service Institute, US Department of State, 1982–83.

Schwab, Susan C. "Building a National Export Development Alliance." *Intergovernmental Perspective* 16 (Spring 1990): 18–20.

Schweke, William, Caril Rist, and Brian Dabson. *Bidding for Business: Are Cities and States Selling Themselves Short?* Washington, DC: Corporation for Enterprise Development, 1994.

– and Robert K. Stumberg. *Could Economic Development Become Illegal in the New Global Policy Environment?* Washington, DC: Corporation for Enterprise Development, July 1999.

Scott, Ian. "The Provinces and Canadian Foreign Policy: Form and Substance in the Policy Making Process." In Elliot J. Feldman and Priscilla Battis, eds, *New North American Horizons: Conference and Survey Report of the Harvard Project on Canadian-United States Relations*, 9–17. Cambridge, MA: University Consortium for Research on North America, 1987.

Scott, James Wesley. "Transborder Cooperation, Regional Initiatives, and Sovereignty Conflicts in Western Europe: The Case of the Upper Rhine Valley." *Publius: The Journal of Federalism* 19 (Winter 1989): 139–56.

– "Cross-border Cooperation in the Baltic Sea Region." *Regional and Federal Studies* 12 (Winter 2002): 135–53.

Segura, Caterina Garcia i. "The Autonomous Communities and External Relations." In Richard Gillespie, Fernando Rodrigo, and J. Story, eds, *Democratic Spain: Reshaping External Relations in a Changing World*, 123–40. London: Routledge, 1995.

– "Les strategies internationals de la Catalogne: Nationalisme politique et pragmatisme économique." *Bulletin d'Histoire Politique* 10 (2001): 99–109.

Seidl-Hohenveldern, Ignaz. "The Relation of International Law to Internal Law in Austria." *American Journal of International Law* 49 (1955): 451–76.

Sharaftutdinova, Gulnaz. "Paradiplomacy in the Russian Regions: Tatarstan's Search for Statehood." *Europe-Asia Studies* 55 (June 2003): 613–29.

Sharman, G. Campbell. "The Australian States and External Affairs: An Exploratory Note." *Australian Outlook* 27 (December 1973): 309.

Sher, Anna, and Alisa Voznaya. "Towards the Neoliberal State: Political Economy of Paradiplomacy and Corporate Control in Tatarstan." In Yildiz Atasoy, ed., *Hegemonic Transitions, the State and Neoliberal Crisis in Capitalism*. New York: Routledge, 2008.

Shulman, Stephen. "National Integration and Foreign Policy in Multiethnic States." *Nationalism and Ethnic Politics* 4 (1998): 110–32.

Shuman, Michael H. "Dateline Main Street: Local Foreign Policies." *Foreign Policy* 65 (Winter 1986–87): 7–13.

– "What the Framers Really Said about Foreign Policy Powers." *Intergovernmental Perspective* 16 (Spring 1990): 27–31.

– *Going Local: Creating Self-Reliant Communities in a Global Age*. New York: Routledge, 2000.

Siegel, Neil S. "International Delegations and the Values of Federalism." *Law and Contemporary Problems* 70 (forthcoming 2008).

Skogstad, Grace. "International Trade Policy and Canadian Federalism: A Constructive Tension?" In Herman Bakvis and Grace Skogstad, eds, *Canadian Federalism: Performance, Effectiveness, and Legitimacy*, 159–77. Don Mills, ON: Oxford University Press, 2002.

Slattery, Thomas F. "World Trade and the Illinois Economy." *State Government* 48 (Winter 1975): 5–7.

Sloan, John W., and Jonathan P. West. "Community Integration and Policies among Elites in Two Border Cities." *Journal of Interamerican Studies and World Affairs* 18 (November 1976): 451–74.

– and Jonathan P. West. "The Role of Informal Policy Making in U.S.-Mexico Border Cities." *Social Science Quarterly* 58 (September 1977): 270–82.

Smith, Nancy Paige. "Paradiplomacy Between the U.S. and Canadian Provinces: The Case of Acid Rain Memoranda of Understanding." *Journal of Borderlands Studies* 3 (1988): 13–38.

Smith, Patrick J. "The Making of a Global City: Fifty Years of Constituent Diplomacy: The Case of Vancouver." *Canadian Journal of Urban Research* 1 (1992): 90–112.

– "Transborder Cascadia: Which Borders Matter?" *Journal of Borderlands Studies* 19 (2004): 99–121.

Sodupe, Kepa. "The European Union and Inter-Regional Co-operation." *Regional and Federal Studies* 9 (Spring 1999): 58–81.

Sohn, Louis B., and Paul Shafer. "Foreign Affairs." In Robert R. Bowie and Carl J. Friedrich, eds, *Studies in Federalism*, 236–95. Boston: Little, Brown, 1954.

Soldatos, Panayotis. "An Explanatory Framework for the Study of Federated States as Foreign-Policy Actors." In Hans J. Michelmann and Panayotis Soldatos, eds, *Federalism and International Relations: The Role of Subnational Units*, 34–53. Oxford: Clarendon, 1990.

– and Hans J. Michelmann. "Subnational Units' Paradiplomacy in the Context of European Integration." *Journal of European Integration* 15 (Winter 1992): 129–34.

Sorensen, Max. "Federal States and the International Protection of Human Rights." *American Journal of International Law* 46 (1952): 195–218.

Spiegeleire, Stephan de. "Gulliver's Threads: Russia's Regions and the Rest of the World." In Kimitako Matsuzato, ed., *Regions: A Prism to View the Slavic-Eurasian World: Towards a Discipline of 'Regionology'*, 293–310. Hokkaido: Slavic Research Center, 1999.

Spiro, Peter J. "State and Local Anti-South Africa Action as an Intrusion upon the Federal Power in Foreign Affairs." *Virginia Law Review* 72 (May 1986): 813–50.

– "Taking Foreign Policy Away from the Feds." *Washington Quarterly* 10 (Winter 1988): 191–203.

– "The Limits of Federalism in Foreign Policymaking." *Intergovernmental Perspective* 16 (Spring 1990): 32–4.

– "The States and International Human Rights." *Fordham Law Review* 66 (November 1997): 567–96.

– "Foreign Relations Federalism." *University of Colorado Law Review* 70 (Fall 1999): 1223–66.

– "Contextual Determinism and Foreign Relations Federalism." *Chicago Journal of International Law* 2 (Fall 2001): 363–70.

– "Globalization and the (Foreign Affairs) Constitution." *Ohio State Law Journal* 63 (2002): 649–730.

– "*Crosby* as Way-Station." *Berkeley Journal of International Law* 21 (Winter 2003): 146–51.

Sridharan, Kripa. "Federalism and Foreign Relations: The Nascent Role of the Indian States." *Asian Studies Review* 27 (December 2003): 463–89.

State International Development Organization. *SIDO Survey 2006: Emerging Trends in State International Business Development*. Washington, DC: State International Development Organization, 2006.

Steinberger, Helmut. "Constitutional Subdivisions of States or Unions and Their Capacity to Conclude Treaties: Comments on Art. 5, para. 2 of the ILC's 1966 Draft Articles on the Law of Treaties." *Zeitschrift für ausländisches öffentliches Recht und Völkerrecht* 27 (1967): 411–28.

Stephens, Beth. "Federalism and Foreign Affairs: Congress' Power to 'define and punish ... offenses against the law of nations.'" *William and Mary Law Review* 42 (December 2000): 447–57.

Stoke, Harold W. *The Foreign Relations of the Federal State*. Baltimore: Johns Hopkins University Press, 1931.

Stone, Alec. "The New Quebec Challenge to North American Diplomacy." *SAIS Review* 3 (1983): 119–31.

Strassoldo, Raimondo. *Frontier Regions*. Strasbourg, France: Council of Europe, 1973.
Stumberg, Robert K. "Preemption and Human Rights: Local Options after *Crosby* v. *NFTC*." *Law and Policy in International Business* 32 (2000): 109–96.
– and Matthew C. Porterfield. "Who Preempted the Massachusetts Burma Law? Federalism and Political Accountability under Global Trade Rules." *Publius: The Journal of Federalism* 31 (Summer 2001): 173–204.
Sullivan, Alan W. "Canadian Federal-Provincial Relations in an International Setting." *Rockefeller Institute Bulletin* 11 (1993): 71–6.
Sutcliffe, John B. "Subnational Influence on the Structural Funds: The Highlands and Islands of Scotland." *Regional and Federal Studies* 12 (Autumn 2002): 102–27.
Swaine, Edward T. "The Undersea World of Foreign Relations Federalism." *Chicago Journal of International Law* 2 (Fall 2001): 337–54.
Swanson, Roger F. "The Range of Direct Relations between States and Provinces." *International Perspectives* (March-April 1976): 18–23.
– *Intergovernmental Perspectives on the Canada-U.S. Relationship*. New York: New York University Press, 1978.
Testa, William A., D.A. Oppedahl, and L.S. Merkel. "The Bi-national Great Lakes Economy." *Chicago Fed Letter* 153 (May 2000): 1–3.
Texas House of Representatives. "The NAFTA's Impact on State Governmental Authority." In *Special House Select Committee on NAFTA and GATT: Interim Report to the 74th Texas Legislature*. Austin: Texas House of Representatives, November 1994.
Thompson, Tommy G. "Going Global: A Governor's Perspective." *Intergovernmental Perspective* 16 (Spring 1990): 15–17.
Thornberry, Chad. "Federalism v. Foreign Affairs: How the United States Can Administer Article 36 of the Vienna Convention on Consular Relations within the States." *McGeorge Law Review* 31 (2000): 107–31.
Tiefenbrun, Susan W. "State and Federal Foreign Affairs Power in the United States." In James E. Hickey and Alexej Ugrinsky, eds, *Government Structures in the U.S.A. and the Sovereign States of the Former U.S.S.R.: Power Allocation among Central, Regional, and Local Governments*, 156–66. Westport, CT: Greenwood, 1996.
Tkachenko, Stanislav. "The Paradiplomacy of St. Petersburg." In Christopher S. Browning, ed., *Northern Europe after the Enlargements*, 161–79. Aldershot, UK: Ashgate, 2005.
Totoricagüena, Gloria. "Diasporas as Non-Central Government Actors in Foreign Policy: The Trajectory of Basque Paradiplomacy." *Nationalism and Ethnic Politics* 11 (2005): 265–87.
Trone, John. *Federal Constitutions and International Relations*. St Lucia: University of Queensland Press, 2002.
Trubowitz, Peter. "Sectionalism and American Foreign Policy: The Political Geography of Consensus and Conflict." *International Studies Quarterly* 36 (June 1992): 173–91.
– and Brian E. Roberts. "Regional Interests and the Reagan Military Buildup." *Regional Studies* 26 (October 1992): 555–68.

Truman, Louis. "Georgia Reaches Across the Globe." *State Government* 48 (Winter 1975): 9–10.

United States Advisory Commission on Intergovernmental Relations. "State and Local Governments in International Affairs: ACIR Findings and Recommendations." *Intergovernmental Perspective* 20 (Fall 1993 – Winter 1994): 33–7.

United States Small Business Administration. *State Export Promotion Activities*. Washington, DC: United States Small Business Administration, October 1984.

Urban, Sabine. "L'intégration économique européenne et l'évolution de part et d'autre du Rhin (Alsace, Bade, Bale)." *Economies et societes* 5 (March-April 1971): 619–28.

Velaers, Jan. "In foro interno et in foro externo: De internationale bevoegdheden van gemeenschappen en gewesten." In Frank Judo and Godfried Guedens, eds, *Internationale betrekkingen en federalisme*, 3–86. Brussels: De Boeck and Larcier, 2006.

Velázquez Flores, Rafael. "La paradiplomacia mexicana: Las relaciones exteriores de las entidades federativas." *Relaciones Internacionales* (2006): 123–49.

Van Ginderachter, Jef. "Les competences internationales des communautés et des regions Belgique." *Studia Diplomatica* 44 (1993): 85–92.

Vandenbergh, Godelieve. "Belgium's Communities and Regions Take on Foreign Affairs." *Federations* 3 (2003): 13–14.

Vázquez, Carlos Manuel. "*Breard* and the Federal Power to Require Compliance with ICJ Orders of Provisional Measures." *American Journal of International Law* 92 (Fall 1998): 683–91.

- "*Breard, Printz*, and the Treaty Power." *University of Colorado Law Review* 70 (Fall 1999): 1317–60.

- "Whither *Zschernig*? New Voices on the New Federalism." *Villanova Law Review* 46 (2001): 1325–40.

Vigevani, Tullo. "Problemas para a atividade internacional das unidades subnacionais: Estados e municípios brasileiros." *Revista Brasileira* Ciências *Sociais* 21 (October 2006): 127–39.

- Walter Wanderly, and Marcelo Passini, eds. *A Dimensao Subnacional e as Relacoes Internacionais*. Sao Paulo: EDUC/Fundacao Editora da UNESP, 2002.

Villiers, Bertus de. *Foreign Relations and The Provinces*. Pretoria: Human Sciences Research Council (HSRC) Publishers, 1995.

Weihe-Lindeborg. *Zum regionalen System: Stellenwert de Versammlung der Regionen Europas*. Marburg: Tectum Verlag, 2005.

Weiler, Conrad. "GATT, NAFTA, and State and Local Powers." *Intergovernmental Perspective* (Fall 1993 – Winter 1994): 38–41.

- "Foreign Trade Agreements: A New Federal Partner?" *Publius: The Journal of Federalism* 24 (Summer 1994): 113–33.

Weyand, Sabine. "Inter-Regional Associations and the European Integration Process." *Regional and Federal Studies* 6 (Summer 1996): 166–82.

Weyreter, M. "Germany and the Town Twinning Movement." *Contemporary Review* 281, no. 1644 (January 2003): 37–43.

Whatley, Chris. *State Officials' Guide to International Affairs*. Washington, DC: Council of State Governments, 2003.

Wildhaber, Luzius. "External Relations of the Swiss Cantons." *Canadian Yearbook of International Law* 12 (1974): 211–21.

– "Switzerland." In Hans J. Michelmann and Panayotis Soldatos, eds, *Federalism and International Relations: The Role of Subnational Units*, 245–75. Oxford: Clarendon, 1990.

Wolff, Stefan. "Paradiplomacy: Scope, Opportunities and Challenges." *BC Journal of International Affairs* 10 (Spring 2007): 141–50.

Wolters, M. "Euregions along the German Border." In U. Bullman, ed., *Die Politik der dritten Ebene: Die Regionen im Europa der Union*. Baden-Baden: Nomos, 1994.

Yoder, J.A. "Bridging the European Union and Eastern Europe: Cross-Border Co-operation and the Euroregions." *Regional and Federal Studies* 13 (2003): 99–106.

Yoo, John C. "Foreign Affairs Federalism and the Separation of Powers." *Villanova Law Review* 46 (2001): 101–8.

Zelinsky, Wilbur. "The Twinning of the World: Sister Cities in Geographic and Historical Perspective." *Annals of the Association of American Geographers* 81 (1991): 1–31.

Zheng, Yu. "Fiscal Federalism and Provincial Foreign Tax Policies in China." *Journal of Contemporary China* 15 (August 2006): 479–502.

Zubiri, Alexander Ugalde. "The International Relations of Basque Nationalism and the First Basque Autonomous Government (1890–1939)." *Regional and Federal Studies* 9 (Spring 1999): 170–84.

Contributors

FRANCISCO ALDECOA is a professor of international relations and Jean Monnet Chair in European Politics at the Complutense University of Madrid. He is also dean of the Faculty of Political and Social Sciences at the same university. He is the author of numerous books and refereed articles on the European integration process, Spanish foreign policy, Latin American politics and integration, regionalism, and subnational diplomacy. He is currently president of the Spanish Association of International Law and International Relations.

PETER BURSENS is currently an associate professor and Jean Monnet Chair in the Department of Political Science at the University of Antwerp, Belgium. He teaches on European integration and federalism. His research interests include European institutions, Europeanization, legitimacy in multilevel systems, and multilevel governance. Dr Bursens holds a PhD in political and social sciences from the University of Antwerp. His publications include "The European Rescue of the Federal State" (2006), with Jan Beyers; and "Europeanization of Subnational Polities: The Impact of Domestic Factors on Regional Adaptation to European Integration" (2008), with Jana Deforche.

NOÉ CORNAGO is an associate professor of international relations at the University of the Basque Country in Bilbao, Spain, where he is also in charge of the master's degree program in peace and development studies. He has published widely on the contemporary transformations of diplomacy, federalism, foreign relations, and multilateralism. He has held visiting positions at Université Laval, Canada; Ohio State University and the University of Idaho, United States; and the Institute for Political Studies in Bordeaux, France.

EARL H. FRY is a professor of political science and Endowed Professor of Canadian Studies at Brigham Young University. He has been a Fulbright Professor at the Sorbonne and the University of Toronto, Enders Professor at McGill University, and special assistant in the Office of the US Trade Representative (USTR). He is the author or co-author of *The Expanding Role of State and Local Governments in U.S. Foreign Affairs* (1998), *The Urban Response to Internationalization* (2004), and *The Politics of International Investment* (1983).

RUDOLF HRBEK holds a PhD from the University of Tübingen (1968), where in 2006 he became Professor Emeritus. He is speaker of the European Center for Research on Federalism, University of Tübingen, and has had visiting professorships at universities in Germany, Italy, Switzerland, Thailand, and the United States. He is currently a visiting professor at the College of Europe, Bruges. Dr Hrbek's research focuses on federalism, political systems in western Europe, and European integration and the EC/EU. He has written and edited approximately 250 books, journal articles, and essays for books. He is a member of the editorial boards of the journals *Integration*; *Regional and Federal Studies*; and *Journal of European Integration*.

EDUARDO IGLESIAS began a professional career with the Argentine Ministry of Foreign Affairs in 1965, becoming an ambassador in 1987 and chief of mission in bolivia and chile. During his career with the ministry, he has occupied numerous posts, including general director of South America, undersecretary of Latin American affairs, undersecretary of consular affairs, general director of Latin American policy, chairman and commissioner at the International Whaling Commission, and most recently delegate of the Ministry of Foreign Affairs in energy-related matters. He has been a United Nations expert with the Committee on Contributions, a position he began in 1999 and for which he has since been reelected twice. He has taught international law and Latin American politics at the School of Law and Social Sciences, Buenos Aires University, and in 2001 became director of the Committee on Provinces and International Relations, Argentine Council for International Relations (CARI).

HAPPYMON JACOB is an assistant professor in the Department of Strategic and Regional Studies, University of Jammu, Jammu and Kashmir, India, where he has been teaching since 2004. He is also a Visiting Fellow at the Nelson Mandela Centre for Peace and Conflict Resolution, Jamia Millia Islamia University, New Delhi, and a guest faculty at the School of International Studies, Jawaharlal Nehru University, New Delhi. His previous appointments include research positions at the Observer Research Foundation, Centre for Air Power Studies, and Delhi Policy Group, all based in New Delhi. Jacob specializes in Indian foreign policy, geopolitics in Southern Asia, security studies, and nontraditional security.

ANDREAS KIEFER is director of the European Affairs Department of Land Salzburg regional administration, Austria. As such, he represents Salzburg in associations and networks like the Assembly of European Regions (AER) and the Regions with Legislative Powers (REGLEG), and he works with the EU's Committee of the Regions as well as with the Council of Europe's Congress of Local and Regional Authorities. He is a former secretary general of the Conference of Presidents of Regions with Legislative Powers and has worked as a common representative of the Austrian Länder in institutional matters in the EU and the Council of Europe since 1999. His lectures and publications focus on regionalism, federalism, subsidiarity, the Committee of the Regions, and interregional cooperation.

JOHN KINCAID is the Robert B. and Helen S. Meyner Professor of Government and Public Service and director of the Meyner Center for the Study of State and Local Government at Lafayette College, Easton, Pennsylvania. He is the editor of *Publius: The Journal of Federalism*, editor of a series of books on the governments and politics of the American states, and an elected fellow of the National Academy of Public Administration. He is the former executive director of the US Advisory Commission on Intergovernmental Relations, Washington, DC, and author of various works on federalism and intergovernmental relations.

ANDRÉ LECOURS is an associate professor in the Department of Political Science at Concordia University. He holds an MA in political science from Université Laval, Quebec, and a PhD in political science from Carleton University, Ottawa. He is the editor of *New Institutionalism: Theory and Analysis* (2005), the author of *Basque Nationalism and the Spanish State* (2007), and a co-author (with Daniel Béland) of *Nationalism and Social Policy: The Politics of Territorial Solidarity* (2008).

FRANCIS KOK WAH LOH is a professor of politics at Universiti Sains Malaysia, Penang. He received his PhD in politics and Southeast Asian studies from Cornell University, New York. His latest publications are *New Politics in Malaysia*, edited with J. Saravanamuttu (2003), and *Southeast Asian Responses to Globalization: Restructuring Governance and Deepening Democracy*, edited with J. Ojendal (2004). He writes regularly on contemporary Malaysian affairs for the *Aliran Monthly*, of which he is a member of the editorial collective. He is a board member of the Asian Regional Exchange for New Alternatives (ARENA) and formerly was a committee member of the Social Science Research Council's (SSRC) Global Security and Cooperation Program (2000–03).

MALCOLM MACLAREN is a *habilitant* in constitutional law and a lecturer in international law at the University of Zurich as well as a postdoctoral fellow at the Swiss National Centre for Competence in Research "Challenges to Democracy in the 21st Century." He holds a doctorate in law (Zurich), an LLM (Frankfurt am Main), an LLB (Toronto), an MA (Oxford, modern history), and a BA (Toronto, English and Latin). He is a member of the Ontario Bar.

FRANÇOISE MASSART-PIÉRARD has a PhD in political and social science from the Université catholique de Louvain, Belgium, where she is currently a professor and director of the Political Science and International Relations unit. Her research interests focus on European integration and the foreign policies of federal regions. Her recent publications include "L'action extérieure des entités subétatiques: Une approche comparée. Union européenne. Amérique du nord" (forthcoming), "Stratégies et jeux de légitimation au sein du système institutionnel de l'Union européenne" (2006), "La Belgique, un modèle évolutif et inédit de gestion des relations internationales" (2006), and "Du local à l'international: Nouveaux acteurs, nouvelle diplomatie" (2005).

AMITABH MATTOO is the vice chancellor of the University of Jammu and a professor of international politics at the Jawaharlal Nehru University, New Delhi. Mattoo holds a PhD from the University of Oxford. He was a member of India's National Security Council's Advisory Board, a member of the task force formed by the Indian prime minister on global strategic developments, and elected to the governing council of Pugwash, the Nobel Prize-winning NGO. He has been a visiting professor at Stanford University, the University of Notre Dame, and the University of Illinois at Urbana Champaign. For his contribution to education and public life, he has been conferred one of India's highest civilian awards, the Padmashree, by the country's president.

HANS MICHELMANN is a professor of political studies at the University of Saskatchewan, specializing in European and comparative politics and international relations. He has held various administrative positions at the University of Saskatchewan. Among his extra-university positions he has been managing editor (1983–97), and editor and associate editor (1997 to present) of the *Journal of European Integration*; director general, Canadian Council for European Affairs (1983–2002); and member, Board of Directors, Canadian Federation for the Humanities and Social Sciences (2002–07). He is a member of the Advisory Board for the *Europe-Asia Journal* and corresponding member of Bayerische Amerika Akademie. He holds a PhD in political science, Indiana University, United States. His publications have centred on administration, politics, and policy of the European Community/Union; Canadian and German government and politics; agricultural trade; federalism; and international relations in federal systems.

Contributors

CHRISTINA MURRAY is a professor of human rights and constitutional law at the University of Cape Town, South Africa. Between 1994 and 1996 she served on a panel of seven experts advising the South African Constitutional Assembly. Since then, her work has focused on constitution making, constitutional design, and the implementation of constitutions. She has also worked in Kenya, Indonesia, Kyrgyzstan, Southern Sudan, and Bolivia. Among her most recently published work is the book, edited with Michelle O'Sullivan, *Advancing Women's Rights: The First Decade of Democracy* (2005) and papers on traditional leadership, ethnicity in South Africa's constitutional design, and government and opposition.

SALIM A. NAKHJAVANI obtained his BCL and LLB from McGill University and holds an LLM in international law from the University of Cambridge, where he was elected Whewell Scholar in International Law in 2002. He served as a legal adviser at the Office of the Prosecutor of the International Criminal Court (2004) and the UN Office of the High Commissioner for Human Rights (2005) before taking up his current appointment as lecturer in law at the University of Cape Town, South Africa, where he remains today. His current research focuses on international criminal law and procedure and international legal theory.

DANIEL THÜRER is a professor of public international, European, and Swiss public and administrative law at the University of Zurich. He holds a doctorate in law from the University of Zurich, an LLM from Cambridge University, and an honorary doctorate in political science from the University of St Gallen. Prof. Thürer is a member of the International Committee of the Red Cross and has been president of its Legal Commission since 1996. He is a past member of the Supreme Court of the Principality of Liechtenstein and a past president of the Zurich Lawyers' Association. He was a founding president of the Swiss Section of the International Court of Justice (ICJ) in 1991.

ANNE TWOMEY is a constitutional lawyer and an associate professor of law at the University of Sydney, Australia. She obtained her LLM in public law from Australian National University and a PhD from the University of New South Wales. She has previously worked for the High Court of Australia, the federal Parliamentary Research Service, the Senate Legal and Constitutional Committee, and the Cabinet Office of New South Wales. She has written widely on federalism, including the book *The Constitution of New South Wales* (2004) and "Australia's Federal Future" (2007), a report prepared for the Council for the Australian Federation.

A Global Dialogue on Federalism

THEME 5: PARTICIPATING EXPERTS

We gratefully acknowledge the input of the following experts who participated in the theme of Foreign Relations in Federal Countries. While participants contributed their knowledge and experience, they are in no way responsible for the contents of this booklet.

Suriani Ahmad, Ministry of International Trade and Industry, Malaysia
Francisco Aldecoa, University Complutense of Madrid, Spain
Hans Altherr, Rechtsanwalt und Ständerat, Switzerland
George Anderson, Forum of Federations, Canada
Céline Auclair, Forum of Federations, Canada
Raja Nazrin Raja Aznam, Setiausaha, Bahagian Adjudikasi dan Timbangtara Kementerian Luar Negeri, Malaysia
Marleen Baetens, Universiteit Antwerpen, Belgium
Gabriela Basualdo, Dirección de Relaciones Internacionales de la Provincia de Corrientes, Argentina
Ralf Baus, Konrad-Adenauer-Stiftung, Germany
Denis Bédard, Government of Quebec, Canada
Louis Bélanger, Université Laval, Canada
Anish Bhasin, University of Sydney, Australia
Jaya Bhasin, Indian Institute of Public Administration, India
Philip Bittner, Bundesministerium für auswärtige Angelegenheiten, Austria
Julie Blase, Principia College, United States
Raoul Blindenbacher, Forum of Federations, Canada/Switzerland
Michael Bliss, Department of Foreign Affairs and Trade, Australia
Geert Bourgeois, Vlaamse regering, Belgium
Matthew Bramley, Pembina Institute, Canada
Dirk Brand, Western Cape Provincial Government, South Africa
Canisius Braun, Konferenz der Kantonsregierungen, Switzerland

Carmen K. Breitwieser, Amt der Oberösterreichischen Landesregierung, Austria
Peter Briner, Ständerat, Switzerland
James Brooks, National League of Cities, United States
Peter Bursens, Universiteit Antwerpen, Belgium
Peter Bussjäger, Vorarlberger Landtag, Austria
Annette Bussman, Auswärtiges Amt, Germany
Annabela Busso, Agencia de Cooperación Internacional de la Provincia de Santa Fe, Argentina
Pedro José Caballero Lasquibar, Basque Government, Spain
Brock Carlton, Federation of Canadian Municipalities, Canada
Pedro Castillo, Consejo Federal de Inversiones, Argentina
James U.H. Chin, Universiti Malaysian Sarawak, Malayasia
Chong Eu Choong, University Tunku Abdul Rahman, Malayasia
Claus-Peter Clostermeyer, Staatsministerium Baden-Württemberg, Germany
Andrés Collado, Ministry of Foreign Affairs, Spain
Noé Cornago, University of the Basque Country, Spain
Don Costello, Department of Foreign Affairs, Canada
David Criekemans, Universiteit Antwerpen, Belgium
Alberto Dalla Via, Cámara Nacional Electoral, Argentina
Régis Dandoy, Université catholique de Louvain, Belgium
Ajita Dayal, Northern Railway, India
Herman De Croo, Président de la Chambre des Représentants, Belgium
Jana Deforche, Universiteit Antwerpen, Belgium
Francis Delpérée, Sénat, Belgium
Alain Demaegd, Cabinet de la Vice-Présidente du Gouvernement de la communauté française de Belgique, Belgium
Kosie de Villiers, De Villiers and Associates, South Africa
Lieven Dewinter, Université catholique de Louvain, Belgium
Ravi Dhingra, Inter-State Council, India
Ben Dornan, University of Sydney, Australia
Mark Duckworth, Department of Premier and Cabinet, Australia
Hugues Dumont, Facultés universitaires Saint-Louis, Belgium
JoAnna Edgerton, City of Kansas, United States
Adrienne Edisis, George Washington University, United States
Bernhard Ehrenzeller, University of St Gallen, Switzerland
J. Isawa Elaigwu, Institute of Governance and Social Research, Nigeria
Freddy Evens, Ministerie van de Vlaamse Gemeenschap, Belgium
Luciano Fabris, Honorable Cámara de Diputados de la Nación, Argentina
Patrick Fafard, Canadian Policy Research Networks, Canada
Alicia Falkowski, Dirección de Asuntos Federales y Electorales del Ministerio de Relaciones Exteriores, Argentina
Azeem Fazwan Ahmad Farouk, Universiti Sains Malaysia, Malayasia
Igor Filibi, University of the Basque Country, Spain

Thomas Fleiner, Institute of Federalism, Switzerland
Earl Fry, Brigham Young University, United States
Anna Gamper, University of Innsbruck, Austria
Caterina Garcia-Segura, University Pompeu Fabra of Barcelona, Spain
Rubén Geneyro, Dirección General de Relaciones Internacionales del Gobierno de la Ciudad Autónoma de Buenos Aires, Argentina
Jose María Gil-Robles, University Complutense of Madrid, Spain
Jean Gillet, Association pour la promotion de l'éducation et de la formation à l'étranger, Belgium
Ramlan Goddos, Yayasan Sabah Head Quarters, Malayasia
Pascal Goergen, Représentant de Bruxelles-Capitale auprès de l'Union Européenne, Belgium
Ellen Golden, Council of State Governments, United States
Parthiban S. Gopal, Universiti Sains Malaysia, Malayasia
Thomas Gossner, Internationalen Bodenseekonferenz, Germany
Eric Gqabaza, Litha Institute, South Africa
Martine Brunschwig Graf, Conseillère nationale, Switzerland
Marcel Guignard, Schweizerischer Städteverband, Switzerland
Mercedes Guinea Llorente, University Complutense of Madrid, Spain
Wajahat Habibullah, Government of India, India
Lim Hong Hai, Universiti Sains Malaysia, Malayasia
Herbert Halbwidl, Amt der Niederösterreichischen Landesregierung, Austria
Stefan Hammer, University of Vienna, Austria
Christa Hareter, Wirtschaftskammer Burgenland, Austria
Mohd. Faisal Syam Abdol Hazis, Universiti Malaysia Sarawak, Malaysia
Low Swee Heong, Knowles Malaysia, Malayasia
Antonio Hernández, Academia Nacional de Derocho y Ciencias Sociales de Córdoba, Argentina
Arno Hibbers, KwaZulu-Natal Office of the Premier, South Africa
Heidi Hobbs, North Carolina University, United States
Devika Hovell, University of New South Wales, Australia
Rudolf Hrbek, Universität Tubingen, Germany
Axel Huelsemeyer, Concordia University, Canada
Syed Ahmad Hussein, Universiti Sains Malaysia, Malayasia
Roberto Ibarguren, Coordinación de Relaciones Internacionales y Comercio Exterior del Gobierno de Salta, Argentina
Abdul Rahim Ibrahim, Universiti Sains Malaysia, Malayasia
Eduardo Iglesias, Consejo Argentino para las Relaciones Internacionales, Argentina
Valeria Iglesias, Consejo Argentino para las Relaciones Internacionales, Argentina
Karl Irresberger, Representative of Austria Federal Chancellery, Austria
Maximiliano Ivanissevich, Organismo Provincial de Turismo de Chubut, Argentina

Happymon Jacob, University of Jammu, India
Jayum Jawan, Universiti Putra Malaysia, Malayasia
Mark Jennings, Attorney General's Department, Australia
Khoo Khay Jin, Universiti Sains Malaysia, Malayasia
Pierre Marc Johnson, Heenan Blaikie, Canada
Petrice Judge, Department of Premier and Cabinet, Australia
Wolfram Karl, Universität Salzburg, Austria
Abigail O. Karos, Ottawa, Canada
Azizah Kassim, Universiti Malaysia Sarawak, Malayasia
Ferry de Kerckhove, Department of Foreign Affairs, Canada
Baudoin de la Kethulle, Federale overheidsdienst buitenlandse zaken, Belgium
Andreas Kiefer, European Affairs Office, Land Salzburg, Austria
John Kincaid, Lafayette College, United States
John Kline, Georgetown University, United States
Arnold Koller, Forum of Federations, Switzerland
Martin Kremer, Auswärtiges Amt, Germany
Chris Kukucha, University of Lethbridge, Canada
Girish Kumar, Indian Institute of Public Administration, India
Alex Kuznetsov, Russian Academy of Science, Russia
Consuelo Laiz, University Complutense of Madrid, Spain
S. Lakshminarayana, Ministry of Home Affairs, Government of India, India
Karl-Heinz Lambertz, Gouvernement de la Communauté germanophone, Belgium
André Lecours, Concordia University, Canada
Tan Pek Leng, Socio Economic and Environmental Research Institute, Malayasia
Ch'ng Teng Liang, LEB Manufacturing, Malaysia
Wolf Linder, University of Bern, Switzerland
Rachel Logan, University of Cape Town, South Africa
Ruth Lüthi, Conseillère d'Etat, Switzerland
Sigisbert Lutz, Schweizerischer Gemeindeverband, Switzerland
David MacDonald, Forum of Federations, Canada
Alfred A. MacLeod, Privy Council Office, Canada
Luzius Mader, Federal Office of Justice, Switzerland
Dumazi Marivate, Department of Provincial and Local Government, South Africa
Françoise Massart-Piérard, Université Catholique de Louvain-la-Neuve, Belgium
Richard Mason, Universiti Sains Malaysia, Malayasia
George Mathew, Institute of Social Sciences, India
Amitabh Mattoo, University of Jammu, India
Maria Mbengashe, Department of Environmental Affairs and Tourism, South Africa

Joe Mbenyane, Mpumalanga Provincial Government, South Africa
Jeremy Meadows, National Conference of State Legislatures, United States
Peter Meekison, University of Victoria, Canada
Federico Merke, Consejo Argentino para las Relaciones Internacionales, Argentina
Hans Michelmann, University of Saskatchewan, Canada
Ernest Mokganedi, Department of Environmental Affairs and Tourism, South Africa
Jutta Moll, Federal Chancellery, Austria
Vanina Mona, Fundación Poder Ciudadano, Argentina
Philippe Monfils, Député à la Chambre des Représentants, Belgium
Manuel Morán, Government of Galicia, Spain
Sindiswa Mququ, City of Cape Town, South Africa
Johannes Müller, Amt der Vorarlberger Landesregierung, Austria
Ute Müller, Bundesrat, Germany
Christina Murray, University of Cape Town, South Africa
Salim Nakhjavani, University of Cape Town, South Africa
Ronel Nel, Nelson Mandela Metropolitan University, South Africa
Matthias Niedobitek, Technische Universität Chemnitz, Germany
Nomusa Nkambule, Mpumalanga Office of the Premier, South Africa
Wan Zailena Noordin, InvestPenang, Malaysia
Kim Richard Nossal, Queen's University, Canada
Markus Notter, Regierungsrat des Kantons Zurich, Switzerland
Theo Öhlinger, Universität Wien, Austria
Tan Lee Ooi, Universiti Sains Malaysia, Malayasia
Wolf Okresek, Department of the Federal Chancellery, Austria
Abu Bakar Omar, Akty Technologies, Malayasia
James Ongkili, Universiti Kebangsaan Malaysia, Malayasia
Beatriz Paglieri, Relaciones Internacionales y Cooperación, Argentina
Sanjay Pande, Jawaharlal Nehru University, India
Luigi Pedrazzini, Direttore del Dipartimento delle istituzioni, Switzerland
Patrick Peeters, University of Leuven, Belgium
Elena I. Peletier, Secretaria de Relaciones Institucionales del ministerio de Gobierno de San Juan, Argentina
Thomas Pfisterer, Ständerat, Switzerland
Mavis Puthucheary, author, Malaysia
Remigio Ratti, Direttore della Radiotelevisione svizerra di lingua italiana, Switzerland
Horst Risse, Bundesrat, Germany
Paloma Román, University Complutense of Madrid, Spain
Andreas Rosner, Verbindungsstelle der Bundesländer, Austria
Jean-François Roth, Ministre de l'économie et de la coopération, Switzerland
Don Rothwell, University of Sydney, Australia

Nicola Roxon, Member of Commonwealth Parliament, Australia
Kim Rubenstein, Australian National University, Australia
Claude Ruey, Conseiller National, Switzerland
Michelle Sager, US Government Accountability Office, United States
Lynette Sait, Free State Provincial Government, South Africa
Janeire Salicio, University of the Basque Country, Spain
Zainal Abidin Sanusi, Universiti Sains Malaysia, Malayasia
Johan Saravanamuttu, Universiti Sains Malaysia, Malayasia
Cheryl Saunders, University of Melbourne, Australia
Peter Schönenberger, Regierungsrat, Switzerland
Achim Schulz, Euregio Egrensis, Germany
Markus Senn, University of Vienna, Austria
Neeraj Sharma, University of Jammu, India
Ulrich Siegrsit, Nationalrat, Switzerland
Miet Smet, Vlaams parlement, Belgium
Murray Smith, Province of Alberta, Canada
Jose Manuel Sobrino Heredio, University of Coruña, Spain
Andrew Southcott, Commonwealth Parliament, Australia
Gerrit Spriet, Advisor to Minister Karel De Gucht, Belgium
Carole Staquet, Assistante parlementaire à la Chambre des Représentants, Belgium
Nico Steytler, University of the Western Cape, South Africa
Peter Stoett, Concordia University, Canada
Robert Stumberg, Georgetown University, United States
Philippe Suinen, Commissariat général des relations internationales de la communauté française Wallonie-Bruxelles, Belgium
Wilfred Madius Tangau, Barisan Nasional Member of Parliament, Malayasia
Khoo Boo Teik, Universiti Sains Malaysia, Malayasia
Daniel Thürer, Institut für Völkerrecht und ausländisches Verfassungsrecht, Switzerland
Hans Martin Tschudi, Regionalleiter Schweizerische Bundesbahnen für die Nordwestschweiz, Switzerland
Anne Twomey, University of Sydney, Australia
Jordi Vaquer, Government of Catalonia, Spain
D.B. Venkatesh Varma, Prime Minister's Office, India
B.G. Verghese, Centre for Policy Research, India
Han Verleyen, Noord-Zuid Koepel 11.11.11, Belgium
Diane Verstraeten, Ministerie van de Vlaamse Gemeenschap, Belgium
N.N. Vohra, Government of India, India
Sven Vollrath, Deutscher Bundestag, Germany
Francis Loh Kok Wah, Universiti Sains Malaysia, Malayasia
Chris Watley, Council of State Governments, United States
Ron Watts, Queen's University, Canada

Heinrich Wedral, Amt der Burgenländischen Landesregierung, Austria
Eveline Widmer-Schlumpf, Regierungsrätin des Kantons Graubünden,
    Switzerland
Gerhart Wielinger, Steiermarkische Landesregierung, Austria
Kay Wilkie, New York State Department of Economic Development,
    United States
Thomas Wobben, Liaison Office of Saxony-Anhalt to the European Union,
    Germany
Toh Kin Woon, Penang State Government Executive Council, Malaysia
Joachim Francis Xavier, Penang Office for Human Development, Malaysia
Chow Kon Yeow, member of Parliament, Malayasia
Mohammad Agus Yusoff, Universiti Kebangsaan Malaysia, Malaysia
Ruslan Zainuddin, Universiti Utara Malaysia, Malaysia

Index

Aeronautics reference (Canada), 120
African National Congress (ANC), 213, 331
Agence wallonne à l'Exportation et aux Investissements étrangers (AWEX) (Belgium), 108, 109, 112n27
agents-general: Australia, 56
Agreement on South Asian Free Trade Area (SAFTA), 171
agricultural policy: Belgium, 106; Canada, 123; European Union, 106; Switzerland, 293n32
AIDS grant: South Africa, 227
Airport Regions Conference (ARC), 79
Alberta, 116; international relations, 116, 127, 128, 130–1
Allison, Graham, 296
anti-Americanism, 301
antiterrorism: Australia, 39, 42
apartheid, 330; South Africa, 212, 213, 214
Argentina, Republic of: agreements vs treaties, 17; border issues, resolving, 13–14; CODEFRO, 22; Committee of Integration, 22; constitutional division of powers, 14–18; constitutional reform, 11; decentralizing trends, 18; Directorate of Federal Affairs, 19, 31; Federal Council of Tourism, 29; federal government's control over provinces, 16–17; federalism, 10–11, 15–16; foreign policymaking, 14–15; geographic and economic features of, 11–12; gross GDP, 13; intergovernmental coordination, 19–21; MERCOSUR, and, 12–14; Ministry of Foreign Affairs, 19–21; municipalities, supporting, 19–20; nature of federalism in, 10–11; questions addressed, 10

Argentine cities: foreign affairs, 19, 20–1; partnerships, 30–1; support for, 19–20
Argentine Constitution, 14–18
Argentine Fund for International Cooperation (FO-AR), 30
Argentine provinces: constituent diplomacy, 23–32; Consultative Forum of Municipalities, Federal States, Provinces and Departments, 13; coordination with federal government, 19–20; CRECENEA-Litoral (NEA), 25, 26; culture and tourism, 28; economic performance, 12; foreign affairs, 23–4; foreign trade, 29–30; Fundación Exportar, 20; hydrocarbon law, 27–8; infrastructure, 28; institutions for foreign affairs, 18–19; international

corporations, 30; international relations, 26–9; international treaties and, 15, 16–17; macro-regions, 25–6; NOA (Region del Noroeste Argentino), 25; overseas technical assistance, 30; participation in intergovernmental organizations, 22–3; Pascua Lama mining project, 27; Patagonian region, 25; population density, 11–12; regional/interregional relations, 24–6; transborder relations, 21–2; Treaty of Economic Integration, 25

armed forces, control of: Argentina, 14–15

arms trade: Belgium, 105; South Africa, 214

ASEAN. *See* Association of South-East Asian Nations

Asian Development Bank (ADB), 202

Asian markets: Argentina, and, 12; Australia, and, 39

Assembly of European Regions (AER), 87n2, 327

Assembly of European Viticultural Regions (AREV), 79

assignment of powers, 6; Argentina, 14–18. *See also* intergovernmental relations

Association of European Border Regions (AEBR), 79

Association of South-East Asian Nations (ASEAN), 39; ASEAN Free Trade Agreement (FTA) (Malaysia), 197, 202; ASEAN Free Trade Area (Malaysia), 192; ASEAN Growth Area (Malaysia), 202–5; ASEAN Regional Forum (Australia), 39

Australia, Commonwealth of: ASEAN, and, 39; border issues, 38; Constitution, *see* Commonwealth Constitution, Australia; constitutional division of powers, 40–6; consultation with states on treaty making, 46–8; defence/security relationships, 39; Department of Foreign Affairs and Trade, 53; economic and geographic features, 37–8; foreign policy, 37, 40–6; intergovernmental affairs (relations), 46–52; international organizations, and, 40; nature of federalism, 38, 40, 43; Principles and Procedures/treaties, 47, 50; ratifying treaties, 50–1; regional trade/culture, 38–9; Standing Committee on Treaties (SCOT), 42–8; trade relations with New Zealand, 38–9; treaty reforms (1996), 48–9; treaty veto, 49

Australia-United States Free Trade Agreement, 52

Australian cities: foreign affairs, 55–6

Australian states: concerns re treaty ratification, 51–2; diplomatic representation overseas, 56–8; foreign affairs institutions, 52, 53; foreign affairs powers, 44–6; foreign policy initiatives, 55–6; international agreements, types of, 44–5; parliaments' role in foreign affairs, 53–4; police force, 42; sister-state relationships, 58; trade and tourism offices, 57–8; treaties, involvement in, 54; treaty implementation, 49–51; treaty reforms (1996), 48–9

Austria, Republic of: civil law enactments, 69; Constitution and foreign affairs, 67–9; Constitutional Court, 72; demographic/economic profile of, 66–7; division of powers, 71; EU sanctions against, 83–5; European politics, 80–2, 85–6; foreign policy, 73–4; foreign trade, 67; international treaties, 73; joint initiatives with *Länder*, 75–6; *Länder*-federation relations re foreign affairs, 73–6; Madrid Convention, 68; Ministry for European and International Affairs, 66; nature of federalism, 66, 71; proxy representation and EU sanctions, 83–4; treaty-making powers, 67–8

Index

Austrian *Länder*, 66, 67, 77–9; bilateral trade, 77–9; civil law amendments, 69; Committee of the Regions (COR), 81–2; common positions of, 71; cooperation agreements, 66, 67, 77–9; Council of Europe, and, 82–5; cross-border cooperation, 68, 69, 77–9; European Court proceedings, 72; external affairs and defence role, 74–5; foreign trade, 77–9: implementing federal and EU legislation, 71–2; participation in EU politics, 80–1, 85–6; presence in Brussels, 81; role in European Union (EU), 69–73; role in international negotiations/organizations, 74; transnational activities, 68, 69; treaty-making powers, 68; uniform position on EU issues, 70–1; working communities, and, 78–9

Austrian municipalities: civil law enactments, 69; cross-border cooperation, 78–9

Aznar, Jose Maria, 246

Baltic Sea Cooperation, 145

Barclays Bank PLC v. Franchise Tax Board (1994) (US), 303

Barisan Nasional (BN) coalition, 189, 194, 331

Basel-City, 271, 286

Basic Law (Germany), 146–50; Article 23, 148, 149, 150, 153–4, 155; cost sharing, 156

Basque Country, 241, 242, 245, 254, 326; diaspora, 257; international activity, 257, 258

Bay of Bengal Initiative for Multi-Sectoral Technical and Economic Cooperation (BIMSTEC), 171, 183

Belgian constituent units: commercial attachés, 101–2; constitutional powers, 95–7; cooperation agreements, 101–2, 105, 108; described, 93; diplomatic representation, 104–5; foreign relations, 107–10; international organizations, joining, 95, 98–9; multilateral relations, 102; regional foreign policy, 98–9; representing Belgian position, 100; substitution mechanism, 97–8; treaty-making powers, 95; veto power, 104

Belgium, Kingdom of: arms trade, 105; cities, 110; common delegations, 105; Community and Region competences, 96; Concertation Committee, 101; constitutional division of powers, 95–7; cooperation agreement on EU policymaking, 99–100; Directorate of European Affairs (DEA), 100; European context and transfer of powers, 106; European Union, and, 94–5, 98–100; Federal Public Service Foreign Affairs, 102; Flemish Community of, 105; Flemish foreign relations, 107–8; foreign relations, context of, 93–5; French Community and OIF, 94, 95, 103; French Community of, 93–4; *in foro interno/externo*, 96, 97–8, 99; intergovernmental relations, 97–106; international cooperation, 94–5; multilateral relations, 102; nature of federation, 93, 101; profile of, 92–3; special laws, 97, 111n9; Wallonia-Brussels Community, 108–9

Benelux, 94; Monetary Union (EU), and, 145

Bjelke-Petersen, Sir Joh, 55

Blair, Tony, 246

border issues/relations, 181–5; Argentina, 13–14, 21–2; Australia, 38; Canada, 118, 127–8; German *Länder*, 145; India, 181–5; South Africa, 214–15, 216, 217, 229–31; Spain, 260; Swiss cantons, 280, 282–3, 285; Swiss cities, 281; US states, 310–11.

boundary disputes: Argentina, 21–2

British Columbia: international relations, 132, 318

British North America (BNA) Act of
  1867 (Canada), 120, 136n16
Brunei-Indonesia-Malaysia-Philippines
  East ASEAN Growth Area (BIMP-
  EAGA), 202, 203–4
Brussels, 110, 149; delegations to, 258
Bush, George W., 246

Canada: Aboriginal population, 116,
  133; BNA Act, 120, 136n16; constitutional division of powers, 119–22; cultural policy, 125; environmental
  policy, 123, 124–5; federalism and
  foreign policy, 115; foreign policy,
  122–5; free trade agreements, 118–19; intergovernmental relations, 122–5; international activities, 117; international relations, powers of, 120–2;
  nature of federalism, 116, 119, 126,
  127, 133; peacekeeping missions,
  117; profile of, 115–17; Quebec nationalism, 115–16; relations with
  United States, 117–18; softwood lumber dispute, 119; treaty-making powers, 120–2
Canada-United States Automotive Products Agreement (Autopact), 123
Canada-United States Free Trade Agreement (CUSTA), 118, 122, 123–4; provincial participation in, 123–4
Canadian cities, international activities,
  133
Canadian provinces: cultural policy,
  125; CUSTA, participation in, 123–4;
  environmental policy, 123, 124–5;
  free trade agreements, and, 118–19,
  123–4; international activities, 115,
  116, 133–4; international relations,
  120–1, 126–33; Kyoto Protocol, 124–5; paradiplomacy, 126, 138n52; relations with federal government on foreign policy, 122–5; softwood lumber
  dispute, 119; transborder issues, 118;
treaty-making powers, 120–2, 125,
  136–7n27
carbon dioxide emissions, 313
Catalan Statute (Spain), 251–2
Catalonia, 241, 242, 245, 251–2, 254,
  326; diaspora, 257; international activity, 257–8
Central American Free Trade Area
  (CAFTA), 302
CENTROPE, 78
Chrétien, Jean, 124
climate change: Australian states and,
  55; UN conference, 123
Cold War, 330
commercial attachés: Belgian constituent units, 101–2
Commissariat général aux Relations internationales de la Communauté
  Française (CGRI) (Belgium), 108–9
Committee of the Regions (COR), 81–2,
  150, 247
Commonwealth Constitution, Australia:
  defence powers, 42; foreign affairs,
  executive/legal powers, 41–2; state
  external affairs power, 44–6
Concertation Committee (Belgium),
  101
Conference of Presidents of Regions
  with Legislative Powers (REGLEG), 79
Conference of the European Regional
  Legislative Parliaments (CALRE), 79
Congress of Local and Regional Authorities of Europe (CLRAE), 83
constituent diplomacy, 4; agents for,
  347; altruistic motives, 7; Argentine
  provinces, 23–32; assignment of powers, trends, 332–3; Austrian *Länder*,
  75–9; Belgium, 95, 97–9, 100, 101–2,
  104–5; by cities, 346–7; conflicts re,
  351; constitutional division of powers,
  331–9; constitutional relations, and,
  6; cooperation with federal governments, 348; developing countries, in,

328; development projects, 348–50; dominant political parties, 331; economic motivation, 7, 347; education and culture, 349–50; ethnic and cultural factors, 326; ethnicity and, 5; EU member states, 328–30; factors affecting, 4–7; FDI and, 347; foreign relations powers, 331–3; geographical setting and, 4–5; high politics and, 350; history, impact of, 330–1; incentives, 347; India, 176–9; intergovernmental relations, 339–46; international agreements, 338–9; offices abroad, 347; political factors, 7; politicians and, 7–8; protecting own interests, 348; regional context and, 326–8; regional organizations and, 348–9; role of Upper Houses, 335–6; Spain, 254–5; Switzerland, 281–8; trade missions, 347; travel abroad, 350; treaty implementation, 337–8; treaty-making powers, 334–5; treaty negotiation, 336–7; US states, 310; wealth and, 325

constituent-unit foreign relations. *See* constituent diplomacy

Constitution: Argentina, 14–18; Australia, 40–6; Austria, 66, 67–9, 70; Belgium, 92, 93, 95–7; Canada, 119–22; Germany, 146; India, 173–5; Malaysia, 194–6; South Africa, 213, 217–20; Spain, 241, 242, 248–52; Switzerland, 274–7; United States, 298–9, 302–5

constitutional context of foreign relations, 6

cooperation agreements: Austrian *Länder*, 66, 67, 77–9; Belgian constituent units, 101–2, 105, 108

cooperation projects: German *Länder*, 145

cooperative federalism: Belgium, 102; Switzerland, 275, 278, 288

Coordination Committee on International and European Environmental Policy (Belgium), 104

coordination mechanisms: Argentina, 19–21; Article 203, Maastricht Treaty, and, 99–100; Canada, 122

Copps, Sheila, 125

COR. *See* Committee of the Regions

Council for the Australian Federation, 55

Council of Europe, 74, 82–5, 247; European Convention for Transborder Cooperation, Spain and, 260

Council of Europe's European Convention for Transborder Cooperation, 327

Council of European Municipalities and Regions (CEMR), 79

creative destruction, 309, 310, 315

Crosby v. National Foreign Trade Council (US), 303

cultural diversity: Spain, 243, 244, 257; Switzerland, 271

culture/cultural policy, 5: Argentine foreign policy on, 28; Canadian provinces, 125, 129; Swiss cantons, 285–6

Cyberjaya (Malaysia), 201

Czech Republic, 144

defence policy/powers: Australia, 39, 42; Austrian *Länder*, 74–5; India, 174; South Africa, 220; Spain, 248; Switzerland, 275

Dehousse, Renaud, 103

Developing Eight (D-8) (Malaysia), 193

development aid: accountability for, 227–8; South Africa, 221–2, 223–4, 227–8; Spanish autonomous communities, 260

development participation: Swiss cantons, 293n36

development projects: constituent diplomacy, 348–50; Malaysia, 193–4;

South African municipalities, 229. *See also* economic development
diplomatic representation: Australian states, 56–8; Belgian constituent units, 104–5. *See also* representative offices abroad
Direction générale des Relations internationales de la Région Wallonie (DRI) (Belgium), 108–9
Directorate of European Affairs (DEA) (Belgium), 100
diversity: Switzerland, 271
Dumont, Hughes, 95

eco-tourism: South Africa, 217
economic development: altruistic motivation for, 7; assignment of powers and, 6; constitutional context of, 6; economic motivation for, 7; intergovernmental relations and, 6–7; political motivation for, 7–8
Elazar, Daniel J., 305
environmental law, jurisdiction for: Argentina, 16, 17
environmental policy: California-British agreement, 313; Canada, 123, 124–5; South Africa, 230
ethnic conflicts: Malaysia, 191
ethnicity, 5
EU Council, 165n15
EU Reform Treaty (2007), 85
Euro-regions, 79
European Coal and Steel Community (ECSC), 94
European Commission, 72
European Common Agriculture Policy, 106
European Court of Justice (ECJ), 72
European domestic policy (*Europäische Innenpolitik*), 85–6
European Economic Area (EEA), 69, 273
European Free Trade Agreement, 273

European Free Trade Association (EFTA), 67
European Grouping for Territorial Cooperation (EGTC), 82, 86
European integration, 331
European Outline Convention on Transfrontier Cooperation between Territorial Communities or Authorities of the Council of Europe, 68
European Union (EU), 4; Argentina, and, 12; Austrian *Länder* participation in, 69–73; Austrian politics, 80–2; Belgium and, 94–5; Belgium constituent units and, 98–9; Committee of the Regions (COR), 81–2; constituent diplomacy and, 328–30; German *Länder* and, 148–50, 153–6; hybrid system, 329; Internal Market, 144, 145; INTERREG, 260; promoting cross-border relations, 260; regional policies, 82; regions with legislative powers, 79; sanctions against Austria, 83–5
export counselling, 347
external affairs: Australia, 42–4; Austrian *Länder*, 74–5. *See also* foreign affairs

FDI. *See* foreign direct investment
Federal Foreign Office (Germany), 151
Federal Public Service Foreign Affairs (Belgium), 102
federalism: virtues of, 316
Ferrero-Waldner, Benita, 75
Financial Equalization Act (Austria) (2008), 87n4
Flanders, 326; foreign relations, 107–8; language union (Taalunie), 94
foreign affairs: Argentine provinces, 23–4; Australia, 41–2; Austria, 67–9, 73–6
foreign direct investment (FDI): US states, 306, 308. *See also* foreign investment

foreign investment: Spanish autonomous communities, 257, 258, 259. *See also* foreign direct investment
foreign policy: Argentina, 14–15; Australia, 37, 40–6; Austria, 73–4; Belgium, 95–7, 101; Canadian intergovernmental relations and, 122–5; foreign relations vs, 312–14; India, 171–2; Malaysia, 192–4, 195; minor foreign policy, 276, 278, 283, 284; Spain, 245, 246, 248; Switzerland, 272, 273; United States, 305–6
foreign relations: Austria, Constitution re, 67–9, 70; Belgian constituent units, 107–10; Belgium, 93–5; 97-8; German intergovernmental relations, 150–6; German *Länder*, 146–7, 157–62; Germany, 146; India, 169, 173, 174; *Länder* within European Union, 69–73; Swiss cantons, 276, 281
foreign trade: Argentina, 19–20, 29–30; Austria, 67; Austrian *Länder*, 77–9; Canada-United States agreements, 118–19; Canadian intergovernmental relations, 123–4; South Africa, 214; Spanish autonomous communities, 257–9; US states, 307–8; Wallonia-Brussels Community, 109. *See also* free trade agreements; trade
Four Motors of Europe, 127, 161, 327
Fox, Vicente, 311
free trade agreements: Agreement on South Asian Free Trade Area (SAFTA), 171; Australia and New Zealand, 38–9; Australia-United States Free Trade Agreement, 52; Canada-United States Free Trade Agreement (CUSTA), 118, 122, 123–4; Central American Free Trade Area (CAFTA), 302; European Free Trade Agreement, 273; North American Free Trade Agreement (NAFTA), 12, 118, 301–2, 303–4, 315, 330, 351; United States, 301–2

Free Trade Area of the Americas (FTAA), 302
Fry, Earl, 344

Gauteng (South Africa), 214
Gauteng Economic Development Agency (GEDA) (South Africa), 226–7
General Agreement on Tariffs and Trade (GATT), 123, 291n14
General Agreement on Trade in Services (GATS), 71, 304
geographical factors, 4–5
Gérin-Lajoie doctrine (Quebec), 121
German cities: municipal diplomacy, 162
German *Länder*: autonomous EU activities, 160–1; Brussels offices, 149; characteristics of, 143; Committee of the Regions (COR), 150; cross-border projects, 145; duty to govern, 148–9; EU Council meetings, 155–6; EU policies, 148–52, 153–6; external relations, 162; foreign relations, 146–7, 157–62; interaction among and within, 151–2; international marketing, 161–2; policy agreements, 158; political statements, 159–60; reform of federalism, 154–5; regional cooperation, 160–1; relations with federal government, 150–6; treaties made by, 157–8; treaty-making powers, 147, 151
Germany, Federal Republic of: Article 23 criticisms, 153–4; Basic Law, 146–50; *Bundesrat*, 148–9, 153; constitutional division of powers, 146–50; country profile, 142–4; EU policies, 148–9, 153–6; European neighbours, and, 144–5; Federal Foreign Office, 151; federation, nature of, 147–8, 152; globalization and, 146; intergovermental relations, 150–6; Law on Cooperation, 155; Lindauer Abkommen, 147, 151, 338; reform of

federalism, 153, 154, 156; treaty-making powers, 147, 151
Ghandi, Indira, 172
globalization, 3, 4, 316; Argentina, 11; challenges of, 310, 311; creative destruction and, 309, 310, 315; economic competition and, 308–9; Germany, 146; India, 177; Malaysia, 192; Quebec sovereignty, and, 129, 139n70; threat to US states, 305, 308, 315
governor general: Australia, 41, 42; Canada, 136n18
Great Lakes Conference of the International Joint Commission on Boundary Water Management, 118
greenhouse gases, 313

harmonization of levels of government: Argentina, 21. *See also* coordination mechanisms
human rights: Australia, 50, 51; Swiss cantons, 291n15; UN committee, 51

ICT. *See* information and communications technology industry
immigration: illegal, Malaysia, 197; illegal migration, India, 181; South Africa, 216–17; United States, 300, 311–12
India, Republic of: border state issues, 181–5; centralized foreign relations, 169, 173, 174; collaboration with states, 181; conflict of laws, 174; conflicts with neighbours, 170; constituent diplomacy, 176–9; Constitution, 173–5; constitutional division of powers, 171–5; cross-border terrorism, 181, 182–3; decentralization demands, 175–6; Department of Economic Affairs, 177; foreign policy, 171–2; globalization, 177; illegal migration, 181; intergovernmental relations, 176–7; legislative powers, 174; limiting state policymaking, 180–1; Ministry of External Affairs, 174, 177; nature of federalism, 173–4; nuclear testing, 172; profile of, 169–70; regional cooperation, 171; regional relations, 184; relations with Pakistan, 170, 182–3; residuary power, 174; strong central government needed, 184–5; WTO agreement, 179
Indian constituent units: decentralization demands, 175–6; foreign economic agreements, 178–9; limits of economic diplomacy, 180–1; smart cities, 179
Indonesia-Malaysia-Thailand Growth Triangle (IMT-GT), 202, 203
information and communications technology (ICT) industry: Penang, Malaysia, 199–202
infrastructure: Argentina, 28; South Africa, 216
Initiative for Integration of the South American Infrastructure (IIRSA), 28
Inter-American Development Bank (IADB), 23
Inter-Ministerial Conference for Foreign Policy (CIPE) (Belgium), 100
Inter-State Council (India), 175
Intergovernmental Policy Advisory Committee (IGPAC) (US), 305
intergovernmental relations: Argentina, 18–23, 339, 340, 344, 345; assessment of, 344–6; Australia, 46–52, 340–1, 345; Austria, 345, 346, 347; Belgium, 342–3, 345, 346, 347; Canada, 122–5, 340–1, 345, 347; formalized procedures, 342–4; Germany, 343, 345, 346, 347; India, 176–7, 339, 340, 344; loosely structured interaction, 340–2; Malaysia, 196–8, 340, 344, 347; national government

dominance, 339–40; patterns of, 339; South Africa, 339, 340, 344, 345, 346, 347; Spain, 339, 340, 341–2, 345, 346, 347; Switzerland, 277–81, 345, 347; United States, 305–7, 344. *See also* assignment of powers
intermestic politics, 316
Internal Market (EU), 144, 145
International Convention on Civil and Political Rights (ICCPR), 51
international corporations: Argentina, 30
international financial institutions (IFIS): Argentine provinces, and, 23
international relations: Argentine provinces, 26–9; Belgium, 97–106; Canadian powers of, 120; Canadian provinces, 126–33; definition of, 296; Spain, 248–9. *See also* external relations; foreign relations
international trade. *See* foreign trade
internationalization: Argentine provinces, 18. *See also* globalization
INTERREG, 145, 327
Interterritorial Commission of Development Cooperation (Spain), 261
Iraq: opposition to US policy in, 313; Spanish support for invasion of, 246; US war in, 302

Jammu-Kashmir, 182, 187n23

Kashmir, 170
Keohane, Robert, 296
Kincaid, John, 217, 324
Klein, Ralph, 124, 128
kleine Aussenpolitik (Switzerland), 276, 278, 282, 283, 284
Klestil, Thomas, 84
Krislov, Samuel, 298
KwaZulu, 230
KwaZulu-Natal, 217, 222, 225, 227
Kyoto Protocol: Australian states support for, 55; Canadian policy, 124–5;

constituent diplomacy and, 350; support for, 313; US disagreements on, 302

La Francophonie. *See* Organisation internationale de la Francophonie (OIF)
Labour Conventions case (Canada), 121
labour policy: Canada, 122–3
Länder, Austrian. *See* Austrian *Länder*
Länder, German. *See* German *Länder*
Land Governors' Conference (Austria), 73, 74, 75
Latin America: MERCOSUR, and, 12–14
Lesotho, 214, 216, 217, 230, 231
Lindauer Abkommen (Germany), 147, 151, 338

Maastricht Treaty, 70, 80; Article 203 provisions, 99
Madrid Convention, 68
Malaysia, Federation of: ASEAN Growth Areas, 202–5; ASEAN ties, 192–3; coercive legislation, 195; constitutional division of powers, 194–6; developing countries, and, 193–4; Economic Planning Unit (EPU), 195; ethnic conflicts, 191; export-oriented industrialization, 191; financial crisis, 191; foreign economic policy, 194; foreign policy, 192–4, 195; foreign trade missions, 197; globalization, 192; HDI ranking, 190–1; illegal immigration, 197; IMT-GT Liaison Secretariat, 203; Institute of Strategic International Studies, 195–6; intergovernmental relations, 196–8; Islamic ties, 193; Ministry of Foreign Affairs, 196; nature of federalism, 195; New Economic Policy, 189, 191–2; Penang, promoting, 199–202; profile of, 190–2; regional relations, 202–5; tourism and trade, 204

Malaysian Business Council (MBC), 196, 208n18

Malaysian states: improving bureaucracy, 199, 208n26; limited foreign affairs role, 189; limited foreign policymaking, 197, 198; socio-cultural foreign affairs, 198; subject to federal authority, 194–5

Malaysian Technical Cooperation Programme (MTCP), 193

Manitoba: international relations, 132

Mercado Común del Sur. *See* MERCOSUR

MERCOSUR, 4, 330; Argentina, 12; Argentine subregions, 25–6; Latin America, 12–14

Mexico: illegal immigrants, 312; US consulates, 311

Ministry for European and International Affairs (Austria), 66

Missouri v. Holland (US), 303

Monetary Union (EU), 145, 154

Montreal, 133

municipal diplomacy: Germany, 162

NAFTA. *See* North American Free Trade Agreement

National Defense Authorization Act (US), 300–1

National Energy Board of Canada, 118

NATO. *See* North Atlantic Treaty Organization

natural resources, controlling: Argentina, 16, 27–8

Nehru, Jawaharlal, 171–2, 175

Neustadt, Richard, 296

New Brunswick: international relations, 131

New Zealand, 38–9

Newfoundland: international relations, 132

Non-Aligned Movement (NAM) (Malaysia), 192, 193

North Atlantic Treaty Organization (NATO), 248

North American Free Trade Agreement (NAFTA), 12, 118, 301–2, 303–4, 315, 330, 351

Northern Cape (South Africa), 214

Nova Scotia: international relations, 132

nuclear testing: India, 172

Nye, Joseph, 296

OIF. *See* Organisation internationale de la Francophonie

Ontario, 116; international relations, 116–17, 127, 131–2

organic farming: Austria, 79

Organisation internationale de la Francophonie (OIF), 94, 95, 129 ; French Community of Belgium, and, 94, 95, 103; Swiss cantons, and, 293n33

Organization of African Unity (African Union) (AU), 213, 215–16

Organization of the Islamic Conference (OIC) (Malaysia), 192, 193

overseas technical assistance: Argentina, 30

Pacific Northwest Economic Region (PNWER), 128

Pakistan: terrorism in, 182–3

partnership. *See* sister-cities; twinning

Patagonia, 28

peacekeeping operations: Canada, 117; South Africa, 217

Penang (Malaysia): bureaucratic delays, 200, 209n32; ICT industry, 199–202; immigration red tape, 201, 209n33

Penang Development Corporation (Malaysia), 200

Penang Skills Development Centre (PSDC) (Malaysia), 201

Phillippart, Eric, 104

Poland, 144, 145
Prince Edward Island: international relations, 132

Quebec, 326; Canadian cultural policy and, 125, 129; Gérin-Lajoie doctrine, 121, 128; international activities, 116; international relations, 116, 126, 127, 128–30, 133–4; Ministère des relations internationals (MRI), 128; nationalist movement, 115–16

Radio Telegraph Convention (Canada), 121
Reconciliation Fund (Austria), 75–6
referendums: Switzerland, 277
regional cooperation: Benelux, 94
regional organizations: constituent diplomacy and, 326–8; developing world, in, 327; EU member states, 328–30
regional relations: Argentine provinces, 24–6; Australia, 38–40; Belgium, 101–2; Benelux, 94; German *Länder*, 160–1; India, 171, 184; Malaysia, 202–5; South Africa, 229–30; Spain, 247–8, 251–2, 253–6
Regulation and Control of Radio Communication in Canada reference, 121
representative offices abroad, 347–8; US states, 307–8, 316. *See also* diplomatic representation

Saskatchewan: international relations, 132
Schengen Agreements, 94, 145
Seamless Songkhla-Penang-Medan (SSPM) Economic Corridor (Malaysia), 203
Second World War, 330, 331
Sectoral Conference Relating to European Union Affairs (SCREU) (Spain), 254, 255
sister-cities: US cities, 314

Sister Cities International, 314
sister-state relationships (Australia), 58
South Africa: apartheid, 212, 213, 214, 215, 216; arms trade, 214; border relations, 214–15, 216, 217; borrowing internationally, 220; centralized federation, 213, 217–18, 220–1, 223; conflict of laws, 218; Constitution, 213, 217–20; constitutional division of powers, 217–20; consultation not required, 222, 223; consultation with provinces, 219; coordinated development initiatives, 221–2, 223–4; development aid, 221–2, 223–4, 227–8; eco-tourism, 217; foreign trade, 214; governmental policy, 222–3; HDI ranking, 215; immigration policies, 216–17; intergovernmental relations, 220–3; international agreements, 218–20; International Relations Coordinating Groups, 222; international roles, 214–17; nature of federalism, 213; peacekeeping operations, 217; policing powers, 220; profile of, 212–14; regional relations, 229–30; role in Africa, 215–16, 234n23; transportation infrastructure, 216; treaty-making powers, 218; veto powers, 218–19, 223
South African Development Community (SADC), 213, 215
South African Municipal International Relations Policy (MIR), 229
South African municipalities: development projects, 229; international agreements, 229; international memberships, 231; international relations, 212, 217, 220, 221; international relations staff, 224–5; regional development priorities, 229–30; twinning agreements, 228, 230
South African provinces: accountability for development aid, 227–8; constitutional powers, 217, 218; consultation

with, 219; implementing national policies, 219, 225; international memberships, 231; international relations, 221, 224; international travel, 225; limited international relations, 212, 217; profile of, 213–14; regional relations, 229–30; trade missions, 226–7; twinning agreements, 224

Spain, Kingdom of: Alliance of the Civilizations, 246–7; autonomous communities, 242; Catalan Statute, 251–2; Conference of Presidents, 256; Constitution, 241, 242, 248–52; Constitutional Court, jurisprudence, 250–2; constitutional division of powers, 248–52; constitutional reform, 243–4; cultural diversity, 243, 244; defence policy, 248; democratic transition, 241, 245, 248; economic transformation, 244; EU membership benefits, 244–5, 247–8; EU subsidies, 247; foreign policy, 245, 246, 248; HDI ranking, 244; intergovernmental cooperation, 253–6; international role, 245–7; isolation of, 245; nationalities vs regions, 242; nature of federalism, 241, 242; profile of, 242–5; regional relations, 247–8, 251–2, 253–6; Sectoral Conference Relating to European Affairs, 263; sectoral conferences, 254–5; support for United States, 246; treaty-making powers, 248–9; US military bases, 248

Spanish autonomous communities: bilateral summits and, 256; Brussels delegations, 258; Catalan statute, 251–2; competition among, 259; Constitutional Court, jurisprudence, 258; cooperation in foreign policy, 249; cross-border relations, 260; cultural distinctiveness, 257; development aid, 260; EU Council of Ministers, 255; EU participation, 247–8, 253; EU working groups and, 254–5; foreign investment, 257, 258, 259; foreign relations power, 249–52; foreign trade and, 257–9; international agreements, 257–8; international program budget, 259; international role, 256–62; limited international success, 261–2; no national representation, 249; profile of, 242; scope of international relations, 251; symbolic concerns, 257; tourism, 257; treaty compliance, 251

Spanish Law on Development Cooperation, 260–1

Special Operations Group (SOG) (India), 182

Statute of Westminster (1931), 40–1, 120

Steinman, Erich, 297

Strauss, Franz-Josef, 76

subsidiarity, principle: Belgium, 97

subsidies: European Union, 247, 347; Canada-US softwood lumber dispute, 119

substitution mechanism: Belgium, 98

sustainable development: South Africa, 230

Swiss cantons: agreements made by, 284–5; competition among, 283; consultation rights, 276, 278–9; cross-border agencies, 285; cultural promotion, 285; diplomacy levels, 285; foreign policy re own concerns, 282–3; foreign policy role, 274, 275–6; foreign relations, 276, 281; GATT participation, 291n14; IGOs and, 272–4, 279; international agreements, 280; joint agreements, 280; joint government commissions, 285; limits on foreign policy of, 283; no foreign representation, 284; OIF, participation in, 293n33; public participation, 287–8; relations between, 279–81;

transborder activities, 280; treaty-making powers, 276, 283; UN Human Rights Committee participation, 291n15
Swiss municipalities: foreign relations, 292n28; municipal relations, 281
Switzerland: accountability, 287; bilateral agreements, 273, 286, 291n11; cantonal cooperation, 277; Conference of Cantonal Governments, 278, 280; constituent diplomacy, 281–8; constitutional division of powers, 274–7, 282; consultation with cantons, 276, 278–9; cooperation in foreign policy, 278–9; cooperative federalism, 275, 278, 288; defence and security powers, 275; Department of Foreign Affairs, 276, 282; diversity of, 271; dualism in foreign policy, 272, 273; European integration, 273; Federal Assembly, 276–7; Federal Council, 275, 276, 288; foreign economic policy, 283, 286; foreign policy tensions, 274, 288; foreign relations powers, 270, 272, 273, 275; IGO membership, 272–4; implementing laws, 277; intergovernmental relations, 277–81; isolation of, 270, 272; joint foreign activities, 279; military independence, 272–3; nature of federation, 274, 288, 289; Presence Switzerland, 294n37; profile of, 271–2; referendums, 277; relationship in the EU, 289

Tayyip Erdogan, Recep, 246
terrorism: India, 181; Pakistan, 182–3
Toonen v. Australia, 51
Toronto, 133
tourism policy/issues: Argentina, 28–9; Australian states, 57; Flanders, 107–8; Malaysia, 204; Spanish autonomous communities, 257; US states, 309. *See also* eco-tourism

trade missions, 347; Malaysia, 197; South African provinces, 226–7. *See also* foreign trade; trade policy/issues
trade policy/issues: Australian states, 57; Malaysia, 202–5; Swiss cantons, 286. *See also* foreign trade
Trade Policy Review Mechanism (TPRM), 180
transborder activities. *See* border issues/relations
transportation system: Argentina, 28; South Africa, 216
Treaty Establishing the European Community (TEC), 80
Treaty Establishing the European Union (TEU) (Treaty of Maastricht), 99
Treaty on the European Community, 99
treaty-making powers, 6; Argentina, 15, 16–17; Australia, 37, 40, 41, 43; Austria, 67–8; Austrian *Länder*, 68; Belgium, 95, 96; Canada, 120–2, 125, 136–7n27; constituent units, 334–5; Germany, 147, 151; minor foreign policy, 276, 278, 283, 284; South Africa, 218; Spain, 248–9
twinning agreements: Alberta, 127; Argentina, 30–1; Austria, 79; Germany, 162; South African municipalities, 228, 230; South African provinces, 224

United Nations (UN): Canadian peacekeeping missions, 117
United Nations Climate Change Conference, 123
United Nations Educational, Scientific and Cultural Organization (UNESCO), 350; Canada, and, 123; Malaysia, and, 198
United Nations Human Development Index (HDI): Malaysia, 190; South Africa, 215; Spain, 244

United Nations Human Rights Committee, 51; Swiss canton participation, 291n15
United Nations Protection Force (UNPROFOR), 193
United States of America: anti-Americanism, 301; Civil War, 299; commerce clause, 302, 303, 304; Constitution, 298–9; constitutional division of powers, 302–5; creative destruction, 315; erosion of state powers, 314–15; federal foreign policy dominance, 313–14; foreign policy, 305–6; foreign policy jurisprudence, 303; foreign policy vs foreign relations, 312–14; foreign relations challenges, 312–16; free trade agreements, 301–2; GDP, 301; global pressure of, 301; globalization, 315; illegal immigration, 300; immigration policy, 311–12; intergovernmental relations, 305–7; intergovernmental tensions, 312–13; intermestic politics, 316; Iraq, war in, 302; Mexican consulates, 311; Native American tribal governments, 297–8; nature of federalism, 297, 298–301; Office of the US Trade Representative, 305; profile of, 297; public-private collaboration, 315; questioning federalism, 315; sanctions against Sudan, 302, 303; sanctuary policies, 312–13; state-federal disagreements, 299–301, 302; States' Federalism Summit, 300; supremacy clause, 302–3, 304; territories of, 297; War of 1812, 299; war on terror, 117–18, 246; Western Climate Initiative, 313
United States of America cities: accelerated foreign relations, 296–7; foreign relations, 317; international programs, 317–18; international relations, 314; sanctuary policy, 312–13; sister-cities, 314; support for Kyoto Protocol, 313
United States of America states: accelerated foreign relations, 296–7; border crossings, 309; border relations, 310–11; California-British agreement re environment, 313; coordinating associations, 306–7; coordination with local governments, 306; dangers of globalization, 305, 308, 315; erosion of authority alleged, 303–4; export promotion, 308; extent of international relations, 303; FDI incentives, 306, 308; foreign policy role, 313–14, 316; foreign relations, 314, 316; governors' diplomacy, 310–11; illegal immigration, 300, 311–12; international programs, 310, 316, 317–18; new business creation, 309–10; offices abroad, 307–8, 316; rights of, 298–301; tourism, 309
Universal Convention on Cultural Diversity (Canada), 125

Vancouver, 133
veto power, treaties: Australia, 49; Belgium, 104; South Africa, 218–19, 223

Wallonia, 326
Wallonia-Brussels Community (Belgium), 108–9
Wallonia-Bruxelles International (WBI) (Brussels), 109
Western Cape (South Africa), 226
Western Cape Investment and Trade Promotion Agency (Wesgro) (South Africa), 227
Western Hemisphere Travel Initiative (WHTI), 309
World Bank, 23; annual GDP estimates, 308
World Health Organization (WHO), 95; Charter, 74

World Tourist Organization, 95
World Trade Organization (WTO), 71; agreement, India, 179; Argentine participation, 22–3; ignoring US federal division of powers, 304; WTO cells (India), 180, 186n12

ZICOSUR (Zona de Integracion del Centro Oeste Sudamericano), 25–6, 28
Zschernig v. Miller (US), 303
Zurich, 286–7